THE CULTURAL AND POLITICAL HISTORY OF GUYANA

THE CULTURAL AND POLITICAL HISTORY OF GUYANA

President John F. Kennedy's Interference in the Country's Democracy

IVAN A. ROSS

Copyright © 2021 Ivan A. Ross.

All rights reserved. No part of this book may be used or reproduced by any means, graphic, electronic, or mechanical, including photocopying, recording, taping or by any information storage retrieval system without the written permission of the author except in the case of brief quotations embodied in critical articles and reviews.

This book is a work of non-fiction. Unless otherwise noted, the author and the publisher make no explicit guarantees as to the accuracy of the information contained in this book and in some cases, names of people and places have been altered to protect their privacy.

Archway Publishing books may be ordered through booksellers or by contacting:

Archway Publishing
1663 Liberty Drive
Bloomington, IN 47403
www.archwaypublishing.com
844-669-3957

Because of the dynamic nature of the Internet, any web addresses or links contained in this book may have changed since publication and may no longer be valid. The views expressed in this work are solely those of the author and do not necessarily reflect the views of the publisher, and the publisher hereby disclaims any responsibility for them.

Any people depicted in stock imagery provided by Getty Images are models, and such images are being used for illustrative purposes only. Certain stock imagery © Getty Images.

ISBN: 978-1-6657-0937-8 (sc)
ISBN: 978-1-6657-0936-1 (hc)
ISBN: 978-1-6657-0938-5 (e)

Library of Congress Control Number: 2021914108

Print information available on the last page.

Archway Publishing rev. date: 09/14/2021

This book is dedicated to Edward Sinclair (Moore). The statement, if we forget the past, we are lost in the present with no vision of the future, is an apt description of Edward's recent years. I had only known him for a few months when he became completely comfortable with my home and friends. Whether I am at home or not, he would enter without knocking. He goes to the fridge, gets a beer, and enjoys it. Often, he would show up with a rack of ribs and proceed to the grill. Gradually he started to lose his memory, and even when he could not remember the words he would like to say, there was always a smile; eventually, he got lost.

No one is born superior to another person. Human superiority is the quality of being better or more powerful than others physically or mentally, and it has to be confirmed upon people; it is not a quality that can be self-imposed based on one's domination of others, accumulated wealth, and properties possessed. -*Ivan A Ross.*

CONTENTS

Preface ix

Chapter 1	*Introduction*	1
Chapter 2	*Guyana*	13
Chapter 3	*The First People of Guyana*	19
Chapter 4	*Colonialism*	39
Chapter 5	*India and its Colonization*	49
Chapter 6	*Africa and its Colonization*	63
Chapter 7	*The Colonization of Guyana*	87
Chapter 8	*Enslaved Africans in Guyana*	101
Chapter 9	*The Berbice Uprising*	109
Chapter 10	*The Anti-Slavery Movement*	117
Chapter 11	*The Abolition of the Slave Trade*	121
Chapter 12	*The Emancipation of Slavery*	125
Chapter 13	*Britain's Slave-Owners Compensation*	131
Chapter 14	*Indentureship*	143
Chapter 15	*The Indentureship of Portuguese*	149
Chapter 16	*The Indentureship of Chinese*	153
Chapter 17	*The Indentureship of Indians*	163
Chapter 18	*Policies and Social Awakenings*	223
Chapter 19	*Political and Social Changes*	227
Chapter 20	*The Formation of Political Parties*	235
Chapter 21	*The First PPP Election of Dr. Cheddi Jagan*	239
Chapter 22	*The Dissolution of the 1953 Legislature*	247
Chapter 23	*The Interim Legislative Council*	257

Chapter 24	Formation of the PNC Party............................267
Chapter 25	The Second PPP Election of Dr. Cheddi Jagan...................... 271
Chapter 26	The Administration of Dr. Cheddi Jagan - 1961 279
Chapter 27	U.S. Government Anti-Jagan Campaign 305
Chapter 28	The Planning of the 1964 Elections..................327
Chapter 29	The Administration of Mr. Forbes Burnham - 1964 415
Chapter 30	The Planning of the 1968 Election 459
Chapter 31	The Administration of Mr. Forbes Burnham - 1968 533
Chapter 32	The Administration of Mr. Forbes Burnham - 1973.. 543
Chapter 33	The Administration of Mr. Forbes Burnham -1980 563
Chapter 34	The Administration of Mr. Desmond Hoyte -1985...573
Chapter 35	The Administration of Dr. Cheddi Jagan -1992 589
Chapter 36	The Administration of Mrs. Janet Jagan -1997...601
Chapter 37	The Administration Mr. Bharrat Jagdeo -1999... 611
Chapter 38	The Administration of Mr. Donald Ramotar - 2011.. 629
Chapter 39	The Administration of Mr. David Granger - 2015...681

Bibliography 695

PREFACE

The world is part of nature and is governed by knowable natural forces and laws. These phenomena can be explained by natural causes and human cognitive, social, and moral characteristics.

Around 60,000 years ago, humans migrated out of Africa and began exploring the earth. In the beginning, they lived as hunter-gatherer nomads foraging for food. Then, about 12,000 years ago, things changed. They started to settle in homesteads and developed methods of farming and the domestication of animals. They acquired the ability to invent and use complex tools for survival and to improve their lifestyles. They lived in natural shelters such as caves and learned to build huts and eventually houses, making it possible for them to live almost anywhere. They became creative and built complex settlements like villages and cities.

As nations developed, humans invented democracy, a political system where everyone has equal rights. Democracy is the people managing their country through elected officials. It was designed to choose the Government through free and fair electoral processes, enable the participation of citizens, the protection of human rights, and a rule of law that applies equally to everyone. If used appropriately, democracy can filter out corruption.

As a Guyanese living in the United States of America, oftentimes, I have been confronted with: Where are you from?

Why are you living in the USA? How privileged it must feel to live in the USA. My response has always been, 'it's a long story.' The story began in 1961 when President John F. Kennedy interfered with my country's democracy. The consequences of the interference are the mass migration of Guyanese, corrupted political behavior, and turmoil that dominates the country to this day, sixty years later.

The legacies of imperialism and colonialism continue to manifest in Guyana. The colonial period was an extension of the era of the industrial revolution. The drive for economic gain from new raw materials for European industries created a scramble for free land and free labor. Corruption thus became part of the divisive strategy of colonialism. The colonizers' divide-and-rule technique enables favoring one ethnic group over another. The dual objectives of the technique are securing the loyalty of one group to the colonial administration and encouraging rivalry among the groups as a strategy for preventing unity. Unity threatens colonial rule.

The information presented in this book teaches the origin of the corruption, deep-seated animosity, and ethnic divisions of our society. Whether we like it or not, we cannot eliminate corruption. It has always been a part of human nature and will continue to infect society. The best we can do is keep it to a minimum.

Ivan A. Ross

CHAPTER 1
Introduction

THE THOUGHTS THAT GUIDED THE COMPILATION OF this book were the documentation of my history. My history is neither from the beginning of my life nor from my parents or grandparents. It is the history of my ancestors and the events that shaped me into who I am. My history was influenced by colonialism, enslavement, indentureship, and imperialism.

If we forget the past, we are lost in the present with no vision of the future. The history of the Indigenous people, enslaved Africans, indentured Portuguese, Chinese, and Indian laborers provides an in-depth view of the evolution of the Guyanese people. It provides evidence of their strong cultural identity and reveals their ambitions, sense of direction, and perseverance to strive for well-being and happiness in the best possible life.

We do not make our history as we please; we make it

under the circumstances given and transmitted from the past. Studying our history is extremely important in understanding who we are so that we can develop a sense of self, a large part of which is learning where we fit into the story of our country and the global community. Cultures originated in ancient times when humans began living in communities. Cultural identity defines our evolutionary identity; it helps us to understand our traditional values and gives us the very meaning of life. All cultures instill moral values in making us the human family that coexist in harmonious societies. We grew up learning our regional culture and the community that shapes our lives, making us unique from cultures in other parts of the world. It is this traditional culture that keeps us bonded to our community.

In 1596 Sir Walter Ralegh described Guyana, (formerly Guiana and British Guiana), as:

> a country that hath yet her maidenhead, never sacked, turned, nor wrought; the face of the earth hath not been torn, nor the virtue and salt of the soil spent by manurance, the graves have not been opened for gold, the mines not broken with a sledge, nor their images pulled down out of their temples.

At that time, Guyana was inhabited by the Indigenous people who have been there for approximately 22,000 years. Shortly after Ralegh's arrival, other Europeans arrived in pursuit of wealth. They attempted to enslave the Indigenous people who resisted and fled from the coastal region to the forested hinterland. The Europeans then brought enslaved people from Africa. After two centuries, they were emancipated, and indentured laborers from Madeira, China, and India took their place on the plantations.

The country was thriving with the European merchants employing the ex-slaves as distributors and retailers of their merchandise. Twelve years out of slavery, 42,000 of the 82,000 Afro-Guyanese laboring population had succeeded in making themselves partly independent of plantation work. They had established 25 communal villages at an aggregate cost of almost $2,250,000. When the indentured Portuguese were liberated, the merchants, themselves Europeans, employed the Portuguese, who quickly took over that role from the Africans.

For generations, we've been unwilling to teach the history of colonialism, enslavement, and indentureship. School teachers are worried about disturbing the children. So, they tell them about the *good* people, like the abolitionists, freedom fighters, and those who escaped to freedom but left out the details of why they were protesting or what they were fleeing. That meant the children became adults with a poor understanding of how colonialism, the ancestral slaves, and the indentured laborers influenced their lives and their country and the powerful and lasting effects they have.

Some have asked why I don't leave my negative history behind. It has also been suggested that my people are too focused on our past and it is preventing us from keeping up with successful societies. Cultural historians have made efforts to study different races to understand how cultures and societies evolve and to guide that process. Still, the physiological and psychological effects of centuries of oppression on generations of enslaved people's thoughts, feelings, and behaviors have been ignored.

The European Society for Traumatic Stress Studies defines trauma as:

> Exposure to an extreme traumatic stressor involving a direct personal experience of an event that involves actual or threatened death or serious injury, or other threat to one's physical integrity; or witnessing an event that involves death, injury, or a threat to the physical integrity of another person, or learning about unexpected or violent death, serious harm, or threat of death or injury experienced by a family member or other close associate.

As experienced in slavery and indentureship, trauma has a recurring effect on subsequent generations who have experienced similar stressors as their ancestors. The trauma explains the persistence of health problems among those whose ancestors were oppressed by colonialism. The success, wealth, and notoriety of some mask the comparatively unfavorable conditions. For example, the incidence of diabetes, high blood pressure, and premature death from heart diseases and prostate cancer are almost double among adults whose ancestors were oppressed compared to those whose ancestors weren't.

Epigenetics is the study of how behaviors and the environment can cause changes that affect how our genes work. Unlike genetic changes, epigenetic changes do not change our DNA sequence, and they are reversible; they can change how our body reads a DNA sequence and which genes would be expressed.

In one study (Dias and Ressler), mice were exposed to a chemical (acetophenone) with a distinct odor. After exposure to the scent, they were given a mild foot shock. Ten days later, after 45 exposures, the mice were mated with females that were not exposed to acetophenone or foot shock. When their young grew up, many of the animals were more sensitive to the odor of acetophenone than to other scents and more likely to be startled by unexpected noise during exposure to the smell. The subsequent offspring, the second generation of the mice trained to fear the scent, also exhibited anxiety in the presence of the odor. Three generations had enlarged M71 glomeruli, structures where acetophenone-sensitive neurons in the nostrils connect with neurons in the olfactory bulb. The exposure changed the genome that affects how the DNA is expressed without altering its sequence.

Another study on the topic (Szyf) concluded that a mother's experience of trauma could change the baby's stress hormone profiles at the genetic level. The research indicates that infant temperament has significant long-term consequences for development, including influencing later personality, social development, and risk of emotional and behavioral problems. The effects on numerous developmental outcomes, including racism, can be transferred intergenerationally through the genes, in which a change can be seen in cortisol levels. An increase in the cortisol levels from the mother changes the threshold of stress for the fetus, making the offspring hyper-responsive to stressors when it is born.

Biologists first observed the transgenerational epigenetic inheritance in plants. Tomatoes, for example, pass along chemical markings that control a crucial ripening gene. There has been evidence that the phenomenon also occurs in rodents and humans. In part, the subject remains controversial. It revokes the discredited assertions of Jean-Baptiste Lamarck's nineteenth-century proposal on the notion that an organism can pass on to its offspring physical characteristics that the parent organism acquired through use or disuse during its lifetime. The process is called the inheritance of acquired characteristics or soft inheritance.

Adaptive coping mechanisms provide an example of a

culturally adapted psychological treatment. Should the coping mechanism be accepted as the treatment for the people to whom the trauma was administered over several generations? Does the adapted treatment restore the physiological and psychological state to where it was before the trauma? There is no simple solution to the trauma associated with people whose ancestors endured the oppression of enslavement and indentureship. The academic community does not consider epigenetics and the concept of inherited race-related trauma as sound science due to the political implications of the subject.

Stereotypes that people of color are unintelligent, subhuman, and lower class still exist and are perpetuated by many families, politicians, and law enforcement. One resolution is, since we cannot change our sordid past, we must not be indifferent to the contemporary suffering linked to that past. The patterns of behavior among the sufferers are a product, not of alien cultural imposition upon a pristine Western environment, but, instead, of social, economic, and political practices deeply rooted in our history. We should not ignore the behavioral problems of those who are struggling, but we should discuss and react to them as if we are talking about our children, neighbors, and friends. It is a tragedy to which we should respond as we would to an epidemic of teen suicide or adolescent drug abuse by embracing, not demonizing, the sufferers.

Our capacity for growth and acceptance of who we are depends on our ability to take responsibility for who we are meant to be; eccentric, strong, weak, distinguished, ordinary, and add our small piece to the great mosaic of life. When we are insecure, we seek power over others as compensation for inadequacy; we take the consequences down upon them and those around them; we take cover in their lives and resist our own fugitive lives projecting onto others. Exerting control over knowledge, the plunder and erasure of identity, and the subjugation to colonizer's rules under repressive means plays a significant role in the moral character of our society.

Unlike reading, writing, and arithmetic, the people of Guyana were not taught their history. They were taught an elitist history; the histories of the colonizers, the British people with power, of Kings and Queens, great leaders of wars, but there was no mention of the ordinary people and the presence of Indians and Africans in the British Empire for centuries. Guyana's more recent cultural and political history cannot be discussed, even among friends, for fear that they would be offended by the conflicting views of what was taught, not through formal education, but by self-serving politicians who were accepted with the credibility of religious leaders.

Humans share over 99 percent of their genetic material with one another. There are more variations among individuals than among ethnic groups. The legacies of racial and ethnic constructs can be recognized in every aspect of life. The melting pot ideal, in which racially and ethnically diverse individuals assimilate into a monolithic culture while losing roots to the culture of origin, has not been successful in Guyana. Rather than encouraging integration, politicians have taken advantage of the divisive concepts of racial and ethnic segregation to shape the population's social, personal, and cultural behavior. Racial and ethnic prejudices have affected the distribution of wealth, power, opportunity and creating enduring social stratifications.

In 1961, the people of the colony of British Guiana elected, through a free and fair election, the first Premier, Dr. Cheddi Jagan. Immediately after assuming duties, Dr. Jagan initiated a discussion on the decolonization of his country. President John F. Kennedy opposed the American-educated dentist whom he labeled a communist. It must be President Kennedy's paranoia of his unsuccessful attempts to overthrow Fidel Castro of Cuba at the time and nightmarish thoughts of having another communist country in the region to humiliate him. Therefore, President Kennedy authorized and funded covert operations to interfere with the country's economic and political developments and the democratic electoral process so that a candidate of his choice could be installed to lead the soon-to-be independent Guyana.

President Kennedy's ruthless subversion of democracy became the policy for subsequent electoral process of using the divisive concepts of racial and ethnic segregation. The concepts shaped the personal, social, and cultural behavior of Guyanese.

Transparency International defines corruption as "the abuse of entrusted power for private gain." Their data shows that 85 percent of humans live under corrupt governments. Corruption traps billions of human beings in poverty and undermines democracy and ethics in society; Justice becomes compromised, and government systems become dysfunctional.

Mahatma Gandhi said: "The world has enough for everyone's needs, but not enough for everyone's greed." As the global economy expanded in the 20th century, the level of corruption increased as well. The World Bank estimated international bribery to exceed US$1.5 trillion annually, which is 2% of global GDP and ten times more than total global aid funds. Other estimates are higher, at 2 to 5% of global GDP. Corruption permeates every level of society, from low-level public servants accepting petty bribes to leaders of nations stealing millions of dollars. Transparency International estimated Indonesia's former president Suharto siphoned off from $15 billion to $35 billion. The Philippines' Ferdinand Marcos, Mobutu Sese Seko of Zaire, and Sani Abacha of Nigeria may have embezzled $5 billion each.

Corruption has become a way of life in many countries. In 2011, two-thirds of Bangladeshis and well over half of Indians paid a bribe during the preceding 12 months. In 2017, one in four people had paid bribes in the previous 12 months to access public service. Nearly 57% of people around the world felt their governments were doing nothing to fight corruption. Only 30% thought their governments were doing well.

Police officers are the most corrupt in Sub-Saharan Africa (47%) and Asia Pacific (39%). The magnitude of global corruption and its constraints on poverty alleviation and economic development is a damaging indictment. In 2017, nearly 10% of Asians, around 400 million, lived in extreme poverty. Corruption siphons off funds intended for poverty alleviation. If developing countries can control corruption and enforce the rule of law, the World Bank estimated *per capita* income could increase fourfold over the long term, the business sector could grow 3% faster, and the infant mortality rate could decrease by 75%.

International financial systems have made it possible for public officials to hide their loot in tax havens. In 2014, the Panama Papers leaked 11.5 million files. They showed that two national leaders among 143 politicians, their families, and close associates from all over the world were using offshore tax havens to hide their wealth. Similarly, the Paradise Papers leaked 13.4 million files from two different offshore service providers and 19 tax haven company registries. It revealed the offshore activities of more than 120 politicians and world leaders and financial engineering of more than 100 multinational corporations.

Strengthening institutions and promptly upholding the rules of law, like Singapore, have shown significant control of corruption. President Xi Jinping of China has declared war on corruption, which has targeted both "tigers and flies," a reference to senior and low-ranking officials. Many powerful Chinese politicians and bureaucrats, who were previously considered untouchables, are in jail for corruption. A 2017 report indicated that nearly 70% of Indians who accessed a public service had to pay a bribe. In India, virtually no prominent political leader has been jailed for corruption. This has given many powerful politicians and senior bureaucrats a license to steal.

Developed countries are not immune to corruption. When a developed country invests in an undeveloped or weaker country for political gain, it is called political imperialism. It advocates the extension of power and dominion to another country by political and economic control. The developed or dominant country invests in infrastructure and social welfare programs giving the impression of sharing the blessings of its civilization. During the nurturing period, the dominant country manipulates the ethnic groups creating ethnic divisions in the weaker country. With the ethnic division and instability, the mission of the dominant country goes unnoticed. The weaker country enjoys the petty benefits, which appear favorable, and eventually creates a dependence on the developed country. Eventually, the developed country achieves its goals and cuts off the blessings.

When slave labor was no longer available in British Guiana, planters had to pay working wages to their former slaves. Sir John Gladstone, a slave owner in Guyana, was also a member of the British Parliament and a prominent figure in the British Government. A protest by the ex-slaves for working wages on his plantations was brutally crushed by the British military. He expelled the workers from his plantations and influenced the British Government, where his son William was Secretary of State for the Colonies, to permit indentured laborers from India as a replacement. He acquired the Indians through false promises and never disclosed to them where they were going. Upon arrival in Guyana, they were not paid for their work on his plantations since they had to pay him for their transportation from India. They had to work under the conditions of slavery in every form, except they were called laborers. Sir John Gladstone received the largest compensation payment made by the Slave Compensation Commission. One group in society is still comfortable with the fact that those who benefited from the atrocities of slavery deserved compensation, but the slaves who suffered the cruelest dehumanizing lives, for generations, deserve no compensation.

The deliberate intent of public authorities to extract personal privileges and monetary rewards at the expense of the public is the most notorious abuse of power. The violation of ethical rules and considerations is progressively worsening the social problems afflicting the world. In Guyana, it has permeated all public and private, governmental and non-governmental institutions. Corruption has become not only a way of life but also a method of acquiring property. It has become an impediment to economic, social, and political development; it intensifies crime and ethnic conflicts and increases poverty, misery, and degradation of society.

CHAPTER 2

Guyana

THE PRECAMBRIAN ROCKS OF GUYANA ARE AMONG THE oldest rocks on earth, dated as more than two billion years old. About 200 million years ago, South America, Africa, India, Australia, and Antarctica were attached to form the Gondwanaland landmass. There were no ice sheets, and plants and animals flourished. Gondwanaland existed from the Neoproterozoic period between one billion and 541 million years ago. The independent continents and countries began breaking apart during the Jurassic period, between 199.6 million and 145.5 million years ago. A warm, wet climate with lush vegetation and abundant animal life was characteristic of the Jurassic period. During that period, a land bridge formed between South America and North America that led to the movement of animals, and eventually humans, between the continents.

Guyana is located in northern South America, bordered by the Atlantic Ocean on the north, Suriname on the east,

Venezuela on the west, and Brazil on the south and southwest. Guyana is the only English-speaking country in South America. It's also named *Land of Waters* by the Indigenous peoples who inhabited it for thousands of years before the arrival of Europeans.

Guyana is north of the equator at 1 to 8 degrees N and 57 to 61 degrees W, where the coastal temperature is an average of 27 degrees Celsius throughout the year. The northeast trade wind keeps the coastline comfortably cool. The rainy seasons are the May-June rains and the December-January or Christmas rains with a total rainfall of approximately 200 centimeters per year.

The coastal plain is heavily cultivated with coconut, rice, sugarcane, and various fruits; livestock – cattle, horses, sheep, goats, and donkeys - wander almost everywhere. Approximately ninety percent of the population lives on the coast that is separated by a belt of white sand from the densely forested hinterland. The aluminum ore, bauxite, is mined from under the white sand.

Beyond the white-sand belt is the dense forest which covers approximately eighty-five percent of the country. The Indigenous people and the p*ork-knockers* who came from the Caribbean islands, especially St. Vincent, to participate in gold and diamond mining populate the forested area.

Among the famous sites in the forested area is the Kaieteur fall. Kaieteur fall has been documented in geologist Barrington Brown's book *Canoe and Camp Life in British Guiana*. In 1887, when descending the Potaro River on geological explorations, Mr. Brown was told by his Native companion that the next day they would come to Old Man Falls, and it is "higher than the trees," so they would have to walk around it. The name given to the falls was based on a legend that an old man was put into a canoe and sent over the falls. For many years the official measurement of the falls was 226 meters, using a barometer. It was discovered that the instrument was affected by the climatic conditions in the gorge, from where the measurement was taken. Measurements by other means revealed the falls to be 244 meters, one of the highest waterfalls in the world.

Beyond the dense forest to the south is the Rupununi savannah. In the south and southwest of the savannah, at the border with Brazil, are the Takatu and Ireng Rivers. The Takatu drains from south to north and the Ireng from north to south. The rivers drain the region via the Rio Branco and Rio Negro Rivers into the Amazon River. Rupununi River drains north into the Essequibo River. At Lake Amuku, the Essequibo and the Amazon waters are mixed.

The Rupununi Savannah was a ranching country described by David Attenborough, Michael Swan, and Stanley Brock. The first cattle were shipped upriver from Brazil in the 1790s. By the 1960s, the herd in the Rupununi had grown to as many as 60,000 heads. From the 1950s, Dadanawa ranch occupied most of the southern savannah. The ranch of approximately 6,475 square km of the country grazed 27,000 heads of cattle and 700 horses. Dadanawa ranch was producing 3,000 marketable steers each year.

The Corentyne River forms Guyana's eastern boundary with Suriname. It is the northern extension of the Amazon River in dense forests and snaking waterways. Large tracts of that area have not been surveyed, nor has there been any actual long-term inhabitation. Unlike other rivers used as international boundaries, the high-water mark on the Guyana side of the river serves as the boundary. Thus, Suriname retains fishing rights. There is a disputed region known as the *New River Triangle*. It is located between the Kutari River to the east and the New River to the west. The southern border extends to a watershed that forms the northern border of Brazil.

An agreement in 1799 established that the border between the predecessor countries of British Guiana and Dutch Guiana would be the Corentyne River. When that agreement was ratified, neither the colonial governments of British Guiana nor Dutch Guiana knew how far the Corentyne River extended into the northern Amazon. Different expeditions surveying the headwaters of the Corentyne reached incompatible conclusions. The differing opinions of those surveys formed the modern boundary dispute over the New River Triangle. Guyana claims the Kutari River, a river breaking from the Corentyne and flowing from a southeast direction, as the true headwater of the Corentyne River, and therefore, the boundary. Suriname claims the New River, a river breaking from the Corentyne and flowing from a southwest direction, as the larger tributary, and therefore, the correct border. The area between those two rivers is the New River Triangle.

The northwestern boundary with Venezuela has been disputed since 1841 when the Venezuelan Government protested alleged British encroachment on Venezuelan territory. Great Britain acquired British Guiana in 1814 by treaty with the Netherlands. Because the treaty did not define a western boundary, the British commissioned Robert Schomburgk, a surveyor and naturalist, to delineate that boundary. His 1835 survey resulted in what came to be known as the *Schomburgk Line*, a boundary that effectively claimed an additional 30,000 square miles for British Guiana. In 1841 Venezuela disputed the British delineation, claiming territorial delineations established at the time of their independence from Spain. Venezuela claimed its borders extended as far east as the Essequibo River, claiming two-thirds of British Guiana's territory.

When gold was discovered in the disputed territory, Great Britain sought to extend its reach further, claiming an additional 33,000 square miles west of the Schomburgk Line. In

1876 Venezuela protested, broke diplomatic relations with Great Britain, and appealed to the United States for assistance, citing the Monroe Doctrine of 1823 to justify U.S. involvement. For the next 19 years, Venezuela repeatedly petitioned for U.S. assistance, calling on its neighbor to the north to intervene by either sponsoring arbitration or intervening with force.

The United States responded by expressing concern but did little to facilitate a resolution. In 1895, invoking the Monroe Doctrine, newly appointed U.S. Secretary of State Richard Olney sent a strongly-worded note to British Prime Minister and Foreign Secretary Lord Salisbury, demanding that the British submit the boundary dispute to arbitration. Salisbury responded that the Monroe Doctrine had no validity as international law. This response was unacceptable to the United States, and in December 1895, President Grover Cleveland asked Congress for authorization to appoint a boundary commission. He proposed that the commission's findings be enforced "by every means." Congress passed the measure unanimously, and talk of war with Great Britain began to circulate in the U.S. press.

Under pressure in South Africa with the Boer War and managing an empire that spanned the globe, Great Britain could not afford another conflict. Lord Salisbury's Government submitted the dispute to the American boundary commission and said nothing else of the Monroe Doctrine. Venezuela enthusiastically submitted to arbitration, confident that the commission would decide in its favor. However, when the commission finally rendered a decision on October 3, 1899, it directed that the border follow the Schomburgk Line. Although rejecting Great Britain's increasingly extravagant claims, the ruling preserved the 1835 demarcation. Disappointed, the Venezuelans ratified the commission's decision.

CHAPTER 3

The First People of Guyana

THE FIRST PEOPLE TO REACH GUYANA MADE THEIR way from Asia, across the Bering Land Bridge, approximately 22,000 years ago. They migrated south into the Americas. From South America, they migrated north to the Guiana region and the Caribbean islands.

Among the locations proposed as early American settlements, well before North America's Clovis culture, is Brazil's Pedra Furada rock-shelter. At that location, archaeologists unearthed burnt wood and sharp-edged stones dated to more than 50,000 years ago. The Pedra Furada's archaeologists Lahaye and Boëda's team also excavated Toca da Tira Peia, a rock-shelter in the same national park as Pedra Furada, from 2008 to 2011. They discovered up to 113 stone artifacts, consisting of tools and tool debris, in five soil layers at that location.

Using a technique that measures natural radiation damage

in quartz grains, the scientists estimated that the last exposure of soil to sunlight ranged from about 4,000 years ago in the top layer to 22,000 years ago in the third layer. Fifteen human-altered stones from the bottom two soil layers were estimated to be older than 22,000 years.

Critics, especially the Clovis investigators, said the Brazilian discoveries could have resulted from natural fires and rock slides. The Toca da Tira Peia location is at the base of a cliff. Archaeologist Gary Haynes of the University of Nevada, Reno, USA, indicated the possibility that crude, sharp-edged stones resulted from falling rocks and are not human handiwork. Another possibility mentioned by archaeologist Stuart Fiedel of Louis Berger Group, an environmental consulting firm in Richmond, VA., USA, stated that capuchins or other monkeys could have produced the tools.

The age of Toca da Tira Peia artifacts has also drawn debate. Dating the artifacts was based on calculations of how long-ago objects were buried by soil. Gary Haynes said that the various environmental conditions, including fluctuations in soil moisture, could have distorted the age estimates. Archaeologist Tom Dillehay of Vanderbilt University in Nashville, TN, USA, saw some of the Toca da Tira Peia artifacts and regards them as human-made implements. He said similar tools had been unearthed at sites in Chile and Peru. His team previously estimated that people settled Chile's Monte Verde site 14,000 years ago and possibly as long as 33,000 years ago.

The absence of burned wood or other finds suitable for radiocarbon dating at Toca da Tira Peia is a problem since it is the standard method for estimating the age of sites up to around 40,000 years old. Also, if people reached South America by 22,000 years ago, "this is the type of archaeological record we might expect: ephemeral and lightly scattered material in local shelters," said Dillehay.

The dates of the Brazil excavations have been a critical factor in the debate over the first migration route from Asia to America. Before the discovery at Toca da Tira Peia, the most popular and widely accepted theory was the overland route, which speculated that the first Americans migrated from Asia across the Bering Strait then dispersed throughout North America. The dates associated with Toca da Tira Peia add mystery to that theory.

Before 22,000 years ago, the Cordilleran Glacier, which covered much of present-day Canada, was not passable enough to reasonably reveal an ice-free corridor for people to travel by foot. Even the Monte Verde radiocarbon dates, which precede 13,000 BCE, could not possibly be accessible or provide enough vegetation to sustain traveling people or herded animals through the vast icy landscape of much of the Americas.

Therefore, the possible routes of migration are either through The Bering Land Bridge or from Polynesia across the Pacific Ocean. The most prevalent theory is the coastal migration hypothesis. This theory argues that people migrated from Asia down along the eastern Pacific Ocean on the western coasts of North and South America. Monte Verde is located 12,875 kilometers south of the Bering Strait. That distance was probably unreasonable to trek on foot, especially on ice. There are remains of 22 varieties of seaweed referenced in regards to this theory.

The Native peoples of the region used those particular seaweed varieties for medicinal purposes. Ethnographic analogy suggests that the Monte Verde residents used those varieties for similar purposes, which further suggests an extensive knowledge of marine resources. With a relative lack of stone tools, it appears that the first settlers were maritime-adapted hunter/gatherer/fishers and not necessarily big-game hunters like the Clovis culture. It is possible that they traveled along the coast by boat or along the shoreline by foot and survived on marine resources throughout their travel south. The presence of objects that were not native to Monte Verde, such as plants, beach-rolled pebbles, quartz, and tar, indicates possible trade networks and other sites of human habitation of similar age.

According to Dr. Dillehay and his team, Monte Verde II was occupied around 14,800 to 13,800 years ago. A tent-like structure made of wood and animal hides was erected on the banks of a creek. It was framed with logs and planks staked into the ground, making walls of poles covered with animal hides. The hides were tied to the poles, using ropes made of local reeds, separating living quarters within the main structure. Two large hearths had been built for community usage outside the tent-like structure, most probably for tool making and craftwork.

Each of the living quarters had a brazier pit lined with clay. Around those hearths, many stone tools and remnants of spilled seeds, nuts, and berries were found. A specimen of the wild potato (*Solanum maglia*), dating back to 13,000 years ago, was also found at the site. It remains the oldest on record for any potato species, wild or cultivated, suggesting that southern Chile was one of the two main centers for the evolution of *Solanum tuberosum*, the common potato. Remains of forty-five different edible plant species were found at the site, over a fifth of them originating from up to 240 km away. That suggested that the people of Monte Verde either had trade routes or regularly traveled in the extended network.

Other important discoveries from the Monte Verde site include human coprolites. A footprint assumed to have been made by a child, stone tools, and cordage. Dr. Dillehay estimated the date for that site using radiocarbon dating of charcoal and bones found at the site. Nine species of seaweed and marine algae were also recovered from hearths and other areas in the settlement. The seaweed samples were directly dated between 14,220 and 13,980 years ago, confirming that Monte Verde-II was occupied more than 1,000 years before the Clovis culture.

Before colonization, many of the Indigenous peoples of South America were hunter/gatherers; many still are, especially in the Amazonian area. Others, especially the Andean cultures, practiced sophisticated agriculture, utilized advanced irrigation, and kept domesticated livestock, such as llamas and alpacas. In the period after the initial arrival of Europeans in the 1490s, the Indigenous population of South America fell rapidly due to a variety of factors, such as disease and warfare.

The agricultural villagers of the tropical forests had more developed exploitative techniques than the hunters and gatherers. Farming, food storage, and transportation by canoe along the rivers made for greater economic sufficiency and the ability to live in large and stable units. The forest-dwelling agriculturalists were mostly the Arawakan and Cariban-speaking peoples. They include the coastal Arawak and the Carib of the Guianas, such as the Barama River Carib and the Macusí.

Tropical-forest farming villagers had socio-cultural units consisting mainly of kin-based populations, structured along age and gender, without much economic, political, or religious ground for social-status differentiation. Social controls were primarily based on kinship rights and obligations of a moral nature. Their richer technology and production of agricultural surpluses enabled villages to remain in the same place for many years.

The depletion of soils necessitated the periodic

re-establishment of new villages and the abandonment of older ones. The nations were supported by a more adequate and dependable food supply, including corn, beans, squash, cassava, and tropical vegetables and fruits. From the rivers, they obtained fish and tortoises along with their eggs. Hunting was essential but subsidiary to agriculture. Rituals surrounding birth, puberty, initiation into men's secret societies, marriage, death, and the shamanistic practices involved in curing illness tend to be similar throughout the region. Many of the rites were similar to those of the more straightforward hunting and gathering peoples.

The United Nations (U.N.) has not adopted an official definition; it relies on self-identification to categorize Indigenous populations worldwide. Many countries do the same. The U.N. declares, Indigenous peoples as inheritors and practitioners of unique cultures and ways of relating to people and the environment. They have retained social, cultural, economic, and political characteristics that are distinct from those of the dominant societies in which they live.

The U.N. Declaration on the Rights of Indigenous Peoples states: "Indigenous peoples have suffered from historic injustices, a result of *'inter alia'*, their colonization and dispossession of lands, territories, and resources." The Organization of American States (OAS) American Declaration on the Rights of Indigenous Peoples repeats the U.N. Declaration language. It adds, "Indigenous peoples are original, diverse societies with their own identities that constitute an integral part of the Americas." According to OAS estimates, more than 50 million people of Indigenous descent live in the Western hemisphere.

There are two South American countries where Indigenous peoples constitute the largest ethnic group. They are Peru, with forty-five percent Indigenous, and Bolivia, with sixty-two percent of people identified as part of an Indigenous group.

The Indigenous population in Guyana is approximately seven percent of the population. The Arawak and the Carib divide into two groups and seven sub-groups: Akawaio, Arekuna, Macusi, Patamona, Wapishana, Warrau, and Wai-Wai.

Arawak

Also known as Arowak and Lokono. They inhabit the Mabaruma, Mattarkai, Moruka, Pomeroon, and Wakapao areas along the Essequibo Coast, Mahaica, Mahaicony, and Berbice Rivers. The Arawaks were pioneer horticulturists.

About 3,500 years ago, they settled at Hosororo on the Aruka River in the country's northwest region. They also resided on the Corentyne River around 2,000 years ago, leaving their unique rock engraving, *Timehri*. To access the rich supply of protein found along the coastal swamps, they invented wooden shovels capable of moving tons of earth to build habitation mounds and raised fields for farming. They cultivated cassava (*Manioc esculenta* or sweet cassava, and *Manioc utilissima* or bitter cassava) on the elevated mounds. Cassava is used in making bread, farina, cassareep (a seasoning and preservative for meats), and poisons used on the tips of arrows. The Arawaks hunted during the rainy seasons when animals migrated from the lowlands in search of higher grounds. Among the animals commonly hunted were deer (*Odocoileus virginianus* and *Mazama Americana*), labba (*Agouti paca*), tapir (*Tapirus terrestris*), peccary, or wild hogs (*Tayassu pecari* and *Pecari tajacu*), agouti (*Dasyprocta agouti*), birds, and tortoises.

Carib

The earliest Caribs inhabited the upper Pomeroon River about 3,000 years ago. This tribe was unique in its mastery of painted ceramics. Their products have been distributed as far as the mouth of the Amazon River. The Caribs are the people who gave the Caribbean area its name. The word '*Carib*' refers to Indigenous groups throughout the Caribbean Islands and the South American mainland, north of the Amazon. Their language can be classified together as the Cariban language family, though certain material culture traits suggest an association with Colombia.

In Guyana, Carib groups are found in the Essequibo Lake District, Pomeroon, and the Northwest Districts, along the Cuyuni, Barama, Barima Rivers, and Demerara and Mahaicony Rivers.

Warau

Also known as Warrau, Warao, Guarao, Guarauno, Araote, Farut, Tirativa, Tivitivi, Uarau, Uarauno, and Uarow. They live in the Pomeroon area, Orealla, and the Corentyne River. The Waraus are believed to be the oldest known inhabitants of Guyana. This tribe is known archaeologically from the shell mounds of the North West Region, some dating back 7,000 years. They live in the low-lying coastal region between the Barima and the Pomeroon Rivers and their tributaries. The Waraus are called the '*water people*' because they built their houses on stilts over or close to the water. The Waraus are excellent fishermen and boat builders; they invented the dugout canoe, which was the earliest seaworthy vessel some 5000 years ago. To them, the palm tree is considered the tree of life. It provides them flour, juice, fruit, lumber for building houses, and leaves for thatching roofs and weaving hammocks.

The Waraus, who believe that their ancestors live in the "Sky Land," are unique in that they are the only representatives of the Warauan linguistic group in South America. Their language is known as an '*isolate*.'

Wapishana

Also known as Wapishana, Vapidiana, Wapixana, they are the most recent Indigenous migrants to Guyana; they arrived in the early 18th century from the Rio Negro area of Brazil. They are located in the Rupununi savannah and are described as the most reliable and industrious Guyanese tribes. They are more agriculturists than hunters and fishers. They were once noted for being the significant traders and canoe makers of the region. They also excel in the weaving of cotton hammocks, a skill they learned from the Macusi tribe. The Wapishana piaiman (shaman) is called '*marinau*,' and he has power over evil spirits, sickness, and diseases. The tribe's religious beliefs are centered on the spirits they call '*Durimas*.'

Patamona

The Macusi or '*Ingarikok*,' are also called: Ingariko, Eremagok, Kapon, Paramona, Paramuni, Partamona, and Patomana or people of the cool, wet place. The Patamonas of Guyana are located in the North of the Pakaraima Mountains. They are known archaeologically from pottery collections in the Yawong valley and the upper Siparuni River. The Patamona nation is the one to which the mystical figure '*Old Kaie*' belongs. Old Kaie is the Patamona Chief in the legend that explains how the magnificent Kaieteur Falls got its name. Kaieteur Falls is also referred to as Kayik Tuwuk or Old Man's Fall in the Patamona language.

After being steadily attacked by the Caribs, the village chief at the time, Kaie, sought a peaceful way out. He prayed humbly to the Makonaima, the great spirit of their people. The Great Spirit does not have a physical form and is never seen by mortal man. Makonaima spoke to Kaie, and he listened. One day in the act of self-sacrifice, Kaie took his wooden canoe and paddled faithfully over the waterfall. This was done in exchange for the protection of his tribe. He selflessly gave up his life in exchange for peace rather than starting a war between the tribes. This behavior is evidence of the harmonious and peace-loving lifestyle of the Patamona people. It is said that Kaie's canoe lies at the bottom of this great fall and has been turned to stone. Descendants of Kaie and his tribe live on the Potaro River, guiding travelers and protecting the life around Kaieteur Falls.

Macusi

Also known as Makushi, Makusi, Makuxi, Macusi, Macussi, Macoushi, Macuchy, Macuxi, Mahuchi, Mokushi, Teweya, and Teueia. This nation is described as the most beautiful one in Guyana; they live in the Northern Rupununi Savannahs and are especially noted for their love of order. They are uniquely skilled in the preparation of the deadly '*curare*' poison. Curare is derived from the plant *Chondrodendron tomentosum*. The alkaloid that curare possesses is *d*-tubocurarine which acts as a neurotoxin, shuts down the nervous system, and produces paralysis. The Indigenous peoples, especially the Macusi in the northern Rupununi savannahs, make a paste from the bark of the curare plant to smear the tips of arrows. Entire lakes or ponds are usually poisoned with the curare plant as a method of harvesting fish.

Arekuna

This nation is archaeologically unknown in Guyana is also referred to as Arecuna and Pemong; they are descendants of the Carib. They once occupied the upper and central Kamarang River from approximately 1839. They are currently concentrated at Paruima. Their outstanding contribution to Guyanese culture is the blowgun, a mysterious and awe-inspiring weapon. They are a powerful nation that produces and supplies cotton to the other tribes, especially the Macusi.

Wai-Wai

The Wai-Wais moved to Guyana from Brazil during the early 19th century. They occupy the headwaters of the Essequibo River. They are also referred to as Wai Wai, Uaiuai, Uaieue, Ouayeone, Parukota, Ouayeome, Ouayeoue, Waiwe, and Woyamana. They are one of the few nations that still use their traditional dress of loincloths and aprons or '*Keweyeu.*' The Wai-Wai tribe is the smallest group in Guyana. They are also included in the Carib-speaking group. The only Wai-Wai community is located in the southernmost region of the country known as Konashen.

The Wai-Wais are skilled weavers and bead workers. The traditional Waiwai architecture, exemplified in the Umana Yana, is considered by many as the embodiment of Indigenous architecture. The Umana Yana is a 55-foot high cone-shaped building (benab) made out of thatched allibanna and manicole palm leaves, wallaba posts, mukru, turu, and nabbi vines. In Guyana, the major vegetation used by the Indigenous peoples for thatched roofing includes the troolie palm, the cokerite palm, and the dhalebanna leaves; the construction of the benab did not require the use of nails. This benab is similar to the Wai-Wai benabs, or shelters found deep in Guyana's interior. It shelters an area of approximately 460 square meters.

Akawaio

Also known as Acewaio, Acawoio, Accawa, Akavais, Akawaio, Akawoio, Akawai, Acahuayo, Capohn, Capong, Kapohn, and Kapon. They are linguistic descendants of the Carib. They inhabit the Upper Mazaruni River basin, Pomeroon, Wenamu, and Upper Cuyuni Rivers and are the peddlers that are found on the coastal reservations. This nation was war-like and aggressive and was also noted for its blowguns. The Akawaios pioneered the occupation of the hinterland forests. Once an Akawaio became a friend, he remained a friend, but once an enemy, is an enemy for life. They were so dreaded that the other nations left them alone, and they became very independent.

The Life of the Indigenous Peoples

Regardless of the Nations of the Indigenous peoples, their commonality is their connection to the earth and the spirits. The Indigenous peoples have been and continue to remain spiritual beings. They are careful with their behavior and attitude toward life, respecting life and other life forces such as water, plants, animals, people, the sun, moon, elements, and ancestors. They are all known for their pride and sensitivity, hospitality, courage, intrepid spirit, dexterity, and connection to their environment. These proud Nations love liberty and have no desire for material wealth.

Approximately 470 million Indigenous people are living throughout the world today. They are referred to by many names: Tribes and Nations, First Nations, First Peoples, Native peoples, Aboriginal peoples, or Original peoples. In the Americas, they are referred to as American Indians. They also have distinct names, words, and phrases in their respective languages and communities to describe themselves. They are diverse and unique, with many distinctive cultures, languages, and traditions influenced by their relationship with each other and the natural world.

It is speculated that the Arawaks and Caribs migrated northward from mainland South America. They first appeared in the Guianas and then in the Caribbean Islands. The Arawaks, mainly cultivators, hunters, and fishermen, migrated to the Caribbean Islands before the Carib and settled throughout the region. The tranquility of the Arawak nation was disrupted by the arrival of the Carib from the hinterland of South America. The war-like Caribs migrated north and made an impact upon their arrival. At the end of the 15th century, the Caribs had displaced the Arawak throughout the islands of the Lesser Antilles of the Caribbean.

One of the legacies of the Indigenous peoples is the word '*Guiana,*' used to describe the region encompassing Guyana, Suriname, and French Guiana, which means '*Land of Waters.*' It is appropriate, considering the area's ocean, rivers, creeks, and lakes.

For administrative purposes, Guyana is divided into 10 regions:

Region 1: Barima/Waini
Region 2: Pomeroon/Supernaam
Region 3: Essequibo Islands/West Demerara
Region 4: Demerara/Mahaica
Region 5: Mahaica/West Berbice
Region 6: East Berbice/Corentyne
Region 7: Cuyuni/Mazaruni
Region 8: Potaro/Siparuni
Region 9: Upper Takutu/Upper Essequibo
Region 10: Upper Demerara/Upper Berbice

The population of the nine Indigenous tribes is scattered all over the country. The distribution is approximately: Akawaio (4,800), Arekuna (1,047), Arawak (16,000), Macusi (7,000), Wapishanas (7,000), Patamona (5,700), Wai-Wai (398), Warrau (4,800) and Carib (4,500). These Tribes belong to three different linguistic groups: the Arawakan, the Cariban, and the Warrauan. The Trio, Atorad, and Taruma are members of other tribes in Guyana. In most cases, they emigrated from neighboring countries and settled in Guyana. One example is the case of the Trio of Cashew Island in the New River area. Some linguistically different groups share common cultural features, while others, although linguistically similar, have nothing in common with culture, social organization, and spiritual life.

The Indigenous population has been subject to changes by the incursions of coastal and foreign mining companies on their traditional lands and the steady out-migration of the young and able-bodied to explore job prospects in neighboring Suriname, Venezuela and Brazil.

The Household Income and Expenditure Survey of 1993

carried out by the Government Statistical Bureau estimated that the Indigenous population of Guyana was 50,222 in a population of 707,458 people; approximately seven percent of the Guyanese population. The majority of the Native communities are located in the hinterland regions, accounting for up to 90 percent of the population. The most inaccessible regions are the Pakaraima and Upper-Mazaruni. Both are part of mountainous areas that spread out into Brazil and Venezuela. A considerable amount of the communities are also located along the rivers on the coast.

Accessibility to the Indigenous communities has improved over time, but because of the conditions of the roads and exorbitant cost of transportation, traveling in the hinterland regions is very challenging. The hinterland physically begins at Bartica, a town on the Mazaruni and Cuyuni Rivers. It is the business town for miners and loggers on their way to and from the hinterland.

The Indigenous people of Guyana still practice fishing, hunting, and agriculture; they live primarily simple, subsistence lives. In some regions, they live in well-established villages on land assigned as reservations. This has partly to do with the availability of services at specific catchment points or changes in the agricultural systems. The colonists introduced Cash-crop agricultural production but never dominated the economic lifestyle of the Indigenous peoples in the country. Despite the many social and cultural changes, the basic Indigenous People's lifestyles stayed intact. Their language, methods of transportation, and the use of traditional medicines have remained unchanged.

The Indigenous Nations of Guyana hold legal land titles. The Lands Commission advised for the recognition of most land titles during the decolonization years of Guyana. Indigenous peoples can claim that it was a condition of

Guyana's independence, lobbied for by Steven Campbell, the national hero of Guyana's Indigenous peoples. More than 16 percent of the national territory has the status of Indigenous land. Seventy-seven areas are designated as *Amerindian people's* land by the *Amerindian people's Act*. Many communities requested the extension of their lands, mainly because of overpopulation, which stresses the available community resources. Many of the lands surrounding their communities are in the hands of mining, large-scale cattle ranchers, and forestry companies.

The hinterland population suffered under structural adjustment because of their small numbers, marginalization, economic poverty, isolation in distant settlements, and high costs of access into the hinterland. In a recent colloquium on poverty in Guyana, Janette Forte of the Indigenous Peoples Research Unit at the University of Guyana described the Indigenous population as "comprising the poorest and most neglected stratum of the Guyanese society."

The levels of diseases, mortality, famine, and inadequacy of primary education are significantly higher than the non-Indigenous groups of the population. The lack of access to higher education, health care, and infrastructure lead to inadequate human resources and leadership qualities to direct communities and manage the appropriate development processes. That also results in high unemployment and abandonment of the culture by the young people who seek employment elsewhere in the country or neighboring countries. Many young men leave their extended families to work as miners or vaqueros far away from home. Even in the Pomeroon area, Indigenous men go to the Mazaruni district searching for employment in the mining or forestry industry. The elderly/ill-bodied and the women stay behind to take care of the farms and the children.

In the hinterland areas, access to health services is minimal. The infant and child mortality rates are higher since many deliveries in remote areas are done traditionally, outside the formal health care system. While the immunization program in the coastal regions is considered very successful, immunization only reaches about 25 percent of the children in the hinterland.

The high incidence of malaria in the hinterland regions has a heavy toll of morbidity, particularly in children. Maternal malnutrition in remote areas by far exceeds the national average. Since the early 1980s, malaria incidence has been limited to the interior regions, precisely those areas where the Indigenous population lives. The figures would have probably led to the declaration of a state of national emergency if they represented rates of infection of the coastal populations. Only a small number of cases occur on the coast, and this is attributed to the fact that the primary carrier, the *Aedes aegypti* mosquito, does not breed on the coast.

In 1990, malaria seemed to be on the wane, with a national total of 22,000 cases recorded. By the end of 1991, with the Dutch NGO Medicins Sans Frontiers winding up its anti-malaria program, the total jumped to 42,000. Concentrated at first in the Rupununi region, which accounted for 77 percent of the cases in 1982, malaria moved north and northwest until all Indigenous areas were affected. In 1992, the North West Region was recorded as having 71.6 percent of the population. In 1984, the incidence of infection was 5.9 percent.

The Wai-Wai living in the remote southern parts of Guyana were struck by malaria more severely than any other country. For the traditional living Indigenous people, malaria comes jointly with new invasions of miners in the Rio Novo area of Brazil. There is a similar pattern between the Indigenous people of Brazil, Venezuela, and Guyana's interior. The Yanomami tribe was struck by invasions of miners in their homelands and consequently malaria.

Tuberculosis screening hardly takes place in the interior, and consequently, the disease has gained ground again in combination with the expansion of malaria. Other diseases which often occur in Indigenous people's communities are gastrointestinal related diseases, intestinal parasites, snakebites, and respiratory infections. Despite the government's efforts, an efficient and effective health network in communication, distribution, and prevention is lacking; not having trained medical personnel, drug supply, and health infrastructure severely constrains effective health care in the hinterlands.

Agricultural production is the backbone of the Indigenous livelihood, as it has been for most people of Guyana. For the Indigenous nations, it also reflects their dependence on the land, a relationship dating back thousands of years. Since Indigenous villages are located in remote areas, transportation and communication costs and food production at the local level directly affect the diet and health of the people living in those parts of the country. Despite the many years of being involved in agricultural diversity and production, outputs continue to be below the national average.

Cassava is the staple food, but also yams, fruits, and cash crops are grown. The men clear and plant the fields, and the women and children are responsible for the maintenance. Most of the Indigenous communities have to rely on their leading crop, cassava, from which they make cassava bread, farina, and the traditional drinks, Parakari and Parawiri. The food security of Indigenous communities has become threatened due to the exhaustion of the natural resources in their environment. Land distribution and structural adjustment have influenced the situation. While many Indigenous communities seek land titles or requests for land extensions, the government sees itself obliged to make more land available for forestry and mining industries and other national economic activities.

As a result of the integration policies during the colonial and post-colonial era, Guyana's Indigenous peoples have become increasingly dependent upon coastal foods. The exploitation of the natural resources, on and in the proximity of Indigenous lands, created a shortage of the fish and meat that once sustained the communities. In some areas, instances of resistance in some communities to conservation parks directly resulted from that exploitation. In the Rupununi, for example, the Rupununi Development Company leased many Indigenous farms in the Kanuka Mountains for cattle raising purposes. When the European Community launched a biodiversity protection program for that mountain region, many Native farmers feared losing their last farmlands.

CHAPTER 4
Colonialism

MARXIST THEORIES CONTEND THAT TRADE EMAnates from colonialism and imperialism. Accordingly, trade implies an oppressor nation exploiting a weaker or oppressed nation. Trade becomes involuntary, leading to asymmetric or one-sided trade gains, with the colonial country achieving all of the trade gains. The colonized country suffers economic loss; that involuntary exploitative trade is far different from mutually beneficial trade.

Colonialism was practiced by empires such as Ancient Greece, Ancient Rome, Ancient Egypt, and Phoenicia (Turkey, Lebanon, Syria, and Palestine). Those civilizations extended their borders into surrounding and non-contiguous areas from about 3550 years ago. They established colonies that drew on the physical and population resources of the people they conquered in order to increase their power.

Modern colonialism began in the fifteenth century when

Portugal started looking for new trade routes and searching for civilizations outside Europe. In 1415, Portuguese explorers conquered Ceuta, a coastal town in North Africa, kicking off an empire that lasted until the end of the twentieth century.

Soon the Portuguese had conquered and populated Madeira and Cape Verde. Then their rival nation, Spain, decided to try exploration. In 1492, Christopher Columbus began looking for a western route to India and China. Instead, he landed in the Bahamas, kicking off the Spanish Empire. Spain and Portugal became locked in competition for new territories and took over Indigenous lands in the Americas, Africa, and Asia. England, the Netherlands, France, and Germany quickly began their own empire-building overseas, fighting Spain and Portugal for the right to lands they had already conquered.

Despite the growth of European colonies, some countries managed to gain independence during the eighteenth and nineteenth centuries, beginning with the American Revolution in 1776 and the Haitian Revolution in 1781.

In the 1880s, European nations focused on taking over African lands, racing one another to coveted natural resources, and establishing colonies that they would possess until decolonization between 1914 and 1975.

Colonial powers justify their conquests by asserting that they had a legal and religious obligation to take over the land and culture of Indigenous peoples. Conquering nations with the role of civilizing barbarous or savage nations, and argued that they were acting in the best interests of those whose lands and peoples they exploited. Despite their claim, the Indigenous people on all continents staged violent and nonviolent resistance to their conquerors. Colonial rule over Indigenous populations relied primarily on open violence, ranging from corporal punishment to full-scale war.

Colonial rule over Indigenous populations was based on structural violence in the context of the rapid transformation of the economy and society in favor of European interests. In frontier areas, individual violence dominated the expansion. The application of violence distinguishes imperialism from peaceful trade relations; it enters the scene and political actions. Extreme forms of violence in imperialism were slavery and massacres, which recent research has increasingly described as genocide.

The Pilgrims, who were decidedly staunch protestant puritans, were forced into exile around 1607 for resisting King James's edition of the holy bible and the Church of England. King James was anxious to populate the new North American colonies, so he let the Pilgrims sail there to practice their religion. Investors financed the voyages, and in return, the Pilgrims would send furs and other goods back to England for sale.

Assailed by storms during the Atlantic crossing, weather forced them north of their intended destination of the British colony of Virginia to land at Cape Cod on November 11, 1620. After finding no suitable home, the pilgrims sailed to Plymouth Bay and settled on an Indigenous American village. The Indigenous Americans of the Patuxent tribe greeted the pilgrims and negotiated a peace treaty with them in which they agreed to provide a mutual defense. That treaty led to the first American Thanksgiving as the Pilgrims celebrated their first harvest in November 1621.

Muslim resistance to colonialism has been documented in Sudan and other parts of Africa, including Senegambia, Somalia, and Northern Nigeria. While profoundly disturbing psychologically, everywhere in tropical Africa, the consequences of colonial rule on Islam's actual spread and institutional development were uneven. Germany's use of Muslims for administrative purposes in East Africa contributed to Islam's progress in the interior. Later, the same practice worked against its advancement by dividing government personnel from the Indigenous people's opposition to foreign domination. The most vigorous opposition to German colonial rule came in rebellion (*maji* in Swahili).

British colonialism replaced the German system after World War I and slowed the progress of Islam in East Africa. The system of indirect rule at the Local Government level protected the power of the local chiefs from being undermined by wealthy Muslim merchants from the coast. Christian schools became the main supply of local administrators, teachers, police, and army personnel. The perception of Christianity as the religion of progress was formed. At the same time, Islam, as it was gradually sidelined, came to be seen as an obstacle to advancement in the modern sector of the economy and politics.

By contrast with East Africa, British colonial rule in Northern Nigeria relied heavily on Muslim personnel to implement the indirect rule and even extended Muslim authority to cover the so-called '*pagan areas.*' Muslim schools were improved, and, as in Sudan, Colleges of Islamic Law were opened. What mainly assisted the spread of Islam during the colonial era was the improvement in communications. Simultaneously, the growing importance of western education was a disadvantage to Islam; it assisted Christianity.

Thailand avoided European colonialism; its modernist reforms were, by contrast, primarily the top-down process in which the brain applies what it knows to fill in the blanks and anticipate what is next. The reforming King Rama IV (Mongkut) reigned from 1852 to 1868. He had spent 27 years as a monk before ascending the throne. He emphasized strict adherence to the Pali canon, excluding later famous works that encouraged the laity to view the Buddha as a miracle worker. Mongkut's monastery was the center of becoming the Dhammayutika Nikaya, a new monastic order that stressed adherence to the Vinaya rules. Increasing centralization led Thailand to the Sangha Act of 1902. The government took effective control of the royal monasteries in the capital and monasteries and monks in Thailand. A national exam syllabus was established with textbooks written by Rama IV's son and the king's half-brother, Prince Wachirayan, who himself became the Supreme Patriarch of the Thai Sangha in 1910.

By the 20th century, a majority of nations were colonized by Europeans at some point. Colonization was linked to the spread of tens of millions from European countries all over the world. In many settled colonies, European settlers eventually formed the dominant power of the population after killing, driving away, or oppressing the Indigenous peoples. Examples include the Americas, Africa, India, Australia, and New Zealand. Those colonies were occasionally called *neo-Europes*. In other places, European settlers formed minority groups with more advanced resources and weaponry to dominate the Indigenous people at their homes.

When Britain started to settle in Australia, New Zealand, and other countries, they regarded the landmasses as '*terra nullius*,' meaning '*empty land*'. Due to the absence of European farming techniques on those lands, the lands were deemed unaltered by man and therefore classified as uninhabited, despite the presence of the Indigenous peoples.

The Indigenous peoples, also known in some regions as First peoples, First Nations, Aboriginal peoples, or Native peoples, are ethnic groups who are the original or earliest known inhabitants of an area. Groups are usually described as Indigenous when they maintain traditions or other aspects of a culture associated with a given region. Not all Indigenous peoples share that characteristic, as many have adopted substantial colonizing cultures, such as dress, religion, and language. Indigenous peoples may be settled in a given region, sedentary, or exhibit a nomadic lifestyle across a large territory. However, historically they are associated with a specific territory on which they depend. Indigenous societies are found in every inhabited climate zone and continent of the world except Antarctica.

Since Indigenous peoples are often faced with threats to their sovereignty, economic well-being, and access to the resources on which their cultures depend, political rights have been outlined in international law by international organizations such as the United Nations, the International Labor Organization, and the World Bank. In 2007, the United Nations issued a Declaration on the Rights of Indigenous Peoples (UNDRIP) to guide member-state national policies to the collective rights of Indigenous peoples, such as culture, identity, language, and access to employment, health, education, and natural resources. Estimates put the total population of Indigenous peoples at approximately 470 million.

Great Britain made its first tentative efforts to establish overseas settlements in the 16th century. The commercial ambitions and competition with France resulted in the establishment of settlements in the Americas. By 1670, British American colonies in New England, Virginia, and Maryland and settlements in Bermuda, Honduras, Antigua, Barbados, and Nova Scotia. Jamaica was obtained by conquest in 1655, and the Hudson's Bay Company established itself in northwestern Canada from the 1670s. The East India Company began establishing trading posts in India in 1600, and the Straits Settlements of Malaysia and Singapore became British through an extension of that company's activities. The first permanent British settlement on the African continent was made at James Island in the Gambia River in 1661. Slave trading had begun earlier in Sierra Leone, but that region did not become a British possession until 1787. Britain acquired the Cape of Good Hope, now South Africa, in 1806, and the South African interior was opened up by Boer and British pioneers under British control.

The early settlements arose from the enterprise of companies and magnates rather than from direct effort on the part of the British crown. The crown exercised rights of appointment and supervision, but the colonies were essentially self-managing enterprises. Thus, the formation of empires was an unorganized process based on piecemeal acquisition, with the British government being a partner in the enterprise.

Britain exercised control over its colonies in the seventeenth and eighteenth centuries, mainly in trade and shipping. Under the mercantilist philosophy, the colonies were regarded as a source of necessary raw materials for England. They were granted monopolies for their products, such as tobacco, rum, cotton, and sugar, in the British market. In return, they were expected to conduct all their trade through British ships and serve as markets for British manufactured goods. The Navigation Act of 1651 and subsequent acts set up a closed economy between Britain and its colonies; all colonial exports had to be shipped on British ships to the British market. All colonial imports had to come by way of England. The slave trade acquired peculiar importance to Britain's colonial economy in the Americas, and it became an economic necessity for the Caribbean colonies.

"There is no more significant pointer to the character of a society than the kind of history it writes or fails to write."-E. H. Carr. It follows that there is no more significant pointer to the character of British society than the exclusion of people of color from its history books. Throughout the centuries of the continuous presence of people of color in Great Britain, a few white people have had all the power in their hands. No person of color has had any influence at all, except the most token kind. White historians, almost without exception, have done their best to deprive people of color of their history, too. They have consistently belittled or wiped out the past of the people of color, which was essentially just another way of depriving people of color of power.

Students of color have seen the primary purpose of Black History as encouragement of Black pride and a feeling of personal worth. In 1899 a former headmaster of Harrow public school, whose task had been to train the sons of the ruling class, summed up his duties in these words:

> An English Headmaster, as he looks to the future of his pupils, will not forget that they are destined to be the citizens of the greatest empire under heaven; he will teach them patriotism... he will inspire them with faith in the divinely ordered mission of their country and their race.

After the end of the colonial empires, the word '*colonialism*' could only refer to a phenomenon from the past and thus fell out of use. Imperialism, however, continued to be used with domination that's comparable to what was practiced by the colonial powers. The word '*neocolonialism*' was also used for that purpose, but it was less successful. After the Second World War, America became the new superpower. Accordingly, imperialism was applied to describe the foreign policy of the United States of America concerning other countries, particularly in Latin America, Asia, and Africa. There was an attempt to make the concept applicable to the policy of the Soviet Union concerning the Central and Eastern European countries that came under its influence after 1945, but that was not very successful. The reason was that imperialism has connotations with capitalism, not with communism, and with overseas possessions, not with adjacent countries. Although there was a Soviet Empire, it was not considered an example of imperialism but traditional power politics. After the end of the Cold War, the word *'imperialism'* lost much of its earlier attraction. Vast, dominated, and politically active populations exist in subaltern positions in post-colonial societies.

In the Cold War atmosphere, Western powers, especially the newly pre-eminent United States, greatly feared radical new states emerging from wars of liberation and preferred to shape successor regimes and constitutions through an orderly pre-emptive process. Decolonization was not a true liberation that the new *Third World* received, but the problem of what would constitute genuine liberation and which groups merit it became increasingly complex. The predicament was for capital-poor ex-colonies by their re-establishment within the formal symmetries and limited liabilities of the United Nations model. From that perspective, the goal of liberation itself became a particular trap, as formally independent and autonomous political standing comes systematically to entail perpetual clientage, expanding debts, and ongoing substantive subservience to outside agencies and agendas.

Like the *free laborer* perceptively critiqued by Marx as free of all access to means of production, the independent states were, by their very freedom and formal equality, radically limiting the life chances of their citizens, especially their subalterns. It has been argued that endemic political violence is a phenomenon of democracy, especially in post-colonial conditions; conditions that engender a spiral of destructive, effervescent leveling crowds. The crowds do not seek liberation but razing, destruction of privileges perceived as unmerited, especially across ethnic lines.

CHAPTER 5

India and its Colonization

THE EAST INDIA COMPANY WAS A BRITISH COMPANY incorporated by royal charter on December 31, 1600, to exploit trade with India. Starting as a monopolistic trading body, the company became involved in politics and acted as an agent of British imperialism in India from the early 18th century to the mid-19th century. The East India Company, set up in 1600, was the first joint-stock company of any importance. Joint-stock Members invested capital is being used jointly and received a share of the profits according to the investment size. It was the East India Company that developed into British rule of India.

In 1608, three of the East India Company's ships visited the city of Surat, 150 miles north of Bombay, and four years later, another of its ships dispersed a Portuguese squadron off Surat. After nearly three years of haggling, the local ruler gave the Company permission to build a '*factory*' or permanent depot at Surat in 1619. From that first base, the English were soon controlling the Arabian Sea and the Persian Gulf. English imports of Gujarati calico pieces soared from 14,000 in 1619 to over 200,000 in 1625. In 1639 English merchants occupied what soon came to be called Madras, and within 20 years, became the most extensive factory on India's east coast. In 1661 King Charles II of England obtained the island of Bombay from the Portuguese. Bombay was a highly convenient trading base; the East India Company leased it in 1668, and the company transferred its headquarters there in 1687.

More than 100 English resident agents were stationed in India. They were able to ensure an average annual profit for the company of 25 percent. The company had its private army, and in 1751, it defeated a French puppet ruler. Three years later, the first British royal troops landed; that was supposed to be a temporary measure. For a large area of India, the combination of British royal troops and British merchant adventurers proved disastrous.

In the 1750s, the ruler of Bengal was trying to get the British out before they got him out. An adventurer named Robert Clive defeated the ruler's troops at the battle of Plassey in 1757. That was the decisive turning-point, not only for British domination of India but also for British extraction of wealth from India. From then on, trade would be supplemented by naked and rapacious plunder, backed by a force of arms. Clive told Pitt in 1759 that there would be little or no difficulty obtaining the absolute possession of those prosperous kingdoms.

In the initial period, before they had the means to plunder India directly, British merchant capitalists had been forced to use some of the profits from elsewhere in the colonial system to pay for the goods they bought from the Indians. At that stage, they had to offer wealth in return. They were offering silver bullion as payment each year. The English trade with India, as written by the economic historian L. C. A. Knowles, "was really a chase to find something that India would be willing to take, and the silver obtained by the sale of the slaves in the West Indies and Spanish America was all important in this connection." The battle of Plassey put an end once and for all to the need to send precious silver to India. Very soon, there was widespread rejoicing at the British army's glorious successes. It was of such proportion that they have been able to carry on the whole trade of India for three years without sending out one ounce of bullion.

For the East India Company, this was a dream come true. Now they could get their hands on India's wealth without having to send wealth in return. The first step was the assumption that they could collect revenue in Bengal, Bihar, and Orissa. There was traditionally in India an intimate relation between harvest and taxation. Before British rule, there was no private property on land. The self-governing village community handed over each year to the ruler or his nominee the King's share of the year's produce.

The East India Company considered this practice barbaric and put a stop to it. Under British rule, a new revenue system was introduced, superseding the traditional right of the village community over land and creating two new forms of property in land: In some parts of the country, landlordism; in others, individual peasant proprietorship. It was assumed that the State was the supreme landlord who introduced a system of fixed tax payments assessed on land. Under the new system, the cultivator had to pay a fixed sum to the government every year whether or not his crop had been successful. In years when the harvest was terrible, the cultivators could only pay their taxes by recourse to moneylenders, whom the British authorities regarded as the mainstay for the payment of revenue and who frequently charged interest of 200 percent annually or more.

A British writer later admitted, "we introduced at one time a method of assessing and cultivating the land revenue which have converted a once flourishing population into a huge horde of paupers." To raise the cash demanded, peasants were forced to sell their produce for whatever price it would fetch. The first effect of British rule in an Indian province was to reduce the incomes of the agricultural classes by 50 percent. The British conquest undermined the rural economy and the self-governing villages.

In 1769 the company prohibited the homework of the silk weavers and compelled them to work in its factories. The company's servants, who lined their pockets by private trading, bribery, and extortion, arbitrarily decided how much each weaver should deliver and how much he/she should receive for it. Weavers who disobeyed were seized, imprisoned, fined, or flogged. Weavers were unable to meet the company's obligations and had their possessions confiscated and sold on the spot. Bengal's ruler complained that the company's agents took away people's goods by force for a quarter of their value. The rulers then compelled the people to purchase from them for five times the value of the goods on pain of flogging or imprisonment.

By the 1770s, Bengal became one continued scene of oppression. Systematic plunder led to a famine in which 10 million people perished: Bengal was left naked, stripped of its surplus wealth and grain. In 1783, the natives of all ranks and orders were reduced to a state of depression and misery. Four years later, a former army officer, William Fullarton wrote:

> In former times the Bengal countries were the granary of nations, and the repository of

commerce, wealth and manufacture in the East. But such has been the restless energy of our misgovernment, that within the short space of twenty years many parts of those countries have been reduced to the appearance of a desert. The fields are no longer cultivated, extensive tracts are already overgrown with thickets, the husbandman is plundered, the manufacturer oppressed, famine has been repeatedly endured, and depopulation has ensued.

A Chancellor of the Exchequer frankly told the Commons in 1858 that "no civilized Government ever existed on the face of this earth which was more corrupt, more perfidious, and more rapacious than the Government of the East India Company from the years 1765 to 1784." The rapacity brought treasure flowing into Britain from the oceans. As India became poor and hungry, Britain became more prosperous than ever before. Clive was penniless when he first landed in India. He returned to Britain with just a third of the revenue he collected and went back home with a personal fortune estimated at £250,000. In that period, the Hindi word '*loot*' entered the English language. It has been estimated that, between the battle of Plassey in 1757 and the battle of Waterloo in 1815, Britain's loot from India was worth between £500 million and £1 billion.

This loot from India furnished the second of those special forced draughts needed to ignite Britain's industrial revolution. Close on the heels of the battle of Plassey came the harnessing of a critical series of inventions and technological advances. Hargreaves's spinning jenny (1764), Arkwright's water-frame (1769), and Crompton's mule (1779) broke with the old hand techniques. In 1785 came the next logical step: the adaptation of Watt's steam engine to drive them. Between 1767 and 1787, the output of cotton goods went up more than fivefold. The increase in productivity was explosive. Nevertheless, Britain's enrichment at the expense of the Indian people had only begun. In the nineteenth century, it was to take new and, in many ways, still more oppressive forms.

When European merchant adventurers first reached India, they found an industrially developed country; not at par with theirs but inferior to advanced European nations. India was a great agricultural country and manufacturing country. It had a prosperous textile industry, whose cotton, silk, and woolen products were marketed in Europe and elsewhere in Asia. It had remarkable and remarkably ancient skills in iron-working and its shipbuilding industry: Calcutta, Daman, Surat, Bombay, and Pegu were important shipbuilding centers. In 1802 skilled Indian workers were building British warships at the Bombay shipyard of Bomenjee and Manseckjee. It was generally acknowledged that the teak-wood vessels of Bombay were significantly superior to the oaken walls of Old England. Benares was famous all over India for its brass, copper, and bell-metal wares. Other important industries included the enameled jewelry and stone-carving of the Rajputana towns and filigree work in gold and silver, ivory, glass, tannery, perfumery, and paper-making.

British rule's long-term consequence was India's deindustrialization; it was forcibly transformed from a country of combined agriculture and manufacturing into an agricultural colony of British capitalism, exporting raw cotton, wool, jute, and oilseeds to Britain. The British annihilated the Indian textile industry with the fury of a forest fire; a dangerous competitor existed, and it had to be destroyed. The shipbuilding industry aroused the jealousy of British firms, and its progress and development were restricted by legislation. India's metalwork, glass and paper industries were likewise throttled. The latter was deprived of its greatest patron when Sir Charles Wood, Secretary of State for India, 1859-66, obliged the British government in India to use only British-made paper. The vacuum created by the contrived ruin of the Indian handicraft industries, a process virtually completed by 1880, was filled with British manufactured goods.

With its explosive increase in productivity in India, Britain's industrial revolution made it essential for British capitalists to find new markets. So in India, the previous monopoly had to give way to a free market. From an exporter of textiles, India had to become an importer of materials. British goods were virtually free entry, but the entry into Britain of Indian manufactured products, especially silks and kinds of cotton, had to be blocked by prohibitive tariffs. Furthermore, direct trade between India and the rest of the world had to be curtailed. By 1840 British silk and cotton goods imported into India paid a duty of only three-and-a-half percent, woolen goods a mere two percent. Equivalent Indian exports to Britain paid import duties of 10 to 30 percent.

The mills of Paisley and Manchester were created by the sacrifice of India's manufacturing industry. The foreign manufacturer employed the arm of political injustice to keep down and ultimately strangle a competitor with whom he could not have contended on equal terms.

There was prosperity for the British cotton industry but ruin for millions of Indian craftsmen and artisans. India's affluent manufacturing towns were blighted: towns like Surat, where it had all begun 200 years before; Decca, once known as the Manchester of India; Murshidabad, Bengal's old capital, in 1757 to be as extensive, populous, and wealthy as London. Millions of spinners and weavers were forced to seek a precarious living in the countryside, as were many tanners, smelters, and smiths. The development of Indian cotton mills in the 1870s, coupled with a trade slump in Britain, led Lancashire textile manufacturers to press for the total repeal of Indian cotton duties. It had given some small protection to the Indian cotton industry and retained labor in the industrial sector which could more usefully be employed to grow cotton for export to Lancashire. The Lancashire capitalists had their way.

In 1879 Viceroy Lytton overruled his entire council to accommodate Lancashire's lobby by removing all import duties on British-made cotton, despite India's desperate need for more revenue in a year of widespread famine. In the last 20 years of the nineteenth century, India's cloth production met less than 10 percent of home demand, while Lancashire products accounted for between one-half and two-thirds of India's annual imports.

Britain's Queen Victoria was proclaimed Empress of India in 1876, made India subservient to British industry, and its needs and was continuing to suck vast wealth out of the sub-continent. Generations of Indian economists and nationalist politicians, supported by a minimal number of British opponents of colonialism, complained of the drain of wealth and analyzed its mechanisms in copious detail. They proved their case with massive evidence from official sources and showed how economic exploitation was the root cause of the Indian people's poverty and hunger.

From time to time, officialdom was forced to curb the worst excesses. One example of that was the inquiry into the plantation system for cultivating indigo. That system began in 1833 when British people were allowed to acquire land in India and set up as planters. Many of those who started to grow indigo in the deltaic area of lower Bengal were experienced sugar planters from the colonies. As one economic historian puts it, the area attracted a rather rough set of planters, some of whom had been slave drivers in the colonies and carried unfortunate ideas and practices with them. Following was the so-called Blue Mutiny of 1859-60, the first strike by Indians against the British. An official inquiry brought to light monstrous abuses by the British planters and their Indian assistants. The Indigo Commission's report revealed the plantation system in Bengal was slavery under another name. Peasants who objected to sowing indigo were murdered; their houses were pulled down; they were kidnapped and locked up; their cattle were seized; their very gardens were grubbed up to make room for indigo. A hundred years later, the word '*indigo*,' to Indians, still stood for British greed, dishonesty, and oppression; unquestionably, that was one of the dark episodes in the history of Britain dealing with a subject people.

Although the abuses were checked from time to time, the abuse continued. Under Britain's imperial rule, the ordinary people of India grew steadily poorer. At the start of the twentieth century, the economic historian Romesh Dutt called Indian poverty "unparalleled." Half of India's annual net revenues of £44 million flowed out of India. The number of famines soared from seven in the first half of the nineteenth century to twenty-four in the second half. According to official figures, 28,825,000 Indians starved to death between 1854 and 1932. The terrible famine of 1899-1900 affected 475,000 square miles with a population of almost 60 million. It was attributed to a process of bleeding the peasants, who were forced into the clutches of money lenders whom the British authorities regarded as their mainstay for revenue payment.

Immediately after the First World War, the Indian national liberation movement began to adopt mass action. The strategy was nonviolent non-cooperation. One proposal by Mahatma Gandhi was that on a particular day, the entire country should observe a *hartal*, which is a day that everyone should stop working for and celebrate that day as a day of fasting and prayer. Following that day was the massacre of unarmed demonstrators at Amritsar on April 13, 1919. Troops commanded by Brigadier Reginald Dyer fired for ten minutes into a dense crowd in a walled enclosure, killing 379 and wounding 1,200. Martial law was proclaimed in Punjab, and there was a government reign of terror, with shootings, hangings, bombing from the air, and harsh prison sentences.

A wave of strikes in 1918-1920 affected Bombay, Calcutta, Madras, Cawnpore, Ahmedabad, and other industrial centers signaled the entry of the Indian working class into the liberation movement. Besides economic strikes, workers staged a political rally against the Rowlatt Act, giving the government power to imprison people without trial. In 1930, Gandhi led a mass movement campaign to boycott imported cloth. Gandhi and 90,000 others were imprisoned.

When the Second World War began, both Gandhi and Nehru expressed sympathy for Britain. However, Subhas Chundra Bose, a former Congress president and leader of the Forward Bloc, supported Congress resolutions opposing the use of Indian resources in the interests of British Imperialism. In August 1942, Gandhi and all other Congress leaders were arrested, and the Congress was declared an illegal body.

The 1943 Bengal famine killed as many as three million people. Recent studies indicate that the responsibility rested squarely on Winston Churchill's shoulders. Most of the famines in India were caused by severe droughts. However, Churchill's wartime cabinet made this one significantly worse, and its decision to plunder India's resources to keep the war machine going. Rice, in particular, was imported to other parts of the empire in significant quantities, and despite multiple warnings and pleas by local officials the country was mainly left without emergency food supplies. So, while India might have survived Japan's conquest of primary rice sources in Myanmar, assorted natural disasters, and bad crops, the British government's decision to leave them without supplies to cushion the blow proved catastrophic.

Britain's decision to strip India of rice was part of their '*denial policy*', which meant that should Japanese forces attempt to invade the region, they would have no supplies readily available. As for Churchill, he reportedly stated that the reason for the famine was that Indians were breeding like rabbits.

That was how it struck the delegation that visited India on behalf of the India League in 1932. The delegation, one of whose members Ellen Wilkinson was later Minister of Education in the 1945 Labor government, spent 83 days in India, meeting Indians of every class and shade of opinion. In their report, *Condition of India* (1934), they said they had been appalled at the poverty of the Indian village. It is the home of stark want. From province to province, conditions vary, but the results of uneconomic agriculture, peasant indebtedness, excessive taxation and rack-renting, absence of social services, and the general discontent impressed us everywhere. In the villages, there were no health or sanitary services; there were no roads, no drainage or lighting, and no proper water supply beyond the village well. Men, women, and children work in the fields, farms, and cowsheds. Everyone works on meager food and comfort and toil long hours for inadequate rectums.

In short, throughout the British occupation, millions of Indians could never get enough food, and at least two-thirds of the people connected, directly or indirectly, with agriculture lived in a state of squalor. On the eve of the British withdrawal in 1947, Jawaharlal Nehru wrote that those parts of India which had been longest under British rule were the poorest: "Bengal, once so rich and flourishing, after 187 years of British rule is a miserable mass of poverty-stricken, starving, and dying people."

The entry into Britain of comparatively small numbers of colored settlers; a few hundred in 1948-1950, about 1,000 in 1951, and 2,000 in 1952 and again in 1953, led to a discussion in the Cabinet. The discussions were not made public until the release of the Cabinet paper. A volume of memoirs published in 1973 stated that early in 1955, Churchill proposed *'Keep Britain White'* as a good slogan for the Election. Churchill was at that time the peacemaker of state racism. In 1952, he inquired if the Post Office was employing colored workers and expressed the risk of such action creating social problems.

The Cabinet asked the Home Secretary to arrange for officials of the Department concerned to examine the possibilities of preventing any further increase in the number of colored people seeking employment in this country. At the same time, the Chancellor of the Exchequer was asked to look into the possibility of restricting people of color obtaining admission to the Civil Service. Churchill was also telling officials of the Ministry of Labor that he would not regard unfavorably proposals designed to restrict the entry of colored workers into Great Britain. Churchill told the Governor of Jamaica, Sir Hugh Foot, that Britain would have a magpie society that would never be accepted.

A Cabinet Working Party on Colored People Seeking Employment in the U.K. was set up in 1953-56. The Cabinet sought information from the Police and staff of labor exchanges. The Police reported that the people of color are work-shy and content to live on national assistance and immoral earnings. The report included that they are poor workmen with a poor mentality who will only work for short periods. Police in industrial areas reported that people of color generally are not suited to many forms of work, Indians and Pakistanis are unscrupulous and usually not successful in work requiring much skill and intellect.

In Newcastle, Glasgow, and Nottingham, the Police condemn Asians as not engaging in practical or productive work. They merely live in the community and produce nothing. West Africans were described as lazy and arrogant, and they associate with prostitutes and are confirmed gamblers. The Police assured the House Secretary that the practice of black men living on the immoral earnings of white women was much more widespread than the number of convictions would appear to indicate. The men of color played a large part in the illicit traffic of Indian hemp. According to Ministry of Labor informants, black workers were more volatile in temperament than white workers. They found it had to accept discipline and were more easily provoked to violence. In the midlands, the view was held by managers of labor exchanges that black workers were physically and temperamentally unsuited to the kind of work available in industrial areas. As for black women, they are slow mentally and find considerable difficulty adapting themselves to working conditions in this country. The speed of work in modern factories is said to be quite beyond their capacity. On the other hand, they have been found to give reasonably reliable service as domestics in hospitals, institutions, and private domestic employment.

CHAPTER 6

Africa and its Colonization

THE EARLIEST AFRICAN EMPIRES SOUTH OF THE Sahara desert were in West Africa. The Empires developed when most of Europe was experiencing the Dark Age, after the fall of the Western half of the Roman Empire around 476. The people of West Africa were smelting iron ore to make tools for warfare and agriculture. Farming tools made of iron made agricultural methods more efficient; that led to improvements in agriculture and greater land productivity; as prosperity grew, the population expanded, giving rise to larger towns. Broad rivers linked people in the larger towns by way of boats. The rivers also maintained the fertility of the soil year-round. At the same time, kingdoms were developing in the region. One of the earliest kingdoms to emerge was Ghana to the far West. By the year 300, the Ghana Kingdom was ruled by about 40 Kings, indicating that its political administration was well developed to allow new kings to take office without destroying the Kingdom by fighting civil wars. The economy of Ghana was based on iron, gold mining, and agriculture. Products were traded with Berber societies north of the Sahara desert.

During the tenth to the fifteenth centuries, the Empires of Ghana, Mali, and Songhay influenced many trade practices. Those powerful empires would extend their power over African trade by directing trade routes through the major cities and taxing the traveling merchants and their goods. Through the power of the empires, many of the trade routes were secured, and the merchant profession became a prosperous one. When traveling, traders could travel individually or in groups or attach themselves to an annual caravan. In addition, local or residential tribes would establish and maintain resting posts for the traveling merchants along the trade routes. The scouts often used those trading posts to guide the caravans along the correct trade routes.

During 1230-1300, the Mali kingdom of the Mande people to the East of Ghana was growing and extending its control of trade in the region. That took the two kingdoms into conflict, and the Mali kingdom took over the Ghana kingdom. The Mali kingdom was able to establish its influence with ease due to the surrounding savannah terrain. It enabled the easy and speedy dispatch of soldiers across the region to conquer neighbors. The adoption of the Islamic faith by the Mali people during the rule of Kankan Musa created a point of unity for the Kingdom.

In 1312 the most famous Malian King, Mansa Musa, came to power. Mansa Musa's reign marks the golden age of the Mali Empire, spreading its territory and fame far and wide. Under Mansa Musa, the empire reached as far as the Atlantic Ocean in the West and past the trading cities of Timbuktu and Gao in the East, encompassing the past Kingdom of Ghana in its entirety, and was home to an estimated five to ten million people.

The twelfth through the sixteenth centuries was known as the *Golden Age* of Africa. West African gold was in high demand. As a result, the Trans-Saharan trade routes were established for trade, travel, and scholarship. Much of what scholars know of the Trans-Saharan trade routes comes from scholars such as Ibn Battuta and Leo Africanus, who crossed the Sahara Desert in the 14th and 15th centuries. Their literary narratives combined with archaeological data provide much insight into the fourteenth-century African trade.

In 1352–1353, Ibn Battuta embarked on a pilgrimage from Morocco to the Mali Empire. Throughout his travels, he described aspects of the Trans-Saharan trade routes he encountered to Mali. He passed through Morocco and much of the Niger Bend. Battuta chronicled everything he saw. The trade routes from Sijilmasa to Walata passed through the salt mines of Taghaza. The town of Takeda in the Niger Bend was a center for copper mining and trade in Egyptian goods. The routes from Morocco to Egypt were large distribution centers for gold.

While trade along the Trans-Saharan trade route was common in the fourteenth century, it depended on the powerful African Empires. The Mali Empire, the Kingdom of Kongo, Benin Kingdom, Hausa City-states, Great Zimbabwe, Ethiopian Empire, Kilwa Sultanate, and the Ajuran Sultanate flourished. The Mali Empire had a cultural flowering centered at the University of Timbuktu.

Timbuktu, one of the world's first universities, dominated the world for producing outstanding scholars. Timbuktu ranked high alongside great empires in Ghana and Songhai. The University of Timbuktu was in a city that was already thriving in the twelfth century. The city of Timbuktu had the largest university of any nation at that time. It was proof of the talents, creativity, and ingenuity of the African people. Timbuktu mystified European explorers for centuries. The ancient mosques, tombs and monuments of the university in Timbuktu comprised the Masajid of Djinguereber, the Masajid of Sidi Yahya, and the Masajid of Sankore. In Islamic tradition, Timbuktu played a significant role in spreading Islam in West Africa starting in 1329.

At its peak, the university at Timbuktu had an average attendance of around 25,000 students in a city of approximately 100,000 people. Within the university's curriculum, various learning degrees were called primary, secondary, superior, and the Circle of Knowledge. Other subjects included literature, science, mathematics, and medicine. Leo Africanus, a sixteenth-century historian, wrote about Timbuktu:

> There are many judges, doctors, and clerics here, all receiving good salaries from King Askia Mohammed of the State of Songhay. He pays great respect to men of learning. There is a great demand for books, and more profit is made from the trade- in books than from any other line of business.

Timbuktu and its literature represent the history that restores self-respect, pride, honor, and dignity that slavery, colonialism, and racism have stripped away from the African people.

Apart from being the epicenter of knowledge, Timbuktu was a prosperous nation that served strategically as the epicenter of global trade routes following the Niger River. It was the center of the world because all gold to the continent of Europe came from there. That was the city where trans-Saharan commerce took place. Merchants from different locations carried out trade between Europe and Mali. Because of its unique geographical position, Timbuktu was a natural meeting point of Songhai, Wangara, Fulani, Tuareg, and Arabs. The inhabitants of Timbuktu traded in gold from the south, salt from the north, and the Divine knowledge came from Timbuktu. Timbuktu was therefore referred to as the crossroads where *the camels met the canoes*. As a result, Timbuktu became an important port where goods from West Africa arrived from the eleventh century onwards.

It took months for merchants to cross the Sahara Desert, and they faced challenges ranging from natural disasters to lost caravans. Travelers who ventured too far away from their caravans and got lost often died from the elements. If scouts died or strayed away from their groups, the caravans would get lost in the desert. Even worse, natural disasters, such as sand storms or fluctuating temperatures, often forced merchants to abandon their goods to save their own lives. In his memoir, Battuta described the Sahara as a "desert haunted by demons."

Mansa Musa's global fame came as a result of his Hajj in 1324 CE. He set out with a vast entourage across the Sahara desert toward Mecca. In Cairo, he initially refused to visit the sultan. Eventually, he made a compromise and bowed before Allah in the presence of the sultan. After the encounter, the sultan honored Mansa Musa by inviting him to sit beside him as an equal. The tradition was for the visitor to bow before him, and Musa believed himself to be of superior rank and power. According to the Islamic writer Al-Umari, Mansa Musa brought no less than 100 camels laden with 300 pounds of gold each and 60,000 people wearing silk, 12,000 servants, and 500 gold-staff bearing slaves before him. Al-Umari stated:

Let me add that gold in Egypt had enjoyed a high rate of exchange up to the moment of their [Mansa Musa's] arrival. The gold medal that year had not fallen below twenty-five drachmas. But from that day onward, its value dwindled; the exchange was ruined, and even now it has not recovered. The mitqal scarcely touches twenty-two drachmas. That is how it has been for twelve years from that time, because of the great amounts of gold they brought into Egypt and spent there.

On his return journey to Mali, Mansa Musa brought many scholars, artisans, architects, and other men of learning. They built many magnificent structures, including the mosque of Gao and buildings in Timbuktu. He also established a diplomatic relationship with the sultan of Morocco, with the two kings mutually sending ambassadors to the other's court. Mansa Musa had a lifelong dedication to education and sent many young men to be educated at the university in Fez, Morocco, who eventually returned and began Quranic schools and universities in many Malian cities. The tale of the wealth of the Mansa of Mali spread far around the globe, making the Malian Empire one of the most famous African empires. Mansa Musa has been claimed to have been the wealthiest person to have ever lived.

By the fourteenth century, empires such as Ghana and Mali had strong ties with the Muslim world, and many of their most prominent leaders practiced the Muslim faith. Mali's most famous ruler, Mansa Musa, traveled across the Trans-Saharan trade routes on his pilgrimage to Mecca in 1325. Islam became so prominent in North and West Africa that Muslim nations controlled many trade routes and caravan networks. During the fourteenth and fifteenth centuries, the primary trading goods along the Trans-Saharan trade routes were gold, salt, precious metals, such as copper and iron, ivory, spices, materials, such as skins, cloth, and leather. Trade among the Sahara Desert was highly influenced by the prominent Western empires and the local people living along the trade routes.

Since the origin of the religion, Islam's influence was evident in the culture where its followers would inhabit. Since religion affects significant aspects of its follower's lifestyle, it influenced family values, social conduct, and even judicial practices of the surrounding communities. As Muslims conquered land, the practices of Islam would spread wherever they went. Islam primarily spread its influence to the Northern and Eastern coasts of Africa.

In 1415, the Spanish Reconquista forced most of the Muslims out of Spain and into North Africa. During that transition from the Almohad Empire to the Muslim tri-state era, trade between Europe and North Africa increased the wealth of the primarily Muslim region and their ability to maintain power in the Sahara. In addition, their control of the gold trade routes led to the rise of the great Mali Empire.

Quarrels over who should succeed the throne and rebellion by the Fulani people in Senegambia and the Songhai people in Gao led to the collapse of the Mali kingdom in the sixteenth century. Songhai became independent of Mali and rivaled it as the supreme power in West Africa. The Songhai had settled on both banks of the middle Niger River. In the 15th century, they established a state that unified much of western Sudan and developed into a brilliant Nation. It was ruled by the dynasty or royal family of Sonni from the thirteenth century to the late fifteenth century. The capital was Gao, a city surrounded by a wall. It was a tremendous cosmopolitan marketplace in which kola nuts, gold, ivory, slaves, spices, palm oil, and precious woods were traded for salt, cloth, arms, horses, and copper.

Islam had been introduced to the Royal Courts of Songhai in 1019, but most people remained faithful to their traditional religion. Sonni Ali reorganized the army, which was equipped with a fleet on the Niger River. Foot soldiers captured the best men of the defeated armies and formed an elite cavalry that was fast and tough. They wore iron breastplates underneath their battle tunics. The foot soldiers were armed with spears, arrows, and leather or copper shields. A group of trumpeters produced military music. The entire army comprised 30,000 infantry and 10,000 equestrians. The Songhai defense system was the largest organized force in western Sudan; it was a political instrument and an economic weapon by its booty. They conquered the cities of Timbuktu and Jenne. Muslim scholars at Timbuktu called Sonni Ali tyrannical, cruel, and impious.

The Sunnis were driven from power by the Muslim Askiya dynasty. The new monarchy based at Gao had centralized and absolute, and sacred power. It was possible to approach him only in a horizontal position. He sat on a raised platform surrounded by 700 eunuchs. People paid taxes to the King in return for internal and external security. The Royal Court was responsible for the administration and the army. Large estates belonging to nobles were worked by laborers that did the fishing, animal raising for milk, meat and skins, and agricultural work.

The Songhai kingdom was the last major one in the region. However, its fall did not bring an end to kingdoms in West Africa. Kingdoms that survived were Guinea, Benin in Nigeria, Ashanti in present-day Ghana, and Dahomey, north of Benin. These kingdoms continued the Trans Saharan trade with the Arab states in North Africa. The Trans Saharan trade was complex. It was not limited to trade and to exchange gold, copper, iron, kola nuts, cloth, and salt. It was also about close cooperation and interdependence between kingdoms south of the Sahara and north of the Sahara. Salt from the Sahara desert was just as crucial to the economies and kingdoms south of the Sahara as gold was for those in the north. Therefore, the exchange of those commodities was vital for the economic and political stability of the region.

Trade significantly influenced the course of history in West Africa. The wealth made through trade was used to build larger kingdoms and empires. The kingdoms built strong armies to protect its interest. Kingdoms that desired more trade control also developed strong armies to expand their kingdoms and protect them from the competition.

Long-distance trade helped the local economy and supported internal trade. For example, merchants traveling between towns across the Sahara needed places to rest and stock up with food for the journey across the Sahara desert. Food would be provided by local markets that relied on local farms for supplies. That practice allowed merchants to plan long trips knowing that local markets would provide food and shelter. Many kingdoms in West Africa encouraged agricultural improvements to meet that need. It meant uniting small farmers, traders, and societies into more substantial trading blocs. For example, in present-day Congo, the Kuba Kingdom brought together different cultures under a single authority and used the Congo River as the main transport link to other distant kingdoms. Smaller traders joined with each other like the Chokwe and Lunda kingdoms under a single broad-based trade. That practice led to an increase in ivory and rubber trade between the kingdoms and Portuguese traders.

The slave trade was also crucial for the economic development of West Africa. For a very long time, West African kingdoms had relied on slaves to carry out heavy work. For example, the Songhai kingdom under the rule of Askia Mohammed used slaves as soldiers. In addition, slaves were trusted not to overthrow their rulers and were given important positions as royal advisers. Songhai rulers believed that slaves could be trusted to provide unbiased advice, unlike other citizens who held a personal stake in decisions. One group of slaves was known as palace slaves or the Arbi; they served mainly as craftsperson, potters, woodworkers, and musicians. Slaves also worked on village farms to help produce enough food to supply the growing population in towns.

The Asante Kingdom of the Akan people grew in the 15th and 16th centuries into a powerful kingdom in the most southern parts of West Africa, present-day Ghana. The growth was made possible by the rich gold mines found in the Kingdom. The Akan people used their gold to buy slaves from the Portuguese. In 1482, the Portuguese interested in obtaining Asante gold had opened a trading port at El Mina. As a result, the first slave trade in West Africa was with the Akan people. The Portuguese brought the slaves from the Kingdom of Benin, near the Niger Delta in Nigeria. Slave labor made it easy for the Akan people to increase agricultural production. The shift transformed the Asante Kingdom into a wealthy agricultural and mining economy.

The Akan people needed slaves to work their gold mines and farms. Passing traders and a growing population in the Asante towns demanded increasing supplies of food. The slave trade with the Portuguese continued until the early 1700s. The Akan people supplied the Portuguese with slaves to work on sugar plantations in Brazil. A small number of slaves were kept in the Asante kingdom. However, by that period, the Atlantic slave trade dominated trade with West Africa. Kingdoms like the Asante and Dahomey used their power to raid societies like the Bambara, Mende, and Fulani for slaves. The Kingdom of Benin is the only known Kingdom in West Africa to abolish slave trading in Benin. The slave trade ban was successful and forced the Portuguese to search for slaves elsewhere in West Africa. However, Dutch traders took over the role, and from the 1600s, the Dutch dominated the West African and Atlantic Slave trade.

The European planter's group dominated political, economic, and social life in the nineteenth century. Although they were the smallest group in terms of numbers, they had links to British commercial interests in London and often enjoyed close ties to the Governor appointed by the monarch. That group also controlled exports and the working conditions of the majority of the population. The following social stratum consisted of a small number of freed slaves, many of mixed African and European heritages, and some merchants. Finally, at the lowest level of society was the majority, the African slaves who lived and worked wherever the plantations were.

There was a great demand from the West Indies sugar plantations for African slaves. The Fon people used their position as sea-merchants to ensure that they held a monopoly of the slave trade. The Dahomey kingdom also relied on its strong military to dominate weaker inland states and conquer coastal states. States looking to trade in the region were expected to pay a fixed tax and fixed prices for slaves. Custom duties were paid in respect of each ship as well.

When Europeans occupied Brazil, the Caribbean, the Guianas, and North America, the need for a massive labor force was greater than in Western Europe. The land was fertile for growing sugar, coffee, and cotton. Large plantations were created to fulfill the ever-growing demand for the crops. The success of those plantations depended on the availability of a permanent, plentiful, identifiable, and skilled labor supply. As Africans were already familiar with animal husbandry and farming in general, had an identifying skin color and could be readily supplied by the existing African slave trade, they became the source of that need. That process set the stage for the expansion of the slave trade into the Americas.

The introduction of grueling labor-intensive crops such as sugar cane, cotton, and coffee demanded the colonists turn to African laborers. Although seeking a trade route to India, the Portuguese also set up forts along the West African coast to export slaves to Europe. Historically, by the year 1500, ten percent of the population of Lisbon and Seville consisted of slaves. Because of the influence of the Catholic Church, which frowned on the enslavement of Christians, European slave traders expanded their reach to the coast of Africa.

The Atlantic slave trade took about 11 million enslaved Africans to the Americas. Africa became Portugal's only concern after signing the Treaty of Tordesillas with Spain in 1494; the two Kingdoms agreed that Spain would have exclusive rights to the western route to the Indies while Portugal would have a monopoly on the African route. Portuguese merchants were, therefore, the lawful providers of enslaved Africans to Spanish colonists in the Caribbean. At first, they received individual asientos, the Spanish royal license to sell slaves in its colonies.

French and Dutch ships were also challenging Spanish supremacy in the Caribbean and the Portuguese control of the Atlantic Slave Trade. However, from the Iberian perspective, they were all pirates. Thus, in 1595 the Spanish Crown tried to regulate the trade by officially giving the Portuguese a monopoly over the asiento.

From the 1620s to the 1650s, England and France claimed their colonial settlements in the Caribbean. However, the importation of enslaved Africans intensified after 1660, when sugar estates began to outpace tobacco farms in British Guiana, St Kitts, Barbados, Antigua, Martinique, and Guadeloupe. As a result, from the 1660s, the number of enslaved Africans transported across the Atlantic more than doubled.

In 1634, the Dutch West India Company occupied Aruba, Bonaire and Curaçao, and Guiana on the mainland of South America. Then, in 1662, after capturing Elmina and other Portuguese trading posts on the West African coast, the Dutch made Curaçao the center of their slave trade in the Caribbean and the source of thousands of slaves heading into French and Spanish colonies. Thus, when France succeeded in putting a member of its ruling Bourbon family on the Spanish throne, it appeared likely that French slave traders would dominate commerce with Spanish colonies.

In 1713, the British gained the Spanish asiento, and with the exclusive rights to this niche market, they raised slave-trading profits to record heights. Thus, European imperial competition over colonial profits in slave trading had a massive impact on the African diaspora in the Caribbean.

In the 1700s, sugar became a mass-market commodity in Europe, a staple of the middle-class diet and eventually for the working classes. Caribbean sugar became the most valuable overseas possessions of France and Britain.

The empires believed that they had to increase the enslaved working population in the colonies to increase sugar production. An example was Santo Domingo, which grew from an abandoned part of Spanish Hispaniola (Haiti) in the early 1600s to become France's most valuable colony globally by the 1780s. Santo Domingo produced more sugar than all the British Caribbean colonies combined, and it was also a leading producer of coffee, Indigo, and cotton. The colony's extraordinary production level was directly related to its enormous population of enslaved Africans. In 1789, ninety-nine slave ships arrived in Santo Domingo, unloading more than 27,000 enslaved men, women, and children. That year, the colonial census stated that 455,000 enslaved people lived together with 31,000 whites and 28,000 free people of color.

By the eighteenth century, the triangular route that European slave ships took was becoming somewhat standardized. American slave ships followed a less triangular course. Most vessels departed from European ports loaded with manufactured goods specifically chosen for the African market, including cloth, iron tools, tobacco, rum, and cowry shells from the Indian Ocean. They traded those with African merchants in exchange for enslaved people and provisions. From that point, captains could stop in the Lesser Antilles or proceed west to Santo Domingo or Jamaica. Those bound for Spanish markets often went to a continental port like Cartagena in Colombia. They sold or traded their enslaved Africans for products like sugar, coffee, cacao, and cotton.

The late eighteenth century was the zenith of buying, transporting, and selling Africans into Caribbean slavery. Changes in ship design and more precise navigation drastically reduced the time to travel across the Atlantic, increasing the number of enslaved people reaching the Americas. The changes even cut the transatlantic mortality rates from about twenty percent in the sixteenth century to less than ten percent. Also, the European governments subsidized the African trade, making it illegal for their colonists to buy from foreign ships. Instead, they used their navies to defend their slave-trading routes and depots along the African coast. While they initially restricted the African slave trade by assigning it to monopolies, by the 1730s, most had opened it up to all of their national merchants in selected ports. More traders hustling the open market in a highly efficient system were satisfying the Caribbean estates' seemingly insatiable labor demands.

In any uneventful ocean crossings, a ship captain took back to Europe a sum many times greater than the initial investment. However, many things could go wrong with this complicated series of voyages, including rebellions, bad market conditions, illness, storms, and hostile ships. Debates over the trade's profits have yielded opposed numbers. Roger Anstey proposed a 10 percent annual profit, while Joseph Inikori's studies suggested an average of 27 percent. The business's risky nature seems to point to high but volatile returns.

Slave traders bound for the Caribbean took about 80 percent of their captives from a vast coastline stretching 5,600 km along the West and Central African coast. They began with the nation of Senegal in the north to Angola in the south. It also penetrated the African interior to 800 to 1,600 km inland. About 20 percent overall came from the region of Mozambique.

The list of African ports involved in commerce changed many times in the long history of the trade. African coastal rulers and merchants controlled the supply of captives, so events in Africa were responsible for most changes in the location of the trade. Leaders involved in wars sold their captives to European ships, and those profits encouraged Africans to fight each other and raid unprotected villages deep in the interior.

After the 1670s, British slave traders outnumbered other European merchants; new coastal areas became significant exporters. The British favored Benin, Nigeria, southeast Niger, and the Gold Coast: Ghana, Burkina Faso, eastern Ivory Coast, and southern Niger. African rulers exchanged captives for guns. Rulers competed with each other, so the acquisition of guns provided an advantage over their rivals and increased their drive to capture and sell slaves. The new availability of guns was a direct consequence of the slave trade. The mass importation of guns for slaves altered warfare in Africa and changed the balance of power between kingdoms. At the height of the Atlantic slave trade, only states equipped with guns could resist attacks from their neighbors. The demand for slaves, combined with the supply of guns, encouraged rulers to attack their neighbors.

Approximately 12 million enslaved Africans were transported across the Atlantic as human property from the sixteenth to the nineteenth century. The most common routes formed what is now known as the *Triangle Trade*, connecting Europe, Africa, and the Americas. For example, from 1560 to 1850, about 4.8 million enslaved people were transported to Brazil; 4.7 million were sent to the Caribbean; at least 388,000, or 4 percent of those who survived the Middle Passage, arrived in North America. Between 1700 and 1808, the most active years of the international slave trade, around 40% of enslaved Africans were transported in British and American ships.

Not all Africans involved in the slave-trading business were victims, nor were Europeans villains or the only villains. Some Europeans were very active in abolishing the slave trade and the emancipation of slavery, though they did so only after two hundred years of slavery. Many African rulers and merchants were also slave-dealers who sold their fellow Africans to the European slave traders. The Europeans took full advantage of the divisions among African rulers. Some were rewarded and encouraged to promote war with their neighbors to create situations to capture and sell their people as slaves.

According to Dr. Walter Rodney, more than 15 million Africans landed in the Americas. However, Africa lost 40-50 million of its population altogether to the slave trade. Dr. Rodney stated:

Rapine and plunder, organized man-hunts, kidnapping that bred more kidnapping, deterioration in the customary law – all these lay behind the façade of relatively orderly and peaceful agreements between European slavers and coastal chiefs. The rulers benefited by receiving the best cloth, drinking the most alcohol, and preserving the widest collection of durable items for prestige purposes. It is this factor of realized self-interest which goes some way towards explaining the otherwise incomprehensible actions of Africans towards Africans.

Dr. Rodney also pointed out that:

> Slaves of West Africa could not be sold except for serious offences. They had their own plots of land and/or right to a proportion of the fruits of their labour. They could marry, and their children had rights of inheritance. They could rise to positions of great Trust. Clearly there is a great difference between this form of servitude and the plantation slavery practised in the Caribbean.

In 1807 the British Parliament abolished the slave trade, and the British Navy began to suppress it. After four centuries of unequal trade, the time had developed Europe and underdeveloped Africa to form a single colonialist system. In the latter part of the nineteenth century, European capitalism's needs were: New sources of raw materials, new markets for manufactured goods, and cheap labor.

British colonies in Africa

As Britain distorted India's economy to obtain as much wealth as possible, it distorted Africa's economy for the same purpose. European traders destroyed the African cloth industry by controlling the distribution of manufactured cloth. As a result, Africa was exporting cotton and importing manufactured cotton products. Moreover, the only technology that Britain was willing to transfer to Africa was firearms; requests for other skills and techniques were rejected.

Following the abolition of the slave trade, there was a scramble for resources where the labor was almost free; the focus was Africa, and Britain grabbed the lion's share. The Gambia was occupied since 1662, Sierra Leone in 1807; Nigeria in 1886; Southern Gold Coast in 1874; The Cape of Good Hope in 1806; Natal in 1843; Basutoland (Lesotho) in 1868; Bechuanaland (Botswana) 1885; Somaliland 1886; Zululand (KwaZulu-Natal, South Africa) 1887; Kenya 1888; Rhodesia (Zimbabwe and Zambia) 1888-93; Zanzibar 1890; Uganda 1890-96; Nyasaland (Malawi) 1891; Ashanti (Ghana) 1901; Egypt 1882; Sudan 1899. The colony of the Gold Coast was established in 1902.

Following the First World War, which was above all a war for the redistribution of loot, Britain received a League of Nations mandate to administer some of the former German colonies in Africa. Britain and Belgium shared the former German East Africa. The British share Tanzania territory. Britain and France shared Cameroon and Togo. German South-West Africa went to the Union of South Africa. Those acquisitions were controlled by capitalist groups and companies such as the United African Company, a subsidiary of Unilever.

Africa's greatest value to Britain's capitalism was its ability to satisfy the need for raw materials such as cotton, rubber, and palm oil. Eventually, the time came when gentlemen's agreements about trading were no longer enough, and that arrangement was replaced by colonial domination.

At a conference in Berlin in 1884-1885, Britain, Germany, Belgium, France, Italy, Portugal, and other European countries met to formulate their plans for the territorial division of Africa. Their goals were pursued with vigor, greed, and devastating fire-power. The Maxim machine gun was invented at the time of the Berlin conference. It was one that the Europeans were not prepared to export to Africa, but for their use to bring 10 million square miles of Africa and over 100 million Africans under their rule. Sir John Scott Keltie said in 1893, "We have witnessed one of the most remarkable episodes in the history of the world. During the past eight years we have seen the bulk of one barbarous continent parceled out among the most civilized powers of Europe."

Colonial domination intensified the underdevelopment of Africa. Mr. Kwame Nkrumah wrote of pre-independence Ghana:

> Under colonial rule, foreign monopoly interests had our whole economy tied up to suit themselves. In a country whose output of cocoa is the largest in the world, there was not a single chocolate factory. While we produce the raw materials for the manufacturing of soap and edible fats, palm products; the manufacture of these items was discouraged. A British firm owning lime plantations here actually expresses the juice from the fruit before shipping it in bulk to the United Kingdom and exporting it back to us, bottled, to retail in stores at a high price. These facts have a kind of Alice in Wonderland

craziness about them. They are implicit in the whole concept and policy of colonialism. It is estimated that during the last thirty years of British colonial administration, British trading and shipping interests out of our country totaled £300,000,000. Just imagine what might have been done by way of development if only part of these gigantic transfers of profit had been retained and used for the benefit of our people by the end of the colonial era, the African continent as a whole remained economically backward. Africa was developed, above all, to supply export crops and raw materials to meet the needs of Europe.

Nigeria was Britain's largest colony. The House of Commons Select Committee on Estimates reported in 1948 that Nigeria had one doctor for every 133,000 people compared to one for every 1,200 in the UK. It has one hospital bed for every 3,700 people compared to one for every 250 in the UK. There were ten dentists in the country. Tuberculosis accounted for an estimated 9 to 10 percent of all deaths, yet the colony had no sanatorium; the disease was treated in ordinary hospitals with long waiting lists. Some patients had to be placed on the floor. Out of 8,000,000 children under the age of 16 years, 7,300,000 received no education at all. In 1934, when 41 Africans were killed in a gold mine disaster, the employers offered £3 to each worker's dependents.

In 1652, a Dutch colony was established at the Cape of Good Hope; eventually, they became migrant farmers Afrikaners. Britain took control of the Cape during the Anglo-French wars of 1793-1815.

In the 1850s, Britain made Natal a native settlement.

The African Bantu-speaking people and San and Khoikhoi, Southern Africa's original inhabitants, were persuaded to move to the settlement. That was the beginning of apartheid, a system where the Native Africans performed manual work for most white settlers on their farms, towns, and villages, and homes at meager wages. Sir Theophilus Shepstone, Secretary for Native Affairs, spent 30 years shaping Natal's racial policy. By 1860, he put the first large-scale segregation policy into operation in which 80,000 Africans were settled in the *Native Reserve*. A commission established eight locations with an area of 1,168,000 acres that was laid down by Britain Colonial Secretary, Earl Grey, as a South African policy that stressed the need for labor from the African communities with the anticipation that the location system would force the Africans to work for the white settlers. In a message to Sir H.G. Smith, Governor of the Cape, Earl Grey wrote:

> I regard it as desirable that these people should be placed in circumstances in which they should find regular industry necessary for their subsistence. Every encouragement should be afforded to the younger natives to become servants in the families of the European settlers. Any native who may have quitted his location to reside elsewhere would become amenable to the general law of the district; but he should not be allowed to leave the location without a pass, and I concur in [the]suggestion, that each adult should be distinguished by a plate or medal, with the number of the station to which they may belong.

Earl Grey also suggested that enough space be provided between the locations to permit the spread of white settlements.

In addition, it would be convenient for European emigrants to have a supply of labor nearby. In 1853 Earl Grey stated:

> If the Africans could be made to exchange their barbarous habits for those of civilized life, the presence of these people would be of greatest possible advantage to the Colonists, by affording them a supply of labor, which is urgently required, and which alone is wanting to render a territory possessing remarkable natural advantages productive, these people could also create a demand for articles of European manufacture which would increase both the trade and revenue of the Colony.

Eventually, the Bantu Kingdoms were subjected to white control; the Xhosa, Griqua, Nguni, Zulu, Sotho, Tswana, Swazi, Mpondo, and Venda were being subjected one way or the other. The Xhosa were driven to desperation by land settlement plans of Sir George Grey, the Governor of the Cape Colony. The communities were divided into small groups and distributed among Afrikaner farmers as apprentices.

Protests by the Natives were dealt with by economic warfare whereby land and mineral rights were bought, and the King and his council were persuaded to sign away the entire country and all rights over future development. The Swazi said, "It was the document that killed us." In 1894, one of Cecil Rhodes biographers described one incident:

> Rhodes travelled down to Pondoland (Eastern Cape) in a coach and eight cream horses, some machine-guns and eight policemen announced that he proposed to annex Pondoland and sent

for Sigcau, the King. He then offered to show Sigcau what would happen to him and his tribe if there was any further unpleasantness, took him to the where the machine-guns were trained on a mealie-field, opened fire on the mealies and brought down the crop, Sigcau noted the lesson, and ceded his country.

Cecil Rhodes famously said: "Remember that you are an Englishman, and have consequently won first prize in the lottery of life."

In the 19th century, British colonial administrations and subsequent South African governments had established '*Reserves*' in 1913 and 1936, intending to segregate Native South Africans from the white British and Dutch settlers. In 1948, the Minister for Native Affairs and later Prime Minister of South Africa, Hendrik Frensch Verwoerd, built on that by introducing a series of measures that reshaped South African society so that whites would be the demographic majority. The creation of the homelands or Bantustans was a central element of that strategy, as the long-term goal was to make the Bantustans independent. As a result, the Native South Africans would lose their South African citizenship and voting rights, allowing whites to remain in control of South Africa.

CHAPTER 7
The Colonization of Guyana

THE NETHERLANDS OBTAINED INDEPENDENCE FROM Spain in the late sixteenth century. By the early seventeenth century, it emerged as a significant commercial power, trading with English and French colonies in the Lesser Antilles. The Netherlands first arrived in Guyana in 1580. They established settlements and built forts at several places in the country. In 1616 they established the first European settlement, a trading post twenty-five kilometers upstream from the mouth of The Essequibo River. Other settlements followed, usually a few kilometers inland on the large rivers.

In 1621 the Government of the Netherlands gave the newly formed Dutch West India Company complete control over the trading post on the Essequibo River. That Dutch commercial concern administered the colony known as Essequibo for more than 170 years. Although the Dutch colonizers were initially motivated by the prospect of trade in the Caribbean, their possessions became significant producers of crops. The growing importance of agriculture was indicated by exporting 15,000 kilograms of tobacco from Essequibo in 1623. The company established a second colony on Berbice River in 1627. Although under the general jurisdiction of this private group, the settlement named Berbice was governed separately. Demerara, situated between Essequibo and Berbice, was not settled until 1741 and emerged in 1773 as a separate colony under the direct control of the Dutch West India Company.

The initial purpose of Dutch settlements was trading with the Indigenous peoples. The Dutch aim soon changed to acquiring territories as other European powers gained colonies elsewhere in the region. Although Guyana was claimed by the Spanish, who sent periodic patrols through the region, the Dutch gained control over the region early in the seventeenth century. The signing of the Treaty of Munster in 1648 officially recognized Dutch sovereignty.

As the agricultural productivity of the Dutch colonies increased, a labor shortage emerged. The Indigenous populations were reluctant to work on plantations. Many of them died from the stressful situations they had to deal with and diseases introduced by the Europeans. The Dutch West India Company turned to the importation of enslaved Africans. The Africans became the critical element in the colonial economy. By the 1660s, the enslaved African population numbered about 2,500. With their arrival, the Indigenous population of about 50,000 retreated into the hinterland.

By the middle of the eighteenth century, the Dutch had established themselves in all sections of the Essequibo region, using Kykoveral and later Fort Island as their bases of operations. Dutch traders and their agents, whom the Director-General appointed, traveled to various locations by foot and canoes. They established contacts with various

Native communities to trade European goods for annatto dye, letter-wood, and crab oil. The Essequibo River was established as the primary communication route. By the third decade of the century, a post was set up at the junction of the Siparuni and Essequibo Rivers. In 1756, the post, known as Arinda, was shifted further upwards to the junction of the Rupununi and Essequibo Rivers.

They established several institutions, including in 1718 a Council of Policy and Justice, to deal with Government and Judicial matters. The Dutch established a Court of Policy in 1732 as the law-making body and was accepted as the first law-making body of the country. On May 26, 1739, a Constitution was established by the Dutch. In 1750, the Council of Justice was separated from the Council of Policy.

Eager to attract more settlers, the Dutch authorities opened the area near the Demerara River to British immigrants in 1746. British plantation owners in the Lesser Antilles were plagued by poor soil and erosion, and many were lured to the Dutch colonies by richer soils and the promise of land ownership. The influx of British citizens was so rapid that by 1760 the English constituted a majority of the European population of Demerara.

During the American War of Independence, which began in 1776, the French joined the Americans in fighting the British. Even though the Dutch remained neutral, they carried out contraband trade and were the American suppliers. Therefore, the British decided to seize the Dutch colonies to prevent them from being used as depots for shipping goods to the Americans. In 1781, the British took control of Essequibo and Demerara without resistance. When they arrived with four privateering ships, the British allowed the settlers to retain their property, but properties of the West India Company were seized.

In Berbice, Governor Pieter Hendrik Koppiers, on learning of the capture of Essequibo and Demerara, organized his small militia to show resistance. However, it could do nothing when the British arrived on the Berbice River and seized Fort St. Andries. As the privateers moved upriver, the crew burned buildings at Plantation Vryheid, where there was some resistance from the Dutch. Shortly after, Fort Nassau was captured. Governor Koppiers reluctantly ceded the colony to a British representative who had arrived from Demerara. As with the case of Essequibo and Demerara, the Dutch planters were allowed to keep their property, and Koppiers continued with the post as Governor. With the British in control of the colonies, there was an influx of British settlers from Barbados. They were given land grants along the coast to cultivate sugar, cotton, and coffee. Since sugar cane proved to be the most lucrative crop, most new settlers abandoned coffee and cotton cultivation and concentrated on sugar cane.

As economic growth accelerated in Demerara and Essequibo, strains began to appear in the relations between the planters and the Dutch West India Company. Administrative reforms during the early 1770s had significantly increased the cost of government. The company periodically sought to raise taxes to cover the expenditures and thereby provoked the resistance of the planters. In 1781 a war broke out between the Netherlands and Britain, which resulted in the British occupation of Berbice, Essequibo, and Demerara.

In 1782, France allied with the Netherlands and seized control of the colonies. The French governed for two years, during which time they constructed a new town, Longchamps, at the mouth of the Demerara River. When peace was established, the colonies were handed back to the Dutch. After regaining power in 1784, the Dutch moved their colonial capital to Longchamps, which they renamed Stabroek. In 1812 that capital was renamed Georgetown by the British.

During their occupation, the British surveyed Essequibo along the coast to a point beyond the Barima River and inside the great mouth of the Orinoco. A map was drafted by the officer in charge of that expedition and was later published in London in 1783. A note on the map indicated the western boundary of the colony as Barima River. However, it was shown that the boundary is Amakura River, which is about fifteen kilometers southwest of Barima River.

By 1786 the internal affairs of the Dutch colony were effectively under British control, although two-thirds of the plantation owners were still Dutch. Towards the end of the eighteenth century, there was much discussion among Spanish officials about the measures to protect their frontier between the Orinoco and the Cuyuni. In 1787, a Spanish missionary in the Orinoco Region, Fray Thomas de Matraro, wrote to Don Miguel Marmion, Governor of Guiana, that "where the Cuyuni and the Yuruan join, there is a convenient site to build a strong house or fort to stop the passage of the Indians so that they might not go to Essequibo, and to prevent the entry of the Dutch to these Missions and savannahs."

On July 10, 1788, Governor Marmion, after setting forth, outlined a scheme for further settlement of the lands upon the frontier. He considered that the south bank of the Orinoco from the point of the Barima, about 100 kilometers inland to the Curucima Creek, being low lying and swampy, should be disregarded as useless. He also proposed that the frontier should run along that creek along the ridge of the Imataka Mountains to south-south-east to Cuyuni River, Mazaruni River, and to the Essequibo. The report added that the frontier should then follow the Essequibo to its source.

Governor Marmion explained that the Dutch traversed

the Cuyuni in canoes and thus carried on their traffic with slaves, merchandise, and other country products. There was no obstacle to prevent them from coming in and going out every time they wished to inspect the Spanish possessions. He urged the Spanish authorities to settle the savannah region on the upper Cuyuni to stop the Dutch, who had already occupied the Cuyuni, from continually extending their colony. He recognized that the frontier settlement could not begin near the boundaries of the Dutch possessions on the Cuyuni because of the cost and difficulty of transporting cattle, provisions, and other necessities to such a distance. It was also challenging to find colonists willing to settle on remote land devoid of communication.

Governor Marmion treated the junction of the Uruan and the Cuyuni as the limit of the Spanish territory in that direction. He considered that by holding the mouth of the Uruan, the Spaniards would secure all the territory they held and all that they could desire to settle. Those areas in the upper basin of the Cuyuni were later awarded to Venezuela by the Arbitral Tribunal in 1899.

Up to the end of the eighteenth century, Spanish control of the district to the east and south of the Orinoco was confined to the sites of their actual settlements and Missions. There was a minimal occupation of outlying territory to the east of the river. There was no attempt to develop the country's resources by opening mines, timber felling, or fishing and hunting. Such enterprises did not fall within the scheme of the Mission. The poor relations between the Spanish missionaries and the Indigenous Peoples outside the Missions would have rendered them impossible.

The return of Dutch rule reignited conflict between the planters of Essequibo and Demerara and the Dutch West India Company. Disturbed by plans for an increase in the slave tax and a reduction in their representation on the colony's

Judicial and Policy Councils, the colonists petitioned the Dutch Government to consider their grievances. In response, a special committee was appointed, which proceeded to draw up a report called the Concept Plan of Redress. That document called for far-reaching constitutional reforms and later became the basis of the British governmental structure.

The plan proposed a decision-making body to be known as the Court of Policy. The judiciary consisted of two courts of justice, one serving Demerara and the other serving Essequibo. The Court of Policy and the Courts of Justice would consist of company officials and planters who owned more than twenty-five slaves.

The Dutch Commission, which was assigned the responsibility of implementing the new system of government, returned to the Netherlands with extremely unfavorable reports concerning the Dutch West India Company's administration. Therefore, the company's charter was allowed to expire in 1792, and the Concept Plan of Redress was put into effect in Demerara and Essequibo. Renamed the United Colony of Demerara and Essequibo, the area then came under the direct control of the Dutch Government. Berbice maintained its status as a separate colony.

In 1795 the French occupied the Netherlands. The British declared war on France and, in 1796, launched an expeditionary force from Barbados to occupy the Dutch colonies. The British takeover was bloodless, and the local Dutch administration of the colony was left relatively uninterrupted under the constitution provided by the Concept Plan of Redress. Both Berbice and the United Colony of Demerara and Essequibo were under British control from 1796 to 1802. The Treaty of Amiens returned the colonies to Dutch control. Peace was short-lived; war between Britain and France resumed in less than a year.

The formation of British Guiana

In 1803 the United Colonies of Essequibo/Demerara and Berbice were seized once more by British troops. At the London Convention of 1814, both colonies were formally ceded to Britain. In 1831, Berbice and the United Colony of Demerara/Essequibo were unified as British Guiana. The colony remained under British control until independence in 1966.

After the Colonies of Essequibo, Demerara, and Berbice were united and became the Colony of British Guiana, the principal Dutch Institutions of the Court of Policy, the College of Financial Representatives, the Court of Justice, the College of Electors, and the Combined Court further continued in existence by the British, although substantially Dutch in character, until 1928.

In 1832, the voting age was lowered from 25 years to 21 years. Two years later, the Public Building was completed and formally handed over to the Committee of the Court of Policy on August 5, 1834. The Public Building became the law-making body of the colony.

In 1835, to be qualified to vote, one must be paying direct taxes of 70 guilders (£5) per annum. In 1836, to be qualified, one must be assessed to pay direct taxes on an income of not less than 2,001 guilders (£143). In 1849, only male British subjects with specific property qualifications were allowed to vote. Voting by women was withdrawn. In 1875, Castellani, an Italian Architect, constructed the coffered ceiling of the Parliament Chamber in the Public Building. It was done in pastel hues of pink, green, blue, and off-white.

In 1889, the Inter-Parliamentary Union began, and in 1891, the British amended the Political Constitution of the colony by the British Guiana Constitution Ordinance, 1891 (No. 1 of 1891). The franchise was lowered. The income qualification for voting, which was reduced from $600 (£125) to $480 (£100) per annum, was further reduced to £75.

Britain's relentless pursuit of its selfish ends was the official version of our history, smugly identified with service to humanity; deeds were glorified, and ulterior motives were attributed to everybody else. The essential racism of the official version of history is seen in its glorification of the British Empire and its arrogant attitude to those who were the *Empire's Subjects*. Throughout the Empire and in Britain, the history of people of color has been the precise opposite of the official myths. By disguising or glorifying the true history of colonialism and writing people of color out of British history, the official historians have marginalized and thus further oppressed those whose history they have distorted or concealed. The distortions and omissions have had the explicit purpose of maintaining the existing segregation.

The Development of the Cities

Georgetown

Shortly after the British seized the colonies, under the command of the Lieutenant Governor and Lieutenant Colonel Robert Kingston, a fort was constructed at the mouth of the Demerara River to protect the harbor. The fort was named Fort St. George, and near to it were the administrative buildings to house the Government of Demerara. The British also began laying out the town in the vicinity of the fort, where a tiny settlement started to develop.

In January 1782, a French fleet arrived, and the British were forced to surrender the colonies. Immediately, the new French administrators set about to build a town at the mouth of the Demerara River. Persons wishing to live in the new town were requested to apply for lots. Slaves dug two parallel canals running east from the Demerara River, and the dirt which was excavated was used to build a dam between the canals. Settlers in the new town built their houses on both sides of the embankment, which was later surfaced with bricks made from burnt clay. The resulting road later became known as Brickdam.

The canals which ran at the back of the houses served as passageways for cargo. The town was first called Longchamps, but the name was changed to La Nouvelle Ville, literally New Town. The French also built two forts at the mouth of the Demerara River; the fort on the eastern side was named Le Dauphin, and that on the western bank was named La Reine.

In Berbice, the French dismissed Governor Koppiers, but they continued the policy of the British of granting lands on the coast for cultivation. When the war ended in 1783, the colonies were handed back to the Dutch, who immediately renamed the new town Stabroek after the West India Company president. Numerous canals were dug to ensure good drainage, and small sluices, called kokers, were built to control the drainage system. Streets were also laid out in a rectangular pattern and were later lined with trees. By 1789, the town had 88 houses and 780 residents.

Between 1783 and 1800, small towns were building up around Stabroek. First was New Town which the French initially established in 1782. American traders set up offices close to the river in that area and built a wharf where American trading ships discharged and loaded their goods. That wharf became known as American Stelling, and the road in the vicinity became known as America Street.

The main street of Stabroek was Brickdam which was about one mile long. A muddy embankment was made to keep back the water of the Demerara River. That embankment became Water Street. Water Street was gradually strengthened by spreading debris from fires on the surface.

The British began to expand road-building in the town

in 1796. In 1797, a road which later became known as High Street was built. Camp Street was laid out in 1805. At that time, Plantation Vlissingen, a coffee plantation, occupied a large area north of Stabroek. In 1804, its owner, Daly, obtained permission to convert part of the plantation into a town. That section was bought by a Mr. Lacy who renamed it Lacytown and built three bridges over the boundary canal to link it with Stabroek and a neighboring new ward, Cummingsburg, initially owned by a Scotsman, Thomas Cumming.

Later, Plantation Vlissingen came under Joseph Bourda, and from that plantation were later carved out Robb's Town (Robbstown) and Newtown. Robb's town was initially known as Bridgetown because of the Barbadians who settled there. However, when John Robb leased a large part of the district and started a housing scheme, the area became known as Robb's Town.

Cummingsburg was originally an estate known as La Bourgade owned by Thomas Cumming, who served as a member of the Court of Policy. He sold off lots along the bank of the Demerara River to merchants who wanted to build warehouses. The area east of Main Street to Cummings Street, divided into residential lots, was named Cummingsburg. In the area occupied by Main Street and Cummings Street, canals were connected by other canals running east-west to the Demerara River. As time went by, some of those canals were filled in to form streets.

Kingston started when barracks were built to house British troops. That ward eventually incorporated a plantation owned by Ms. Eve Leary. Soon the elite of the society set up residences in that locality. Werk-en-Rust was initially a plantation south of Stabroek. Towards the end of the eighteenth century, the owners began selling land close to Demerara River to saw millers. Initially, people did not want to live in Werk-en-Rust because a cemetery was there. However, as the demand for living space arose, people decided to settle there, and by 1799, it became an extension of Stabroek.

As the urban area expanded, there came a need for the establishment of various services. J.C. de La Coste attempted in 1790 to publish a newspaper. He imported a printing machine, but the newspaper business was not successful. The government set up a post office in 1796. In the same year, the idle newspaper printing machine was bought by Mrs. Volkerts, who employed two Barbadian printing technicians and obtained contracts to print Government notices. Not too long after, she began publishing the first known Guyanese newspaper, the *Royal Essequibo and Demerara Gazette*.

Medical services were first organized during the French occupation (1782-83). However, the British built the first hospital in 1796 to treat British troops afflicted by yellow fever. A Guyana store was later built at that site. A few years later, a hospital for sailors was built at the site occupied by the Museum.

When the British re-occupied Guyana in 1803, the entire urban area at the mouth of the Demerara River was referred to as Stabroek; in 1812, it was renamed Georgetown. Like the *Burgs,* Stabroek became *Wards* of the newly renamed capital of Essequibo/Demerara.

Major General Hugh Lyle Carmichael was appointed Governor of Demerara/Essequibo in 1812. In May of that year, Stabroek became Georgetown after the heir to the British throne, who later became George IV. Then in October, on behalf of the government, he purchased an area of land in Cummingsburg for a Parade Ground. Towards the end of the century, half was used to develop the Promenade Gardens, while the other half remained as the Parade Ground.

New Amsterdam

In 1784 when Berbice was restored to the Dutch, engineer Herlin was sent from Amsterdam to build a town in the growing settlement at the Berbice and Canje Rivers junction. The land was cleared of the forest and divided into quarter-acre lots, and soon a few houses were erected. By 1791, the town, named New Amsterdam, was firmly established and became the new capital of Berbice; soon, Governor Van Batenburg moved into a newly built Government House.

The States-General of the Netherlands was concerned that the trading activities of both the West India Company and the Berbice Association were conducted more for the benefit of those two organizations than for the Dutch nation. As a result, the company's charter failed to win renewal in 1791, and Essequibo/Demerara was placed under the control of a Council of Colonies, a Dutch government department. Four years later, the charter of the Berbice Association was canceled, and the colony was put under the control of a Committee of Colonial Affairs in Amsterdam.

In 1796, Essequibo/Demerara and Berbice were seized by the British. Governor Van Batenburg retained his position as Governor of Berbice, and the British continued granting land to settlers who migrated from Barbados. Over a hundred new cotton plantations were established, and slaves were imported in more significant numbers. The slave population grew from 8,232 to 17,885 during the period 1796-1802. Large land areas were also put up for sale by the colony's government, and much of those were bought by Lord Seaforth, who became Governor of Barbados in 1801.

CHAPTER 8
Enslaved Africans in Guyana

THE GUIANAS, THE *WILD COAST*, BETWEEN THE Amazon and Orinoco Rivers, was fought over by French, British, and Dutch colonists. Sugar, coffee, cotton, and cocoa plantations thrived in the Dutch West India Company districts administered outposts at Demerara, Essequibo, and Berbice.

The exact date of the first arrival of enslaved Africans in Guyana is unknown, but it is believed that the first group was brought by Dutch settlers as early as 1630. By 1674, the West India Company shipped approximately 84,000 slaves from Africa to Brazil, Guiana, and Curaçao. However, the drive for colonies and the years of war against Spain and Portugal had exhausted the West Indian Company's capital and brought it close to bankruptcy.

The Middle Passage trip between the African and American continents took roughly 80 days on ships ranging from small schooners to massive, purpose-built slave ships. Humans were packed on and below decks without space to sit up or move around, without ventilation or sufficient water. Approximately fifteen percent of them became sick and died on the voyage.

In addition to the physical violations the enslaved people suffered, they were torn from their families, homelands, social positions, and languages. Still, despite the vast cultural and linguistic diversity, they found ways to understand each other. Those who endured the journey of the middle passage were unable to record their stories; their names and identity were lost from historical records. In the New World, Africans transformed elements of their cultures into the creolized societies of the African diaspora. Widespread southern and Caribbean food traditions, music, and religious rituals in the New World have been traced back to African roots.

In 1562 the Englishman John Hawkins assembled a group of financiers to invest in the slave trade. He set sail for the African coast, where he hijacked a Portuguese slave ship near Sierra Leone. Hawkins took the enslaved Africans and sold 301 of them to Spanish colonists in the Caribbean. The extraordinary profits he took home generated English interest in the slave-trading business.

From the 1650s, the West India Company was haunted by financial problems that made it almost impossible to invest in the Atlantic trading network. When several plans to reform the company failed, the State's General finally decided to dissolve the West India Company in September 1674. However, the slave trade to the Guiana colonies and Caribbean islands remained under the company's control until the 1730s. Between 1674 and 1739, the West India Company shipped approximately 187,000 slaves from Africa to the colonies. Of those, 5.1% from Senegambia, 15.8% from Sierra Leone, 17.8% from the Windward Coast, 68.5% from the Gold Coast, 28.8% from Benin, 16.1% from Biafra and Guinea, 91.4% from the West Coast, and 35.5% from elsewhere, arrived in British Guiana.

As plantations expanded on the coast of Guiana, more slaves were brought from Western Africa, and there were occasions when planters bought slaves smuggled from the West Indies by other traders. On the arrival of a slave ship at different ports in Berbice, Essequibo, and Demerara, auctions were held, and planters came from all over to find bargains. The slaves were exposed naked and were closely inspected by the prospective buyers to determine if they were healthy. They were made to jump, swing their arms and legs, and were examined like farm animals. Entire families were auctioned, but buyers showed no concern over family bonds by making purchases that separated husbands and wives and children from parents. Friends and relatives were also separated from each other in the process.

The slaves were housed in buildings that were some distance away from the master's house on the plantations. Most of the slave houses were thatched roofs and walls of old boards or wattle and mud. The floors were the earth itself, and there was no furniture except some rudimentary pieces that the slaves, over time, managed to make.

While the slaves were provided with certain foodstuffs by their masters, they raised their subsistence crops. Vegetables, plantains, and root crops were grown on small garden plots that the master allowed them to use. However, they could only do their farming on Sundays when they were not required to work on the plantation. They also took the opportunity to fish on Sundays in the nearby canals, rivers, or oceans. Each adult slave was given one pound of salted codfish every Sunday by the plantation owner. The salted codfish was imported from North America. A child slave was given a smaller allocation.

On special Christian holidays, there was an additional allowance of about a pound of beef or pork, some sugar, and a quantity of rum.

The slaves also obtained a clothing allowance roughly every year. The men received a coarse woolen jacket, a hat, about six yards of cotton, and a piece of canvas to make a pair or two of trousers. Women received the same allowance as the men, but children received none. The children remained naked until they were about nine years old or were given cast-off clothing that their parents managed to find or were able to purchase.

The workday of the slaves began even before daybreak. They were marched to the fields by slave drivers who controlled them with whips. Slave drivers were themselves slaves who the white plantation owners specially selected. A white overseer supervised the entire operation. With farm implements allocated to them, the slaves worked in the fields and were occasionally whipped by the slave drivers if they attempted to idle. Around the middle of the day, they were given an hour's break to refresh themselves. The workday ended at about eight in the evening. The slaves who worked at the sugar mills during the grinding season were forced to work even longer hours.

Slaves were punished in various ways. For striking a white man, a hand could be cut off. Whipping was the most common form of punishment, and that was inflicted liberally and in the cruelest form. A slave driver did the whipping under the watchful eye of a white overseer, and it was not unusual for victims to be beaten to death.

The white plantation owners used various methods to maintain complete control over their slaves. Their principal process was that of divide and rule. Members of the same tribe were separated on different plantations to prevent communication among them. The aim behind that was to avoid plans to rebel. The separation, however, created a problem of communication since the plantation would have different groups of slaves speaking other languages. Therefore, the planters had to find a way to communicate with their slaves. Soon a new language, known as Creole-Dutch, developed, which became a common tongue among the slaves. When the British took control of Guiana in the nineteenth century, English words were injected into the language, and it became the basis of the Guyanese Creoles language.

Slaves were prevented from practicing their religions. Some slaves were Muslims, while many had their own tribal beliefs. Since the Christian planters saw non-Christians as pagans, they ensured the slaves could not gather to worship in the way they were accustomed to when they lived in Africa. Later Christian missionaries were permitted on the plantations to preach to the slaves on Sundays. Eventually, many of them were converted to Christianity. The general belief that the converted slaves became docile and they were less willing to support rebellion on the plantations.

Another means of control was the creation of a class system among the slaves. Field slaves formed the lowest group, even though some of them had special skills. There were the factory slaves who worked in the sugar boiling process. Higher up were the artisan slaves such as blacksmiths, carpenters, and masons, who were often hired out by the planters. Those slaves also had opportunities to earn money for themselves on various occasions. Higher up were the drivers who were specially selected by the white planters to control the other slaves. The domestic or house slave had a special place in the arrangement. They worked in the master's house, and because at times they received special favors from the master, they held other slaves in contempt. Usually, the slaves in the lowest rung of this social ladder were the ones who rebelled; frequently, the domestic slaves were the ones who betrayed them by reporting the plots to the masters.

There were also divisions based on skin color. It was relatively easy for an African to rise to the level of a driver. Mixtures occurred through the birth of children as a result of unions between white men and African slave women (mulatto), white men and mulatto women (mestee), and mulatto men and African women (sambo). Thus, some slaves of succeeding generations had lighter complexion, and the white planters discriminated in favor of them. The slaves with white fathers or white relatives were placed in positions above those of the field slaves. That was the beginning of color discrimination in society. Of course, in all of this, the European whites occupied the highest rung of the social ladder. They found willing allies among the mixed or colored population who occupied the intermediate levels. The pure Africans remained at the lowest level.

Except for earnings enjoyed by the artisan slaves, most slaves depended on obtaining money by selling surplus produce from their gardens and the sale of their livestock. On Sundays, the village markets were held, and the slaves seized the opportunity to barter or sell their produce. On those occasions, the slaves purchased a few pieces of clothing and other items for their homes. The Sunday markets were also when slaves from different plantations were able to socialize and exchange news and gossip. There were times of recreation. Those were usually at the end of the harvesting, at Christmas, and on public holidays when the slaves were allowed to hold dances that had to end by midnight.

Slaves were allowed to purchase their freedom through the process of manumission. However, by the time slaves saved up enough money to buy their freedom, they would have already become old and feeble. In some cases, female slaves who bore the master's children were manumitted while still relatively young.

During colonization, many slaves escaped from the brutal conditions on the plantations to the jungle. The term maroon was used throughout the region. It is derived from cimarrón, a Spanish word for runaway slaves. The Indigenous Peoples welcomed the maroons and helped them to survive in the forest. They were taught to grow and harvest their staple crop, cassava, and the use of medicinal plants. The Maroons eventually formed their communities and gradually displaced the Indigenous peoples, who moved further in the hinterland. The maroons are primarily in the South Eastern region of Guyana.

The early seventeenth century saw the establishment of a plantation economy in the Guiana region of South America based on African slave labor. The African slaves were brought from Senegambia, Sierra Leone, the Gold Coast, and Benin. They belonged to several tribes, spoke different languages, and had different religious beliefs. The Fulani-speaking slaves from Senegambia practiced Islam and were taken to British Guiana, lacking the leadership of Imams and the possession of the Quran.

The plantation life did not support prayers at fixed times, fasting at prescribed periods, or feasting on holidays which did not coincide with those observed by the plantocracy. The plantations that were geared exclusively to sugar production gave the slaves no scope for involvement in religious activities, as they did in their homeland. The white slave owners felt that the Africans were incapable of religious sentiment. The Fulah people of West Africa subsequently became descriptive of indentured Indian Muslims and their descendants. On the other hand, Indigenous African religious beliefs were eventually labeled as '*Obeah*' and survived the difficulties of plantation life. The beliefs underwent significant changes, although they remained clearly African in structure.

CHAPTER 9
The Berbice Uprising

THE AFRICAN SLAVE POPULATION GREW AS THE PLANtations expanded. The main concern of the white plantation owners was to extract the greatest amount of labor from the slaves. Little effort was ever made to improve the wretched and degrading living conditions under which the slaves were forced to live. With the harsh treatment and brutal punishments inflicted on them by their owners, some of them rebelled while others, from time to time, escaped into the forests. Those who were recaptured suffered horrible deaths as punishment. The punishment was meant as a deterrent to others who might have also planned to escape. Some of those in Berbice who escaped managed to reach Suriname, where they joined up with Bush Negro colonies.

In 1762, a slave rebellion of thirty-six male and female slaves occurred in the Dutch colony Berbice. After the slaves rebelled, a militia force was sent by Governor Van Hoogenheim, and the rebellion was finally repressed by a stronger influence of the Dutch militia. Some of the slaves escaped but at least one was executed. The repressive techniques of the planters were bringing matters to a boiling point, and just a few months later, around February 23, 1763, a more organized revolt took place. The uprising became known as the Berbice Slave Rebellion. It lasted ten months and marked the first attempt by many enslaved people to win their freedom. Significantly, it was also the first organized attempt to win freedom on the entire American continent. Despite the division in the ranks and the eventual failure of the rebellion, it emerged as the first group of Guyanese revolutionary heroes who initiated the struggle against colonial oppression.

The uprising initially broke out at Magdalenenburg, a plantation on the upper Canje River owned by a widow, Madam Vernesobre. The slaves killed the manager and the carpenter, burned the owner's house, and moved on to neighboring plantations as far as the Corentyne. They urged support from the slaves at the other plantations. Some of them attacked their owners and either joined them or escaped into the forest.

Very quickly, the rebelling Africans were organized as a fighting force by Mr. Coffy, who was a house slave on another Canje plantation, Lilienburg, where the slaves had also rebelled. Mr. Coffy had been taken to that plantation as a child and was trained as a cooper by Barkey, the plantation owner.

On hearing the uprising news, Governor Van Hogenheim immediately sent all available military assistance to the planters in Canje. The military was made up of 12 soldiers and 12 sailors from one of the five ships in the harbor. The entire colony had only 346 whites, including women and children, and 3,833 African slaves. Mulattos, who also formed a section of the population, generally sided with the whites throughout the rebellion.

The rebellion, which began on privately owned estates, soon attracted the slaves on plantations owned by the Berbice Association. The rebels burned buildings and cane fields and attacked and killed a white person. Soon they reached plantations on the Berbice River. Among the plantations attacked were Juliana, Mon Repos, Essendam, Lilienburg, Bearestyn, Elizabeth, Alexandria, Hollandia, and Zeelandia. Slaves from those and other plantations joined the rebel forces, which moved steadily towards the capital of Berbice, Fort Nassau, located 56 miles up the Berbice River on its right bank. Whenever they attacked the plantations, they seized gunpowder and guns belonging to the owners.

The European population who escaped sought refuge on the five ships in the Berbice River, Fort Nassau, Fort St. Andries at the mouth of the Berbice River, and in a brick house Plantation Peerboom, about 70 miles upriver on the left bank. Others, in panic, fled through the forest to Demerara. The feeling of hopelessness was compounded by an epidemic of dysentery, which affected the Europeans instantaneously.

On March 3, a rebel group, numbering over 500, led by Mr. Cosala, launched an attack on the brick house at Peerboom, which white defenders heavily fortified. The rebels threw balls of burning cotton on the roof, which began to burn, but the defenders could put out the fire. During a period of inaction, the manager of Plantation Bearestyn demanded to know why the Africans were attacking Christians. Mr. Cosala shouted back that they would no longer tolerate the presence of whites or Christians in Berbice since they were now in control of all the plantations.

After a period of negotiations, the rebels agreed to allow the whites to leave the brick house unharmed and depart for their boats in the river. However, as the whites were leaving, the rebels opened fire, killing many of them and taking many prisoners. Among the prisoners was the wife of Plantation Bearestyn, whom Mr. Coffy kept as his wife.

As the rebellion leader, Mr. Coffy, accepted by all the rebels, declared himself Governor of Berbice and set up his administration at Hollandia and Zeelandia. He selected Mr. Akara as his deputy and set about drilling his troops and establishing discipline. Two other leaders who emerged were Mr. Atta and Mr. Accabre, the latter being very disciplined and military-conscious. Other military leaders included Mr. Cossala and Mr. Goussari. Work crews among the Africans were organized to farm the estate lands to produce food supplies to sustain the population.

From the beginning, Coffy encountered difficulties with his forces as some sections felt that defeating the Europeans meant that they could now act as they pleased. Small groups roamed across the countryside plundering abandoned estates, while others spent most of their time drinking rum and dressing up in European clothing looted from the plantations. Several creole slaves - those born in the colony - did not wholeheartedly support the rebellion. They gave themselves up to plantations that were far removed from the area of rebel activity.

Meanwhile, the Dutch Governor, Van Hoogenheim, and other whites at Fort Nassau were undecided on what they should do. The Governor wanted to defend the colony, but the Court of Policy voted for abandonment. Morale was very low. On March 8, 1763, Fort Nassau was abandoned after the buildings were burned and the cannons spiked. The whites traveled by boats to Fort St. Andries, which Van Hoogenhiem quickly found inadequate for housing and defense. Also, there was no food and fresh running water. He had preferred to stop at Dageraad, a plantation about 16 kilometers down the river from Fort Nassau, but the others did not agree.

At Fort St. Andries, Van Hoogenheim finally agreed to allow the whites to abandon Berbice when an English ship with 100 soldiers arrived from Suriname. Van Hoogenheim immediately withdrew his decision to abandon the colony and began to re-organize his defense. He dispatched 25 soldiers to Plantation Fredericksburg up the Canje and left a small group with two ships to guard the mouth of the Berbice River. With the remaining larger group and volunteers among the whites, they sailed with three armed vessels to Dageraad.

Van Hoogenheim fortified the previously abandoned buildings and arranged the three ships so that their guns would defend the new position. The rebels, led by Mr. Akara, immediately launched three successive attacks on the Europeans, but they were driven back.

Mr. Coffy, who did not approve those attacks immediately after, on April 2, 1763, wrote to Governor Van Hoogenheim saying that he did not want a war with the whites. He also proposed the partition of Berbice between the whites and blacks, with the whites occupying the coastal area and the blacks in the interior. Mr. Coffy wrote:

> Coffy, Governor of the Negroes of Berbice, and Captain Akara send greetings and inform Your Excellency that they seek no war; but if Your Excellency wants war, the Negroes are likewise ready. Barkey and his servant, De Graff, Schook, Dell, Van Lentzing, and Frederick Betgen, but more especially Mr. Barkey and his servant and De Graff, are the principal originators of the riot, which occurred in Berbice. The Governor (Coffy) was present when it commenced and was very angry at it. The Governor of Berbice asks Your Excellency that Your Excellency will

come and speak with him; don't be afraid, but if you don't come, we will fight as long as one Christian remains in Berbice. The Governor will give Your Excellency one half of Berbice, and all the Negroes will go high up the river, but don't think they will remain slaves. Those Negroes that Your Excellency has on the ships, they can remain slaves.

The Governor greets Your Excellency.

Maintaining his delaying tactics, Van Hoogenheim insisted in his correspondence to Governor Coffy that he was still awaiting a response to the partition proposal from Holland. By the end of March, the Director-General of Essequibo and Demerara, Laurens Storm van Gravesande received information about the rebellion. He instructed the Commander of Demerara to seek assistance from the Caribs, Arawaks, and Akawaios to mount an attack on the Berbice rebels from the south. Van Gravesande also wrote to the Zeeland Chamber and the Directors of the Berbice Association in Holland and the Governor of St. Eustatius, seeking military assistance for the Europeans in Berbice. Eventually, two well-armed ships with 158 soldiers arrived in Berbice.

By this time, Governor Coffy had lost his patience with Governor Van Hoggenhiem, and on May 13, 1763, he agreed to an attack on Dageraad with a force that numbered about 2,000 while the whites had about 150 armed men. The three ships in the river maintained a steady firing of their heavy guns on the attackers, and by mid-afternoon, they were forced to withdraw after suffering a loss of 58 dead. Eight whites died during this conflict.

After this defeat, Governor Coffy wrote to Governor Van

Hoogenheim again, offering his partition proposal to bring peace with honor. In a very firm statement, he insisted that "in no case will we be slaves again."

The defeat of the slaves helped to open up divisions in their ranks. Those who had been field-slaves began to express disapproval of Governor Coffy, who was a house slave. Mr. Atta was the leader of the field slave faction. Tribal jealousies emerged, and fights broke out between members of different tribes. Creole blacks, at times, attacked those who recently arrived from Africa. Those divisions seriously undermined the military strength of the rebels and helped to encourage the whites to regroup their forces.

Interestingly, soon after their arrival, a group of Dutch soldiers, including Jene Renaud and Sergeant De Niesse, who had mutinied and deserted the post on the Corentyne, were captured and employed by the rebels to train the troops, and make weapons. Governor Coffy used them for training his forces, and some led small bands in guerrilla attacks on plantations controlled by the whites. Due to distrust, some of those Dutch deserters were killed by the Africans.

Meanwhile, the differences between Governor Coffy and Mr. Atta continued to grow, and eventually, Mr. Atta challenged him for leadership. The opposing supporters fought each other, and after Mr. Atta's faction won, Governor Coffy killed his close supporters before shooting himself.

Mr. Atta, now the new leader, appointed Mr. Accabre as his military commander, and three other leaders, Mr. Quacco, Mr. Baube, and Mr. Goussari, rose among the ranks. By that time, reinforcements were arriving to support the whites. A combined Amerindian force was already moving through the forest from the south. From December 19, 1763, soldiers from Holland moved up the Canje and Berbice Rivers and took back control of the plantations. Large numbers of Africans surrendered while others fled into the forest. Some mounted resistance, but the Dutch soldiers quickly suppressed them. However, in two battles, including one at Wikki Creek, the African forces could score victories.

Mr. Atta and Mr. Akara were soon taken prisoner, but Mr. Accabre resisted the Dutch forces with a disciplined band by using innovative military strategy. Eventually, he was betrayed by Mr. Akara and Mr. Goussari, who were prisoners of the Dutch. Overwhelmed by the superior number of the Dutch soldiers, Mr. Accabre was captured. When he was brought before Governor Van Hoogenheim, he proudly admitted his role as a rebellion leader.

Mr. Accabre, Mr. Atta, Mr. Akara, Mr. Quacco, Mr. Baube, Mr. Goussari, and many other slaves who fought for their freedom were executed. Between March and April 1764, forty slaves were executed, 24 broken at the wheel, and 24 burned to death. Others rounded up, were re-enslaved and put back to work on the plantations, and returned to their white owners' control.

CHAPTER 10

The Anti-Slavery Movement

I N 1787 THE QUAKERS OF PORTSMOUTH MADE THEIR ANti-slavery campaign official by forming The Society for Effecting the Abolition of the Slave Trade and joined forces with prominent abolitionists such as William Wilberforce. They were so organized in their methods of activism, such as civil disobedience, research, and evidence-gathering, that they set the blueprint for many future lobbying organizations. One of their most effective actions was to commission an illustration of the Liverpool slave ship the Brookes, named after its owner, Joseph Brookes, and present it to the nation in poster form. It appeared in newspapers, pamphlets, books, and coffee houses. The horror that it produced quickly established the illustration as a hugely influential part of the abolitionists' anti-slavery campaign.

The architect of the use of the Brookes as political propaganda was the Quaker abolitionist Thomas Clarkson. In the history of the rise, progress, and accomplishment of the abolition of the African slave trade by the British Parliament (1808), he stated that the print seemed to make an immediate impression of horror upon all who saw it and was therefore instrumental, in consequence of the wide circulation given it, in serving the cause of the injured Africans. Clarkson's choice of the Brookes proved to be a revelation to large numbers of people. As he traveled around England, galvanizing the anti-slavery campaign, he was attacked in Liverpool in 1787 and almost killed by a gang of sailors paid to assassinate him.

Over 25 years, Brookes' ship made ten Atlantic crossings, carrying in total 5,163 enslaved Africans. Of those, 4,559 survived, meaning that over ten percent of its prisoners died. Records from The Trans-Atlantic Slave Trade Database indicated that on its 1785-86 voyages, it carried 740 enslaved Africans, 258 more than the 1788 poster showed. In 1788 The Regulated Slave Trade Act was passed. It became the first British legislation to regulate slave shipping and limit the number of slaves an individual ship could transport.

Although Liverpool was late entering the slave trade, by 1740, it had surpassed Bristol and London as the slave-trading capital of Britain. In 1792, London had 22 transatlantic sailing vessels, Bristol had 42, and Liverpool had 131. The Brookes was built at the height of Liverpool's slave-trading empire. By that time, the city's shipbuilders had mastered the art of constructing custom-built slave ships. In the early 18th century, the average size of a slave ship was 70 tons; by the end of the century, it had tripled to 200 tons.

Liverpool was so dominant in the North Atlantic slave trade that one in five enslaved Africans crossing the ocean was carried in a Liverpool slave ship. The city could build ships to the exact specifications and requirements of the slave merchants. Consequently, the industry employed 3,000 shipwrights, alongside other ancillary trades, such as rope makers, gun makers, and those who supplied comestibles to be carried on board.

Liverpool's economy and the economies of neighboring Lancashire and Yorkshire benefited, too. Ships bound for Africa would be laden with goods to appeal to African traders to make the outbound journey profitable. Textiles from Lancashire and Yorkshire mills were the most attractive commodity. They made up about 50 percent of the outbound cargo, alongside guns and knives, brass cooking pots, copperware, clay pipes, beer, and liquor. Local craftspeople and small industries supplied the ships. Estimates suggested that one in eight of Liverpool's population of 10,000 were dependent on trade with Africa, and forty percent of its income was derived from the trade.

The slave trade was the backbone of the city's prosperity. The reinvestment of proceeds gave stimulus to trading and industrial development throughout the northwest of England and the Midlands. Liverpool's Rodney Street was built between 1782 and 1801 and provided townhouses for many elite merchants, including John Gladstone, father of Prime Minister William Ewart Gladstone. It was named after Admiral Rodney, who defeated the French in St Lucia in 1782 to preserve the British influence in the West Indies. Rodney supported the slave trade. Elsewhere in the city, the Port of Liverpool buildings displayed stone carvings of slave ships and dolphins on its façade. The Cunard building carries sculptures of a Native American and an African man and woman.

The Liverpool Street immortalized by the Beatles in their song *'Penny Lane'* takes its name from the slave trader James Penny, objection to the abolition movement. Eager to protect his business, he boldly claimed in evidence to the Lords Committee of Council in 1788 that: "The slaves here will sleep better than the gentlemen do on shore." He was not the only Liverpool figure to campaign in the build-up to the 1788 Act. Liverpool slave traders submitted 64 petitions to Parliament arguing against the abolition of the slave trade.

In 1999 Councilor Myrna Juarez proposed that Liverpool City Council debate a motion to express remorse for the effects of the slave trade on millions of people worldwide. Some protested the incongruity of the debate in a town hall where images of African slaves were molded into the plasterwork. The motion unleashed a controversy. Nevertheless, the council acknowledged Liverpool's involvement in the slave trade, and a formal apology was made. The city acknowledges its slave-trading history with the International Slavery Museum, which opened in 2007 as part of the Maritime Museum.

Support was growing for a British slavery museum in the capital after the Mayor of London, Sadiq Khan, backed the proposal, arguing that it would help tackle racism. Other institutions have also acknowledged the role of slavery in their history, such as Harewood House in Yorkshire. In September 2018, Glasgow University, in a welcome move, published a report into its historical links to slavery, acknowledging that, although the university did not invest directly in the slave trade, it did receive donations from those who did.

In 1807 The Slave Trade Act saw the official end of the slave trade in Britain. As the anniversary of that act on March 25 approaches once more, taking the lead from Liverpool, it is time that more individuals and institutions are transparent about the legacy that slavery has left on the planet.

CHAPTER 11

The Abolition of the Slave Trade

IN 1807 THE INTERNATIONAL SLAVE TRADE WAS ABOLished in the British Empire. Colonial life changed radically by the demise of the slave-trading business. Slavery, however, continued until the Demerara rebellion of 1823. At that event, ten to thirteen thousand slaves in Demerara and Essequibo rose against their oppressors. Although the rebellion was quickly crushed, the momentum for abolition remained, and in 1838 total emancipation was granted.

In 1807, the British Parliament passed the Slave Trade Act of 1807, which outlawed the international slave-trading business, but not slavery itself. The legislation was timed to coincide with the expected prohibition of 1808 of the international slave trading by the United States, Britain's chief rival in maritime commerce. The legislation imposed fines but did little to deter slave-trading participants. A new Member of Parliament successfully introduced the Slave Trade Felony Act in 1811, which at last made the overseas slave-trading business a felony act throughout the empire.

The Royal Navy established the West Africa Squadron to suppress the Atlantic slave trade by patrolling the coast of West Africa. It did suppress the slave trade but did not stop it entirely. Between 1808 and 1860, the West Africa Squadron captured 1,600 slave ships and freed 150,000 Africans. They resettled many in Jamaica and the Bahamas. Britain also used its influence to coerce other countries to agree to treaties to end their slave-trading business and allow the Royal Navy to seize ships involved in slave trading.

Between 1807 and 1823, abolitionists showed little interest in abolishing slavery itself. Mr. Eric Williams presented economic data in *Capitalism and Slavery* to show that the slave trade itself generated only small profits compared to the much more lucrative sugar plantations of the Caribbean. Therefore, slavery continued to thrive on those estates. However, from 1823 the British Caribbean sugar industry went into a terminal decline, and the British parliament no longer felt they needed to protect the economic interests of the West Indian sugar planters.

The Anti-Slavery Society was founded in London in 1823. Members included Joseph Sturge, Thomas Clarkson, William Wilberforce, Henry Brougham, Thomas Fowell Buxton, Elizabeth Heyrick, Mary Lloyd, Jane Smeal, Elizabeth Pease, and Anne Knight. Jamaican mixed-race campaigners such as Louis Celeste Lecesne and Richard Hill were also members of the Anti-Slavery Society.

During the Christmas holiday of 1831, a large-scale slave revolt in Jamaica, known as the Baptist War, broke out. It was organized initially as a peaceful strike by the Baptist minister Samuel Sharpe. The rebellion was suppressed by the militia of the Jamaican plantocracy and the British garrison ten days later in early 1832. Because of the loss of property and lives in the 1831 rebellion, the British Parliament held two inquiries. The results of those inquiries contributed significantly to the abolition of slavery with the Slavery Abolition Act of 1833. Sugar planters from the British colonies of Jamaica and Barbados formed a body of resistance against the abolishment of slavery. The West India Lobby, which later evolved into the West India Committee, purchased enough seats to resist the overtures of abolitionists. However, The Reform Act of 1832 swept away their seats, clearing the way for most House of Commons to push through a law to abolish slavery itself throughout the British Empire.

The Act had its third reading in the House of Commons on July 26, 1833, three days before William Wilberforce died. It received the Royal Assent a month later, on August 28, and came into force the following year, on August 1, 1834.

In practical terms, only slaves below the age of six were freed in the colonies. Former slaves over the age of six were redesignated as apprentices, and their servitude was abolished in two stages: The first set of apprenticeships came to an end on August 1, 1838, while the final apprenticeship was scheduled to end on August 1, 1840. The Act expressly excluded *'the Territories in the Possession of the East India Company, or to the Island of Ceylon, or to the Island of Saint Helena.'* The exceptions were eliminated in 1843.

CHAPTER 12

The Emancipation of Slavery

WITH THE PASSING OF THE ABOLITION OF THE Slave Trade Act by the British Parliament in 1807, the attention of campaigners against the slave trade switched to slavery itself. Although the slave trade had been banned, nothing had been done to free the existing enslaved Africans in the British Empire. In 1823, religious groups, politicians, and supporters from around the country came together to form the Anti-Slavery Society.

By 1824, more than 200 branches of the Anti-Slavery Society in Britain indicated the increasing support for the fight against slavery. The campaign was one of many tremendous economic and social changes in Britain and the British colonies. It was increasingly evident that the plantation system in the British colonies needed reform and transformation. Factory owners in England were being forced to consider the rights and needs of workers. British planters were facing new forms of competition in a changing world market. Moreover, deprived of their cargoes of enslaved Africans, British ships now crossed the Atlantic fully laden with raw materials such as cotton and sugar on the return journey only. Thus, the abolition of slavery in Britain was waged in a society already in a state of economic, political, and social flux.

A strong network of women's anti-slavery associations developed. The Birmingham Society played a particularly active role in helping to promote and establish local groups in many parts of Britain. Influenced by the Birmingham Society, over 73 women's associations were founded between 1825 and 1833, which supplied a constant stream of information to rouse public opinion against slavery. Women found a basis from which they could pursue their liberation. They were able to use the terminology of the anti-slavery campaign as a way to articulate the inequalities that they suffered.

While Mr. William Wilberforce and others pushed the debate forward in parliament, enslaved people in the British colonies continued to fight for their freedom. As the reporting of the campaign gained momentum in the press, both in Britain and throughout the British colonies, rebellions and resistance increased. In Demerara, in 1823, over 13,000 slaves joined a rebellion because they felt that the local plantation owners had refused to obey British orders to give them their freedom.

Planters in the colonies, their supporters, and pro-slavery representatives in the British Parliament continued to argue for slavery. From time to time, the opposition erupted into violence, and in some cases, missionaries in the colonies which were in favor of emancipation found their churches burned by aggrieved planters. In the 1830s, several Acts were passed that fundamentally changed British society and the lives of millions of people living in British colonies. The Reform Act of 1832 brought an end to the old system. Most Members of Parliament were allowed to purchase their seats in parliament.

The new Parliament of 1833 included men (women were not allowed to become MPs) connected with Britain's textile industries. In August 1833, the Slave Emancipation Act was passed, giving all slaves in the British Empire their freedom, albeit after a set period of years. Plantation owners received compensation for the *loss of their slaves* in the form of a government grant of £20,000,000. In contrast, the enslaved people received no compensation and continued to face much hardship. They remained landless, and the wages offered on the plantations after emancipation were extremely low.

The 1833 Act did not come into effect until August 1, 1834. The first step was the freeing of all children under six. However, although the many thousands of enslaved people in the British colonies were no longer legally slaves after August 1, 1834, they were still made to work as unpaid apprentices for their former masters. These masters continued to ill-treat and exploit them. Enslaved people in the British colonies finally gained their freedom at midnight on July 31, 1838.

The planters were afraid that the ex-slaves would not want to work on the plantations, even for wages. The planters cut down fruit trees, destroyed gardens, banned them from fishing to deny them any source of food that might compete with plantation work. The ex-slaves turned to three sources of livelihood: small-scale trading, skilled trades, and subsistence farming. Thousands of ex-slaves were settling on vacant backlands. Six years later, the slave population on the plantations about a third of what it was in the last years of slavery. The planter's only option was to recruit a new labor force that is cheap and obedient.

When apprenticeship came to an end in 1838, two years earlier than initially intended, Britain had control of Jamaica,

Barbados, Trinidad, Tobago, the Leeward and Windward Islands, the Bahamas, the Turks, and Caicos Islands, British Honduras, and British Guiana. In Barbados, all available land was occupied. However, in several other colonies, an independent peasantry came into being by a remarkable process of self-help and solidarity. It was not at all to the taste of the planters, who did their best to put a stop to it. The movement was most potent in British Guiana. Despite a decision that land should not be sold to the emancipated slaves, many pooled their resources to buy abandoned estates. First to do so were 83 ex-slaves, five of them women, who in 1839 bought a 500-acre cotton plantation for $10,000. There was a tradition that they took the money to the vendors in wheelbarrows in small denomination coins.

By 1850, of a total Afro-Guyanese laboring population of 82,000, over 42,000 had succeeded in making themselves at least partly independent of plantation work. They had established 25 communal villages at an aggregate cost of almost $2,250,000, a staggering achievement for a people just twelve years out of slavery. The authorities stepped in and limited the number of joint purchasers, first to 20 in 1852 and then to 10 in 1856. The planters controlled the legislature, and their main aim was the command of the labor market. They did not want the peasants' settlements to succeed. As the planters intended, poverty forced many into partial dependence on the plantations as a source of livelihood.

Similar settlements, following the end of the apprenticeship, sprung up in Jamaica and Trinidad. In Jamaica, by 1843, some 19,000 ex-slaves had bought land and built their cottages. Nevertheless, in Trinidad, estate managers and the government collaborated to make land prices too high for most would-be settlers.

The overwhelming majority of the populations of those

colonies, whether of African or Asian descent, had no say whatsoever in making decisions that affected their lives. Representative government was out of the question, as that would have meant giving black people the vote. Furthermore, this was something the British were not prepared to do. They said so quite openly. The Duke of Newcastle, soon to become Colonial Secretary, told the House of Lords in 1858 that responsible government for the colonies was only applicable to colonists of the *'English race.'*

In 1897, a royal commission admitted that they had placed the laboring population where it is, and created for it the conditions under which it exists, those conditions being distress and difficulty in finding a livelihood.

CHAPTER 13
Britain's Slave-Owners Compensation

THE SLAVE COMPENSATION ACT OF 1837 AND THE London Society of West India Planters and Merchants provided for payments to slave-owners. Under the terms of the Act, the British Government paid out £20,000,000 to compensate some 3,000 families who owned slaves to lose their property in Britain's colonies. That figure represented a staggering 40 percent of the treasury's annual spending budget and calculated as values equate to around £16.5 bn in today's terms. The British Government took on a £15 million loan to finance the payments, finalized on August 3, 1835, with banker Nathan Mayer Rothschild and his brother-in-law Moses Montefiore; £5 million was paid out directly in government stock. The British taxpayers did not pay that money back until 2015 when the British Government decided to modernize the gilt portfolio by redeeming all remaining undated gilts. The long gap between this money being borrowed and its repayment was due to the type of financial instrument used rather than borrowed money.

Dr. Draper from University College London (UCL), who studied the compensation papers, said there was a feeding frenzy around the compensation. As much as twenty percent of the wealthy Victorian Britons derived all or part of their fortunes from the slave business. As a result, there are wealthy families all around the UK who are still enjoying the proceeds of slavery where it has been passed on to them. The accurate scale of Britain's involvement in the slave trade has been laid bare in documents revealing how the country's wealthiest families received the modern equivalent of billions of pounds in compensation for participating in the world's most atrocious business.

Academics from UCL, including Dr. Draper, spent three years drawing 46,000 records of compensation given to British slave-owners into an internet database to be launched for public use. However, he emphasized that the claims were not just from affluent families but included many ordinary men and women and covered the entire spectrum of society. Dr. Draper added that the database's findings might have implications for the reparations debate. Barbados was currently leading the way in calling for reparations from former colonial powers for the injustices suffered by slaves and their families.

Ten million pounds went to slave-owning families in the Caribbean and Africa, while the other half went to absentee owners living in Britain. The biggest single payout went to James Blair, a member of parliament, who had homes in Marylebone, Central London, and Scotland. He was awarded £83,530, the equivalent of £65 million today, for 1,598 slaves he owned on the plantation he owned in British Guiana.

Among those revealed to have benefited from slavery are the Prime Minister, David Cameron, former minister Douglas Hogg, authors Graham Greene and George Orwell, poet Elizabeth Barrett Browning, and the new chairman of the Arts Council, Peter Bazalgette. Other prominent names which feature in the records include scions of one of the nation's oldest banking families, the Barings, and the second Earl of Harewood, Henry Lascelles, an ancestor of the Queen's cousin. George Orwell's great-grandfather, Charles Blair, received £4,442, equal to £3 million today, for the 218 slaves he owned. Henry Phillpotts, the Bishop of Exeter, with three others as trustees and executors of the will of John Ward, First Earl of Dudley, was paid £12,700 for 665 slaves in the West Indies, Henry Lascelles, 2nd Earl of Harewood received £26,309 for 2,554 slaves on six plantations.

The amount was dwarfed by the amount paid to Sir John Gladstone, the father of Prime Minister William Gladstone. He received £106,769 (modern equivalent £83 million) for the 2,508 slaves he owned on nine plantations. His son, who served as Prime Minister four times during his 60-year career, was actively involved in his father's claims.

Mr. Cameron is revealed to have slave owners in his family background. The compensation records showed General Sir James Duff, an army officer and MP for Banffshire in Scotland during the late 1700s, was Mr. Cameron's relative. Sir James, the son of one of Mr. Cameron's great-grand-uncle, the second Earl of Fife, was awarded £4,101, equal to more than £3 million today, to compensate him for the 202 slaves forfeited on the Grange plantation in Jamaica.

Another illustrious political family that still carried the name of a prominent slave owner is the Hogg dynasty, which includes the former cabinet minister Douglas Hogg. They are the descendants of Charles McGarel, a merchant who made a fortune from slave ownership. Between 1835 and 1837, he received £129,464, about £101 million in today's terms, for the 2,489 slaves he owned. McGarel later brought his younger brother-in-law Quintin Hogg into his hugely successful sugar business, which later used indentured laborers on plantations in British Guyana established under slavery. Furthermore, Quintin's descendants continued to keep the family name in the limelight, with both his son, Douglas McGarel Hogg, and his grandson, Quintin McGarel Hogg, becoming Lord Chancellors.

Dr. Draper said that seeing the slave-owners' names repeated in 20th-century family naming practices is a stark reminder about where those families saw their origins. In this case, he was thinking about the Hogg family. To have two Lord Chancellors in Britain in the 20th century bearing the name of a slave-owner from British Guiana, who went penniless to British Guyana, came back a very wealthy man and contributed to the formation of this political dynasty, which incorporated his name into their children in recognition. It seems to be an illuminating story and a potent example. Mr. Hogg refused to comment, saying that he did not know anything about it. Mr. Cameron declined to comment after a request was made to him.

Another demonstration of the extent to which slavery links stretched into modern Britain is Evelyn Bazalgette, the uncle of one of the giants of Victorian engineering, Sir Joseph Bazalgette, and ancestor of Arts Council boss Sir Peter Bazalgette. He was paid £7,352 (£5.7 million in today's money) for 420 slaves from two estates in Jamaica. Sir Peter said that it had always been rumored that his father had some interests in the Caribbean, and he suspected that Evelyn inherited that. So, he heard rumors, but the payment confirms it. It is the sort of thing wealthy people did in the 1800s. He could have put his money elsewhere, but regrettably, he put it in the Caribbean.

Many of the country estates, grand buildings with hundreds of rooms stuffed with antiques and arts from across the globe; tourist love them, and they are a guarantee for the box office as Downton Abbey and Pride, and Prejudice can attest are indelibly linked to the brutal legacies of slavery, indentureship, and colonialism. While their grim origins may have been overlooked, there are debates over how Britain reckons with its imperial past. At the center of the controversy is the National Trust, a heritage body created in 1895 to preserve the natural beauty and historical significance across England, Wales, and Northern Ireland. Ninety-three places have been identified. Approximately one-third of them benefited from or connected to the humanitarian atrocities of slavery, indentureship, and colonialism. They include Chartwell, Winston Churchill's former home in the southeastern county of Kent, Devon's spectacular Lundy Island, where convicts were used as unpaid labor, and Speke Hall, near Liverpool, whose owner, Richard Watt traded rum made by slaves. He purchased a slave ship in 1793 that trafficked slaves from Africa to Jamaica.

About 29 properties benefited from compensation after owning slaves was abolished in Great Britain in 1837, including Hare Hill in Cheshire, where the owners, the Hibbert family, received the equivalent of £7 million ($8.8 million) to make up for the loss of slaves. John Orna-Ornstein, the National Trust's Director of Culture and Engagement, said that at a time when there is an enormous interest around colonialism, more broadly and indeed slavery more specifically, it felt very appropriate, given that they care for so many of these places of historical interest, to commission a report that looks right across them and try to assess the extent of those colonial legacies still reflected in the places that are looked after. Not everyone agrees. Moreover, in some cases, the responses have been of indignation and fury.

When the National Trust first published its report and highlighted the connections to mark UNESCO's Day for Remembrance of the Slave Trade, there was an inevitable backlash. Replies detailed how mahoganies felled by enslaved Africans were used to build furniture for stately homes were swift in their disdain. Some said they were canceling their National Trust membership in protest. Others said that the past could not be changed and historic buildings are to be enjoyed, no matter their past.

It was mentioned that they did not want the National Trust to ram it down their throats, while others talked darkly of history being erased. Opinion pieces in newspapers decried supposed attempts by the Trust to somehow talk Britain down by revealing the truth about its past. Former newspaper editor Charles Moore, writing in the right-leaning Spectator magazine, accused the Trust of creating a shameful manifesto that rejects objectivity in favor of a binary interpretation of history designed to make its members ashamed to be British. The report's mention of revered wartime leader Winston Churchill in connection with contentious colonial era governance has drawn particular ire.

Oliver Dowden, the UK's Culture Minister, told the Daily Telegraph newspaper that the organization should focus on preserving and protecting the British heritage that Churchill is one of Britain's greatest heroes. He told the paper that he rallied the free world to defeat fascism, and it will surprise and disappoint people that the National Trust appears to be making him a subject of criticism and controversy.

For its part, the National Trust says that it is merely providing historical context. "The role of the National Trust is a very clear one," says Orna-Ornstein. "Our role is to be as open and honest as we can, to tell the full history of the places and collections that we care for and to not do more than that." Despite threats to cancel memberships, people have expressed interest in hearing more about those connections, he said. On both sides, the debate is passionate and, to some extent, polarized. He was confused by the response of some people saying that they are erasing history. Journalist and commentator Seun Matiluko said that it is not like they are taking anything away; they are just saying that this is part of history and adding context to a particular artifact. It is adding something. He struggled to find a way to be offended by it. Matiluko believes that it is vital that the National Trust does not find itself dragged into a debate about its report and that they need to listen to what their board and members are saying and not focus too much on the media.

Trevor Burnard, a professor specializing in slavery and emancipation at the UK's Hull University, said that it is a little bit surprising that anybody would respond to it because it seems to be a very non-controversial thing to discuss. It was known for a very long time that Britain was heavily implicated both in slavery and colonialism. He said the Trust's report not only gave vital context to those buildings and estates but made them more attractive. He thinks they have moved a long way from hiding things about the past to preserve some propriety that no longer exists, and as long as it is not done didactically, they should not expect people in the past to have attitudes that correspond to their own. Any organization should be looking at its history from a broader perspective than is currently done.

Anshuman Mondal, professor of Modern Literature at the University of East Anglia, feels the National Trust's report and its reaction spoke to a lack of racial literacy in Western countries. He also believed the connections run even more profound than the Trust's report indicated. "A headline figure might say one thing, but nearly every country house built in that period had some relationship to the wealth generated by slavery," he says. "And not just slavery but by both, firstly, mercantile colonialism and secondly, territorial imperialism." Mondal criticized the arguments of some who said that Britons are unfairly made to feel embarrassed about their history. "I think we should be embarrassed about it," he says. "We should be ashamed of it. Now obviously, this doesn't mean you then try to forget about it, but the attitude you take to the past is the key question. If you say we shouldn't be embarrassed about it, well, what are people really saying? We should be proud of these people?" Orna-Ornstein said that while he was shocked at the scale of the links between properties and slavery, especially Hare Hill, it is not hugely surprising that such links existed in the first place. Orna-Ornstein said:

> When you think that a lot of the places that the National Trust cares for saw their greatest development in the 17th, 18th and 19th centuries...a period when colonialism was absolutely intertwined with society and the world was becoming increasingly international and a part of that international trade was through colonial relationships, in that sense it is much less surprising.

Mondal believes that the National Trust's report, coupled with Black Lives Matter and other movements looking to bring down statues of slave owners in the UK, reflects a broader point. "If you think about indirect links to slavery, our entire society is structured by that," he said." The Industrial Revolution was made possible by the profits by slavery." Speaking about the adverse reaction on social media,

Seun Matiluko said it revealed, "That some people are scared of approaching history that might make them look bad." She argued that such attempts to reckon with the past are not exercises in dismantling national pride. "At this point, to move forward, we just need more rational conversations and not to get stuck in the binary of 'Britain's good or Britain's bad.' Just say 'this is what happened' and ask 'how do we feel about it?'"

The National Trust started to act on the report and making the historical links between its places and slavery and colonialism clearer. "We've already updated interpretations on our website or in the places themselves, about 30 so far," said Orna-Ornstein. "Over time, we plan to do that more widely." He also highlighted an existing project, Colonial Countryside, run in conjunction with the University of Leicester that aimed at educating younger people about the links between the British Empire's colonies, slavery, indentureship, oppression, and the homes that were built as a result. The places themselves are not changing. The houses will still be opulent. The gardens perfectly tended the atmosphere as English as afternoon tea and complaining bitterly about the weather. However, by providing more context, the chances are that on the next visit to a National Trust property, one will come away knowing more about how it was built and from where the money used to build it was derived.

The TV chef Ainsley Harriot, who had slave-owners in his family, said he was shocked by the amount paid out by the Government to the slave-owners. "You would think the Government would have given at least some money to the freed slaves who need to find homes and start new lives, it seems a bit barbaric. It's like the rich protecting the rich."

Rulers of Colonized British Guiana

1760 – 1820 George III (father of George IV, William IV, and Edward III).

1820 – 1830 George IV.

1830 - 1837 William IV (son of George III).

1837 - 1901 Victoria (daughter of Edward III, mother of Edward VII).

1901 – 1910 Edward VII (son of Victoria).

1910 – 1936 George V (son of Edward VII, father of Edward VIII and George VI).

1936 – 1936 Edward VIII (son of George V).

1936 – 1952 George VI (son of George V and father of Elizabeth II).

1952 –1966 Elizabeth II (daughter of George VI).

In the 1930s, Eric Williams of Trinidad wrote, "after three centuries of British rule, the tropical farms' main crops were extreme poverty, hardship, disease, illiteracy, and slum housing." In 1937, every adult over twenty years of age was affected by deficiency diseases, and the working population was reduced to at least one-half. With the mothers debilitated by starvation and internal parasites, the infant mortality for Trinidad was 120 per 1,000 live births; for Jamaica 137; Antigua 171; St Kitts 187; Barbados 217; Great Britain 58.

In 1938-39 another Royal Commission, chaired by Lord Moyne, investigated social conditions in British Guiana, Barbados, Trinidad, Jamaica, British Honduras, and the Leeward and Windward Islands. The report was such a revealing document that the British Government thought it should not be published until the Second World War was over; it did not appear until June 1945. According to the report, rates for agricultural laborers had advanced little beyond the shilling-a-day introduced after emancipation. The rate per day was: British Guiana - 52 cents for men and 31 cents for women; St Kitts – 28 cents for men and 24 cents for women; Grenada and St Lucia - 30 cents for men and 24 cents for women; Trinidad – 44 cents for men and 24 cents for women; Jamaica – 44 cents.

On July 20, 1939, at a banquet for West Indian sugar planters, Winston Churchill said that Britain's possession of the West Indies and India provides Britain with more capital wealth and reserve than any European nation. The wealth enhanced their success in the Napoleonic wars and took them through the eighteenth and nineteenth centuries; it laid the foundation for Britain's commercial and financial dominance globally.

CHAPTER 14

Indentureship

INDENTURED SERVITUDE IS DATED BACK TO MEDIEVAL times in England. The ordinance of laborers, passed in June 1349, declared that all men and women under sixty who did not practice a craft must serve anyone requiring their labor. Parliament updated the law in 1495 and 1563, with the latter version, the Statute of Artificers, still being in effect when the English founded Jamestown, Virginia, USA. Between 1520 and 1630, England's population more than doubled, from 2.3 million to 4.8 million. The Parliament expected that the 1563 statute might banish idleness and deal with the overwhelming number of poor and unemployed citizens. The founding of Virginia was partially in response to that problem. In his Discourse on Western Planting in 1584, Richard Hakluyt argued to Queen Elizabeth that new American colonies would energize England's decayed trades and provide work for the country's multitudes of loiterers and idle vagabonds.

In England, an indenture, or labor contract, was a *'Covenant Merely Personal'* and could apply either to farm laborers or apprentices learning a trade. Contracts generally lasted a year, after which terms were renegotiated. Sir George Peckham, a merchant, and adventurer, noted in 1583 that young children were sometimes bound to service by parents who might not otherwise afford their upbringing. At the same time, there was not necessarily a strong stigma attached to indentureship. First in England and then in Virginia, the institution temporarily transformed free men and women into chattel or property to be bought and sold.

Under indentureship, the contract stipulated that the worker was borrowing money for traveling and would repay the lender by performing a certain kind of labor for a set period. Skilled laborers were usually indentured for four or five years, but unskilled workers often needed to remain under their master's control for seven or more years. Most workers who became indentured laborers were males, generally in their late teens and early twenties. However, thousands of women also entered into these agreements and often worked off their debts as household employees or domestic servants.

Indentureship in the U.S. began in the early 1600s in Virginia, not long after the settlement at Jamestown. Early American settlers needed cheap labor to help manage their large estates and farmland. Landowners agreed to fund the passage of European immigrants to Virginia in exchange for their labor. Approximately 300,000 European workers immigrated to the American colonies in the 1600s as indentured laborers. Indentureship continued throughout much of the 1700s but at a slower pace.

Other parts of the world engaged in some version of indentureship at around the same time it was happening in the United States. People went to the Caribbean to work as indentured laborers on sugar plantations. The immigrants entered indentureship contracts of their own free will, unlike slavery, where they were not given a choice in the matter. Treatment of indentured laborers differed significantly from one master to another. Some masters considered their laborers' personal property and made them work difficult jobs before their contracts expired.

Other masters treated their slaves more humanely than their indenture because slaves were regarded as a lifetime investment, whereas servants would be gone in a few years. European indentured laborers also feared better than slaves in other respects; they had access to the courts and were entitled to own land. However, masters retained their right to prohibit their servants from marrying and had the authority to sell them to another master at any time.

A specific similarity between slavery and indentured laborers is that indentured laborers could be sold, loaned, or inherited, at least during their contract terms. As a result, some indentured laborers performed work for the landowners who paid for their passage across the Atlantic. The British colonizers, who lived in what would later become the United States, used indentureship and enslavement to get enough people to farm crops such as tobacco and cotton in the Southern part of the country.

People who survived their period of indentureship went on to live free lives in the colonies, often after receiving some small compensation like clothes, land, or tools to help set them up. That was the incentive for poor whites to indenture themselves and their families and move to the so-called New World.

Some Africans who were indentured were often captured and taken to the USA against their will. That is what happened to the holder of Casor's indenture, Anthony Johnson.

Johnson served out his contract and went on to run his tobacco farm and hold his indentured laborers, among them Casor. At that time, the colony of Virginia had very few black people; Johnson was one of the original 20.

After a disagreement about whether or not Casor's contract has lapsed, a court ruled in favor of Johnson, and Casor saw the status of his indenture turn into slavery, where he, not his contract, was considered property. Casor claimed that he had served his indenture of seven or eight years and seven more years on top of that. The court sided with Johnson, who claimed that Casor was his slave for life. Casor became the first person to be arbitrarily declared a slave for life in the USA. An earlier case had ended with John Punch having been declared a slave for life as a punishment for trying to escape his indentured servitude. His fellow escapees, who were white, did not receive the same punishment.

In 1661, Virginia made it a state law allowing any free white, black, or Indian to own slaves and indentured laborers. When Johnson died in 1670, his race was used to justify giving his plantation to a white man rather than to his children by his wife, Mary; A judge ruled that he was not a citizen of the colony because he was black.

Indentureship is one of the arrangements in which a variety of misinformation manipulates individuals. It is an institution that reflected a fairly common practice whereby landlords were assured that others worked to feed them and were held down, legally and economically, while doing so. The arrangements were enacted into law to provide labor under controlled and specified conditions. Indentureship was one of the various guises in which individuals across the globe were conscripted to provide labor for the development of the capitalist mode of production that developed Europe. It continued to exploit the world it had *discovered* and, more germanely, conquered from the 1490s.

The British East India Company conquered India between 1657 and 1818. The British passed laws that changed the rules on land taxes and crops that should be cultivated. Consequently, millions died from famine. Those who survived were pushed off the land to become the excess labor exported to other parts of the British Empire as needed. Under the new racism, Indians were lower intrinsically than Europeans. Indentured Indians were first used within India in the tea plantations of Assam and then to the newly acquired islands of Reunion and Mauritius.

After the emancipation of enslaved Africans in the British Empire, rather than moving to *free labor,* as was promised, they introduced *unfree* indentured labor by law. The contracts of the indentures were structured to keep them bound to their employer. If they were not in the fields, they had to be either in jail or in hospital. Infractions of their contract were subjected to criminal penalties, and those were liberally applied.

The indentureship system in India was a kind of serfdom. Recruited by agents at Calcutta and Madras, who toured villages where crops were failing and told of more accessible work for higher wages, the Indians signed contracts. The laws were heavily weighted against them; they were held criminally liable for even the most straightforward breach of the contract. Though they left India ignorant of the conditions under which they were traveling and the work that they would be required to do, the laborers had no freedom to withdraw from the contract once it was signed.

The indentured Indians saved the sugar economy in British Guiana and Trinidad and contributed significantly to Britain's wealth. The system was built on the foundation laid by the slavery system that it so closely resembled. Overseers pride themselves as disciplinarians and claim to always have their indentures at work, in the hospital, or prison. Hugh Tinker said that indenture did, indeed, replicate the actual conditions of slavery. For almost eighty years, British politicians and administrators were confronted with evidence that the planting interest was exploiting Indian workers in ways that a decent, humane society could not tolerate.

Nevertheless, they continued to assure themselves that these wrongs were mere abuses and irregularities which could be amenable to reform. The system came to an end as a result of an outcry from Indian public opinion. The British authorities thought it wise to make such a concession when the nationalist movement was gaining strength.

CHAPTER 15

The Indentureship of Portuguese

AFTER ABOLISHING THE SLAVE TRADE IN 1807, THE planters were in desperate need to substitute the free and reliable labor force. To fill the ranks of the soon-to-be-liberated African slaves, they were initially interested in seeking a labor force from Europe since they realized a decreasing proportion of whites in the colonies. They felt that the imbalance could be remedied by recruiting indentured labor from European countries. In addition to strengthening their security, they wanted to have an alternative labor force to compete with the ex-slaves for plantation jobs after emancipation, forcing down employment costs.

In late 1834, a small group of Portuguese was recruited from the Portuguese island of Madeira. On May 3, 1835, forty indentured peasants arrived from Madeira on the ship Louisa Baillie. The arrivals were brought in through the private enterprise of the planters who were made aware of the great

149

poverty and political instability on the island of Madeira. The hard-pressed Madeiran peasants were most likely eager to seek their fortune in the land referred to as El Dorado. By the end of the year, others had arrived and were contracted as indentured laborers to various sugar plantations. The Madeiran peasants were capable farmers born on a small and mountainous island where every square meter of the soil was precious. Their recruitment was part of a migration scheme based on a bounty system. Under that system, public money made available by the British Government was used to pay the planters for each immigrant transported to the Colony.

In addition to the Portuguese who arrived in 1835, small groups of Germans and English farmers were also recruited. In 1836, 44 Irish and 47 English laborers landed in British Guiana, and in the following year, 43 Scottish laborers arrived from Glasgow. In 1839, 209 Maltese and 121 Germans were added to the population. Many of those laborers did not adapt well to the climate. They suffered, resulting in high mortality. The Maltese, who were indentured to Hibernia in Essequibo, suffered severely. Their social conditions deteriorated so rapidly that the Governor canceled their indentures and arranged for them to be shipped back to Malta.

Between 1836 and 1839, the planters did not recruit any more Portuguese. That situation changed in 1840 when 15 Portuguese from Madeira arrived, followed by 4,297 in 1841. The first arrivals suffered from a deficiency in the diet, inadequate accommodation, and overwork in a rigorous climate to improve their economic status. Neither suffering nor death deterred them. After their indentureship, thirty of the original emigrants returned to Madeira with their earnings and encouraged their families, relatives, and friends to migrate to British Guiana. The later arrivals from Madeira seemed to be less impoverished, acclimatized better, and suffered less.

The year 1841 proved to be a bad year for the immigrants as yellow fever raged in British Guiana. Among the children, measles spread rapidly with fatal results. The British Guiana Government concern over the high death rate of the Portuguese, set up a commission of inquiry to investigate the reasons for the sickness and mortality among the emigrants.

Based on the results, instructions were sent to the recruiting agent in Madeira to discontinue sending emigrants to British Guiana after March 1, 1842. Migration was also halted when the Governor and the Bishop of the island began a scare campaign warning those who are desirous of going to British Guiana to be branded and sold as slaves on arrival. That caused the emigration to slow down. Despite the mortality and the subsequent discontinuation of emigration from Madeira, more than 1,200 Portuguese arrived between 1842 and 1846. A turn-around occurred in 1846 when a Famine struck the island in 1846, and a turn-around occurred. It encouraged over 6,000 of the inhabitants to migrate to British Guiana under the bounty system. By 1848, an additional 4,000 left the island for British Guiana. Migration was halted again in 1848 due to a high mortality rate among the new immigrants. It resumed in 1850. From then on, small numbers of Portuguese continued to arrive until 1882, when the last group of 182 arrived. From the inception of Portuguese migration, 30,645 indentured Portuguese arrived mainly from Madeira, while smaller groups came from the Azores, Cape Verde, and Brazil.

The indentured Portuguese rarely remained on the sugar plantations after they completed their period of indentureship. They found it physically challenging to carry out the tasks in the sugarcane fields. The popular opinion also influenced them that working in the sugarcane fields was akin to slavery. In addition, they felt uncomfortable working alongside Africans and Indians, whom the whites regarded as socially inferior. Being white also felt below their dignity to associate themselves with such a menial position in colonial society. The planters, themselves whites, were uncomfortable ordering people of their ethnic group to do strenuous fieldwork. The planters suggested that the Portuguese be given the status of British citizens, but that never happened.

They moved off the plantations and their small plots of land as soon as their indentureship period of two to four years ended. Some of them got into the huckster and retail trades. The European merchants in Georgetown employed many of them as agents to retail imported goods to the rural areas. They quickly took over that role from the Africans and mulattos who were initially given that task. As retailers, they established shops and supplied basic supplies to the plantation workers who were, by that time, mainly indentured Indians. A few of them also began importing their goods, including famous Portuguese Port wines from Madeira.

The Portuguese readily adapted to commerce. During their indenture, they worked hard and saved their earnings which they invested mainly in their businesses. By 1851, 173 out of the 296 shops in Georgetown belonged to the Portuguese. In New Amsterdam, they owned 28 of the 52 registered shops, while in the villages; they had 283 of the 432 shops. By the end of the nineteenth century, large Portuguese firms appeared on Water Street in Georgetown.

The Portuguese contributed significantly to the country's economy as they moved into every type of business. They eventually formed a significant section of the growing merchant class and became a buffer class between the non-white and English expatriate populations. However, they were generally regarded by the English planters and civil servants as belonging to a slightly lower social status. The Englishmen soon classified them as a different ethnic group from that of Europeans.

CHAPTER 16

The Indentureship of Chinese

EVEN THOUGH THE PLANTERS IN BRITISH GUIANA expressed interest in introducing Chinese laborers since emancipation, it was not until 1851 that such recruitment began. Because of the long travel distance from China, Chinese were not recruited since it was cheaper to transport Indians. However, Indian immigration was suspended between 1848 and 1851. It cost a planter thirteen British pounds to transport an Indian laborer from Calcutta or Madras. The cost was fifteen pounds to transport a Chinese laborer from any of the ports of China. With the growing need for laborers at the sugar estates, the planters decided to recruit Chinese.

In August 1851, the British Guiana Government agreed to pay the planters a bounty of $100 for each Chinese who landed on the Colony. The following month George Booker, one of the sugar plantation owners, arranged for the first shipment of Chinese to work as indentured laborers. The 115 men and

39 boys were transported from the port of Amoy on Lord Elgin. The ship departed on July 23, 1852, and after a journey of 177 days, arrived in Georgetown on January 17, 1853. On this challenging voyage, sixty-nine of the passengers died.

Another ship, the Glentanner, chartered by Hyde, Hodge & Co, left Amoy with 305 men and boys and arrived in Georgetown on January 12, 1853. A total of fifty-one passengers died on the journey. The same Company recruited another 352 men and boys later in the year. They were shipped from Amoy on the Samuel Boddington on November 25, 1852, and arrived in Georgetown on March 4, 1853, after a voyage that lasted only 98 days. On this voyage, fifty-two passengers died. On this journey, the Chinese mutinied and almost managed to take control of the ship.

Most of the Chinese who arrived during this period were assigned to estates in West Demerara. However, the British Guiana Government expressed concerns about the physical quality of the Chinese recruited and the large number of boys who were passed off as adults. Subsequently, the Government withdrew the bounty payment to the recruiting planters on August 1, 1853. Earlier that year, James White, the recruiting agent for the British Guiana Government in India, was appointed as Emigration Agent for the British West Indies in China. However, he was dismissed in June of the following year mainly because he failed to recruit Chinese laborers.

The Chinese proved to be good workers on the estates they were indentured for five years. Subsequently, the planters influenced Governor Philip Wodehouse to appeal to the British Government on their behalf to allow the transport of Chinese to British Guiana through private enterprise. At first, that was not supported by the British Government, but eventually, in 1857, permission was granted for recruitment for one year. Towards the end of 1858, two ships overloaded with 761 passengers, collected from *Baracoons*, left Hong Kong for Georgetown to arrive in March and May 1859. On those two ships, 60 persons died on the long voyage.

In 1858 the authorities in the Chinese provinces of Kwangtung and Kwangsi, served by the city of Canton, encouraged people to migrate. That enabled the recruiting agents to contract females who were part of entire families. Thus, on December 24, 1859, the Whirlwind sailed from Hong Kong with 304 men, 56 women, seven boys under 15 years, and four girls under 13 years of age. The voyage lasted 78 days, and not a single life was lost.

From 1859 to 1860, five more ships left Hong Kong and Canton for British Guiana. There were 1549 men, 298 women, 53 boys, 26 girls, and 18 infants. In the succeeding years, ships continued to sail from Hong Kong, Canton, Amoy, Swatow, and Whampoa with Chinese laborers who included a disproportionate amount of women. The Dartmouth, which made the final voyage, sponsored by Hyde, Hodge & Co., started from Hong Kong on December 24, 1878. After 81 days, it arrived in Georgetown with 515 passengers: 436 men, 47 women, 18 boys, five girls, and nine infants. In that group were about 70 Christian converts. Thus, for the entire period of 1853 to 1879, 13,541 Chinese landed in British Guiana.

Contract of an indentured Chinese person in 1873

Agreement between *Soo Acheong*, a native of China, and Theophilus Sampson, Esq., Acting as Agent for the Government of the Colony of British Guiana in the West Indies.

Whereas the said T. Sampson has opened an Emigration Office at Canton for obtaining Chinese for the Colony of British Guiana, I the said *Soo Acheong* agree to go onboard ship and to go the British Guiana and there to work on the terms set forth below:

1. *I agree to work in British Guiana as I may be directed by the Government Immigration Agent or for any person to whom he may transfer this contract.*
2. *The period of service is five years commencing from the day I begin to work, or if on my arrival I am too ill to work, then it shall commence eight days after my recovery.*
3. *I agree to do any kind of work that I may be lawfully directed to do, whether in town or country, in fields, in factories, in private houses, etc.*
4. *I shall not be required to work on Sundays unless I am employed as a domestic servant or to take care of cattle; in such cases, I must work on Sunday in all cases in which it is the local custom to do so. In all other cases, my time during Sunday shall be entirely at my own disposal.*
5. *A day consists of 24 hours, and I may not be required to work more than nine and a half hours in one day. If I work more than nine and a half hours one day, I may work an equal length of time on another, or if not, then my employer shall compensate me.*
6. *At the end of the five years' service, my master will give me $50 in lieu of a return passage to China. If at the expiration of the term of the contract I do not wish to return to China, and if the Authorities of the place still permit me to reside in Guiana, in that case, my master shall give me the $50 stipulated in the contract for my own use; but if I wish to enter into another agreement for five years, half of the above sum namely $25 will be given to me by my master as a bonus, and at the end of the second five years the original sum of $50 will be paid to me in lieu of a return passage to China.*
7. *If after arrival I become incurably ill so as to be unable to work, my master shall at once pay me the fifty dollars to assist me to return to China, if my master does not do so, I may*

> petition the Authorities who shall on their part recover the money for me.
> 8. Wherever I may work, or in whatever family I may be employed, I must obey the lawful regulations there in force; on the other hand, should I at any time feel aggrieved at the conduct of my master towards me, all reasonable facility shall be afforded me, for laying my complaint before the proper officers of the Colony.
> 9. When the contract shall have been signed, and I have embarked, I cannot again return to the shore.
> 10. It is distinctly agreed that this contract binds the Indian to go as a laborer to no other place than British Guiana.
> 11. During the five years beginning on the day agreed in the contract, the wages shall be four dollars a month or the equivalent in gold, for which my master shall be responsible. The wages shall be paid every month and shall not be allowed to fall into arrear.
> 12. Every day, food will be issued as follows; 8 oz. salt meat and 2½ lbs. of other articles, all of which shall be good and wholesome.
> 13. In case of illness, medical attendance and medicines, and proper food will be provided free of expenses till recovery; no matter what such medical expenses may amount to, the master may make no deduction on account of them from the Indian's wages.
> 14. Each year they will be given me one suit of clothes and one blanket.

The fourteen thousand Chinese arrived in British Guiana between 1853 and 1879 on 39 vessels bound from Hong Kong filled the labor shortage on the sugar plantations endangered by the abolition of slavery. A smaller number of Chinese arrived in Trinidad, Jamaica, and Suriname. The Chinese achieved considerable success in the colonies. Most were bound under a five-year indentureship to work on the sugar plantations. Eighty-five percent of them were men, and most returned to China or immigrated to other parts of the Guianas and the Caribbean after completing or escaping their indentures. Those who remained subsequently turned to trade, competing effectively with the Portuguese and Indians, who had also entered as indentured laborers.

In 1853, the British Government had decided to support a government-sponsored recruitment program. However, by May 1854, the British Guiana Government decided to halt immigration from China due to the transportation costs that had increased by over 66 percent and the failure to recruit women. With the absence of Chinese women among the immigrants, many men established conjugal relations with African women. The mixed children born out of those unions were referred to as *Chinese-duglas.*

Unlike other overseas Chinese communities, the Chinese of British Guiana swiftly abandoned traditional Chinese customs, religion, and language. Their acceptance of Christianity contrasted with the strong attachment of other overseas Chinese communities to their ancestral religions. Many of the first-generation Chinese-Guyanese were Christians in China, and they converted readily on arrival. They built and maintained their Christian churches throughout the Colony and paid their Chinese-speaking catechists. In 1860, Mr. Lough Fook, who had come from China to spread the gospel among the immigrants, established The Chinese Baptist Church of British Guiana, first at Peter's Hall and later at Leonora. Wu Tai Kam, an Anglican missionary, arrived in the Colony from Singapore in 1864 and successfully proselytized immigrants. He was given a government stipend as a missionary to the

Chinese immigrants and was instrumental in establishing the Chinese settlement at Hopetown, West Coast Berbice.

For those who were lucky enough to marry the few Chinese women in The Colony or migrated as families, domestic life was characterized by a sense of good breeding in familial relations. They always hung curtains in their rooms and decorated them with mirrors and pictures. Their homes were regarded as models of cleanliness and comfort. The descendants of the Chinese spoke and wrote English fluently. By the 1920s, there was no longer a need for Chinese-speaking pastors. In the first years of the 20th century, prosperous Guyanese Chinese began sending their sons and daughters to England for university education.

By the mid-twentieth century, the descendants of the original immigrants had assimilated so entirely into mainstream British colonial culture that they had become uninteresting to anthropologists. Anthropologist Morton Fried found them entirely at home in European culture and its local manifestation, with no ancestral cult, no ancestral tablets, no ceremonial burial ground or permanent record of genealogy, and no trace of Chinese medicine. The grandchildren and great-grandchildren of the original immigrants did not even know the Chinese characters for their names. The young anthropologist declared with exasperation, "These people are scarcely Chinese."

The Chinese continued to prosper in the retail trades. They contributed substantially to the Colony's gold, diamond, and bauxite resources, its professional community, and its political life. The three pillars of the community were the Chinese Association, the Chinese Sports Club, and St. Savior's Church, an Anglican house of worship founded, funded, and pastored by the Chinese-Guyanese.

On arrival in British Guiana, the Chinese immigrants agreed to the following terms of employment:

1. *Payment was at the same rate as indentured laborers - $4 a month, with sufficient food.*
2. *The working period would be seven and a half hours per day, except Sundays and holidays.*
3. *Free housing and medicines would be provided by the estate owner.*
4. *One dollar per month would be deducted from the wages for monetary advances made in China.*
5. *Every immigrant could terminate his contract at the end of a year, on payment, for each unexpired year of the contract, of a sum equal to one-fifth of the amount of the passage money.*
6. *Every female Chinese immigrant was required to live on the same estate with her husband or with her father if she was single and would not work unless she agreed.*

Those terms were discussed with the Chinese immigrants who signed agreements with the recruiting agents in China before they departed for British Guiana. The first Chinese batch was assigned to Plantation Blankenberg, West Coast Demerara, then to other estates on the West Bank Demerara. Those who arrived later were distributed to other estates, including to a few in Berbice and Essequibo. Working conditions were relatively good on most estates, but some Chinese laborers complained from time to time of unethical treatment.

The Chinese came from many regions, and they spoke different dialects. They also had varying skills and religious beliefs. Many of them were social outcasts picked up from the streets, while others emigrated to escape misery and war. They were concerned about maintaining their language and forms of their culture. Some of them, who had a relatively good level of education, organized night schools on the sugar plantations to teach the boys writing and singing. Eventually, like the Portuguese, the Chinese forsook the plantations for the retail trades and soon became assimilated into the Guyanese society.

CHAPTER 17

The Indentureship of Indians

IN THE NINETEENTH CENTURY, AFTER ABOLITION OF THE slave trade, two million Indians were transported to labor in British colonies as a substitute for slave labor. The system expanded after the emancipation of slavery in the British Empire in 1833, in the French colonies in 1848, and in the Dutch Empire until 1863. Indian indentureship lasted until the 1920s and resulted in the development of a large Indian diaspora in the Caribbean, Guyana, Natal, Réunion, Mauritius, Sri Lanka, Malaysia, Myanmar, and Fiji.

In 1807, Britain had some 2.5 million slaves and the same number as indentured laborers. By the 1830s, slaves on British plantations began to exercise their right to freedom. Africa could not remain the catchment area for replacements. The eyes of the British Government turned to its most lucrative colony, British India. British rule had extended up to Bhojpuri-speaking Bihar in the north and between Madras and Mysore in the south. Lord Cornwallis '*Permanent Settlement*' taxation killed millions in Bengal and left those who survived on the edge of famine and desperation. The famines that resulted from that pool produced the new slaves.

During the period of unpaid apprenticeship, following the emancipation of slaves in 1833, many liberated Africans left their former masters. The planters who required a regular, docile, and free-labor force appeared to be an economic disaster. Britain was forced to look elsewhere for cheap labor and turned its attention to Madeira and China for a brief period, then to India.

The solution came in the form of a new system of forced labor, which in many ways resembled enslavement. Indians, under an indenture or contract labor scheme, began to replace enslaved Africans on plantations across the British Empire.

A planter of Trinidad proposed the large-scale importation of free laborers from India in 1814. He soon won the support of the Governor of the colony. The Gladstone family, who received the largest compensation of £85,606 for 2,183 slaves set free in British Guiana and Jamaica, enthusiastically sponsored the idea. From 1838 about 238,000 Indians were shipped to British Guiana, 145,000 to Trinidad, and 21,500 to Jamaica.

The first Indians arrived in British Guiana under a scheme ordered by Lord Stanley, Secretary of State for the Colonies. A civil contract between Britain and Indian workers was drawn up for an initial period of five years. Indians were treated the same as the African slaves in the early phase. As with African slaves who were held in forts awaiting transportation, Indians were held in depots. They were often deceived about the work on offer. They were hustled aboard waiting ships unprepared for the long and arduous four-month sea journey. William Gladstone, who also imported Indians for his plantations in British Guiana, was Secretary of State for the Colonies. Officials informed him that the Indians had no idea of the place they agreed to go to or the length of the voyage they were undertaking.

Within two years, Charles Anderson, a British magistrate in British Guiana, unable to contain his anger, wrote to the Colonial Secretary declaring that the Indians were treated with great and unjust severity, by overwork and personal chastisement. Whipping, imprisonment, and death were common, often through starvation. Nothing had changed except for the ethnicity of the slaves. Plantation owners enforced the regulations so harshly that, according to the Historian Hugh Tinker, the decaying remains of immigrants were frequently discovered in cane fields. If laborers did not work, they were not paid or fed; they simply starved to death. In 1840 the importing of contract labor from India was suspended.

After the supply of Indian contract laborers was cut off, a few Europeans were imported, but they were by no means sufficient for the tasks. Lord Stanley experimented with a few schemes that yielded few results. He reinstated immigration from India. This time an Act was passed to protect the well-being of the Indian immigrants. Provision was made for basic housing, food rations, clothing, and wages for the immigrants on a task basis.

Slavery had powerful allies, including the Church of England, which used slaves on its sugar plantations and lobbied against abolition in Parliament. An alliance of the Church and the City had to be appeased, and it was. By 1844, after fruitless attempts to find Chinese laborers from Malacca and Africans from Sierra Leone, London decided that commerce was more important than morality. The *loot* of India resumed, and it soon began to fill the British Empire cash-crop havens of Mauritius, British Guiana, Fiji, Jamaica, and Trinidad first, followed by Natal, Malaysia, Ceylon, and Myanmar. Women were picked up to solve sex starvation and learned the meaning of slavery when British crews raped them *en route*. Those who died in the squalor and disease on the ships were thrown overboard. By the 1880s, destitution in Bihar and Avadh had forced even high caste Brahmins into indentured labor, making them a powerful community in places like Fiji. The patois of Mauritius includes a heavy strain of Bhojpuri; its music is a fascinating blend of Bihar, Britain, and France.

Most indentured laborers were drawn from the agricultural and laboring classes of the Uttar Pradesh and Bihar regions of north India. A comparatively smaller number was recruited from Bengal and various areas in south India. Approximately 85 percent of the immigrants were Hindus, and 14 percent Muslims. Despite the adverse conditions experienced under the indentured system, about 90% of the Indian immigrants chose to make British Guiana their permanent home at the end of their contracted periods of indentureship. The predominant age group of the immigrants was 20-30 years. While most came as unmarried individuals, some came as small family units.

The debate surrounding the nature and workings of the system of Indian Indentureship in India is multifaceted and relatively open-ended. Much ambiguity has marked the system, especially during the first three decades of operation. These include the recruitment process in India and the British role in the impoverishment of nineteenth-century India. It is still unclear whether the indentured Indians were fully cognizant of the real nature and details of what they were embarking on or their level of awareness that they were leaving Indian soil.

Initially, the journey from India to British Guiana averaged about three months. It became substantially shorter and less turbulent with the opening of the Suez Canal in 1869.

Conditions on board the ships were cramped and depressing, and there were frequent outbreaks of such diseases as cholera, typhoid, dysentery, and measles which led to high mortality rates on some of the journeys.

The first two decades of the system were highly experimental, lacking in rules and conditions. There were two central and constant features of the system: Immigrants were contracted for long periods with a single employer, and there were penal sanctions for breaches of the contract. From the Immigration Ordinance of 1854 until 1917, the system remained relatively consistent with a few notable changes, the most significant of which was granting Crown land in place of the free return passage between 1869 and 1880.

Life on the estates was bound by the terms and conditions of the contract that the indentured immigrants had signed, even though most were illiterate in all three languages in which the contract was formulated. In effect, the Indians were not free during their periods of indenture. They could not demand higher wages, leave the estate without permission, live off the estates, or refuse the work assigned to them. As stipulated in the contract, the basic minimum wage was 25 cents per day or task for adult males and 16 cents for adult females. Although this amount could not be reduced legally, the plantation often lengthened the task. Wages also varied according to the type of work, season, and area. The contract stipulated a 45-hour workweek, but it could be six days a week with nine hours each day during crop time. Sunday was always a holiday.

A most troublesome feature of the system for the indentured laborers was the fact that they could be and were prosecuted as criminals for what were civil offenses; the slightest breach of contract and immigration laws. Indians leaving the boundaries of their respective estates were required to carry a pass stating that they had been granted permission to do so.

Many Indians were imprisoned for vagrancy or being found at large if found off the plantation without a pass or ticket of leave. Such unlawful absence from the estate could result in a maximum sentence of seven days in jail. Absence from the estate for three or more days was termed *'Desertion'* and could earn the immigrant a maximum of two months in prison. Official investigations revealed that the everyday occurrences of both absenteeism and desertion were deeply connected to the question of management on the estates, the harsh treatment of the immigrants, and unscrupulous employers conniving for desertion by unfit or unwanted persons.

To deal with the issues of absenteeism and desertion, Indians who had completed their periods of indenture were still required to carry their Certificates of Industrial Residence to prove that they were not deserters seeking employment; their word did not suffice. Other offenses carrying sentences included willful disobedience, threatening or verbally insulting the employer, and deception in performing work. The courts were heavily weighted against the Indians, and excessive sentences were often unfairly imposed upon them. Very few Indians understood the Immigration Ordinances, could defend themselves or pay for legal aid. By the 1870s, Immigration Laws were becoming increasingly arbitrary and confusing for the immigrants. Also, each revision of the law saw penalties becoming more stringent and comprehensive.

While, in theory, there were several apparatus put in place for the well-being and protection of the immigrants, these were more often than not very ineffective. The Immigration Department was headed by the Protector of Immigrants/Agent-General, who was supposed to be representing the interests of the Indians via its regulations and regular estate inspections. The immigration department even acted as a court of the last appeal. It was highly vulnerable to pressure from the planters and often failed to protect the immigrants' duties.

Too few immigrants lodged complaints due to fear of victimization and the impartiality of the magistrate's court, which was often inclined to accept the evidence of the estate authorities over that of the Indians. Those, together with an all-pervading influence of the planters, overarching administrative weaknesses, and general complacency in the operation of reformed laws, led to excessive exploitation being an integral aspect of the system of Indian indenture. However, the ultimate sanction against the maltreatment of the immigrants was the power of the Governor to remove even an entire gang from an estate.

Despite the safeguards put in place by the British Parliament to prevent indentured workers from suffering a new form of enslavement, plantation owners continued to abuse their Indian workers. At the end of the nineteenth century, Mahatma Gandhi argued with the Colonial Government in Natal, South Africa, for Indian rights. Through Gandhi's efforts and intervention by the Indian Government, the indenture scheme finally ended. By then, the number of Indians shipped to British Colonies worldwide was estimated to be 2.5 million.

Under a system of agreement, an order in the Council of Britain was passed on July 12, 1838, making provision for Indians to serve as indentured laborers in British Guiana for five years. On January 13, 1838, the Whitby left the shores of India with 249 laborers and arrived in British Guiana on May 5, 1838. After the voyage of 112 days, five Indians died. The Whitby proceeded first to Berbice and unloaded 164 of its passengers at Hilbury, East Bank Berbice, nearly 12 miles from New Amsterdam. On the same day, it sailed to Vreed-en-hoop, West Demerara, and unloaded 80 passengers. The 244

Indian laborers that arrived on the Whitby were 233 men, five women, and six children. The first man to step onshore in Berbice was Anant Ram, while in Demerara; the first man to disembark was Nutha Khan.

On January 29, 1838, the Hesperus sailed from Calcutta with 165 Indian laborers on board. It arrived at Port Georgetown on the night of May 5, 1838. Two Indians fell overboard, and 13 died during the voyage. The 152 Indians on board the Hesperus were 135 men, six women, and 11 children. On January 26, 1845, Lord Hunger left Calcutta with 162 Indians and arrived in Georgetown on May 4, 1845, with 152 Indians. The ship Success arrived on July 21, 1845, with 231 Indians. Fourteen died on the way. Nester arrived on December 26, 1845, with 233 Indians together with 500 bags of rice.

On February 2, 1846, the ships Manchester, Thetis, Tamerlane, Martin Luther, and Troy in succession, then the John Wickliffe, Bussorary Merchant, Aurora, Lady Mekennaway, and SS Ganges set sailed with Indian laborers from India to British Guiana. During those 79 years, 238,979 indentured Indians served the colonial administration of British Guiana. They were distributed to various plantations on the coastline of Guyana.

On arrival in Guyana, they were quarantined and then assigned to the various estates for the contracted three-year period. That was followed by a two-year period which completed the industrial residence of five years. At the end of these five years, the Indian immigrants would be granted a Certificate of Industrial Residence, a freedom paper certifying that the individual was no longer under indentureship. However, to qualify for the free return passage back to India, the Indians had to re-indenture themselves for five years. However, they were free to choose both employer and occupation. The only alternative for returning to India without completing the full ten years of labor in the colony was at one's own expense.

The plantation system and the living conditions were unfavorable for human existence; the laborers worked from sunrise to sunset and were paid just enough to survive. They labored to provide a luxurious living for their masters. The Indians were disciplined and found satisfaction in honest and productive work. They were kind, hospitable, and generous as they strive to live contented lives with the continuation of the rich culture and heritage they brought with them.

The foremost characteristic of the struggle of the Indian laborers against the indentureship and plantation system was their unity. Those who traveled on the same ship were considered ship brothers and sisters, *Jahaji*. A further contributing factor to unity was that everyone maintained their inter-faith mind of mainly Hindus and Muslims. There was also the belief that the caste system has been lost through the crossing of the oceans. Through the years, the community spirit has manifested itself in various situations, such as forming groups singing Ramayan Bhajanas, reading the Holy Quran, observing the various festivals and Holidays.

The plantation owners and the colonial administration feared the workers' unity and used several techniques to obstruct it. There was evidence that the Indian laborers were being mistreated. Far more significant were the uprisings that frequently led to tragic deaths of laborers protesting illegal wages, bad conditions, and exploitation of women. There were eight prominent disturbances on sugar plantations leading to shooting by colonial police from Devonshire Castle in 1872 to Enmore in 1948. At Vreed-en-hoop, West Bank Demerara, an English nurse Betsy Ann testified that she had witnessed the flogging of Indian laborers with the cat-o-nine tails. Another woman, Elizabeth Caesar, witnessed a flogging under the manager's house, after which the salt pickle was rubbed onto their backs. One out of every five laborers was brought before the courts, not for offenses of a criminal nature but for resistance to a plantation system that was supported by the judiciary and colonial administration.

By the 1870s, Indians had proven themselves the virtual backbone of the sugar industry in British Guiana. For the Indians, estate life had become irrevocably unattractive. Indians began moving off the estates in large numbers to become independent farmers, settling on and cultivating lands granted to them through the land commutation scheme or what they had purchased from the State.

Throughout the entire Indian indenture system, the living conditions on any given estate were hardly agreeable, often in highly subhuman conditions. On the estates, Indians were assigned barrack-type quarters. These were frequently the same barracks used to house the formerly enslaved Africans. Each room of the barrack building measured 10 feet square and 8 to 10 feet high. The partitions between rooms did not reach the roof so that there was a total lack of privacy. Ventilation was always inadequate. Each such room accommodated a married couple and their children or two to four single adults. Cooking was usually done on the outside.

Two persistent problems on the estates were sanitation and the provision of drinking water. Although some estates had wells and manual water pumps, the facilities for storing rainwater on the estates were inadequate. Even when there was adequate storage, the water was still often polluted since both employers and laborers were careless about preserving the purity of the drinking water. The Indians themselves further exacerbated the situation by drinking water from the streams, ponds, and canals. Until the twentieth century, stagnant drains and the absence of latrines created serious sanitation problems on most of the estates. Indians had to resort to using the fields. Thus, dysentery, cholera, and other parasite-related diseases as intestinal parasites, ground itch, and anemia were rampant on almost all estates. Indians were also victims of occasional epidemics of yellow fever and smallpox.

According to the law, each of the estates had to have a hospital to cater to the Indian indentured laborers, which the District Medical Officers visited at fixed times. However, the condition of these hospitals fluctuated from good to deplorable. In the latter situation, the Indians had to stay in their barracks and hospital when the doctor visited. The Indians had such distaste for staying under the dilapidated conditions that they would run away from the hospital. A law had to be passed that imposed jail sentences on those who ran away from the hospital. Despite steady attempts at improving the health of the laborers, investigations have revealed that an indentured laborer was ill for up to four weeks per year. The high infant mortality rate was a significant source of concern throughout indenture.

Due to the combined factors of the general lack of privacy in the living arrangements and the disappearance of the extended family system, there was a loosening of conjugal bonds, and family life on the estates suffered tremendously. Throughout the entire duration of the indenture system, there was an acute imbalance in the ratio of male to female laborers. The eventual scarcity of Indian women had a severe impact on family life on the plantations since most Indian men refused to marry or cohabitate with African women. Competition for Indian women led to the erosion of caste restrictions and generated severe tension, which often erupted in violence and sometimes loss of life against unfaithful women. Traditional Indian male-female dynamics eroded. The practice of dowry in the Hindu marriage ceremony where the bride's party gave gifts to the groom was reversed and replaced by the bride price, where the prospective groom had to pay for his bride. Marriages were noticeably unstable, and keeper unions were quite common, with their stability residing primarily in the satisfaction of the female. Inter-caste marriages and Hindu/Muslim marriages were common on the estates.

A wide cross-section of the Indian caste system manifested itself among the indentured laborers. Hardly surprisingly, about 38 percent came from the agricultural castes, 31 percent from the low and laboring castes, and about 13 percent from the Brahmin/priestly caste. These figures, however, carry with them a deep-seated ambiguity on the issue of authenticity of caste proclamations by the indentured Indians. There are many stories of individuals changing their castes from the time they arrived at the depots in India. However, there was a significantly rapid attenuation and reworking of the Indian social system, which could not reproduce itself under extremely variant social, political, economic, ethnic, and religious composition. Thus, rather than the system itself, some elements of caste ideology and practices survived on the estates in variously attenuated and diluted forms.

The process of caste disintegration and dilution began in the depots in India, where all the indentured, regardless of caste classification, had to share common space and facilities. That process continued on the estates where shared living facilities and consequent indiscriminate contact among all the laborers further diluted many traditional taboos such as those associated with eating and touch. All of the laborers, except a few, were reduced to the same social status. Occupation, instead of being dictated by caste, was now determined by the estate overseer. Though small in number, high caste men, or those with claims to a high caste, continued to wield influence among the others. The Brahmins, due to their role in religious and ritual performance and preservation, would emerge at the front of Indian socio-cultural and even socio-political life on the estates.

In general, life on the plantations focused on the maximum extraction of labor was not conducive to the substantial reconstruction of any aspect of religious, cultural, or family life. In addition to the highly labor-intensive days, there were many rules and regulations that directly curtailed Indian religious and cultural practices. For example, Hindus were prohibited from beating drums at their wedding ceremonies traditionally held at night since they disturbed the peace. Nevertheless, despite the many encumbrances, Indian religion and culture elements were eventually evident on almost all estates.

By the 1860s, rudimentary 2-3 feet tall structures, the earliest Hindu temples, began dotting the plantations. Similarly, the Muslims set up prayer spots. Simple domestic ceremonies such as the puja, with or without an animal sacrifice, were being conducted. Daily recitation from religious texts such as the Ramayana became a common occurrence after a long day's work. Those rituals provided the laborers with much-needed respite and solace from their otherwise horrible and drudging situation. Even communally observed festivals took birth on the plantations in the Muharram/Hosay celebration and the Ramleela festival.

The intense social, religious, and cultural diversity due to the vast sweep of migration developed a reconstruction process; it was highly creative and marked by substantial telescoping, adjustment, and substitution levels. Syncretism was also evident in the growing participation of Hindus in highly ritualistic Christian and Muslim religious practices.

Life on the plantations hardly took into account the particularities of Indian social life. Thus, Indian marriages, both

Hindu and Muslim, were not recognized as legal unless registered with the District Immigration Agent, and the children born of such unions were deemed illegitimate. Consequently, there were persistent problems over the inheritance of property. Governors had to re-grant lands to the children of Crown grantees who failed to register their marriages and had died intestate. For the Indians, their religious ceremony was all the validation needed for a marriage. The Colonial authorities only recognized those officially registered unions, which was not part of the Indians' tradition.

Hindus had to resort to burying their dead since permission was not granted for the traditional cremation method. Alcohol and ganja consumption was quite common among the Indians, and, unsurprisingly, many ordinances and laws were implemented to curb the widespread and increasing drunkenness. It was indeed that unity of principle and action that brought overwhelming success to their lives in Guyana.

How the Indians were induced to British Guiana

Under a Bill for protecting the Indian laborers, it was proposed to legalize their importation into the colonies. The manner that the Slave-trade crept in under the shadow of Parliamentary regulation became a race between abuses and legislation. The legislation was always in the rear, and so it was with the Indian trade. The same circle of the most poignant misery was followed year after year with the same result; in the case of the new, as of the old, the only path of safety lies in absolute prohibition.

LONDON: Harvey and Darton, Gracechurch Street; Ball, Arnold and Co., 31, Paternoster Row; Hatchard and Son, 187, Piccadilly; and at the Office of the British and Foreign

Anti-slavery Society, 27, New Broad Street. (The pamphlet was printed initially by Johnston and Barrett, Printers, 13 Mark Lane, London).

This pamphlet was drafted by the British Foreign and Anti-Slavery Society in response to Lord John Russell's announcement that his cabinet was considering that the ban on importing Indian laborers to Mauritius is lifted. The pamphlet described John Scoble's account of the abuses directed towards Indians uncovered during his trip to the West Indies for the Central Emancipation Committee. The pamphlet, written in February 1840, also attempted to display the Mauritian planter's circumvention of Crown directives concerning the importation of slaves and Indian laborers. Although Russell met with a delegation of the abolitionists, he confirmed that the Government would proceed with its intention of reopening the exportation of Indian laborers. With a few exceptions, the exportation of indentured Indian laborers to various British colonies lasted until January 1, 1920, when the last indentured Indians in Fiji were released from their contracts. Transportation of indentured Indians to British Guiana ended in 1917.

The following statement to the press was to fill the hiatus left in the papers recently presented to the House of Commons regarding the Hill Indians in British Guiana, which Mr. William Gladstone moved on February 18. It appeared desirable that the country should know that a large amount of information respecting the general treatment of the Indians in that colony existed besides the very partial, and, I have no hesitation in saying because I am personally familiar with the facts, most unfair representations made to the Home Government on the whole subject.

Before I visited Guiana in the early part of 1839, the concealment system was adopted with admirable success. When, however, concealment was no longer possible, palliation and apology were resorted to; and to me, were it not a source of deep sorrow that the exposure of the hardships and sufferings of the wretched Indians were treated with lightness, and that an attempt was made thereby to impose on the British public, it would be infinitely amusing to observe the attempts of Governor Light, to account for his ignorance of the facts brought to light, the silence of his magistracy, and the conduct of the parties implicated in the guilty transactions to which reference is made. The ridiculous attempt of his Excellency to fasten unworthy motives on me, in part I felt it to be my duty to take in the affair. I pass by as unworthy of observation. However much it may please the planters, it cannot injure me.

It was not my intention to have added my name to the statement, now given to the public - not judging it to be necessary; but having submitted it to the perusal of some friends after it was in type, they suggested the propriety of my doing so, and this must be my apology for the form in which it appears.

JOHN SCOBLE
London, February 28, 1840.

Origin of the Indian Slave Trade

On January 4, 1836, John Gladstone, Esq., addressed a letter to Messrs. Gillanders, Arbuthnot & Co., of Calcutta, in which he said:

> You will probably be aware that we are very particularly situated with our negro apprentices in the West Indies, and that it is matter of doubt and uncertainty, how far they may be induced to continue their services on the plantations after their apprenticeship expires in 1840. This, to us,

is a subject of great moment and deep interest in the colonies of Demerara and Jamaica. We are, therefore, most desirous to obtain and introduce laborers from other quarters, and particularly from climates similar in their nature.

After giving a most glowing account of the colony, the lightness of the labor required, and the repose enjoyed by the people, their "schools on each estate for the education of children; and the instruction of their parents in the knowledge of their religious duties" - (there were no schools on Vreed-en-Hoop or Vriedestein!!) he sums up all by observing, "It may be fairly said they pass their time agreeably and happily." Full of fears, however, for the future, he adds, "It is of great importance to us to endeavor to provide a portion of other labourers, whom we might use as a set-off, and, when the time for it comes, make us, as far as possible, independent of our negro population." He then gives an order for 100 Indians - "young, active, able-bodied people," to be bound to labor "for a period not less than five years, or more than seven years," the wages not to "exceed four dollars per month," to provide themselves! To which communication Messrs. Gillanders & Co., gave the following "encouraging" reply, on June 6, 1836; "within the last two years, upwards of 2000 natives have been sent from this to the Mauritius, by several parties here, under contracts of engagements for five years. The contracts, we believe, are all of a similar nature; and we enclose a copy of one, under which we have sent 700 or 800 men to the Mauritius; and we are not aware that any greater difficulty would present itself in sending men to the West Indies, the Natives being perfectly ignorant of the place they agree to go to, or the length of the voyage they are undertaking." They then go on to state that the men selected for Mauritius, have "hardly any ideas beyond those of supplying the wants of nature;" and, therefore, we suppose, more likely to become the dupes of the cunning knaves who would entrap them into engagements, of the nature of which, they would be entirely ignorant. The "Dhangurs," they add, in a subsequent part of their letter, "are always spoken of as more akin to the monkey than the man. They have no religion, no education, and, in their present State, no want, beyond eating, drinking and sleeping; and to procure which, they are willing to labour." Healthy subjects, honestly, to be made slaves and cultivate the estates of John Gladstone, Esq., in Demerara! Now what reply was made to the proposition of Gillanders and Co.?

Did the wealthy planter express his indignation that the Indian laborers were to be spirited away from their native land, under the idea that they were going to the "Company's Rabustie, to be engaged in gardening? Did he express his disgust that his agents should select such ignorant and wretched creatures as the Dhangurs to practice deceit upon? No! On the March 10, 1837, he and his friend, John Moss, Esq., of Liverpool, gave Messrs. Gillanders & Co. to understand, that in the following May, they intended to forward the good ship Hesperus to take Indians to Demerara," to the number of 150, and that should they have children to take with them, fifteen or twenty may be sent in addition. "In Demerara," Mr. Gladstone adds:

> The females are employed in the field as well as the men; and if the female Indians will engage to work there, a larger proportion may be sent, say two women to three men, or, if desired, equal numbers; but if they will not engage to work there, then the proportion sent to the Isle of France, of one female to nine or ten men, for cooking and washing, is enough.

It is enough to give these quotations to show the origin of the Indian slave-trade: and all we need to add, is, that "Andrew Colville, Esq., (a near connexion of Lord Auckland's) and Messrs. Davidsons, Barkley & Co. of London," joined their friend Mr. Gladstone in a similar commission to Messrs. Gillanders & Co.

Proceedings of the Government

It became necessary, in consequence of the State of the law in British Guiana, which restricted contracts for labor to three years duration, that Mr. Gladstone and his friends should be accommodated with an Order in Council to sanction their contracts for five years, commencing on the arrival of the Indians in Demerara. This had been granted them by Lord Glenelg, with the concurrence of Sir John Hobhouse, and of course, the whole of Her Majesty's then ministry. Under the date of May 20 1837, Mr. Gladstone wrote Gillanders & Co. "I have now made the necessary arrangements with the colonial department, and an Order in Council corresponding with them will be immediately published." He then increases the order for Indians from 150 to 200 (stating the tonnage of the "Hesperus" to be 334,) but he adds, "If that number should be considered too many, do not reduce it under 150," And remember, "one-third for the Messrs. Moss, two-thirds for me." The Order in Council was of the most objectionable kind. It gave carte blanche to every villain in British Guiana and every scoundrel in India to kidnap and inveigle into contracts for labor for five years, in a distant part of the world, the ignorant and inoffensive Hindu!

The Order in Council was issued July 12, 1837, but it was not until January 3, 1838, that the public in this country became aware of its existence, when it was denounced in the *British Emancipator* as giving birth to new slave-trade. In May, intelligence was received through the medium of the Calcutta papers of the most painful nature, detailing the infamous conduct of the Chokedars who were put on guard over the Indians, shipped for Demerara on board the Hesperus. One man died as a consequence of his having been kept below; and the Indians were made to pay by the Chokedars for the privilege of coming on deck! The same papers state that "the agent for shipping these poor unfortunate people has stated that he is authorized to ship TEN THOUSAND!"

Private letters also corroborated the fact that the Indians "had to be forced on board" the Hesperus - that "the hatches were bolted down," and that one man died from suffocation. It was stated also in the same communication that Whitby found difficulty in inducing the natives to go, and that force was required to accomplish the object. These statements were made on the authority of the Rev. Mr. Boaz, a Missionary in Calcutta. It was subsequently discovered that the trade of kidnapping Indians had been extensively carried on and that prison depôts had been established in the villages near Calcutta for the security of the wretched creatures, where they were most infamously treated, and guarded with the utmost jealousy and care, to prevent their escape until the Mauritian and Demerara slave-owners were ready for their reception.

A complete account of the discovery of the kidnappers, their modes of procuring Indian laborers, and their places of the retreat was inserted in the *Asiatic Journal of Calcutta*, July 5, 1838, copied from the authenticated report of Sergeant Floyd to the magistrates. It further appears that through the exertions of a Mr. Dias, a magistrate, twenty of the kidnappers were punished, and one hundred and twenty-five Indians released from their grasp that was described as highly delighted with their deliverance; and "as each group left the office, they gave three or four hearty cheers, and showered down blessings on the magistrate's head." Ought not the agents who employed these execrable kidnappers to have been punished? They most righteously deserved to have been placed by the side of the villains they employed.

The arrival of Indians in British Guiana

According to the official account, the number of Indians shipped from Calcutta, per *Hesperus*, was 155 men, five women, and ten children, in all 170 persons for Messers. Gladstone and Moss; per Whitby, they were shipped, 250 men, seven women, and ten children, in all 267 persons, to the care of James Matthews, Esq., attorney to Andrew Colville, Esq., and John Cameron, Esq., agent to Messrs. Gillanders & Co., of Calcutta. The Indians consigned to Mr. Cameron and were disposed to Messrs. Davidsons, Barkley & Co., and James Blair, Esq. During her voyage, the mortality on board the Hesperus was fourteen, of which number two were represented to have been drowned (suicides?). The mortality on board the Whitby amounted to four. From both vessels, 419 Indians landed, and they were distributed in the following manner:

Plantation Owners	Males	Females
Vreed-en-Hoop (John Gladstone, Esq.)	65	5
Vredestein (John Gladstone, Esq.)	31	0
Anna Regina (Moss)	46	3
Belle-Vue (*A. Colville, Esq.*)	79	3
Waterloo (James Blair, *Esq.*)	47	0
Highbury (Messers. Davidsons & Co.)	117	11
Total	**385**	**22**

A total of 407 persons, according to the official returns of the special magistrates, printed by order of the House of Commons, February 21, 1840, No. 77, pp. 51, 52. There was a difference in the numbers of Indians landed and located at the plantations; the discrepancies cannot be accounted for from the papers.

On August 30, 1838, Governor Light, having made the tour of the colony, wrote to Lord Glenelg, as follows: - "From the reports I have received, and from my personal observation, the Indians appear satisfied with their position, and have not disappointed their employers." In another dispatch, dated November 19, 1838, his Excellency states that "the general good health of the emigrants from India, is equal to that of any other labourer in this colony," the Creole Negros, of course not excepted. In this view, the Assistant Colonial Secretary, Mr. Wolseley, concurs, for he appends to his general report on the State of the immigrants, "The Indians have acclimatized well, and have suffered no disadvantage by emigrating to this colony." At a still later period, January 11, 1839, Governor Light, in a dispatch to Lord Glenelg, observes, "If my information be correct, the Hill Indians were accustomed to a marshy soil, to very low wages, and precarious scanty food, and though on limited wages, in comparison with the free labourer, yet are as carefully protected from oppression, and their complaints redressed as speedily, as those of other labourers!" He adds, "The Indians on Mr. Gladstone's property, are a fine healthy body of men; they are beginning to marry or cohabit with the negresses, and take pride in their dress; the few words of English they know, added to signs common to all, prove that `Sahib' was good to them."

On January 30, 1839, Mr. Special Justice Coleman inspected the Indians on plantation Vredestein, John Gladstone, Esq., and gave a most favorable report of their condition.

The labor required of them, only two-thirds of that expected from the late apprentices; and that "always of the lightest work going on." Their allowances are as per contract. To be sure, their houses were "not in good repair," but that is a matter of little importance in a colony where the climate is so "genial!" and where Governor Light firmly believed they had "more means of enjoyment than in their own country." Vreed-en-Hoop, another property of Mr. Gladstone's, was visited by Mr. Special Justice Delafons, on February 20, 1839; who reports that the Indians were "cheerful and contented;" but, unlike their brethren on Vriedestein, they were compelled to perform the same description of labor as the negro gang, and had one and a-half-guilder stopped out of their wages monthly, to be paid on their completing their servitude, as per agreement. The deaths on Vriedestein, in eight months, two males; on the sick list ten: and on Vreed-en-Hoop, in nine months, four males; on the sick list four.

On January 31, 1839, Mr. Special Justice Coleman inspected the Indians on Belle-Vue, the property of Mr. Colville, and reports that they were "lodged in a large *logie* built purposely for them," and were not required, or expected, to perform more than "two-thirds of the tariff of labour for seven hours and a-half." He states the number of deaths in eight months to nine males and one female child: on the sick list twenty. Mr. Special Justice Mure reports, the Indians at Anna Regina, belonging to Messrs. Moss, appear to be "very cheerful and contented," and that only one death had occurred in eight months. Mr. Special Justice Rose reports that the Indians on Waterloo, the property of James Blair, Esq., "are apparently quite satisfied," and that during eight months, there had been four deaths, and fifteen were on the sick list. On plantation Highbury, belonging to Messrs. Davidsons & Co., visited by Mr. Special Justice Macleod, on January 31, 1839, he reports, the Indians "cheerful and contented," and the number of deaths fifteen males, and two females, with from ten to fifteen on the sick list. It thus appears that the mortality during a period of rather more than eight months after arrival, on 419 Indians had been thirty-eight, *viz.*, thirty-five males and three females, and that seventy were usually on the sick list.

Up to this period, there was not a whisper to be heard in the colony of the ill-treatment of the Indians, although it must have been known to the special justices of the various districts in which the Indians were located that they were frequently in the habit of running away from the plantations, on the ground of alleged ill-treatment and anxiety to return to their native land. It was known that a large number had fled from Belle-Vue and were found on plantation Herstelling, on the opposite side of the river, where they declared that, in consequence of the severity of the treatment they had endured from their manager, Mr. Young, who accompanied them from India, they would rather die than go back. When the promise was given that the individual complained of should be discharged, they returned to the estate. It was also known that many fled at different times from plantation Vreed-en-Hoop, and that two "Jummun and Pulton, who left on October 11 1838, were never found". The bodies of two strange men were discovered about that time at Mahaica. They were found dead in the bushes; no doubt they were the missing Indians. The female child, about ten years old, who was reported dead in Mr. Special Justice Coleman's report, perished from the terrible effects resulting from the forcible violation of her person. An account of those incidents and much more that might be mentioned were carefully excluded from the reports.

The actual condition of the Indians was brought to light in consequence of a paragraph that appeared in the columns of the British Emancipator of January 9, 1839, which had reached the colony. James Matthews, Esq., after allowing three weeks to elapse to put his house in order, requested the Governor to appoint a commission of inquiry into the condition of the Indians on Belle-Vue, with the view of proving that the statements in the Emancipator were false and scandalous. It was to have been a very tight affair, but Mr. Scoble, being at that time in the colony and privately informed of the intended investigation, was determined to be present at the proceedings.

The evidence was taken by the Commissioners, although of the most partial and limited nature, established that the general accuracy of the report which had been made and was the means of bringing to light the hidden horrors of the system pursued on Belle-Vue. To detail, the whole of the iniquities practiced on the wretched Indians on that estate would fill a volume. It will be sufficient to say that the general manager of the estate, Mr. Russell Sharlieb, the manager of the Indians, and Dr. Nimmo, a relation of Mr. Gladstone, the medical man of the estate, as well as of Vredestein and Vreed-en-Hoop, were all indicted and convicted of brutal assaults, before the Inferior Criminal Court of British Guiana, and either fined or imprisoned!

One incident, however, connected with the sick-house on Belle-Vue must not be omitted; it is taken from an account given by an eyewitness of the melancholy scene. He wrote: "The spectacle presented to the observer in the sick-house was heart-rending! The house itself was wretchedly filthy, the persons and the clothes of the patients were filthy also; the poor sufferers had no mats, nor mattresses to lie on; a dirty blanket was laid under them and their clothes wrapped together formed a kind of a pillow. In one room where there were raised boards for the accommodation of seven persons only, eleven were confined, four of them lying on the floor. The squalid wretchedness of their appearance, their emaciated forms, and their intense sufferings from disease and sores, were enough to make the heart bleed! In the second room were found a worse class of patients. The scene in this chamber beggars description; out of the five confined there, two were dead, and one of the remaining three cannot long survive; should the others ultimately recover, it will be by a miracle - their bones appeared ready to protrude through their skins! (the three died shortly after.) When the magistrate inquired by signs of the miserable creature who appeared to be near death, what food he was allowed - he pulled out some hard-brown biscuit from under his head and exhibited it!! The Indians confined in other apartments appeared in the same State as those confined in the first chamber; in one of them was a man whose limbs have become contracted by disease since he came to the estate. In fact, you may suppose, that it must have been misery in perfection to have drawn from Mr. Wolseley this observation: I never saw such a dreadful scene of misery in my life as is now to be seen in the sick-house. I have been in a great many hospitals on various estates for the last twenty years; but I never saw such a melancholy scene!!"

But lest it should be suspected that the description is overwrought, attention is called to the remarks of Sir M. McTurk, one of the Commissioners appointed by the Court of Policy, to visit the estates on which the Indians were placed and to report thereon. In his place in the Court of Policy, he said:

> He would now say that, before that inquiry, it had often been his lot to witness scenes of distress, of acute bodily suffering, and deep affliction; but such unalleviated wretchedness, such hopeless misery as he beheld in that hospital, never before had he seen, nor could he have imagined that it existed in this colony. The

Indians in it were not suffering merely from sores; they had mortified ulcers, their flesh rotting on their bones, their toes dropping off. Some of them were in a dangerous state from fever, and all were in the utmost despondency.

The Commissioners corroborated the appalling statement in their official report. On Belle-Vue, they stated:

> Twenty have died from diseases contracted in the colony, and twenty-nine are now in a wretched state from ulcers, many of whom, in all probability, will die; and should they survive, they will (some of them) be rendered unfit to support themselves, from the loss of their toes, and part of their feet - the sick-house presents a spectacle pitiable to behold. These poor people are in a state of great misery, and from whatever cause it may have sprung, the effects are so appalling, that humanity calls loudly for the interference of the executive.

The consequence of this appeal was, after considerable opposition from Mr. Matthews, the attorney of the estate, and Dr. Nimmo, the medical attendant, they were removed to the colonial hospital and placed under the humane care and skillful treatment of Dr. Smith, the physician of the establishment.

It is to be regretted that Mr. Colville, to whom the Government imparted the information relative to the treatment of the Indians on his estate, instead of expressing his warm indignation against the brutal system of oppression practiced there by his agents, should have sought to extenuate, if not to justify, their criminal deeds. That gentleman should be told that when his portion of the Indians arrived in Demerara, there was no building prepared for their reception; that the sick-house was emptied of its patients, to make room for them; and that in four rooms in that sick-house, the whole eighty-two Indians were thrust, men, women, and children, without regard to delicacy or decency, together; and kept in that loathsome den for nearly three months, before a shed could be erected for their shelter!

And let that gentleman be told also that the whip, the bamboo, and the dungeon, were constantly resorted to compel labor or to gratify revenge. And further, he should know that the schoolmaster Berkley, who first hinted the cruelties that were practiced on miserable Indians, after having his stock killed, has been driven from the estate, without payment of the miserable sum due to him for salary; and is now the victim of most bitter persecution on the part of every manager in the district!

Happily, however, for the cause of humanity, and probably, for the interests of Mr. Colvile, the atrocious conduct of his agents has been partly made known, but who shall say that similar atrocities may not again be perpetrated? There are not always to be found in the colony men who have the courage to expose and denounce the evils which exist. The last report of the special magistrate dated November 1, 1839, states the mortality to have been, up to that period, twenty-two males, besides the murdered girl!

Let us now take a glance at Vreed-en-Hoop, the property of Mr. Gladstone. We find that in consequence of a communication made to the Governor that the Indians on that estate were ill-treated, an inquiry was ordered into the circumstances. The result of the first inquiry is summed up by Mr. Young, the Government Secretary, in a letter, addressed, by order of his Excellency, to James Stuart, Esq., the attorney to the property; and is as follows:

Government Secretary's Office, May 2, 1839

A report having reached the Governor that the Indians of Vreed-en-Hoop had been flogged, and that two of them, in consequence of ill-treatment, had fled from the estate, and had since perished in the neighborhood of Mahaica, his Excellency directed a court of inquiry, consisting of three stipendiary magistrates, to be assembled for the purpose of ascertaining the truth of the report. I am now directed to recapitulate to you the facts elicited by the investigation; to inform you of the ultimate measures which have been determined on; and to suggest to you such a course of proceeding, on your part, towards the individuals whose conduct is implicated in these transactions, as, in his Excellency's opinion, humanity towards the Indians, and a due regard of the reputation of the colony at large, render just and necessary.

As you were yourself present at the court of inquiry, it is not, perhaps, necessary to set forth in detail the whole of the evidence, (of which, however, you may obtain a perusal at this office, should you desire it); in the margin will be found the names of the witnesses who speak to the facts which I am now to recapitulate.

> The Indians were locked up in the sick-house; saw them the day after they were flogged; their backs were swollen; they were in the sick-house for two days after the flogging. - *Will Clay.*
>
> When they run away and are stubborn, they get two or three lickings; they are flogged with a cat-o'-nine-tails; they were tied with a rope round the post, and were licked on the bare back. - *Alexander.*

They appeared to me as severely punished as my matties were, during the apprenticeship; when flogged, they were flogged with a cat, the same as was formerly in use; they brought all from the sick house together, and took them to the negro-yard to be flogged; they were tied to a post. - *Rose*.

The Indians were locked up in the sick house, and next morning they were flogged with a cat-o'-nine-tails; the manager was in the house, and they flogged the people under his house; they were tied to the post of the gallery of the manager's house; I cannot tell how many licks; he gave them enough. I saw blood. When they were flogged at manager's house, they rubbed salt pickle on their backs. - *Elizabeth Caesar*.

I think two of the Indians were brought into the hospital to have their backs dressed; I rubbed them with camphor and high wines; the backs were bruised. The first time seven Indians were locked up; the second, six Indians. - *Betsey Ann, Sick Nurse*.

Their hands were tied behind their backs; they were beaten with a rope; ten times they licked them; heard them complain to the manager; Mr. Jacobs licked Modun every day. When licked, they put the breast to the post with hands stretched out; some tie the hands before, some behind. Indians run away because they are licked. - *Narrain*.

His Excellency desires me to observe that although some of the other witnesses, as well as those whose names are mentioned in the margin, in other parts of their evidence, give a description, perhaps, somewhat less revolting than that contained in the foregoing extracts, yet the fact of flogging and confinement having been inflicted is proved beyond all dispute.

The minutes of the court were referred to Stipendiary Justice Coleman (who was not on the commission of inquiry) in a letter, of which I annex a copy, and you will perceive that he has been instructed to adjudicate upon the cases, or to refer them, for trial, before the Supreme Court of Criminal Justice, as may be most consistent with his own judgement, and the laws in force.

The Sheriff of Berbice, who was acquainted with the Hindustani language, has been summoned from Berbice, in order to assist in interpreting the complaints of the Indians, and for the purpose of conveying to them an explanation of the punishment which Captain Coleman is enabled, by law, to award against anyone who shall, in future, at any time, commit similar outrages on their persons. His Excellency confidently expects your entire concurrence in the above measures, for the punishment of the wrongs these strangers have hitherto sustained; and, under this expectation, I am to suggest to you, that, although a legal tribunal can visit Mr. Sanderson and Mr. Jacobs (either or both, as the evidence may appear to the court to justify such a sentence) with punishment for what the Indians of Vreed-en-Hoop have, hitherto, wrongly suffered, yet, that the most efficient protection, for the future, can best be afforded, by your dismissal of Messrs. Sanderson and Jacobs.

Mr. Sanderson, as the resident manager, either did know, or ought to have known of these transactions; under the most charitable supposition, his ignorance must be esteemed highly culpable.

Of Mr. Jacobs' unfitness to retain any authority over the Indians of Vreed-en-Hoop, there cannot be a doubt; and it is reported that, pending the investigation, he brutally assaulted one of them, and that he is, at this moment, on his trial, before Stipendiary Magistrate Mure, for the offence. It has also been reported to the Governor, that the wages due to the Indians, are paid to the interpreter Jacobs, on their behalf, a practice which his Excellency considers may have been a source of discontent. I have, &c.

(Signed) *HEF YOUNG,*

James Stuart, Esq., Government Secretary.
Attorney of Plantation Vreed-en-Hoop.

To this communication, the attorney sent a scornful reply, and refused to accede to his Excellency's request. The investigation, however, led to the trial and conviction of Jacobs for assault on the persons of five Indians, and the sentence of the court, was a fine of £20 sterling, and one month's imprisonment in Georgetown Jail. Subsequently to this, Jacobs was again tried for another assault on an Indian and fined 30 shillings by the court. A third assault was proved against him, and a fine of forty shillings inflicted.

Those convictions were deemed sufficient by those who originated the proceedings, and to establish the fact that as part of the regular discipline of the estate, the wretched Indians were most cruelly whipped and injured. But this was only part of the system: Jacobs was also proved to have mulcted the Indians of their money, which the wretched creatures paid to him instead of a threatened beating. A list of thirty-one cases is given in the report of the Commissioners, who were thus robbed of their hard-earned money to the extent of 28½ dollars at various times. The amount of punishment inflicted on the Indians first and last, must have been enormous, and yet because there was no legal evidence to prove that

Sanderson, the general manager of the estate, had personally directed the flogging, either in the house or in the field, he was retained in his situation.

To suppose that for twelve months, these things could have occurred under his own eye, and he did not know it, must be to disqualify him for the situation he holds, and ought of itself to have been a sufficient reason for his immediate dismissal from office. But he is too good a manager, in the colonial sense of the term, to be lost, so he still represents his wealthy master on plantation Vreed- en-Hoop. And now what does Mr. Gladstone do, when put in possession of the documents, forwarded to him by the Government, containing the melancholy details referred to? Why, like Mr. Colville, he has not one word of commiseration to expend on the Indians; but a great deal of indignation against Messrs. Scoble and Anstie, to whom reference no doubt is made, in the following passage:

> The people continued cheerful and contented; but evil disposed persons have recently gone among them, and have endeavored to create a bad and dissatisfied feeling, in which they have partially succeeded, as it is at present too generally the case in England, where similar effects are produced by the Chartists and others, among the lower classes.

Perhaps, as the letter which contains this paragraph, was addressed to the Marquess of Normanby and to his noble colleague in office, Lord John Russell; so that Mr. Scoble, and his friend, Mr. Anstie, find themselves in grand company indeed, and, of course, will thank Mr. Gladstone for the honor done them!

The number reported dead on Vreed-en-Hoop, on

November 1, 1839, was nine, and two absent, who, no doubt, perished in the bush at Mahaica, eleven in all; and thirteen were then on the sick list. The general treatment of the Indians on Vriedestein has been the same as on Vreed-en-Hoop, and the mortality greater, in proportion to the number settled there, viz.: eight males, to November 1, 1839, when there were five on the sick list. The original number placed the two estates, the latter end of May, 1838, was 104, and the mortality has been nineteen in a period of eighteen months, in addition to the fourteen who perished on the voyage from Calcutta, and who formed part of the original number of 170 shipped on the joint account of Messrs. Gladstone and Moss.

In reviewing the foregoing facts, one cannot fail being struck, first, by the circumstances, that so much oppression, cruelty, and misery, escaped the attention of managers, attorneys, magistrates, and even the executive itself, for nearly twelve-months; that it should have been left to a visitor to the colony to expose the horrid truths which were submitted to public attention.

Secondly, those things should have occurred on the estates of two men of princely wealth, who affirm that they gave their agents the most positive instructions -- that the Indians entrusted to them should be treated with the greatest imaginable tenderness and care!

Thirdly, that when the facts of the inhumane treatment of the Indian laborers were reported to those gentlemen, they either affect to palliate or deny them, or to justify their agents; and to characterize those who have been providentially the means of dragging the offenders to justice, as among the most infamous men.

Fourthly, they should have had the audacity to appeal to the Government of this country, to allow them, and others like them, to introduce, *ad libitum*, as many thousands of the natives of Hindustan, as will enable them effectually to coerce the labor of the negro freemen, and still further, to enrich themselves at the expense of the liberty and happiness of mankind.

On plantation Highbury, notwithstanding the favorable reports of the treatment of the Indians there, the mortality has been very great, viz. seventeen males and one female, and twelve reported on the sick list, November 1 1839. From that estate, as well as those already mentioned, the Indians have repeatedly run away. On one occasion, sometime in April or May last year, upwards of twenty of them cut their way, due east, for many miles through the bush, in the hope of reaching Bengal. When in the presence of those they know to be their friends, and really interested in their welfare, they give full vent to their feelings, and exhibit their real sentiments, and with tears and clasped hands, and in broken English, entreat to be sent back to their native country and to their kindred from whom they have been wantonly separated.

On plantation Anna Regina, the deaths were two, and on plantation Waterloo, five are reported dead, and three on the sick list, on November 1 1839. Thus, then, it appears from official documents, that out of the 437 Indians shipped at Calcutta, eighteen died on the voyage to Demerara; and that out of the 419 settled on the various estates referred to in May, 1838, sixty-four have died from various diseases, two have perished in the bush, and one has been murdered; making a total of sixty-seven deaths in eighteen months, being about one-sixth of the whole. It may be added that there is no legal provision made for the restoration of such Indians as may survive the period of their Indentures to India.

In consequence of the facts brought to light in the early part of the year 1838, as to the true character of the Order in Council of July 12, 1837, and the public indignation felt at the proceedings of the planters, in Mauritius and elsewhere, and their agents, and kidnappers in India, the Government declared its intention on the July 20, of that year, to rescind the obnoxious Order in Council. In the course of the last session of Parliament, Sir John Hobhouse stated that not only had Her Majesty's ministers put an end to the traffic of Indians but that the Governor-General of India had anticipated them and had issued a prohibition against the further exportation of Hill Indians. The humanity and justice of these measures were not less honorable to the Government than they were satisfactory to the public.

Notwithstanding the Order in Council of July 12, 1837, admitting the introduction into British Guiana of Indians, under indentures of five years, had been rescinded, the proprietary body in the early part of last year, obtained a vote through the financial representatives of the colony, seconded by the zealous exertions of the Governor, of the enormous sum of £400,000 sterling, to be devoted exclusively to the increase of their stock of laborers; subsequently, an ordinance similar to the Colonial Passengers' Bill was passed, now under the consideration of the House of Commons, with the view of securing the concurrence of the Home Government, in their gigantic immigration scheme.

Their object was not merely to draw laborers from the smaller West India colonies and Europe, but principally from Africa and Hindustan. Hence, they had provided for the support of a resident agent in Calcutta and another on the western coast of Africa. That scheme was recommended to the acceptance of the Home Government, with all the zeal of a partisan by the executive, but it did not meet with the anticipated success. Lord Normanby, in a dispatch, dated August 15, 1839, which did him honor, conveyed the intelligence to the colony that her Majesty had been pleased to disallow the immigration ordinance, and, about that part of it which proposed to import Africans and Hill Indians, observes:

> With regard to the introduction of labourers from India, more than enough has already passed to render Her Majesty's Government decidedly hostile to every such project, and the laws now in force in different presidencies would effectually prevent the execution of this part of the scheme. We are not less opposed to the plan of recruiting the negro population of the West India colonies from Africa. No precaution which has been, or which could be devised would prevent such a measure from giving a stimulus to the internal slave-trade on that continent, or from bringing discredit on the sincerity of the efforts made by this nation for the suppression of that system of guilt and misery.

On what grounds then, we ask, does the Government now propose to relax the prohibition on the export of Indians in the case of Mauritius? Are the planters of that colony more worthy of the confidence than those of Guiana? Are they more honorable and humane? We assert not: then why the preference?

The restless activity of this powerful body, supported as it is by a corrupt and venal press in the colonies and by a well-paid band of agents in this country, was never more manifest than at the present moment or directed to more unworthy objects. Convicted again and again, of the grossest misstatements respecting the conduct of the free negroes, the state of the crops, and the general prosperity of the colonies, they continue to assert the absolute ruin of these possessions of the

Crown, and call upon the Government to give them laws to coerce labor under a state of freedom, and to place the administration of the laws entirely in their own hands by the removal of the Stipendiary Magistrates; to allow them to import, to an unlimited extent, and under contracts of service for five years, the natives of India, that they may be able to reduce the wages of their late slaves to the minimum point, and thus force them, once more, under their cruel and despotic sway.

In consequence of their exertions and misrepresentations, there is the most imminent danger at the present moment, that the Indian slave-trade will be revived and that the measures for which the abolitionists of this country have striven so long, and so zealously, will give place to others of the most objectionable kind. Already has it been announced in Parliament, by Lord John Russell, that the restriction imposed on the exportation of Hill Indians, so far as they relate to Mauritius, are to be abandoned, and the intimation has been received with unbounded joy by the felon-planters of that colony. In the papers, which have just been printed by order of the House of Commons, we learn by a letter, dated Mauritius, June 11, 1839, that the planters received the gratifying intelligence, that Sir William Nicolay submitted a dispatch to the Council here, by which it appears that the ministry apprises him of a bill which would be laid before Parliament, authorizing the introduction of Indians, and permitting them to engage for FIVE YEARS. "This intelligence," it is added, "has spread universal joy throughout the colony, and `nous sommes saurés,' escapes the lips of the least sanguine!" Whatever might have been the intention of the ministers of the Crown, they were not able, during the last session, to carry such a measure. Neither the house nor the country would have permitted such an iniquitous scheme to be carried into effect.

One fact is clear, however, that the admirable Order in

Council of September 7, 1838, regulating contracts in the Crown colonies, and which limited their duration to *one year*, and provided that where the laborers had been "induced to enter into the same by ANY FRAUD, MISAPPREHENSION, MISREPRESENTATION, OR CONCEALMENT," the same should be void; and which further required, that all contracts, to be valid, must henceforth be made, not at Calcutta and elsewhere, but in the colonies to which the laborers might resort, in the presence of the proper authorities, and under the forms therein set forth, was to be set aside in Mauritius, within a few months after it had gone into effect! Moreover, now what the Government dared not, or could not do the last session, they propose to do this: Lord John Russell will relax the restrictions on this infamous traffic in the persons of men, and throw open India, once more, to the Mauritians, who have ever shown themselves as destitute of every human sympathy, as they have proved themselves regardless of all laws human and divine!

In the papers which have been recently laid before Parliament, which embrace but a very small part of the proceedings relative to the Hill Indians in Mauritius, and are consequently extremely defective in the information they contain, will be found enough to convince the most skeptical of the inhumanity and wickedness of the doings of the Mauritian planters. The whole system has been characterized by the grossest fraud and cruelty, and has been sustained by the most infamous tyranny and oppression.

How were the Indians in Mauritius obtained previously to the restrictions being laid on? Mr. F.R. Prinsep, Secretary to the Government of India, in an official report on the subject, states: "The methods adopted for procuring labourers to engage for service in colonies and places beyond sea, are productive of serious frauds, and have led to much oppression, and," he further observes, "the system is a source of injury and abuse, rather than of benefit to the labourers, in the form in which it is at present carried on." The Governor, Sir William Nicolay, in referring to the same subject in a dispatch to Lord Glenelg, dated May 21, 1839, observes, "That very nefarious practices have been resorted to, in many instances, in order to procure labourers for embarkation for this island, is beyond all doubt." Mr. Special Justice Anderson asserts in one of his letters to the Governor that "many of them have actually been KIDNAPPED from their own country, which," he adds, "they have ALL been induced to leave, under circumstances of GROSS FRAUDS." To go into the history of all those "frauds," would be to detail circumstances, second only in atrocity to those connected with the African slave trade. The fact is established beyond dispute that multitudes have been kidnapped, forced into prison depots until the Mauritian slavers were ready to receive them, hurried on board, put under hatches and guards, robbed and pillaged of the advances made to them by the Mauritian agents in Calcutta, shipped in large numbers onboard vessels, without the requisite accommodation, food, or medical attendance, brought under the most fraudulent contracts to labor for years on scanty wages, and scanty fare, separated from their families and their homes, compelled to perform the hardest agricultural labor known, at the discretion of their masters and without the protection of an upright, impartial, and efficient magistracy.

It is difficult to ascertain when the first shipment of Indians to Mauritius took place, or the exact number of them introduced at various periods. It appears that from August 1, 1834, to October 24, 1838, there were 13,243 Indians, *viz.*, 12,994 men; 198 women; and fifty-one children. From June 1, 1837, to June 22, 1838, there were shipped from *Cochin* 308 Indians, supposed to be all males. From June 1, 1837, to June

24, 1838, there were shipped from *Pondicherry* 5058 Indians, all males. From June 1, 1837, to August 25, 1838, there were shipped from *Rajahmundy* 441 Indians, viz., 434 men and seven women; making a total of 19,050 -- viz., 18,794 men, 205 women, and fifty-one children.

However, it is pretty clear, from the petition addressed to her Majesty by the planters and others, dated May 18, 1839, that many Indians had been introduced. The 100 persons who signed that document stated that within the "last four years," they had "caused to be brought from British India upwards of 20,000 native Indian laborers." It is stated, by some parties, that the whole number introduced cannot be much short of 30,000.

Concerning the mortality that has occurred since the arrival of the Indians at Mauritius, the statements vary. It is, however, admitted by the Governor to have been great and to have been "the source of deep regret" to him. In a dispatch, dated December 31, 1838, the Colonial Secretary (Mr. Dick) thus wrote:

> The mortality which has prevailed among the Indian laborers, as well on their voyage as after their arrival here, and more particularly on some estates and establishments, has been the source of deep regret to his Excellency. Mr. Special Justice Anderson, states the mortality of the Indians in Port Louis, to amount to eight or nine per cent, per annum! This would be equal to the destruction of the whole number of Indians introduced every twelve years.

Out of the 19,050 Indians introduced, we have an account in the papers, and only 205 were women! It is easy to conceive that, from this frightful disparity of the sexes, the most horrible and revolting depravity and demoralization must necessarily ensue; and that such large masses of ignorant and degraded beings must carry with them a most corrupting influence on others.

As to the general treatment of the Indians in Mauritius, one opinion can be entertained by the friends of humanity. Independently of the evidence derived from private sources, on which implicit reliance can be placed, which represents the state of the Indians as deplorably wretched, and their hardships and sufferings even greater than those endured, by the negroes when slaves, the fact of their having become the prey of the Mauritian planters would be sufficient to justify the worst apprehensions that could be entertained on that point. One honest functionary in Mauritius, Mr. Special Justice Anderson, has spoken out upon this point in opposition to those who would have us believe that the Indians in that colony are treated with "humanity and kindness;" and, we have no doubt, in opposition to his interests and personal ease and comfort.

In his letters to Governor Nicolay, dated the 19th and 30th of November, 1839, he states, that those whom he had examined in Port Louis, were "overworked," were subjected to severe "personal chastisement," were without proper shelter and "lodging accommodation," were deprived of necessary medical attendance and care when suffering from disease, and in other ways seriously injured and abused, insomuch that he says, "it is a source of astonishment to me, that anybody of freemen, whatever may have been their former condition, should have borne, with the patience and forbearance which the Indian labourers at Port Louis have displayed, the bitter disappointment which must have attended their introduction into this island," and, he adds:

To induce them to come here, their ignorance is worked upon in India by the most false and deceitful representations, and the robbery and pillage which has been practiced on them at Calcutta, would scarcely be credited, if the fact was not established by the most convincing testimony. They reach this colony after having been robbed of six months' pay, which is advanced, (or said to be advanced,) in India; and when here, their comfort is in every way neglected, while they are compelled by the engagements to which their own ignorance, or the avarice of others have bound them, to toil during five years for a recompense bearing no proportion to the work to which they are subjected, when compared with the common estimation of the value of labour in this colony, or to the sum which they would earn if they had the free disposal of their own time.

Because of these facts, the writer of this article would earnestly call on every philanthropist in the kingdom to use his utmost exertions and influence, in public and in private, to prevent the relaxation of the restrictions to which reference has been made; and to urge on the Government the paramount importance of maintaining, in all its integrity, the Order in Council of September 7, 1838; and to demand that all the fraudulent contracts into which the Indians have been induced to enter, whether in Mauritius or Guiana, shall be immediately canceled, and the unfortunate victims of cupidity be permitted to return home. And that the parties, whether in India, who have been guilty of entrapping them into fraudulent contracts, or in the colonies, who have injured and oppressed them, shall be brought to condign punishment. This would be a valuable lesson to the planters. It would teach them to husband their resources. It would procure for the emancipated negroes the consideration and care which are their due, for so long as the planters in the British Colonies can calculate upon the cultivation of their estates by the introduction of adult laborers, they will be as careless of the general welfare of their peasantry, in future, as they have been reckless of the lives of their slaves in times past.

The Parliamentary Papers which should be consulted on the subject, treated in the preceding statement, are as follows, viz., No. 180, March 2, 1838; No. 232, in continuation; No. 463, 1839. Hill Indians in British Guiana, No. 77, 1840, in continuation, and No. 58, 1840, Mauritius; and to the information contained in these documents should be added, that which may be found in the columns of the British Emancipator, from the May 29 to October 2, 1839, and in Number 4, of the British and Foreign Anti-Slavery Reporter, dated February 26, 1840.

P.S. Whilst the foregoing statement was passing through the press, the Committee of the British and Foreign Anti-slavery Society presented a Memorial to Lord John Russell on the subject to which it refers. The deputation which presented the Memorial to his Lordship were as follows, viz.: Sir Charles Style, Bart., M.P.; Daniel O'Connell, Esq., M.P.; Edward Baines, Esq., M.P.; Dr. Hodgkin, and Messrs. W. Ball, G. Stacey, H. Tuckett, D. Turnbull, C.F. Brown, J. Beaumont, R. Russell, C. Phipps, John Scoble, and J.H. Tredgold. In the interview with his Lordship, it was understood that the Government would persevere in their intention of relaxing the restrictions on the exportation of Indians to Mauritius within certain limits. This is deep to be regretted; let the friends of humanity be on the alert, and the design may yet be defeated.

The following is a copy of the Memorial presented: To the Right Honorable Lord John Russell, M.P., Her Majesty's Principal Secretary of State for the Colonies.

My Lord,

The Committee of the British and Foreign Anti-Slavery Society, have learnt with deepest regret, that it is your Lordship's intention to recommend to the Queen in Council, to relax the existing restrictions upon the exportation of Hill Indians from Hindustan, so far as they affect Mauritius, and that initiative measures have already been introduced to the attention of the House of Commons for the accomplishment of that purpose.

In approaching your Lordship, for the purpose of respectfully submitting to your Lordship's consideration, the reasons which induced them to give to the contemplated measure, their most earnest and determined opposition, the Committee beg to assure your Lordship, that they are governed only by a sincere desire to secure the native Inhabitants of the East from injustice and oppression, and the recently emancipated Negroes in Mauritius, the full enjoyment of that liberty which has been obtained for them at so costly a sacrifice to the British nation.

(1) The Committee would remind your Lordship of the fact, that the Mauritian Planters have always been conspicuous for their daring violation of the laws under which they are placed; for their disloyalty to the Crown of these realms; and for their unwearied opposition to the humane measures of the Home Government, intended for the benefit and protection of their late bondsmen, as a decisive proof that no confidence can be placed in their good faith and honor, and that no substantial justice can be obtained at their hands for the Asiatic Laborer, or the emancipated Negro; and they are

further confirmed in this view of the case by the notorious fact, that for the most part, the Authorities in Mauritius are influenced by the predominant party there, which is known to be hostile to British Laws and to British Rule, and to be violently opposed to the full and fair development of the great measure of freedom lately bestowed on the Negroes.

(2) The opposition to the facts which have come to their knowledge, the Committee can place no reliance whatsoever on the general statements put forth by interested parties, representing the Indians at present in Mauritius, as happy in their condition, and as having no wish to change it. Independently of other evidence, in their opinion, it is impossible to conceive, that these wretched persons can be contented with their lot, when it is remembered that large numbers of them were conveyed to Mauritius, under the most fraudulent pretenses; without regard to the equality of sexes, to the separation of families to their social elevation, or to their moral welfare, and forcibly brought under contracts for labor, for long periods of time at the smallest rate of wages. And in their judgement also, it would be contrary to the universal experience of mankind, to believe that they can be happy, when it is known, that the parties who introduced them into that colony, were influenced only by the sordid purposes of gain, and by the avowed intention of coercing the labor, and of keeping down the wages of the Negroes in a state of freedom.

(3) As the Committee would earnestly deprecate the further introduction of Hill Indians into any of the emancipated colonies, as fraught with the most injurious consequences morally as well as otherwise, to the existing laboring population, and as, therefore, calculated immeasurably to impede their advance in civilization and religion; they would respectfully submit to your Lordship that, on this ground also, the Mauritian planters are least of all fit to be entrusted with

the care of the ignorant and degraded natives of Hindustan, inasmuch as they have shown themselves not only utterly regardless of, but entirely opposed to the education of their late slaves in morals and religion.

(4) The Committee are firmly persuaded that the proposed measure, instead of inducing the Mauritian planters to act upon just and equal laws, and to depend on the exercise of humane treatment and good faith towards their present laborers, for the cultivation of their estates, will cause them to rely on unjust and adventitious expedients for the accomplishment of their objects, and will have the effect of reviving the traffic in the persons of men which no enactments in this country, however humanely intended, can prevent, or even control. It appears also to the Committee, that the necessary consequence of the relaxation of the restrictions on the exportation of Indians to Mauritius, must lead to a similar measure in favor of British Guiana and Trinidad; an event, which they would greatly deplore, as fatal to the interests of humanity and destructive of the hopes they have cherished in connection with the freedom of the slave.

(5) The pretense that the natives of India would be benefited by the proposed measure, the Committee venture respectfully to deny. In order effectually to relieve the suffering and oppressed Hindus, they humbly conceive a series of enlightened, humane, and comprehensive laws that must be substituted for those which exist; and the present system of misgovernment be entirely abandoned. All partial expedients to relieve the misery which so extensively prevails in that vast country, can, in their judgement, only have the effect of retarding the introduction of those searching reforms which the exigencies of the people, and the prosperity and security of the empire so immediately and peremptorily require.

(6) The distance of Mauritius from the controlling power

of the home government, and the consequent difficulty and delay in obtaining information relative to the evils which exist in that colony, and of applying early and efficient remedies to them, has been felt by your lordship's predecessors in office; whilst the signal success of the Mauritian planters, in carrying on their nefarious schemes in frustrating the measure of government, and in displacing its officers and in obtaining an immense sum of money as compensation for slaves which had been feloniously introduced, by means the most fraudulent, fully justify, in the opinion of the Committee, the alarm they feel as to the consequences which will result from the projected measure.

(7) For these reasons the Committee earnestly entreat your Lordship, and your Lordship's colleagues in office, not to advise her Majesty, to sanction the relaxation of the restrictions referred to, but to maintain them inviolate; and to order such measures to be immediately taken, as shall restore to their families and to their homes, those wretched Indians who have been fraudulently introduced into Mauritius, and are held to service contrary to the Order in Council of the 7th September, 1828.

Signed W. BALL,
Chairman of the Committee.
British and Foreign Anti-Slavery Society,
27, New Broad Street, 28th February 1840.

Letter from John Gladstone, Esq. to Messrs. Gillanders, Arbuthnot & Co., Liverpool, 4th January 1836.

Dear Sirs,
I met with an accident here about three weeks ago, which confined me to the house, from which I am now recovering,

and hope in a few days to be able to return to Edinburgh; this will account to you for using my son's pen for writing in place of my own.

I observe by a letter which he received a few days ago from Mr. Arbuthnot that he was sending a considerable number of a certain class of Bengalese, to be employed as laborers, to the Mauritius. You will probably be aware that we are very particularly situated with our Negro apprentices in the West Indies, and that it is a matter of doubt and uncertainty how far they may be induced to continue their services on the plantations after their apprenticeship expires in 1840. This to us is a subject of great moment and deep interest in the colonies of Demerara and Jamaica. We are therefore most desirous to obtain and introduce laborers from other quarters, and particularly from climates something similar in their nature. Our plantation labor in the field is very light; much of it, particularly in Demerara, is done by task-work, which for the day is usually completed by two o'clock in the afternoon, giving to the people all the rest of the day to themselves.

They are furnished with comfortable dwellings and abundance of food; plantations, the produce of the colony, being the most common, and preferred generally by them; but they have also occasionally rice, Indian corn, meal, ship's biscuits, and a regular supply of salt cod-fish, as well as the power of fishing for themselves in the trenches. They have likewise an annual allowance of clothing sufficient and suitable for the climate; there are schools on each estate for the education of the children, and the instruction of their parents in the knowledge of religious duties.

Their houses are comfortable, and it may be fairly said they pass their time agreeably and happily. Marriages are encouraged, and when improper conduct on the part of the people takes place, there are public stipendiary magistrates, who take cognizance of such, and judge between them and their employers. They have regular medical attendance whenever they are indisposed, at the expense of their employers.

I have been particular in describing the present situation and occupation of our people, to which I ought to add, that their employment in the field is clearing the land with the hoe, and, where required, planting fresh canes. In the works a portion is occupied in making sugar, and in the distilleries, in which they relieve each other, which makes their labor light. It is of great importance to us to endeavor to provide a portion of other laborers, whom we might use as a set-off, and, when the time for it comes, make us, as far as it is possible, independent of our negro population; and it has occurred to us that a moderate number of Bengalese, such as you were sending to the Isle of France, might be very suitable for our purpose; and on this subject I am now desirous to obtain all the information you can possibly give me. The number I should think of taking and sending by one vessel direct from Calcutta to Demerara would be about 100; they ought to be young, active, able-bodied people. It would be desirable that a portion of them, at least one-half, should be married, and their wives disposed to work in the field as well as themselves.

We should require binding them for a period not less than five years or more than seven years. They would be provided with comfortable dwellings, food, and medical assistance; they would also, if required, be provided with clothing, or wages to provide themselves, which, for the able-bodied, would not exceed four dollars per month, and in that proportion for females and their children as they grow up; a free passage would be given to them to Demerara, where they would be divided, and 20 to 30 placed on one plantation. I do not know whether the class referred to are likely to be of a particular caste, and under the influence of certain religious feelings, and also restricted to any particular kind of food; if so, we must endeavor to provide for them accordingly. You will particularly oblige me by giving me, on receipt, all the information you possibly can on this interesting subject; for, should it be of an encouraging character, I should immediately engage for one of our ships to go to Calcutta, and take a limited number to Demerara, and from thence return here. On all other subjects I refer you to letters from the house; and always am.

Dear Sirs, yours truly
John Gladstone.

Since writing so far it has occurred to me that in bringing Lascars from India security is required that they shall be returned to the country. I do not know whether this would extend to any particular caste being brought to the West Indies, or whether it is applicable in the instance you have mentioned of those sent to Mauritius. Several importations from Madeira and Azores have taken place into Demerara, and so far with good effects on the minds of the blacks.

Copy of letter from Messrs. Gillanders, Arbuthnot & Co. to John Gladstone, Esq. Calcutta, 6th June 1836. (Parliamentary Papers, LII No. 180, 1837-38. MF41.413-414).

Dear Sir,

We beg to acknowledge your letter of the 4th January, referring to your desire to procure natives from this part of the world to work upon your estates in the West Indies, and in some degree render you independent of the Negro population at the termination of the present system; and it is with regret that at the time the letter under reply was written you were suffering from an accident, the effects of which, however, we hope ere this are entirely gone.

Within the last two years more than 2,000 natives have been sent to Mauritius, by several parties here, under contracts of engagement for five years. The contracts, we believe, are all of a similar nature; and we enclose copy of one, under which we have sent 700 or 800 men to the Mauritius; and we are not aware that any greater difficulty would present itself in sending men to the West Indies, the natives being perfectly ignorant of the place they agree to go to, or the length of the voyage they are undertaking. The tribe that is found to suit best in the Mauritius is from the hills to the north of Calcutta, and the men of which are all well-limbed and active, without prejudices of any kind, and hardly any ideas beyond those of supplying the wants of nature, arising it would appear, however, more from want of opportunity than from any natural deficiency, of which there is no indication in their countenance, which is often one of intelligence. They are also very docile and easily managed, and appear to have no local ties, nor any objection to leave their country.

In the event of your determining to introduce these people in the West Indies and sending a ship for them, a contract such as the one enclosed, if approved of, or modified or enlarged as you may think necessary, may be entered into with any number of men you would wish us to procure, and this contract upon landing the men in the West Indies and being registered at the Police-office, would, we conclude, give your managers sufficient power to insist upon their performing any reasonable task they may be set to. Such has been the case in Mauritius, and in one or two instances where the men have been idle or lazy, they have been punished by the competent authority. It would perhaps avoid after-discussion were the currency in which the men will be paid, and its equivalent value with the rupee as stated in the contract. The best period for procuring and shipping the men is in our cold season, between the months of November and April, and the instruction to procure the men should precede the ship about two months, to give time to collect them; we should of course not be able to find a cargo for the ship, but some morghy rice might be sent, which with a little care would keep for three years.

The security taken by government here upon taking natives to England is to protect the East India Company from loss in the event of natives being left in England without the means of subsistence or of finding their way back, in which case the Company are bound to provide for them until a passage to India can be procured, but no guarantee is required upon sending men elsewhere; as however the colonial government will probably make the importer enter into an agreement that these men shall be no burden to the colony, a provision is made in the contract to withhold so much of their allowances as will pay their passage back, should it be found necessary to discharge them before their period of service has expired.

We fear we should not find so many as half of the number provided with wives; as, however, our friends at the Isle of France have always discouraged the men being so accompanied, we are not very well able to say how far the women might be induced to go.

Our letters from the Isle of France speak very favorably of the men hitherto sent, many of whom our friends write to us have their task completed by two o'clock, and go home, leaving the Negroes in the field. We are not aware that we can say any more on this subject, unless we add, that in inducing these men to leave their country, we firmly believe we are breaking no ties of kindred, or in any way acting a cruel part.

The Hill tribes, known by the name of Dhangurs, are looked down upon by the more cunning natives of the plains, and they are always spoken of as more akin to the monkey than the man. They have no religion, no education, and, in their present state, no want beyond eating, drinking, and sleeping; and to procure which they are willing to labor. In sending men to such a distance, it would of course be necessary to be more particular in selecting them, and some little expense would be incurred, as also some trouble; but to aid any object of interest to you, we should willingly give our best exertions in any manner likely to be of service.

We are, &c.

Gillanders, Arbuthnot & Co.

P.S. You will observe, upon reading over the form of our contract, that it is registered in our Police-office, and authenticated by one of the magistrates, in whose presence the document is signed, after the nature of it has been explained to the parties in their own language.

(signed) G., A. & Co.

The Chartist Movement

The first mass movement driven by the working classes grew following the failure of the 1832 Reform Act to extend the vote beyond those owning property.

In 1838 a People's Charter was drawn up for the London Working Men's Association (LWMA) by William Lovett and Francis Place, two self-educated radicals, in consultation with other members of LWMA. The Charter had six demands:

All men have the vote (universal manhood suffrage).

Voting should take place by secret ballot.

Parliamentary elections every year, not once every five years.

Constituencies should be of equal size.

Members of Parliament should be paid.

The property qualification for becoming a Member of Parliament should be abolished.

From the British Emancipator of January 9, 1839. (Parliamentary Papers, LII No.232, 1837-38. MF41.413-14).

I SEE the British public has been deceived with the idea that the Indians are doing "well," such is not the fact; the poor friendless creatures are miserably treated, at least I can speak confidently of plantation Bellevue. On this estate they have made two attempts to escape, as they say, to go to Calcutta. In the first, 22 succeeded by night to cross the river, landing on the opposite shore; they attempted to explore the woods, but after undergoing much fatigue and hunger, they were retaken at the back of plantation Herstelling, and conveyed again to the estate. In the last attempt they were discovered by the watch of the night and driven back. I saw a gang of them last week in custody of the police, who were taking them to the public buildings; their offence I did not learn. I inquired of Mr. Berkeley, who is a teacher on the place, respecting food; he said they had enough of rice, and I think "fat" or lard.

Deaths, he said, more than ten have died in this place, Bellevue, and the manager (Russell) refuses to give a rag of clothes to bury them in. I had one of these Indians in my own place, who is capable of saying a few words in English; he told me, "Russell no good; Indian sick salt, salt no more." He was all but naked; and a friend present gave him a few old raiments, which seemed highly to please him. They are paid here with the Company's rupees, five rupees a month. Is this not scandalous? They have been offered by the merchants, two bits a piece for them. I do not believe they can get its value in the colony.

Ought not the planters to be compelled to give their value in Demerara silver currency? I have also heard that two from Gladstone's estate escaped through the bush, and were captured by Captain Falant, at Fort Island, in the Essequibo River, and brought back to the plantation. Surely these things are far from being "well," the one alluded to above told me, "Calcutta better."

Copy of Letter from Andrew Colvile, Esq., to the Right Honorable Henry Labouchere, 9 Fenchurch-buildings (Parliamentary Papers, XXXIX No. 463, 1839. MF42.266-67). 29th July 1839.

My Dear Sir,

I have to acknowledge the receipt of the papers relating to the state of the Indians on Bellevue estate, which I have read with attention.

In the absence of that further information which may be expected by the next packet, I do not feel competent to form a decided opinion upon the medical treatment of the patients; but I understand, from a gentleman who has recently arrived from the colony, and who was there during the investigation of the 9th March, that Dr. Nimmo complains of the evil effects of an order issued by the late Governor, Sir J.C. Smith, declaring that, according to the construction of the Abolition Act, neither the manager nor the medical attendant on an estate were at liberty to confine the sick to the wards of the hospital. The consequences of this are stated to be the absence of everything like hospital regulations, and great difficulty in inducing the sick to follow out any regular course of treatment, either in point of medicine, food, or regimen; and, if this be so, I am glad to learn that the poor people have been removed to the public hospital in George Town, where, I presume, they will be subject to proper hospital regulations. I have learnt farther, from the same gentleman that the assault of which I regret to find Dr. Nimmo guilty arose from this state of things: I am told that, upon visiting the estate, he met one of the patients to whose sores he had applied a certain dressing. Upon examining him he found that not only had he left the hospital in disregard of his advice, but he had removed the medical dressing, and had applied one of his own.

In his irritation Dr. Nimmo, very improperly, no doubt, struck him a single blow with his riding cane, and desired him to go back to the hospital, and have his wound properly dressed. With respect to the more serious assaults by the interpreter, I regret both that this should have happened, and that the necessity for his services should have saved the individual from part of the punishment awarded to him; but I cannot omit to observe, with reference to the memorandum dated 14th May 1839, and signed H.E.F. Young, that the declaration of the interpreter there referred to was made by him in a private examination, when anxious to bring forward everything that might extenuate his offence, and justify his release from confinement; that he was wholly silent upon this point when confronted with Mr. Russell on his trial; and that upon the trial his want of veracity was proved by his denial of having confessed to Mr. Russell that he had beaten the Indian. When I oppose this declaration, so made by the interpreter, the denial upon oath, by Mr. Russell, of his having ever authorized him to beat the Indians, I cannot consider the interpreter entitled to much credit.

With respect to any suspicion which may exist of want of care on the part of the manager, it should not be forgotten that the extreme jealousy exercised against everything like restraint or coercion of the people, by the manager of an estate, would render it difficult, or rather impossible, for him to enforce that cleanliness and early attention to the extraction of the chigoes, which, if it had been adopted, would have prevented the bad sores, with which so many of the Indians have been unhappily afflicted.

I take the liberty to enclose extracts from my letters to my agent, containing the instructions which I have from time to time given regarding the Indians. If you will be kind enough to take the trouble to read them, I hope you will consider that I have not been deficient in taking precautionary measures for their proper care and comfort; though I sincerely lament the extent of the mortality and sickness, from whatever causes they may prove, upon a minute and careful investigation, to have arisen.

I have, &c.
(signed) A. Colvile.

Chartists and Abolitionists. (*Parliamentary Papers*, XXXIX, No. 463, 1839. MF42.266-67).

This reference from Colvile refers to the Chartist movement which demanded universal male suffrage, ballot voting, annual parliaments and equal representation, and an end to property requirements for members of Parliament. In 1838, with the publication of the People's Charter, this movement had considerable strength among the working class throughout Great Britain. The connection between Chartists and Abolitionists varied between antagonism and support. On occasion, Chartists had disrupted anti-slavery meetings to bring awareness to their issues. Anti-slavery movements were seen to be strongest among the middle class, and Chartists voiced the opinion that the Abolitionists cared more for the black slave than the working poor in Britain. However, while some antagonism existed, both movements shared a similar philosophy, and both caused shared members. For instance, Joseph Sturge, one of the founders of the British and Foreign Anti-Slavery Society, was also involved with the Chartist movement.

Sir John Cam Hobhouse

Lord Broughton served as president of the board of control for India from 1835 to 1841 and again from 1846 to 1852. During the early establishment of the indenture system Sir Hobhouse was not opposed to the scheme, and replied to Gladstone that the Indian Government would not interfere with his plans.

Lord John Russell

A member of the Whig Party, John Russell became head of the Colonial Office in September 1839 from Lord Normanby. He believed that while the export of labor to British Guiana had been a failure, sufficiently stringent regulations should protect Indians going to Mauritius under a one-year contract of indenture. This belief was based on the opinion that Indians travelling to Mauritius would receive higher wages and better conditions than what were available in India.

CHAPTER 18

Policies and Social Awakenings

THE CONSTITUTION OF THE BRITISH COLONY FAVORED the European planters. The planters' political power was based in the Court of Policy and the two Courts of justice established in the late eighteenth century under Dutch rule. The Court of Policy had legislative and administrative functions and was composed of the Governor, three colonial officials, and four colonists, with the Governor presiding. The courts of justice resolved judicial matters, such as licensing and civil service appointments, brought before them by petition.

The Court of Policy and the Courts of Justice were controlled by the plantation owners and constituted the center of power in British Guiana. The colonists who sat on the Court of Policy and the Courts of Justice were appointed by the Governor from a list of nominees submitted by two electoral colleges. In turn, the seven members of each College of Electors were elected for life by those planters possessing twenty-five or more slaves. Although their power was restricted to nominating colonists to fill vacancies on the three central Governmental councils, the electoral colleges provided a setting for political agitation by the planters. Raising and disbursing revenue was the responsibility of the Combined Courts, which included members of the Court of Policy and six additional financial representatives appointed by the College of Electors. In 1855, the Combined Court also assumed responsibility for setting the salaries of all government officials. This duty made the Combined Court a center of intrigues resulting in periodic clashes between the Governor and the planters.

Guianese began to demand a more representative political system in the nineteenth century. Pressure from the new Afro-Guianese middle class was growing towards a constitutional reform in the late 1880s. There were desires to convert the Court of Policy into an assembly with ten elected members, to ease voter qualifications, and to abolish the College of Electors. Reforms were resisted by the planters, led by Mr. Henry K. Davson, owner of a large plantation. In London, the planters had allies in the West India Committee and also, in the West India Association of Glasgow, both presided over by proprietors with major interests in British Guiana.

Constitutional revisions in 1891 incorporated some of the changes demanded by the reformers. The planters lost political influence with the abolition of the College of Electors and the relaxation of voter qualification. At the same time, the Court of Policy increased to sixteen members; eight of those were elected members, whose power would be balanced by the eight appointed members. The Combined Court also continued, consisting, as previously, of the Court of Policy and six financial representatives who were elected. To ensure that there would be no shift of power to the elected officials, the Governor remained the head of the Court of Policy; the executive duties of the Court of Policy were transferred to a new Executive Council, which the Governor and planters dominated. The 1891 revisions were a great disappointment to the colony's reformers. As a result of the 1892 elections, the membership of the new Combined Court was almost identical to that of the previous.

The next three decades saw additional, although minor, political changes. In 1897 the secret ballot was introduced. A reform in 1909 expanded the limited British Guiana electorate, and for the first time, Afro-Guianese constituted a majority of the eligible voters.

Political changes were accompanied by social change with various ethnic groups involved. The British and Dutch planters refused to accept the Portuguese as equals and sought to maintain their status as foreigners with no rights in the colony and voting rights. The political tensions led the Portuguese to establish the Reform Association. After the anti-Portuguese riots of 1898, the Portuguese recognized the need to work with other disenfranchised groups of the Guianese society, particularly the Afro-Guianese. By the early 20th century, organizations including the Reform Association and the Reform Club began to demand greater participation in the colony's affairs. Those organizations were essentially the instruments of a small but articulate emerging middle class. Although that new middle class sympathized with the working class, the middle-class political groups were hardly representative of a national political or social movement. Working-class grievances were usually expressed in the form of riots.

CHAPTER 19

Political and Social Changes

THE SEVERITY OF THE OUTBURSTS OF THE RUIMVELDT riot in 1905 reflected the widespread dissatisfaction of the workers with their standard of living. The uprising began in November 1905 when the Georgetown stevedores went on strike demanding higher wages. The strike grew confrontational, creating the country's first urban-rural worker's alliance. On November 30, people took to the streets of Georgetown, and by December 1, the situation was out of control. At Plantation Ruimveldt, a crowd of porters refused to disperse when ordered by a police patrol and artillery detachment. The colonial authorities opened fire, and four workers were seriously injured.

Word of the shootings spread throughout Georgetown. Hostile crowds began roaming the city and taking over several buildings. By the end of the day, seven people were dead and seventeen badly injured. In a panic, the British administration called for help. Britain sent troops, who finally calmed the uprising. Although the stevedores' strike failed, that uprising planted the seeds of the trade union movement.

World War I was fought far beyond the borders of British Guiana, but the war altered Guianese society. The Guianese who joined the British military became the nucleus of an elite Guianese community upon their return. The war also led to the end of the East Indian indentured service. Britain's concerns over political instability in India and criticism by Indian nationalists that the program was a form of human bondage prompted the British government to outlaw indentured labor in 1917.

In the years of World War 1, the colony's first trade union was formed. The British Guiana Labor Union (BGLU) was established in 1917 under the leadership of Mr. H. N. Critchlow and led by Mr. Alfred A. Thorne. The union was formed at a time of widespread business opposition. The BGLU initially represented Guianese dockworkers. By 1920, the membership stood at around 13,000. It was granted legal status in 1921 under the Trades Union Ordinance. The BGLU was an indication that the working class was becoming aware of their rights and concerns.

The second trade union, the British Guiana Workers' League, was established in 1931 by Mr. Alfred A. Thorne, who served as the League's leader for 22 years. The League sought to improve the working conditions for people of all the ethnic groups who were brought to the colony under a system of forced or indentured labor.

After the war, economic interest groups began to clash with the Combined Court. The colony's economy became less dependent on sugar and more on rice and bauxite. The producers of the new commodities resented the sugar planters' continued domination of the Combined Court. The planters were feeling the effects of lower sugar prices and wanted the Combined Court to provide new drainage and irrigation programs to improve production.

In 1928, the Colonial Office announced a constitution that would make British Guiana a crown colony under the tight control of a Governor appointed by the Colonial Office. A Legislative Council replaced the Combined Court and the Court of Policy with a majority of appointed members. The new constitution represented a step backward and a victory for the planters to middle- and working-classes and political activists.

On March 28, 1928, the British Parliament enacted the British Guiana Act, making provision for the Colony's Government. On July 13, 1928, the British Guiana (Constitution) Order in Council, 1928, was made by the King in Council, and on July 7, 1928, the Court of Policy met for the last time. On July 18, 1928, the new British Crown Colony Constitution – The British Guiana (Constitution) Order in Council, 1928 – came into operation. British Guiana became a British Crown Colony. The British established the first Legislative Council and replaced the Dutch created Court of Policy and the Combined Court.

The Legislative Council was composed of 30 Members: The Governor, 2 Ex-Officio Members, 8 Nominated Official Members, 5 Nominated Unofficial Members, and 14 Elected Members from 8 Constituencies. The Elected Members were 14, and the others were 16. The following were the first 30 Members of the First Legislative Council of the Colony of British Guiana:

The Governor

Brigadier General Sir Frederick Gordon Guggisberg.

Ex-Officio Members

Crawford Douglas Douglas-Jones, *Colonial Secretary.*
Hector Archibald Josephs, *Attorney General.*

Nominated Official Members

Thomas Millard, *Colonial Treasurer.*
William Bain Gray, *Director of Education.*
William Ernest Horatio Bradburn, *Inspector General of Police.*
John Cormack Craig, *Director of Public Works.*
Bernard Reader Wood, *Conservator of Forests.*
Sydney Howard Bayley, *Managing Director, Colonial Transport Department.*
John Mullin, *Commissioner of Lands and Mines.*
William George Boase, *Acting Surgeon General.*

Nominated Unofficial Members

Arthur Piercy Gardiner Austin.
Thomas Traill Smellie.
Francis Dias.
James Smith.
Sydney Howard Seymour.

Elected Members

Robert Edward Brassington, *Senior Member for North West Essequibo.*
Stanley McDonald DeFreitas, *Junior Member for North West Essequibo.*
Robert Victor Evan Wong, *Senior Member for southeast Essequibo.*
Edmund Fitzgerald Fredericks, *Junior Member for southeast Essequibo.*
Eustace Gordon Woolford, *Senior Member for New Amsterdam.*
Joseph Eleazar, *Junior Member for New Amsterdam.*
Nelson Cannon, *Senior Member for Georgetown.*
Percy Claude Wight, *Junior Member for Georgetown.*
Joseph Gonsalves, *Other Member for Georgetown.*
Hubert Chester Humphrys, *Member for East Demerara.*
Alfred Victor Crane, *Member for West Demerara.*
Edward Alfred Luckhoo, *Senior Member for Berbice.*
Albert Raymond Forbes Webber, *Junior Member for Berbice.*
Arnold Emanuel Seeram, *Member for Demerara.*

The Legislative Council met for the first time on November 28, 1928. Prayers were read by the Rt. Rev. Oswald H. Parry, Bishop of British Guiana. Members were made and subscribed to the Oath. The Chief Justice administered the Oath to the Governor. The Governor administered the Oath to the Members. Standing Rules and Orders were considered and approved.

The 1930s brought a period of deep depression and economic hardship to all segments of Guianese society. All of the major exports - sugar, rice, and bauxite - were affected by low prices and high unemployment. The working class found itself without a political voice during a time of worsening economic conditions. By the mid-1930s, British Guiana and the whole British Caribbean were marked by labor unrest and violent demonstrations. In the aftermath of riots throughout the British West Indies, a royal commission under Lord Moyne was established to determine the reasons for the riots and to make recommendations.

The Moyne Commission questioned the people, including trade unionists, professionals, and representatives of communities. The commission pointed out the deep division between the country's two largest ethnic groups, the Afro-Guianese and the Indo-Guianese. The Indo-Guyanese's larger group consisted primarily of rural rice producers or merchants; they had retained their culture and did not participate in national politics. The Afro-Guianese was largely urban workers or workers at the bauxite mine; they adopted European culture and dominated national politics. To increase the representation of the majority of the population in British Guiana, the Moyne Commission called for increased government democratization and economic and social reforms.

The Moyne Commission's report in 1938 urged the extension of the franchise to women and persons not owning land and encouraged the emerging trade union movement. Many of the Moyne Commission's recommendations were not implemented because of World War II's outbreak and because of British opposition.

The period of World War II was marked by continuing political reform and improvements to the national infrastructure. The Governor, Sir Gordon Lethem, created the country's first Ten-Year Development Plan, led by Sir Oscar Spencer, the Economic Adviser to the Governor, and Mr. Alfred P. Thorne, Assistant to the Economic Adviser. The plan reduced property qualifications for office holding and voting and made elective members a majority on the Legislative Council in 1943. Under the aegis of the Lend-Lease Act of 1941, a modern airbase,

Atkinson field, was constructed by United States troops. By the end of World War II, British Guiana's political system had been widened to encompass more members of society. The economy's foundations were strengthened by increased demand for bauxite.

CHAPTER 20

The Formation of Political Parties

A T THE END OF WORLD WAR II, POLITICAL AWAREness and demands grew in all segments of society. The immediate postwar period witnessed the founding of British Guiana's major political parties. When Dr. Cheddi Jagan returned home from studying dentistry in the U.S.A., he established his dentistry clinic and was soon immersed in politics.

While visiting the clinic for dental services, a patient who was also a worker at a sugar plantation expressed to Dr. Jagan the grievances of workers at the sugar plantation. At that time, The Man Power Citizens' Association (MPCA), led by Ayube Mohamed Edun, was providing organized leadership for the sugar workers and workers of the bauxite mine. After the Leonora sugar workers' strike in 1939, its popularity grew significantly. By 1943, it became the largest trade union with more than 20,000 members. Dr. Jagan joined the MPCA and became the treasurer in 1945. He eventually became part of the management team for one year. During his tenure, he frequently clashed with the more moderate union leadership over policy issues. That position allowed him to meet other union leaders in British Guiana and throughout the English-speaking Caribbean.

In 1946, Dr. Jagan organized the Political Affairs Committee (PAC) and was elected a Legislative Council member in 1947. The Political Affairs Committee was formed as a discussion group. The new organization published the *PAC Bulletin* to promote its ideology of liberation and decolonization. The PAC's outspoken criticism of the colony's poor living standards attracted followers as well as detractors. In the November 1947 general elections, the PAC put forward several members as independent candidates. The PAC's major competitor was the newly formed British Guiana Labor Party, which, under Mr. J. B. Singh, won six of the fourteen seats contested. Dr. Jagan won one seat, and he joined the Labor Party. He had difficulties with the party's center-right ideology and soon left.

The Labor Party's support of the policies of the British Governor and the inability to create a grass-roots base stripped it of liberal supporters. The Labor Party's lack of a clear-cut reform agenda left a vacuum, which Dr. Jagan moved to fill.

Disturbances on the colony's sugar plantations gave Dr. Jagan an opportunity to achieve national standing. After June 16, 1948, police shootings of five Guianese workers at Enmore, the PAC, and the Guiana Industrial Workers Union (GIWU) organized a large and peaceful demonstration, which enhanced Dr. Jagan's standing with the Guianese population.

From 1928 to 1964, the First-Past-The-Post Constituency system was the electoral system used in British Guiana. Under the First-Past-The-Post system, the country was divided into

Constituencies and candidates contested as individuals in a constituency. The voters voted for a candidate. The candidate who received the highest number of votes won the seat.

After the PAC, Dr. Jagan's next step was founding the People's Progressive Party (PPP) in January 1950. Using the PAC as a foundation, Dr. Jagan created a new party that drew support from all communities. To increase support among the Afro-Guianese population, Mr. Forbes Burnham was brought into the party. Earlier in Dr. Jagan's political career, he publicly supported Marxist politics that was sometimes at odds with the reality of the Guianese race-class situation. While Marxism proved to be philosophically valuable to the Caribbean decolonization and nationalist struggles, Caribbean leaders failed to apply it to their policies.

The PPP's initial leadership was multi-ethnic and non-revolutionary. Dr. Jagan became the PPP's parliamentary group leader, and Mr. Burnham assumed the responsibilities of party chairman. Other key party members included Mrs. Janet Jagan and the PAC veterans Mr. Brindley Benn and Mr. Ashton Chase. The party's first victory was in the 1950 municipal elections, in which Mrs. Janet Jagan won a seat. Dr. Jagan and Mr. Burnham failed to win seats, but Mr. Burnham's campaign made a favorable impression on many Afro-Guianese citizens. From its first victory in the 1950 municipal election, the PPP gathered momentum. However, the party's anti-colonial message made the British Government uncomfortable and labeled his political ideology as Socialism.

A British commission in 1950 recommended universal adult suffrage and the adoption of a ministerial system for British Guiana. The commission also recommended that power be concentrated in the executive branch, that is, the Governor's office. Those reforms presented the parties with an opportunity to participate in national elections and form a government but maintained power in the hands of the British-appointed Chief Executive. The arrangement annoyed the PPP and saw it as an attempt to curtail the party's power. Colonial officials showed their displeasure with the PPP in 1952 when, on a regional tour, Dr. and Mrs. Jagan were designated prohibited immigrants in the British colonies, Trinidad and Grenada.

CHAPTER 21

The First PPP Election of Dr. Cheddi Jagan

IN 1953, A NEW CONSTITUTION WAS INTRODUCED IN British Guiana conferring adult suffrage, an elected House of Assembly, elected Ministers, and women were allowed to be legislators for the first time. Similar constitutions had already been granted to Jamaica in 1944 and Trinidad in 1950. Any attempt to postpone a similar step for British Guiana would have presented an unpleasant effect on British Guiana and the rest of the West Indies.

With the new Constitution, the Office of Speaker and a Ministerial system of Government were created for the Colony of British Guiana. A new bicameral Legislature, a State Council, and a House of Assembly were also introduced. Once the new Constitution was adopted, an election was set for April 1953. In the 1953 general elections, the PPP won 18 of the 24 seats in the new House of Assembly. The National Democratic Party won 2 seats, and Independent Candidates won 4 seats. Six PPP Members of the Assembly were elected on May 18, 1953, to be Ministers and were assigned portfolios. Three women became legislators for the first time, and one was elected to be the first deputy Speaker. The Governor appointed the first Speaker.

The PPP, with elements of both ethnic groups' middle sectors, made for a formidable constituency. Conservatives branded the PPP as communist, but the Party campaigned on a platform that appealed to growing nationalism. The other major Party participating in the election, the National Democratic Party (NDP), was largely an Afro-Guianese middle-class organization with middle-class Portuguese and Indo-Guyanese. The PPP soundly defeated the NDP and the United Farmers, the Workers Party, and the United National Party. Trevor Munroe stated, "Dr. Cheddi Jagan had won a massive election victory in 1953, the first Marxist to win a majority in democratic elections – Allende was not the first in the hemisphere..."

On April 7, 1953, Sir Eustace Gordon Woolford was appointed by Governor Sir Alfred William Lungley Savage to be the Speaker of the new House of Assembly. He was the first Speaker for British Guiana and held office until June 30, 1957. A new Constitution (*Waddington*) was introduced.

On April 27, 1953, General Elections were held under the First-Past-The-Post Constituency system for 24 seats in the new House of Assembly and for the first time under universal adult suffrage. The People's Progressive Party polled 77,695 or 51% of the valid votes and obtained 18 of the 24 seats in the House of Assembly. The National Democratic Party won 2 seats, and Independent candidates won 4 seats.

The First Members of the new House of Assembly:

The Speaker

Sir Eustace Gordon Woolford.

Ex-Officio Members

John Gutch, *Chief Secretary.*
Frank Wilfred Holder, *Attorney General.*
Walter Ogle Fraser, *Financial Secretary (Acting).*

Elected Members (24).

People's Progressive Party (18).
Ministers (6).
Cheddi Jagan, *Leader of the House and Minister of Agriculture, Forests, Lands, and Mines*
(No. 23 – Corentyne Coast).
Linden Forbes Sampson Burnham, *Minister of Education* (No. 14 – Georgetown North-East).
Ashton Chase, *Minister of Labor, Industry, and Commerce* (No. 10 - Georgetown South).
Sydney Evanson King, *Minister of Communications and Works* (No. 16 – Central Demerara).
Joseph Prayag Lachmansingh, *Minister of Health and Housing* (No. 8 - East Bank Demerara).
Jai Narine Singh, *Minister of Local Government and Social Welfare* (No. 7 – West Bank Demerara).

Deputy Speaker

Janet Jagan (No. 3 – Western Essequibo).

Other Members

Fred Bowman (No. 6 – Demerara-Essequibo).
Clinton Reginald Wong (No.11 – Georgetown South Central).
Jessie Irma Sampson Burnham (No.12 – Georgetown Central).
Frank Obermuller Van Sertima (No.13 – Georgetown North).
Ram Karran (No. 15 – West Central Demerara).
Jane Phillips-Gay (No. 17 – East Central Demerara).
Chandra Sama Persaud (No. 18 – Mahaica-Mahaicony).
Samuel Mahabali Latchmansingh (No. 19 – Western Berbice).
Ajodha Singh (No. 21 – Berbice River).
Robert Stanley Hanoman-Singh (No. 22 – Eastern Berbice).
Mohamed Khan (No. 24 – Corentyne River).

National Democratic Party

William Oscar Rudyard Kendall (No. 20 – New Amsterdam).
Eugene Francis Correia (No. 5 – Bartica and Interior).

Independents

William Alfred Phang (No. 1 - North West).
Thomas Sherwood Wheating (No. 2 - Pomeroon).
Theophilus Lee (No. 4 – Essequibo Islands).

Charles Albert Carter (No. 9 - Upper Demerara River).

On May 18, 1953, the House of Assembly held its First Sitting with the following First Members of the First State Council:

The President.

Sir Frank McDavid.

Ministers without Portfolio appointed by the Governor:

William John Raatgever.
Lionel Alfred Luckhoo.
William Alexander Macnie.
Rahman Bacchus Gajraj.
Alan John Knight.

The State Council held its First Meeting on May 25, 1953. The Ceremonial Opening of the Legislature took place on May 30, 1953. Since the election, British Guiana elected Ministers has been under strong anti-colonial democratic influences. The verdict of the electorate was acceptable. The Party had its chance to govern the Colony, despite the risks involved. The Governor was hoping to influence the Ministers against any form of extremism in the Party, but the responsibilities of the office were, therefore, to modify their views. It was clear that they had taken every opportunity to undermine the British Constitution and to further the democratic and anti-colonial cause. Typical of the actions was the refusal to move a loyal address to '*Her Majesty*' on the first meeting of the House of Assembly and to send a delegation from the House to meet Her Majesty the Queen in Jamaica.

They were the moving force behind the strike for better

working conditions on the sugar plantations, which paralyzed the sugar industry of the territory for four weeks. At one time, there were signs of it spreading to the entire country. The conservative business communities criticized the actions. Their sole aim appears to be the representation of the working class in the territory. In the colonists' view, they were seeking to achieve by the classical Communist technique, supporting trade unions for the working class.

The leading figures were in contact with the World Federation of Trade Unions in Vienna. In those circumstances, Britain felt that there was no doubt that a halt must be called and the powers of the Ministers be taken away and the leading figures imprisoned. On September 25, 1953, it was proposed to advise Her Majesty to make the necessary Orders in Council. Troops and emergency legal powers were arranged. On October 9, 1953, the Constitution was suspended. The State Council and the House of Assembly were prorogued. The portfolios of the six elected Ministers were removed. They became Ministers without Portfolios. On December 2, 1953, the Secretary of State for the Colonies announced in the British House of Commons the appointment of the following to comprise the Constitutional Commission:

Sir James Robertson, *Chairman.*
Sir Donald Jackson.
George Woodcock.
R.E. Radford, *Colonial Office Secretary.*

On December 21, 1953, the Legislature, the State Council and the House of Assembly, was dissolved. The British Prime Minister said that arresting and detention without charge of the People's Progressive Party leaders was a serious step, and the Cabinet ought to be made aware of the grounds on which it was justified. The Colonial Secretary said that the authorities in British Guiana were faced with a dilemma. If they made no arrests until violence or bloodshed had occurred, they would be accused of weakness and share some of the responsibility for the subsequent suffering and disorder. If arrests were made to forestall serious trouble, it could be said that the arrests had not been justified.

The Governor was entitled to make such arrests under the emergency powers conferred on him by Order-in-Council. It would be a mistake to deprive him of all discretion in exercising his function of preserving law and order. The Governor was urged to take steps to restrain the leaders of the PPP short of arresting them. However, when the Governor indicated that the leaders were organizing illegal meetings and obstructing the Governor's efforts to restore normal conditions in the Colony, the Colonial Secretary authorized him to make the arrests.

As a result of intimidation, witnesses required by the prosecution were not coming forward. The Colonial Secretary urged the Governor to take all possible administrative means to bring the PPP leaders to trial. The Lord Chancellor expressed that, while the Governor could not reasonably be criticized for exercising his emergency powers in the way he did, there was a limit to the period for which persons could reasonably be held under such powers without being brought to trial. The Colonial Secretary indicated that he was curious if his colleagues shared his view and if it would be right for him to accept an interview with the former leader of British Guiana during his visit to Britain. He would, of course, confine himself to listening to what Dr. Jagan has to say to him.

It was the general view of the Cabinet that the Colonial Secretary would be well advised to accord interviews both to the representatives of the PPP in London and also to the representatives of the Opposition Parties in British Guiana. Already skeptical of Dr. Jagan and the PPP's perseverance, conservative forces in the business community were further distressed by the new administration's expanding the State's role in the economy and the society. The PPP implemented its reform program rapidly, which brought the Party into a confrontation with the Governor and high-ranking civil servants, who preferred more gradual changes.

The issue of civil service appointments also threatened the PPP from within. Following the 1953 victory, appointments became an issue between the predominantly Indo-Guyanese supporters of Dr. Jagan and the Afro-Guyanese supporters of Mr. Burnham. Mr. Burnham threatened to split the Party if he were not made sole leader of the PPP. A compromise was reached in which members of Mr. Burnham's faction received ministerial appointments.

The PPP's introduction of the Labor Relations Act provoked a confrontation with the British. That law aimed to reduce intra-union rivalries but would favor the GIWU, which was closely aligned with the ruling Party. The opposition charged that the PPP sought to gain control over the Colony's economic and social life and was moving to stifle the opposition. The day that the act was introduced to the legislature, the GIWU went on strike supporting the proposed law.

The British Government interpreted the intermingling of party politics and labor unionism as a direct challenge to the Constitution and the Governor's authority. The socio-economic reforms along with the strikes and demonstrations, prompted the British authorities to dismiss Dr. Jagan from office.

CHAPTER 22

The Dissolution of the 1953 Legislature

A MEETING OF THE FOLLOWING CABINET WAS HELD at 10 Downing Street, S.W.1, on Thursday, October 8, 1953, at 6 p.m.

The Right Hon. Sir Winston Churchill, M.P., *Prime Minister (in the Chair).*

The Right Hon. Anthony Eden, M.P., *Secretary of State for Foreign Affairs.*

The Most Hon. Lord Simonds, *Lord Chancellor.*

Lord The Right Hon. H. F. C. Crookshank, *Chancellor. M.P., Lord Privy Seal.*

The Right Hon. *the Earl Alexander of Tunis, Minister of Defense.*

The Right Hon. Oliver Lyttelton, M.P., *Secretary of State for the Colonies.*

The Right Hon. Sir Walter Monckton, Q.C., M.P., *Minister of Labor and National Service.*

The Right Hon. Harold Macmillan, M.P., *Minister of Housing and Local Government.*

The Right Hon. Sir Thomas Dugdale, M.P., *Minister of Agriculture and Fisheries.*

The Right Hon. the Marquess of Salisbury, *Lord President of the Council.*

Secretariat:

The Right Hon. Sir Norman Brook.

Mr. R. M. J. Harris.

1. The Cabinet considered the latest developments in British Guiana. The Colonial Secretary said that it had hitherto been intended that, as soon as British troops were deployed in the territory, the Governor should take the following action:

(i) Assume emergency powers under the Order-in-Council made at Balmoral on October 4.

(ii) Remove the Ministers' portfolios under the emergency powers.

(iii) Publish a statement of Her Majesty's Government's policy and announce the intention to suspend the Constitution.

(iv) Arrest the leaders of the People's Progressive Party.

Suspension of the Constitution could not be effected without Parliamentary action at Westminster and must, therefore, await the reassembly of Parliament. Under the emergency powers available, however, the Ministers could, in the meanwhile, be relieved of their responsibility, although they would technically remain Ministers so long as the Constitution remained in force. The Royal Welch Fusiliers landed at Georgetown. Their reception was friendly, and the situation in the town was entirely calm. In the circumstances, the Governor urged that, while an action under (i)-(iii) above should be taken as planned, no arrests should be made unless there were further developments in the situation. The Colonial Secretary remained of the opinion that there was ample justification for immediate arrests. However, he agreed that it would be inexpedient to make the arrests at that moment when there was no public disorder in the Colony. Therefore, with the Prime Minister's approval, he instructed the Governor to proceed with the action summarized in (i)-(iii) but to wait for developments before making any arrests and, if possible, to refer to him before making them.

Colonial Office telegram No. 78 to Sir A. Savage of October 8. The Prime Minister said that he did not doubt that removing the Ministers' portfolios and suspension of the Constitution could be abundantly justified on the ground that Ministers were given a fair trial but had demonstrated that their management of the Colony's affairs could only lead to its ruin. It would, however, be very much harder to justify arresting and detaining men who would of necessity remain Ministers for the time being if they were not to be charged with any specific offense and conditions in the Colony remained quiet.

There was general support in the Cabinet for the course it is proposed to follow. However, it was recognized that it might well make it necessary for the troops to remain in the territory for a more extended period. It was also recognized that if the Ministers were left at liberty after being relieved of their functions, they were likely to make as much capital as they possibly could out of the position and might seek to stir up disaffection by agitation and possibly strike action. While it was agreed that it would not be political to arrest them at the moment, Ministers considered that they should not be allowed indefinitely to flout the Government of the Colony and Her Majesty's Government before the eyes of the world. The Minister of Defense asked whether the battalion of Argyll and Sutherland Highlanders which was about to leave for Georgetown should still proceed thither or be diverted to Jamaica and whether the move of the battalion of the Gloucestershire Regiment, which was due to sail from Liverpool on October 14 for Jamaica, should be canceled.

The Cabinet:

(a) Endorsed the instructions sent to the Governor of British Guiana in Colonial Office telegram No. 78 of October 8.

(b) Agreed that the Argyll and Sutherland Highlanders' projected move to Georgetown should proceed on the understanding that they could be diverted to Jamaica *en route* if the development of the situation in British Guiana appeared to justify this course.

(c) Agreed that no overt action should be taken for the time being regarding the proposed move of the First Battalion of the Gloucestershire Regiment to Jamaica, on the understanding that the position should be reviewed in three to four days.

2. The Foreign Secretary said that the British and United States Ambassadors in Rome and Belgrade had now made the initial communications to the Italian and Yugoslav Governments following the plan, approved by the Cabinet on October 2, for bringing about a *de facto* settlement of the Trieste problem. These communications had been received reasonably well. Tito's response, in particular, had been less violent than might have been expected: He had not threatened to annex Zone B of the Free Territory. The Colonial Secretary stated:

> The elected Ministers in British Guiana were under strong Communist influences. They were taking every opportunity to undermine

the Constitution and to further the Communist cause. Some of them had been the moving force behind the strike which had paralyzed the sugar industry, and they were seeking to establish a totalitarian dominance over the territory by penetrating the trade unions and local government.

The main reason is that they were in touch with the World Federation of Trade Unions in Vienna. It was necessary to take away the Ministers' powers, imprison the leading figures and suspend the Constitution at the earliest possible moment.

In August 1949, USA President Truman signed the North Atlantic Treaty, which marked the beginning of NATO. Two years earlier, he requested $400 million in aid from Congress to combat communism in Greece and Turkey. The Truman Doctrine pledged to provide American economic and military assistance to any nation threatened by communism.

On March 29, 1951, Julius and Ethel Rosenberg became the only two American civilians to be executed for espionage-related activity in the USA. They were convicted of conspiring to sell U.S. atomic secrets to the Soviet Union and executed by electric chair at Sing Sing Prison, Ossining, New York, USA, in 1953, despite outrage from liberals who portrayed them as victims of an anti-communist witch hunt.

The U.S. government used the Rosenbergs case to prove to the public that communism threatened the American way of life and claimed that fighting communism required that human rights and civil liberties take a back seat to national security. Lori Clune's book, *Executing the Rosenbergs: Death and Diplomacy in a Cold War World*, wrote that the Rosenbergs case remains "emblematic of the tragic consequences that result when actions are driven by paranoia and fear." "Few cases in American history have stirred emotions, generated debate in and out of government and the judicial system, and have had as enduring and divisive a political impact as the prosecution of the Rosenbergs." - Sam Roberts, reporter, New York Times. Martin Sherwin, Professor of History, George Mason University stated:

> The Rosenberg case and the United States' Cold War policies will always be the subjects of lively academic debate. The release of the Rosenbergs grand jury records would advance this important debate and enlighten the public about the Rosenbergs case, and more generally, about the development of the United States' controversial Cold War policies.

Mrs. Janet Jagan's biography stated that she was born Janet Rosenberg in Chicago, Illinois, USA, and claims no relation to Ethel and Julius Rosenberg, whose parents migrated from the USSR. Mrs. Jagan's maternal grandparents, Adolph and Rosa Kronberg (née Appelbaum), were also immigrants. Adolph immigrated to Chicago from Romania, and Rosa came from Hungary. Adolph and Rosa Kronberg had four children - Mary, Kate, Laura, and Leo. Kate was the mother of Mrs. Jagan; her parents were Charles and Kate Rosenberg. At age 22, while working as a student nurse, she met Cheddi Jagan, a Dentistry student at Northwestern University. They married and moved to British Guiana, where Dr. Jagan set up his dental practice.

The association of Dr. Jagan with communism became a controversy from the time he entered the Guianese political scene in the late 1940s. Dr. Jagan supported a Marxist system as the best strategy for the people of his country who were oppressed by colonization. He was an alleged Communist, although he denied it. His wife was a member of the Young

Communist League while she was a university student. She also denied allegations that she was a Communist.

On October 9, 1953, the British suspended the Constitution, discontinued the State Council and the House of Assembly without dissolving them, and removed the ministers' portfolios. It would have been much harder to justify arresting and detaining men who would of necessity remain Ministers for the time being if they were not to be charged with any specific offense, and conditions in the Colony remained quiet. There was general support in the Cabinet for the proposed course. However, it was recognized that it might make it necessary for the troops to remain in the territory for a more extended period. It was also recognized that if the Ministers were left at liberty after being relieved of their functions, they were likely to make as much capital as they possibly could out of the position, and they might seek to stir up disaffection by agitation and possibly strike action.

While it was agreed that it would not be political to arrest them, the Ministers considered that they should not be allowed indefinitely to flout the Government of the Colony and Her Majesty's Government before the eyes of the world. The Minister of Defense asked whether the battalion of Argyll and Sutherland Highlanders which was about to leave for Georgetown should still proceed thither or be diverted to Jamaica and whether the move of the battalion of the Gloucestershire Regiment, which was due to sail from Liverpool on October 14, for Jamaica, should be canceled. The Cabinet agreed that the Argyll and Sutherland Highlanders' projected move to Georgetown should proceed on the understanding that they could be diverted to Jamaica en route if the development of the situation in British Guiana appeared to justify this course.

It was agreed that no overt action should be taken regarding the proposed move of the First Battalion of the Gloucestershire Regiment to Jamaica, on the understanding that the position should be reviewed in three to four days. The final advice was that the situation was deteriorating daily, and the Governor doubted whether more than 50 percent of the police were not reliable. He felt, however, that if a British battalion arrived on the spot at an early date, the police would remain loyal. He, therefore, proposed that a battalion of the Royal Welch Fusiliers should proceed at once to British Guiana, from Jamaica, in a cruiser and two frigates. They would arrive in Georgetown on October 9. The cruiser would have to station fifteen miles off the port, and the frigates would land the troops. As soon as the troops landed, the Governor would take action under emergency powers to imprison the leaders and suspend the Constitution. In discussion, the following points were made: In operations of this kind, the risk of bloodshed was much less if overwhelming force was deployed at the outset. That consideration suggested that it would be preferable to send two battalions to Georgetown rather than one. On the other hand, an additional battalion could not reach there before October 20. By that date, the situation would have deteriorated further, and the police might no longer be reliable.

A supplementary force of one battalion could be brought to readiness in the United Kingdom. It could sail with some of its vehicles in an aircraft carrier on about October 8 or 9. The only battalion immediately available for that duty was at half-strength. However, there were three full-strength battalions in the Infantry Brigade held as reinforcement for Egypt.

No information on intentions was given to the Governments of other Commonwealth countries or the United States. It was, however, proposed that the Government of Canada, which had important commercial interests in British Guiana, should be told of the plan twenty-four hours before it was put into operation. It was suggested that Australia, New Zealand, the United States, and possibly Venezuela should also be told about twelve hours before the plan took effect. It was unlikely that there would be any adverse reactions in the United States, where anti-colonial sentiments would, in this case, be offset by anti-Communist sentiments. The Governments of India, Pakistan, and Ceylon should not be informed until the operation has begun.

The Cabinet approved the Colonial Secretary's proposals for suspending the Constitution of British Guiana. The Minister of Defense was invited to arrange for a battalion of the Royal Welch Fusiliers to proceed at once to British Guiana, from Jamaica, with a naval force of one cruiser and two frigates; and to make all the necessary preparations to enable a further battalion to be sent at full-strength from the United Kingdom, in an aircraft carrier, if reinforcements proved to be needed.

Within six months of the election, the British suspended the Constitution, discontinued the State Council and the House of Assembly without dissolving them, and removed the ministers' portfolios. The Constitution was suspended to prevent the '*Subversion of Government*' of what has been referred to as '*the extremist leaders of the Party*.' The Legislature, the State Council and the House of Assembly, was dissolved. All persons ceased to be Ministers and legislators from 1954 to 1957. An Interim Legislative Council was made up by the British. An amendment to the 1953 Constitution was established as a new Wholly Nominated Single Chamber Interim Legislative Council and became effective from 1954 to 1957.

CHAPTER 23

The Interim Legislative Council

GOVERNOR SAVAGE SUSPENDED THE CONSTITUTION, removed Chief Minister Dr. Jagan from office, and declared a state-of-emergency on October 9, 1953. British government troops were brought in from Jamaica to maintain order. The British Government appointed a three-member Constitutional Commission headed by Sir James Robertson on December 2, 1953, and appointed an interim government on December 27, 1953.

Governor, Sir Alfred William Lungley Savage, addressed the Interim Legislative Council at the first meeting on January 5, 1954. The former Speaker, Sir Eustace Gordon Woolford, continued as Speaker of the new Legislative Council. Following the dissolution of the Legislature on December 21, 1953, Temporary Constitutional Provisions were introduced. A new Executive Council was established. An Interim (Wholly Nominated Single Chamber) Legislative Council consisting of 28 Members: A Speaker, the Chief Secretary, the Attorney General, the Financial Secretary, and twenty-four Nominated Members, was established. No Members were nominated from the People's Progressive Party.

The members of the new body were nominated by the Governor and consisted of a small group of conservative politicians, businessmen, and civil servants. No Members of the elected People's Progressive Party were nominated. There were changes in the composition of the successive Legislative bodies and the Presiding Official of the Legislative bodies. There were changes in the elections system, the franchise, the constituencies, and the dress code for male Members attending sittings. The legislation was enacted for the payment of salaries and superannuation benefits for legislative service.

The following were the First Members of the Interim Legislative Council:

The Speaker

Sir Eustace Gordon Woolford.

Ex-Officio Members

John Gutch, *Financial Secretary*
Frank Wilfred Holder, *Attorney General*
Walter Ogle Fraser, *Financial Secretary*

Members with Portfolio (They were not designated, Ministers).

Sir (Edwin) Frank McDavid, *Member for Agriculture, Forests and Lands and Mines.*

Percival Augustus Cummings, *Member for Labor, Health, and Housing.*

William Oscar Rudyard Kendall, *Member for Communications and Works.*

George Arthur Cyril Farnum, *Member for Local Government, Social Welfare and Co-operative Development.*

Members without Portfolio (They were not designated, Ministers).

Geoffrey Haward Smellie (Resigned from 1.1.56).
Rahman Bacchus Gajraj.
Rupert Clement Tello.

Nominated Official Members

Wellesley Trevelyan Lord, *Commissioner of Lands and Mines.*
James Isaac Ramphal, *Commissioner of Labor.*

Nominated Unofficial Members

William John Raatgever, (Deputy Speaker to August 1, 1956).
Theophilus Lee.
William Alfred Phang.
Lionel Alfred Luckhoo.
William Alexander Macnie, (Deputy Speaker from 3.8.56).
Charles Albert Carter.
Eugene Francis Correia.
Douglas Campbell Josiah Bobb.
Hamid Rahaman.
Gertrude Hyacinth Collins.
Esther Elizabeth Dey.

Hugh Arthur Fraser.
Lt. Col. Ernest James Haywood.
Rupert Bramwell Jailal.
Sugrim Singh.

The Robertson Commission, appointed to inquire into those events, recommended an indefinite marking time in constitutional matters. In January 1954, the Members of the Robertson Constitutional Commission arrived in Guyana and commenced their work. On April 3, 1954, Dr. Cheddi Jagan was arrested by police at Mahaicony and sentenced to six months imprisonment with hard labor on April 4, 1954. Dr. Jagan was released from prison on September 12, 1954. The People's Progressive Party boycotted the Commission. In September 1954, the Constitutional Commission submitted its Report dated September 1, 1954, to the Secretary of State for the Colonies. It was announced in November 1954 that Her Majesty's Government accepted the recommendation but intended to do everything possible to fit the Colony for return to representative Government.

Since the suspension of the Constitution, efforts to improve conditions in the Colony and develop its resources have been intensified. Progress has not been as good as was hoped, but the ground was prepared for carrying through the practical program of development announced for 1956/60.

In the political field, the most significant development has been a split in the PPP. One faction, led by Dr. Jagan, derived his support mainly from the Indo-Guianese in the sugar plantations and rural districts. The other, led by Mr. Burnham, supports the Afro-Guianese community and is stronger in Georgetown and urban areas. The Interim Government did not secure any measure of popular support; its members had no political future.

The National Labor Front, a new political party led by Mr. Lionel Luckhoo, the Mayor of Georgetown, was formed. It provided a practical focus for Opposition to the extremist wing of the PPP. Against that background, Governor Sir Patrick Renison, who assumed duty in October, considered resuming constitutional advancement. As a first step, he relaxed restrictions on political meetings imposed under the Emergency Powers. There has been a marked heightening in political interest and considerable speculation about the elections' prospects.

The Governor was satisfied that he should maintain the initiative and put forward proposals for a limited and safeguarded step toward restoring a representative Government. He proposed an elected element into the Legislative Council and appointed elected members on the Executive Council with portfolios. There was no question of elections being held before April 1957. The plan was to leave the date open as an opportunity for a new National Labor Front buildup. If that proves successful, it will open up the possibility of an effective coalition of anti-Communist forces in which the Burnham faction of the PPP could join. The Governor discussed how the Constitution would work in that event since it would be expected that he would offer them an appointment to the Executive Council. He was confident that the PPP leaders could not risk provoking a breakdown in the Constitution again without forfeiting their support in the country; it was likely that they would prove co-operative if appointed to the Executive Council. There was evidence that Dr. Jagan personally, as distinct from the convinced Communists in his group, was anxious to secure some political future for himself and may be concerned about the possibility of disenfranchisement. That was a reasonable prospect of the experiment, providing the basis for further progress in the political field.

It was clear to proceed cautiously with full safeguards against Communist extremism; there was no expectation of any severe loss of confidence in the business communities. At the worst, the Constitution could be reverted at the discretion of the Governor. There would be a company of United Kingdom troops in the Colony to safeguard against any disturbance.

Mr. Burnham, leader of the Opposition, who was associated with Dr. Jagan in the misdemeanors of the Government that led to the suspension of the Constitution in 1953, supported Dr. Jagan's demands; he did so with the hope that Dr. Jagan's administration would get in a mess and that he would benefit at the next elections.

Request for Amendment of British Guiana Act, 1928, was made partly because the Guianese, through their misconduct, had one Constitution suspended and was nervous of having any future Constitution suspended and in part for prestige reasons at home. The assurance offered by the Colonial Secretary that he would not advise the exercise of the power save for constitution-making or in a grave emergency seems sufficient. This was not a sticking point for the delegation.

As a result of the poor performance of the Interim Government, even its mouthpiece, the *Daily Chronicle*, on November 27, 1955, complained in an editorial:

> Two years have gone by and we are no better off than we were before the political debacle. We have had more houses built, we have had self-aided schemes, a little of this and a little of that, but the population is increasing faster than ever, unemployment is increasing and the cost of living continues to rise. We submit to marking time politically, and even here we expect the time has come for some closure to that,

but must we submit to marking time where the economic development of the country is concerned? Must we continue to live as we are living, or should we say existing? Let there be an end to this nonsense.

W.J. Raatgever, President of the Georgetown Chamber of Commerce and a member of the Interim Government, during a debate in the Legislative Council in November 1955 declared: "So far as I have seen - and I have gone around quite fairly - there has been no developmental work done in this country." Jock Campbell, Chairman of Bookers and champion of British colonialism, had been forced to admit in August 1955 that there was "a very unsatisfactory state of affairs" existing in the country and that there could be no progress in a "political vacuum."

The UDP saw their participation in the puppet Interim Government as a chance to be in *power*. Many of their members, who held leading positions in the administration, such as John Carter, Lionel Luckhoo, and W.O.R. Kendall, were fearful of any forthcoming election. On October 26, 1956, during discussions in the Executive Council on a date for the general election under the Renison Constitution, Kendall, the Minister of Communications and Works, called for a delay in the election to allow the Interim Government to win some support. Kendall stated that the Interim Government needed more time to allow its projects to impact a large part of the population.

W.T. Lord, another nominee to the Legislative Council, complained about December 21, 1956, that the Minister of Agriculture, Lands, and Mines, Frank Mc David, had failed to formulate a policy concerning either land or agriculture and that "not one constructive idea has been produced." Clearly, the Interim Government was suffering from inertia. Money available for development in 1954-55 was under-spent because the Government members could not agree on using it. Of the $44 million earmarked for that period, only $26 million was actually spent.

Faced with a deteriorating economic situation, the British Government sought an electoral solution after it felt that the PPP would lose if the electoral boundaries were manipulated. The British Government probably also developed the opinion that PPP supporters were either disillusioned because of many of their leaders being imprisoned or had moved away to join with the Burnham group after the split in the Party in February 1955. The British Government was apparently convinced that the Burnham group would win the election or join with the UDP in a coalition government, forcing the PPP into Opposition.

The colonial authorities also wanted a commitment by an elected government on the issue of the West Indian Federation. In a statement, Governor Renison explained: "If British Guiana was still without any form of representative government which would decide whether not to join the Caribbean Federation, it would be a disappointment." The leaders of Barbados, Jamaica, and Trinidad also influenced the British Government to decide to hold a general election since Burnham's propaganda line convinced them that he would win any forthcoming election and lead Guyana into the West Indian Federation. The West Indian leaders, Grantley Adams, Norman Manley, and Patrick Solomon of Barbados, Jamaica, and Trinidad, respectively, apparently gave Burnham their unilateral support when they met with him in Ghana in March 1957.

The Governor admitted that the period of the Interim Government was a "frustrating period of marking time". That was not strange since dictatorial and non-democratic rule by puppets appointed by the British Government could not generate any form of progress. Finally, a new constitution was drawn up by the Secretary of State for the Colonies, Alan Lennox-Boyd, announced on April 25, 1956. It was even more backward than the one proposed by the Robertson Commission, which met in 1954 to rationalize the overthrow of the PPP Government. It provided a single-chamber Legislative Council of 12 elected members counterbalanced by eight nominated and four ex-officio members; an Executive Council of 5 elected members counterbalanced by four ex-officio members and one nominated. The Robertson Commission, though providing for similar control of the Executive Council by the Governor, had recommended that the legislature should have, as in 1953, an elected majority. The House of Assembly proposed 25 elected seats, one more for Rupununi than in 1953.

The PPP and other political parties immediately registered Opposition to the constitutional proposals. The PPP demanded that the new Constitution must introduce a considerable measure of self-government. Shortly after the announcement of the proposals was made, the Governor left for London for consultations. On his return in October 1956, he announced that the legislature would be modified to have 14 elected seats instead of 12, three ex-officio members, and 11 other nominated members.

Mr. Burnham broke away from Dr. Jagan in 1955. He told of a crude interpretation of ideological differences between him and Dr. Jagan. As far as his party is concerned, since his separation from the PPP, signs of racial awareness have been observed. However, that awareness has not developed into conscious or active hostility between the Indo-Guianese and the Afro-Guianese. At the general election of 1957, *'Appan Jhaat'*, meaning support your people, was uttered for the first time.

CHAPTER 24

Formation of the PNC Party

MR. BURNHAM WAS ONE OF THE FOUNDING LEADers of the People's Progressive Party, which was launched on January 1, 1950. The Indo-Guyanese labor leader Dr. Jagan became Leader of the party, and Mr. Burnham became its chairman. In 1952 Mr. Burnham became the party's affiliated trade union president, the British Guiana Labor Union. In 1953, the PPP won 18 of 24 seats in the first election by the Universal Adult Suffrage Franchise permitted by the British Colonial Government. According to property, income, and literacy qualifications, previous elections were based on a limited suffrage franchise. In the short-lived PPP government that followed, Mr. Burnham served as Minister of Education.

In 1955, there was a split in the PPP between Mr. Burnham and Dr. Jagan. The results of the 1957 elections came as a severe shock to Burnham and his followers. As an independent candidate, Sydney King joined Burnham's party, which was renamed the People's National Congress (PNC).

The division between Mr. Burnham and Dr. Jagan resulted from the differences in ideological perspectives. Dr. Jagan was said to support a Socialist path, and Mr. Burnham claimed to be a proponent of Moderatism. Neither the USA nor Britain wanted a communist government controlling a South American country. The powers, therefore, unaware of his communist leanings, supported Mr. Burnham through misguided naiveté.

At a special congress held on October 5-6, 1957, at the Astor Cinema in Georgetown, the following officers were elected: Forbes Burnham, Leader; Dr. Lachmansingh, chairman; Francis Da Silva, first vice-chairman; Jai Narine Singh, general secretary; Andrew Jackson and Jessie Burnham, assistant secretaries; Stanley Hugh, treasurer. The executive council also included Dr. J.A. Nicholson, George Young, Mrs. Mentore, Curtis Charles, Brentol Blackman, M. Edinboro, Sydney King, and Jane Phillips-Gay. Jessie Burnham eventually resigned from the PNC in 1958 and two years later rejoined the PPP.

The election of Sydney King, who was regarded as a Black nationalist, did not seem to win the support of Jai Narine Singh, an Indo-Guianese in the party's leadership structure. Early in 1958, Singh resigned from the PNC and organized his party called the Guiana Independence Movement. Sydney King was then named general secretary. By his inclusion in the top leadership, the PNC was able to win the support of the majority of Afro-Guianese on the East Coast Demerara; that certainly helped to polarize the politics along racial lines.

The PPP, in the meantime, continued to command the support of a significant proportion of the Afro-Guianese population. That proved to be worrisome for Mr. Burnham, who decided to form an alliance with the Afro-Guianese middle class he previously received little support. He planned to organize the influential anti-PPP Afro-Guianese politicians under his banner with the hope of attracting them.

Mr. Burnham learned an essential lesson from the 1957 elections. He could not win if supported only by the lower-class, urban Afro-Guianese. He needed middle-class allies, especially those Afro-Guianese who backed the moderate United Democratic Party (UDP). Mr. Burnham worked to balance maintaining the backing of the Afro-Guyanese lower classes and gaining the support of the more capitalist middle class. Mr. Burnham's stated preference for socialism did not bind the two groups against Dr. Jagan. Race seems to be a more practical choice. Mr. Burnham appealed to race and proved highly successful in bridging the divide. That strategy convinced the powerful Afro-Guianese middle class to accept a more radical leader than they would have preferred to support; it neutralized the objections of the Afro-Guianese working class to enter an alliance with those representing the more moderate interests of the middle classes.

Those differences did not go very deep. It was remarked that there were three Afro-Guianese Ministers in Dr. Jagan's Cabinet. The counsel of the PPP at the inquiry was an Afro-Guianese Lawyer. Some of Dr. Jagan's most substantial opposition in the proceedings was Indo-Guianese. Mr. Luckhoo, the counsel for the Chamber of Commerce, Mr. Ramphal, the counsel for the Trade Unions, and Mr. Jai Narine Singh, the counsel for the National Democratic Party, were all Indo-Guianese. One of the most vigorous opponents of Dr. Jagan is another Indo-Guianese, Mr. Sankar, the Trade Union leader.

There was no clear-cut division between the races, although Dr. Jagan's supporters were, for the most part, Indo-Guianese, and the supporters of PNC were mostly the Afro-Guianese.

The difference was not racial but economic and vocational. As was known, the Indo-Guianese, for the most part, was agriculturists, and they are the supporters of Dr. Jagan. In the towns, the percentage of Afro-Guianese residents is greater than the percentage of Indo-Guianese. The town dwellers supported the PNC not because their Leader is an Afro-Guianese. However, some of the Socialistic policies of Dr. Jagan appear less favorable for town dwellers than for the rural population. Those policies were dictated, not by racialism, but because in British Guiana, agriculture is of primary importance. Its development tends to promote agriculture in a more considerable measure than industrial schemes.

Before general elections were announced for August 1957, Mr. Burnham declared that his group would contest all 14 seats. The UDP also made a similar announcement. On the other hand, the PPP continued to pursue changes in the proposed constitution and finally decided to contest 13 of the seats after it could not get the other political parties and groupings to form a united front to contest the election.

The PPP convincingly won 9 seats at the general election, while Burnham's group won 3, the UDP 1 and the NLF 1. After the election, Burnham's group merged with the UDP to form the People's National Congress. With the formation of the PPP Government, even though with limited powers, the period of the Interim Government came to an unlamented end.

CHAPTER 25

The Second PPP Election of Dr. Cheddi Jagan

THE 1957 ELECTIONS WERE HELD UNDER A CONSTITU-tion that demonstrated the extent of the growing ethnic division within the Guianese electorate. The revised Constitution provided limited self-government, primarily through the Legislative Council. Of the council's twenty-four delegates, fifteen were elected, six were nominated, and the remaining three were ex-officio members from the interim administration. The two wings of the PPP launched vigorous campaigns, each attempting to prove that it was the legitimate heir to the original party. Despite denials of such motivation, both factions made a strong appeal to their respective ethnic constituencies. Dr. Jagan's PPP faction convincingly won the 1957 elections. Although his group had a secure parliamentary majority, its support was drawn more from the Indo-Guyanese community.

On August 12, 1957, General Elections were held for 14 seats for the 14 Constituencies in the Legislative Council. The Legislative Council consisted of 24 Members: A Speaker, 3 Ex-officio Members, 14 Elected Members, and 6 Nominated Members.

Four Political Parties contested the elections and were allocated the following seats: PPP (J) 9 seats, PPP (B) 3 seats, NLF 1 seat, and UDP 1 seat.

On August 21, 1957, Sir Donald Edward Jackson was appointed by the Governor, Sir Patrick Muir Renison, to be Speaker of the new Legislative Council. He was the Second Speaker and held the office until July 17, 1961.

The Members of the new Legislative Council were:

Speaker

Sir Donald Edward Jackson.

Ex-Officio Members

Francis Derek Jakeway, *Chief Secretary*
Anthony Mordaunt Innis Austin, *Attorney General*
Francis William Essex, *Financial Secretary*

Elected Ministers (PPP) (Jagan)

Dr. Cheddi Jagan, *Minister for Trade and Industry (No.1 – Eastern Berbice)*.

Brindley Horatio Benn, *Minister of Community Development and Education* (No. 12 – Essequibo River).

Edward Balkaran Beharry, *Minister of Natural Resources* (No. 5 – Eastern Demerara).

Janet Jagan, Minister of Labor, Health, and Housing (No. 13 – *Western Essequibo*).

Ram Karran, *Minister of Communications and Works* (No. 11 – Demerara-Essequibo).

Other Elected Members (PPP) (Jagan).

Fred Bowman (No. 10 – Demerara River).
Balram Singh Rai (No.6 – Central Demerara).
Sheik Mohamed Saffee (No. 4 – Western Berbice).
Ajodha Singh (No. 3 – Berbice River).

Other Elected Members (PPP) (Burnham)

Linden Forbes Sampson Burnham (No. 8 – Georgetown Central).
Andrew Leonard Jackson (No. 7 – Georgetown North).
Jainarine Singh (No. 9 – Georgetown South).
William Oscar Rudyard Kendall (*UDP*) (No. 2 – New Amsterdam).
Stephen Campbell (NLF) (No. 14 – North Western District).

Nominated Members

Rahman Baccus Gajraj (Deputy Speaker from April 17, 1958).
Rupert Clement Tello.
Robert Elliot Davis.
Anthony Martin Fredericks.

Henry Jocelyn Makepeace Hubbard.
Anthony Greaves Tasker.

The Legislative Council held its First Meeting on September 10, 1957. At that Meeting, a Mace was put into use in the Legislature for the first time. The Governor, Sir Patrick Muir Renison, addressed the Legislative Council.

In October 1957, the People's National Congress (PNC), led by Mr. Forbes Burnham, was formed and replaced the Burnhamite faction of the People's Progressive Party. The United Democratic Party (UDP), led by Mr. John Carter, merged with the new People's National Congress. Mr. Burnham's move was accomplished by merging his PPP faction and the United Democratic Party into a new organization, the PNC. The middle-class Afro-Guianese was represented by the UDP, led by John Carter. Burnham started negotiations with the UDP.

The leaders of the PNC believed in different ideologies. Some were Socialists, while others, particularly the former UDP members, were strongly Conservative and Pro-capitalist. Their conflicting views were often expressed at the public meetings, obviously generating confusion among the rank and file supporters. The party had great difficulty formulating an official policy statement. It did not arrive at one until early 1961 when Mr. Burnham invited Rawle Farley, a Guyanese economist at the University of the West Indies, to mediate with the executive committee members.

In March 1959, the two parties held a joint congress in Georgetown. The UDP disbanded itself and merged with the PNC. The joint membership elected a new executive committee. Burnham was elected Leader, and the executive committee included his close supporters, Sydney King, and Andrew Jackson. Prominent members of the disbanded UDP such as

John Carter, Eugene Correia, and Neville Bissember were also elected.

In November 1960, a new party, the United Force, was inaugurated by Mr. Peter D'Aguiar, chosen as its Leader. As stated by Mr. D'Aguiar and Senator Ann Jardim, the political differences between the UF and the PPP were nothing more than a narrative of personal frustration. The UF supported the movement towards independence, but when the proposal for appointing a Constitution Committee was mooted in the Legislative Assembly, Mr. D'Aguiar and his party staged a walk-out. The UF wanted a referendum to be held on the question of independence. They objected to the words *Freedom Year* being stamped on mail sent through the Post Office. They also objected to 1962 being described as the Freedom Year in documents issued from Government offices.

The political professions of the PNC were somewhat vague, and there was a tendency to give a racial tinge to its policy. Mr. Burnham expressed the opinion that it was Dr. Jagan who was responsible for that unfortunate development. He referred to the murder of an Afro-Guianese supporter of the PNC at Port Mourant, which is the birthplace of Dr. Jagan. The Senior Information Officer suppressed the report of that event at the request of the Government. He also referred to other acts of violence against the supporters of the PNC, especially in the rural areas where the Indo-Guianese population was predominant. There was not much substance in the contention of Mr. Burnham, and it seems that whatever racial differences existed was brought about by political propaganda.

In 1961, the United Force was formed with Mr. Peter D'Aguiar as the Leader. On July 18, 1961, the Legislative Council was dissolved and a new Constitution – The Constitution of British Guiana – annexed to The British Guiana (Constitution) Order in Council 1961 that was made on June 26, 1961, by Her Majesty by and with the advice of Her Privy Council, came into operation.

The new Constitution revoked the 1953 Constitutional Instruments and its amendments. Provision was made in the new Constitution for a Premier, and a Council of Ministers called the Executive Council or the Cabinet. Provision was also made for a two-chamber Legislature – a Senate and a Legislative Assembly. The Senate consisted of 13 Members. The Legislative Assembly consisted of a Speaker to be elected by the Assembly and 35 Members elected under the system in operation, i.e., the First-Past-The-Post System with 35 constituencies. The 1961 Constitution established the Office of Premier.

The primary issue and challenge for that PPP was the ending of colonialism. The only way to derail the plans of the Colonial Office was for one party to secure a majority of seats. Such a party can then make the demands of Dr. Eric Williams of Trinidad. Dr. Williams's party demanded the right to appoint two of the five nominated seats. That was granted after the Secretary of State for the Colonies, in a dispatch to the Governor, declared that the principle of the nominating members must not be utilized to frustrate the will of the people. That was regarded as the accepted British constitutional practice in Mauritius, Malaysia, and Trinidad. That new constitutional development prompted the imperialists to unite to prevent any party from securing a majority of seats. To achieve that, they have changed the constituency boundaries and voting methods to favor other parties.

The PPP believed that trade unions were essential for the working people to have their rights and fair wages and working conditions guaranteed. The party promised to encourage the unification of the trade union movement and eliminate rivalry. The party believed that trade unions that have the workers' confidence should be recognized as the representative of the workers.

In the late 1950s, the British Caribbean colonies were actively negotiating the establishment of a West Indies Federation. The PPP welcomed the new Federation but regretted that the Colonial office saddled it with a Colonial Constitution. The colonists supported British Guiana's participation based on dominion status for the Federation and internal self-government for each territory. The PPP agreed to commit to the Federation only after the Guianese people expressed, through a referendum, the desire to enter the Federation.

The racial riots and attacks on communities during that period made the situation ugly for British Guiana and the people's everyday life. Dr. Jagan and his wife Janet had a hard time moving around in the capital city. There was not much more Dr. Jagan could have done to confront racism in the population. The day-to-day life of politics exposed him to some of the advantages that came with partisanship.

History has taught that the PPP split played into the hand of the colonizer and undermined the prospect of a *'New Society'* and a *'New Guyana'* based on racial understanding and national unity. The legacy of Dr. Jagan is in the air for large sections of the Afro-Guianese population who see him as responsible for many of the racial problems of British Guiana. However, neither Dr. Jagan nor Mr. Burnham created the racial order in British Guiana. It was created by colonization, including the invitation of competing labor groups and the integration of Afro- and Indo-Guyanese peoples into the economy and society very differently. The seeds for conflict and exploitation in the colony have always been there. The trauma and problems of racism in British Guiana continue to this day.

CHAPTER 26

The Administration of Dr. Cheddi Jagan - 1961

THE 1961 ELECTIONS WERE CONTESTED BY THE PPP, the PNC, and the United Force. The UF was a conservative party representing the business industry, the Roman Catholic Church, the Indigenous population, the Chinese and Portuguese voters. The elections were held under a new constitution that marked a return to the degree of self-government that existed briefly in 1953. It introduced a bicameral system boasting a wholly elected thirty-five-member Legislative Assembly and a thirteen-member Senate appointed by the Governor. The post of Prime Minister was created and was to be filled by the majority party in the Legislative Assembly. With the strong support of the Indo-Guyanese population, the PPP won by a substantial margin, gaining twenty seats in the

Legislative Assembly, compared with eleven seats for the PNC and four for the UF. Dr. Jagan was named Premier.

The Legislative Assembly and the Senate

On August 21, 1961, General Elections were held, for the last time under the First-Past-The-Post system, for 35 seats in the Legislative Assembly. The results were as follows:
People's Progressive Party, 20 seats (42.6% of the votes).
People's National Congress, 11 seats (41% of the votes).
United Force, 4 seats (16.2% of the votes).
The People's Progressive Party formed the Government and Dr. Cheddi Jagan was appointed the Premier, and full internal self-government was granted.

The Members of the Legislative Assembly were:

Speaker

Rahman Baccus Gajraj, *People's Progressive Party.*

Ministers

Dr. Cheddi Jagan, *Premier, and Minister of Development and Planning.*
Brindley Horatio Benn, *Minister of Natural Resources.*
Ram Karran, *Minister of Works and Hydraulics.*
Balram Singh Rai, *Minister of Home Affairs.*
Ranji Chandisingh, *Minister of Labor, Health, and Housing.*
Charles Ramkissoon Jacob, Jnr., *Minister of Finance.*
Fenton Harcourt Wilworth Ramsahoye, *Attorney-General.*
Earl Maxwell Gladstone Wilson, *Minister of Communications.*

Parliamentary Secretaries

George Bowman, *Parliamentary Secretary to the Ministry of Natural Resources.*

Lawrence Everil McRansford Mann, *Parliamentary Secretary to the Ministry of Works and Hydraulics.*

Other Members

Sheik Mohamed Saffee.
George Lakey Robertson.
Moses Bhagwan.
John Bernard Caldeira.
Victor Downer.
Abdul Maccie Hamid.
George McLinton Henry.
Derek Chunilall Jagan.
Goberdhan Harry Lall.
Mohamed Shakoor.

People's National Congress

Linden Forbes Sampson Burnham.
William Oscar Rudyard Kendall, *Deputy Speaker.*
John Carter.
Eugene Francis Correia.
Neville James Bissember.
William Alexander Blair.
Rudolph Stanislaus Stanley Hugh.
John Gabriel Joaquin.

Robert James Jordan.
Claude Alfonso Merriman.
Henry Milton Shakespeare Wharton.

United Force

Peter Stanislaus D'Aguiar.
Stephen Campbell.
Randolph Emanuel Cheeks.
Edward Eyre Melville.

The first meeting of the Legislative Assembly was held on October 5, 1961. The Legislative Assembly elected Rahman Baccus Gajraj to be the Speaker. He was not an elected Member of the Assembly. He was the Third Speaker and the First Speaker to be elected by the Legislative body. He held the office until September 24, 1964.

The First Members of the Senate

Ashton Chase.
Cyril Victor Too Chung.
Claude Christian.
Mooneer Khan.
Cedric Vernon Nunes.
Christina Ramjattan.
Herbert Thomas.
Anne Jardim.

The First Meeting of the Senate was held on October 5, 1961. The Senate elected Ashton Chase to be President of the Senate. The Senate elected Cyril Victor Too Chung to be Vice-President of the Senate. The Ceremonial Opening of the new Legislative Assembly and the new Senate took place on October 6, 1961. It became the Second Sitting of the Legislative Assembly and also the Second Sitting of the Senate. The Governor, Sir Ralph Grey, addressed the Legislature.

Both Houses of the Legislature passed a Resolution asking Her Majesty's Government to fix a date for independence in 1962. The Resolution was approved by a substantial majority and unanimously by the two main parties with 85% of the votes in the recent General Elections. On December 13, Dr. Jagan asked the Colonial Secretary to give effect to the Resolution. Because the British Government undertook to consult further with the United States Government, the Colonial Secretary told Dr. Jagan that although the 1960 Constitutional Conference formula represented the agreed position, the Legislature's Resolution was a new development in so far as at the 1960 Conference. There was no unanimity on the Guianese side on the question of independence.

The Colonial Secretary proposed to consult his colleagues early and would inform Dr. Jagan of Her Majesty's Government's decision early in the New Year. Dr. Jagan was profoundly disappointed and took the question to the United Nations. His address to the Fourth Committee led to the draft Resolution inviting Her Majesty's Government to resume negotiations with British Guiana. This Resolution was due to be debated when sessions resumed the following January.

President John F. Kennedy's Administration

In his 1961 inaugural address, President John F. Kennedy proclaimed:

> Let every nation know, whether it wishes us well or ill, that we shall pay any price, bear any

burden, meet any hardship, support any friend, oppose any foe, in order to assure the survival and the success of liberty.

At the time, African Americans in the Southern United States were denied the right to vote, barred from public facilities, subjected to insults and violence, and could not expect justice from the courts. In the Northern United States, African Americans also faced discrimination in housing, employment, education, and many other areas.

In 1954, the Supreme Court ruled unanimously, in *Brown v. Board of Education*, that racial segregation in public schools was unconstitutional. Many southern political leaders claimed the desegregation decision violated the rights of states to manage their systems of public education, and they responded with defiance, legal challenges, delays, or token compliance. As a result, school desegregation proceeded very slowly. By the end of the 1950s, fewer than 10 percent of African American children in the South were attending integrated schools.

The pace of civil rights protests rose sharply in response to the Supreme Court's decision. Martin Luther King Jr. led a boycott that ended segregated busing in Montgomery, Alabama. In 1957, National Guard troops under orders from President Dwight D. Eisenhower enforced the desegregation of Little Rock Central High School in Arkansas. However, even after Little Rock, school integration was painfully slow, and segregation, in general, remained largely untouched.

In February 1960, four African American college students sat down at a Woolworth's lunch counter in Greensboro, North Carolina, and asked to be served. They were refused service, and they refused to leave their seats. Within days, more than 50 students had volunteered to continue the sit-in, and within weeks the movement had spread to other college campuses. Sit-ins and other protests swept across the South in early 1960, touching more than 65 cities in 12 states. Roughly 50,000 young people joined the protests that year.

During the 1960 presidential campaign, civil rights had emerged as a crucial issue. A few weeks before the election, Dr. Martin Luther King Jr. was arrested while leading a protest in Atlanta, Georgia. Mr. John F. Kennedy phoned Dr. Martin Luther King's wife, Coretta Scott King, to express his concern, while a call from Robert Kennedy to the judge helped secure her husband's safe release. The Kennedys' intervention led to a public endorsement by Mr. Martin Luther King Sr., the influential father of the civil rights leader. Across the nation, more than 70 percent of African Americans voted for Kennedy, and those votes provided the winning edge in several key states. When President Kennedy took office in January 1961, African Americans had high expectations for the new administration.

Kennedy's narrow election victory and small working margin in Congress left him cautious. He was reluctant to lose southern support for the legislation by pushing for civil rights legislation. Instead, he appointed some African Americans to high-level positions in the administration and strengthened the Civil Rights Commission. He spoke out in favor of school desegregation, praised several cities for integrating their schools, and put Vice President Lyndon Johnson in charge of the President's Committee on Equal Employment Opportunity. Attorney General Robert Kennedy focused his attention on voting rights.

President Kennedy was reluctant to push ahead with civil rights legislation, but millions of African Americans would not wait. Eventually, the administration was compelled to act. Seating on buses, bus stations, waiting rooms, restrooms, and restaurants was segregated. In May 1961, the Congress of Racial Equality, led by James Farmer, organized integrated

Freedom Rides to defy segregation in interstate transportation. Freedom Riders were arrested in North Carolina and beaten in South Carolina. In Alabama, a bus was burned, and the riders attacked with baseball bats and tire irons.

In 1962, James H. Meredith Jr., an African American Air Force veteran, was denied admission to the University of Mississippi, known as *Ole Miss*. Meredith attempted to register four times without success. Long telephone conversations between the President, the attorney general, and Governor Ross Barnett failed to produce a solution. When federal marshals accompanied Meredith to campus in another attempt to register for classes, rioting erupted. Two people died, and dozens were injured. President Kennedy mobilized the National Guard and sent federal troops to the campus. Meredith registered the next day, attended his first class, and segregation ended at the University of Mississippi.

In the spring of 1963, Dr. Martin Luther King Jr. launched a mass protest campaign in Birmingham, Alabama, which King called the most segregated city in America. Initially, the demonstrations had little impact. Then, on Good Friday, King was arrested and spent a week behind bars, where he wrote one of his most famous meditations on racial injustice and civil disobedience. One of Dr. King's young followers, James Bevel, summoned African American youths to march in the streets at the beginning of May. Birmingham City Commissioner Eugene Connor used police dogs and high-pressure fire hoses to put down the demonstrations. Nearly a thousand young people were arrested. The violence was broadcast on television to the nation and the world.

Governor George Wallace of Alabama had vowed at his inauguration to defend "segregation now, segregation tomorrow, and segregation forever." In June 1963, he upheld his promise to "stand in the schoolhouse door" to prevent two

African American students from enrolling at the University of Alabama. To protect the students and secure their admission, President Kennedy federalized the Alabama National Guard. Furthermore, on June 11, the President addressed the nation. He defined the civil rights crisis as moral, as well as constitutional and legal. He announced that civil rights legislation would be submitted to Congress to guarantee equal access to public facilities, end segregation in education, and provide federal protection of the right to vote.

President Kennedy entered the presidency determined to re-energize foreign policy. To that end, he assembled a team of young White House and National Security Council advisers, the so-called *best and the brightest*, which included McGeorge Bundy, Walt Rostow, Ted Sorenson, and Arthur Schlesinger, Jr.

Kennedy selected Dean Rusk as his Secretary of State. Rusk had served in several positions at the Department of State, including Deputy Under-Secretary of State and Assistant Secretary of State for East Asian and Pacific Affairs. Rusk believed that the Secretary of State served at the President's pleasure and thus did not seek control of foreign policy. Kennedy selected Robert S. McNamara, the President of Ford Motor Company, as his Secretary of Defense. Harvard's Dean, McGeorge Bundy, served as his National Security Adviser. The Director of the Central Intelligence Agency, Allen W. Dulles, continued in that position, which he had held since 1953.

In April 1961, a few months into his administration, Kennedy authorized a secret invasion of Cuba by a brigade of Cuban exiles. The operation collapsed in two days due to faulty intelligence. Anti-Castro forces were defeated and captured at the Bay of Pigs. The spectacular failure of that confrontation was a setback for Kennedy and one he became determined to overcome. Though he took full responsibility for the failed operation, the CIA's reputation was tarnished, and Kennedy soon replaced Allen W. Dulles with John A. McCone. The Bay of Pigs fiasco affected Kennedy's respect for the Joint Chiefs of Staff's advice and placed a strain on the civil-military relationship.

Premier Cheddi Jagan's visit with President Kennedy

With expectations of independence from British colonization, Premier Jagan went to the White House at Washington, DC on October 25, 1961, to meet with President John Kennedy. Dr. Jagan was seeking financial aid to assist with the transition of the soon to be independent country: "I went to see President Kennedy to seek the help of the United States and seek his support for our independence from the British." He said in an interview:

> He was very charming and jovial. Now, the United States feared that I would give Guyana to the Russians. I said if this is your fear, fear not. We will not have a Soviet base. I raised the question of aid. They did not give a positive response. The meeting ended on this note.

The meeting was recorded by the historian Arthur M. Schlesinger Jr. in *A Thousand Days*, his memoir of the Kennedy's White House. "Dr. Jagan was unquestionably some sort of a Marxist," he wrote, but also "plainly the most popular leader in British Guiana," adding, "The question was whether he was recoverable for democracy. Another question was whether he and his nation of 600,000 represented a threat to the United States".

In Washington, some American political leaders were already describing Dr. Jagan as a communist. They were worried that even though he was the most popular Guianese Leader, he would not follow the democratic path. As such, the US administration had already implemented plans to undermine his Government, even though the British Government had insisted that Dr. Jagan was a more responsible leader than Mr. Forbes Burnham. The British had communicated their feelings to the Americans at the highest level, explaining that both governments should give Dr. Jagan economic support to prevent him from making approaches for support from the communist bloc.

When Dr. Jagan arrived in Washington, he appeared on the *Meet the Press* television program. Because he made no critical remarks of the Soviet Union, the Kennedy administration immediately felt less enthusiastic about providing any economic assistance. President Kennedy, who watched part of the *Meet the Press* show, told his advisers that he would not commit until he met with Dr. Jagan.

At the meeting, President Kennedy was accompanied by his special assistant Mr. Arthur Schlesinger, Jr., and Mr. George Ball, the Assistant Secretary for Economic Affairs at the State Department. Dr. Jagan outlined the economic issues of British Guiana and explained that he believed state planning would be most instrumental in overcoming the economic and developmental problems facing his country. President Kennedy replied that the United States was not interested in forcing private enterprise in countries where it was not relevant. He added that the primary purpose of American aid was to support national independence and encourage individual and political freedoms. For the United States, he said, it was important for a country to maintain its national independence. "So long as you do that, we don't care whether you are socialist, capitalist, pragmatist or whatever," Kennedy declared. "We regard ourselves as pragmatists."

Dr. Cheddi Jagan interpretation of Marxism and Communism:

There are various definitions of communism. If one looks at the United States Immigration Act, one finds a definition of communism there and if I were to be asked, do I agree with this definition, and would, you would tell me that I am a communist. I would say I am not a communist. In the law, the Suppression of the Communist Act, in South Africa for example, to criticize the policy of apartheid is regarded as communism. In such a situation I would consider myself a communist.

If you look in a Webster dictionary, one would find there a definition of communism which will compel me to say that I am not a communist because the assumptions there are that liberties on freedoms will be denied under such a set up. And therefore, I feel that in this complicated question of communism there are many sides, many views, but in this country the people who have been accusing us for many years on this question have always assumed that communism is evil. That is why I have always refused to give a yes or no answer to this very complicated question. I have always said that I am a Marxist, if I am to be tagged, because Marxism is a philosophy.

Marxism is a science of the laws of development of society from one stage to the next. There could be various stages to this, the national democratic independence level - the stage that we are in; the socialist level, and then ultimately, the so-called communist level. Now, Sir, by saying that I am a Marxist, I could be at one and the same time anti-colonialist, an anti-imperialist, a democrat, a socialist, a humanist, and a communist. I wish to make this very clear, because already statements are being made as a result of what I said...to smear me.

As a passionate anti-colonialist, I am interested in the independence of my country - political independence; as an anti-imperialist, I am interested in putting an end to the domination and subjection of the economy of my country; as a democrat, I am interested in preserving the liberties and freedom of the people - not only in preserving, but in enlarging them; as a socialist, I am interested in the creation of a new society which will lay the basis for the end of exploitation. I believe the tenets of communism to be for each according to his ability, to each according to his need. I believe in that.

The two leaders discussed the issue of nationalization. President Kennedy said that the U.S. had no problem with that but would expect compensation to be given. A lively exchange on Dr. Jagan's political ideas followed, and the British Guianese Premier spoke of his commitment to parliamentary democracy. President Kennedy said that the United States would be supportive of genuine non-alignment but would be opposed to a total commitment by British Guiana to the communist bloc. He then questioned Dr. Jagan about his views regarding relations with that group. The Guianese leader retorted by asking him if the U.S. would view a trade agreement between British Guiana and the USSR as an unfriendly act. Kennedy responded by saying that it would be a matter of concern if such an agreement compromised the economic independence of the (*weaker*) country. According to former U.S. President Harry Truman, "Socialism is a scare word they've hurled at every advance the people have made. Socialism is what they called public power, social security, deposit insurance, and independent labor organizations. Socialism is their name for anything that helps all people."

In terms of aid to Guyana, Kennedy did not discuss specific amounts, leaving that matter to be dealt with by Mr. Schlesinger, Mr. Ball, and other officials at follow-up meetings. Before meeting with President Kennedy, Dr. Jagan had requested the U.S. $40 million in aid. That amount, the Americans felt, was out of proportion for such a small country as British Guiana. Latin American countries with larger populations and more politically friendly to the U.S. were also competing for American economic assistance. After the discussions with the President, the Americans finally decided not to give any specific commitment to Dr. Jagan. They told him that they would have to examine the relative merits of each project.

Dr. Jagan was disappointed over the development and requested another meeting with Kennedy. However, President Kennedy did not agree to another meeting. He instructed Mr. Schlesinger to meet with Dr. Jagan. Since the British Government was concerned that Dr. Jagan should not return home disappointed, President Kennedy suggested to Mr. Schlesinger that a satisfactory statement could be drawn up which would not commit the United States to any immediate funds. President Kennedy was convinced that Dr. Jagan would cease being a parliamentary democrat. He told Mr. Schlesinger:

> I have a feeling that in a couple of years he will find ways to suspend his constitutional provisions and will cut his opposition off at the knees. With all political jockeying and all the racial tensions, it's going to be almost impossible for Dr. Jagan to concentrate the energies of his country on development through a parliamentary system.

On October 26, Mr. Schlesinger met with Dr. Jagan at the Dupont Plaza Hotel in Washington. He expressed disappointment that the United States was not prepared to announce a commitment to British Guiana's development program. He was, however, satisfied that the U.S. was willing to work out a joint statement on the meetings. The document was finalized on the following day and stated that the United States "looked forward to closer association between a free and democratic British Guiana and the nations and organizations of the Hemisphere." It committed Dr. Jagan "to uphold the political freedoms and defend the parliamentary democracy which is his country's political heritage." It indicated that the United States would send a mission to Guyana to examine what forms of economic assistance could be provided for development projects.

After Dr. Jagan left Washington, President Kennedy met in secret with his top national security officials, and a pragmatic plan took shape. Declassified documents indicated a direct order from the President to unseat Dr. Jagan. Though many Presidents have ordered the CIA to undermine foreign leaders, they said the Jagan papers are a rare smoking gun; a clear written record, without veiled words or plausible denials, of a President's command to depose an elected leader of a country. In short order, things started to go badly for British Guiana. Sixty years later, Guyana cannot recover from the subversive actions of President John F. Kennedy.

Financial difficulties during the administration of Dr. Cheddi Jagan

In December 1961, the Government introduced currency restrictions, prohibiting the export of liquid assets from the country. British Guiana was part of the sterling currency and also a member of the Eastern Caribbean Currency Board. The currency was, therefore, a regional one. At that time, the holders of Eastern Caribbean dollars in British Guiana could only change them into foreign currencies per the exchange control regulations that were enforced in the colony. The new regulations suspended the conversion of the British Guiana dollar into sterling. The action of Dr. Jagan's Government in suspending convertibility into sterling, without prior consultation with the Eastern Caribbean Currency Board, gave rise to considerable alarm.

In addition to those difficulties, the Finance Minister was faced with the immediate need for $15 million for extraordinary expenses and to meet increases in the cost of some services. The Government agreed to increase the salaries for civil servants, and for that purpose, an additional $3.5 million was required. The Government also needed $2.5 million to repay loans, $1.5 million for expenditure on sea defenses, the maintenance of roads, and improvements to the aerodrome, which were long overdue.

Provision had to be made for money by some means during 1962. Mr. Kaldor, a well-known economist of considerable experience who served on the United Kingdom Tax Commission and had advised the Governments of India, Ceylon, Mexico, and Ghana, was invited by Dr. Jagan to consider the problem and suggest ways of raising revenue. The budget for 1962 was prepared based on his recommendations. On January 31, 1962, that budget was presented to the Legislative Assembly by Dr. Jacob, Minister of Finance, who opened his speech by declaring that the ground was "being laid to strengthen our economic position and raise living standards by accelerating the rate of economic growth through our own efforts."

Dr. Jacobs pointed out that external aid was an absolute necessity. Self-help was even more critical because foreign aid was no substitute for self-determination. He mentioned that the prevailing tax structure was biased in favor of the richer and owners of properties. Therefore, an impartial progressive taxation system that distributes the burden equitably between those who derive income from the property and those who get their incomes from work was necessary. He, accordingly, proposed new taxes, the burden of which would fall on the higher income groups only. He proposed a capital gains tax, an annual property tax, and a tax on gifts.

In addition to those, he proposed specific measures for preventing the evasion and avoidance of taxes. He also proposed a new model of assessing the minimum measure of income tax concerning commercial transactions. He proposed that the minimum income should be 2 percent of his annual turnover irrespective of whether the business had shown a profit or a loss. However, wherever there was a loss, it was set off against profits in the subsequent years. It will be seen, at once, that this measure was aimed at dishonest business people who reported a loss year after year although their business continued to flourish.

Another unusual provision in the Bill was reducing the advertising allowance to one-quarter of one percent of the total turnover. That was intended to prevent unnecessary waste on prestige advertising and reduce the income tax payable. A scheme of compulsory savings was also introduced to increase the flow of resources for development purposes. That scheme contemplated a deduction equivalent to a contribution of five percent of wage and salary income over $100 a month and 10 percent of other income instead of Government bonds redeemable after seven years. Those measures were not calculated to yield the total additional $15 million required, and the balance was still to be raised.

The Minister of Finance proposed an increase in the import duty on certain goods which he considered not necessities, e.g., alcoholic drinks, tobacco, concentrates for non-alcoholic drinks, tea, motor spirit, perfumes, cosmetics, the more expensive dress fabrics, footwear, glassware, chinaware, jewelry, radios, refrigerators, and motor cars. He also proposed increases on certain foods for which adequate substitutes were available in the country, e.g., meat, fish, butter, cheese, fruit, fruit juices, and jams. There was also an increase in the excise duties on rum and other spirits and on beer.

The Minister pointed out that those duties and taxes would not impose any hardship on the lower-income group's people; an increase in the urban consumer price index would be only one percent. He hoped, in that manner, to increase the country's revenues by about $8 million. He also scaled down the figure of $15 million, which was necessary to meet the increase in the recurrent expenditure in his initial estimate.

The opposition used the budget to excuse sustained and increasingly hostile demonstrations against Dr. Jagan's Government. The budget won immediate approval from many persons. The *New York Times* said in an editorial that the budget was courageous and economically sound. *The London Times*, in a leading article, observed the immediate problem for Dr. Jagan is how to win some acceptance for his economic proposals, which were courageous and certainly not far from what British Guiana must-have. Sir Jock Campbell, Chairman of Booker Bros., said, "It clearly was in intention a serious attempt by the Government to get to grips with the formidable economic problems of the country by a hard program of self-help. It was radical." Senator Tasker of Bookers in British Guiana gave his opinion about the budget by saying, "*we* assessed it as a realistic attempt to grapple with the economic problems of British Guiana."

One concern of the opposition was the Minister of Finance, who, in his speech in the Legislative Assembly on October 9, 1961, expressed his own beliefs, indicating that he believed in the Marxist creed. In the course of his speech, Dr. Jacobs said:

> My honorable friend, who is a member of Georgetown Central (Mr. D'Aguiar) has attempted on the floor of this House to refute Marxism. This is a futile attempt. Learned university professors, of course of the bourgeois tradition, professional mercenaries, politicians, common vilifiers, have all tried to refute the unassailable logic of Marxism. They have all failed. We will attempt to build a new society, a society which exists in more than one third of the world today; a society in which there will be freedom and plenty for everybody. That is a genuine socialist society.

The Daily Chronicle and the *Argosy*, which were under the control of Mr. D'Aguiar, leader of the UF, were hostile to Dr. Jagan. They opened their assault on the day following the introduction of the budget. The Chronicle said that the Government was going to squeeze dollars from every worker. A few days later, it carried the headline 'Tax Avalanche Will Crush Working Classes.' Another headline stated 'Slave Whip Budget' and went on to say that the budget is "*Marxist.*" A week after introducing the budget, The Chronicle printed a letter on the 'Iniquitous Budget,' which contained the exhortation 'Stir yourselves, down with this shameful budget, down with the Government.' Two days later, another letter proclaiming 'Budget will bring misery to the country' and ending 'This is a trodden democracy. Let's unite and fight for our rights'. The agitation grew throughout 1962 and 1963. Dr. Jagan said:

> A fire was set in the center of town, the wind fanned the flames, and the center of the city burned. There are still scars. Then they changed their tactics. This is where the CIA support came in full. They imposed a full blockade on shipping and airlines. We were helpless. We had no power.

The CIA engineered the disturbances and maintained that the intense internal dissatisfaction with his administration was attributable solely to outside influences. The establishment of an independent government in British Guiana under leadership that had been markedly receptive to Marxist ideas would create an intolerable situation for the United States.

The cover which the CIA used was a London-based international trades' union secretariat, the Public Services International. As Coups go, it was not expensive: Over five years, the CIA paid out something over £230,000. For British Guiana, the result was about 370 deaths, untold hundreds wounded, and approximately £10 million worth of damage to the economy.

Special Group/303 Committee-approved funds were used again between July 1963 and April 1964 in connection with the 1964 general strike. When Dr. Jagan's and Mr. Burnham's supporters clashed in labor disputes on the sugar plantations that year, the United States joined with the British Government in urging Mr. Burnham not to retaliate with violence but rather to commit to a mediated end to the conflict. At the same time, the United States provided training to anti-Jagan forces, enabling them to defend themselves if attacked and boost their morale.

From 1961 to 1964, Dr. Jagan was confronted with a destabilization campaign conducted by the PNC and UF In addition to domestic opponents of Dr. Jagan, an important role was played by the American Institute for Free Labor Development (AIFLD), which was a front for the United States of America Central Intelligence Agency. Various reports indicated that AIFLD, with a budget of U.S. $800,000, maintained anti-Jagan labor leaders on its payroll and an AIFLD-trained staff of 11 activists who were assigned to organize riots and destabilize the Dr. Jagan government. Riots and demonstrations against the PPP administration were frequent, and during disturbances in 1962 and 1963, mobs destroyed part of Georgetown, inflicting approximately $40 million in damage.

To counter the MPCA with its link to Mr. Burnham, the PPP formed the Guyanese Agricultural Workers Union. That new union's political mandate was to organize the sugarcane field workers. The MPCA immediately responded with a one-day strike to emphasize its continued control over the sugar workers.

The PPP government responded to the strike in March 1964 by publishing a new Labor Relations Bill almost identical to the 1953 legislation that had resulted in British intervention. Regarded as a power play for control over a critical labor sector, the introduction of the proposed law prompted protests and rallies throughout the capital. Riots broke out on April 5; they were followed on April 18 by a general strike. By May 9, the Governor was compelled to declare a state of emergency. Nonetheless, the strike and violence continued until July 7, when the Labor Relations Bill was allowed to lapse without being enacted. To end the disorder, the Government agreed to consult with union representatives before introducing similar bills. Those disturbances exacerbated tension and animosity between the two major ethnic communities and made reconciliation between Dr. Jagan and Mr. Burnham impossible.

Dr. Jagan's term had not yet ended when another round of labor unrest rocked the colony. The pro-PPP GIWU, which had become an umbrella group of all labor organizations, called on sugar workers to strike in January 1964. To dramatize their case, Dr. Jagan led a march by sugar workers from the plantation to Georgetown. That demonstration ignited outbursts of violence that soon escalated beyond the control of the authorities. On May 22, the Governor finally declared another state of emergency. The situation continued to worsen, and in June, the Governor assumed total power. British troops were brought in to restore order and proclaimed a moratorium on all political activity. By the end of the turmoil, 160 people were dead, and more than 1,000 homes were destroyed.

To quell the turmoil, the country's political parties asked the British Government to modify the constitution to provide more proportional representation. The colonial secretary proposed a fifty-three-member unicameral legislature. Despite opposition from the ruling PPP, all reforms were implemented, and new elections were set for October 1964.

As Dr. Jagan feared, the PPP lost the general elections of 1964. The PPP won 46 percent of the vote and twenty-four seats, making it the largest single party but short of an overall majority. However, the PNC which won 40 percent of the vote and twenty-two seats, and the UF, which won 11 percent of the vote and seven seats, formed a coalition. The socialist PNC and capitalist UF joined forces to keep the PPP out of office for another term. Dr. Jagan called the election fraudulent and refused to resign as Premier. The constitution was amended to allow the Governor to remove Dr. Jagan from office. Mr. Burnham became Premier on December 14, 1964.

Dr. Jagan's pragmatism and administrative skills eventually matured into a more cohesive and praxis-based analysis. His book *The West on Trial: My Fight for Guyana's Freedom* is a fine example. Colonial overlords of Guyana and Western journalists continued portraying him as a communist. Dr. Jagan's support for his Marxist pronouncements was his best personal leadership choice to free the working and poor people from British colonization. Dr. Jagan's deep loyalty to the principle of political freedom made him reluctant to disavow his sympathies with communism and communist organizers globally. He grew tired of the countless attacks in the media, splits between the party, and imperial hostility by the West. He began focusing more on a cross-class nationalist message. Critics saw him as a dogmatic Marxist or one who rejected the label for political opportunity.

Unlike most of the leaders of the Caribbean, Dr. Jagan long described himself as a Marxist, and his ideologies grew with time:

> As a passionate anti-colonialist, I am interested in the independence of my country – political independence; as an anti-imperialist, I am interested in the end to the domination and subjection of the economy of my country; as a Democrat, I am interested in preserving liberties and freedom of all the people – not only in preserving but in enlarging them; as a Socialist, I am interested in the creation of a new society which will lay the basis for the end of exploitation.

The destabilization campaign conducted by the PNC and UF, with the support of the United States of America and Britain continued towards Dr. Jagan. There was a tremendous increase in racial tension. The potential for conflict came from a week of strikes and riots that shook the capital city of Georgetown in mid-February 1962. The immediate cause of the strikes was alleged to be Premier Jagan's budget bill. However, the riots developed into racial antagonism and the dissatisfaction of urban groups, notably public service employees and business people, with the policies of the PPP government. As the disturbances spread, they took on the character of a struggle between the Afro-Guianese urban community and the Indo-Guianese Government and its rural supporters.

Paradoxically, the February crisis strengthened Dr. Jagan by consolidating the support of his Indo-Guianese followers. At the same time, it reduced his stature and tarnished his prestige as a national leader. His economic and financial problems were more acute than before the riots. The government was hard-pressed to meet current expenditures. Whereas, before the riots, almost 20 percent of the labor force was out of work, an even larger number were unemployed due to the destruction in Georgetown.

Dr. Jagan's plans for economic development were set back, partly because he was forced to trim his tax measures and partly because uncertainties about the country's political stability were inhibiting the flow of outside public assistance, on which development is heavily dependent. The February events discouraged foreign investment. Extensive capital flight was in progress, and foreign investors were doing no more than attending to existing operations. Many city merchants were inclined to cut and run rather than to stay and rebuild.

The crisis also left the opposition with reduced prestige. Several leaders acted carelessly. The unions, which were predominantly Afro-Guyanese, actively collaborated with the opposition parties. The rank and file of the largest single union, chiefly Indo-Guianese, did not. There were rumors of dissension in the PPP and reports that the opposition might try to win some of Dr. Jagan's legislators away from him. However, sufficient defections to cause the legislative defeat of the Dr. Jagan government are not considered probable under the existing circumstances.

On May 28, 1963, by a Resolution of the Legislative Assembly, Dr. Jagan, Premier and Minister of Development and Planning, and three other Members of the Assembly were suspended for refusing to apologize for discourteous conduct at the previous sitting of the Assembly. On September 25, 1964, the Legislature was dissolved.

CHAPTER 27

U.S. Government Anti-Jagan Campaign

INFLUENCING ELECTIONS OF ANOTHER COUNTRY IS THE most blatant form of foreign interference. Jessica Brandt, Head of Research and Policy for the Alliance for Securing Democracy, wrote, "Freedom from foreign interference is not a Democratic or Republican value; it is deeply American, rooted in the country's founding." In 1788, Alexander Hamilton, an American statesman born in the Caribbean, warned that "the desire in foreign powers to gain an improper ascendant in the United States is one of the most deadly adversaries of republican government." Daniel Byman said, "Russian interference in the 2016 election was one of the most effective and dangerous foreign operations ever conducted against the United States."

Throughout the Cold War, the United States of America had difficulty appreciating how different forms of politics and economic systems are applied in different countries and that *Marxism* is not a monolithic Soviet-led international movement. In the 1960s, President John F. Kennedy used his Central Intelligence Agency to replace the democratically elected leader of British Guiana with a person of his choice. That was the extent of the infatuation with communism. The United States/United Kingdom alliance did not keep Washington from political intervention in a country that answered to an American ally. Mr. Arthur M. Schlesinger, Jr., President Kennedy's historian and adviser on Latin America, wrote, "We misunderstood the whole struggle down there."

In 1961, President Kennedy ordered the Central Intelligence Agency to subvert the country's leader. The leader fell, and the country was under the administration of the person that the United States favored. The CIA's men accomplished their task and moved on to another. Eventually, the cold-war ended; with its end, the fallen leader was again democratically elected to lead his country.

That event of 60 years ago was filed away, the four Presidents who were involved passed on, but it is still fresh in the memories of those who lived through it. Mrs. Janet Jagan said, "They made a mistake putting Mr. Burnham in, the regrettable part is that the country went backwards. One of the better-off countries in the region 30 years ago, Guyana today is among the poorest. Its principal export is people."

The chain of events began in 1953 when British Guiana, a colony inhabited by the Indigenous Peoples and descendants of enslaved Africans, indentured Portuguese, Chinese, and Indian laborers, elected its first native-born leader, Dr. Jagan. The British Prime Minister, Winston Churchill, suspended British Guiana's Constitution and ordered the dissolution of the Government, imprisonment of the elected leader, his wife, and members of his cabinet as they were too leftist for Churchill's taste. Throughout Cheddi Jagan's career in British Guiana, which included his nomination to lead the colony in 1953, 1957, and 1961, opponents claimed that he and the leading members of the People's Progressive Party were Communists.

Dr. Jagan and officials of the party habitually spoke well of Communist countries and their leaders; they never found reason to criticize them even when asked directly if they belonged to international Communist-front organizations. That was enough to convince the U.S. government under the leadership of President Kennedy that Dr. Jagan was a Communist bent upon taking independent Guyana into the Soviet Bloc. In an extensive study of the U.S. and British national archives, historian Stephen Rabe's, *U.S. Intervention in British Guiana* clearly stated that Dr. Jagan was a democratic Marxist socialist whom the United States government had misunderstood and therefore reflexively worked to remove from power. "Maybe, one day, the CIA will open its archives and let the public read the damning evidence that one of the agency's spies collected in British Guiana," Rabe wrote. "The declassified intelligence record currently does not sustain charges that Jagan intended to take his country into the Soviet camp."

During the USA administration of President Bill Clinton, he appointed the AFL-CIO's William Doherty, Jr. as U.S. Ambassador to Guyana. Dr. Jagan rejected Mr. Doherty and assumed that President Clinton was unaware of Mr. Doherty's British Guiana activities during President Kennedy's administration.

According to the United States Freedom of Information Act, it was time to declassify the documents that detailed President Kennedy's involvement in British Guiana. Dr. Jagan insisted that the documents be released so that history can be revised. The State Department and the CIA said they should remain classified since the record might anger Dr. Jagan or embarrass the United States. Dr. Jagan explained:

> Everybody in Guyana knows what happened; I don't understand why they should be kept secret. I'm not going to use these documents to blackmail the United States. Maybe President Clinton doesn't know our history, but the people who advise him should at least know their own history.

Mr. Schlesinger wrote, "it was idle to suppose that communism in Latin America was no more than the expression of an Indigenous desire for social reform." Dr. Jagan became isolated in Kennedy's administration and eventually ceased to oppose the CIA's project. Mr. Schlesinger said:

> He wasn't a Communist. The British thought we were overreacting, and indeed we were. The CIA decided this was some great menace, and they got the bit between their teeth. But even if British Guiana had gone Communist, it's hard to see how it would be a threat.

The whole story, he said, proved the truth of Oscar Wilde's witticism: "The one duty we owe to history is to rewrite it." That background indicates the U.S. infatuation with Dr. Jagan's political orientation almost from the moment he emerged as the Guianese leader. It also introduces the political competitor Mr. Forbes Burnham, who would become the CIA's instrument against Dr. Jagan in President Kennedy's project. On May 5, 1961, at a National Security Council (NSC) meeting, it was agreed to have the Cuba task force look for ways to avoid a communist takeover of British Guiana. The U.S. Secretary of State, Mr. Dean Rusk, wrote to British Foreign Secretary Lord Home on August 11, 1961, asking if anything could prevent Dr. Jagan's electoral victory. The British minister said no, and advised that it would be a better option to educate Dr. Jagan. By the end of August, the State Department was advocating offers of nudging Dr. Jagan into a pro-American direction, combined with a covert operation to expose and destroy communism in British Guiana. On September 3, 1961, President Kennedy approved that essential program. Mr. Schlesinger complained about a document that referred to Dr. Jagan as a *'possible sleeper'* agent in a cable.

"British Guiana," White House, Arthur Schlesinger Jr., Special Assistant to the President, memorandum for U. Alexis Johnson, State Department, September 7, 1961.

Mr. Arthur Schlesinger criticized Secretary of State Rusk's characterization of Dr. Jagan as a "sleeper," explaining that "sleeper is a technical term meaning a disciplined agent who pretends to be one thing and then, at a given moment, tears off his mask and reveals himself as something entirely different. I have not heard this seriously suggested about Dr. Jagan." Instead, Schlesinger notes that Dr. Jagan is "probably something more dangerous than a sleeper - he is a muddlehead. Confused idealists have caused the world far more trouble than conspirators." Nonetheless, Schlesinger hopes that U.S. Ambassador Mr. David Bruce does not give the British a "misleading impression" of the U.S. position on British Guiana and Dr. Jagan. The President's special assistant also stresses that diplomacy should be given a chance, "my guess is that the President has been thinking in terms of a cordial try at bringing British Guiana into the hemisphere."

A round of U.S./British talks took place in London during that September. The general idea was to provide technical economic assistance on one hand, with a covert intelligence gathering project proceeding alongside it. The CIA Director, Mr. Allen W. Dulles, worked on that concept. Ambassador David Bruce led the American delegation with Mr. Frank G. Wisner, CIA station chief and former head of the operations directorate, at his side. The British stipulated that the U.S. must in fact try and work with Dr. Jagan.

Dr. Jagan was aware that others were curious about him. He arranged a visit to the United States and England at the end of October. The State Department announced that he would meet with President Kennedy. The meeting was scheduled for October 25, and a briefing memo for the president was prepared. At the meeting, Dr. Jagan represented himself as a socialist in the style of British politician Aneurin Bevan. The American participants found him evasive on matters of his Marxist ideology. The White House announced that the U.S. would provide British Guiana with technical assistance. Dr. Jagan then went on to New York and London.

FBI informants supplied details of Dr. Jagan's comments at social events in New York, and U.S. diplomats followed his movements in London. Early in December, Mr. Schlesinger met with a Guianese labor leader and one from the United Steel Workers of America. They contemplated covert operations that were taking form as a political action. The leaders acted unilaterally and not in a democratic manner.

With the economic problems of early 1962, Dr. Jagan introduced a budget that included a tax increase, allegedly, without consultation with the opposition, that led to a strike and rioting in Georgetown. Several buildings in the city were burnt. Seeing flames from his official residence, the Red House, Dr. Jagan was convinced that the CIA had fomented the riots. That was disputed because the labor organizers, who were allied with the agency representing the Americans linked to the Guianese opposition, were not in the colony at the time.

What actually happened was the U.S. officials used the Georgetown riots as the excuse to write off Dr. Jagan. On February 19, with smoke still rising from burnt buildings, Secretary of State Mr. Dean Rusk wrote to Lord Home calling for "remedial steps" to counter Dr. Jagan's "Marxist-Leninist policy" and adding that "I have reached the conclusion that it is not possible for us to put up with an independent British Guiana under Dr. Jagan." At the White House, Mr. Schlesinger countered that Dr. Jagan was not a communist but a naïve "London School of Economics Marxist filled with charm." The tax scheme, he added, was not socialist but orthodox, something suitable for Britain. British official views mirrored those that Mr. Schlesinger expressed. London resisted moving against Dr. Jagan.

"Labor Situation in British Guiana," Department of State, Memorandum of Conversation, December 4, 1961.

White House meeting between Schlesinger and Wendell Bobb, the general secretary of the British Guiana Mine Workers Union, outlines the latter's views on labor politics in British Guiana as well as possible courses of action for the U.S. Bobb began by explaining that the "Dr. Jagan government was actively pushing to enter the labor field and, if possible capture political support from the trade union." Schlesinger asked about rumors regarding "an impending separation of Janet Jagan and her husband," to which Bobb argued that it would be politically insignificant but then changed his mind, noting that it would "hamper substantially the PPP's effort to penetrate British Guiana's trade union movement." Schlesinger also asked about Mr. Burnham, given British concerns regarding "Mr. Burnham's reliability and financial honesty," to which Bobb responded by explaining that "there was no alternative to Mr. Burnham."

Concerning U.S. aid to British Guiana, Schlesinger explained the paradox:

> If the U.S. should extend assistance, it would to some degree help Dr. Jagan politically. On the other hand, if the U.S. should deny any assistance to British Guiana, it would mean that the legitimate needs of the people would not be met and those who are fighting for freedom would not receive help.

Bobb argued in favor of U.S. aid but to "make every effort to prevent Dr. Jagan from and the PPP from getting all the credit."

President Kennedy was more impressed by the case put forward by London than by the meeting at Foggy Bottom, Washington, DC. On March 8, 1962, he issued an order on British Guiana, which he sent to Secretary Rusk and the Director of Central Intelligence, John A. McCone. The Special Group meeting minutes indicated some hesitation in the U.S. approach until they can get the British on board. Alexis Johnson explained to the Group's members that "Secretary Rusk wants action deferred on this matter until he has an opportunity to discuss it further with Lord Home." Johnson explained that he recommended Rusk to "Press Lord Home to agree to a joint U.S./British examination of alternatives to the present situation," and handed out an INR intelligence assessment of the opposition parties in British Guiana. The Group agreed to the suggestions until after a meeting between Rusk and Home.

In February 1962, opposition political parties and the Trades Union Council (TUC) mounted street demonstrations against the budget introduced by the People's Progressive Party Government, the demonstrations culminating in riots, arson, and looting on Friday February 16. The disturbances were part of a series of politically motivated activities which continued through 1963 and 1964. The objective was primarily to destabilize the PPP Government.

The U.S. anti-communist trade unions and other organizations were covertly involved in providing financial and propaganda assistance to the TUC and the opposition political parties. The United States Government itself was deeply involved in the effort. At the highest level, it encouraged the British Government to change the electoral system for the 1964 elections so as to provide the results that they desired.

Propaganda inciting February 16, 1962 demonstration

On Sunday, February 18, 1962, two days after *Black Friday*, the transcript of a tape was found, and the Police seized an illegal transmitting set. Before its seizure, the illegal radio was heard by Guianese over the wavelengths inciting the people against the Government. The radio tape was a threat against the lives of PPP leaders, namely, Dr. Jagan and Messrs. Benn, Kelshall, and Jacob. It is interesting to note the false news which was spreading and which was meant to inform people that foreign ships were outside Guiana, ostensibly waiting to come in and cause trouble. What is even more significant is the line "We want a new Indian leader." The voice on the tape was that of a woman:

This is Free Guiana speaking to you, Radio Free Guiana. Listen to the truth. Our country stands face to face with destruction and disaster. The City of Georgetown is little more than a smoking ruin. Over 60 businesses have been destroyed by fire;

countless others have been looted of all they once held. The heart of our capital city is a charred and blackened ruin. How did it happen? All over Guiana, people are asking themselves this question: How did it happen? On Monday, February 12, the first public protest against the budget presented began when workers walked out of their jobs, and Water Street firms were forced to close. From Monday to Friday, demonstrations and public meetings were held to voice the mass protest against the Government's policies. These demonstrations were peaceful. There was no violence. People exercised their democratic right of protest against a Government which had ceased to act in the people's interest.

> On Friday, February 16, the Government instructed the Police to fire tear gas at a harmless crowd near the Electricity Corporation. An eye witness says that when the first bombs were thrown the crowd was talking and laughing. There was no violence. Women and children were in that crowd. It was not a mob bent on destruction. Houses full of innocent people were gassed by the Police on the instructions of Kelshall, Benn, Jacob and Jagan. When those bombs were thrown the Government betrayed themselves. They had proved themselves to be the ferocious communists that many people had so long suspected them to be. The Government, by first using violence deliberately, incited violence. They smashed a democratic protest and laid the foundation of the riot which followed.

On Saturday, the *Evening Post* published this statement, and it must be remembered that the Evening Post has always supported the Government:

British Guiana licks its wounds today after the blackest Friday in its history. Blackened and battered by violent hands of a maddened, Georgetown presents a pitiful and painful example of what can happen when authority is misused. The blame for the mad violence which was let loose upon Georgetown yesterday, in our opinion, must be laid on the shoulders of the administration. It was the thorough indiscriminate and foolish use of tear gas bombs which incensed the mob and provoked the retaliation and rage which was unleashed upon the City. It was a terrible misjudgment on their part, on the pent-up fury in the hearts of the people, and their ability to meet action with counter action. The control which the Unions and the two political parties opposed to Government had succeeded in exercising over the people maddened by the budget proposals and the turn of force in the country, was completely shattered by ill-advised action, and it will be noted that it was a certain element of the Georgetown crowd which broke loose. It was rather fortunate that they were neither aided nor abetted by the Unions or the political parties, or the blow delivered yesterday could have been country-wide.

Imperialist troops are already there. The very troops Dr. Jagan scorned and vilified in 1953. Imperialism is keeping him in power; it's a measure of his control. He cannot control this country any longer. Kelshall, Benn, Jacob and Jagan, you are communists and you have lost. Not all your imperialism will put Guiana together again. Nothing you can do will heal the wounds. We do not want you. You are responsible for the violence, the shooting and the burning. You have incited it. Your PYO thugs and criminals have looted and burnt buildings of men who opposed you. You have stirred up the mobs that went mad because you had lost control and were desperately trying to save yourselves. You are trying to destroy us, but we will not be destroyed. You are asking the Governor to suspend the constitution because you are ignorant and afraid, and your communist friends cannot send their rockets yet. Kelshall, go back to your yacht and your palace in Trinidad. You have helped your fellow fools to ruin our country.

Five warships are now in the Demerara River. Four Dutch ships are stationed in the Corentyne, and a Cuban battleship is waiting outside. We are about to become a battleground for the greater glory of Kelshall, Benn, Jacob, and Jagan. Our lives are to be lost for the sake of these men, but these men are sick and stupid. They are not worth the life of a rat, much less the life of a man.

Kelshall, Benn, Jacob, and Jagan, you have done enough. The time is late. Please get out and leave us to a rebuild in the confidence that your wickedness will never rise again. We want a new Indian leader, Jagan, a man who is strong in himself, who is not dominated by a white

Trinidadian, and a clique of stupid self-seekers. We do not want you, or Kelshall, or Benn or Jacob. We warn you to go before the time comes when you no longer can.

After the culmination of the riots, arson, and looting on Friday, February 16, the Government of Guiana requested a Commission of Inquiry that the British Government appointed to investigate the disturbances. The Report by the Commission was reproduced in full. A Memorandum of the PPP was presented to the Commission; a review of the Commission's findings was originally published in *Thunder*, the weekly newspaper of the PPP, on October 6, 1962.

Commission of inquiries of the causes of the demonstration

The Commission did not probe deeply into all aspects of the disturbances and the events leading up to them and did not agree with some conclusions. They were able to identify those responsible for the disturbances and held them up to public view.

Regarding the budget which was supposed to have been the cause of the disturbances, there was nothing deeply vicious or destructive of the economic security of the budget; it had been drawn up on the advice of an experienced economist, who could not be said to have any Communist prepossessions. They pointed out that the budget won immediate approval from many persons and sections of the press - Senator Tasker, Sir Jock Campbell, the New York Times, and the London Times. They pointed out that Dr. Jagan, fully cognizant of the economic needs of British Guiana and of the inadequacy of the country's internal resources to meet them, made strenuous efforts to obtain economic aid from abroad to develop the country but such aid was not forthcoming. They pointed out that it was in the light of the failure to get foreign aid that the budget was introduced.

The Commission agreed that the budget was a genuine attempt to grapple with the economic problems of British Guiana, but as they pointed out, that there was a section of the press in British Guiana itself which was strongly, almost viciously critical of the budget. They pointed out that the Daily Chronicle, which is under the effective control of Mr. D'Aguiar, Leader of the United Force, and the Argosy, which is also hostile to Dr. Jagan, opened their assault on the budget the day following its introduction.

The Commission pointed out that the opposition to the budget was motivated by political considerations. The budget was used as an excuse. Speaking of the United Force, the Commission said that the list of grievances given by Mr. D'Aguiar and Senator Ann Jardim against the PPP is "little more than a narrative of personal frustration." Speaking of the PNC, they said: "The real motive force behind Mr. Burnham's assault (on the budget) was a desire to assert himself in public life and establish a more important and more rewarding position for himself by bringing about Dr. Jagan's downfall." The Commission pointed out that Mr. Burnham tried to say that the budget contained measures calculated to inflict hardships on the working classes by increasing the cost of living. That the Commission said was far from true. They pointed out that the attitude of the United Force in that matter was "more honest" than that of the PNC, for the United Forces represented the businessmen and the middle classes. They were affected by the new taxes on capital gains, gifts, and property holdings.

The Commission also indicated that on the publication of the budget, many commercial industry members raised the prices not only on those goods upon which import duty had been increased but also on other goods that did not come within the purview of the budget. They pointed out that the increases were in almost every instance more than the actual increase in the import duty. They have shown how some businessmen, like Mr. H. B. Gajraj, advocated that businessmen should stop dealing in commodities which had not been taxed, like sugar, flour, and oil, and that they should stop all credit facilities to their customers in order "to cripple the people and bring tremendous pressure on the Government."

The Report clearly showed that the trade union leaders were influenced in their opposition to the budget by political considerations and by personal animosity to Dr. Jagan and his Government. The Report spoke of the acrimonious hostility and stated that the Commission did not believe Mr. Richard Ishmael's statements in no uncertain terms. It stated that all individuals and organizations that had grievances against the Government combined to form a veritable torrent of abuse, recrimination and vicious hostility directed against Dr. Jagan and his Government.

The Commission of inquiry showed how the maneuvers of the two opposition parties led directly to the events of Black Friday. The contravention of the Proclamation showed how Mr. Burnham worked his supporters up into "a state of frenzy" and how Mr. D'Aguiar "seized every opportunity of attacking Dr. Jagan's Government and inciting the crowds during the week of the disturbances." It pointed out that Mr. D'Aguiar repeatedly lied to the Commission of Enquiry. Mr. D'Aguiar told the Commission that on the morning of February 16, he did not tell the crowd that the child who had been affected by the tear gas had died. Nevertheless, the Commission remarked that many witnesses had given evidence that Mr. D'Aguiar had told the crowd that the child had died. At that stage, the Commission remarked:

> We are constrained to observe that his being wedded to truth did not impose so stern a cloisteral isolation upon him as not to permit an occasional illicit sortie, in order to test the seductive and politically rewarding adventure of flirting with half-truths.

They also remarked that Mr. D'Aguiar had stated under cross-examination that the crowd had compelled him to take the initiative on eight occasions. The Commission found that the false rumor that a child had been killed by tear gas provided the immediate stimulus to violence and that Mr. D'Aguiar had passed on the false information to the crowd.

The Commission investigation of the Chamber of Commerce showed how its members encouraged and fostered the strike of their employees. Mr. Nascimento, a personal assistant to Mr. D'Aguiar and general manager of the Daily Chronicle, which the Commission described as an "unashamed and remorseless protagonist of the United Force," suggested that employers pay their employees who went on strike, thus subsidizing the strike. Messrs. Figueira, Bettencourt-Gomes, and Gajraj were even more enthusiastic about supporting the strike than Nascimento. The Commission pointed out that while the Chamber, as such, did not sponsor a lock-out; it "turned a blind eye to the attitude and intentions of its members." The Chamber's President explained that it could not regulate its members' actions by saying that the Chamber was a democratic body. The Commission's comment on that matter was worthy of note: "This lamentable confession of impotence scarcely redounds to the credit of a responsible body incorporated by special ordinance and professing the lofty aim of promoting the interest of trade and commerce."

The Commission noted that, though the Minister of Finance had invited the trade union leaders to discuss the budget and the meeting had been fixed for February 13, the Trade Union Council decided to call a general strike. The Commission described their action as "a breach of faith and a display of irresponsibility," The Commission drew attention to "the strange unfeeling attitude of the political leaders when the passions aroused by them had been let loose on the town."

The Governor asked Mr. Burnham to use his influence and advise the crowds to desist from acts of violence. Mr. Burnham refused. The Commission described his attitude as "callous and remorseless." It stated: "We may at this stage draw attention to the strangely unfeeling attitude of the political leaders when the passions aroused by them had been let loose on the town." The Governor asked him to employ his loudspeaker system and ask the crowds to leave the streets. "Mr. Burnham, however, replied that he would consult his Executives. Strangely enough, the Executives could not see their way to accede to the Governor's request." Mr. Burnham dealt with the matter in his statement before them:

> We could not help. There were too many obstacles, one was that we were very short of petrol and we felt that if we went all around Georgetown using up this petrol at the Governor's request, we would have no petrol for the vehicles to carry out Party work. We also considered it ill-advised to go and tell people to desist from what they were doing when we had nothing to do with the starting of it. The man who calls off the dog owns the dog.

That callous and remorseless attitude was reminiscent of Mark Antony's observation, 'Mischief, thou art afoot. Take thou what course thou wilt.' As regards Mr. D'Aguiar, all he could think was asking the Governor to protect his wife and family. He telephoned the Governor and said that, "he could not see his way to making an appeal for peace to the riotous crowds of Georgetown."

The Commission mentioned how enemies of the Government propagated wild and false rumors. The civil servants, for instance, went on strike because of a rumor that the Premier had stated in a broadcast that all civil servants who went on strike would be dismissed. It was established that the Premier did not make any such threat. It was significant that the persons involved were Mr. Richard Ishmael, whose statements the Commission stated that they could not believe, and one Mr. Hill, whom the Commission described as a "wholly unreliable witness." They have noted that it was Mr. D'Aguiar who gave the crowd the false information that a child had been killed, the information that was supposed to have incited them to violence and led directly to the outbreak of violence.

The Commission said they do not believe the events of February 16 were part of a plot to overthrow the Government by the use of force, overlooking all the evidence of the organized plan presented to them and the fact that the Premier had foretold with remarkable accuracy the course of events of the week that culminated on Black Friday. They omitted all references to the secret transmitter, the pirate broadcasts, and seditious tapes. They promised to deal with those aspects of the Report in subsequent issues.

In conclusion, they could not do any better than to compare the impression which the Commission had of Burnham, Ishmael, Gajraj, and D'Aguiar, as given above, with the impression that they had given of Dr. Jagan, as seen in the following:

"There was certain glamour about him, emanating from his youthful exuberance and a zeal which is characteristic of dedicated men. He seemed to possess a sense of purpose and a determination to work for his countrymen's freedom and their material progress."

Dr. Jagan's testimony to the Commission:

"As a passionate anti-colonialist, I am interested in the independence of my country - political independence; as an anti-imperialist, I am interested in putting an end to the domination and subjection of the economy of my country; as a democrat, I am interested in preserving the liberties and freedom of the people - not only in preserving, but in enlarging them; as a socialist, I am interested in the creation of a new society which will lay the basis for the end of exploitation. I believe the tenets of communism to be from each according to his ability, to each according to his need. I believe in that."

Mr. Luckhoo (Consul for the Georgetown Chamber of Commerce) - "This is your conception of the tenets of communism and you believe in that?"

Dr. Jagan - "Yes."

Mr. Luckhoo - "That represents your communist belief."

Dr. Jagan - "Yes."

Dr. Jagan's more critical remarks to the Commission on questioning - "I have never subscribed to racialism in this country. I have always fought against it, and will always continue to fight against it. I am referring to persons who dominate society here. For instance, there is a society here called the Defenders of Freedom. I am referring to persons like Mr. Willems who is the head of that group who, when I was President of the Sawmill and Forest Workers' Union, refused to allow me, the Secretary of the Union, and others to go on Government property to organize workers to fight for workers' rights."

Mr. Luckhoo – "Before I take my seat I want to put this to you, that you primarily and your party are the cause of the disturbances of Black Friday by a course of conduct in which you and your Organization have been following a communist pattern in which you have created fear in the minds of the people, in which they feel that their monies, their property, and their securities are going to be confiscated. The people fear their families are threatened and that growing fear all accumulated and ended with Black Friday."

Dr. Jagan – "That is not so. I would like, Sir, to elaborate on this answer. It is not today that this question of communism has come up in British Guiana. This question has been aired from the moment I entered politics in this country from 1946 when I and a few others got together and organized a Committee called the Political Affairs Committee. If there have been fears as a result of our activity, day by day, or year after year to struggle for democratic liberty in this country, for people in this country, this has been due to the fact that many individuals, the press, leaders in political parties - I remember in 1953."

Chairman - "Do not make a speech. You said no to the question. I cannot allow you to make a political speech."

Dr. Jagan - "Sir, the question has taken a great deal of my time and a great deal of your time. I have to put it in its proper perspective Mr. Luckhoo is suggesting that my party led to the disturbance."

Sir Edward Asafu-Adjaye (Member of the Commission) - "You have already said no."

Dr. Jagan - "And I wish to prove otherwise - to the contrary - that there were activities, such as ones in which Mr. Luckhoo was leader of a political party, organized these fears in the minds of the Guianese people."

Dr. Jagan - Sir, it is because I have stood up for the working class that they have voted for me. I have not put a bayonet on their backs and said 'Come vote for me.

Counsel (for the Commission) - "If there were no division of power, as I imagine it would be after independence, do you really think that you would have been better able to deal with the situation which arose last February?"

Dr. Jagan - "Certainly."

Question - "In what respect?"

Dr. Jagan - "Under the present constitution, prosecutions are in charge of the Director of Prosecutions. The question of control of armed forces is a question which is completely in the hands of the Governor, the Head of State. Under an independent constitution armed forces will be under, too, the Head of State, but he will be working with the advice of the Government."

Question - "What could you have done if there had been no division of power?"

Dr. Jagan - "I could have brought into the country, at that stage immediately the armed forces which were at Atkinson Field."

Question - "On Thursday morning?"

Dr. Jagan - "Yes, Thursday morning or evening."

Question - "Or perhaps even on Wednesday?"

Dr. Jagan - "At that stage, probably it was not reached. But as soon as it became clear that the leaders of the people in the opposition were deliberately disregarding the law and deliberately breaking it, the situation at that stage had become very explosive and therefore I would have brought in whatever support - military support - there was for the civil power, immediately."

Mr. Farnum (Counsel for the United Force) - "Would you agree that Mr. D'Aguiar's products were to be boycotted because he opposed your views which represent the views of the people?"

Dr. Jagan - "Because he deliberately tried to use measures which were unconstitutional to overthrow a government which was a people's Government."

Question - "And your paper Thunder is today urging that the boycott continue?"

Dr. Jagan - "Yes."

Question - "Is it a form - an effort to punish?"

Dr. Jagan - "Not to punish; not to support an individual to get rich and wealthy at the expense of the people whose interests he is generally against."

CHAPTER 28

The Planning of the 1964 Elections

"The Situation and Prospects in British Guiana," Special National Intelligence Estimate (NIE) No. 87.2-62, April 11, 1962.

E XPANDING ON THE MARCH 1962 INTELLIGENCE ESTImate, this NIE is more assertive in its conclusion that Dr. Jagan was a communist, "The PPP leadership has a clear record of Communist association and of Communist-line policies, but the evidence does not show whether or to what extent they are under international Communist control. We believe, however, that Dr. Jagan is a Communist, though the degree of Moscow's control is not yet clear." The evidence presented against Dr. Jagan is slim. As the report concludes, he appears to follow in the footsteps of other post-colonial leaders, "We believe that a Dr. Jagan government in the post-independence period would be likely to identify itself as it has in the past with anti-colonialist and independence movements. It would probably follow a policy of nonalignment and seek to benefit from relations with both the West and the Communist countries, but would probably lean in the Soviet direction."

The report is also more skeptical about the possibility of Dr. Jagan losing elections in the near term given that, "The February crisis strengthened Dr. Jagan by consolidating the support of his East Indian followers with sufficient defections to cause the legislative defeat of the Dr. Jagan government are not considered probable in the near future under existing circumstances."

As such, new elections under the same legal structure would likely "return a Dr. Jagan government again, even in the face of a PNC-UF electoral coalition."

"Minutes of the Special Group Meeting", April 19, 1962. Memorandum for the Record.

These meeting minutes showed deliberations over expenditures for a CIA project [*project and country remain redacted*] to "achieve the objectives of the project through the 1964 election." The project likely referred to British Guiana's expected elections. A goal of the operation is that "there would be no knowledge on the part of the recipients as to the true source of the funds."

"Summary of Development of (REDACTED) Operation Concerning British Guiana," CIA, c. June 1962.

The CIA contacted the two main opposition figures in British Guiana, Mr. Linden Forbes Burnham, and Mr. Peter D'Aguiar, and "they both agreed to insist on an electoral system of proportional representation for British Guiana at the Constitutional Conference, which began in London on October 23." The CIA was able to get the support of both men "in return for a promise of financial assistance." Furthermore, in the U.S., there was an effort to revitalize the Help Guiana Committee, a small organization of British Guianese in New York.

"Eyes only for the Secretary from the President." White House Memorandum from President John F. Kennedy to Secretary of State Dean Rusk, c. June 15, 1962.

JFK informs his secretary of state to write a letter to British Prime Minister Harold Macmillan explaining that an independent British Guiana led by Dr. Cheddi Jagan "disturbs us seriously" and making it clear that the President of the United States believes that:

> We must recognize that Dr. Jagan is now thoroughly distrustful of our own motives. We have concluded, therefore, that it is unrealistic to hope that a British Guiana led by Dr. Cheddi Jagan could be kept on the side of the West through a policy of cooperation as was envisaged during the talks held in September of last year. We must be entirely frank in saying that we simply cannot afford to see another Castro-type regime established in this Hemisphere. It follows that we should set as our objective an independent British Guiana under some other leader.

"British Guiana," with attached "Action Program for British Guiana" Secretary of State Dean Rusk Memorandum for President John F. Kennedy, July 12, 1962, Two versions, A and B, showing different redactions.

This alarming memo by Secretary Rusk warns the President that U.S. intelligence, as well as recent statements made by Dr. Jagan, prove that he is a communist; therefore, "I believe we are obliged to have our policy on the premise that, come independence, Dr. Cheddi Jagan will establish a 'Marxist' regime in British Guiana and associate his country with the Soviet Bloc to a degree unacceptable to us for a state in the Western Hemisphere. A policy of trying to work with Dr. Jagan, as urged by the British, will not pay off. Dr. Jagan is already too far committed emotionally and suspicious of our intentions."

Rusk makes it clear that the only alternative is to make sure Dr. Jagan does not emerge as the leader of a newly independent British Guiana, "My conclusion, therefore is that we should set as our objective the replacement of the Dr. Jagan government prior to the independence of British Guiana which it now seems will take place in 1963" (version B). Rusk recommended that the President should approve that an "objective of U.S. policy" should be "to bring about the replacement of the government of Dr. Cheddi Jagan by one friendly to West, prepared to follow multi-racial policies and to carry out a realistic economic and social development program" (version B). Rusk also recommended that "we inform the British of our intentions." (Version A) and "initiate [REDACTED] discussions of political action with Mr. Burnham, Rai and D'Aguiar" (version A).

The attached action program explained that, "our objective of replacing Dr. Jagan will, therefore, probably be resisted by the British. They will mistrust the efficacy of a U.S. political action program in the Colony and fear that the result could require reinstitution of direct British rule. Nonetheless, [w]hile further consultations are unlikely to result in agreement; we hope to secure British acquiescence" (version A)."

The attachment outlines several political actions to oust Dr. Jagan with new elections. These include "Tacit election arrangements between Mr. Burnham and D'Aguiar to avoid election conflicts..." (Version A). As for an independent campaign by former PPP member Balram Singh Rai, "[w]e believe that he could carry with him an appreciable number of moderate Indian voters... his influence is needed to swing the balance against the PPP" (version A). Finally, there would be an effort to flip six competitive seats in the Legislative Assembly to deny Dr. Jagan a majority: "it is in those constituencies that our efforts would be focused" (version A).

"British Guiana," National Security Council, McGeorge Bundy memorandum for President John F. Kennedy, July 13, 1962.

After reading Rusk's "hard" memo to JFK recommending presidential approval for getting rid of Dr. Jagan, Bundy cautions the President against such a decision, explaining that, "while the papers make a clear case against supporting Dr. Jagan, or even trying to sustain peaceful coexistence with him, the case for the proposed tactics to be used in opposing him is not so clear. In particular, I think it is unproven that the CIA knows how to manipulate an election in British Guiana without a backfire." Bundy wants a final decision to be delayed and recommended that Secretary Rusk not "go to the British Ambassador with the proposed talking paper until we are a little sure of our own capabilities and intentions." Furthermore, if the President decides to approve the anti-Jagan project, it should not be Rusk who should sell the policy to the British but, "I think you may want to go all out with David yourself on this one."

"British Guiana," Department of State, William H. Brubeck memorandum for McGeorge Bundy, National Security Council, August 8, 1962.

This memo to Bundy explains that Alexis Johnson and Richard Helms agreed that they should make a proposal to the British for British Guiana with the goal "to bring matters to a head by forcing a consideration of political factors [REDACTED]." The agenda should include the "Nature of a successor government to Dr. Jagan."

"British Guiana," National Security Council, McGeorge Bundy memorandum for Arthur Schlesinger Jr., September 19, 1962.

A conspiratorial memo from Bundy to Schlesinger in which the national security adviser explained that the British have responded satisfactorily to American requests on British Guiana. However, President Kennedy wants to make sure "that its exact character is not put on paper anywhere. He has also asked that it be kept away from the State Department [REDACTED]." As a consequence, Bundy told Schlesinger that "we are not cluing the State Department below the highest levels, and we are all enjoined by the President to keep out of it ourselves other than for the transmission of traffic to those who are directly concerned."

National Security Council, Carl Kaysen memo to McGeorge Bundy on cataloguing important papers for the President to read, October 5, 1962.

The high interest that JFK and his top advisers placed on British Guiana, in preparing the President's weekend reading material, NSC Deputy Carl Kaysen writes to Bundy that on matters of British Guiana, "I think you know about the most interesting developments here."

"Meeting on CIA Matters with the President's Foreign Intelligence Advisory Board," CIA, Cord Meyer Jr. Covert Action Staff, Memorandum for the Record, April 17, 1963.

Details of a briefing by the CIA to the President's Foreign Intelligence Advisory Board (PFIAB) concerning covert actions and likely including British Guiana. The memo explained that the State Department was "putting considerable pressure on the [REDACTED] regime to persuade it to hold the elections scheduled for [REDACTED] 1963." Nonetheless, the CIA acknowledged that "despite the pressure, there was still considerable doubt whether the elections would actually take place." The memo also described U.S. "covert support" to some political parties for the forthcoming parliamentary elections. Murphy, representing PFIAB, was surprised with the decision of supporting some political elements and described it "as quite a switch."

He also issued the same directive as National Security Action Memorandum (NSAM) 135. It was highly unusual for a covert action instruction to appear as both a NSAM and a directed missive, and suggested that the President was trying to stop something he felt was out of control. As it happened, the same day British Guiana was up for discussion at the 5412 Special Group. The contents of Kennedy's order reinforced the impression of urgency, and the 5412-discussion showed that the commanders of the secret wars followed the President's instructions. NSAM-135 declared, "No final decision will be taken on our policy toward British Guiana" until after further discussions. Kennedy, further, delineated three questions to answer before any decision was made.

Within a few weeks of NSAM-135, the CIA weighed in with a pair of intelligence estimates on the Caribbean Colony. In a memorandum to Director McCone of the Office of National Estimates (ONE) commented on the Georgetown riots, agreeing that the tax bill had been the main catalyst, marking the PPP as "Communist-oriented" and the PNC as "Socialist," and portraying the British as much less concerned over the political orientation of Dr. Jagan and the PPP than was Washington. The CIA acknowledged that Dr. Jagan was not under Soviet control, but that did not satisfy some policymakers. The ONE followed in April with Special National Intelligence Estimate (SNIE) 87.2-62, discussing the short-term outlook for British Guiana. The estimate argued that the "PPP leadership" had a clear record of "communist-line policies" and that Dr. Jagan was a communist.

The CIA estimates answered two of President Kennedy's three key questions in which the agency projected that Dr. Jagan would win the next election, even if opposed by a coalition of Mr. Burnham's PNC and the United Force party. The SNIE also estimated that there was no prospect that a Dr. Jagan's government would agree to a coalition with the other parties, which it far outnumbered in the Guianese assembly. A Dr. Jagan administration could be expected to follow a non-aligned foreign policy to some degree friendly to the communist bloc.

Kennedy's third question concerned the British - would they delay independence for British Guiana and provide for new elections. Secretary Rusk held talks with Lord Home on the sidelines of a meeting in Geneva in mid-March. With British reluctance so evident, he reported back that covert action with or without London was necessary. Nevertheless, a program designed to bring about the removal of Dr. Jagan became one option included in a State Department policy paper released on March 15. At the 5412 Special Group session on March 22, Director McCone was asked to assess the chances of various lines of covert action that could be adopted. The State options paper specified a covert political action. The main instrument for such a gambit would be international labor unions cooperating with the CIA. A month later, CIA support for labor operations would be the lead item at the 5412 Special Group, in a meeting attended by CIA operations chief Richard Helms and Deputy Director Marshall S. Carter.

During May 1962, President Kennedy and British Prime Minister Harold Macmillan held direct talks, while the Guianese opposition leader Mr. Forbes Burnham visited Washington. The meetings cleared away some of the obstacles to covert action. Senior officials decided that Mr. Burnham's socialism was preferable to whatever-it-was that Dr. Jagan believed. Equally important, the British decided to delay independence, leaving an opening for a CIA operation. One key indicator of the crumbling of opposition to a covert operation would be when Mr. Arthur Schlesinger told Mr. Jack Kennedy, on June 21, that a Forbes Burnham government would cause much fewer problems for the U.S. than one led by Dr. Jagan.

On June 14, the 5412 Special Group considered a CIA paper outlining a covert political action but deferred judgment pending solution of the basic political problem. That same day Mr. Dean Rusk sent the meeting minutes, State Department intelligence and FBI reports, and a draft action program to Kennedy. Included with the documents was the comment that replacement of the Dr. Jagan government should be set as the U.S. objective. That was the first formal request for a British Guiana covert operation.

President Kennedy dictated a reply sent to Secretary Rusk. He expressed general agreement with Rusk's position but preferred for the time being to follow the British line. Rusk temporarily withdrew his covert action proposal. In subsequent London talks, he then got the British to agree that Guianese independence would be delayed, and they began thinking more positively of a fresh election conducted by means of "proportional representation," rather than a direct ballot. U.S. experts held that to be the only way to defeat Dr. Jagan at the polls. The U.S. plan was to change the electoral rules, then work to ensure Dr. Jagan's party could not win an election.

On July 12, Mr. Rusk proposed that the United States aim to overthrow the Dr. Jagan government. State presented essentially the same package with a more elaborate action plan that included diplomatic aspects, steps to influence the colonial congress about to take place in London, political action and propaganda in the Colony, and economic aid for the opposition.

A letter to President Kennedy from Prime Minister Macmillan, July 18, 1963

The British advised us of their decision "to impose a system of proportional representation without a referendum and then to hold elections under a new system". This letter also informed us of a British expectation to "renew direct rule for a period of six months to a year while a new constitution is introduced and new elections held under it." The latter assertion was made on a British assumption that Dr. Jagan would resign when informed of the new electoral system at a Constitutional Conference held October 22–31. He did not do so but repeatedly stated that he does not feel bound to accept the British decisions.

Dr. Jagan seems uncertain and a little desperate, but he is unlikely to resign voluntarily. No occasion has yet arisen to show whether he will obstruct the carrying out of the decisions, but probably he will try to hang on, temporizing and avoiding flagrantly illegal acts. His regime has been organizing a protest march on Georgetown as well as secretly promoting a rash of arson in the countryside. The regime is likely to try to foster an atmosphere of intimidation and potential terror in an effort to attract international attention and more particularly to discourage opponents of the regime.

While the UK agrees as to the importance of getting rid of Dr. Jagan, it is reluctant to impose direct rule unless Dr. Jagan's actions so clearly call for such a course as to pose no presentational problems for the UK. In addition, the UK tends to put somewhat less weight than we do on the advantages of such a step. The UK believes that Dr. Jagan would pose as a martyr and could be more dangerous in opposition than as Premier.

In view of the above circumstances, we think it desirable that the UK increase security and interpret its reserved powers in the foreign affairs field broadly in order to frustrate communist aid to the Dr. Jagan regime.

The assassination of President John F. Kennedy

President John Kennedy was assassinated on November 22, 1963, at 12:30 p.m. while riding in a motorcade in Dallas, Texas, during a campaign visit. After being shot in the neck and head, Kennedy was pronounced dead at 1:00 p.m. He was 46 years of age. At 2:15 p.m., Lee Harvey Oswald, an employee at the Texas School Book Depository, was arrested for President Kennedy's assassination. Oswald was born in New Orleans, Louisiana, in 1939. His father died of a heart attack two months before he was born. After living on and off in orphanages as a boy, he moved with his mother to New York at age 12, and there he was sent to a youth detention center for truancy. It was during this time that he became interested in Socialism. After moving back to New Orleans, he joined the Marines in 1956, where he earned a sharpshooter qualification and discovered Marxism. Upon receiving an early honorable discharge from the Marines in 1959, he migrated to the Soviet Union for two and a half years. He was denied USSR citizenship but was allowed to live in the country. Upon learning that Oswald defected to the USSR, the Marines downgraded his 1959 discharge from "honorable" to "undesirable" in 1962. Oswald returned to Texas with his Russian wife and daughter.

Later that year, he allegedly attempted to shoot retired United States Major General Edwin A Walker, a staunch critic of Communism. In 1963, Oswald was denied passage to Cuba and the USSR and started a job at the Texas School Book Depository in Dallas.

These are the words of President John F. Kennedy, written for the speech that he had planned to deliver at Austin, Texas on the evening of November 22, 1963:

Here in Austin, I pledged in 1960 to restore world confidence in the vitality and energy of American society. That pledge has been fulfilled. We have won the respect of allies and adversaries alike through our determined stand on behalf of freedom around the world, from West Berlin to Southeast Asia - through our resistance to Communist intervention in the Congo and Communist missiles in Cuba - and through our initiative in obtaining the nuclear test ban treaty which can stop the pollution of our atmosphere and start us on the path to peace. In San José and Mexico City, in Bonn and West Berlin, in Rome and County Cork, I saw and heard and felt a new appreciation for an America on the move - an America which has shown that it cares about the needy of its own and other lands, an America which has shown that freedom is the way to the future, an America which is known to be first in the effort for peace as well as preparedness.

For this country is moving, and it must not stop. It cannot control, for this is a time for courage and a time for a challenge. Neither conformity nor complacency will do. Neither the fanatics nor the faint-hearted are needed. And our duty as a party is not to our party alone, but the Nation, and, indeed, to all mankind. Our duty is not merely the preservation of political power but the preservation of peace and freedom.

So let us not be petty when our cause is so great. Let us not quarrel amongst ourselves when our Nation's future is at stake. Let us stand together with renewed confidence in our cause - united in our heritage of the past and our hopes for the future - and determined that this land we love shall lead all mankind into new frontiers of peace and abundance.

Following the assassination of President John F. Kennedy, President Lyndon B. Johnson continued the Kennedy administration's policy of working with the British Government offering encouragement and support against the democratically elected leader of British Guiana.

"British Guiana," CIA, Richard Helms memorandum for McGeorge Bundy, National Security Council, December 5, 1963.

Richard Helms summarized recent decisions by the British government to change the electoral system of British Guiana, making it likely that Dr. Jagan will not be reelected after independence. Duncan Sandys, the British colonial Secretary, declared a series of decisions, which Helms explains, "do not involve British Guianese legislative action. Instead, HMG (Her Majesty's Government) Orders in Council will be used. Four are now contemplated to cover electoral registration, the special force, the new electoral system, and the ultimate constitution (except for the electoral provisions. The letter would become effective after independence)."

Helms wrote that Dr. Jagan was not cooperating with British authorities but was also not taking any provocative actions. Helms concluded by assessing British thinking, "My net impression of the Colonial Office thinking is as follows: While not sure how Dr. Jagan will act in the future, the Colonial Office is working on the assumption that direct rule will become necessary. But since such action is likely to heighten domestic (particularly from the Labor party) and international criticism of British handling of the British Guiana situation, HMG will wait until Dr. Jagan's actions provide clear-cut justification... but will not try to deliberately force him into a corner or find a pretext to oust him."

"Meeting on British Guiana," National Security Council, McGeorge Bundy, Memorandum for Record, December 6, 1963.

A memorandum indicating that the U.S. is still frustrated with British hesitation to re-establish direct rule over British Guiana. Helms, Bundy, and others agreed that "all hands would apply as much heat as possible to Mr. Ambler Thomas (British Colonial Office), showing him all the agreeable ways and means of finding causes for the resumption of direct rule." They also agreed to think of recommendations for how JFK should approach the matter with the British prime minister in the future.

Memorandum from Secretary of State Rusk to President Johnson Washington, February 6, 1964.

Drafted by Burdett on February 5, and forwarded to McGeorge Bundy under cover of a February 7 memorandum in which Burnett assumed Bundy would "wish to talk to the President personally" about it.

SUBJECT: Visit of British Prime Minister Home, British Guiana.

I recommend you make the following points to Sir Alec Home regarding British Guiana: You are as concerned as President Kennedy over British Guiana Emergence of another Communist state in this hemisphere cannot be accepted; there is grave risk of Dr. Jagan's establishing a Castro-type regime should he attain independence. Prime Minister Macmillan and President Kennedy agreed that British Guiana should not become independent under Dr. Jagan and that a change of government is inevitable. Dr. Jagan must be defeated in the next election. Suspension of the constitution and imposition of direct rule would help defeat Dr. Jagan. Direct British control over internal security, strengthening the police, and a broad interpretation of the powers reserved to the UK in foreign affairs to prevent entry of personnel and funds from Cuba would help overcome the atmosphere of intimidation by Dr. Jagan. Sir Alec will probably (a) confirm the Macmillan/Kennedy understanding, (b) endorse the importance of assuring Dr. Jagan's defeat, (c) question the feasibility of a resumption of direct UK rule unless the grounds can be publicly shown to be fully justified.

Washington, February 12, 1964, 4:30 p.m.

PARTICIPANTS:

United Kingdom

Sir Alec Douglas-Home, *Prime Minister of the United Kingdom.*
R. A. Butler, *Secretary of State for Foreign Affairs.*

Sir Harold Caccia, *Permanent Under-Secretary, The Foreign Office.*
Sir David Ormsby Gore, *British Ambassador.*
Sir Timothy Bligh, *Principal Private Secretary to the Prime Minister.*
Sir Burke Trend, *Secretary to the Cabinet.*

United States

The President.
The Secretary of State.
Governor Harriman, *Under Secretary of State for Political Affairs.*
David K. E. Bruce, *Ambassador to Great Britain.*
McGeorge Bundy, *Special Assistant to the President on National Security Affairs.*
William R. Tyler, *Assistant Secretary, EUR.*
Richard I. Philips, *Director, P/ON.*
Willis C. Armstrong, *Director, BNA.*

[*2 lines of source text not declassified*] they were now engaged in registering parties, and he gathered that there had been some problem in the development of splinter parties. Mr. Bundy remarked that people were engaged in party cultivation, but that it was stony ground. The Secretary noted that the East Indians who don't like Dr. Jagan are reluctant to come forward. It was understood that party activity was being closely observed. The Secretary went on to say that it was very important not to let Dr. Jagan take over in a situation of independence. [*11/2 lines of source text not declassified*] The Prime Minister said that at some point there would have to be an election, and he thought December might be a good time.

On a February 27 memorandum for the record, Burdett

noted that Bundy stated that the President and Prime Minister had discussed British Guiana privately during the latter's visit and that they had reaffirmed the agreements existing between President Kennedy and Prime Minister Macmillan, and in particular, the understandings reached at Birch Grove the previous summer. Kennedy and Macmillan met at Birch Grove, England, on June 30, 1963, where the British proposed, and Kennedy agreed, that independence should be delayed, that a proportional representation electoral system be established, and that the alliance between the leading politicians opposed to Dr. Jagan be supported.

Drafted by Thomas M. Judd, Officer-in-Charge of UK Affairs. The meeting was held in Tyler's office. This memorandum is part 2 of 2; (part 1 was not found), Washington, February 19, 1964, 10 a.m.

PARTICIPANTS:

United States

William R. Tyler, *Assistant Secretary for European Affairs.*
William G. Burdett, *Deputy Assistant Secretary, EUR.*
Willis C. Armstrong, *Director, BNA.*
Thomas N. Judd, *BNA.*

United Kingdom

Patrick Gordon Walker, *Labor "Shadow" Foreign Minister.*

Mr. Tyler asked Mr. Gordon Walker what he thought about British Guiana. Gordon Walker replied that he knew Mr. Tyler was thinking of an article which appeared in The Reporter on February 13 which purported to represent Gordon Walker's views. Since the article had come out, he had been giving considerable thought as to what he had really said to the man who had written the article. To the best of his recollection, he had made the following points which, he emphasized, were his own views which had not been fully checked out with the Labor Party:

It made the Labor Party uncomfortable not to grant independence to any country when the situation is ripe. He recognized the primacy of U.S. interests in British Guiana. Labor believed there would be social revolutions in Latin America. Some of those would be ugly ones which would not fit in with the pattern of the Alliance for Progress. Some Nasser-type governments would undoubtedly emerge.

Labor would like to find a way to give independence to British Guiana without affronting or injuring the U.S. Britain of course cannot afford to appear as an agent of the U.S. The way in which the Douglas-Home government was trying to do this was completely unacceptable to the people of British Guiana because it makes the entire country into one constituency. Some other form of proportional representation might well be considered by Labor.

At a Constitutional Conference in London in October 1963, the major British Guiana party leaders asked British Colonial Secretary Sandys to devise a constitution, "since they were unable to agree among themselves." Sandys then decreed a new registration and general election under proportional representation for a single house legislature. "Dr. Jagan was furious at being outsmarted."

There was a discussion of the menace represented by Dr. Jagan. Mr. Tyler said they were seriously concerned with the way Dr. Jagan conducted himself. They could not live with a

Castro-type government on the South American continent. Mr. Gordon Walker thought the U.S. exaggerated the menace of Dr. Jagan. There was a limit to what he could do, in view of the racial division in British Guiana; for example, he could hardly have complete control in a situation where the capital of the country was against him.

Mr. Tyler added that they were worried about the Castro aspects - that British Guiana would be used as a base for subversion on the continent. Mr. Gordon Walker replied that a bit of that sort of thing was bound to develop in Latin America. However, if a way could be found for the U.S. to put its troops into British Guiana, the Labor Party would not object. Britain did not want to keep its troops there indefinitely. Britain had no real reason of its own to stay. Furthermore, its troops were spread too thin. One battalion now in British Guiana was not enough.

Memorandum from the Deputy Director for Plans of the Central Intelligence Agency (Helms) to the President's Special Assistant for National Security Affairs (Bundy), Washington, March 18, 1964.

Reference was made to the memorandum of March 7, 1964, concerning the efforts of the Dr. Jagan-controlled Guiana Agricultural Workers' Union (GAWU) to gain control of the sugar workers in British Guiana. During the past week the strike continued and the situation was still serious. The intimidation by GAWU forced workers to remain away from their jobs, and Ministers of Dr. Jagan's government, including Dr. Jagan himself, gave their full and open support to the strike. Thus far the management group has remained firm in not recognizing the GAWU, but events may force the companies at least to allow a poll of the sugar workers to determine which union they wish to represent them. That in itself would be a defeat for the anti-Dr. Jagan Manpower Citizens' Association (MPCA), which represented the sugar workers, and further withdrawals from the MPCA could result in its complete loss of control of the sugar workers.

In this memorandum to Bundy, Helms reported on GAWU-inspired violence and killings. The police force was vigorous in its efforts to control the intimidations and demonstrations, but the force is not large enough to handle the situation completely. British troops have not yet been used. [2 *paragraphs (221/2 lines of source text) not declassified*]

A copy of this memorandum is being sent to Mr. Burdett. RH

Department of State, Telegram from Georgetown on Developments in the Meakins Case, March 27, 1964.

The State Department explains that it concurs with the "approach Congen [Consul General] has made to the Governor expressing concern about the regime's policy trying to bar foreign labor leaders unfriendly to PPP." Of particular interest to the U.S. is the Eugene Meakins case, but the AFL/CIO has informed the embassy that the union "prefer[s] continue to pursue possible legal steps without any US Govt. intervention." The U.S. seeks clarification on the probability that legal recourse will work and explains, "In any case BG TUC [Trade Unions Council] and American trade unionists concerned with matters intended to maximize propaganda advantages should Meakins be deported."

Memorandum from the Deputy Director for Plans of the Central Intelligence Agency (Helms) to the President's Special Assistant for National Security Affairs (Bundy), Washington, May 1, 1964.

An essential element to winning the next general elections in British Guiana and forming a successful coalition government after the defeat of Premier Cheddi Jagan is the behind-the-scenes co-operation of Mr. Linden Forbes Burnham, leader of the People's National Congress (PNC), and Mr. Peter S. D'Aguiar, leader of the United Force. Although the two opposition leaders worked closely together at the London Constitutional Conference in October 1963 and agreed to continue joint discussions when they returned to Georgetown, those discussions have not taken place, and there has been no co-operation.

Memorandum to Bundy, Helms reported that [*text not declassified*] had informed the CIA that the new general elections in British Guiana would be held during the last 3 months of 1964 and that [*text not declassified*] had agreed that [*text not declassified*] could inform the leaders of the two main opposition parties [*text not declassified*] of this timing.

In April 1964 [*less than 1 line of source text not declassified*] sent a political adviser for each party to British Guiana to assist with preparations for voter registration and secondly to work out a [*less than 1 line of source text not declassified*] understanding between Mr. Burnham and Mr. D'Aguiar for co-operation during the election campaign and for the future coalition government. Those advisers have arranged for two meetings between Mr. Burnham and Mr. D'Aguiar, one on April 24 and the second on April 28. Thus far Mr. Burnham and Mr. D'Aguiar have agreed to the following:

(a) To share poll watchers in certain areas and to share the costs of challenges in these areas.
(b) To cooperate in a joint publicity campaign before and during the registration period.
(c) To refrain from attacking the other party during the election campaign outside of "honest politicking."
(d) To review their progress at mid-point in the registration period and consult on any corrections that might need to be made.
(e) To decide if specific areas of responsibility are desirable, based on the results of the registration.
(f) The two leaders have also discussed cabinet posts for a future coalition government, but have not yet reached agreement on this matter. The advisers report that the meetings have been harmonious.
(g) A copy of this memorandum is being sent to Mr. William C. Burdett of the Department of State.

Research Memorandum from the Deputy Director of Intelligence and Research (Denney) to Acting Secretary of State Ball, Washington, Outlook for More Violence in British Guiana, May 12, 1964.

In an effort to prevent the holding of a UK-imposed proportional representation election, expected to be held late this year, the Dr. Jagan regime has been resorting to intimidation and violence. What began some 12 weeks ago as a strike by the pro-Jagan sugar workers' union has developed into a campaign of beatings, bombings, and arson in which 19 persons have been killed and more than a million dollars' worth of property and sugar cane have been burnt. The violence has exacerbated the racial tensions between the majority East

Indians and the minority Negroes to such an extent that some officials fear that the situation may get out of hand.

Contributing to that concern has been the agitation of activists in the Dr. Jagan regime, who have attacked not only members of the competing sugar workers' union but also the opposition parties, which are composed mainly of Negroes and other non-Indians. Local police have uncovered arms buried by members of Dr. Jagan's youth organization. [*3 lines of source text not declassified*]

As the proportional representation election which threatens to oust him from office draws nearer, registration began on May 8, Dr. Jagan's despair is deepening. In the hope that the election may be postponed, he has invited Prime Minister Williams of Trinidad to try to mediate the differences between him and the leaders of the opposition parties. It seems unlikely, however, that the opposition parties, hopeful of victory in a proportional representation election, will agree to Williams' proposals. As the Dr. Jagan's regime grows more desperate, its extremist elements may well be tempted to undertake more ambitious acts of terrorism. Such acts could provoke the threatened Negro minority into large-scale retaliation.

Telegram from the Department of State [*text not declassified*] to the Consulate General in British Guiana. Washington, May 13, 1964.

Following is a [*less than 1 line of source text not declassified*] State [*less than 1 line of source text not declassified*] cable for Carlson [*less than 1 line of source text not declassified*]:

(1) We concur with Mr. Burnham not to resort to counter-violence and that he can be assured that if PPP makes an effort to take over the country by force the U.S. Govt. will not stand by and see opposition

crushed by terror, and Carlson's comments on arms to Mr. Burnham.

(2) We are now exploring the possibility of giving counterterrorism training to selected members of the opposition. While this will not have any immediate positive effect on containing violence, it may give a boost to opposition. We will inform you when final decisions and plans are made. [*Less than 1 line of source text not declassified*].

In an April 30 memorandum to Bundy, Helms wrote that if the situation deteriorated "to the extent that it is decided to furnish the trainees with the necessary material, this would be furnished to them [*text not declassified*] British Guiana." A marginal note in Bundy's handwriting reads "Approved by phone. May 7."

Meanwhile, we suggest you discuss [*less than 1 line of source text not declassified*] steps which could be taken to control violence. It is our view that frequent use of [*less than 1 line of source text not declassified*] mechanism should be made not only to work out local solutions to problems but also to give a true picture to the Governor so he will in turn influence Coloff. Request cable summary of all [*less than 1 line of source text not declassified*] meetings [*less than 1 line of source text not declassified*].

In a March 23 memorandum to Bundy, Helms reported that "the Colonial Office has taken note of the request by the Department of State that the British Guiana elections not be held prior to the U.S. Presidential elections on November 3 1964."

Memorandum from Helms to Bundy, May 21.

[*less than 1 line of source text not declassified*] Wished that influence could be brought to bear on Richard Ishmael, president of the Manpower Citizens' Association (MPCA), which is the anti-Jagan sugar workers' union, to co-operate with the pro-Jagan arbitration committee which has been set up to mediate the dispute. [*less than 1 line of source text not declassified*] representatives pointed out to [*less than 1 line of source text not declassified*] that this would be giving in to Dr. Jagan and that Ishmael probably would not follow [*less than 1 line of source text not declassified*] advice in this matter. [*less than 1 line of source text not declassified*] agreed with this, but said that he would not like [*less than 1 line of source text not declassified*] to urge defiance from Ishmael.

In view of the above, a [*less than 1 line of source text not declassified*] State [*less than 1 line of source text not declassified*] cable has been sent to the Consul General [*less than 1 line of source text not declassified*] in Georgetown, giving [*less than 1 line of source text not declassified*] the following guidance:

(a) Our principal objective is to defeat the PPP in the forthcoming elections and to bring into power a coalition government of the People's National Congress, the United Force, and alternative East Indian party(ies), headed by Mr. Burnham. While retaining tactical flexibility, all our moves must be directed at the attainment of this objective.

(b) We believe that in terms of accomplishing our objective, things at this time are going well despite the current wave of violence. Registration of voters to date and the increasing nervousness of the PPP support this assessment.

(c) Therefore, we should make every effort to adhere to the present schedule, i.e., elections under proportional representation in early November, and to avoid being deflected from our present course. The PPP is clearly making every effort to upset this schedule.

(d) We believe that resumption of direct British rule at this stage would impede the attainment of our objective. Resumption could delay elections, make it easier for the British Labour Party, if it comes to power, to tamper with Sandys' decision, and give the PPP additional campaign issues.

(e) We share the view of the Governor that the declaration of a state of emergency probably will be required to cope with the security situation. The British may have to buttress the declaration by dispatching additional troops to British Guiana. We see advantages in the declaration resulting from the '*advice*' of the Ministers. If '*advice*' from the Ministers is not forthcoming, declaration by a special Order in Council may well be necessary.

In telegram 298 to Georgetown, May 22, the Department reported that the British Embassy in Washington had informed it that, under pressure from the Governor and the Commissioner of Police, Dr. Jagan had notified the Governor that he would "advise" the Governor to declare a state of emergency on May 22 or 23.

(f) Tactically we would prefer to allow HMG on its own initiative, without urging by the U.S., to arrive at the conclusion that a declaration of emergency and probably the dispatch of additional troops are required.

(g) We agreed with your reasons that it would be disadvantageous for the MPCA to consent to co-operate with the committee to investigate the sugar dispute, which is obviously stacked in favor of the PPP. We also agree that Ishmael is not likely to cooperate. In discussions locally you should continue to take the position that Ishmael should be allowed to make his own decision.

(h) [*1 line of source text not declassified*]"

A copy of this memorandum is being sent to Mr. William C. Burdett of the Department of State. Ambassador Bruce in London has been informed of the above.

Memorandum from the Deputy Director of Plans of the Central Intelligence Agency (Helms) to the President's Special Assistant for National Security Affairs (Bundy), Washington, May 22, 1964.

On May 21, 1964, the Consul General in Georgetown [*less than 1 line of source text not declassified*] reported that [*3 lines of source text not declassified*] it was now evident that the security situation had reached the point where it would be essential for a state of emergency to be declared. The Governor has urged both Cheddi and Janet Jagan to end the strike on the sugar estates and to give him the necessary advice of the Council of Ministers to declare a state of emergency, as reported in my memorandum of May 21. The Governor has reported that Premier Dr. Jagan would be prepared to give him the advice of his Ministers on either May 22 or 23; he said the legal documents were ready for the emergency order, but there were still a few decisions yet to be made. However, the Dr. Jagan emergency order may not contain sufficient powers to control the situation, such as the right to search and detain without a warrant. [*text not declassified*] State [*text not declassified*] telegram from Georgetown, unnumbered, May 21. [*file name not declassified*] Progress Report [*file name not declassified*] State Memos).

Call on Premier Dr. Cheddi Jagan, Georgetown, Memorandum of Conversation, May 25, 1964.

Premier Dr. Cheddi Jagan of British Guiana.
Delmar R. Carlson, *American Consul General, British Guiana.*
William B. Cobb, Jr., *British Guiana Desk Officer, Washington.*

We were received by Premier Dr. Jagan in his darkened, air-conditioned office. Dr. Jagan explained that because of astigmatism his eyes suffered from the intense glare and therefore he was more comfortable in a dim office. Dr. Jagan said he was most discouraged about the situation in British Guiana. The efforts of the sugar workers to throw off the burden of the company union had led to tension in the community and racial animosities had been aroused. He did not know what would happen now. The struggle against the company union and the BGTUC is nothing but a company union nowadays, should be resolved and he had appointed a committee to try to resolve it but only the sugar workers were willing to cooperate.

On the political scene he was also discouraged. The British Government had imposed PR although it was admittedly a most unsatisfactory voting method and he wondered what it might lead to. The British had pushed him around since he first organized the PPP and had changed the system on him time and again gerrymandering districts, changing the number of districts, and now even PR. It was most discouraging and Indian voters might well become disenchanted with the so-called parliamentary system of democracy and turn elsewhere if the Guiana experience was any example. Perhaps it was a result of the cold war tensions but parliamentary and democracy seemed on the way out. In Latin America for example there are many more dictatorships today than ever before since World War II.

"No matter what I try to do," Dr. Jagan said:

> I can get nowhere. I am opposed by everyone, including the CIA which I suppose is the American Government. I laid my cards on the table to President Kennedy, and he gave me to understand that he would help me but he didn't and I can only conclude that he was a liar or that he was influenced to change his decision. The people in BG know that I am trying to help them. They are not dumb. But they see that I am being frustrated at every turn. When I see newspaper correspondents, they distort what I tell them. I am being maligned by a press agency in Miami, presumably run by Cuban refugees, who has distributed an article saying that I advocated wiping out the Negroes in B.G. This is completely untrue, it's a deliberate distortion.

Telegram 403 from Georgetown, May 30, reported Carlson's observations of the meeting with Dr. Jagan, including Dr. Jagan's view that the United States turned against him after what he thought had been a successful visit to Washington, presumably because "pressure had been brought on President by right wing groups or by CIA." Dr. Jagan visited the United States and met with President Kennedy on October 25, 1961. Dr. Jagan also felt the only answer to the present situation was a grand coalition but that "speaking man to man, Mr.

Burnham would not join in because the United States would not let him." Carlson reported that he responded that he could not believe that the Premier, or Mr. Burnham, or Mr. D'Aguiar were or could be puppets of anybody.

In his rambling exposition, Dr. Jagan mentioned that he often listened to the VOA, and referred specifically to a panel program which discussed the situation in Vietnam. He said that one of the speakers pointed out that the war in Vietnam was being lost because it was not supported by 80% of the population. He inferred that the turmoil in South East Asia was a direct result of American involvement.

The Wismar Massacre

The event at Wismar has been a prohibited event for discussion because of the atrocities that took place. The victims don't want to relive their thoughts, and those who instigated and participated are too embarrassed to discuss it. Guyana continues to deny its seriousness and refuses to accept the public denunciation as a part of any possible reconciliation. Every national election is a reminder and fear of being intimidated, attacked, robbed, and sexually assaulted. The national political leadership of the PPP and PNC allowed the Wismar incident to remain a prohibited subject instead of history. Not only have Guyanese failed to record and thoughtfully document that critical part of their history, but the previous generations have not passed on this information.

Wismar and Christianburg are two villages where approximately 2,000 Indo-Guyanese resided among 18,000 Afro-Guyanese. Wisma and Christianburg are in the mining town of Mackenzie, located 105 kilometers up the Demerara River from the capital city, Georgetown. The destruction began at

Wismar on Sunday, May 24. For 38 hours, the 18,000 Afro-Guyanese residents armed with cutlasses, sticks, gasoline bombs, and guns burnt and destroyed over 230 Indo-Guyanese homes and businesses. Indo-Guyanese who thought they could find shelter in their own homes were confronted and beaten by large mobs of Afro-Guyanese screaming "kill de Indians" as their houses were burnt. One family whose home was on fire was confronted by a large gang who assaulted the wife until she was unconscious, repeatedly stabbing the husband, and then kicked and molested the two small children. Families escaped from the villages into the nearby forest, where they were hunted like animals. However, they had a better chance of survival in the forest than in the villages.

In addition to the mass burning and looting, over 1,500 Indo-Guyanese became homeless. In the indiscriminate beating of Indo-Guyanese men, women, and children, eight women, including two girls, were raped. Some of the women were repeatedly raped as the marauding band took turns on the Indo-Guyanese women. No one knows the actual number of women who were assault since Guyanese women who were victims of rape seldom admit or report such brutality due to the shame associated with it. One man was burnt alive.

Mr. Ramjattan, a supporter of the PPP, was found decapitated. Injuries were in the hundreds, ranging from gunshot wounds, stab wounds, burns, broken bones, and mutilated bodies. One Indo-Guyanese man had both of his legs and feet broken. An employee from the Demerara Bauxite Company said: "The Indians never had a chance." An Afro-Guyanese woman showing no remorse said: "De ga wa dem deserve." The evacuation of Indo-Guyanese from the massacre sites did not occur until the evening of May 25, when two river steamers were commissioned to take the first batch of 1300 refugees to Georgetown, where they were called humiliating names, stoned, and further humiliated by Afro-Guyanese as they arrived. A Red Cross worker said of the survivors: "Few wept, but the hundreds of children appeared terrified and frightened." Out of the 1,300 that arrived in Georgetown, 300 found shelter with relatives while the rest slept on the concrete floor of the pier warehouse in Georgetown. A temporary shelter was soon set up at a factory outside Georgetown. Eventually, homes were provided for them in predominantly Indo-Guyanese communities. For the rest of May 26, 27, and 28, about 500 Indo-Guyanese emerged from hiding in the forest and were safely transported to the refugee camps in Georgetown.

Obviously, the massacre could have been significantly reduced or even avoided if the 75 members of the Mackenzie Police and Volunteer Force were not all Afro-Guyanese. The entire armed forces detachment at Mackenzie was heavily armed but took no action while many friends, family, and neighbors carried out the atrocities. Many police and Volunteer Forces members took part in the looting, beating, and assault of Indo-Guyanese. In one incident, two Afro-Guianese members of the Volunteers Service refused to intervene when two Indo-Guyanese women were being raped. Instead, the women were rescued by employees from DEMBA. In another case, the Volunteer Force shot a young Indo-Guyanese man to death because he refused to stop at their command. In those 38 hours, no Afro-Guyanese was arrested, but bullets wounded two.

Mrs. Janet Jagan, then Minister of Home Affairs, on June 1, in a speech to the Guyana Parliament, equated the suffering at Wismar to genocide since the Police had done nothing to prevent the massacre. She said:

Is it possible for anyone to believe that, with the widespread violence, arson, rape, and murder, there could have been no show of force by the armed Police and armed volunteers. Since this is impossible to accept, one can only come to the conclusion that planned genocide of a village was carried out with the connivance of all concerned.

She then resigned to protest the British Police Commissioner not responding to her orders. After 24 hours of violence, British troops arrived. Their suggestion was to evacuate the area. However, they were powerless to stop the violence, and they imposed a curfew with bands of marauding Afro-Guianese hunting Indo-Guianese families who had taken refuge in the surrounding forests and continuing to burn houses. The colony's Governor, Sir Richard Luyt, announced that 250 more men of the Devon and Dorset regiment would be flown in from Britain within 48 hours. The curfew did manage to quiet the situation, but most of the killing, rapes, burning, and assault had already taken place.

In September 1964, the Governor of British Guiana, Sir Richard Luyt, appointed a commission to investigate the causes of the violence. The Commission concluded that the disturbances were politically and racially inspired. They noted that "the thorough destruction of East Indian property, and the fact that the security forces were in no case able to apprehend arsonists, force us to conclude that the destruction . . . was organised, and well organised".

The Police and the British Guiana Volunteer Force did not protect the Indo-Guyanese population. It was not until British soldiers arrived on the scene late in the evening that there was some relief in the attacks.

According to the Commission, the plot started on Wednesday, May 20, 1964, when the home of Pandit Ramlackhan was bombed. There was a strike at Demba on Thursday, May 21, and Friday, May 22. On May 22, Daniel Persaud's house was set on fire, and there was an explosion at Ibrahim Khan's home. Three people were injured in that blast. The arson escalated on Saturday, May 23, and Sunday, May 24. Between 7 a.m. and 8 a.m. on May 25, the situation deteriorated rapidly. There was widespread violence, arson, and looting. The stage was set for a day of unmitigated tragedy. At about 8.00 a.m., it was rumored that an Indo-Guyanese man kicked an Afro-Guyanese boy. The Police subsequently investigated the incident and found it to be untrue.

On the day of the disturbances at Wismar-Christianburg, there were 57 cases of assault, including rape. Two persons were killed, and at least 197 houses were destroyed, and several instances of looting. The majority of the Afro-Guianese laughed at the Indo-Guyanese, blood-stained and battered, raped and naked, shocked and destitute, helplessly went to the Wismar Police Station for refuge. Afro-Guyanese women played their part in the events to the fullest extent.

On May 26, the R.H. Carr and the M.V. Barima were made available to transport evacuees to Georgetown. Some went by air. The presence of Afro-Guyanese police officers and volunteers at the disembarkation point in Georgetown caused fear in the evacuees, who felt safe with assurances by officials of the B.G. Sanatan Dharma Maha Sabha.

The British troops, imposing a curfew, restored order. As darkness fell, fires were still seen in the area, and sporadic attacks on Indo-Guyanese life and property continued. On May 26, Isaac Bridgewater, the father of Senator Christina Ramjattan, was murdered and his place burnt. Arson took place on the Mackenzie side on May 27, and on June 2, Indo-Guyanese houses at Cara Cara were burnt. Toolsie Persaud's gasoline installation at Section C, Christiansburg, was destroyed on July 25.

On July 6, an explosion occurred at Booradia on a launch named *Sun Chapman*, taking goods and passengers from Georgetown to Wismar. About thirty-eight persons perished in that disaster. The echo of the Sun Chapman disaster was immediately felt at Mackenzie when five Indo-Guyanese were murdered and seven seriously injured. Before the official report of the Sun Chapman tragedy reached the Police and British army, Afro-Guyanese were on the rampage again. The implication was that the explosion was PPP retaliation for the Wismar Massacre. Police investigations found no evidence of that.

The International Commission of Jurists (ICJ) recommendations, which the PNC government agreed to implement, declare that the Guianese armed forces will ensure that no *ethnic cleansing* will reoccur.

After independence from Britain, the name of the bauxite town was changed from Mackenzie to Linden. The PNC leader Mr. Linden Forbes Burnham named it after himself. Did Mr. Burnham change the town's name from Mackenzie to Linden because he wanted to remove the colonial legacy and substitute a local term for a foreign or colonial one? If that were truly Mr. Burnham's intention, he would have renamed Georgetown, named after King George of England. The sentiment of those who suffered at Wismar is that Mr. Burnham renamed the town that has been the scene of his greatest political triumph; he gave it his name to symbolically establish his stamp and mark over a massacre where he had reigned supreme over Indo-Guyanese. Is *Linden* a message to Indo-Guyanese that if they challenged him, they could expect the same fate as they experienced on May 24, 25, and 26, 1964?

Mr. Burnham's move to change the name from Mackenzie to Linden was only one of his many acts to show his supremacy and superiority over the Indo-Guyanese community. He humiliated the victims by recommending May 26 as Guyana's Independence Day. The PPP initiated and fought desperately for the decolonization of Guyana. At the end of British rule, the PPP did not participate in the independence celebrations with the same enthusiasm with which it fought for it.

In *The West on Trial*, Dr. Jagan wrote about his objections to May 26, being chosen by Prime Minister Burnham for Guyana's independence. He felt it was insensitive and immoral. Burnham, of course, had no such compunctions. President Jagan omitted the date from the national calendar of holidays during his time in office, and stated: "If it is to be a national holiday, May 26, should stand as a day of remembrance for the victims and survivors of the Wismar Massacre - lest we forget this instance of man's gravest inhumanity to man that visited our country." A subsequent PPP/C Administration reinstated the holiday.

The Commissioners stated:

> We have come to the conclusion that the disturbances which took place in the Wismar-Christianburg-Mackenzie area on May 25, 1964 were politically and racially inspired…. and the fact that the security forces were in no case able to apprehend arsonists, forces us to conclude that the destruction was not 'spontaneous', but was organized, and well organized. It was a diabolical plot, ingeniously planned and ruthlessly executed.

Mr. Forbes Burnham, on May 27, commented on the response of the Police and government towards Wismar said, "I am surprised and amazed that similar action has not been taken at certain areas on the West Coast of Demerara where murder, rape, arson and intimidation has become the order of the day for the last 14 weeks, and in spite of the declaration of emergency…"

Memorandum from Gordon Chase of the National Security Council Staff to the President's Special Assistant for National Security Affairs (Bundy), Washington, May 25, 1964.

I talked to Bill Burdett today about the situation in British Guiana. Bill made the following points:

(1) The present unrest in British Guiana is still a long way from being serious. Only a few people have been hurt and the British response has been as needed to be only a moderate one. The unrest, in part, is a sign that we are on the right track; Dr. Cheddi Jagan and/or his people are beginning to feel that they are on their way out and are stirring up trouble in the hope that they can reverse the trend. We will see more of this sort of thing over the next few months.

(2) We should keep our eye on November. A postponement of elections might give a Labor Government in the UK an opportunity to throw a monkey wrench into our effort to get rid of Dr. Jagan. In a May 28 memorandum Chase reported to Bundy that he had spoken to Burdett about preparing for a Labor Party victory. Burdett advised against talking to Labor before the election, but also recommended that, if Labor won, "our Ambassador should immediately talk to the new Prime Minister." Chase added that he would talk to Burdett's replacement, J. Harold Shullaw, about the need for further contingency planning with respect to a Labor victory. A marginal note in Bundy's handwriting next to this sentence reads "good."

(3) Our policy with respect to BG is the right one and we should stay with it. With a little luck, the events

between now and November will be controllable. With a little more luck, events after November, with Dr. Jagan in opposition, will also be controllable.

(4) There does seem to be an area where some useful work can be done. We probably can usefully do more planning with respect to the moves we will take once Dr. Jagan is gone. (I will look into this one—to see what planning has been done and what else needs to be done). A marginal note in Bundy's handwriting next to this sentence reads: "Also contingency planning for a Labor victory in the United Kingdom."

Memorandum from the Deputy Director for Plans of the Central Intelligence Agency (Helms) to the President's Special Assistant for National Security Affairs (Bundy), a copy of this memorandum is being sent to Mr. J. Harold Shullaw of the Department of State, Washington, June 9, 1964.

(1) On June 3, 1964 Linden Forbes Mr. Burnham, leader of the People's National Congress proposed in the Legislative Assembly that a three-party coalition government be formed to run British Guiana until elections are held under proportional representation (PR) later this year. Mr. Burnham's reasoning for suggesting a coalition now with the People's Progressive Party and the United Force was that it would lessen tensions and allow for more vigorous police action to control the situation. He believed that acceptance of an interim coalition would mean that Dr. Jagan had acknowledged PR as the voting system. Mr. Burnham, however, indicated that he would go no further with

this idea unless it was accepted by Peter D'Aguiar, leader of the UF.

(2) Mr. D'Aguiar refused to join the coalition. Meanwhile, Dr. Jagan was preparing a counter proposal for a coalition of the PPP and PNC, excluding the UF. Dr. Jagan's proposal was contained in a letter sent to Mr. Burnham on June 6. His coalition would last for two to four years before new elections were held; the elections would be held under a combination of PR and the old voting system of first-past-the-post. Dr. Jagan proposed that the ministries be equally divided between the two parties, with Dr. Jagan as Prime Minister and Mr. Burnham as Deputy Prime Minister. Dr. Jagan suggested that the coalition continue after independence when the Ministries of Home Affairs and Defense would be divided between the two parties. Between then and independence, Dr. Jagan asked that a United Nations presence be introduced in British Guiana and that the UN and Commonwealth nations be asked to aid in the creation of security and defense forces.

(3) In reporting the above, Consul General Carlson, [*less than 1 line of source text not declassified*] in Georgetown, said that [*less than 1 line of source text not declassified*] Dr. Jagan found that to be the expedient moment to propose such a coalition government: G.W.Y. Hucks, British electoral commissioner, announced publicly on June 4, that voter registration had been very high in the Corentyne, a Dr. Jagan stronghold, and low in Georgetown, where Mr. Burnham is strongest. [*less than 1 line of source text not declassified*] Dr. Jagan may have been encouraged over his chances in the coming election, or simply believed that it was psychologically

an opportune time to press ostensibly reasonable terms of a coalition government on Mr. Burnham, hoping that he will panic into settling for half now rather than risk losing it all later on. [*3 paragraphs (141/2 lines of source text) not declassified*]

Memorandum from Gordon Chase of the National Security Council Staff to the President's Special Assistant for National Security Affairs (Bundy), Washington, June 13, 1964.

The Governor of BG has taken over the emergency powers from the Council of Ministers and started to pick up some of the people who were suspected of being responsible for the recent violence. The action by the Governor does not detract from the other responsibilities of the Ministers, which remain intact.

Telegram 422 from Georgetown, June 13, not attached, reported Governor Luyt's new Order-in-Council "which in effect puts him rather than Dr. Jagan regime in charge of emergency."

A June 12 memorandum to Bundy reported that a number of prominent PPP leaders were scheduled for immediate arrest under the secret and about-to-be-invoked Order-in-Council emergency regulations, which permitted the detention of persons suspected of being involved in terrorist activity.

Harry Shullaw, (Bill Burdett's successor) stated that the State (Harry, Alexis Johnson, and Bill Tyler) feels that the Governor is the best judge of the present situation and that his step may give us a breather for a while. Harry feels that there are few negatives involved in the move. Dr. Jagan's forces may try to use the development as a new reason for postponing the elections, but unrestrained violence probably works toward this end even more effectively.

The Committee of 24 at the UN has been hearing appeals from the Dr. Jagan forces, and renewed appeals can probably be expected. The British will probably be able to continue to stall off a UN inquiry on the grounds that BG is an internal British matter and that the British are already working towards a solution (i.e. PR). Neither we nor the British favor a UN inquiry since such an inquiry could conceivably lead to a UN recommendation that PR be substituted by another scheme.

In general, I think the situation in BG is still tolerable. It merits close watching, however, and I will continue to keep an eye out.

Telegram from the Consulate General in British Guiana to the Department of State, Georgetown, June 27, 1964.

Premier Jagan called me to his office late afternoon June 26 and talked for over an hour along the following lines. For the first time he is seriously worried about what is happening in BG and where it is going. Several years ago, he thought BG had a bright future; there was much waiting to be done in the way of economic development and possibility to help solve problems outside BG. For example, Jamaica, Barbados and Trinidad were all facing pressing economic problems resulting partly from exploding populations. They were trying to solve this by some industrialization but would never be able to keep up. In fact, all these places were just barely keeping the lid on. (He apologized at this point for digressing.)

Now in British Guiana there was this deplorable violence, senseless retaliation, and there seemed no end in sight. A few days ago he had to take his daughter out of school in Georgetown because of harassment by classmates. Several times he asked somewhat rhetorically "what can be done?" I asked if he were satisfied that he and the two opposition leaders had done everything that was within their power, individually as well as collectively, to stop the violence. He said he thought so but that everybody could not be controlled. He said he wanted this to be a very frank discussion. I asked him if he believed people in Mazaruni had anything to do with violence. He quickly replied that he did not think so but there was this theory of a plan. He said he wished to talk about solutions.

He said as I knew he had been seeking a coalition but his efforts had come to nothing. In the past few days he had been talking with the Governor about such a possibility and now he wished to talk with me. As long as the U.S. was opposed to having PPP in coalition or in government at all, Mr. Burnham would refuse. During coalition negotiations with Mr. Burnham when Ghanaian delegation was here, Dr. Jagan had made concession after concession, including parity in cabinet, but Mr. Burnham always had another demand. This experience and subsequent ones simply illustrate that Mr. Burnham will not go against the wishes of the U.S.

He had thought many times about what caused his relations with the U.S. to "go sour." He still did not know specifically how this happened. He used to go annually from 1957 to 1961 to the U.S. and personal relations were very good. In 1961 he had talks with President Kennedy, Chester Bowles, Schlesinger, and other top officials. They had probed him very deeply and he had every reason to believe that he had passed the test. He had been quite frank with them about his socialist views. Generally speaking he was inclined to think there were two reasons for the deterioration: opposition leaders in BG had effectively spread word in the U.S. that he was Communist and secondly, there had been U.S. trouble with Cuba. These two elements, in interacting ways, had given the impression that he was a potential menace to the U.S. This was a myth but was now a fact of life in the U.S. which he must recognize. In actual fact, he said, the U.S. need have no concern on this score.

Recently he had talked with various elements in Georgetown including Pres. Chamber of Commerce, businessmen, Catholic Church, etc. about possible solutions to the BG problem. Several had told him that he and the PPP were Communist, that there was fear of regimentation, exclusion of private enterprise, and, if independent, of invitation by him to Soviets and Cubans to come in. He told them in essence that his record belied any danger to private enterprise. He had publicly pledged to keep his hands-off sugar and bauxite industries, and as for regimentation, there could be ironclad guarantees in the constitution and he was not fool enough to try to tear up the constitution with opposition being so strong in BG. As for Soviets and Cubans, he was prepared to have a treaty of neutrality, e.g., along Austrian lines. If the U.S. wanted, it could have the right to intervene. This was in fact unnecessary because he realized the U.S. would intervene in any event if its security were threatened. Some businessmen had mentioned BG might be another Zanzibar, but he realized BG is in the same hemisphere as the U.S. and events which take place in Africa would not be permitted to take place here.

Dr. Jagan said in final analysis only three courses were possible in BG: coalition, civil war and partition. He thought the coalition was dependent on the U.S. He thought partition was no solution and recalled difficulties and suffering which ensued when India was partitioned. Economically partition would not make sense, but BG already is drifting toward partition. (I agreed that partition would not represent progress.) He could see no end to violence without a coalition. Uncontrollable groups were now operating. I asked whether when he said coalition, he meant all three parties. He said no, he meant PPP/PNC because their objectives were more similar and, in any event, there should be an opposition party. I asked whether he had in mind a coalition now before the election or after or both. He did not see much value in the coalition before the election, since ministers would just be settling into their jobs "when the dog fight of elections would start in October or November," but he was willing to consider it. He was more interested in an agreement for coalition after elections. While he much preferred postponement of elections to give time to work out problems, he was willing to consider acceptance of no postponement. He added that the PPP had not yet decided whether to contest those elections.

He asked where the U.S. stood and what my views were. I told him that the U.S. was assuming that the course of events would be determined by elections in implementation of Colonial Secretary's decisions and that after the elections we would presumably know what government we would be dealing with. In the meantime, pending basic political decisions by the electorate, we were in effect simply waiting. I indicated incidentally that he placed far too much weight on the view that Mr. Burnham acted on the basis of what he thought the U.S. wanted. In my experience, politicians of all kinds were guided primarily, if not entirely, by what they thought would get votes and how they would fare at polls. I suggested that what happens in BG is for parties here to decide and matters of coalition or no coalition were not matters for the U.S. to determine but could and undoubtedly would be decided by political leaders here. I mentioned that if he wished I would report his views exactly insofar as possible as presented to me. He was extremely pleased. I cautioned however that there would not necessarily be any response but that channels of communication were open and I would faithfully report his views at any time.

Comment: Dr. Jagan gave a controlled performance. He was purposely calm, reasonable, most courteous, and earnest. Only sign of tension was slight shaking of hands at times; otherwise he seemed relaxed. It is obvious that he would give almost anything to obtain U.S. support and will leap at any possibility of favorable response. We can probably expect some more peace feelers.

Memorandum for the Record, Washington, June 30, 1964.

Mr. Tyler; Mr. Cobb; Mr. Helms; [2 *names not declassified*]; Mr. McGeorge Bundy; Mr. Chase. The meeting was called at Mr. Tyler's request, primarily to discuss recent messages about the situation in BG.

Dr. Jagan's coalition proposal

The groups agreed with the Consulate General's assessment that we should steer clear of a coalition government. We are on the right track and should press ahead towards the elections. If necessary, we should stiffen up Governor Luyt who has given some indications that he may be weakening on the coalition issue - *i.e.* the Governor is very concerned about the security situation, and may feel that a coalition will reduce the terrorism.

Dr. Jagan's emissary to the US

While a dialogue with Dr. Jagan might conceivably cool down the BG security problem, it was decided that we should not accept a visit from a Dr. Jagan emissary. We would be able to get no meaningful concessions from Dr. Jagan and the fact that we talked to a Dr. Jagan emissary would probably help Dr. Jagan's cause. Moreover, it would be difficult to keep a dialogue going, for purposes of cooling down the security situation, since we would have very little to say to Dr. Jagan.

A telegram to London, July 2, reported that Dr. Jagan wished to send Attorney General Ramsahoye to Washington to discuss the British Guiana problem with Department officers. The Department requested that the Colonial Office have the Governor decline to transmit Dr. Jagan's request.

UN trusteeship

The group discussed Eric Williams' proposal that BG be made a UN trusteeship for five years. The group did not think this was a good idea since at best it would only delay a bad situation, and at worst might make the Communist menace even tougher to control.

The group agreed on the following actions:

First, the State [*less than 1 line of source text not declassified*] would cable Georgetown and tell our people that we agree with their assessment and are against a coalition and emissary.

Second, the State will tell Ambassador Bruce to talk to the British about the BG situation. Bruce will try to get the British to apply whatever force is necessary to control the security situation in BG.

Third, at a somewhat lower level, the U.S. Government and

HMG will get together in the near future to compare notes and ensure that we are still on the same wavelength.

An undated telegram to Georgetown advised "we do not believe coalition talk should be encouraged" and "we have no intention of receiving any envoy from British Guiana for we do not wish to give Dr. Jagan any encouragement." It also stated that Dr. Jagan should be advised that the U.S. Government was in no position to direct Mr. Burnham to accept or reject a coalition and that any question of an envoy should be taken up with the Governor, the official responsible for external affairs.

In an undated telegram to London for Ambassador Bruce, Tyler requested that Bruce inform the Colonial Office that "we are anxious that every effort is made to hold elections in November under proportional representation as planned," that additional UK forces be sent to British Guiana, and that all possible steps be taken to put down further violence there. A telegram from London to Tyler, July 2, reported that the Colonial Secretary, Duncan Sandys, responded that HMG intended to go forward with the elections as planned, was most reluctant to send more troops to British Guiana, and had reached no conclusion about the possibility of a coalition, but would consult with the United States before doing so.

Memorandum from the Deputy Director for Plans of the Central Intelligence Agency (Helms) to the President's Special Assistant for National Security Affairs (Bundy), Washington, July 17, 1964.

The US/UK talks on British Guiana on July 16 chaired by Sir Hilton Poynton, Permanent Undersecretary of the Colonial Office, produced basic agreement on an assessment of the security situation, electoral prospects, and the need to proceed on course with elections in late November or early December. There was agreement on both sides that, although results might be close, registration figures indicated that Premier Jagan, at best, could get no more than 48 percent and probably would not get more than 46 per cent of the vote. This calculation did not presume that an alternative East Indian party would have any strength, and both sides agreed every effort should be made to keep them from falling by the wayside.

In a July 11 memorandum to Ball, Tyler reported that he and Shullaw intended "to discuss tactics" with the British and that "our objective continues to be the holding of elections later this year under a system of proportional representation which hopefully will result in the formation of a new Government replacing the Dr. Jagan regime." Tyler added that the threat to this objective "arises from the deteriorating security situation and from Dr. Jagan's efforts to exploit a situation for which he and his followers are primarily responsible, so as to secure a postponement of the elections."

The British maintained that the principal threat to elections comes from the deteriorating security situation. They suggested that even with one division peace and order could not be guaranteed. The situation in Georgetown is particularly critical in that violence there could force the postponement of elections. The British urged that Mr. Forbes Burnham, leader of the People's National Congress, be counselled to exercise all possible restraint on his supporters in Georgetown. They noted that the London papers played up the killing of Indian children, omitting African deaths and arson.

The British said the Governor had suggested he be authorized to try to obtain a PNC/People's Progressive Party coalition as a means of reducing tension in the pre-electoral period. They acknowledged that assurances of success were limited, but thought that failure might be attributed to Dr.

Jagan served to discredit him. We explained the bases of our opposition and found that the British did not take issue with them.

On the assumption a non-Jagan government could be formed, we said we would be prepared to extend the same financial assistance we agreed to last October. The British suggested the formation of a US/UK/Canada joint development commission to work out a long-term plan. We made it clear that US aid was predicated on Dr. Jagan is not included in the post-election government.

When the British inquired what policy might be should Dr. Jagan win, we reiterated that such a situation would be politically intolerable in the United States.

On the question of the envoy to the United States the British said they could not oppose if Dr. Jagan came in a private capacity and expressed hope he would be received. We said we had made no plans to receive him or any other emissary and hoped the situation would not arise.

The question of possible steps to assist in the security problem was discussed at length and the British agreed to explore with the Governor, who will be recalled for consultation soon:

(a) The possibility of establishing under the emergency regulations communal peace committees, seeking to obtain the public support of Dr. Jagan and Mr. Burnham for the same.
(b) Announcing the date of elections at this time as an indication of their firmness of intention to proceed.
(c) The formation of a national government in which all three parties would participate.
(d) Both sides agreed that little leverage existed to force Dr. Jagan to cooperate in the elections since he had everything to lose and nothing to gain.

"Bombing of Freedom House and the Guyana Import/Export, Ltd., During a Meeting of the Three Political Leaders," Central Intelligence Agency, Intelligence Information Cable, July 18, 1964.

This intelligence memo describes the reactions of the three national leaders of British Guiana, Dr. Jagan, Mr. Burnham, and Mr. D'Aguiar, to a series of bombings that occurred as the three men were gathered to discuss the country's growing troubles. The bombings took place at Freedom House, the headquarters for the People's Progressive Party, and at the Guyana Import/Export, Ltd. Dr. Jagan "turned white and became incoherent and extremely nervous when told that Gimpex and Freedom House had been bombed." D'Aguiar seemed to want to exploit the situation as he "extended his sympathy, but told Dr. Jagan that this was all the more reason to halt the violence and urged Dr. Jagan to act on the recommendations he and Mr. Burnham had been making." Mr. Burnham "jocularly suggested that Mr. D'Aguiar's business had been destroyed." The CIA speculated that the bombing was of the PPP's own making, given that "the timing of the blasts while the meeting was in progress suggested that it might have been a plot of the PPP, especially since Dr. Jagan had initiated the meeting and the PPP knew exactly what time it was taking place."

Memorandum for the Record. Washington, July 27, 1964.

William Tyler, Harold Shullaw, William Cobb, Richard Helms, [name not declassified], McGeorge Bundy, Peter Jessup, Gordon Chase.

The meeting was called to discuss the attached cable from

Georgetown. The cable reported Consul General Carlson's apprehension about telling Dr. Jagan we are not ready to receive an envoy. The group agreed that a visit to the U.S. by a Dr. Jagan emissary would be a bad thing. At worst, such a visit would be interpreted to mean that the U.S. supports Dr. Jagan; at best it would be interpreted as a sign that we can live with him. The visit would hurt the opposition parties in BG and would not help us domestically.

The group then discussed whether it would be advisable to send a lower-level official down to BG to talk to Dr. Jagan as well as to the two opposition leaders. The advantages of this would be that we would appear reasonable, "willing to listen", and that it might allow us to stall for time and reduce the rate of violence in the months between now and the BG elections. The main disadvantage is that any talks with Dr. Jagan will probably be misinterpreted by the uncommitted voters in BG - which number about 10%; such talks might indicate to these voters that "perhaps the U.S. does not think Cheddi is so bad."

The group agreed that Dr. Jagan's request to send an envoy to the U.S. should be turned down and that we should not offer to send someone down to BG. However, we should use gentler wording than the flat assertion now under consideration, *i.e.* "This proposal has been informally discussed with the Americans and they see no useful purpose for it. Therefore, it would be better if the proposal were dropped." Instead, a more flexible position should be adopted which offers a *quid pro quo* - *i.e.* when the violence stops, we will reconsider the proposal. The group decided that a cable should be drafted in this sense and sent to London, /3/ with an information copy to Georgetown.

An attached undated telegram to London requested the Embassy to ask the Colonial Office to modify its instructions to the Governor to the following:

This proposal has been informally discussed with the Americans who see no useful purpose in it at this time. The Americans are obviously influenced in this point of view by the continuing pattern of violence in British Guiana and widespread belief in British Guiana, as elsewhere, that PPP as governing party bears heavy responsibility for this state of affairs. Their subsequent attitude toward the question of emissary naturally would be influenced by the course of events in British Guiana.

According to an August 1 telegram from Carlson to Shullaw, the Governor delivered the message to Dr. Jagan on July 30, but omitted the part suggesting that the PPP was responsible for the violence. Dr. Jagan made no objection, observing that "it means then that if things stay quiet the emissary will be received" to which the Governor responded that he could not speculate beyond the wording of the message. (file name not declassified).

"British Guiana Meeting, July 27, 1964," White House, National Security Council Memorandum for the Record, with attached telegram from Consul General Carlson re envoy from British Guiana, July 29, 1964.

Consul General Carlson warned of his "apprehension about telling Dr. Cheddi Jagan we are not ready to receive an envoy." Carlson stresses that officials should be aware of the potential costs of revealing that Dr. Jagan's "last faint hope of peace ... is dashed by the governor's message to the effect that the U.S. will not even listen." Carlson expects Dr. Jagan's response will be: "The U.S. will become principal villain" and violence against U.S. targets could follow. The envoy advises that the "question therefore arises whether any consideration should be given to keeping Dr. Jagan slightly on hook." The participants at the staff meeting, including Helms, Bundy, Chase, and Jessup largely disagree with Carlson's recommendations, concluding that, "a visit to the U.S. by a Dr. Jagan emissary would be a bad thing." The group believed that "[a]t worst, such a visit would be interpreted to mean that the U.S. supports Dr. Cheddi Jagan; at best it would be interpreted as a sign that we can live with him. The visit would hurt the opposition parties in BG and would not help us domestically."

Bundy and Helms also reject a proposal to send a lower-level official to British Guiana because uncommitted voters-about 10 percent of the electorate-might incorrectly presume that, "perhaps the U.S. does not think Cheddi is so bad." Taking some of Carlson's warnings into consideration, the group recommends that the U.S. should tone down its language when responding to Dr. Jagan: "Instead, a more flexible position should be adopted which offers a quid pro quo *i.e.* when the violence stops, we will reconsider the proposal."

Action Memorandum from the Assistant Secretary of State for European Affairs (Tyler) to Secretary of State Rusk, Washington, July 31, 1964.

Duncan Sandys has written to you stating that he believes order and security in British Guiana can only be restored through an all-party coalition government. He asks for our support in bringing about such a coalition. The attached July 30 message from Sandys stated that the British were not certain they would be able to restrain racial violence sufficiently to hold elections and they were satisfied that the only method of restoring order and security was to bring about a temporary all-Party coalition to bridge the period to the elections.

During my talks in London with British officials July 16 and 17, I outlined the reasons why we thought a pre-election coalition of Dr. Jagan's party and the two opposition parties was of doubtful value so far as security is concerned and dangerous from the point of view of our political objectives in British Guiana. The British officials with whom we talked were unable to make a convincing case for the coalition. Despite this, Sandys has come down on the side of a coalition. I continue to believe this is an unwise and unnecessary move.

Recommendation

That you approve the attached message to Sandys which reiterates our doubts about a coalition and asks for further consideration before the Governor is given instructions to try to bring one about.

Message from Secretary of State Rusk to the British Colonial Secretary (Sandys), Washington, August 4, 1964.

I fully appreciate your concern at continuing violence in British Guiana and your desire to find some way of preventing a situation developing which could necessitate postponement of the elections you intend holding in the colony later this year. I also sympathize with your capable and courageous Governor in his efforts to carry out his responsibilities under such trying conditions. In the circumstances I am somewhat hesitant to raise again the doubts and misgivings about a pre-election coalition which we expressed to your people at the recent London talks. Since, however, we are in complete agreement on the constructive objectives we are pursuing in British Guiana, I have no hesitation in doing so.

In the first place we seriously doubt that Dr. Jagan, who has been using violence for political purposes, would be likely to forgo such tactics if a coalition were formed. Apart from that consideration there is, in our opinion, the very real possibility that a pre-election coalition would adversely affect the electoral prospects of the PNC and the UF by confusing the supporters of those two parties. A coalition of the PPP and PNC excluding the UF would endanger the hope for a post-election PNC–UF coalition which at the moment is the only possibility of replacing the Dr. Jagan Government. In short, we share your view of the importance of holding the elections later this year but are concerned that nothing be done in the pre-election period in the quest for order and security which would jeopardize the currently hopeful electoral results.

Since the London talks on July 16 and 17, there have been several developments in British Guiana which may be relevant. The strike of the sugar workers ended in what amounted to a defeat for Dr. Jagan. Whether this will result in any immediate improvement in the security situation, of course, remains to be seen. I also understand that Dr. Jagan has broken off his "unity" talks with Mr. Burnham and D'Aguiar. In the course of those talks he clearly indicated that the coalition he seeks has as its objective postponement of the elections. He showed no interest in a coalition limited to a brief pre-election period but insisted on a five-year coalition.

I would be most grateful if you would give further consideration to these very real concerns on our part about the dangers of such a course of action.

Warm regards,
Dean Rusk

In a personal message to Rusk, attached to an August 17 covering note from the British Embassy, Sandys' deputy, Sir Hilton Poynton, reported that the risk of violence was diminished and the case for a temporary coalition was therefore less strong. Poynton stated that he was sure that Sandys would agree, upon his return from holiday, that the idea should not be pursued under these circumstances. If, however, violence was to set in again at the pitch it reached in June and July, a temporary coalition might be reconsidered.

Memorandum for the Record, Washington, September 11, 1964.

Messrs. William Tyler; Harold Shullaw; Delmar Carlson; William Cobb; [name not declassified]; McGeorge Bundy; Gordon Chase. The meeting was called so that Consul General Carlson could brief the group about the current situation in BG.

(1) Election Prospects - Mr. Carlson said that the election prospects are good. The Justice Party seems to be doing surprisingly well and everyone, including Dr. Jagan, seems to think that the anti-PPP forces will win. At the same time, the PPP is likely to get a plurality. The group agreed that something would have to be done if the PPP did win. The general feeling was that, despite his conciliatory noises, Dr. Jagan is the same rehabilitated bad egg he has always been; he has not really been educated by the US/Cuban experience.

(2) Security Situation - Mr. Carlson said that the security situation is fairly good these days. He added that this is the thing to watch before and after the elections.

If the security situation gets very bad before elections, the Governor will be inclined to push for a PPP/PNC coalition. Assuming Mr. Burnham wins the election, a deteriorating and uncontrollable security situation could conceivably push Mr. Burnham and the Governor towards accepting the formation of a PPP/PNC coalition.

(3) Mr. Burnham - Mr. Carlson made these points relating to Mr. Burnham: First, while Mr. Burnham is now getting on very well with the leaders of other opposition parties, we should not expect this to last forever. The anti-PPP forces are bound to have plenty of problems with one another in the future. Second, Mr. Carlson noted that Mr. Burnham and the British do not get along. The Governor does not like Mr. Burnham, who twists the lion's tail whenever he can. We can expect to see a growing British/Mr. Burnham problem. Third, Mr. Carlson said that while he is trying to build a relationship with Mr. Burnham, it is tough to do so. Mr. Burnham, a racist and probably anti-white, remembers slights and repays them; at the same time, he takes advantage of people who treat him softly. A recent frank exchange between Carlson and Mr. Burnham, however, proved at least partly satisfactory. Mr. Burnham said that if he gets into power, he will not recognize the USSR and that he will have nothing to do with Cuba so long as he can find other people to buy British Guiana's rice.

(4) Other - Mr. Carlson reported that Mr. Burnham had said that it would be helpful if, during his campaign, he could promise the voters something concrete (*e.g.* the East-West road and the airport terminal). The group agreed that we should go along with Mr.

Burnham on this. The group discussed briefly the future of Atkinson Field. Mr. Tyler agreed to call DOD's John McNaughton to get a reading on how important the facility is to us.

In a May 12, 1965, memorandum to Howard Meyers, Director of Operations for the Office of Politico-Military Affairs (G/PM), Shullaw reported that the Government of British Guiana wanted to resolve the status of Atkinson Field, and asked again for a reading from the Department of Defense regarding its retention. Shullaw stated that Carlson had reported that if the United States was prepared to agree to release the field unconditionally, the Government of British Guiana in return would probably be willing to agree to unrestricted authorization for the United States to use the field whenever it wished.

Telegram from the Assistant Secretary of State for European and Canadian Affairs (Tyler) to the Ambassador to the United Kingdom (Bruce), Washington, September 14, 1964.

In our view, following considerations argue for desirability of expediting preparations for elections and setting election date as early in November as feasible with appropriate announcement earliest:

(1) Possible complicity of Mr. Burnham in Georgetown violence and conceivably his indictment (*which the Governor is considering*).

(2) Likelihood of attempts by Jaganites and others to use such prospects to delay elections and seek alternative courses of action.

(3) Uncertainty of opposition groups over the date of election.

(4) Adverse effect of any late date on the present momentum of opposition parties. FYI: Our primary aim with above is to avoid substantial interval when efforts might be made toy with Sandys' decision in some fashion, especially if Mr. Burnham under indictment for conspiracy commit murder.

Telegram from the Consulate General in British Guiana to the Department of State, Georgetown, October 3, 1964.

[*Less than 1 line of source text not declassified*] Pass following message from Carlson to Shullaw.

In discussions with Mr. Burnham at his initiative early this week I found him relaxed and confident. He apparently believes elections are largely a matter of getting votes out and having organized to do so along lines of the U.S. party he foresees no particular problem. Every week or so he plans to spend a few days in the countryside talking to small groups and has already done so in African pockets of Corentyne. He preferred this method rather than mass meetings in order to minimize the problem of security. He planned no concentrated campaign with mass meetings until the last 3–4 weeks before the December 7 election. His party manifesto will appear at the start of that phase of the campaign. In the meantime he plans to issue separate pamphlets about unemployment, education, roads, and rice.

Burnham was especially interested in any ammunition we could provide to counter Dr. Jagan's exploitation of the theme that Cuban rice market depends on his continuation in office.

I told him we were aware of this problem and would see what we could develop.

Mr. Burnham was also much interested in what specifics he could promise in the way of projects. I suggested (1) improvement of East Coast road; (2) maintenance of seawall; (3) airport improvements, including new terminal building; (4) Berbice Bar cut. Re: sea wall I pointed out he could claim the regime jeopardized lives and property by failure to do maintenance work over the last few years. He could call attention to the break in wall and flooding near Buxton early this year. He picked this up with alacrity. He also apparently liked Berbice Bar cut (which incidentally may improve his relations with New Amsterdam PNC boss Kendall who is not always enthusiastic about Mr. Burnham). He was all for the East Coast road, but also suggested desirability improving the road from New Amsterdam to Skeldon in Corentyne, saying the need was especially great because not only is the road in miserable condition but also there is no railroad. He also wanted Atkinson–Mackenzie road (estimated total cost U.S. $8 million) and mentioned desirability developing road to Potaro and eventually on to Brazil. He thought this road would open up agricultural areas. Although he sought my immediate approval to road in Corentyne and Atkinson/Mackenzie road,

I made clear I was not in position to go beyond East Coast road without further authorization. He asked me to look particularly into possible authorization of Corentyne road. He has in mind after very brief respite following the election to announce a full-scale program. He would like during four-year term to complete as many short-range projects as possible and to have made sufficient start on a number of long-range projects that the public can clearly see what future portends from Mr. Burnham administration. Shortly after announcing his program he apparently wishes to make tour abroad, not only for purposes of prestige or recognition but also to collect commitments for financial or economic assistance. He did not specify what countries he has in mind but it will undoubtedly include Germany and the U.S. He mentioned that Dr. Jagan had apparently been given much attention when he visited Washington in 1961. I have little doubt that Mr. Burnham will expect to be received by the President and that he is already leading up to this suggestion.

Comment: It would be politically desirable for Mr. Burnham to advocate Corentyne road since it would so clearly benefit Indian community as well as have immediate impact as an adjunct of East Coast road. This road passes through rice and sugar areas from New Amsterdam to Skeldon and is 48 miles long. In 1949–1953 this road was rebuilt and paved reportedly at a cost of about U.S. $3 million, but because of faulty engineering and construction it deteriorated almost completely after 4 years. Since then it has been occasionally patched. It is estimated that rehabilitation and paving with asphalt could be done for about U.S. $1.5 million. It is suggested that the Department explore the feasibility of permitting me to inform Mr. Burnham Corentyne road may also be improved.

The Department may wish to consider whether to touch base with the Colonial Office to obtain their concurrence to substitute Corentyne road for some other project or projects of equivalent value now on U.S. /U.K. agreed list. (Actually, this road could be considered part of the East Coast road.) Mr. Burnham will doubtlessly be raising matters of both Corentyne and possibly Atkinson–Mackenzie road with me shortly in order to start preparing pamphlets on roads. Therefore, sooner we can decide whether we bless Corentyne road at least in principle the better.

In an unnumbered telegram to Carlson dated October 7, Shullaw reported that Mr. Burnham could be assured that the United States would assist British Guiana in road improvement projects and that this would include East Coast roads at least as far as Skelton. Regarding the Atkinson–McKenzie road, Shullaw said that "assurances must be hedged at this time," due to the question of how best to finance all the road projects.

Backchannel Message from the Department of State to the Embassy in the United Kingdom, Washington, October 14, 1964.

There follows a paper on our interest in British Guiana which you may draw on in talking with Harold Wilson, should he become Prime Minister. Wilson will undoubtedly have.

In an October 13 memorandum to Bundy, Chase stated that this cable was redrafted to delete mention of a possible Johnson/Wilson telephone call and instead stressed the need for Bruce to talk personally to Wilson, who was "sensitive to the US/UK Alliance." A notation in Bundy's handwriting on the memorandum reads "OK, MB."

A very tight schedule and countless other problems but we believe it would be best to go straight to him personally on this subject rather than to his Colonial Affairs Minister. So far as we can tell developments in BG are in accordance with our policy objectives and we hope Wilson will agree to continue along the charted course.

Talking paper for Ambassador Bruce

(May be left with Mr. Wilson should he request it)

Since August 1961 the problems of British Guiana as it approaches independence have been discussed at the highest levels of our two governments with a view to seeking ways whereby the colony may obtain independence without posing a threat to the security of its neighbors in the Western Hemisphere. As you know, Latin America is an area of the greatest importance to us. The establishment of an independent government in British Guiana under leadership which has been markedly receptive to communist ideas and vulnerable to communist subversion would create an intolerable situation for the United States and other countries in the Hemisphere. Previous British Governments have shown an understanding of this situation [*1 line of source text not declassified*] affording a full opportunity for the United States to express its views. [*2 1/2 lines of source text not declassified*] The President hopes you will share with him the conviction that it should continue along present lines.

It is the opinion of the United States Government that the proposed elections in British Guiana under Proportional Representation, despite the difficulties entailed, provide a democratic means through which the aspirations of all the people and races of British Guiana can be faithfully reflected. We believe that if the electorate participates fully in the elections the results can provide a basis for the formation of a representative government in which the possibility of communist infiltration will be significantly reduced. It is our intention to do what we can to assist a non-communist government in British Guiana so that the country at the earliest practicable date may attain independence with economic and social stability and have the prospect of playing a useful role in the hemisphere and in the community of free nations.

Bruce did not get an opportunity to talk to Wilson personally (the British Labor Party won the general parliamentary elections of October 15 and Harold Wilson, as party leader, became Prime Minister) and transmitted this message, but did give it to Patrick Gordon Walker, the new Labor Foreign Secretary.

A few miscellaneous items on British Guiana, Memorandum from Gordon Chase of the National Security Council Staff to the President's Special Assistant for National Security Affairs (Bundy), Washington, October 17, 1964.

(1) The election prospects still look good. One of the things we are concentrating on is ensuring that the opposition parties turn out to vote on Election Day; to this end the CIA, in a deniable and discreet way, is providing financial incentives to party workers who are charged with the responsibility of getting out the vote. Another thing worth concentrating on is the job of ensuring that intimidation, threats, and violence do not hamper the conduct of the BG elections; attached is a cable from Carlson which describes British planning in this area.

(2) With respect to the impact on the BG situation of the Labor victory, State feels that the election was sufficiently close so that Labor will be chary of tampering with the present course of events in BG. While this takes some of the edge off our worry, you may still want to talk about BG with Lord Harlech the next time you see him.

(3) We are going ahead with our contingency planning for a likely Mr. Burnham victory. In this regard, Harry Yoe, the AID man working on BG, will make a quiet trip to BG between November 4 and November 12 to evaluate projects which we may want to initiate immediately after the BG elections.

Two notations in Bundy's handwriting relating to this paragraph appear on the memorandum: one reads "Bruce and Walker talked recently," and the other reads "I did it. He assures me the new Govt. will know of our interest."

From Ambassador Bruce to Secretary Rusk. Backchannel Message from the Embassy in the United Kingdom to the Department of State, London, October 19, 1964.

Have had no opportunity to deliver a message as instructed to Harold Wilson, if elected, on British Guiana. I did, however, take the subject up with Gordon Walker this morning, who will shortly discuss it with the Prime Minister. Foreign Secretary said the present HMG had never approved a policy predecessor on BG. They recognized, however, USG's particular interest in safeguarding BG against Communist takeover. He will be prepared to give an answer during the Washington trip. [1 paragraph (11/2 lines of source text) not declassified].

(1) I think HMG will permit proposed December elections under proportional representation to take place. [1 line of source text not declassified].
(2) Appointment of Greenwood as Colonial Secretary bodes no good for us later on in this affair. Nevertheless, I believe the Prime Minister will keep him under strict control.

Memorandum from the Assistant Secretary of State for European Affairs (Tyler) to Secretary of State Rusk, Washington, October 20, 1964.

We have just learned that Dr. Jagan is flying to London on October 21 to urge the British to postpone the elections scheduled for December 7 in British Guiana. We also have a message from Ambassador Bruce who has taken up British Guiana with Patrick Gordon Walker, who says he will discuss it promptly with the Prime Minister. Gordon Walker says he will be prepared to discuss British Guiana in his forthcoming visit and to give us his Government's position at that time. In view of the fact that we got to Gordon Walker first, we think it unlikely that the British will take any decision regarding postponement without consulting with us.

In an October 20 memorandum to Bundy, Chase reported that, in his *Weekly Gabfest on BG*, that morning with Richard Sampson and William Cobb, the latter had stated that the Labor government was very unlikely to postpone the elections. Our real difficulties are likely to arise after the December 7 elections, since at that time Colonial Minister Tony Greenwood will naturally expect to play an important role in British Guiana developments.

Memorandum from the Director of the Office of British Commonwealth and Northern European Affairs (Shullaw) to the Assistant Secretary of State for European Affairs (Tyler), Washington, October 27, 1964.

Several weeks after the Anglo/US consultations in July 1964 violence in BG came to a virtual halt with the end of the sugar workers strike, and the beginning of the election campaign. In mid-August a new East Indian party was formed - the Justice Party - and Dr. Jagan announced that the PPP would participate in the elections "under protest."

The campaign is now in full swing with the deposit of electoral lists October 26, and the three major parties, as well as several new parties are active. As the campaign intensifies the likelihood of violence increases but every effort is being made to maintain security. To this end the US has just supplied 20 radio transmitter receivers and 10 jeeps for the police.

Dr. Jagan's actions indicate that he is on the defensive. He is blaming his government's failure to receive assistance on reactionary elements in the U.S. and the U.K., and he maintains that the intense internal dissatisfaction with his administration is attributable solely to outside influences. The most recent estimate from the Colonial office suggests Dr. Jagan would get only 40% of the vote if elections were held today. Last July, we thought he would get from 45% to 48%.

We are preparing to move ahead with an assistance program for a non-Jagan government in BG. The program would consist of road rehabilitation, maintenance of the seawall, making a cut through the Berbice Bar to open up the New Amsterdam area, and construction of a road from Atkinson field to the interior. An AID representative will go to BG November 4 to investigate the degree to which the BG administrative services can be used in implementing the projects.

We must anticipate that if Dr. Jagan loses by a close vote HMG will press us to agree to a Dr. Jagan/Mr. Burnham coalition government after elections. They may argue that only in a PPP/PNC coalition can the major groups in the population be represented; that a government which does not contain the PPP will be under continuing attack designed to keep it from governing effectively; and that an African dominated Mr. Burnham government will seek to intimidate and repress the East Indians.

We believe a PPP/PNC coalition after the elections would only add to BG's problems. It would be politically impossible for the US to assist a government in which Dr. Jagan and his colleagues played a role. Intense personal rivalry between Dr. Jagan and Mr. Burnham would contribute to instability and intensify racial antagonisms. We hope that a coalition government can be formed without the PPP and that it will be genuinely multi-racial. We will use the influence we have in support of such a government.

Telegram 125 from Georgetown, October 26, reported a 2-hour discussion between Carlson and Mr. Burnham on October 23, during which the latter spoke of his thoughts about whom he wanted for the various cabinet positions in his coming government, with United Front and Justice Party leaders slotted for minor positions. Carlson reported that Mr. Burnham's "current thinking somewhat disturbing because may indicate intention to make coalition government unduly PNC dominated with other parties' participation kind of sham," which Carlson said would be "very divisive" and would lead to a Mr. Burnham administration of "one term or less."

Memorandum of Conversation, Washington, October 27, 1964, 10 a.m. Drafted by Shullaw. The meeting was held in Secretary Rusk's office. The memorandum indicates it is an advance copy; no final or approved copy has been found.

PARTICIPANTS:

United States.

The Secretary.
William R. Tyler, *Assistant Secretary for European Affairs.*
J. Harold Shullaw, *Director, EUR/BNA.*

United Kingdom

Patrick Gordon Walker, *Foreign Secretary.*
The Lord Harlech, *British Ambassador.*

Sir Harold Caccia, *Permanent Undersecretary, Foreign Office.*

By way of background the Secretary described the great problem in the Western Hemisphere of ensuring that the long overdue social and economic revolution is carried out democratically and without communist exploitation. He noted that the long tradition of the Monroe Doctrine means the strongest possible feeling in the United States against foreign intervention in this Hemisphere. In the case of Cuba, the two non-negotiable points are the Soviet presence and Cuban interference in the affairs of other Hemisphere countries. Castro has shown no willingness to cease this interference although the Cubans have suffered reverses in the case of Venezuela and the recent election in Chile.

The prospect that the United Kingdom might leave behind an independent British Guiana a second Castro regime would be a major concern to the United States. Dr. Jagan has received aid from Castro and has meddled in Suriname. We cannot take a chance on him [*1 line of source text not declassified*]. Proportional Representation offers the possibility of unseating Dr. Jagan and obviating the need for direct British administration. We are prepared to give substantial assistance to a noncommunist, non-Dr. Jagan government. The Secretary described the British Guiana problem as a gut issue on which we need the help of the British Government. He expressed the hope that the elections in British Guiana would be held as scheduled. [*11/2 lines of source text not declassified*]

In his reply, the Foreign Secretary remarked that a Labor Government could not do less than the Conservatives with respect to trade possibilities with Cuba. He said, however, that he would look into the suggestion made earlier by the Secretary that Britain, as an alternative to trading with Cuba, attempts to improve its trade ties with other Latin American countries. The Secretary said he would send the Foreign Secretary a message on what we thought might be done to strengthen UK relations with the Hemisphere.

With respect to British Guiana, the Foreign Secretary gave the assurance that his Government would proceed with the elections as scheduled. [*2 lines of source text not declassified*] The Foreign Secretary said he had a very unfavorable opinion of Mr. Burnham who is a thoroughly unreliable person. Regardless of the outcome, the election will provide no answer to the problem of racial conflict and therefore there is little prospect of early independence emerging from it.

The previous Government committed itself to an early post-election conference on independence, which in the view of the Labor Government, was not desirable. He thought the preferable course of development would be along the lines of self-government with a Commonwealth Court consisting perhaps of Indians, Nigerians and Canadians to deal with the racial conflict. The actual date for independence could be fuzzed. The Foreign Secretary expressed the hope that even if British Guiana does not obtain early independence, it will nevertheless be possible for the United States to furnish aid. He added that Eric Williams on a recent visit to London had advised strongly against early independence.

The Secretary replied that we would be quite happy to see an indefinite continuation of British authority in British Guiana. Perhaps the Organization of American States might ask the British Government not to grant independence while racial strife continues.

Mr. Tyler added the comment that a Mr. Burnham/Dr. Jagan coalition would make it impossible to get Congressional approval of aid for British Guiana. The Foreign Secretary indicated that he recognized a Mr. Burnham/Dr. Jagan coalition would not work although the British Government could not take a public position to this effect. [*1 paragraph (3 lines) of source text not declassified*]

Dr. Jagan Backchannel, Central Intelligence Agency, Memo from Bruce to Taylor on Greenwood, October 30, 1964.

Dr. Jagan's attempts to have the British government "suspend elections and organize Commonwealth or UN commissions to visit BG to recommend constitutional changes replacing the PR electoral system." Dr. Jagan charged that the British had not lived up to their original commitments. He claimed that the police had "suppressed" reports that the PNC had engaged in terrorism. If he had known, Dr. Jagan asserted, he would have never agreed to join Mr. Burnham in "accepting constitutional solution by Sandys, and he felt that had Sandys or the governor been aware of the nature of these reports, HMG would not have imposed any procedure by which Mr. Burnham and PNC could come to power." Greenberg responded to Dr. Jagan by explaining "it is much too late to change now."

Mr. Burnham pretended to cooperate but dragged his feet with allies. His PNC was also violent. The Police Special Branch had collected evidence on PNC political violence back to 1962. As Home Affairs Minister, the reports would have gone to Mrs. Janet Jagan, so Dr. Jagan's protestations of ignorance in the fall of 1964 rang hollow. A United Force activist even suggested a coup d'état be mounted against Dr. Jagan's government. By the middle of the year, houses were being torched at a rate of five or more a day. More than 2,600 families (15,000 persons) had been forced from their homes. The political season brought nearly two hundred murders and a thousand persons wounded. That was real violence. Dr. Jagan,

Mr. Burnham, and Mr. Peter D'Aguiar were actually conferring one day in August 1964 on tamping down the violence when, down the street, the PPP headquarters and the import export company it ran were bombed, "My God, it's Freedom House!" Dr. Jagan exclaimed.

By the latter part of 1964, Dr. Jagan had offered concessions. The violence was being widely attributed to Afro-Guianese (PNC), and the CIA's Indo-Guianese political party project that they installed. The British continued to worry that Dr. Jagan would win anyway. At the end of July, a high-level U.S. group rejected any visit by a Dr. Jagan emissary. Then, to top it all, in October a British election threw out Douglas-Home's Conservative Party government and installed a Labor cabinet headed by Harold Wilson. Lord Home had been reluctant to play with the CIA in British Guiana; the position of the leftist Laborites was even more in doubt.

Very promptly, Anthony Greenwood, colonial secretary in the new Wilson government, rendered his account of the first Labor meeting with Dr. Jagan to the American embassy in London. The new government shut out Dr. Jagan. Greenwood rejected the Guianese leader's protest; he would never have agreed to the Sandys Plan had he known the extent of Mr. Forbes Burnham's meddling. The British replied that he should have known, and defended the police performance in British Guiana. It was too late to postpone the election or take other action.

Something occurred that froze the Labor government into its position. The *Smithers affair* remains obscure to this day. It concerned remarks from Peter H.B.O. Smithers, parliamentary undersecretary of state at the Foreign Office, which the Wilson government considered having been openly denounced by Colonial Office officials in British Guiana. Smithers was a Conservative Member of Parliament. The Americans considered it important. In Washington, on November 2, the CIA sent a memorandum to the State Department clearly based upon "OPERATIONAL IMMEDIATE" reporting in agency channels. Frank Wisner, London station chief, had been approached by James Fulton, a senior aide to MI-6 director Sir Dick White, with an appeal for Ambassador Bruce to take up the *Smithers affair* with the Foreign Office, taking it out of intelligence channels and putting it into policy ones. Apparently, there was a feeling at MI-6 that British diplomats were more flexible than the Colonial Office on a joint CIA/MI-6 role in British Guiana, while Anthony Greenwood had less political strength in the cabinet than his predecessor. By then, however, the election was just about a month away and it is not clear what a "CIA/MI-6" role could have been.

"British Guiana," Central Intelligence Agency, Memo for J. Harold Shullaw, November 2, 1964.

This memo to the State Department's desk officer for the United Kingdom shows the CIA concerned about how the British were handling the Smithers affair. The agency appears to distrust the British Colonial Office and prefers an intervention by the Foreign Office, at least in part because "the foreign office is more sympathetic towards a coordinated US/UK position and CIA/MI-6 role than are certain persons in the Colonial Office." Despite the inability to recover the content of what Smithers said, this document provides a revelatory glimpse into the depth of CIA concern with British Guiana.

Airgram from the Consulate General in British Guiana to the Department of State, Georgetown, November 5, 1964.

This report is intended to make a matter of record, certain assurances given to me by L.F.S. Burnham, Leader of the People's National Congress, concerning the foreign policy of a Mr. Burnham administration in an independent British Guiana. These assurances (which I conveyed orally during consultation in the Department in September) arose out of a very frank conversation in which I pointed out that while the general trend of Mr. Burnham's thinking was known to us, some important foreign policy aspects were unspecified. In the ensuing discussion and in response to my questions, Mr. Burnham assured me categorically that:

He would not recognize the USSR.

He would not recognize or associate in any way with the Castro regime.

He would cut off all trade with Cuba if asked to do so, provided that the U.S. arranged an equally good market for British Guiana's rice.

He would join the OAS.

In a discussion of some adverse impressions among some parts of the local community about Mr. Burnham, he denied any intention to permit racial considerations to decide policy; to take over the trade union movement, or to establish a dictatorial regime.

Comment: *When Mr. Burnham gave these assurances, he was under the impression that I was being suddenly called to Washington for consultation about the British Guiana situation, including his role here.*

"British Guiana," Central Intelligence Agency, Memo from Richard Helms to McGeorge Bundy, November 18, 1964.

This memo from the CIA deputy director for plans gets straight to the point: "Barring any unforeseen circumstances between now and the elections on December 7 which might adversely affect the situation, a coalition of the opposition parties should win a majority of votes cast." Helms predicted that if Dr. Jagan loses he will "play a wait-and-see game for two to three months in the hope that the PNC/UF/JP coalition will collapse." But if the coalition proves viable and, "if U.S. financial support moves swiftly into British Guiana, [REDACTED] Dr. Jagan may resort to violence in order to prevent Mr. Burnham from governing and to bring about his downfall." Helms ends by explaining that if violence occurs the British have two battalions in British Guiana and two additional ones that could easily be moved into the country.

Prime Minister Dr. Jagan saw his future passed before him. The CIA field report on November 6, observed that he was very much concerned about the prospects for his People's Popular Party. Dr. Jagan had no desire to form a coalition government with Mr. Burnham and the People's National Congress.

Others were looking at the prospects too. The CIA did a number of assessments of the election's likely outcome. In his stream of reports to the White House, Richard Helms took a guardedly optimistic view. The CIA foresaw that Dr. Jagan's and Mr. Burnham's parties would each take about 40 percent of the vote and D'Aguiar's United Force would carry about 15 percent. The CIA's false-flag East Indian group, the Justice Party, would take about 5 percent.

The big day was December 7, 1964. The Americans thought it started well but then became more and more anxious. The election can usefully be viewed through the eyes of Gordon Chase, who was the NSC staff officer for intelligence activities. On the day, Chase reported very high turnout, perhaps even more than 90 percent, commenting "this is a good thing, assuming everybody votes the way we think." By the next day the outlook was not quite so rosy: "Cheddi is doing much better than expected," and "this promises to be a real cliff hanger". Suddenly, the odds that a potential Mr. Burnham coalition might have a majority of even one seat were judged no better than 6 to 5. On December 8, it finally looked like a defeat for Dr. Jagan and his PPP, and so it turned out to be.

"British Guiana - Election," White House, National Security Council, Memo from Gordon Chase to McGeorge Bundy, December 7, 1964.

This memo updates the national security adviser on preliminary assessments of the elections in British Guiana. Gordon Chase explains that voter turnout appears to be higher than 90 percent, which "is a good thing." Chase then explains that the "estimate, before the polls opened," was that the PPP would get 22 seats; the PNC, 19; the UF, 9; the Justice Party, 2; and another party, one. For Washington this would be a delightful outcome. "For no particular reason, I feel in my bones that the margin of victory won't be this large; hopefully, I'm wrong."

Memorandum of Conversation, Washington, December 7, 1964, 1:10 p.m. Drafted by Tyler and approved in the White House on December 16. The meeting was held in the Cabinet Room at the White House.

PARTICIPANTS:

United States

The President.
Secretary Rusk.
Secretary McNamara.
Ambassador David Bruce.
Mr. George Ball.
Mr. McGeorge Bundy.
Mr. William R. Tyler.

United Kingdom

Prime Minister Wilson.
Patrick Gordon Walker, *Foreign Secretary.*
Denis Healey, *Secretary of State for Defense.*
Lord Harlech, *British Ambassador.*
Sir Harold Caccia, *Permanent Undersecretary of State.*
Sir Burke Trend, *Secretary to the Cabinet.*
Mr. D. J. Mitchell, *Private Secretary to the Prime Minister.*

The President and Prime Minister Wilson joined the group at about 1:10 p.m. The President said that he had had a very enjoyable meeting with the Prime Minister, and that both of them had discussed how to get re-elected. Mr. Wilson said that he had very much enjoyed their talk which had related to principles, objectives and political background. They had not tried to get into any arguments for or against any particular solutions. The President said that he and the Prime Minister had whole-heartedly agreed that our objectives and hopes stand upon having a proper understanding of each other. It was better to talk across the table than in the columns of newspapers. He had told Wilson that "a burned child dreads fire," and that he didn't intend to pressure Mr. Wilson, and he felt sure that Mr. Wilson did not intend to pressure him.

The President went on to say that he thought it would be useful for our two governments to continue to "reason together," as recommended in Isaiah. He felt that this meeting was a continuation of previous meetings which would permit both sides to explore their common problems and discuss them. Nothing would emerge from this meeting that was black on white or of a nature to make other countries feel that a blueprint of action had been developed by our two governments. We were not undertaking to provide answers to our problems at this meeting. The President said that he had to be very careful because of what the press tended to write.

The Secretary reported to the President very briefly on the discussions at Ministerial level which had been held while the two principals were talking alone that morning. It had been decided that we would discuss defense questions this afternoon, also Southeast Asia, Southwest Africa, and other matters. Mr. Wilson said that he wanted to talk to the President about British Guiana. He had told Dr. Jagan that whoever wins in BG, the UK would not grant BG independence as there would be a bloodbath if it did so. He thought that if both Mr. Burnham and Dr. Jagan (the latter of whom he described as a naive Trotskyite) were out of BG it would be so much the better. He didn't think a government could be entrusted to either of them and the UK rather felt that the U.S. placed excessive trust in Mr. Burnham who was just as bad in his own way as Dr.

Jagan was in his. Gordon Walker interjected, "they are both horrors." Mr. Wilson said that it would be necessary to arrange for a Canadian or an Australian distinguished judicial figure to go down to British Guiana in order to lay the groundwork for the organization of the judiciary, eventually.

A December 7 memorandum of conversation reported Rusk's discussion with Foreign Secretary Walker that morning concerning British Guiana. Walker said that HMG would not "go toward independence in the foreseeable future. Perhaps some steps toward increasing self-government could be devised." The Foreign Minister added that he thought that the U.S. Government "had an excessively favorable estimate of Mr. Burnham."

In a December 6 memorandum to the President, Ball urged Johnson "to demonstrate your personal interest" in British Guiana to Wilson by emphasizing that the United States attached great importance to a satisfactory outcome, that independence should not be granted prematurely, that the United States could not provide assistance to any government which included Dr. Jagan, and that it was hoped that close cooperation and aid would contribute to a racially peaceful, democratic, and non-Communist British Guiana.

Editorial note

December 7, 1964, elections in British Guiana resulted in Dr. Jagan's Peoples' Progressive Party gaining 45.6 percent of the popular vote and 24 seats in the legislature. Mr. Burnham's Peoples' National Congress (PNC) won 40.5 percent of the popular vote and 22 seats in the legislature. However, in accordance with the constitutional tradition in the United Kingdom and the Commonwealth, the Governor offered the

Premiership to Mr. Forbes Burnham as the person commanding the most confidence of the legislature as a whole. Mr. Burnham was asked to form a government, and he did so by placing his party in coalition with Mr. Peter D'Aguiar's United Force, which had won 12.5 percent of the popular vote and 7 seats in the legislature. It took several weeks for the PNC and the UF to agree on terms for a coalition.

Dr. Jagan initially refused to resign as Premier but he did so after an Order in Council was issued in London authorizing his removal. Dr. Jagan later held a press conference in which he promised strong but non-violent opposition to the new government.

In a telegram from Georgetown, December 10, Carlson reported that the most striking aspect of the election was the extent of racial voting. He reported that "in one district after another the number of votes for Dr. Jagan's PPP was approximately the same as the number of registered Indian voters." Carlson said that the cause of "such complete racial voting by Indians apparently stems from fear and distrust of African-led government" and that the PPP's propaganda and pre-election violence played on those fears and "created psychology which made Indians impervious to reason. Thus, Indians deserted the United Force with its advocacy of multi-racial approach, non-violence, and prosperity. Likewise rejected was Justice Party leader Rai's logical appeal to Indian self-interest to obtain a share in non-PPP administration which was certain to come about as a result of the election." Carlson concluded that the consequence of this racial voting was that the PNC/UF coalition would have to govern without significant Indian representation.

Considering the future, Carlson was pessimistic about the depth of the racial cleavage in British Guiana. He speculated that while the Mr. Burnham administration would probably try to "demonstrate responsibility, improved government, and assistance" to all Guianese, it seemed unlikely that such an approach would lead to Mr. Burnham's reelection within the next few years, "especially in view of increased number of eligible Indian voters at that time. Therefore, it might be expected before another election Mr. Burnham administration may seriously toy with more radical solutions, possibly e.g. seeking to obtain independence in order to tamper with the electoral system."

"British Guiana Election," White House, National Security Council, Memo from Gordon Chase to McGeorge Bundy, December 8, 1964.

In this memo, Chase warns Bundy that the CIA projection for the elections indicates "Cheddi is doing much better than expected, and the odds are probably no better than about 6 to 5 that the opposition parties will win by one seat."

"British Guiana Election," White House, National Security Council, Memo from Gordon Chase to McGeorge Bundy, December 9, 1964.

Chase provides mixed news. On the one hand, "It looks as if the election is pretty much in the bag for the opposition parties." However, the Mr. Burnham coalition will only have a 1-3 seat majority. The main problem concerns the solidification of the Indian vote by the PPP. "One disturbing element is that the Justice Party will probably not win a seat... This means that we may want to figure out some other way to bring East Indians into the Government. One possibility might be to try to bring into a PNC/UF coalition a couple moderate 'goodie' PPP members (not including Dr. Jagan, of course)." J. Harold Shullaw, State Department desk officer for the United Kingdom, and Chase will meet to discuss these issues. In the end Chase concludes on a happy note, "Assuming the above projections are correct, we have not done too badly. While I would have preferred to see a less impressive PPP showing and a more impressive Justice Party showing, the main objective has been accomplished-i.e. beating Dr. Jagan."

Without manipulation, in the 1961 election the PPP received 43 percent of the vote, and that had sufficed to obtain 20 seats in the assembly. Despite CIA's political action efforts in the 1964 election, the PPP votes increased to 46 percent. That was sufficient for only 24 seats in an expanded parliament. Mr. Burnham's PNC got the same share of votes in both elections, 41 percent, despite heavy gerrymandering of Guianese expatriate votes. With that relative failure, the number of PNC representatives nevertheless doubled, from 11 in 1961 to 22 in December 1964. The United Force party got 12 percent of the vote and 7 seats in the assembly. The Justice Party got no seats. Dr. Jagan won the popular vote. Under the proportional representation scheme his party obtained more seats in parliament. The British governor turned away, however, offering Mr. Burnham the chance to compose a coalition in which Mr. Peter D'Aguiar became finance minister.

An October 1965 memorandum by CIA's chief analysts looked ahead to the approaching days of independence. Conceding Mr. Burnham's weaknesses, the estimators also acknowledged Dr. Jagan's continuing strength. The analysts believed that after independence Mr. Burnham would no longer need to show unity, and differences between the PNC and UF would emerge. The CIA indicated that Mr. Burnham would need to gain only a little support from the Indo-Guianese to be successful and that could be done through development projects favoring them. He would then obtain financial aid from the United States, United Kingdom, and Canada to accomplish that.

During the Johnson administration, the U.S. Government continued the Kennedy administration's policy of working with the British Government to offer encouragement and support to the Pro-West leaders and political organizations of British Guiana as that limited self-governing colony moved toward total independence. The Special Group/303 Committee approved approximately $2.08 million for covert action programs between 1962 and 1968 in that country.

U.S. policy included covert opposition to Dr. Jagan, who was labeled by the US as, "a pro-Marxist leader of British Guiana's East Indian population". A portion of the funds authorized by the Special Group/303 Committee for covert action programs was used between November 1962 and June 1963. The U.S. Government successfully urged the British to impose a system of proportional representation in British Guiana with the hope that it would be beneficial to the anti-Jagan forces. The US also urged the British to delay independence until the anti-Jagan forces could be strengthened. Through the Central Intelligence Agency, the United States provided Mr. Burnham's and Mr. Peter D'Aguiar's political parties, which were in opposition to Dr. Jagan, with both money and campaign expertise as they prepared to contest the December 1964 parliamentary elections. The U.S. Government's covert funding and technical expertise were designed to play a decisive role in the registration of voters likely to vote against Dr. Jagan. Mr. Burnham's and Mr. D'Aguiar's supporters were registered in large numbers, helping to elect the anti-Jagan coalition.

Special Group/303 Committee-approved funds were again used between July 1963 and April 1964 in connection with the 1964 general strike in British Guiana. When supporters of Dr. Jagan and Mr. Burnham clashed in labor strife in the sugar plantations that year, the United States joined with the British Government in urging Mr. Burnham not to retaliate with violence, but rather to commit to a mediated end to the conflict. At the same time, the United States provided training to certain anti-Jagan forces to enable them to defend themselves if attacked and to boost their morale.

Following the general strike, the 303 Committee-approved funds were used to support the election of a coalition of Mr. Burnham's Peoples National Congress and Mr. D'Aguiar's United Force. After Mr. Burnham was elected Premier in December 1964, the U.S. Government, again through the CIA, continued to provide substantial funds to both Mr. Burnham and D'Aguiar and their parties. In 1967 and 1968, the Group/303 Committee-approved funds were used to help the Mr. Burnham and Mr. D'Aguiar coalition contest and win the December 1968 general elections. When the U.S. Government learned that Mr. Burnham was going to use fraudulent absentee ballots to continue in power in the 1968 elections, it advised him against such a course of action, but did not try to stop him.

Telegram from the Department of State to the Consulate General in British Guiana, for Carlson from Shullaw, Washington, December 10, 1964.

We believe it would be helpful if you were to talk with Mr. Burnham soonest while he is considering the composition of the cabinet and make the following points.

(1) We were gratified by the election outcome for in our view it provides a basis on which BG can move forward toward independence without the danger of communist domination.

(2) We were pleased by the report from our Consul General that in his view a PNC/UF coalition appeared certain. We think this is of vital importance as a means of maintaining the broadest possible support for the new government. We do not hold any brief for any specified United Force representation, that is, we hold no brief for including D'Aguiar himself in the cabinet. The important thing is UF representation.

In telegram 193 from Georgetown, December 10, Carlson reported that Mr. Burnham had admitted to him that the United Force commanded much of the managerial talent in the country, "which the new administration would need." Mr. Burnham's main concern was the "means to overcome what he called Jaganism." Carlson reported that Mr. Burnham "urged desirability of early independence and appealed to me to persuade the USG to use its influence to that end," and that Mr. Burnham said that he did not want to be "hampered" by British "fair play" and that "if we do not down this 'ogre Dr. Jagan' before too long we will never be able to do so."

(3) We were pleased to hear that Mr. Burnham was studying ways to include East Indians in the government. We have heard that he is considering Rai for an important appointive position to head a commission and we think this is a wise move. We also think there would be much merit in having an East Indian Attorney General and perhaps this could be achieved

with Ramsahoye by changing the constitution so that the Attorney General would not be a member of the government.

(4) We would not be opposed to Mr. Burnham trying to bring one or two moderate PPP Indians into his cabinet but in this connection, it must be clearly understood that the United States would not be able to provide assistance for a government which involved a PPP/PNC coalition of any kind or which included Dr. Jagan or his henchmen. We assume that Mr. Burnham will be on guard against approaches by Dr. Jagan to get the nose of his camel under the tent. For your information in our talks in London we will take the position that the election outcome is advantageous to our joint interests.

While we are disappointed at showing of JP, GUMP, *etc.*, we do not think idea of alternative EIP should be dropped. We anticipate that the UK may seek our support for a PPP/PNC coalition but we will resist this appeal. Our position is that the new government without Dr. Jagan should be given a chance to demonstrate capacity and work for racial harmony and this best achieved by not including PPP members who provoked racial strife for their own ends. We plan to counsel Mr. Burnham toward moderation and assist him where possible. To include Dr. Jagan and PPP in a coalition would probably lead to strife and jeopardize this assistance.

In a telegram from Georgetown to London, December 11, to the attention of Ericson for Shullaw, Carlson reported Mr. Burnham's basic agreement with the U.S. advice. Carlson stressed to Mr. Burnham the importance of reaching a coalition agreement with the UF quickly; otherwise the new administration would be vulnerable to claims that it was only a minority government, "and that it would be wise to ensure that UF accepts responsibility for the new government." Carlson also advised that UF participation would encourage the business community and private investors.

In a telegram from Georgetown to London, December 17, to the attention of Ericson for Shullaw, Carlson reported that he had urged that UF leaders be included in the list of original cabinet appointments, after Mr. Burnham had stated that "having UF in the cabinet would evolve in a month or two."

CHAPTER 29

The Administration of Mr. Forbes Burnham - 1964

THE FIRST VOTE TO SCAR THE GUYANESE PEOPLE took place in 1964 and involved America. Washington funded opposition groups challenging Dr. Jagan, the country's Premier, in its final colonial years. According to U.S. State Department archival documents, $2.08 million was spent on "covert action programs" in Guyana between 1962 and 1968. In the lead-up to the poll, the CIA and AFL-CIO were on the ground, allegedly inciting racially charged strikes and riots. "The U.S. fostered violence and death in British Guiana," historian Stephen G. Rabe, author of U.S. Intervention in British Guiana: A Cold War Story, said: "U.S. money fueled this violence and death."

Dr. Jagan's party won a majority in that election, held two years before independence. Still, British and American officials instituted a proportional representation system that allowed the PNC to take power. The British Governor invited Mr. Burnham to form a coalition with a small capitalist third party, giving him the combined votes to unseat Dr. Jagan. Although officials on both sides of the Atlantic worried that Mr. Burnham bore the marks of a demagogue, he was not the doctrinaire socialist that Dr. Jagan was; little else mattered.

On December 7, 1964, General Elections were held for the first time under Proportional Representation for 53 seats in the House of Assembly. Under the Proportional Representation System, there were no constituencies. Parties submit lists of candidates, and voters vote for the list of their choice. The votes were counted and assigned to the parties. Parties were allocated seats in proportion to the votes they received. Parties then extract the number of names from their lists, and those persons become Parliamentarians.

Fifty-three members were elected from the results of the General Elections. Two were elected by the National Congress of Local Democratic Organs, and ten were selected by the Regional Democratic Councils – one from each Council.

People's Progressive Party 109,332 votes, 24 seats (Dr. Cheddi Jagan).

People's National Congress 96,657 votes, 22 seats (Linden Forbes Sampson Burnham).

United Force 29,612 votes, 7 seats (Peter Stanislaus D'Aguiar).

Justice Party 1,334 votes, 0 seats (Balram Singh Rai).

Guyana United Muslim Party 1,194 vote, 0 seats (Mohamed Hoosain Ganie).

Peace, Equality & Prosperity Party 224 votes, 0 seats (Kelvin Wesley DeFreitas).

National Labor Front 177 votes, 0 seats (Cecil Gray).

The People's National Congress (with 22 seats) and the

United Force (with 7 seats) formed the Government through a coalition. On December 14, 1964, Mr. Linden Forbes Sampson Burnham (PNC) was appointed Premier.

Members of the House of Assembly:

Speaker

Aubrey Percival Alleyne (PNC)

Members of the Government (28)

Ministers (13) (PNC & UF)

Linden Forbes Sampson Burnham, *Premier, Minister of Development and Planning, and Attorney General.*
Dr. Ptolemy Alexander Reid, *Minister of Home Affairs.*
Neville James Bissember, *Minister of Health and Housing.*
Randolph Emanuel Cheeks, *Minister of Local Government.*
Eugene Francis Correia, *Minister of Communications.*
Peter Stanislaus D'Aguiar, *Minister of Finance.*
Mrs. Winifred Gaskin, *Minister of Education, Youth, Race Relations & Community Development.*
C.M. Llewellyn John, *Minister of Agriculture.*
Robert James Jordan, *Minister of Forests, Lands, and Mines.*
Mohamed Kasim, *Minister of Works and Hydraulics.*
William Oscar Rudyard Kendall, *Minister of Trade and Industry.*
Deoroop Mahraj, *Minister without Portfolio.*
Claude Alfonso Merriman, *Minister of Labor and Social Security.*

Parliamentary Secretary (1)

Stephen Campbell, *Parliamentary Secretary, Ministry of Home Affairs.*

Other Members (14)

David Brandis DeGroot
William Alexander Blair
Jagnarine Budhoo
Charles Frederick Chan-A-Sue
Oscar Eleazar Clarke
Royden George Basil Field-Ridley
John Gabriel Joaquin
Hari Prashad
Thomas Anson Sancho
Rupert Clement Tello, *Deputy Speaker*
James Henry Thomas
Cyril Victor Too Chung
Rev. Alex Benjamin Trotman
Henry Milton Shakespeare Wharton

Members of the Opposition (24)

Dr. Cheddi Jagan
Brindley Horatio Benn
Ram Karran
Ranji Chandisingh
Henry Jocelyn Makepeace Hubbard
Dr. Charles Ramkissoon Jacob, Jr.
Cedric Vernon Nunes
Dr. Fenton Harcourt Wilworth Ramsahoye

Earl Maxwell Gladstone Wilson
George Bowman
Sheik Mohamed Saffee
Ashton Chase
Moses Bhagwan
John Bernard Caldeira
Abdul Maccie Hamid
Derek Chunilall Jagan
Goberdhan Harry Lall
Yacoob Ally
Lloyd Linde
Joseph Rudolph Spenser Luck
Reepu Daman Persaud
Mohendernauth Poonai
Dr. Subhan Ali Ramjohn
Eugene Martin Stoby

The House of Assembly held its first meeting on December 31, 1964. The Members of the PPP did not attend the First Sitting. Aubrey Percival Alleyne (PNC), an elected Member of the House of Assembly, was elected by the House of Assembly to be the Speaker. Immediately after his election, he resigned as a Member of the House of Assembly and vacated the Speaker's Office. He was then re-elected as Speaker. He was the Fourth Speaker. The vacancy in the House of Assembly was filled by Philip Duncan, a PNC Member, who made and subscribed to the Oath in the Assembly on January 27, 1965. The Ceremonial Opening took place on March 29, 1965. The Governor, Sir Richard Edmonds Luyt, addressed the Assembly.

On May 18, 1965, the Members of the PPP attended the Assembly. An amendment to the Constitution provided for the Office of Prime Minister instead of Premier. Linden Forbes

Sampson Burnham, who was the Premier, became the First Prime Minister.

On January 26, 1966, the Flag for an Independent Guyana, designed by Whitney Smith, Director of the Flag Centre, Florida, USA, and approved by the House of Assembly. In February 1966, Queen Elizabeth visited British Guiana. On February 25, 1966, the Coat of Arms for an Independent Guyana, designed by Edward Burrowes, Stanley Greaves, and Alvin Bowman, was selected on the recommendation of the National History and Arts Council and approved by the College of Arms in England, was accepted by the House of Assembly. On April 21, 1966, the Guyana National Anthem, composed by Robert Cyril Gladstone Potter, was approved by the House of Assembly.

On May 26, 1966, British Guiana attained Independence as Guyana. A new Constitution came into operation. The Office of Governor-General replaced the Office of Governor. The Governor, Sir Richard Edmonds Luyt, became the Governor-General. The House of Assembly became the National Assembly of the Parliament of Guyana. The Members of the House of Assembly became the Members of the new National Assembly of the Parliament. The Office of the Legislature was renamed the Parliament Office. Two new Offices of Clerk of the National Assembly and Deputy Clerk of the National Assembly were established by the Constitution, outside of the Public Service. They replaced the Public Service Offices of Clerk of the Legislature and Assistant Clerk of the Legislature. The designation *Marshal* was changed to *Sergeant-at-Arms*. During 1966, Sir Richard Edmonds Luyt, Governor-General, left Guyana and was replaced by Sir Kenneth Sievewright Stoby.

On June 4, 1966, the Government published a Notice designating Members of the National Assembly as Members of Parliament, with the letters *MP* after their names. On November 15, 1966, a Speaker's Chair was presented as an Independence gift from the Government and People of India to the Parliament of Guyana. From December 17, 1966, to 1969, Sir David James Gardiner Rose was the Governor-General. He was killed in an accident in London on November 10, 1969.

On August 4, 1967, the Speaker of the National Assembly, Aubrey Percival Alleyne, died. On February 16, 1968, Rahman Gajraj was elected by the National Assembly to be the Fifth Speaker of the National Assembly. On October 22, 1968, a Clerks' Table, three Clerks' Chairs, and a Sergeant-at-Arms' Chair were presented as Independence Gifts from the British House of Commons to the Parliament of Guyana. On November 5, 1968, the First Parliament of Guyana was dissolved.

Following independence, social benefits were provided through foreign aid to a broader population, specifically in health, education, housing, road and bridge building, agriculture, and rural development. During Forbes Burnham's last years, however, the Government's attempts to build a socialist society caused a massive emigration of skilled workers and other economic factors, leading to a significant decline in the overall quality of life in Guyana.

Memorandum from the Director of the Office of British Commonwealth and Northern European Affairs (Shullaw) to the Assistant Secretary of State for European Affairs (Tyler), Washington, December 21, 1964.

The talks were from our standpoint most satisfactory. We found that in the British view so long as Dr. Jagan continues as the leader of the Indian community racial harmony cannot be re-established without a rapprochement between him and Mr. Burnham. You will note that we took issue with this concept pointing out that Dr. Jagan's record does not justify any assumption that he can serve as a basis for the establishment of racial harmony. I believe we have in effect bought time which Mr. Burnham can use to try to allay the Indian fears. If Mr. Burnham's actions bear out the intentions of his speeches, there may be some basis for hope.

The agreed minutes of the U.K./U.S. consultations reported that U.S. officials made the case that "the Justice Party could continue to serve a useful purpose" as an alternative for Indian voters and that Indian confidence could be won by including Indians in the government and in other public bodies, especially in the police force.

On the question of prompt action to start a vigorous assistance program in British Guiana, it was found that HMG was in such a state of indecision regarding the role of its new Ministry of Overseas Development that authority was not given for Mr. Yoe to precede to Georgetown on January 1. A willingness to give this authority at an early date was indicated. The power play between the Ministry of Overseas Development and the Colonial Office may create a number of problems before responsibilities are finally divided between the ministers.

In a telegram to Ericson in London for use at the U.S./U.K. conference, December 8, Shullaw reported that the AID program proposed for British Guiana for the 1965 calendar year included $5.8 million in grants for road and sea defense maintenance; $.825 million in grants for technical assistance; $5.0 million in a development loan for the Atkinson–McKenzie road; and $3.5 million in loans for public works, small industries, and housing.

The record of the U.S./U.K. meeting on economic aid

to British Guiana was reported in a memorandum of conversation, dated December 18. In a telegram from Georgetown to London on December 17, to the attention of Ericson for Shullaw, Carlson reported that the Governor thought that the "program looked fine."

Memorandum of Conversation, Washington, January 4, 1965

Michael N. F. Stewart, *Minister, British Embassy;* Iain J. M. Sutherland, *First Secretary, British Embassy;* William R. Tyler, *Assistant Secretary;* Harold Shullaw, *Director, BNA* .

In the absence of Lord Harlech, Mr. Stewart was asked to meet the Secretary on the subject of British Guiana. Mr. Tyler explained that the Secretary had been obliged to go to the White House and had instructed him to convey his views to Mr. Stewart.

We believe that Mr. Burnham has not done badly since taking office and that he has adopted a moderate and constructive line in his public statements regarding racial conciliation. We are under no illusions about Mr. Burnham's weaknesses and shortcomings. He is not ideal, but nevertheless he is the only alternative at present to Dr. Jagan and the PPP.

We have told Mr. Burnham that we would move ahead rapidly on an aid program immediately after the British Guiana elections. We are ready to do so and wish to send an AID official, Mr. Yoe, to Georgetown to work out details. Any delay, we are convinced, would have extremely adverse consequences. Such delay would destroy Mr. Burnham's confidence in us and make his relations with Governor Luyt difficult.

We are asking, therefore, with great urgency that the Prime Minister and Foreign Secretary authorize our going ahead with the implementation of our aid program. We have had a formal request from Mr. Burnham dated December 29 which he stated was submitted with the agreement of the Governor. We have instructed our Embassy in London to give copies of the letter of request to the Colonial Office and the Ministry of Overseas Development. To get the program under way at the earliest date, we are proposing that Mr. Yoe and an engineer proceed to Georgetown on or about January 10.

At a January 8 meeting, Stewart told Tyler that "HMG warmly welcomes the U.S. (AID) proposal." In response to Mr. Stewart's question, Mr. Shullaw said that we had outlined our proposed aid program during our talks with British officials in London on December 17 and 18. We had also at that time said that we would like to send Mr. Yoe to Georgetown at the beginning of January. Mr. Stewart said that he would report immediately to London on this conversation and our request for clearance for Mr. Yoe's visit.

In a January 23 letter to Crockett, Harry W. Yoe (AID) reported that he had arrived in British Guiana on January 15 and met with Mr. Burnham and Finance Minister D'Aguiar. He was impressed that they and other figures in the government and the civil service had a "sincere desire to utilize the assistance given in the most efficient manner," but that work on the roads and sea wall was hampered by a shortage of machinery and trucks. Yoe suggested that equipment could be obtained quickly from "ready stocks of the Navy."

Memorandum from Gordon Chase of the National Security Council Staff to the President's Special Assistant for National Security Affairs (Bundy), Washington, February 8, 1965.

[*11/2 lines of source text not declassified*] there is a note of optimism in BG these days, even among East Indians; [*less than*

1 line of source text not declassified] the Governor is pleasantly surprised by Mr. Burnham's performance thus far, and [*less than 1 line of source text not declassified*] the two men seem to be getting along quite well with each other; [*less than 1 line of source text not declassified*] we can expect the PPP to come up with some kind of shenanigans during Greenwood's visit to BG, now scheduled for about February 12–15. [*text not declassified*] British Guiana, visited the country January 16–19. He did not meet with Mr. Burnham during this trip, but met with him on February 3 in New York. Mr. Burnham was en route to British Guiana from the United Kingdom, where he met the new Colonial Secretary, Anthony Greenwood, whom Mr. Burnham found "not as pro-Dr. Jagan as he had originally assumed." [*file name not declassified*]. [*text not declassified*] reported PPP intentions "to assume a more aggressive attitude" toward the new Mr. Burnham government.

BG Rice Exports - There is a glut of rice in BG these days and we are working [*less than 1 line of source text not declassified*] on ways of moving some of it into the export market. This is important; as you may recall, one of Cheddi's major claims during the campaign was that only the PPP was able to dispose of BG rice grown primarily by East Indians.

In a February 26 memorandum to Deputy Director Helms, Assistant Secretary Tyler requested [*text not declassified*] on a project involving the disbursement of up to $550,000 to subsidize the clandestine purchase of 5,000 tons of rice from British Guiana.

Memorandum from the Officer-in-Charge of British Guiana Affairs (Cobb) to the Director of the Office of British Commonwealth and Northern European Affairs (Shullaw), Washington, February 19, 1965.

The Greenwood visit was very successful from our point of view. Dr. Jagan behaved like a petulant adolescent, while Mr. Burnham and D'Aguiar made favorable impressions.

In a telegram from Georgetown, February 15, Carlson reported a discussion with Greenwood, who agreed that Mr. Burnham had done well but thought that "sooner or later Cheddi would win an election." Greenwood said, "I don't subscribe to the view, you know, that Cheddi is a Communist," he was "in his way brilliant although rather incompetent. He then remarked: 'On the other hand, here is this other man who knows relationships so quickly, where British Guiana fits in the wider scheme of things, procedures, etc., whereas Cheddi just does not grasp those things." Dr. Jagan is reportedly going to Leipzig to get bloc funds but whether his line of credit with the bloc is still good remains to be seen.

Reynolds metals signed a 25-year contract with the government on February 16. It would double production to 600,000 tons annually and Reynolds paid $500,000 in advance income taxes. Total taxation of the bauxite industry will be 50% of profits this year according to D'Aguiar.

Rice is still our number one problem. An American rice broker arrives in British Guiana February 22 to try to arrange a sale with Peru but the Rice Marketing Board may not do business since it seems to insist on a premium price. Puerto Rico's Governor is seeking ways to help out also. An American rice growing specialist will go to British Guiana in March.

Mr. Burnham told Carlson he had asked the Police Commissioner to give us a list of the equipment needed to modernize the police force. We sent a message stressing that we could provide no equipment until we conducted a public safety survey and that we would not conduct a survey unless HMG requests it. I doubt we should be in the police business so long as the UK is in BG.

In a telegram from Georgetown, February 24, Carlson agreed but added that the situation was "so different from that elsewhere" that it merited special consideration and suggested supplying the police with vehicles and motorcycles after obtaining U.K. approval.

In response to a request from D'Aguiar for financial advice we indicated we could send on a short visit an FSR and an FSO who might be helpful.

HMG was not amused by public reference to John Carter as next BG Ambassador to the U.S. and asked us to discourage the same.

To get the AID program going we need to buy road machinery in a hurry. Gordon Chase is checking with Defense to see if they have stocks which we might tap (the Navy Department told us it does not have) and AID has been asked to assemble the machinery and trucks as quickly as possible but it looks as if we will have a 90-day delay which isn't good.

One hundred thousand (100,000) pounds of dried milk was shipped from Panama in early February and this should keep the glasses filled until the shipment from New Orleans arrives. Carlson has asked for a PL480 adviser since the BG Red Cross wants to get out of the milk business July 1. The specialist who recently worked out a program for Jamaica will be available to go down in late March or early April.

At the Canadians' request Harry Yoe is going to Ottawa to coordinate assistance planning for BG. I advised the U.K. Embassy.

Telegram from the Department of State to the Consulate General in Georgetown, Washington, February 25, 1965.

Follow up for Carlson from Shullaw: Your message re: Greenwood visit extremely enlightening was apparently more productive than we anticipated. We agreed with the Governor that it is important to take advantage of Greenwood's good will and provide him with a basis for [garble—convincing?] The Labor Party that Mr. Burnham has been more responsible than many Laborites have believed. You should therefore, after briefing the Governor on our views, pass them onto me. Burnham in a manner you judge most likely to be effective.

(1) U.S. heard very favorable report about Greenwood's visit from HMG, and is aware that Mr. Burnham's astute statesmanship was major factor in visit's success.

(2) The U.S. believes that if Mr. Burnham agrees now to authorize Greenwood to establish a commission to examine the question of racial imbalance, he will in effect speed up setting a date for a constitutional conference.

A February 18 memorandum to Bundy indicated that Greenwood had been very impressed by Mr. Burnham, "commenting that he had no idea that he was a man of such stature," while the performance of Dr. Jagan and his party was "lamentable." Greenwood no longer believed a coalition of Dr. Jagan's party and Mr. Burnham's party would work. Greenwood reportedly felt that if the racial imbalance question in the security forces could be resolved, then a constitutional convention to prepare the way to independence could be held.

(3) If Mr. Burnham drags his feet on authorizing the appointment commission, he will retard setting a date for the conference.

In a February 25 telegram from London to Shullaw, Ericson reported that the Foreign Office insisted on cooperation from Mr. Burnham on the Commission to study racial imbalance. However, much of Greenwood's attitude toward Mr. Burnham and Dr. Jagan had changed, Greenwood was "politically committed here to commission ideas and could not sell independence conferences or return of emergency powers to his Labor colleagues unless Mr. Burnham accepted commission." [*Department of State, INR/IL Historical Files, Carlson, Department Messages [file name not declassified], Vol. 3, 1/1/65–7/6/65*].

(4) While Mr. Burnham no doubt disappointed over emergency powers, he has gained far more than he realizes, and rather than be discouraged he should build on his gains. For example, securing Greenwood's agreement to amend the constitution to permit the appointment of Mr. Ramphal as Attorney General is a master stroke and real achievement. Tactically Mr. Burnham should play this appointment up as a major step toward racial harmony and betterment relations between races. Mr. Burnham might wish to announce further that he will no longer press for lifting emergency powers. Will ask the new Attorney General to undertake thorough study conditions and thereafter advise the Governor, Premier and Cabinet when emergency might be lifted. That was suggested as one way of getting over that hurdle and avoiding any "horse trade."

(5) U.S. hopes Mr. Burnham will seize this chance to make progress toward independence by in effect providing Greenwood the tools he needs to do the job, *i.e.*, authorize Greenwood to go ahead with commission to examine racial imbalance, and work with him toward this end. We urge him to send Greenwood a message giving the authorization Greenwood requested.

Telegram from the Consulate General in British Guiana to the Department of State, Georgetown, April 11, 1965, 4 p.m.

Following is course of developments over past 36 hours in Mr. Burnham/D'Aguiar budget crisis since the telephone conversation in London, in which I indicated grave threat to continued coalition. This threat now appears to have been brought under control and an impasse resolved after intensive pressure by ConGen.

In a telegram from Georgetown, April 9, Carlson reported his talk with D'Aguiar earlier that day about the latter's intention to resign. D'Aguiar told Carlson he had "no political future," the PNC intended to merge with or swallow up his party, and that, therefore, he would direct all his efforts towards doing a "good job as finance minister." D'Aguiar thought that since "there is no hope in hell of balancing the budget" due to PNC politically inspired spending increases, that the only hope for the country was "in providing an image which will attract private investment" through a good budget, "especially by the abolition of property tax."

During the Mayor's reception evening April 9 for newly appointed BG commissioner to the UK, Lionel Luckhoo, Minister of Works and Hydraulics Kassim told me that at the cabinet meeting scheduled that evening it was anticipated that a decision would be made for D'Aguiar to leave cabinet. Kassim did not know whether other UF ministers would remain but thought they would. That meeting apparently went far into the night but without real results. D'Aguiar did not attend but other UF ministers did with his permission.

On the morning of April 10, at briefing on rice problem by Dr. Efferson (Dean of School of Agriculture, Louisiana State University) in Mr. Burnham's office which was attended by Kassim, Minister of Trade and Industry; Kendall, Minister of Agriculture; John, and by myself and other US representatives, message was received about one hour later from Mr. Burnham summoning key ministers to special meeting at his residence. On the way out I urged Kendall, whose political judgment Mr. Burnham respects, to see that if D'Aguiar had to go that it be done smoothly on grounds personal and health reasons, preferably with commendatory letter of appreciation from Mr. Burnham, but sought impress on Kendall importance of retrieving situation if at all possible. I also spoke with Kassim, who seemed uncertain and depressed. Gave him the same advice along with the view that D'Aguiar's departure from government would be damaging but departure of UF would be disastrous and consequently every effort must be made to retain D'Aguiar's services.

Toward midnight April 10, I learned [*less than 1 line of source text not declassified*] that UF executives had held meeting at which D'Aguiar claimed matter of principle and substance was involved on which he felt strongly: that party's choices were: (1) for him to resign with other UF ministers remaining; (2) for all UF ministers to resign; and (3) for all UF members to resign from legislative assembly. After lengthy discussions the executives voted for all ministers to resign and to defer the question of leaving the assembly (7 members) until constitutional aspects could be determined. Report also indicated that D'Aguiar scheduled to meet with Mr. Burnham at 9 a.m. April 11 for the final session.

I immediately sought to reach Mr. Burnham without success. I called D'Aguiar early in the morning on April 11. He was just arising so invited him to breakfast. [Less than 1 line of source text not declassified] Decided to try a combination of flattery, pleading, and strong language related to horrible consequences of breakdown anti-Jagan forces. Told D'Aguiar how much US entities appreciated his contributions to Mr. Burnham administration, what favorable impact his presence in government had on various visitors, e.g., that American businessmen usually say after seeing ministers that they are good but D'Aguiar is really outstanding.

D'Aguiar usually makes a better impression than any other minister on businessmen. Told him one main reasons for USG support and confidence in BG was coalition and constructive role D'Aguiar was playing; everyone knew he was outstanding member of cabinet and counting on him; that Washington would not be able believe that on issue of abolition of property tax worth about $1 million he would hand BG to Dr. Jagan on a silver platter; that I had just been to Washington and had given optimistic appraisal stability Mr. Burnham administration, and USG on basis such reports had gone to extraordinary lengths to expedite aid and to make it substantial; that because of this stability and his presence in cabinet potential foreign investors were being encouraged; that I could not believe that after all effort put into saving BG from communism, including strenuous efforts by D'Aguiar (all those miles and all those speeches), it was going to be thrown away.

I stressed it would be bad enough if he felt he must leave government but to permit UF to leave was to sell his country out; that with all trouble spots Secretary and senior officers had to cope with, such as Vietnam, Russians, Castro, Chinese, were we now going to have to add BG to the list? I asked him to think about consequences in BG itself which would doubtless see a return to violence, possibly against his own supporters.

Then suggested that there must be compromise and that he must realize Mr. Burnham could not give way totally under an ultimatum of resignation. Mr. Burnham must save face and D'Aguiar must give at least a little bit. I asked if he would accept the idea of a moratorium if I could obtain Mr. Burnham's agreement, or some kind of depletion allowance which would permit the government to collect property taxes with one hand and refund it with the other.

We discussed matters and arrived at a compromise whereby existing industries could deduct the cost of any expansion or capital improvements from taxes owed or, if the company did not qualify in this way, purchase of government debentures would be regarded as paying tax. New industries would be exempt from tax. (First $50,000 is not taxable in any event under existing legislation.) At my insistence he also reluctantly authorized a moratorium of two years but only as last resort if Mr. Burnham rejected the above.

At this point, with D'Aguiar's concurrence, I informed Mr. Burnham that 9 a.m. meeting with D'Aguiar was postponed if agreeable and I would meet with Mr. Burnham first. He agreed. D'Aguiar said he also wished to have Mr. Burnham's agreement to downward revision of income tax rates and to simplifying tax structure by decimal system. This tax now ranges from 6 percent on the first $1,000 to 70 percent on $13,200 and above. Total cost of D'Aguiar's plan would be about $125,000 BWI. He was prepared not to inaugurate it until 1966 but wished to make some allusion to possibility in the budget message scheduled April 14.

Finally, D'Aguiar confided other matters which have been

bothering him in coalition, some of which are petty annoyances which probably loom much larger than otherwise in view his fatigue: there were too many long cabinet meetings at night with important matters decided at late hours; lack of expeditious handling of agenda items, inadequate air conditioning, and belief that no one but he felt free to be critical. I offered to talk to Mr. Burnham about reducing the number of night sessions or possibly exempting D'Aguiar in some fashion, as well as proposing more personal consultation with D'Aguiar. D'Aguiar thought it would be a good idea to have a committee with each side represented on a party basis to express freely to the other any matters of concern. I did not commit myself to support this idea as I am not certain that it would be productive. D'Aguiar, throughout the whole first part of discussion, kept reiterating desire to resign, but by the end of discussion had specifically agreed to stay indefinitely and to give it another try.

I saw Mr. Burnham immediately afterward and informed him of the likelihood of UF ministers resigning, possibility of UF leaving the legislative assembly and recalled a series of serious consequences previously drawn to his attention. Told him it seemed essential to keep D'Aguiar in government at least at this stage and to settle this tax issue at any cost. Told him Washington had been given favorable view of stability his administration during my recent visit, that USG would find collapse of coalition over tax involving $1 million incomprehensible, that if events should take this disastrous turn, I had little doubt USG would have to reevaluate its aid program since there would be little point in improving country for Dr. Jagan. D'Aguiar was now willing to accept the tax issue and Mr. Burnham readily accepted it, even claiming he had proposed most of it to D'Aguiar yesterday. (This may be more face-saving.) Told Mr. Burnham that more than just taxes were involved here: D'Aguiar was tired, unsure he was really wanted or appreciated, and Mr. Burnham should pat him on the back occasionally.

I outlined D'Aguiar's complaints and suggested Mr. Burnham find ways to ameliorate them. I suggested he call D'Aguiar at least once each week and talk over important matters personally, making clear that D'Aguiar was not just another minister. In short, although Mr. Burnham might find it distasteful, he should turn on some of his charm.

In order not to risk agreement coming apart in Mr. Burnham/D'Aguiar meeting, I suggested that no meeting be held but that either Mr. Burnham or I simply inform D'Aguiar of Mr. Burnham's concurrence with tax compromise. Mr. Burnham agreed and telephoned D'Aguiar, who said he wished to see Mr. Burnham anyway "to thrash out a few things." Mr. Burnham then asked me to remain during this session. D'Aguiar made notes on all major tax changes in the new budget, asking Mr. Burnham in each case to agree. Mr. Burnham was considerate, readily agreed, although offering occasional language changes.

Mr. Burnham exempted D'Aguiar from cabinet meeting evening April 11 or any meeting April 12 to free him to work on budget. He agreed to try to operate cabinet meetings more expeditiously, to consider farming out items to subcommittees, to have better air conditioning in cabinet rooms, and to have more personal consultation. D'Aguiar suggested periodic special committee meetings on a party basis in which criticism would be freely offered on any subject without thought of offense. Mr. Burnham agreed but suggested it be limited to cabinet officers and parliamentary secretaries. D'Aguiar agreed and read back all of his notes. By this time three hours had passed and Mr. Burnham invited us to sample his bar.

Information Memorandum from the Deputy Assistant Secretary of State for European Affairs (Davis) to Secretary of State Rusk, Washington, May 21, 1965.

The question of holding a constitutional conference and fixing a date for independence is becoming an increasingly serious issue in British Guiana. Premier Mr. Burnham is becoming suspicious of both the United States and the United Kingdom and his suspicions have been intensified by press stories in Britain to the effect that the United States Government is opposed to early independence on the grounds that an independent British Guiana might go communist.

In a telegram from Georgetown for Shullaw, May 17, Carlson reported that he assured Mr. Burnham that the press stories were completely false. The British have informed us that they expect to hold the promised constitutional conference as early as practicable, presumably, if all goes well sometime toward the end of this year, but they have not been willing to be this explicit to Premier Mr. Burnham. Instead they have told him that the conference could not be scheduled until there had been time to study a report on racial imbalance in the public services which the British Guiana Government has requested from the International Commission of Jurists.

In a telegram from Georgetown for Shullaw, May 22, Carlson reported that the Governor had confirmed his earlier assurance that the "only stipulation [concerning timing] was that of time to 'study' ICJ report before constitutional conference and that there was no mention of requiring its implementation."

Our Consul General in Georgetown has been told to try to allay Mr. Burnham's suspicions of foot-dragging on the part of the British and to deny press reports that the United States opposes independence. We have suggested to the British that a more forthcoming reply to Mr. Burnham's request for a constitutional conference in September might be helpful. Specifically, we have suggested that since it is their intention to convene this conference this year Premier Mr. Burnham might be advised of this fact.

In a telegram from Georgetown for Shullaw, June 1, Carlson reported that Mr. Burnham was "quite unimpressed" with and unconvinced by U.S. arguments that the United Kingdom was not dragging its feet on independence. Carlson stressed to Mr. Burnham that the United States did favor early independence.

In a telegram to Georgetown for Carlson, May 21, Shullaw reported that he had called in John Killick of the British Embassy and "suggested that HMG might wish to consider being somewhat more forthcoming," and that there could be "considerable gain were HMG to tell Mr. Burnham that the conference would be held this year."

Memorandum from Gordon Chase of the National Security Council Staff to the President's Special Assistant for National Security Affairs (Bundy), Washington, June 23, 1965.

(1) In a June 22 memorandum to Rusk, Assistant Secretary of State for European Affairs John M. Leddy recommended informing Dean "We believe it is absolutely essential we continue as necessary our covert financial support to the anti-Jagan political parties in British Guiana" and that it would be appreciated if the Ambassador would convey to Prime Minister Wilson and Foreign Secretary Stewart "our deep concern ... [*less than 1 line of source text not declassified*].

(2) Rusk spoke to Ambassador Dean yesterday and made a hard pitch.

(3) Harry Shullaw called me this afternoon to say that we have indications that we may be getting a negative answer from the British. Toward this off, your help is needed. He offered the following possibilities:

    (a) You could call Ambassador Dean and, without mentioning the fact that we know the British are thinking negatively, refer to the Secretary's conversation with the Ambassador yesterday and indicate that the White House (the President, if you can say it) is also very interested in an early affirmative answer. The words *'early affirmative'* was underlined and a marginal note in Chase's handwriting reads: "FYI we need to write some checks for Mr. Burnham." Also, you want the Prime Minister and Foreign Minister to know this.

    (b) You could authorize the State Department to make the above point to the British on your behalf.

(4) Shullaw feels that a direct call from you to Dean will be most effective and that the sooner you make the call, the better (the British may be replying to us any time now). I agree with Harry on both accounts. According to a July 9 memorandum of conversation Dean advised Rusk that [*text not declassified*] had approved the U.S. covert support program.

I will call Dean as per Paragraph 3(a).

A marginal note next to this paragraph reads: "done."

Tell the State to make the pitch on behalf of the White House.

See me.

Memorandum from Gordon Chase of the National Security Council Staff to the President's Special Assistant for National Security Affairs (Bundy), Washington, July 14, 1965.

In response to your question, here are some reasons why the announcement of a Constitutional Conference seems a good thing. Since we can in no way be assured that the British will stay in BG for 5 or 10 years, it is probably better to get the British out of BG sooner rather than later. In a telegram from London, July 14, the Embassy reported that Greenwood would announce the next day in Parliament that he had proposed November 2 as the date for the British Guiana constitutional conference in London.

(a) With the British in BG and the East Indian population growing, there is always the chance that the British will change the rules of the game (*e.g.*, coalition, a new election). In this regard, it is probably true that Dr. Jagan feels he still has a chance so long as the British are around. With the British gone, Dr. Jagan himself may decide to bug out.

(b) With the British gone, it is highly likely that Mr. Burnham will do what is necessary to ensure that Dr. Jagan does not get back into power on the wings of a growing East Indian population (*e.g.*, import West Indian Africans; establish literacy tests for voters - these would hurt the PPP).

(c) The chances for violence probably won't increase significantly with independence. Generally speaking, the East Indians are timid compared to the Africans and, without the British to protect them; they might be even more timid. Also, it is conceivable that a British military presence could be maintained even after independence.

(d) If Mr. Burnham does not get fairly early independence, his credibility as a national leader will be questioned *i.e.*, not able to deliver on his big promises. Once we assume that relatively early independence is probably not only inevitable but also desirable, it would seem to make sense to announce it. In this regard, it should be noted that Mr. Burnham has been pressing the British very hard to live up to their previous commitment on a Constitutional Conference, and British reluctance (until now) to agree to a specific date strained Mr. Burnham/British relations; this, in turn, has, on occasion, led Mr. Burnham to suspect that we were encouraging the British in their stand. In short, an unpleasant situation, all around, was building up. GC PS - Best guess on date of independence is mid-1966.

Paper Prepared in the Department of State, Washington, July 30, 1965.

The Department reported receipt of a brief on British policy in British Guiana on July 23 from the British Embassy in Washington in preparation for the first of a series of "periodic discussions on policy toward British Guiana as it approaches independence." The British brief was enclosure 1 to the airgram. The first meeting was held on July 30 between representatives of the British Embassy in Washington and Department of State officers led by Deputy Assistant Secretary Richard H. Davis, during which this paper was given to the British.

The United States comments on Britain's Policy on British Guiana

The United States Government studied with interest the brief on the British policy in British Guiana which was received on July 23, 1965. The United States welcomed the intention of the British Government to convene the constitutional conference in November which would, among other tasks, fix the date for independence. The United States shared with the British Government the view that the Indian community should be represented at the conference. It would normally be expected that Dr. Jagan and his party attend the conference even though they might not wish to see independence granted under the present government, just as Mr. Burnham and Mr. D'Aguiar represented their parties at earlier constitutional conferences under somewhat similar circumstances.

Dr. Jagan's behavior since the election in December gave rise to the question whether he appreciates the responsibilities of the role of the incumbent upon him as leader of the opposition. His failure to resign the office of Premier, his failure to meet jointly with the Colonial Secretary and present Premier to discuss racial imbalances, his announced intention to refuse to cooperate with the Commission of Inquiry of the International Commission of Jurists, and his erratic pattern of attendance at sessions of the House of Assembly may indicate that no matter what steps are taken he would find some pretext to refuse to attend the Conference. It was therefore suggested that consideration should now be given to the possibility that other persons in the Indian community in British Guiana may have to be invited in order to assure that the important section of the community be represented at the conference.

In a brief on British policy in British Guiana on September

3, the British doubted whether they could invite other persons to represent the Indian community if the PPP refused to attend, since these special invitees could hardly claim to be democratically elected representatives.

The United States also shared the British view of the importance of allaying Indian fears for the future, and hoped that the report of the ICJ Commission would contribute toward that objective. They noted that the British Government is anxious that Dr. Jagan's party cooperate with the Commission in order so that the report would not be opened to criticism and that evidence was tendered from one side only. Should Dr. Jagan's party fail to avail itself of the opportunity offered by the ICJ Commission it would seem to bear out the view that the leaders of the party were not genuinely interested in alleviating alleged imbalances and discrimination but have used this charge as a smoke screen for their political objectives.

The United States Government believes that the racial fears in British Guiana would be difficult to assuage, based as they are on deep racial cleavages. They are not easily susceptible to rapid transformation and several generations may be required to effect more than marginal progress toward that objective. While efforts of the government make a contribution toward this task, it should not be assumed that any government, no matter how well intentioned, would be able to eradicate long standing suspicions. Only years of education, association, and understanding can break down the wall of segregation on which racial fears rest. Nevertheless, there was a major role for the security forces in British Guiana to play in the task of seeking stable conditions. The presence of British troops in British Guiana provides ample evidence for that conclusion. If British troops can remain after independence until adequate local forces are recruited, trained, and equipped to meet the security requirements of the area, that would contribute substantially to allaying Indian fears.

Since the maintenance of internal security and stability would be no small task, the nature, composition and objectives of the British Guiana security forces would not, we hope, have to take into account the possibility of a foreign threat. The United States hoped that problems arising from the Venezuelan boundary claim can be resolved amicably between two such good friends as Her Majesty's Government and the Government of Venezuela. It would be unfortunate if a continuation of that claim was to be used as the pretext for establishing an Army in British Guiana or for recruiting security forces in excess of the Government's domestic requirements and of a nature not suitable to the countries' needs, thereby imposing a possibly excessive burden on the developing economy.

The United States welcomes this opportunity to exchange views on B.G. and looks forward to receiving additional briefing on British policies in the Colony.

Memorandum from the Deputy Director for Operations of the Central Intelligence Agency (Helms) to the President's Special Assistant for National Security Affairs (Bundy), Washington, August 6, 1965.

The coalition government of Forbes Mr. Burnham's People's National Congress (PNC) and Mr. Peter D'Aguiar's United Force, installed as a result of the December 1964 elections was having some success in restoring responsible government to British Guiana. The coalition is not an easy one, however, since Mr. Burnham and Mr. D'Aguiar neither like nor trust each other and hold conflicting political views. They are united by their opposition to Dr. Jagan. Dr. Jagan's opposition People's Progressive Party is suffering from increased factionalism caused by conflicting personal ambitions and differences of opinion concerning its role as an opposition party. There is no evidence to indicate that Dr. Jagan has lost the political support of the vast majority of the Indian population. Some evidence is coming to light of increased Chinese Communist interest in the PPP, and a number of party leaders recently visited China including two leaders of the militant group within the PPP which reportedly wishes to break away from Dr. Jagan and form a Communist Party of British Guiana. Dr. Jagan has taken a public position opposing the granting of independence to British Guiana under Mr. Burnham, and this also has caused him some difficulties.

The International Commission of Jurists is now conducting an inquiry in British Guiana into the question of racial imbalance in the public service, including the security forces. It is expected to produce a report about October 1, 1965. The British Government has informed Mr. Burnham of its intention to convene a conference in London to devise a constitution for British Guiana and to set a date for independence. This conference would take place once the International

A Commission of Jurists' report has been submitted, and a date of November 2, 1965 is tentatively established. If this sequence of events is not interrupted, it is expected that British Guiana will achieve independence in the spring of 1966.

The security situation in the country remains disturbed and Dr. Jagan was believed to be directing arson and sabotage activities, attempting to increase those to such an extent that the British Government would be forced to delay the independence conference. The leadership of the Guiana Agricultural Workers' Union (GAWU), which is loyal to Dr. Jagan, plans a major strike effort on the sugar estates during August and September. This could lead to racial violence, and it may be

Dr. Jagan's intention to utilize the strike for that purpose. Local security forces continued to be less than adequate, and the presence of 1300 British troops was still required to ensure internal security.

The United States Government is providing approximately $12,000,000 in financial aid to the Burnham government, some of these funds being useful for attacking unemployment in the Georgetown area. The economic situation is slightly improved in British Guiana although the government's inability to find a market for its rice crop is causing some unrest, particularly among the Indian population, and provides Dr. Jagan a handy criticism of the government. The [*less than 1 line of source text not declassified*] program in British Guiana had three objectives:

(1) To obtain intelligence on the PPP's capabilities and intentions, particularly Dr. Jagan's plans in the immediate future.
(2) To keep Mr. Burnham and D'Aguiar working together in the coalition government, and to keep their parties organized in support of the coalition government and prepared for a quick election if one should be necessary.
(3) To counter Dr. Jagan's efforts to gain control of organized labor in British Guiana. [*1 paragraph (8 lines of source text) not declassified*]

The following items were suggested for discussion at the forthcoming meeting:

(a) The current situation in British Guiana.
(b) Current United States Government policy with respect to British Guiana.

(c) Anticipated problems in the immediate pre-independence and post-independence period. The withdrawal of British troops from British Guiana and the inadequacy of local security forces are of immediate concern.

(d) [*less than 1 line of source text not declassified*] Maintaining covert channels to Mr. Burnham and Mr. D'Aguiar and how that should be carried out.

Telegram from the Consulate General in British Guiana to the Department of State, Ref: Message for Shullaw (info Brubeck) from Carlson, September 15, 1965.

Had a long and useful discussion with Mr. Burnham on the evening of September 15 lasted until well after midnight, after which he still planned to do some work at his office. He is not looking as well as he should, probably due to overwork and possibly because of a recent crash dieting program which took off about 30 pounds. At the moment he also has what seems to be a painful sacro-iliac condition.

Opportunity arose early in conversation to seek to determine how he views the central problem of assuring re-election in 1968. It is clear that he prefers to hope that a significant fraction of Indians can be won over to his party or to one he can work with. If, however, it appears that such development is not occurring he then strongly favors a program for importation of West Indian Negroes and while conceding there would be practical problems, believes they could be overcome. If such a program is not possible, I gather he would be willing to consider such ideas as unitary statehood with Barbados or, conceivably, disenfranchisement of illiterates. He finds such thoughts very distasteful but believes he would do so if convinced there is no other way to survive politically against PPP.

This topic enabled me to raise the matter of anxiety in some quarters, such as UF, regarding his ultimate intentions and to talk to him along the following lines. Impression is that there is increasing anxiety within UF that Mr. Burnham might establish a police state. This is undoubtedly having an effect on D'Aguiar but apparently that is only one aspect of what is bothering him. Indications are that he is becoming dissatisfied again and while the situation has not reached the stage of crisis comparable to the weekend when the coalition was in danger of collapse, time to do something about this reviving potential danger is now. It is essential to seek to improve relations with D'Aguiar and to try to go to London in general accord.

In addition to concern over Mr. Burnham's intentions, D'Aguiar apparently feels that he is not being consulted sufficiently, is too often overridden in cabinet on fiscal matters that expenditures are higher than should be and sometimes include unnecessary items, as well as projecting increased expenses next year. His concern is understandable. It is natural for there to be anxiety about intentions in periods of great uncertainty when a country is emerging as independent. Such apprehension should be recognized and steps taken to cope with it. One must remember that UF regards itself not as a junior partner but as key. On the fiscal side, D'Aguiar's services are needed. He is probably more inflexible than necessary on occasion but perhaps Mr. Burnham is too much the other way.

In any event, substantive points should be talked out and cultivating D'Aguiar, in my opinion, would have great effect in facilitating agreement on substantive matters. D'Aguiar is a man who needs to be appreciated. Complimenting him is effective. I realize this course of action may be disagreeable but politicians - and diplomats - sometimes have disagreeable tasks. Mr. Burnham can do this job. I suggested that he might wish consider some of the following approaches: consult D'Aguiar much more frequently; reassure him at appropriate stage soon about intentions; be frank and genuine on this subject; perhaps have him to dinner or other private meeting weekly until London conference; seek his opinion and advice on various subjects, even if your mind is already made up; compliment him privately and perhaps publicly in press conference just before leaving for London, in course reviewing accomplishments your administration; consider asking him to visit United States and talk to business groups (I told Mr. Burnham that if this useful I will be prepared give D'Aguiar invitation at USG expense); refrain, at least for present, from raising items involving expenditures which D'Aguiar most likely regard as unnecessary.

In a September 16 telegram for Shullaw, sent earlier in the day, Carlson reported that D'Aguiar had told him that morning that he was generally concerned by Mr. Burnham's tentative 1966 expenditure plans, and that "there would be a balanced budget for 1966 'or else'." Mr. Burnham agreed with my analysis and prescription and indicated intention to begin this operation soonest. Plan to see D'Aguiar if possible, today.

Memorandum from Gordon Chase of the National Security Council Staff to the President's Special Assistant for National Security Affairs (Bundy), Washington, October 5, 1965.

Today I had lunch with Del Carlson who is presently in town for consultations. Here are some of the points which came up.

(1) BG Security Forces - The way matters now stand, independence is likely to come in April 1966 and the British will want to take out their troops a few days before independence. Unfortunately, the local BG security forces will not be in a position to handle the security job effectively before September, 1966. The problem: delaying independence (not likely) or to keep the British troops in place after independence. Del said that the British have not yet made a firm decision on that matter and that we might be able to convince them to keep troops in BG after independence. I indicated to Del that we will be happy to lend a hand in this effort when he and State give us the word. He assured me that he and State will have our offer clearly in mind.

In a September 21 memorandum to Chase, Cobb reported that during the next exchange of views with the British Embassy, the Department of State planned to present the advantages of keeping British forces in British Guiana until September 1966.

(2) Mr. Burnham's Visit - Mr. Burnham is expected to come to the United States sometime in early December. Del emphasized that the trappings of the visit are as important as the visit itself. He urged that, in addition to the appointment with the President (which is a must); we should try to give Mr. Burnham some red-carpet treatment. For example, it would be wonderful if we could get Mr. Burnham into Blair House. A marginal notation in Bundy's handwriting next to this sentence reads: "This should be easy." I told Del that we will be as helpful as we can.

(3) Venezuela/British Guiana Border Dispute - Del said that the Venezuelan claim against British Guiana

(Venezuela is claiming about one-half of BG as its own) irritates the hell out of Mr. Burnham and that the Venezuelans seem to be getting more serious as time goes on. Del thought that we should look very hard at this one in the fairly near future to see if we should be doing anything. For example, we could urge both parties to go to the International Court of Justice; [*4 lines of source text not declassified*] I told Del that I would look into the matter to see if there is anything that we should be doing at this stage of the game.

At a meeting between Secretary Rusk and Venezuelan Foreign Minister Irabarren Borges on October 7 Rusk "expressed the hope that the Venezuelan Government would pursue this matter bilaterally with the U.K. and not seek to involve the U.S. at this point 'since we have more than enough other problems."

(4) East Indians - Del said that we are so far getting nowhere with respect to building up an alternative East Indian party. He went on to say, however, that the situation is still very fluid and that we should probably wait until after independence before we get to work on this problem in earnest. The big hope is that we can locate an alternative East Indian leader; so far no one of any stature appears to be on the horizon. A lesser hope is that Mr. Burnham will, by sensible and progressive policies, be able to win the East Indians over to his side. Mr. Burnham, however, is not at all confident that he can ever translate East Indian acceptance of his regime into East Indian votes. Neither is Del.

Del added that even if the East Indians cannot be wooed away from Dr. Jagan, Mr. Burnham will probably do whatever is necessary to win the election in 1968. This could take the form of importing Negroes from other Caribbean countries or, in a pinch, establishing literacy tests for Guianese voters. Literacy tests would hurt the East Indian population more than the Negro population.

(5) Carlson's Availability - Carlson will be in Washington for the next week or so; he will, of course, be delighted to come over and talk to you if you want to get an up-to-date briefing. Are you interested? Yes. Set it up. Not this time.

Memorandum of Conversation, Washington, October 18, 1965, 11 a.m.

PARTICIPANTS

United States

The Secretary
J. Harold Shullaw, *Director, BNA*

United Kingdom

Anthony Greenwood, *Secretary of State for the Colonies.*
Sir Patrick Dean, *British Ambassador.*
Ian Wallace, *Assistant Undersecretary of State, Colonial Office.*
C. G. Eastwood, *Assistant Undersecretary of State, Colonial Office.*

The Colonial Secretary said he believed Dr. Jagan and the

PPP would attend the Constitutional Conference scheduled to begin in London on November 2 although they would probably walk out at some point in the proceedings. Mr. Greenwood expressed satisfaction with the course of developments in British Guiana during the past year under Mr. Burnham's leadership. He also expressed an optimistic view of the Conference prospects and satisfaction that Mr. Burnham is prepared to accept the recommendations in the report of the International Commission of Jurists. Mr. Greenwood said this was not easy for Mr. Burnham to do, but it should be a helpful gesture on the eve of the Constitutional Conference.

The Secretary expressed concern at the security situation in British Guiana following independence and asked if it would be possible for the UK to leave some military forces after independence. Mr. Greenwood replied that in view of our concern he would be prepared to recommend retention of British forces for a limited period of time after independence. He stressed that there was no precedent for doing so. Mr. Greenwood said Mr. Burnham was being pressed to get on with the creation of local security forces, but it would be a year from now before such forces would be able to take on the job of security. While Mr. Burnham was asking for independence in February, Mr. Greenwood thought June or July would be more realistic. The Colonial Secretary added that Mr. Burnham is agreeable to British forces staying on for a period after independence.

In a meeting later that day at the White House with Bundy and Chase, Greenwood said that to shorten the gap between independence and the readiness of local security forces the British would delay independence until June or July and institute a phased withdrawal of British troops. Bundy expressed continuing Presidential interest in British Guiana. Greenwood complimented Bundy on the U.S. Consul General in Georgetown. Bundy responded "we have taken particular pains in our selection of personnel for all agencies operating in British Guiana."

At a meeting on November 27, Dean informed Rusk that the British Cabinet, acting upon Greenwood's recommendation, had decided to allow British troops to remain in British Guiana after independence on May 26, 1966, until October 1966 when Guyanese forces would be prepared to assume their responsibilities.

In response to the Secretary's question about the Venezuelan claim Mr. Greenwood said the claim was without a sound legal basis and for that reason Venezuela would be uninterested in referring the dispute to the International Court. The Secretary expressed the hope the matter could be resolved before independence since otherwise the existence of the dispute would constitute a bar to membership for Guiana in the OAS. The Secretary asked whether there was any possibility of minor border adjustments. Both Mr. Greenwood and Mr. Wallace replied that any territorial concession to Venezuela would be exploited by Dr. Jagan against Mr. Burnham.

The Colonial Secretary in the course of the conversation described Mr. Burnham as a "good Prime Minister" whose performance has been above expectations. He suggested that Mr. Burnham has made some progress in reassuring the small, well-to-do Indian business community and noted the return of Indians to areas which they had left during the racial disturbances. The Colonial Secretary's references to Dr. Jagan were unsympathetic. He believes Dr. Jagan's position has deteriorated in the past year as his party has suffered from internal differences.

Memorandum from the Deputy Director for Operations of the Central Intelligence Agency (Helms) to the President's Special Assistant for National Security Affairs (Bundy), Washington, December 10, 1965.

(1) The British Guiana Independence Conference concluded in London on 19 November 1965 by setting the date of 26 May 1966 for the independence of what will be known as the state of Guyana. The conference also produced an agreement on a draft constitution for the new state and stipulations in the conference record for consultations between the leaders of the two parties in the coalition government. A number of compromises were worked out between Premier Forbes Mr. Burnham and Finance Minister Peter D'Aguiar which, hopefully, will ease some of the strains between them. The conference did not, however, succeed in bringing the two leaders much closer together; they remain basically incompatible on both personal and political grounds and are united only in mutual defense against the threat posed by Dr. Jagan.

(2) [*5 lines of source text not declassified*] It was generally agreed that the basic division of the country along racial lines would continue, that Dr. Jagan and the PPP would continue to enjoy the support of the vast majority of the Indian population and that this would continue to pose a serious threat to the government of independent Guyana. [*less than 1 line of source text not declassified*] informally indicated that the British Government was alert to the possibility of racial violence breaking out following independence and would continue to be sensitive to any developments

which might bring into question the good judgement of the British Government in granting independence to a government led by a representative of a minority racial grouping in the circumstances now prevailing in British Guiana.

(3) Apart from the conference, the British Government and Premier Mr. Burnham made some progress in negotiating other agreements, primarily with respect to the internal security of the country. The British have agreed to maintain troops in Guyana until the end of October 1966 and to train and provide a cadre for the newly formed Guyana Defense Force. This force and the augmented Guyana police forces were to be brought to a sufficient level of capability to permit the withdrawal of British troops in October 1966. The adequacy of this solution cannot be judged at this time.

(4) In a conversation [*less than 1 line of source text not declassified*] on 20 November, Forbes Mr. Burnham stated that his immediate objective is to launch his economic development plan so that he will be able to induce large numbers of West Indians of African descent to settle in Guyana prior to the December 1968 elections. His purpose is radically to alter the racial balance now existing in the electorate in sufficient time to enable him to win a plurality in the 1968 elections. Mr. Burnham stated that he will seek aid from both the British and American Governments for this purpose. He said further that he was confident his scheme was feasible and that it was the only possible course of action which would prevent Dr. Jagan returning to power with the support of the Indian community.

An unattributed memorandum, dated November 26, reported that [*name not declassified*] met with Mr. Burnham on November 20. Mr. Burnham said that the British had rationalized the outcome of the Conference "to solve their own consciences," fully expecting that the constitutional safeguards would inevitably lead to East Indian control by constitutional methods, which he said was "not going to come about." The report highlighted not only Mr. Burnham's plans for West Indian immigration, but also his idea "that under the new constitution absentee voting would be permissible."

(5) A copy of this memorandum is being made available to Mr. J. Harold Shullaw at the Department of State.
Richard Helms.

National Intelligence Estimate of the prospects for Guyana over the next year or two, Washington, April 28, 1966.

(1) British Guiana will probably make a relatively smooth transition to independence, but racial suspicions between East Indians and Negroes will continue to dominate Guyanese politics.

(2) When (or whether) these tensions break out again into violence will depend in large measure on the conduct of Prime Minister Burnham, leader of the Negro party, and of Dr. Jagan, leader of the East Indian party. For over a year, Mr. Burnham has governed with considerable restraint and Dr. Jagan has refrained from violent opposition. But new elections are due by late 1968, and between now and then tensions will rise and may at some point get out of hand.

(3) Even after British troops depart in October 1966, Guyanese security forces can probably cope with sporadic violence. If violence got out of control, Mr. Burnham would probably call for a return of British troops. If US consent was forthcoming and British troops were available, we believe that London would comply.

(4) The governing coalition of Mr. Burnham, a professed but pragmatic socialist, and the conservative United Force leader, Peter D'Aguiar, will continue to be a tenuous one. Friction between the partners over patronage and fiscal issues will probably be intensified after independence, but chances are that a common fear of Dr. Jagan will hold the coalition together.

(5) Guyana's economy will need substantial foreign capital, much of it from the US. The need for aid will keep Mr. Burnham on tolerable terms with the US, UK, and Canada, though his administration will incline toward a neutralist posture in foreign affairs. If Dr. Jagan came to power, he could, because of his Marxist sympathies and his connections in Communist countries, count on some help from these countries. However, they probably would furnish only token quantities of aid.

CHAPTER 30

The Planning of the 1968 Election

Telegram from the Ambassador to Guyana (Carlson) to the Department of State, Georgetown, July 15, 1966, 2:30 p.m.

[*TELEGRAM NUMBER NOT DECLASSIFIED*] PLEASE PASS THE following to Mr. Cobb from Ambassador. Proposed action program designed to ensure government victory in the next general election.

1. It is believed that the action proposed in this paper, designed to ensure a victory in the next general election (1968–69) for the parties of the coalition government led by Prime Minister Forbes Burnham, must be tempered and weighed in light of the following basic considerations:
    (a) Present indications are that the East Indian people, as a whole, dislike the African, distrust him,

especially fear him, and believe that they must stay together, particularly as a voting unit, if their rights are to be protected and their aspirations achieved.

(b) The East Indians, generally, believed that if they maintain their solidarity, they can, by virtue of their rapidly increasing numbers, win any future election.

(c) Most East Indians do not now think, and will not easily be convinced, despite a plethora of anti-Communist and anti-Jagan propaganda, that Dr. Jagan is anything less than an altruistic leader who, although perhaps capable of error, loves his people and is motivated by a desire to act in their best interests. His charismatic appeal continues basically undiminished, although apparently some of the gloss has gone from his image.

(d) Within the PPP, those relatively few East Indians who question Dr. Jagan's motives and leadership and might even welcome a replacement are most reluctant to oppose him openly for fear of intimidation – which the government cannot prevent. The February 1966 murder (undoubtedly inspired by Dr. Jagan's People's Progressive Party) of Ackbar Alli, a PPP activist who turned on Dr. Jagan, is one of many incidents that have made a strong impression on the East Indian mind. The few PPP leaders who oppose Dr. Jagan also realize that the mass of party supporters is likely to favor Dr. Jagan over them in any open contest.

2. As sobering as the foregoing observations may be, the seemingly solid East Indian, Dr. Jagan-built wall must inevitably develop some cracks. There are a few indications that economic improvement, especially the

road program, is making a favorable impression on some East Indians. It is too early to tell how significant this may be. The following proposals are of the type which seem best designed to hasten the development of East Indian disaffection from Dr. Jagan, enhance the position of the government and provide a much-needed assist to the economy of the country, which if not improved can only further complicate the political situation:

(a) Intensify and expand the road building program, giving special emphasis to the predominantly East Indian areas such as the Corentyne. The major artery from New Amsterdam to Crabwood Creek (the last village in the Corentyne) should be paved before the election.

(b) By means of a soft loan, assist with the reorganization and modernization of the rice industry. While this effort may not attract any new support for the government, it is needed as a means of stabilizing a major industry of importance to the economy.

(c) Give consideration to special assistance to the anti-Jagan ManPower Citizens' Association (MPCA), the largest labor union in the country and the one officially representing some 20,000 sugar workers. Such assistance might include establishment of a credit union to assist the predominantly East Indian MPCA-affiliated worker to satisfy his basic needs. Obviously, it would enhance the position of the MPCA and weaken its arch rival, the Guyana Agricultural Workers' Union - Dr. Jagan's principal pirate labor arm. Most important, it would give the East Indian tangible evidence that his individual lot was being improved under the government, actively assisted by the U.S.

(d) Carefully examine the extent of need and the feasibility of making grants or soft loans to expand the government's credit facilities in the agricultural sector. Again, if the small farmer, who is predominantly East Indian, can perceive tangible benefits under the present administration, in a manner he has not known before, considering his basically pecuniary nature, he might consider severing his ties with Dr. Jagan. This might also be an opportunity to promote a diversification program in agriculture by giving priority consideration to the farmer willing to plant some of the basic agricultural commodities which the country is now forced to import. A new rural credit agency, initially endowed by Guyana by the U.S. and geared to give rapid small loans to the farmer on a non-racial basis, might have merit.

(e) Explore assisting the government in the construction and renovation of small school buildings in the rural areas. This would include assistance in the acquisition of basic educational tools such as books.

(f) Assist with the modernization and expansion of medical facilities in the small medical stations in the rural areas. Again, in this effort the East Indian would receive considerable benefit.

(g) Consider assisting the government to greatly expand its present youth program, including a CCC-type project involving rehabilitation, training and trail building in the interior.

3. Activities of a less orthodox nature which are recommended or are now being conducted would include the following:

   (a) Consider giving financial assistance and active encouragement on a selective basis to East Indian individuals or groups which might emerge and show promise of being able to politically influence a significant segment of the East Indian population. (At the present time, the prospects in this area are not particularly encouraging. The anti-Jagan East Indian Justice Party and the Guyana United Muslim Party have been discredited, and consequently offer little, if any, hope of being able to contribute substantially to any future anti-Jagan effort. However, if nothing new appears before 1968, and there is reason to believe that these basically defunct organizations can still play a useful role, consideration should be given at that time to pumping new blood into their emaciated bodies. It is not believed that any action in this regard is justified at present.)

   (b) Continue to promote the growth and attempt to extend the influence of the small moderate group within the PPP in the hope that its members might succeed in replacing the Dr. Jagan leadership or gain sufficient strength to break away and form a new viable East Indian party.

   (c) Encourage the government to consider the feasibility of exiling Cheddi and Janet Dr. Jagan. Without them the PPP, as presently constituted and oriented, would be hard-pressed to continue. The exiling of Janet alone would probably not be sufficiently useful in the light of the problems involved, including that of splitting a family. While she is highly important as the organizer, Cheddi is the vote getter and could probably keep the Indian community largely intact. As a practical matter, the government is not likely to take any such action unless the Jagans provide it with some good pretext; and this may never happen.

(d) Encourage the government, and assist where necessary, to conduct a survey of its supporters who live abroad for the purpose of ascertaining their exact numbers and qualifications to cast absentee ballots in the next election. Government offices in London, Washington, New York, and Ottawa should be able to assist by requesting Guyanese in their areas to register.

(e) At the Washington level, have election experts conduct a study and make detailed recommendations as to how best (preferably in the simplest and most fool-proof manner) the government might proceed to rig, if necessary, the next election. Particular attention should be given to the absentee ballot which would seem to lend itself to manipulation, as well as to any maneuver in Guyana.

(f) Consider the possibility of buying East Indian votes. (Circumstances do not now appear to lend themselves to this practice. For fear of being exposed to the wrath of the PPP, the East Indian would most likely immediately denounce to the PPP any such attempt to influence his vote, or, at best, quietly take the money and then proceed to vote as his bloodline dictated.)

(g) Continue to assist the coalition parties of the government to maintain their organizational structures; and be prepared in the next election to give all the support necessary to enable these parties to register all their potential supporters, conduct a vigorous campaign and ensure that all their people arrive at the polls on time.

(h) Continue to encourage the government to pursue a benign policy toward the East Indian, attempting to convince him of the government's impartiality and genuine desire to improve his standard of living, etc.

4. Prime Minister Mr. Burnham is reasonably convinced that West Indian (Negro) immigration might well solve his electoral problem. More objective observers tend to be more skeptical, primarily because there is not enough time before the next election. While there is no doubt that additional human resources will be required to subdue the extensive Guyana wilderness, with local unemployment still high (at least 15 percent of the total work force) it would seem that immigration cannot proceed in the next year or so at an inordinate rate. The East Indians are, understandably, solidly against this migration scheme and many of Mr. Burnham's supporters will oppose it unless they first have jobs. As a short-term election device, immigration does not seem to be very practical. In fact, Mr. Burnham might easily lose more supporters from within than he hopes to gain from without - particularly if he immediately pushes for the fifteen-twenty thousand immigrants he has in mind.

5. Mr. Burnham is pressing for some type of Caribbean grouping and envisions himself as a likely leader of whatever might emerge. Also, he has entertained the possibility of putting together some form of unitary

state with Barbados or Antigua, or one or several of the smaller islands. (Mr. Burnham told the U.S. Ambassador on July 4, that Grenada and St. Lucia had recently expressed an interest in merging with Guyana.) This plan might prove workable, but again there is no assurance that anything will materialize within the next two to three years. Arrangements of this nature, obviously, cannot be unduly pushed; but they should certainly be discreetly encouraged where possible.

6. Best estimates available indicate that the domestic non-East Indian voting population in 1968–69 will still exceed the East Indian electorate by five to eight thousand. No provision is made in these estimates for new immigrants. Absentee voters probably number between ten and fifteen thousand, with the non-East Indian in the majority. Balanced against this apparent margin in favor of the government, is the fact that the government could easily lose the votes of as many as ten thousand of its nominal supporters. They would be the dissatisfied and the disgruntled might well refuse to go to the polls or in some cases conceivably even vote for the PPP. Facing a contest such as this, a man as astute as Mr. Burnham, will probably want to enter the game with at least a few extra aces. (In 1964 the PPP received 109,000 votes; the coalition parties a total of 126,000; the total vote was 238,530 out of 247,495 registered, the projected registration in 1968–69 is estimated at 284,387.)

7. Mr. Burnham was not considering calling an election before 1968, and apparently there was no great advantage in doing so. Prior to that time, he will not be able to demonstrate major accomplishments, such as

substantially reducing unemployment, etc. In short, he can probably afford to give Dr. Jagan a few more votes conceivably by virtue of the greater numbers of East Indians who will have arrived at the voting age by 1968, in the hope that by waiting, he, Mr. Burnham can not only better satisfy his own supporters but hopefully wean away a few of the East Indian voters.

8. Mr. Burnham has confided to close colleagues that he intends to remain in power indefinitely, if at all possible, by constitutional means. However, if necessary, he is prepared to employ unorthodox methods to achieve his aims. In these circumstances, probably the best that can be hoped for at this time is that he might respond to guidelines and thus take the most effective and least objectionable course to attain his goals.

Mr. Forbes Burnham meeting with US President Lyndon B. Johnson

Letter from the Ambassador to Guyana (Carlson) to the Assistant Secretary of State for Inter-American Affairs (Gordon). Georgetown, August 4, 1966.

Dear Mr. Gordon:

1. I trust you may have seen my telegram (Georgetown 99) reporting how impressed Prime Minister Burnham was with his visit to the United States. He was especially taken with President Johnson and believes that the President strongly supports him. I thought you would be interested in the Prime Minister's brief confidential

summary to me of the topics discussed with the President privately.

Mr. Burnham had a private meeting with President Johnson at 5:11 p.m. on July 22 at the White House. They were joined from 5:32 to 6:00 p.m. by Guyanese Ambassador Sir John Carter, Assistant Secretary Lincoln Gordon, and Ambassador Carlson. According to a notation in the President's Daily Diary, Rostow and Bowdler said that there was no substantive reason for this meeting.

(a) The President expressed appreciation for Mr. Burnham's congratulatory telegram on the successful flight of Gemini 10.

(b) Mr. Burnham raised the subject of Viet Nam, apparently indicating support of the United States and expressing wonder as to how the Communists always seem to get away with their case before much of the world.

(c) After the discussion of Viet Nam, which was relatively short, the conversation turned to civil rights. Mr. Burnham expressed admiration for all that had been accomplished to promote Negro voting rights and education. His remarks were complimentary of the President's achievements in this field. It was not clear from Mr. Burnham's rather sketchy account whether it was at this point, earlier, or as seems probable later, that the President said something along the following lines: "Remember you have one friend in this corner going for you and his name is Lyndon Johnson."

(d) Finally, Mr. Burnham related to the President the idea of migration from the over-populated British West Indian islands to Guyana and the needed

electoral benefit to the Mr. Burnham administration. The President's subsequent inquiry to you as to whether we are "on top" of this idea has been interpreted as a very significant indication of the President's sympathetic attitude toward it.
2. While I assume that this private meeting was intended as off-the-record, I thought it might be useful for you to have the highlights as they appear from this end. If no record of any sort is appropriate, please destroy this letter and so advise me. I am not sending a copy to anyone else but you may wish to let John Hill and Bill Cobb see it.
3. Incidentally, I noted that the Prime Minister's account corresponds to a considerable extent with my prediction about the points which he would raise, as reported in Bill Cobb's memorandum of July 22 to Bill Bowdler, and that he did not raise any of a variety of specific economic matters more appropriate to lower levels.

Best regards,
Sincerely, Del

Prime Minister Burnham's plans for 1968 elections, Memorandum Prepared for the 303 Committee, Washington. March 17, 1967.

It is established U.S. Government policy that Dr. Jagan, East Indian Marxist leader of the pro-Communist People's Progressive Party in Guyana, will not be permitted to take over the government of an independent Guyana. Dr. Jagan has the electoral support of the East Indians, who are approximately 50% of the total population of Guyana. It is believed that Dr. Jagan has a good chance of coming to power in the next elections unless steps are taken to prevent this. Prime Minister Mr. Burnham, leader of the majority People's National Congress in the coalition, is aware of the problem, and has stated that he is fully prepared to utilize the electoral machinery at his disposal to ensure his own re-election.

Mr. Burnham has initiated steps for electoral registration of Guyanese at home and abroad, and has requested financial assistance [*less than 1 line of source text not declassified*] for the PNC campaign. It is recommended that he and his party be provided with covert support in order to assure his victory at the polls. At the same time, it is believed that support to Peter D'Aguiar and his United Force, the minority party in the coalition government, is also essential in order to offset Dr. Jagan's solidly entrenched East Indian electoral support. It is recommended that the 303 Committee approve the courses of action outlined in this paper at a cost of [*less than 1 line of source text not declassified*].

In a meeting [*text not declassified*] on September 16, 1966, Mr. Burnham requested money for various political purposes and outlined his plans to issue identification cards to all Guyanese above the age of 10, and to identify and register all Guyanese of African ancestry in the United Kingdom, Canada, and the United States in order to get their absentee votes in the next elections. "Conversely, Mr. Burnham acknowledged with a smile, East Indians living abroad may have trouble getting registered and, if registered, getting ballots."

According to an April 10 memorandum for the record, the 303 Committee approved this proposal at its April 7 meeting. [*text not declassified*] emphasized during the Committee's discussion the importance of starting early in the implementation of the proposal to prevent the election of Dr. Jagan in the next elections in Guyana.

Origin of the Requirement

Under the Guyana Constitution, new elections for the National Assembly must take place before March 31, 1969, and can take place at any time should the Prime Minister bring about the dissolution of the Parliament. Prime Minister Forbes Burnham of Guyana is aware that the U.S. Government is opposed to Dr. Jagan's assumption of power in Guyana. He is also acutely conscious of the racial factors in the country which work to Dr. Jagan's advantage, and he realizes that he must immediately initiate a vigorous campaign if he is to defeat Dr. Jagan.

Mr. Burnham has personally undertaken the task of reorganizing the PNC, which has not functioned in many areas since the last elections. He plans to establish campaign headquarters in Georgetown and other urban areas where the African vote is concentrated, and will also send organizers throughout Guyana to re-enlist PNC supporters who have been inactive in party affairs since the last elections. At the same time, Mr. Burnham is sending a trusted political adviser abroad to survey the potential absentee vote which he can expect from Guyanese residing in the U.S., the U.K., Canada and the West Indies.

Mr. Burnham believes that he would have great difficulty ensuring his own re-election without support from the U.S. Government. He has requested financial support [*less than 1 line of source text not declassified*] for staff and campaign expenses, motor vehicles, small boats, printing equipment, and transistorized public address systems. He also wishes to contract for the services of an American public relations firm to improve his image abroad and counteract Dr. Jagan's propaganda in the foreign press.

Since we believed that there is a good likelihood that Dr.

Jagan can be elected in Guyana unless the entire non-East Indian electorate is mobilized against him, we also believed that campaign support must be provided to Peter D'Aguiar, the head of the United Force and Mr. Burnham's coalition partner.

The U.S. Government determined in 1962 that Dr. Jagan would not be acceptable as the head of government in independent Guyana. When elections were scheduled for December 1964, [*less than 1 line of source text not declassified*] was instructed to ensure Dr. Jagan's defeat by the provision of guidance and support to Mr. Burnham and D'Aguiar, leaders of Guyana's two anti-Dr. Jagan political parties. That was accomplished. Mr. Burnham and Mr. D'Aguiar established a coalition government which is now in power. That is; however, an uneasy arrangement and Mr. Burnham desires a PNC majority in the Assembly to result from the forthcoming election. While we are not yet persuaded that Mr. Burnham's objective is feasible, we believe it is essential that he wage a vigorous campaign against Dr. Jagan from this moment on.

Action to remove Dr. Jagan from power in British Guiana was considered by the Special Group during the period April 6, 1961– May 23, 1963. [*less than 1 line of source text not declassified*] financial support to the British Guiana Trades Union Council during the strikes of 1962 and 1963 was approved. The Special Group did not approve other political action against Dr. Jagan during that period because of British Government concern. Since early 1963, political action operations in Guyana have not been the subject of Special Group consideration.

Pertinent U.S. Policy Considerations

U.S. policy towards Guyana since 1962 has been to prevent the return to power of a government headed by Dr. Jagan.

Operational Objectives

To prevent the installation of a Dr. Jagan-led government in Guyana by providing support to the PNC and the UF for the purpose of assuring an electoral victory for the non-Dr. Jagan parties.

Risks Involved

Dr. Jagan has consistently and publicly accused the U.S. and U.K. Governments of having undermined him and of having aided Mr. Burnham. It is expected that he will continue to reiterate these charges and to accuse the U.S. and U.K. of supporting Mr. Burnham, regardless of what course of action Mr. Burnham may follow. Dr. Jagan has cried wolf so often in the past that a reiteration of the same charges is not expected to carry much impact, particularly if the timing of the operation is handled appropriately. In this connection, Mr. Burnham is thinking of utilizing voting machines in certain districts in Guyana, knowing that this will attract Dr. Jagan's attention and lead to charges of fraud. Since Mr. Burnham does not intend to rig the machines, and the tallies will in fact be accurate, he believed that would not only divert Dr. Jagan's attention during the election campaign but will add credibility to the results after the fact.

Mr. Burnham has been made aware that the U.S. Government will attach the utmost importance to tight security practices in the event that support is provided to him as proposed in this paper. He recognized that any exposure of that support would reflect on him as well as on the U.S. Government, and he was prepared to deny receipt of any such aid. American and British press coverage of the 1968 elections must be expected to be relatively intensive, and it was likely that some British and American correspondents may be favorably predisposed to Dr. Jagan. For this reason, it will be essential that Mr. Burnham not only counter Dr. Jagan's assertion that Mr. Burnham represents a minority of the electorate, but also that the U.S. Government's involvement not be revealed in any way.

Recent publicity resulting from the ramparts exposures led to charges in the press that AFL/CIO assistance to the British Guiana Trades Union Council during the general strike of 1964 was in fact CIA action to overthrow the Jagan government. There has been no allegation in the aftermath of the Ramparts exposures that the U.S. Government was involved in the December 1964 election. Therefore, it is believed that since the AFL/CIO is not involved in this proposed course of action in any way, and since there has been no exposure of U.S. Government involvement in the 1964 elections, necessary risks involved in the proposed course of action can be undertaken with appropriate safeguards.

The present security forces in Guyana are considered adequate to contain limited or sporadic violence. However, should Dr. Jagan resort to large-scale violence such as occurred during the 1962–64 period, the present security forces would not be adequate. If this should occur, it would be problematic as to whether the U.K. could be persuaded to send in British troops, even if Mr. Burnham so requested. In any event, the British would have difficulties in sea-lift and logistical support.

In recent months various methods for dealing with Dr.

Jagan's problem have been considered by the Department of State [*less than 1 line of source text not declassified*], and discussed with representatives of the British Government. The proposed course of action outlined in that paper was believed to represent the most desirable course of action under current circumstances. Should it appear, as the election campaign develops, that if this proposed course of action is not sufficient other actions may become necessary to supplement the proposal? Whichever courses of action are pursued, it is believed necessary that we anticipate that elections will be held in Guyana no later than March 1969 and support Mr. Burnham for the PNC and to D'Aguiar for the UF is essential in any case. [*less than 1 line of source text not declassified*] will continue to monitor the Guyana situation to permit identification and evaluation of other courses of action should Dr. Jagan depart from his current strategy or should it appear that he is likely to win an election despite our best efforts to prevent this. These other courses of action are outlined in Tab C.

Timing of the Operation

[*61/2 lines of source text not declassified*] For this reason, we recommend the immediate and continuing injection of fiscal support to both the PNC and the UF, and we propose to maintain close contact with Mr. Burnham and D'Aguiar and their principal associates in order to influence the course of the election wherever necessary. This should be initiated at the earliest possible date, so that alternate tactics can be considered.

Recommendation

It is recommended that the 303 Committee approve the proposed course of action at a level not to exceed [*less than 1 line of source text not declassified*].

Telegram from the Ambassador to Guyana (Carlson) to the Department of State, Georgetown, June 1967.

In the course of discussion with Prime Minister Burnham last night I raised the subject of the coming elections and explained that election mathematics at my disposal tended to show that the PNC majority over the PPP and the UF would require a minimum 60,000 votes additional. Even Prime Minister Burnham does not consider that overseas vote can be blown up to that extent; even 50,000, the figure used by him very hypothetically and 30,000 accepted as more realistic (Embassy finds in excess of 25,000 not believable).

Earlier Prime Minister Burnham said that overseas vote figures could be manipulated pretty much as he wished and he tentatively had in mind say 25,000 for a new coalition government and 5,000 for the PPP. When pressed by these mathematics, Prime Minister Burnham said he "would not break his lance" over the PNC majority, meaning that if the U.S.G. made an issue of it he would not pursue it. Clearly however he intends to follow a number of election tricks to add to the PNC totals and detract from the PPP votes. Accumulated total of these may well produce a surprisingly good showing for the PNC, though falling short of absolute majority. Adds that he is well aware of the need that these election tricks are done smoothly and without controversy.

Prime Minister Burnham appreciated the point of view that the motive behind his pining for majority lies in great part in difficulties doing business with Finance Minister Peter D'Aguiar. I suggested that the solution to this problem lay less in engineered majority than it did in arranging for D'Aguiar's honorable withdrawal from politics and government after the election was won and a new coalition government formed. Mr. Burnham would have much less trouble with remaining UF officials. Mr. Burnham was receptive to the idea but saw no UF official on horizon who could take over. I suggested this would be UF problem which could be arranged, provided D'Aguiar withdrawal was affable and in constructive agreement with Prime Minister Burnham.

Memorandum from the Deputy Director for Coordination of the Bureau of Intelligence and Research (Trueheart) to the Director (Hughes) and Deputy Director (Denney), Washington, December 6, 1967.

A review of recent 303 Committee actions on Guyana provided operational background that you may find of use in your review of SNIE 87.2–67. The 303 Committee action has been predicated on the assumption that Dr. Jagan is a Communist or an accurate facsimile of one, and that his becoming Prime Minister of Guyana would be disastrous for Guyana, would prove a dangerous stimulus to Castro, and would introduce an unacceptable degree of instability in the Caribbean area.

The final paragraph of the Estimate, on the significance of a Dr. Jagan victory, has therefore attracted a good deal of attention in ARA, and CIA/DDP as it has gone through its several revisions. In its earlier forms the paragraph reflected a judgment inconsistent with that which motivated the policy decisions of the 303 Committee; in its latest form the inconsistency has considerably diminished. For its part, DDC finds the current version acceptable.

On 10 April 1967 the 303 Committee approved a proposal to provide Prime Minister Forbes Burnham of the Guyanese People's National Congress with covert support in the next national elections. The cost of the assistance necessary to assure a Mr. Burnham victory over Dr. Jagan of the People's Progressive Party was estimated at [*less than 1 line of source text not declassified*]. Some of this was to go to Mr. Burnham's coalition partner, the United Force.

Committee approval was grounded in the belief that as Prime Minister, Dr. Jagan would be an instrument of Communist influence in Latin America. The [*less than 1 line of source text not declassified*] paper embodying the proposal noted that during Dr. Jagan's years (1961-1964) as head of the government, some 50 PPP youths were trained in Cuba in guerrilla warfare, a *Guyana Liberation Army* was organized and equipped largely with Cuban weapons, and $3,000,000 of Soviet bloc funds entered Guyana for the support of the PPP. The paper also stated that some 90 PPP youths were currently being trained (educated?) in Bloc countries and that in Guyana Dr. Jagan's Accabre College was training Guyanese youth in Marxist thought.

The paper forecast that the vote would be an extremely close thing even if Mr. Burnham had our assistance. The [*less than 1 line of source text not declassified*] suggestion, adopted by the Committee, was to make 12 equal monthly payments to Mr. Burnham to help him in revitalizing his party and in organizing his absentee vote strength. If Mr. Burnham's electoral prospects appeared bleak, [*11/2 lines of source text not declassified*]. These measures, it was hoped, would forestall the necessity of exile of Dr. Jagan, or his detention, or coup d'état after the elections.

The Committee's approval was attended by a

recommendation by the Executive Secretary for a quarterly progress report on the progress of the campaign. On 7 August [*less than 1 line of source text not declassified*] reported to the 303 Committee that some [*less than 1 line of source text not declassified*] of the original sum had been committed, that a [*21/2 lines of source text not declassified*].

In oral presentation an [*less than 1 line of source text not declassified*] representative noted that the vote might go as high as 350,000 (instead of the 278,000 previously predicted) and that the increase was expected to be largely Indian and therefore pro-Jagan. The race, he said, would be nip-and-tuck all the way. The [*less than 1 line of source text not declassified*] disposition at the moment, and that of ARA, is to continue to rely on the electoral process in Guyana (no matter how much that process will need adjustment), [*2 lines of source text not declassified*]. If it does, the issue will be submitted to the 303 Committee for review.

The minutes of the meeting of the 303 Committee of August 7 reported [*text not declassified*] the estimated voting figures. The minutes recorded that Rostow and [*text not declassified*].

Special National Intelligence Estimate, Washington, December 7, 1967.

According to a note on the cover sheet this estimate was prepared in the Central Intelligence Agency with the participation of the intelligence organizations of the Departments of State and Defense, and the National Security Agency. The United States Intelligence Board concurred in this estimate on December 7, to consider the prospects for Guyana, with particular attention to problems and consequences of the coming parliamentary election.

Conclusions:

1. Voting in the coming election, which according to the Constitution must take place by the end of March 1969, will again be predominantly along racial lines. Dr. Jagan, the East Indian leader and an enthusiastic Marxist-Leninist, has a basic advantage: The East Indians are now probably a slight majority of the population. The Negroes, almost all of whom support Forbes Mr. Burnham, the present Prime Minister, constitute about 44 percent.
2. Mr. Burnham, whose coalition with the small, conservative United Force has always been fragile, and is working on various schemes to enlarge the Negro vote. He will try to obtain a substantial number of absentee votes from Negro Guyanese residing abroad. Beyond this, he is exploring means to merge Guyana with one or another Caribbean island (most likely St. Vincent) so as to increase the proportion of Negro voters. D'Aguiar resigned from the Cabinet on September 26 despite Carlson's best efforts to dissuade him. An October 24 memorandum from Trueheart to Hughes reported that the move to associate with St. Vincent would probably not succeed. It stated that "we understand that the Commonwealth Relations Office in London is negatively disposed."
3. If Mr. Burnham became convinced that such arrangements would not suffice to keep him in power and Jagan out, he would probably rig the election. In any case, he would have to rely on the small civilian police and Guyana Defense Force (GDF), both of which are predominantly Negro, to maintain order. They

probably could do so, except in the unlikely event of a major East Indian uprising.

4. Prospects for a second Mr. Burnham Administration would depend in major part on how he won. A merger with St. Vincent, for instance, would almost certainly raise fears, among East Indians and UF supporters, of discrimination and possibly even of persecution under a government completely controlled by Negroes. Such fears could produce unrest and some violence. If Mr. Burnham returned to power as head of a coalition in an election that appeared reasonably fair, prospects would be good for continuing stability and further gradual economic progress. The need for outside economic aid would nonetheless continue.

5. If Dr. Jagan's party won, he would probably not be permitted to exercise power. Mr. Burnham could use force to keep him out, or suspend the Constitution and rule by fiat, or even press for a grand coalition which he himself would seek to head. Alternatively, he could permit Dr. Jagan to take office, only to subvert his government at a later date.

6. In the unlikely event that Dr. Jagan did take and hold power, the Communist orientation of his government, more than its actual capabilities, would make it a new disturbing factor in hemispheric affairs, especially in the Caribbean area. Communist countries would make considerable propaganda capital of the fact that such a government had come to power by free elections. The USSR and some other Communist governments would move quickly to establish diplomatic or trade missions in Georgetown. Both the Soviets and Castro would probably provide Dr. Jagan with small amounts of economic aid.

7. A Jagan administration would, however, be beset by powerful internal opposition and would not have the resources for an adventuresome program abroad. Thus, Dr. Jagan would not try to launch an independent Communist revolutionary effort on the continent or in the Caribbean, though he probably would cooperate in the overt and clandestine activities sponsored by the USSR or Cuba. Such actions would encourage Venezuela to press its territorial claims against Guyana and perhaps even to undertake military action.

Omitted here is the Discussion portion of the estimate including sections on Background, the Mr. Burnham Government, Pre-election Maneuvers, and Security Forces.

Post-election Prospects:

If Mr. Burnham wins, the post-election prospects will depend in major degree on how he manages to do so. If he were returned to office as head of a coalition, and as a result of a more or less normal and reasonably fair contest, the prospects for his government would be good. He would require continuing economic aid from the US, and if he got it, Guyana would almost certainly make gradual further economic progress. He would more than likely again have trouble within the coalition, and opposition on the part of Dr. Jagan and the East Indians Guyanese would become increasingly bitter. But there probably would not be disorders and violence of such magnitude that the Guyanese security forces could not control them.

If, however, he blatantly rigs the election, or if he wins by means of a merger with St. Vincent or another Caribbean island, the political situation is likely to be more unstable. Should Guyana join with St. Vincent, for example, the additional number of Negro voters in the new nation would produce fears among East Indians and UF members alike that the Mr. Burnham government would become solely a Negro-run institution and that they would be excluded from power indefinitely. Dr. Jagan would be the first to claim that the merger was engineered by the US and would use it in his anti-US propaganda in Guyana and abroad. At least initially, some unrest and violence would be likely. The Guyanese security forces would probably remain loyal to Mr. Burnham and be capable of preventing violence from getting out of hand.

If, in spite of Mr. Burnham's pre-election activities, Dr. Jagan's PPP gained a majority of seats in the Assembly, Cheddi probably still would not be permitted to form a government. Mr. Burnham might call upon the security forces to keep Dr. Jagan out, or suspend the Constitution and rule by fiat, or even try persuading Dr. Jagan to join in a grand coalition which he, Mr. Burnham, would head. Any of these actions, with the possible exception of the last, would raise racial tensions and produce danger of violence, both probably more inflammatory than the merger possibility discussed above.

It is possible that for appearances' sake Mr. Burnham would let Dr. Jagan take office, only to subvert his government at a later date. It is unlikely that Mr. Burnham would go into loyal opposition, but if he did, Dr. Jagan would still face a highly troubled tenure. The Negroes in opposition would probably be more militant than the East Indians have been, and Dr. Jagan could not count on the security forces.

However, determined Dr. Jagan was to take measures to favor the East Indians or to carry out Marxist economic policies, he would be severely inhibited by circumstances. Sooner or later, he would have to make numerous concessions to the Negroes or risk being deposed. He has talked of nationalizing the important foreign enterprises, but he is probably aware that expropriation of the foreign aluminum companies or of the big British-owned sugar properties would be disastrous economically. He would, in any case, encounter certain economic difficulty. There would be a loss of confidence on the part of private investors, and most of the economic assistance from which the Mr. Burnham government has benefited would probably not be forthcoming to Dr. Jagan. His friends among the Communist countries would probably provide some help, but less. Cuba would most likely give Dr. Jagan a favorable price for Guyana's rice and the USSR would probably give limited credits. In 1965–1966, the US committed $18 million in aid to Guyana of which $13 million has been drawn down.

In the unlikely event that Dr. Jagan did take and hold power, the Communist orientation of his government, more than its actual capabilities, would make it a new disturbing factor in hemispheric affairs, especially in the Caribbean area. The USSR and other Communist countries would make considerable propaganda capital of the fact that such a government had come to power by free elections, and the Dr. Jagan government would support the Communist nations in international forums on basic issues. The Soviets and some other Communist governments would move quickly to establish diplomatic or trade missions in Georgetown. Yet a Dr. Jagan administration would be beset by powerful internal opposition, and its internal weakness would require it to move cautiously in order to retain power while trying to strengthen its political base. It would not have the resources to carry out an adventuresome program abroad. Thus, Dr. Jagan would not try to launch an independent Communist revolutionary effort on the continent or in the Caribbean. He probably would cooperate in the overt and clandestine activities sponsored by the USSR or Cuba. All actions of this kind would encourage Venezuela, certain to be suspicious of Dr. Jagan regardless of his policies, to press its territorial claims against Guyana and perhaps even to undertake military action.

Memorandum from James R. Gardner of the Office of the Deputy Director for Coordination of the Bureau of Intelligence and Research to the Deputy Director for Coordination of the Bureau of Intelligence and Research (Trueheart), Washington, January 22, 1968, 11:25 a.m.

Drafted by Bowdler and approved in the White House. The meeting was held in the President's office. Mr. Burnham visited Washington for medical care at the Bethesda Naval Medical Center. A Department of State briefing paper prepared for the meeting recommended the President congratulate Mr. Burnham on 3 years of stability and racial peace, assure him of the high priority of the AID program in Guyana and that "we have also selected our best people to send to Georgetown," and be aware that Mr. Burnham might request that the United States influence the Government of Venezuela to ease its border dispute pressures on Guyana.

PARTICIPANTS
The President
Prime Minister Forbes Burnham of Guyana.
Sir John Carter, *Ambassador to the United States from Guyana.*
Mr. Robert M. Sayre, *Acting Assistant Secretary of State.*
Mr. William G. Bowdler, *the White House.*

Two substantive issues were discussed in Prime Minister Mr. Burnham's 20-minute meeting with the President. In the Guyanese elections, the Prime Minister thought he would have to go to elections by November 1968. He said he was "calmly confident" about the outcome. The President stressed the importance of maintaining his coalition strong.

A January 20 memorandum for the President from Rostow noted that Guyana's uneasy coalition partnership had become shaky over appointments and budgetary issues and stressed that "a word from you on the importance of maintaining uneasy political combinations in election years would be useful."

The Prime Minister described his border difficulties with Venezuela during the past year. He referred to Venezuela's having blocked Guyana from eligibility to sign the Latin American Nuclear Free Zone Treaty at the UN last session. He asked the President if the United States could use its influence with Venezuela to be less "bellicose" about the boundary problem. Mr. Sayre explained that we had been active with both sides in keeping the dispute quiet. The President asked Mr. Sayre for a memorandum on the subject.

The Treaty for the Prohibition of Nuclear Weapons in Latin America was signed at Mexico City on February 14, 1967, and entered into force on April 22, 1968. The United States was not a signatory, but was party to two Additional Protocols dealing with matters concerning non-Latin American nuclear powers.

Memorandum of Conversation, Washington, January 23, 1968, 10:30 a.m.

Drafted by Hill and approved by Shlaudeman. The meeting was held in the Secretary's office. The memorandum is part 1 of 5. Part 2, Caribbean Regional Problems, and part 5, World Situation. Sayre sent Rusk a January 22 briefing memorandum for this meeting. Call of Prime Minister Mr. Burnham Electoral Situation in Guyana

PARTICIPANTS:

Foreign

L. Forbes Mr. Burnham, *Prime Minister of Guyana.*

H.E. Sir John Carter, *Guyanese Ambassador to the United States.*

United States

The Secretary

Mr. Robert M. Sayre, *Acting Assistant Secretary for Inter-American Affairs.*

Mr. John Calvin Hill, Jr., *Director, North Coast Affairs.*

Following his release from a physical check-up at Bethesda Naval Hospital, Prime Minister Mr. Burnham paid a 45-minute courtesy call on the Secretary. After an exchange of pleasantries, the Secretary asked the Prime Minister how he saw the situation in Guyana. Mr. Burnham replied that he was "quietly confident" about the outcome of the elections, which could be held at any time before the end of March 1969. Amplifying on this at a later stage in the conversation, he said he thought that the government had picked up support and that, while it would be untruthful to suggest that there was a landslide of defectors from the PPP, there were some who had gone over to the government in some areas. He might pick up 3% to 4% of the East Indian vote. He was also counting "heavily" on the overseas absentee ballots, which were concentrated in the U.K. and, secondly, in the U.S. He said that last year's U.S. Supreme Court decision which had the effect of allowing Guyanese citizens who had also become naturalized U.S. citizens to vote without losing their U.S. citizenship would be helpful. The

Secretary expressed some uncertainty whether the decision contemplated voting by such citizens while they were resident in the U.S. and whether electioneering in this country would present problems. He said we would look into this. Mr. Burnham indicated that no objectionable electioneering was contemplated and, in substantiation of his assessment that his electoral prospects were good, pointed out that Dr. Jagan was already setting the stage among his followers for a defeat by claiming the elections would be rigged, he would not be allowed to assume power.

Memorandum of Conversation, Washington, January 23, 1968, 10:30 a.m.

Drafted by Hill and approved by Shlaudeman. The memorandum is part 3 of 5; regarding parts 1, 2, 4, and 5. The meeting was held in the Secretary's office.

SUBJECT: Call of Prime Minister Mr. Burnham of Guyana Border Disputes
PARTICIPANTS:

Foreign

Mr. Burnham, *Prime Minister of Guyana.*

H.E. Sir John Carter, *Guyanese Ambassador to the United States.*

United States

The Secretary

Mr. Robert M. Sayre, *Acting Assistant Secretary for Inter-American Affairs.*

Mr. John Calvin Hill, Jr., *Director, North Coast Affairs*.

The Prime Minister alluded to the border dispute with Suriname which had flared up before his departure and reported that, in the interval, Sir Lionel Luckhoo, the Guyana High Commissioner in London, had taken the matter up in The Hague with the Foreign Minister when he was presenting his credentials as Ambassador to the Netherlands. Sir Lionel was in the process of returning to report in detail, but he had gained the impression that the Netherlands was not backing the Government of Suriname and that the matter could be settled quietly.

The border dispute with Venezuela was more worrisome, especially as it was also an election year in Venezuela with the consequent temptation to agitate the issue. The saving factor was the Venezuelans were pledged not to use force and that they seemed to realize the problems which would result from a hostile government on their frontiers. The Mixed Commission was now working satisfactorily (except that the Ankoko Island question remained unsolved) and it was setting up a Subcommittee to look into economic cooperation. Guyana appreciated the efforts that the U.S. had been making to keep matters cool on the Venezuelan side and was counting on the U.S. to continue those efforts, as the Opposition in Guyana was only too anxious to cry "sell out" at any sign of failure to maintain the nation's sovereignty. The Secretary commented that border issues were often agitated in political situations but that it was contrary to Venezuela's traditions and objectives in the OAS and UN to settle matters by force. He remarked that, in the 40 or so border disputes around the world, it was our observation that those in possession seemed to win out and that the thing to do was for all to remain cool.

In 1966 Venezuela moved to occupy the border island of Ankoko, half of which was claimed by Guyana, according to a background paper attached to a January 22 briefing memorandum from Sayre to Rusk. That paper also described how Venezuela had "effectively blocked Guyana from becoming a party to the Organization of American States by the Act of Washington which bars admission to American States that have unresolved border disputes with a member state."

Memorandum of Conversation, Washington, January 23, 1968, 10:30 a.m.

Drafted by Hill and approved in S on January 23. The memorandum is part 4 of 5; regarding parts 1–3 and 5. The meeting was held in the Secretary's office.

PARTICIPANTS:

Foreign

Mr. Forbes Burnham, *Prime Minister of Guyana.*

H.E. Sir John Carter, *Guyanese Ambassador to the United States.*

United States

The Secretary

Mr. Robert M. Sayre, *Acting Assistant Secretary for Inter-American Affairs.*

Mr. John Calvin Hill, Jr., *Director, North Coast Affairs.*

The Secretary invited the Prime Minister to take five minutes or so to say frankly what he thought the U.S. should be doing in Guyana. The Prime Minister noted with appreciation that the U.S. had been in the forefront of contributors of assistance to his development effort but that, as he had indicated at the Donor's Conference in Georgetown, his principal problem had been to raise sufficient local currency financing to make use of the external financing offered. In fact, part of last year's British assistance had to be foregone because local cost financing could not be raised. He understood the Congressional and U.S. balance of payments considerations which put constraints on U.S. assistance for local costs, but it would be useful to have the utmost flexibility in this regard. Meanwhile, he had been exploring with the U.S. the possibility of a PL 480 program (for instance, Guyana was importing $15 million or more in U.S. wheat) which would provide a counterpart which could be used for local cost purposes. The Secretary indicated sympathy with regard to the local cost financing problem, which emanated from our balance of payments, and with regard to PL 480. He indicated he would want to take up the PL 480 problem with Messrs. Hill and Sayre later. There followed a brief discussion of the recent U.S. balance of payments problems, in which the Secretary emphasized the effort which had been taken to avoid an adverse impact on investments in and trade with the less developed countries.

Information Memorandum from the President's Special Assistant (Rostow) to President Johnson, Washington, Guyana's Border Dispute with Venezuela, January 25, 1968.

During Prime Minister Burnham's call, he asked for our help in persuading Venezuela to be less "bellicose" about the border dispute.

The dispute, involving some 5/8 of Guyana, goes back to colonial times. We became involved in the 1890s in an arbitration effort between the British and Venezuelans. The award generally corresponds to Guyana's present boundaries. Venezuela has never accepted it.

Venezuela allowed the case to lie dormant until Guyana approached independence. Thinking that it could get more concessions out of a Britain anxious to get rid of a problem colony than an independent new nation, the Venezuelans began agitating their claim. They blocked Guyana from joining the OAS and becoming part of the Latin American Nuclear Free Zone.

In 1966, at Geneva, the British and Venezuelan Governments agreed to establish a Mixed Guyana/Venezuela Commission to discuss the dispute. The agreement provides that if the dispute has not been resolved by 1970, the Commission will be dissolved and the problem taken to the United Nations.

The Commission has not made any progress toward resolving the boundary question but it has succeeded in draining off some of the political heat. Last year there was a small flare-up when Venezuela occupied the border island of Ankoko, half of which is claimed by Guyana. We have made it clear to both governments that they should use the Mixed Commission to work out their differences. We follow the controversy closely and counsel restraint when things get unsettled. After the Ankoko incident interrupted the dialogue, we encouraged President Leoni to receive an emissary from Guyana to resume bilateral talks. Venezuela eventually agreed to that, and offered to consider joint economic development projects in Guyana under the aegis of the Mixed Commission. Prime Minister Burnham accepted that suggestion with the understanding that the projects would not be limited just to the disputed territory.

The prospects for reaching a solution to the border controversy in the near future are not bright, unless there is a sharp change in attitude by the Venezuelans. For internal political reasons, they now find it convenient to agitate the issue from time to time. Our strategy is to use our influence to restrain the Venezuelans from further adventures along the frontier and from too much politicking at home. We have repeatedly reminded the Venezuelans that if they undermine Mr. Burnham, they run the risk of getting a communist bridgehead at their back door under Dr. Jagan.

Walt

Electoral Assistance to Guyanan [sic] Prime Minister Burnham - Progress Report. Memorandum from the Assistant Secretary of State for Inter- American Affairs (Oliver) to the Deputy Under Secretary of State for Political Affairs (Bohlen), Washington, February 13, 1968.

Attached is a [*less than 1 line of source text not declassified*] memorandum of January 22 reporting the progress that has been made in putting into effect the 303 Committee's decision of April 1967 to provide anti-Jagan forces in Guyana with covert support for the next national elections, which are scheduled for late 1968 or early 1969. The bulk of the assistance, whose total cost was estimated at [*less than 1 line of source text not declassified*], was to go to Prime Minister Forbes Burnham of the People's National Congress (PNC); a lesser amount was to go to the PNC's junior partner in the government coalition, the United Force.

The attached memorandum reported that the PNC claimed to already have 20,000 overseas Guyanese registered, [*text not declassified*], and that, "*according* [*less than 1 line of source text not declassified*]," Cheddi and Janet Jagan and a small hardcore group of Marxists around them had purged the PPP of the majority of its moderate leaders at the party congress in late August 1967.

The Committee's decision was grounded in the belief that as Prime Minister, Dr. Jagan would be an instrument of Communist influence in Latin America. He is a declared Marxist, and during his years as head of government in 1961–64 demonstrated in a number of ways his close sympathy with both the Soviet Union and Cuba. The [*less than 1 line of source text not declassified*] memorandum of proposal that formed the basis of the Committee's April decision pointed out that in these years some 50 members of his People's Progressive Party were trained in guerrilla warfare in Cuba; that some 90 PPP youths were currently being educated in Bloc countries; that the Soviet Union, during Dr. Jagan's premiership had given over $3,000,000 in direct support of the PPP; and that Dr. Jagan's Accabre College, which he established in Guyana in 1965, is a base for Marxist indoctrination of PPP members.

The attached memorandum notes a number of steps that have been taken to implement the 303 Committee decision. A PNC training program in organizational and campaign techniques is in progress [*4 lines of source text not declassified*] to publicize Guyana's progress and thus attract the maximum number of these voters.

A nation-wide registration of all Guyanese over 15 has been all but completed; the information it yields will be helpful in indicating likely areas and groups for PNC campaign effort. For its part, the UF has begun working in both urban and rural areas and among its potential supporters in American Indian settlements. Of the [*less than 1 line of source text not declassified*] originally authorized, [*less than 1 line of source text not declassified*] was committed in FY '67. Of the [*less than 1 line of source text not declassified*] programmed for FY 1968 only [*less than 1 line of source text not declassified*] has been committed thus far, but the report anticipates an early quickening in the pace of outlays.

Despite these endeavors, the election still promises to be a nip-and-tuck affair. The country's vote will once more be cast almost completely along ethnic lines, and there is no solid assurance that Mr. Burnham's Negro supporters, even with their strength supplemented by their overseas compatriots, will carry the day against the East Indian supporters of Dr. Jagan. The feasibility of Mr. Burnham's design to affect a pre-election merger with St. Vincent and thus take advantage of that island's largely Negro vote is still uncertain. Guyana's border problems with Venezuela and Suriname are being vigorously exploited by Dr. Jagan, as are charges that the United States, and especially the CIA, is involving itself in Guyana's internal affairs. But although prospects are thus unclear, they are bright enough to justify keeping to our present course.

I recommend that the attached memorandum be noted in the next 303 Committee meeting.

Dr. Jagan charged that the Shoup Registration System International of Pennsylvania was a front for the CIA and would help with the rigging of the coming elections, according to a December 17, 1967, *New York Times* article, a copy of which was attached but not printed.

Secretary of State Rusk met with Guyana Deputy Prime Minister/Minister of Finance Dr. Ptolemy Reid on May 24, 1968. Dr. Reid's primary purpose in coming to the United States was to generate electoral support for the People's National Congress (PNC) among Guyanese living in the United States. Reid took over as Minister of Finance from United Force leader, Peter D'Aguiar, in late September 1967, after the latter's resignation. Ambassador Carlson estimated that Reid's Guyana would assume the leadership of the anti-Jagan forces in Guyana in the event of Mr. Burnham's death or incapacitation.

Dr. Reid had progressively assumed more responsibility for economic development matters in Guyana and his visit occasioned a review of the U.S. Aid program in Guyana. The briefing memorandum prepared for his visit reported that the U.S. Agency for International Development (AID) program in Guyana "has been progressing well with inputs of grants, loans, and PL 480 foods of roughly $10 million per year since the Mr. Burnham government took office in December 1964." These memoranda stated that substantial improvements had been made in the main coast road, and that Morrison-Knudson was preparing to begin work on the last remaining unimproved coastal road section, on the Corentyne in the eastern part of the country, financed by a $7.5 million AID loan. Another AID project was the building of a 50-mile road from Atkinson Field to the previously isolated mining town of Mackenzie, begun in 1966 and finished the summer of 1968. Major improvements were made through AID funds to the international airport developed at Atkinson Field. An AID loan was also planned for Guyana's rice industry, to construct drying/storage centers at a number of sites along the coastal rice growing areas, to modernize Guyanese rice mills, to establish a rice research station, and to provide technical assistance. The loan was approved in November of 1968.

Memorandum Prepared for the 303 Committee, Washington, support to Anti-Jagan Political Parties in Guyana, Progress Report, June 5, 1968.

On 7 April 1967 the 303 Committee approved a proposals to support anti-Jagan political parties in Guyana in the national elections scheduled for late 1968 or early 1969. Previous progress reports on this activity were considered by the 303 Committee on August 7, 1967 and February 16, 1968.

The 303 Committee meetings on August 7, 1967, and February 16, 1968, were reviewed as discussion, rather than decision, meetings. The facts noted in Document 431 and in the January 22, memorandum cited in footnote 2 thereto were among the topics reviewed at the February 16 meeting.

This progress report describes current and projected activities in the election campaigns of the People's National Congress (PNC) and the United Force, notes a new turn in Prime Minister Forbes Burnham's electoral strategy and describes the current state of Guyana's border disputes with Venezuela and Suriname.

This report also refers to the previous progress report on this activity, considered by the 303 Committee on 16 February 1968, which stated that of the [*less than 1 line of source text not declassified*] originally approved by the Committee, approximately [*less than 1 line of source text not declassified*] were spent in FY 1967 and [*less than 1 line of source text not declassified*] were programmed for FY 1968. This report further points out that these funds have now been spent and it is estimated that an additional [*less than 1 line of source text not declassified*] will be needed for the remainder of FY 1968 and [*less than 1 line of source text not declassified*] will be needed in FY 1969. Approval for the expenditure of this amount is recommended. The [*less than 1 line of source text not declassified*] are available [*less than 1 line of source text not declassified*]. Of the [*less than 1 line of source text not declassified*] needed for FY 1969, [*less than 1 line of source text not declassified*] are available or programmed [*less than 1 line of source text not declassified]*; the remaining [*less than 1 line of source text not declassified*] would have to be provided from the [*less than 1 line of source text not declassified*] Reserve for FY 1969.)

According to the minutes of the July 12 meeting of the 303 Committee, [*name not declassified*] acknowledged "the seemingly high costs for such a 'postage stamp' country election but indicated that known Cuban or Soviet subsidies to Dr. Jagan are on almost the same scale." The additional funding was approved by the Committee.

Preparations for the elections are proceeding satisfactorily with the following activities now under way:

Campaign in Guyana

The campaign organizations of the People's National Congress (PNC) led by Prime Minister Forbes Burnham and the United Force led by Peter D'Aguiar have been set up in Guyana and both these parties are now engaged in their electoral campaigns. Due to its larger size and the wider and more varied activities demanded of it, the PNC is more advanced in its state of organization than is the UF. PNC offices have been set up at the precinct level throughout the populated areas of the country and party activists have begun to canvas potential voters. The UF began its campaign later than the PNC due to its smaller size and the somewhat more restricted area in which it must organize. However, the UF campaign is now beginning to get underway, party organizers are canvassing urban areas where most UF voters are located and are also making an increasing number of visits to the interior, where Amerindian voters, who made up approximately one third of the UF vote in 1964, are located. The UF and the PNC each have a campaign manager in Guyana [*less than 1 line of source text not declassified*]. Both of these are professional political organizers and are doing an excellent job in getting the parties organized for the elections.

According to a July 2 memorandum from Oliver to Bohlen, part of the additional funds was for PNC and UF motor vehicles and boats to reach Amerindian voters and funds to contact overseas voters.

Guyana National Census and Voter Registration

The Government of Guyana is carrying out a census of all citizens 14 years of age and over who reside in Guyana. The names of Guyanese of voting age will be drawn from the census list to compose the voter registration lists for the elections. All three parties, the PNC, the UF and the PPP led by Dr. Jagan, are now working to make sure that their adherents are properly registered. [*3 lines of source text not declassified*] The Government of Guyana at one time planned to have the census completed in early 1968; however various delays have occurred and the government recently said privately that the census will not be completed until the end of July, at which time registration will be closed. Due to these delays, the government's contract with the company expired, company representatives who were in Guyana returned to the US, and Guyanese are completing the census without the company's help. Prime Minister Burnham recently said that he believes the registration can be completed in time to permit elections to be held in early December 1968 but there is a possibility that they may not be held until February 1969. According to the constitution, elections must be held by the end of March 1969.

Registration of Overseas Voters

The main thrust of present PNC and UF efforts overseas is to get potential voters registered. This will be strictly a registration of voters as no census is being conducted in overseas areas. This registration effort is going slowly but reasonably satisfactorily in the US and Great Britain but has run into snags in Canada. Steps are being taken to correct this problem. It is difficult to estimate what the total number of overseas registrants will be as there are no figures to be used as a basis for such an estimate. There may be as many as 20,000 potential voters in Great Britain and possibly 15,000 in the US and Canada, as many as 25,000 of these may be supporters of the PNC and the UF.

New Developments

[*less than 1 line of source text not declassified*] representatives met with Prime Minister Forbes Burnham in late April to discuss operational matters related to the electoral campaign. At that meeting Mr. Burnham stated unequivocally that he plans to conduct the registration and voting in such a manner that the PNC will emerge with an absolute majority in the Guyana National Assembly. Mr. Burnham said that he will never again allow the life of his government to depend upon his coalition partner Peter D'Aguiar and that if the voting should turn out in such a manner that he could not form a government without the help of D'Aguiar, he would refuse to form a government. Mr. Burnham said that he plans to register 17, 18, 19 and 20-year-old PNC adherents (minimum voting age is 21 years) to make up part of the vote he needs and will direct his campaign in such a way as to attract enough additional East Indian voters to put the PNC approximately on a par with the PPP in Guyana. The additional votes he would need to give the PNC an absolute majority would come from overseas Guyanese. On the other hand, Ambassador Carlson [*less than 1 line of source text not declassified*] in Georgetown commented that they believe this is wishful thinking by Mr. Burnham. They believe Mr. Burnham would encounter insurmountable administrative and organizational difficulties in attempting to rig the elections to the extent necessary to assure the PNC an absolute majority.

It should be noted that Mr. Burnham's plans to get an absolute majority in the elections constitute a basic change in strategy. Planning heretofore had been based upon the PNC and UF running separately but re-forming the coalition after the elections. Mr. Burnham will probably still be willing to have a coalition government after the elections but wants an absolute majority so that the coalition will be formed on his terms and so that the life of his government will not depend on the UF and Peter D'Aguiar.

[Omitted here are sections 4–8, "Additional Development," "Security," "Coordination," "Future Plans," and "Recommendations."]

Memorandum from Secretary of Agriculture Freeman and Administrator of the Agency for International Development Gaud to President Johnson, Washington, June 21, 1968.

Public Law 480 Program with Guyana

We recommend that you authorize us to negotiate a PL480 sales agreement with Guyana to provide approximately 1,500 tons of edible vegetable oil, 2,000 tons of wheat/wheat flour, 100 tons of tobacco and 3,000 tons of potatoes for which the current export market value (including applicable ocean transportation costs) is approximately $1.0 million. The proposed terms are payment in dollars of 5 percent on delivery and the balance in approximately equal installments over 20 years; interest will be 2 percent per annum during a two-year grace period and 2.5 percent thereafter. The Departments of State and Treasury concur in this recommendation.

Need for Program

The Guyana (Mr. Burnham) Government has undertaken with help from the United States Agency for International Development and the British and Canadian Governments an ambitious economic development program over the past three years. We have given particular priority to assisting this government in its effort to demonstrate what a democratic government can achieve following the years of difficulties under the rule of communist-oriented Dr. Jagan. The Mr. Burnham government is making a special effort to accelerate its development projects, particularly for agriculture, but local currency costs for development have placed a substantial strain on the Burnham government's budget.

This agreement would assist the Burnham Government to sustain its record of economic achievement and progress, which is important at this time since national elections were held in Guyana prior to March 31, 1969, with Dr. Jagan again opposing Mr. Burnham.

Self-Help Efforts

In negotiating this agreement, we will seek the following commitments from the Government of Guyana: The local currency generated from the sale of the commodities in the importing country shall be made available for development of agriculture as follows:

(1) For the construction and improvement of roads connecting rural areas with the market cities and also for planning and construction of access roads in the Atkinson/McKenzie land settlement project.
(2) For the modernization of agriculture through the expansion of adaptive research and extension and increasing the means for storage, processing and distribution of basic food crops and for land development and water control in farming areas along the coast.
(3) For the improvement of facilities and operation of the government maternity and child health centers, especially for projected family planning, and including vaccinations for polio, etc.
(4) For strengthening systems of collection, computation and analysis of statistics to better measure the availability of agricultural inputs and progress in expanding production and marketing of agricultural commodities.
(5) For other improvements in the agricultural sector to be agreed upon by the USAID Mission and the Government of Guyana.

Military Expenditures Review

With respect to Section 620(S) of the Foreign Assistance Act, State/AID has concluded that U.S. developmental assistance is not being diverted to military expenditures and that Guyana's resources are not being diverted to military expenditures to a degree which materially interferes with Guyana's development.

Orville L. Freeman
William S. Gaud.

Telegram from the Ambassador to Guyana (Carlson) to the Department of State, Georgetown, June 28, 1968. [File name not declassified], Vol. 4, July 7, 1965–February 14, 1969. Secret, for Hill ARA/NC from Amb. Carlson.

(1) Had long discussion with Prime Minister Burnham June 27 on variety subjects but my primary purpose was to assess his attitude re dimension of possible electoral results and whether reports referred to in your message to me of June 21 should be viewed as definitive. In a June 21 telegram Hill had advised Carlson to warn Mr. Burnham not to rig the election so extreme as to show an African majority in the population.

(2) I first touched on status of possibility SA loan mentioning that while great progress had been made toward authorization and I was hopeful, it was at the moment still not certain. There was, however, another matter involved in this which was of concern to me. Some of the friends of Guyana in Washington had recently become apprehensive as to whether the Prime Minister might plan Tammany Hall tactics on such a massive scale as to taint the results, raise questions of legitimacy, and embarrass the U.S. I was sure that he would no more want to have us all in the funny papers than would our friends in Washington. I said I assumed that Sonny Ramphal had already mentioned to him that John Hill had expressed this anxiety to Ramphal in New York. In addition, an

ingredient in the discussion in Washington of my request for SA funding had been the question as to whether election was to be so fixed as to make such funding unnecessary thereby saving us several million dollars. (Mr. Burnham seemed impressed by this point.) Also because of our strong support of Mr. Burnham's administration in the past, which was well known, and the closeness of GOG/USG relations, what he does will also inevitably affect our image.

Supporting Assistance loans could provide over $2 million for small public works projects, reducing unemployment and resulting in maximum political impact during the pre-election period. In a June 28 telegram [*text not declassified*], on Carlson's behalf, requested [*name not declassified*] immediate intercession, since the loan agreement had to be signed prior to the end of the fiscal year (June 30) and Gaud was reluctant to proceed. Carlson planned a direct appeal to the Secretary of State "if day's events require," but the loan was approved without this proving necessary.

(3) Mr. Burnham asked what these people thought was reasonable and I told him the matter was not one of any precise equation but simply one of dimension. We wanted him to win; we had backed him to the hilt; neither of us wanted a scandal. He agreed. I asked him what he really expected electorally. He said he foresaw the PNC in about the same range of votes in Guyana as the PPP; *i.e.*, roughly even, perhaps not quite as much as the PPP, or perhaps slightly more but in general about the same order of magnitude. Mr. Burnham told me he expects to work hard on Muslims and hopes to have some success as well

as with various other non-Africans so as to give PNC more multi-racial image. He hoped part of this process could take place before the election and mentioned various individuals including Kit Nascimento and Ann Jardim.

(4) As far as overseas was concerned, he thought registration of as many as 50,000 was within the realm of possibility because of ease with which persons can qualify as Guyanese, i.e., descendants if mother was Guyanese and even foreign wives of Guyanese under the law qualify. He was urging his agents to work vigorously toward this large registration but he thought the prospect was not good for high voter participation overseas. He expected not more than about 30,000 to vote if registration went as high as 50,000. We agreed that the overseas vote should be heavily PNC, i.e., 75–90% (with him more inclined to the latter figure). We agreed that it was entirely logical that it should be heavily PNC.

(5) Since all indications from collateral reporting showed that his intentions were much more reasonable than had been feared, this was as far as I thought it necessary to go. Our conversation generally tended to confirm reports from several other sources a few days before [*less than 1 line of source text not declassified*] that Mr. Burnham is not planning or expecting a massive rig. [*less than 1 line of source text not declassified*] reports that he is mentally prepared to accept plurality and is hoping for 26 seats with thought that if coalition is not reestablished (presumably due D'Aguiar on scene trying set terms) that he will be able persuade at least two if not three UF legislators to join him in forming majority.

Circular Telegram from the Department of State to All American Republic Posts. Washington, Guyana/Ven. Confidential. Drafted by Luers and George F. Jones, cleared by Hill and Richard A. Frank (L/E), and approved by Sayre. Repeated to London, USUN, USCINCSO, and Montevideo for Assistant Secretary Oliver, July 17, 1968.

Following is summary developments of the Guyana/Venezuela border dispute that can be drawn on as appropriate.

(1) Dispute originates in the 1899 Arbitral Award of territory west of Essequibo River (about five-eighths of what is now Guyana) to Great Britain. GOV has since 1962 maintained officially that the arbitral award was the result of a "fraudulent deal" between British and Russian members tribunal and therefore the award is null and void. In the period immediately prior to British granting independence to Guyana, Venezuela pressed for reopening the question of where the boundary should lie in belief that Venezuela could more easily twist the tail of British lion than of its small, newly sovereign neighbor. In February 1966 at Geneva UK, British Guiana and Venezuela Governments signed an agreement establishing a Mixed Commission to discuss disputes arising out of Venezuelan claims. Since Guyana's independence in May 1966, the Mixed Commission has met 9 times and has generally served as a useful channel for diversion of the political heat generated in both countries.

(2) Mixed Commission meetings have been frustrating to GOV, however, since it apparently saw a Mixed Commission to redraw the boundary, whereas Guyana

saw it as a forum to examine validity Venezuelan allegations concerning Arbitral Award. In an effort to break the impasse, GOV offered to contribute to joint economic development of disputed territory. GOG expressed willingness to discuss Venezuelan economic assistance but broke down when it became clear to GOG that GOV wanted to exercise more authority over the project than normal for economic assistance donors.

(3) Last year Venezuela occupied the tiny border island Ankoko, half of which was claimed by Guyana. As dispute boiled over *'Ankoko Affair'* early summer 1967 we encouraged President Leoni to receive Guyana emissary. Talks resulted in easing of tensions and assuring GOG that Venezuela did not intend to use force in the dispute and that matter would be played in low key during the pre-electoral period in Guyana.

(4) In May 1968 Venezuela reiterated a 1965 warning that any commercial concessions GOG might grant to foreign firms in disputed territory would not be recognized by GOV. (GOV has a policy not to grant new concessions for mineral exploration in territory it controls.) This brought angry charges from the Guyana Government that Venezuela violated the Geneva Agreement by publicizing its claim outside the Mixed Commission and committing "economic aggression" against Guyana. In late June GOV withdrew from sub-commission for economic development following refusal GOG entertained joint development of disputed territory.

(5) On July 9 Venezuelan President issued a decree claiming 9 miles of territorial sea beyond the 3 miles claimed by Guyana off the coast of disputed territory.

"Explanatory note" published with degree pointed out Venezuela claims 12 miles of territorial sea off its own coast and wished to record its claim to similar areas off disputed territory. However, since Guyana does not claim a zone from 3 to 12 miles Venezuela feels free claim zone and, "explanatory note" implies, exercise immediate sovereignty over it by some unstated "physical act of possession" or "concrete act of dominion." GOV member Mixed Commission told press foreign merchant ships would have the right to innocent passage through the zone (which includes major shipping lanes) but no fishing rights. Naval vessels could pass with GOV permission. GOV FonMin told the US Ambassador privately he "assumed" GOV would institute naval patrols of the zone.

(6) On July 13, Under Secretary asked explanation decree's meaning from Venezuelan Ambassador in Washington stating that if Venezuela intended exercise rights of sovereignty in 3 to 12 miles zone off Guyana US would take "most serious" view situation. Under Secretary pointed out:

  (a) In addition to the fact that the USG does not recognize 12 miles of territorial seas, the US does not accept the decree's validity if it implies actual exercise of sovereignty and if matters came up in an international forum; we could not support Venezuela.

  (b) We viewed decree's explanatory note with allusions such as "physical act of possession" as more disturbing than decree itself and wondered about GOV intentions in view of earlier assurances from Venezuelan President that GOV would not resort to force.

Telegram 206210 to Georgetown, July 20, reported that Under Secretary Katzenbach met with Prime Minister Burnham earlier in the day and assured him "that the U.S. viewed the decree as invalid under international law and had so informed GOV firmly."

Telegram 206216 to Georgetown and Caracas, July 20, reported that President Leoni of Venezuela, in the presence of Foreign Minister Iribarren, gave Ambassador Bernbaum assurances that "no incidents would occur and that the right of innocent passage would be honored." The telegram reported that these assurances were conveyed to Mr. Burnham following his meeting with Katzenbach.

(c) (c) We concerned that GOV actions might erode Mr. Burnham electoral strength and divert his attention from campaign prior to crucial electoral confrontation with Dr. Jagan which will possibly take place in December this year.

Telegram 7021 from Caracas, July 20, reported that after Bernbaum's conversation with Leoni and Iribarren (*see footnote 3 above*) Foreign Office Director of Political Affairs Herrera Marcano met with Carlson who outlined the effect GOV's actions were having on Guyana's domestic political situation stressing how they were helping Dr. Jagan and hurting Mr. Burnham. Carlson pointed out that Dr. Jagan's position had been on ebb, but that Mr. Burnham had felt compelled to bring him in to consult on Guyana's position in order to present a united front, thus lending Dr. Jagan some new respectability. Carlson also said that "*recent Government of Venezuela 'provocations' distracted Mr.*

Burnham " and they could have a significant effect on Mr. Burnham's campaign effort.

(7) The US has consistently maintained a neutral stance on the merits of the dispute itself and has informed GOV and GOG. We may, however, be compelled to make our position public at a future date on legal aspects of the recent decree and its implications for peace in the area. We will attempt to avoid making public our legal position until GOV responds to the Under Secretary's inquiry.

(8) GOG has undertaken at the UN present case to regional groups and particularly seeks support from LA countries. Mr. Burnham was also contemplating bringing matters to UNSC.

(9) Press reports implying US favors GOV inaccurate and to date press reports of GOV military or naval movements also appear inaccurate.

(10) Foregoing can be used as background in discussion with government officials provided such action would not be interpreted as lobbying for interests of either government.

Rusk advice on Mr. Burnham's U.S. visits, July 24, 1968. Memorandum to the President.

Rusk advised that although Mr. Burnham's U.S. visit was private and unofficial, he had come to Washington to discuss his government's concerns about Venezuela's recent territorial waters decree with Katzenbach. Rusk recommended that Johnson meet with Mr. Burnham for a brief courtesy call because "Mr. Burnham needs to demonstrate in Georgetown that he has received highest level consideration of the Guyana position on the recent Venezuelan decree," adding that Dr. Jagan's newspapers "have taunted Mr. Burnham that U.S. silence on the decree constitutes tacit approval of this new Venezuelan claim."

Prime Minister Forbes Burnham, accompanied by Ambassador John Carter, paid a courtesy call on the President. Assistant Secretary Oliver was also present. After an exchange of greetings, the Prime Minister described the Venezuelan decree claiming nine miles of territorial waters beyond the three-mile limit off the disputed territory of Essequibo. Mr. Burnham also mentioned the Venezuelan warning to firms seeking concessions in the disputed territory. He said the warning had already scared off one Canadian investor. In making the presentation, the Prime Minister gave no indication that he was seeking Presidential help.

In a July 23 memorandum to Johnson, Rostow stated that the appointment "must be handled in such a way that it does not offend our Venezuelan friends. This is manageable and the Prime Minister will certainly play ball." Rostow added that "The State is doing all possible to defuse the incident without taking sides on the territorial dispute. So far, these efforts seem to be meeting with success." The President inquired about the outlook for the elections in Guyana. The Prime Minister expressed optimism. While no date has been set for the election, he thought it would be in early December.

The President, mentioning his interest in regional integration, asked the Prime Minister how he saw the Caribbean Development Bank shaping up. The Prime Minister described past difficulties with Jamaica. He noted that recently there seemed to be a change in the Jamaican attitude which gives some reason to hope they would join the Bank and bring the Bahamas and British Honduras with them. Mr. Burnham added that on his way back he is expecting to talk to Prime Minister Shearer about the Bank.

The President said he would like to be as helpful to Guyana as he could. He told the Prime Minister he could give careful consideration to any proposals he wished to make. Mr. Burnham thanked him for his understanding and willingness to support him.

Support to Anti-Jagan Political Parties in Guyana, Memorandum Prepared for the 303 Committee, Washington, Progress Report, November 21, 1968.

(1) On April 7, 1967 the 303 Committee approved a proposal to support anti-Jagan political parties in Guyana in the national elections scheduled for late 1968 or early 1969. Previous progress reports on this activity were considered by the 303 Committee on August 7, 1967; February 16, 1968 and July 12, 1968. The report noted that the elections have been set for December 16, 1968; describes progress in the election campaigns of the People's National Congress led by Prime Minister Forbes Burnham and the United Force led by Peter D'Aguiar, noted the outcome of the national census and voter registration effort in Guyana and describes the problems facing Mr. Burnham stemming from his having padded the registration lists in the United Kingdom excessively in an attempt to win an outright majority in the elections. The report also noted the security implication arising from Peter D'Aguiar being aware of this padding and his efforts to counter it.

The progress report also stated that somewhat under half of the funds approved for that activity for fiscal year 1969 were obligated by mid-November 1968. [*Omitted here are sections 2–6, Current Activities, Date of Elections, New Developments, Additional Pertinent Developments, including Border Problems, the MPCA, the PNC/UF Coalition, and U.S.–U.K. Discussions, Security, and Coordination.*]

(7) Future Plans [*less than 1 line of source text not declassified*] will continue to provide financial support and electoral guidance to the PNC and the UF for their campaigns in Guyana and overseas. The PNC contracted with a U.S.-based motion picture company to produce newsreel films showing the progress made by the Mr. Burnham government; the first two of a projected ten films are now being shown in Georgetown and depict Mr. Burnham inspecting self-help projects in small villages and the visit of Indian Prime Minister Indira Gandhi to Guyana.

The United States government will continue to exert all possible influence to persuade Mr. Burnham to pursue a moderate and statesmanlike course toward the PPP and the UF with regard to the registration problem and to the objections of these parties to the electoral law. To date, Mr. Burnham has not responded in the manner desired to U.S. advice to avoid an overly large false registration and to U.S. urging to plan for the formation of another coalition government after the elections. He feels that his own pride, self-respect and competence as a leader are called into question when he is urged to continue his cooperation with Peter D'Aguiar, whom he hates. Racial considerations are most likely a significant ingredient in Mr. Burnham's attitude. Thus, we have no assurance that he will accept our guidance in this regard. Peter D'Aguiar also is an extremely difficult person to deal with and so far, has rejected our attempts to persuade him to take a more moderate and flexible line toward Mr. Burnham.

D'Aguiar was in close touch with Dr. Jagan regarding the lawsuit that each of their parties was instituting and at one point it appeared that the two parties would cooperate closely in the suits. Dr. Jagan and Mr. D'Aguiar have now agreed to consult and cooperate in their attacks on Mr. Burnham and the government. D'Aguiar continued to maintain a strong anti-Communist attitude and told Dr. Jagan that he dislikes his Communist sympathies and will work with him only to obstruct any government plans for electoral chicanery. However, D'Aguiar despises Mr. Burnham passionately and has a paranoid streak in him; this combination may well induce him to take attitudes and to pursue courses of action that a better-balanced man would avoid.

Of the [*less than 1 line of source text not declassified*] approved for this activity for fiscal year 1969, a total of approximately [*less than 1 line of source text not declassified*] has been obligated through mid-November 1968.

(8) In a December 18 memorandum to Bohlen, Trueheart reported that Rostow read the memorandum for the 303 Committee and asked that the other 303 Committee principals see it and note it at the next Committee meeting, but that it is not formally placed on the agenda. Trueheart added that the memorandum reported that [*text not declassified*],

with 303 Committee approval, had contributed some [*text not declassified*] to the electoral campaign of the PNC and the UF.

Loan for Guyana Rice Industry Bill, Action Memorandum from the President's Special Assistant (Rostow) to President Johnson, Washington, November 23, 1968, 10:40 a.m.

Gaud is asking urgently for your approval of a $12.9 million loan to modernize the rice industry in Guyana (Tab B). Charlie Zwick recommends your approval (Tab A). The Treasury has no problem on balance of payments grounds.

The critical elections in Guyana will take place December 16. Prime Minister Burnham has done a very good job of preparing the political ground to fend off Dr. Jagan's challenge at the polls. Although the East Indian population outnumbers Mr. Burnham's predominantly black following, some of Dr. Jagan's supporters have been won over by Mr. Burnham's good government record. The outlook is for a very narrow Mr. Burnham victory, barring last-minute surprises.

This rice loan project plays a key part in Mr. Burnham's electoral strategy. The government's efforts to modernize Guyana's rice industry, well publicized for over a year, will help split Dr. Jagan's almost solid political support among the small rice farmers, all of whom are East Indian. The project has been delayed for technical reasons long past the intended starting date. Nonetheless, the announcement of the loan within the next few days will still have important political benefits for Mr. Burnham and help to guarantee his election. That was a good project on its economic merits. The overriding argument, however, is that it provides important political support for Mr. Burnham at this crucial point. Ambassador

Carlson urges your approval in time for an announcement to be made in Georgetown early next week. I recommended that you approve authorization of that loan.

In an introduction to the collection of declassified documents, the Historian of the US State Department wrote that the Special Group/303 Committee of the National Security Council approved approximately USD 2.08 million for covert action programs towards the 1964 and 1968 elections in Guyana. A good proportion of that covert funding was given to the PNC and the UF, in 1963 and 1964, when they were trying to overthrow the PPP government. The Historian stated:

> After Mr. Burnham was elected Premier in December 1964, the U.S. Government, again through the CIA, continued to provide substantial funds to both Mr. Burnham and Mr. D'Aguiar and their parties. In 1967 and 1968, the 303 Committee-approved funds were used to help the Burnham and D'Aguiar coalition contest and win the December 1968 general elections. When the U.S. Government learned that Mr. Burnham was going to use fraudulent absentee ballots to continue in power in the 1968 election, it advised him against such a course of action, but did not try to stop him.

The provision of covert electoral funds by a foreign government to political parties was a breach of Guyana's laws. In the campaign to keep the PPP out of government, the provider and the receiver of such illegal donations had no qualms about stepping beyond the bounds of law.

Mr. Burnham's rigging plans were hatched shortly after Guyana became independent in 1966. Delmar Carlson, the

United States Ambassador to Guyana, reported in a telegram to the State Department on July 15, 1966 that:

> Mr. Burnham has confided to close colleagues that he intends to remain in power indefinitely, if at all possible, by constitutional means. However, if necessary, he is prepared to employ unorthodox methods to achieve his aims. In these circumstances, probably the best that can be hoped for at this time is that he might respond to guidelines and thus take the most effective and least objectionable course to attain his goals.

It was apparent that the United States government wanted Mr. Burnham to be re-elected and it began to give a positive view to the idea of providing his party with financial support despite his plans to utilize "unorthodox methods" to gain re-election. The 303 Committee, in a memorandum prepared on March 17, 1967, reported:

> Prime Minister Forbes Burnham, leader of the majority People's National Congress (PNC) in the coalition has stated that he is fully prepared to utilize the electoral machinery at his disposal to ensure his own re-election. Mr. Burnham has initiated steps for electoral registration of Guyanese at home and abroad, and has requested financial assistance for the PNC campaign. It is recommended that he and his party be provided with covert support in order to assure his victory at the polls. At the same time, it is believed that support to Peter D'Aguiar and

his United Force (UF), the minority party in the coalition government, is also essential in order to offset Dr. Jagan's solidly entrenched East Indian electoral support. It is recommended that the 303 Committee approve the courses of action outlined in this paper.

The amount of money recommended still remains as classified information. "In a meeting on September 16, 1966, Mr. Burnham requested money for various political purposes and outlined his plans to issue identification cards to all Guyanans (sic) above the age of 10, and to identify and register all Guyanans (sic) of African ancestry in the United Kingdom, Canada, and the United States in order to get their absentee votes in the next elections 'Conversely, Mr. Burnham acknowledged with a smile, East Indians living abroad may have trouble getting registered and, if registered, getting ballots."

The March 1967 memorandum also noted that Mr. Burnham was planning to establish his campaign headquarters in Georgetown and other urban areas where the Afro-Guyanese votes were concentrated. He was also sending "a trusted political adviser" abroad to survey the potential absentee vote which he can expect from Guyanese residing in the U.S., the U.K., Canada and the West Indies. It added:

Mr. Burnham believes that he would have great difficulty ensuring his own re-election without support from the U.S. Government. He has requested financial support for staff and campaign expenses, motor vehicles, small boats, printing equipment, and transistorized public address systems. He also wishes to contract for the services of an American public relations firm to improve his image abroad and counteract Dr. Jagan's propaganda in the foreign press. Since we believe that there is a good likelihood that Dr. Jagan can be elected in

Guyana unless the entire non-East Indian electorate is mobilized against him, we also believe that campaign support must be provided to Peter D'Aguiar, the head of the United Force (UF) and Mr. Burnham's coalition partner.

The Committee examined the risks involved in the US political assistance to Mr. Burnham. It stated that, because Dr. Jagan had consistently and publicly accused the American and British Governments of having undermined him and of having aided Mr. Burnham, it was expected that he would continue to make those claims. It added that "Dr. Jagan has cried wolf so often in the past that a reiteration of the same charges is not expected to carry much impact, particularly if the timing of the operation is handled appropriately." It was apparent that the 303 Committee was privy to Mr. Burnham's plans. It pointed out:

> Mr. Burnham is thinking of utilizing voting machines in certain districts in Guyana, knowing that this will attract Dr. Jagan's attention and lead to charges of fraud. Since Mr. Burnham does not intend to rig the machines, and the tallies will in fact be accurate, he believes this will not only divert Dr. Jagan's attention during the election campaign but will add credibility to the results after the fact.

Mr. Burnham was also made aware that the American Government would attach the utmost importance to tight security practices in the event that he received American support for the elections. The memorandum explained:

> He recognizes that any exposure of this support will reflect on him as well as on the US

Government, and he is prepared to deny receipt of any such aid. American and British press coverage of the 1968 elections must be expected to be relatively intensive, and it is likely that some British and American correspondents may be favorably predisposed to Dr. Jagan. For this reason, it will be essential that Mr. Burnham not only counter Dr. Jagan's assertion that Mr. Burnham represents a minority of the electorate, but also that the US Government's involvement not be revealed in any way." The Committee concluded: "we recommend the immediate and continuing injection of fiscal support to both the PNC and the UF, and we propose to maintain close contact with Mr. Burnham and D'Aguiar and their principal associates in order to influence the course of the election wherever necessary. This should be initiated at the earliest possible date, so that alternate tactics can be considered.

Ambassador Delmar Carlson, met with Mr. Burnham in early June 1967, and in a telegram sent to the State Department he revealed that Mr. Burnham's plans to rig the votes in the next elections:

> In the course of discussion with Prime Minister Mr. Burnham last night I raised the subject of the coming elections and explained that election mathematics at my disposal tended to show that the PNC majority over the PPP and the UF would require a minimum 60,000 votes additional. Even Prime Minister Burnham does

not consider that overseas vote can be blown up to that extent; even a 50,000-figure used by him very hypothetically and 30,000 accepted as more realistic (Embassy finds in excess of 25,000 not believable). Earlier Prime Minister Mr. Burnham said that overseas vote figures could be manipulated pretty much as he wished and he tentatively had in mind say 25,000 for a new coalition government and 5,000 for the PPP. When pressed by these mathematics, Prime Minister Mr. Burnham said he 'would not break his lance' over the PNC majority, meaning that if the U.S.G. made an issue of it he would not pursue it. Clearly however he intends to follow a number of election tricks to add to the PNC totals and detract from the PPP votes. Accumulated total of these may well produce a surprisingly good showing for the PNC, though falling short of absolute majority. Adds that he is well aware of the need for these election tricks to be done smoothly and without controversy.

During that meeting, Carlson also suggested to Mr. Burnham that he should continue to work closely with D'Aguiar and his United Force. Mr. Burnham was already having difficulties working with D'Aguiar, and the ambassador suggested that the solution to this problem "lays less in engineered majority than it did by arranging for D'Aguiar's honorable withdrawal from politics and government after the election was won and a new coalition government formed." Despite Carlson's best efforts to encourage a working relationship with Mr. Burnham, D'Aguiar resigned from the cabinet on September 26, 1967. Earlier, on August 7, 1967, some of the original sum proposed for assistance to the PNC and UF was committed by the US government. Part of the funds was to be used for the PNC and UF to contact overseas voters and also for these parties to purchase motor vehicles and boats to reach the Indigenous voters in the remote areas of the country.

On December 6, 1967, William Trueheart, the Deputy Director for Coordination of the Bureau of Intelligence and Research of the State Department, sent a memorandum to Thomas Hughes and George Denney, the Director and Deputy Director, respectively, of the Bureau of Intelligence and Research of the State Department, in which he reported that the 303 Committee on April 10, 1967 approved a proposal to provide Mr. Burnham "with covert support in the next national elections" to assure a PNC victory over Dr. Cheddi Jagan and the PPP. Some covert monetary assistance was also to go to the United Force.

Trueheart's memorandum predicted that the result of the elections would be very close even with assistance provided to Mr. Burnham. It revealed that the 303 Committee decided to "make 12 equal monthly payments to Mr. Burnham to help him in revitalizing his party and in organizing his absentee vote strength." According to the Committee, if Mr. Burnham's electoral prospects appeared bleak, certain measures (not revealed) would be implemented. In an ominous revelation, Trueheart stated: "These measures, it was hoped, would forestall the necessity of exile of Dr. Jagan, or his detention, or coup d'état after the elections."

The Venezuelan government, in 1964 was prepared to support the overthrow of Dr. Jagan, and to seek US support for this venture. According to that plot, Mr. Burnham and D'Aguiar would be encouraged to form a "Revolutionary Government" after a coup initiated with the assistance of 100 trained men given 30 days special training in Venezuela; and at the same time Cheddi and Janet Jagan would be kidnapped and taken to Venezuela. A memorandum from William Tyler, Assistant Secretary of State for European and Canadian Affairs, to Secretary of State Rusk on July 10, 1964 gave details of this arrangement. Apparently, a similar plan, according to Trueheart's memorandum, remained in active consideration in the event of a Dr. Jagan victory in 1968.

A CIA report prepared on December 7, 1967, with the participation of the intelligence organizations of the Departments of State and Defense, and the National Security Agency stated that Mr. Burnham was working on various schemes to enlarge the Afro-Guyanese votes for his party. He was trying to obtain a substantial number of absentee votes from Afro-Guyanese residing abroad. Beyond that, he was also exploring means to merge Guyana with one of the Caribbean islands, most likely St. Vincent, so as to increase the proportion of Afro-Guyanese voters. The report continued:

> If Mr. Burnham became convinced that such arrangements would not suffice to keep him in power and Dr. Jagan out, he would probably rig the election. In any case, he would have to rely on the small civilian police and Guyana Defense Force (GDF), both of which are predominantly Negro to maintain order. They probably could do so, except in the unlikely event of a major East Indian uprising. If Dr. Jagan's party won, he would probably not be permitted to exercise power. Mr. Burnham could use force to keep him out, or suspend the Constitution and rule by fiat, or even press for a grand coalition which he himself would seek to head. Alternatively,

he could permit Dr. Jagan to take office-only to subvert his government at a later date.

Mr. Burnham visited the United States in January 1968 for a medical check-up at the Bethesda Naval Hospital. After his release from the hospital, he held a 45-minute discussion with Secretary of State Dean Rusk at the State Department on January 23. Mr. Burnham informed Rusk that he was confident about the outcome of the elections which had to be held before March 1969. He said he was also counting "heavily" on the overseas absentee ballots concentrated in the UK and in the US. He said that the US Supreme Court decision in 1967 allowing Guyanese nationals who had become naturalized US citizens to vote without losing their US citizenship would be helpful. Mr. Burnham stated that there would be objectionable electioneering in the US and pointed out that Dr. Jagan was already setting the stage among his followers for a defeat by claiming the elections would be rigged. Rusk also met with Deputy Prime Minister and Minister of Finance Dr. Ptolemy Reid on May 24, 1968. Reid's primary purpose in coming to the United States was to whip up electoral support for the People's National Congress (PNC) among Guyanese residing in the U.S.

A memorandum prepared for the 303 Committee on a progress report on "Support to Anti-Dr. Jagan Political Parties in Guyana" and dated June 5, 1968, set out clearly the plan by Mr. Burnham to rig the forthcoming elections. The relevant part of the document stated:

[*less than 1 line of source text not declassified*] representatives met with Prime Minister Forbes Mr. Burnham in late April to discuss operational matters related to the electoral campaign. At this meeting Mr. Burnham stated unequivocally that he plans to conduct the registration and voting in such a manner that the PNC will emerge with an absolute majority in the Guyana National Assembly. Mr. Burnham said that he will never again allow the life of his government to depend upon his coalition partner Peter D'Aguiar and that if the voting should turn out in such a manner that he could not form a government without the help of D'Aguiar, he would refuse to form a government. Mr. Burnham said that he plans to register 17, 18, 19 and 20-year-old PNC adherents (minimum voting age is 21 years) to make up part of the vote he needs and will direct his campaign in such a way as to attract enough additional East Indian voters to put the PNC approximately on a par with the PPP in Guyana. The additional votes he would need to give the PNC an absolute majority would come from overseas Guyanese. On the other hand, Ambassador Carlson, in Georgetown has commented that they believe this is wishful thinking by Mr. Burnham. They believe Mr. Burnham would encounter insurmountable administrative and organizational difficulties in attempting to rig the elections to the extent necessary to assure the PNC an absolute majority. It should be noted that Mr. Burnham's plans to get an absolute majority in the elections constitute a basic change in strategy. Planning heretofore had been based upon the PNC and UF running separately but re-forming the coalition after the elections. Mr. Burnham will probably still be willing to have a coalition government after the elections but wants an absolute majority so that the coalition will be formed on his terms and so that the life of his government will not depend on the UF and Peter D'Aguiar.

Burnham's plan to rig the elections was amplified in another memorandum prepared on June 12, 1968 by Thomas H. Karamessines, Deputy CIA Director for Plans, for Walt W. Rostow, Special Assistant to President Johnson. The document, titled "Plans of Guyana Prime Minister Mr. Forbes

Burnham, Leader of the People's National Congress (PNC), to rig the elections scheduled for late 1968 or early 1969", showed US government complicity in this arrangement. Even though it had knowledge of Mr. Burnham's plans, it did absolutely nothing to prevent the fraud and actually provided full encouragement. The memorandum, copied to Paul H. Nitze, Deputy Secretary of Defense, and Ambassador Covey T. Oliver, Assistant Secretary of State, made the following revelation:

(1) (a) In a meeting of high-level government and People's National Congress leaders Mr. Forbes Burnham, Prime Minister of Guyana and leader of the PNC, gave instructions to rig the election scheduled for late 1968 or early 1969 in order to permit the PNC to win a clear majority. In the last elections, held in December 1964, the PNC won 40.5 per cent of the total vote; the United Force won 12.4 per cent; and the People's Progressive Party made up principally of East Indians, won 45.8 percent. Mr. Burnham said that the registration of East Indians, who traditionally vote for the People's Progressive Party, should be strictly limited in order to keep their number of eligible voters as low as possible. He also gave instructions to his party leaders to increase the size of the PNC electorate by registering some PNC adherents who are between the ages of 17 and 20 years of age, although the minimum age for voting is 21 years of age. He said he planned to have written into the electoral law a provision for increasing the use of proxy votes.

(b) Through those means and by campaigning diligently, Mr. Burnham said he hopes the PNC will receive approximately half of the total vote cast in Guyana. In order to provide the winning margin for the PNC, he has arranged for Guyanese who reside overseas to vote in the Guyanese elections. He believes that there are sufficient PNC adherents overseas to give the PNC a clear majority. If it appears that the overseas registration is not sufficient to provide this majority, Mr. Burnham said he has instructed his campaign organizers overseas to provide enough false registrations to give the PNC the desired majority. The PNC was conducting registration of overseas voters principally in the Caribbean, the United Kingdom, Canada, and the United States.

(2) The above information further clarifies Mr. Burnham's intentions regarding the forthcoming elections in Guyana. In April 1968 Mr. Burnham stated that he would not form a government if he had to continue to depend on his coalition partner, Peter D'Aguiar, leader of the United Force, after the elections. In order to avoid having to depend on D'Aguiar, Mr. Burnham said that he will rig the elections in such a way that the PNC will win a clear majority. After winning a majority, he said he would welcome a coalition with the UF, because he would not have to depend on the UF to maintain the government.

Thomas H. Karamessines,
Deputy CIA Director for Plans

There was some concern about the extent of the planned rigging. In a June 21 telegram Mr. John Calvin Hill, Jr., Director for North Coast Affairs, Bureau of Inter-American

Affairs, Department of State, advised Ambassador Carlson to warn Mr. Burnham not to rig the elections so extremely as to show an African majority in the population. According to a telegram sent to the State Department on June 28, 1968, Carlson had a long discussion with Mr. Burnham the day before "to assess his attitude" on the "dimension of possible electoral results."

Carlson seemed to be somewhat worried about the rigging plans. He reported:

> Some of the friends of Guyana in Washington had recently become apprehensive as to whether the Prime Minister might plan Tammany Hall tactics on such a massive scale as to taint the results, raise questions of legitimacy, and embarrass the U.S. I was sure that he would no more want to have us all in the funny papers than would our friends in Washington. I said I assumed that Sonny Ramphal had already mentioned to him that John Hill had expressed this anxiety to Ramphal in New York.

Mr. Burnham asked what these people thought was reasonable and was told the matter was not one of any precise equation but simply one of dimension. They wanted him to win, they had backed him to the hilt; neither of them wanted a scandal. He was asked what he really expected electorally. He said he foresaw the PNC in about the same range of votes in Guyana as the PPP; i.e., roughly even, perhaps not quite as much as the PPP, or perhaps slightly more but in general about the same order of magnitude.

Mr. Burnham said that he expects to work hard on Muslims and hopes to have some success as well as with various other non-Afro-Guyanese so as to give PNC a multi-racial image. He hoped part of that process could take place before the election and mentioned various individuals including Mr. Kit Nascimento and Ms. Ann Jardim. "As far as overseas was concerned, he thought registration of as many as 50,000 was within the realm of possibility because of ease with which persons can qualify as Guyanese, i.e., descendants if mother was Guyanese and even foreign wives of Guyanese under the law qualify. He was urging his agents to work vigorously toward this large registration but he thought the prospect was not good for high voter participation overseas. He expected not more than about 30,000 to vote if registration went as high as 50,000. We agreed that the overseas vote should be heavily PNC, i.e., 75-90% (with him more inclined to the latter figure). We agreed that it was entirely logical that it should be heavily PNC. Since all indications from collateral reporting showed that his intentions were much more reasonable than had been feared this was as far as I thought it necessary to go. Our conversation generally tended to confirm reports from several other sources a few days before that Mr. Burnham is not planning or expecting a massive rig. He is mentally prepared to accept plurality and is hoping for 26 seats with the thought that if coalition is not reestablished (presumably due D'Aguiar on scene trying set terms) that he will be able persuade at least two if not three UF legislators to join him in forming a majority."

A final progress report on "Support to Anti-Jagan political parties in Guyana", prepared for the 303 Committee on November 21, 1968 by the State Department, noted that the elections would be held on December 16, 1968. The report described "the problems facing Mr. Burnham stemming from his having padded the registration lists in the United Kingdom excessively in an attempt to win an outright majority in the elections. This report also notes the security implications arising from Peter D'Aguiar having become aware of this padding and his efforts to counter it." It further stated that the US authorities would continue to provide financial support and electoral guidance to the PNC and the UF for their campaigns in Guyana and overseas.

The PNC contracted a US-based motion picture company to produce newsreel films showing the progress made by the Mr. Burnham government. The first two of a projected ten films were shown in Georgetown and depict Mr. Burnham inspecting self-help projects in small villages and the visit of Indian Prime Minister Indira Gandhi to Guyana. The report concluded:

> The United States government will continue to exert all possible influence to persuade Mr. Burnham to pursue a moderate and statesman-like course toward the PPP and the UF with regard to the registration problem and to the objections of these parties to the electoral law. To date, however, Mr. Burnham has not responded in the manner desired to U.S. advice to avoid an overly large false registration and to U.S. urging to plan for the formation of another coalition government after the elections. Racial considerations are most likely a significant ingredient in Mr. Burnham's attitude. Thus, we have no assurance that he will accept our guidance in this regard.

CHAPTER 31
The Administration of Mr. Forbes Burnham - 1968

T HE PEOPLE'S NATIONAL CONGRESS OF PRIME Minister Burnham won 30 of the 53 seats in Parliament in the December 16 elections. Mr. Burnham won 50.7 percent of the domestic vote and a heavy majority overseas, raising his total to 55.8 percent of the registered voters. The United Force party emerged with four seats in Parliament. The People's Progressive Party won 19 seats.

Ambassador Carlson reported that Mr. Burnham "was somewhat disappointed at not making greater inroads into the East Indian community (Dr. Jagan got almost all of their votes) in view of his four-year record of peace, stability and economic progress." (Telegram 2201 from Georgetown, December 20) Mr. Burnham named members of the PNC Parliamentary delegation on December 24 and named his new cabinet on December 31.

Elections for the 53 seats in the National Assembly of the Second Parliament of Guyana were held on December 16, 1968, under proportional representation. The following seats were allocated:

PNC 30 seats
PPP 19 seats
UF 4 seats

Mr. Linden Forbes Sampson Burnham became the Prime Minister. The Second Parliament commenced when the National Assembly met on January 3, 1969, with the following members:

Speaker of the National Assembly

Rahman Baccus Gajraj

Members of the Government (30)

Elected Ministers (4)
Linden Forbes Sampson Burnham, *Prime Minister.*
Dr. Ptolemy Alexander Reid, *Minister of Finance.*
Robert James Jordan, *Minister of Agriculture and Natural Resources.*
Mohamed Kasim, *Minister of Communications.*

Non-Elected Ministers (3)
Shridath Surendranath Ramphal, *Attorney General and Minister of State.*
Martin Wylde Carter, *Minister of Information.*
Hamilton Green, *Minister of Works and Hydraulics.*

Other Members (26)

Joseph Nathaniel Aaron
Margaret Matilda Ackman
Kenneth Berkeley Bancroft
Neville James Bissember
Jagnarine Budhoo
Winslow George Carrington
Leonard Ignatius Chan-A-Sue
Oscar Eleazer Clarke, *Deputy Speaker*
Eugene Francis Correia
Malcolm Corrica
Philip Duncan
Eugene Hugh Allan Fowler
William Haynes
Hugh Desmond Hoyte
John Gabriel Joaquin
Clifton Mortimer Llewellyn John
Patricia Anita Limerick
Shirley Merle Patterson
Bishwaishwar Ramsaroop
Sheik Mohamed Saffee
Abdul Salim
David Arthur Singh
Jeffrey Ronald Thomas
Ralph Chesterfield Van Sluytman
Conrad Egerton Wrights
Mohamed Zaheeruddeen

Members of the Opposition (23)

People's Progressive Party (19)
Dr. Cheddi Jagan, Leader of the Opposition
Ranji Chandisingh

Earl Maxwell Gladstone Wilson
Ram Karran
Dr. Fenton Harcourt Wilworth Ramsahoye
Derek Chunilall Jagan
Mohamed Yacoob Ally
Reepu Daman Persaud
Eugene Stoby
Goberdhan Harry Lall
Abdul Maccie Hamid
Ivan Remington
Bhola Persaud
Vincent Teekah
Regina Philomena Sahoye
Roshan Ally
Edgar Lealand Ambrose
Balchand Persaud
Lilian Maud Branco

United Force (4)
Peter Stanislaus D'Aguiar
Randolph Emanuel Cheeks
Marcellus Feilden Singh
Cyril Victor Too-Chung

Rahman Baccus Gajraj was elected to become the Fifth Speaker, and Oscar Eleazer Clarke was elected Deputy Speaker. The ceremonial opening of the second Parliament took place at the second sitting of the National Assembly on February 4, 1969. The Governor-General of Canada, Roland Michener, and Mrs. Michener visited the Parliament on February 17, 1969.

In April 1969, following the recommendation of a Representative Committee of the National Assembly, the S*hirt Jac* was introduced as an alternative form of dress for male Members of the Assembly.

The full-bottomed wig and the ceremonial gown used by the Speaker and the bob wigs and gowns used by the Clerks, on formal occasions, and the bob wig and gown which the Speaker in all other circumstances used, were no longer used.

On June 19, 1969, the Standing Orders of the National Assembly were approved by the Assembly.

On November 10, 1969, Sir David Rose, the Governor-General, was killed in London.

Edward Victor Luckhoo acted as Governor-General from 1969 to 1970.

On February 23, 1970, Guyana became a Republic and ceased to be part of Her Majesty's dominions but continued to be a Commonwealth Member. The National Assembly elected Arthur Chung to be the First President.

On January 4, 1971, Mr. Sase Narain was elected to be the Sixth Speaker. On May 14, 1973, a new Public Address system with microphones and speakers was presented to the Parliament of Guyana by the German Democratic Republic.

The votes from the diaspora determined the 1968 election. Investigating voting lists compiled by Mr. Burnham's diplomats in Britain and The United States of America uncovered hundreds of invented names and fake addresses. Instead of Guyanese voters, Granada TV found two horses in a Manchester field, a boarded-up butcher's shop in Brooklyn, a stretch of railway in London, and many bemused homemakers who had never heard of the voters purportedly at their addresses. Of 900 names checked in Britain, just over 100 were genuine. In New York, four in every 10 were real. Mr. Peter D'Aguiar, who briefly allied with Mr. Burnham, called it "a seizure of power by fraud, not an election."

The State Department's declassified documents revealed the methods used to impose the anti-democratic election on the Guyanese people. No amount of whitewashing can ever remove the stain left on the country and its people. Within months of taking office, Mr. Burnham decreed new national security laws, which permitted unlimited search-and-seizure powers and detention without trial for up to 90 days. Despite much of his socialist rhetoric, he remained closely allied with the United States and Great Britain.

The 1968 elections allowed the PNC to rule without the UF. However, many observers claimed the elections were marred by manipulation and coercion by the PNC. The PPP and UF were part of the political landscape but were ignored as Mr. Burnham began to convert the machinery of the state into an instrument of the PNC. After the elections, Mr. Burnham's policies became more leftist as he announced he would lead Guyana to socialism.

The CIA got its way, but the United States of America lost in its covert operation. Mr. Forbes Burnham turned out to be corrupted, arbitrary, and self-dealing. After the 1968 election, with the CIA subsidizing Mr. Burnham, the leader increasingly turned away from the United States. In 1970, despite all the CIA aid, Mr. Burnham turned to the left and adopted the very politics the United States had sought to prevent. In that year, he abruptly changed direction and promoted Guyana's alliance with Cuba, the Soviet Union, and other communist nations.

He consolidated his dominance of domestic policies through gerrymandering, manipulation of the balloting process, and politicization of the civil service. A few Guyanese of Indian ancestry were co-opted into the PNC, but the ruling party was unquestionably the embodiment of the Afro-Guyanese political will. Although the Afro-Guyanese middle class was uneasy with Mr. Burnham's leftist direction, the PNC remained a shield against Indo-Guyanese dominance.

A challenge to the newly independent government came at

the beginning of January 1969, with the Rupununi Uprising. In the Rupununi region, in southwest Guyana along the Brazilian border, two European settlers and their native employees rebelled against the central government. Five Guyanese policemen were killed. Valerie Hart MP, the daughter-in-law of one of the settlers and spokesperson for the rebels, declared the area independent and asked for Venezuela's aid. Troops arrived from Georgetown within days, and the rebellion was quickly put down. Although the uprising was not a significant affair, it exposed underlying tensions in the new state and the natives' marginalized role in their political and social lives.

The 1970s belonged essentially to Mr. Burnham. On February 23, 1970, Guyana was declared the Co-operative Republic. It was in that era in the history of Independent Guyana that Mr. Burnham became transformed from the "intellectually gifted" and cunning politician into the pragmatic but overtly vainglorious national leader. No English-speaking Caribbean personality wielded more power in the region. Until 1970, he steered a moderate course, seeking foreign investment and keeping his distance from Cuba and the socialist countries. In 1970, however, he veered sharply to the left, declaring Guyana a *Cooperative Republic*. He established diplomatic relations with Cuba, the Soviet Union, and other communist countries and sought leadership among Third World nations. Between 1971 and 1976, the Canadian- and American-owned bauxite mines and British-owned sugar plantations and refineries were nationalized. By 1979, nationalization policies had reduced the private sector's share in the economy to 10 percent.

Nationalization of assets of all foreign industries, the prohibition of imports into the nation, extensive electoral fraud, political repression, party paramountcy, cult activities, IMF/World Bank intervention, mass migration, and

Mr. Burnham's own *Cooperative Socialism* all became tenets of a political landscape substantially reflecting the leader's dreams. Mr. Burnham was not disillusioned, nor was his plans altogether impractical. In 1970, Guyana became the world's first Cooperative Republic by ceasing ties with Britain, thus, replacing the Governor-General with an Executive President. The Guyana National Cooperative Bank was opened to help finance cooperative ventures, particularly the Sanata Textile Mill, the hydroelectric plant on the Mazaruni River, and the Yarrowkabra Glass Factory at Timehri.

The cooperative, Mr. Burnham said, would be the "principal instrument for achieving socialism...making the small man the real man." Under that theory, the cooperative sector was to become the dominant sector. He imported a successful economic model of production used in Puerto Rico. He began nationalizing companies with heavy foreign interest, such as the Demerara Bauxite Company (DEMBA), a subsidiary of the Canadian bauxite company ALCAN. The massive sugar industry was nationalized in 1975. An External Trade Bureau was established to monitor imports and exports. All seemed well for the citizens.

Guyana's status in international affairs was elevated. World-recognized leaders such as Indira Gandhi and Fidel Castro visited Guyana. Burnham hosted the first Caribbean Festival of the Arts (CARIFESTA) in 1970, importing luxurious cars as part of the grand arrangement for the historic occasion. A key-person behind the formation of CARICOM in 1973 was Mr. Burnham, who played host to the Conference of Foreign Ministers of Non-aligned Countries in 1972. That same year, relations with Cuba were reinstated. Later in the 1970s, Mr. Burnham granted permission for the Cuban Army to use Guyana as a transit point on its way to Angola, a bold move since Barbados had withdrawn its support due to US protest, and Trinidad announced that it would not honor such a request if it were made. Unquestionably, Mr. Burnham's image was greatly improved, especially in Cuba, Eastern Europe, and the West Indies.

Setting out to realize his cooperative socialist revolution, Mr. Burnham gathered technocrats and skilled intellectuals *par excellence* to his ranks. Mr. Vincent Teekah, a former senior PPP member, defected to become a minister under Mr. Burnham. Mr. Teekah was mysteriously murdered. Another Indo-Guyanese intellectual, Mr. Shridath Ramphal, was Attorney General before becoming General Secretary for the Commonwealth, a position used to cushion Mr. Burnham's messages. The military expanded as defense allocation increased from $8.76 million in 1973 to $48.72 million in 1976 (500% increase). The Guyana National Service (GNS) was formed in 1974 and the Guyana People's Militia in 1976.

The establishment of the 1763 Monument became a key national symbol. Mr. Burnham ordered and partook in the supervision of the construction of the Enmore Martyrs Monument in 1976. Mr. Burnham proclaimed that his progressive cooperative socialism would feed, house and clothe Guyana by that same year, Guyanese had good hopes.

In the early 1970s, electoral fraud became blatant in Guyana. PNC victories always included overseas voters, who consistently and overwhelmingly voted for the ruling party. The police and military intimidated the Indo-Guyanese. The Army was accused of tampering with ballot boxes.

CHAPTER 32

The Administration of Mr. Forbes Burnham - 1973

THE 1973 ELECTION WAS CONSIDERED A LOW POINT in the democratic process. An amendment to the Constitution abolished legal appeals to the Privy Council in London. After consolidating power on the legal and electoral fronts, Mr. Burnham turned to mobilize the masses for what was to be Guyana's Cultural Revolution. A national service program was introduced that emphasized self-reliance, loosely defined as the population feeding, clothing, and housing itself without outside help.

From the inception, Mr. Burnham's agenda was overloaded with much of his own will, and by the end of the seventies, his dream became a nightmare. His 1973 elections campaign began unofficially with the seizing of paper stock from the PPP newspaper, *Mirror*. Days before the July elections, the

Government announced that ballots would be transported for their *protection*, by the armed forces and government bodies to army headquarters at Thomas Lands, Georgetown. They remained there for more than twenty-four hours.

Fatal violence also scarred that election. In Berbice, a PPP stronghold of rice farmers, fishermen, and cane cutters, violence erupted when party activists tried to escort ballot boxes to counting stations. The army killed two Indo-Guyanese poll workers, who became known as the *Ballot Box Martyrs*. While the police harassed and intimidated Indo-Guyanese voters outside, PNC party members and government officials at the polling stations employed manipulations to curtail the PPP vote. The overseas vote was again padded; proxy and postal voting gave the dead, under-aged, and fictional a say while disenfranchising the real Guyanese people. In a telegram, US Embassy officials told the State Department that ballot boxes were stuffed while at army headquarters: "As US had in past devoted much time, effort, and treasure to keeping Dr. Jagan out," it read, "we should perhaps not be too disturbed at results of this election."

Elections were held on Monday, July 16, 1973, under proportional representation for 53 Members of the National Assembly. The Ceremonial Opening of the Fifth Parliament took place at the Eleventh Sitting of the National Assembly on October 29, 1973. President, Arthur Chung, addressed the Assembly.

The following votes were received and seats allocated:

PNC, 243,803 votes, 37 seats
PPP, 92,374 votes, 14 seats
LP, 9,580 votes, 2 seats

PDM, 2,053 votes, 0 seats

Speaker

Sase Narain

Members of the Government – People's National Congress (49)

L.F.S. Burnham, *Prime Minister*
Dr. P.A. Reid, *Deputy Prime Minister and Minister of National Development and Agriculture*

Senior Ministers (7)

H.D. Hoyte, *Minister of Works and Communications*
SS Ramphal, *Minister of Foreign Affairs and Justice*
H. Green, *Minister of Co-operatives and National Mobilization*
H.O. Jack, *Minister of Energy and Natural Resources*
F. E. Hope, *Minister of Finance*
Dr. K.F.S. King, *Minister of Economic Development*
SS Naraine, *Minister of Housing*

Ministers (5)

W.G. Carrington, *Minister of Labor*
S.M. Field-Ridley, *Minister of Information and Culture*
B. Ramsaroop, *Minister of Parliamentary Affairs and Leader of the House*
C.L. Baird, *Minister of Education*
Dr. O.M.R. Harper, *Minister of Health*

Ministers of State (9)

M. Kasim, *Agriculture*
O.E. Clarke, *East Berbice/Corentyne*
P. Duncan, *Rupununi*
C.A. Nascimento, *Office of the Prime Minister*
M. Zaheeruddeen, *Essequibo Islands/West Demerara*
C.V. Mingo, *Internal Security*
W. Haynes, *Mazaruni/Potaro*
A. Salim, *East Demerara/West Coast Berbice*
F.U.A. Carmichael, *North West*

Parliamentary Secretaries (8)

J.R. Thomas, *Ministry of Housing*
C.E. Wrights, *Ministry of Works and Communications*
M.M. Ackman, *Office of the Prime Minister, and Government Chief Whip*
E.L. Ambrose, *Ministry of National Development and Agriculture*
K.B. Bancroft, *Hinterland, Ministry of National Development and Agriculture*
S. Prashad, *Ministry of Co-operatives and National Mobilization*
J.P. Chowritmootoo, *Ministry of Education*
R.H.O. Corbin, *Ministry of Co-operatives and National Mobilization*

Other Members (18)

J.N. Aaron
L.M. Branco
M. Corrica

E.H.A. Fowler
J. Gill
W. Hussain
S. Jaiserrisingh
K.M.E. Jonas
M. Nissar
L.E. Ramsahoye
J.G. Ramson
P. Rayman
E.M. Stoby
S.H. Sukhu
C. Sukul
H.A. Taylor
R.C. Van Sluytman
L.E. Willems

Members of the Opposition

PPP (14)
Dr. C. Jagan, *Leader of the Opposition*
Ram Karran, *Deputy Speaker*
Narbada Persaud
Clinton Collymore
Janet Jagan
Sheik Feroze Mohamed
Reepu Daman Persaud
Lallbachan Lalbahadur
Basil James
Cyril Calvin Belgrave
Roshan Ally
Dalchand
Dindayal

Harry Persaud Nokta
Liberator Party (2)
G. Kumar
M.F. Singh, *Deputy Speaker*

The Third Parliament of Guyana commenced when the National Assembly met on July 26, 1973.

The PPP did not attend and did not participate in the work of Parliament until May 24, 1976. On July 10, 1978, a referendum was held in Guyana. On July 21, 1978, a Constituent Assembly, comprising all Members of the National Assembly, was established by the Assembly to prepare a new Constitution for Guyana. The Members from the PPP did not participate in the work of the Constituent Assembly. In February 1980, the Constituent Assembly presented its Report to the National Assembly.

The new Constitution was set out in Act No. 2 of 1980, which the National Assembly passed on February 14, 1980, and assented to by the President on February 20, 1980. On October 6, 1980, the new Constitution came into operation. Arthur Chung ceased to be President. Linden Forbes Sampson Burnham became President.

Sase Narain was elected Speaker of the National Assembly, and M.F. Singh was elected Deputy Speaker of the National Assembly. On March 14, 1974, Marcellus Feilden Singh resigned as Deputy Speaker of the National Assembly and was appointed Leader of the Opposition. On March 28, 1974, Ralph Chesterfield Van Sluytman was elected Deputy Speaker.

Mr. Burnham declared 1973 as the year of the breakthrough, claiming that the PNC won the Indian votes in Berbice. He also proclaimed the birth of the *New Guyana Man* back in the office. The *Founder Leader* crystallized his prominence in his *Declaration of Sophia* speech in 1974. He declared that the PNC "apologetically assumes its paramountcy over the government which is merely one of its executive arms." Consequently, the Government created the Office of the General Secretary of the PNC and the Ministry of National Development (OGSMND) in 1975. As the name suggests, it became a conduit between the PNC party and the PNC government, making government business and resources available to those of the PNC party. A party card became essential for access to social benefits, civil service positions, contracts, and such things as business permits. By the mid-seventies, an estimated 80% of the economy fell under the eyes of the PNC government, whose workforce more than doubled since 1964, becoming replete with PNC party members.

Government authoritarianism increased in 1974 when Mr. Burnham advanced the paramountcy of the party. All organs of the state would be considered agencies of the ruling PNC and subject to its control. The State and the PNC became interchangeable; PNC objectives were now public policy. Mr. Burnham's consolidation of power in Guyana was not total; opposition groups were tolerated within limits.

Dr. Jagan's political presence continued to decline in the 1970s. Outmaneuvered on the parliamentary front, the PPP leader tried another tactic. In April 1975, the PPP ended its boycott of parliament with Dr. Jagan stating that the PPP's policy would change from non-cooperation and civil resistance to critical support of the Mr. Burnham regime. Dr. Jagan appeared on the same platform with Prime Minister Burnham to celebrate ten years of Guyanese independence on May 26, 1976.

Despite Dr. Jagan's conciliatory move, Mr. Burnham had no intention of sharing powers and continued to secure his position. When overtures intended to bring about new elections and PPP participation in the Government were brushed aside, the sugar industry workforce went on a bitter strike. The strike was broken, and sugar production declined steeply in 1976 and 1977.

The PNC postponed the 1978 elections, opting instead for a referendum to be held on July 10, 1978, proposing to keep the incumbent Assembly in power. The referendum was poorly received. Although the PNC government proudly proclaimed that 71 percent of eligible voters participated and that 97 percent approved the referendum, other estimates put turnout at 10 to 14 percent. The low turnout was primarily caused by a boycott led by the PPP, WPA, and other opposition forces.

On July 21, 1978, a Constituent Assembly, comprising all Members of the National Assembly, was established by the Assembly to prepare a new Constitution for Guyana. The Members from the PPP did not participate in the work of the Constituent Assembly.

In February 1980, the Constituent Assembly presented its Report to the National Assembly. The new Constitution was set out in Act No. 2 of 1980, which the National Assembly passed on February 14, 1980, and assented to by the President on February 20, 1980. On October 6, 1980, the new Constitution came into operation. Arthur Chung ceased to be President. Linden Forbes Sampson Burnham became the First President with executive powers. On October 25, 1980, the Third Parliament was dissolved.

In the referendum held in July, with electoral results widely fraudulent, Mr. Burnham sought to strengthen his party's nearly total control of the Government. The election was condemned internationally as fraudulent. Mr. Burnham's quasi-socialist policies led to economic stagnation in the 1980s. The country could not export sufficient amounts of sugar, bauxite, and rice to earn the foreign exchange needed for vital imports.

Mr. Burnham's policies were designed to help Guyana. Still, instead, his authoritarian rule spurred a wave of emigration, especially after his 1974 decree that essentially established one-party practice in the country. In seeking other sources of much-needed revenue, Mr. Burnham struck exceptional deals, such as one with a controversial religious leader in San Francisco named Jim Jones, who had a large group of African-American followers. In 1974 Jim Jones paid Mr. Burnham $2 million to lease four thousand acres of land near Port Kaituma. Four years later, the mass suicides of the Peoples Temple occurred after a US congressional delegation arrived to investigate human-rights abuses.

Mr. Burnham's control over Guyana began to weaken when the Jonestown massacre brought unwanted international attention. In the 1970s, Jim Jones, leader of the People's Temple of Christ, moved more than 1,000 of his followers from San Francisco to form Jonestown, a utopian agricultural community near Port Kaituma in the northwestern region of Guyana. Members of the Guyanese Government regarded the People's Temple of Christ as a model farming community that shared its vision of settling the hinterland and its view of cooperative socialism.

The People's Temple was well equipped with openly flaunted weapons that hinted that the community had the approval of members of the PNC's inner circle. Complaints of abuse by the cult leader prompted United States congressman Leo Ryan to fly to Guyana to investigate. The San Francisco area representative was shot and killed by members of the People's Temple as he boarded an airplane in Port Kaituma to return to Georgetown. Fearing further publicity, Jim Jones and more than 900 of his followers died in a massive communal murder and suicide. The November 1978 Jonestown massacre suddenly put Burnham's Government under intense foreign scrutiny, especially from the United States. Investigations into the killings led to allegations that the Guyanese Government had links to the fanatical cult.

Was it the intention of the PNC, not only to allow Jim Jones to carry out his shady deals to obtain strongly armed cultists to assist the regime in putting down any popular uprising, and also to use the settlement and the cult for causing Venezuela to think twice before it could invade Guyana? The reasoning behind that contention was that the Jonestown settlers were American citizens, and Venezuela would be cautious not to attack them or occupy their settlement. In case of a Venezuelan invasion, the USA would be forced to support Guyana since American citizens would also be under attack. Venezuela itself would not want any military confrontation with the USA.

In October, shortly before the Jonestown murder-suicide, President Carlos Andrez Perez of Venezuela paid a two-day visit to Guyana, at a period when relations between Guyana and Brazil were becoming friendly. His itinerary included a visit to Jonestown, but this was canceled at the last moment. The Guyana Government gave no reason for the cancellation of Perez's visit to Jonestown. Some media reports indicated that Venezuela was against the settlement of the People's Temple in that area. An editorial in the January 30, 1979 issue of the *Mirror* expressed a similar view when it stated:

> Another reason may be that Guyana did not fare so well during the last high-level meeting with Venezuelan President Perez, and failed to reach an agreement. The Jonestown affair had not made relations any better, particularly with the strong suggestions that Jonestown was set up with the consent of the Guyana Government as a buffer in the disputed territory.

In May 1979, the *Caribbean Contact* printed an extract of a lecture on the Jonestown tragedy, delivered at the University of the West Indies (UWI) Cave Hill Campus in Barbados by the UWI historian, Professor Gordon Lewis. Professor Lewis claimed that the Jonestown commune could be seen as a deliberate attempt by the PNC regime to have the settlement act to firmly establish Guyana's ownership to the territory claimed by Venezuela, with similar motives as the Israeli's establishment of settlements on the so-called disputed West Bank of the Jordan River. However, the PNC denied any such strategy and maintained that the Jonestown settlers were merely agriculturalists intent on developing the interior.

Two days after that tragedy - on November 20, 1978 - the Guyana Minister of Information, Shirley Field-Ridley, stated at a press conference that the followers of the People's Temple subscribed to some of the objectives of the PNC. The Government, she said, had no problems with the Temple whose members had "established a reputation for themselves as being good farmers, industrious and hardworking." A complete denial of the involvement of the PNC regime in the Jonestown affair was made by Mr. Christopher Nascimento, the Guyana Minister of State in the Office of the Prime Minister. In a letter published in the *Caribbean Contact* of June 1979. Mr. Nascimento, commenting on the publication by Professor Gordon Lewis the previous month in the newspaper, said, "in historical terms, a legitimate parallel might not be drawn between the settlement of the Pilgrims in Massachusetts in 1620 and the People's Temple of Guyana in 1974".

Although the bloody memory of Jonestown faded, Guyanese politics experienced a violent period. Some of the violence was directed against the WPA, which had emerged as a vocal critic of the State and Mr. Burnham in particular. One of the party's leaders, Dr. Walter Rodney, and several professors at the University of Guyana were arrested on arson charges. The professors were soon released, and Dr. Rodney was granted bail. The WPA leaders then organized the alliance into Guyana's most vocal opposition party.

In 1979, the level of violence continued to escalate. In October, the Minister of Education Vincent Teekah was mysteriously shot to death. The following year, Dr. Walter Rodney was killed by a bomb while sitting in his car. The PNC government quickly accused Dr. Rodney of being a terrorist who had died at the hands of his bomb and charged his brother Mr. Donald Rodney with being an accomplice. The later investigation implicated the Guyanese Government. However, the circumstances of Rodney's death damaged Mr. Burnham's image with many leaders and intellectuals in other countries who earlier had been willing to overlook the authoritarian nature of his Government.

On October 24, 1979, Mr. Vincent Teekah, the Minister of Education, was killed by a bullet wound. It was apparent that the shot was fired at close range and from an angle that cannot be explained if he was sitting, as he was, according to his companion. Mr. Teekah was in the company of an American dentist, Dr. Oswaldene Walker, who lived in Takoma Park, Maryland, and was visiting Guyana as the private dentist for Prime Minister Burnham.

According to Dr. Walker's testimony, two men attacked them as Teekah showed her the sights, and he was shot while they parked on the East Bank Demerara roadside, just south of Georgetown. After calling for help, she reported that a man helped her shift the body over from the driver's seat, and he accompanied her to the hospital. While Mr. Teekah's body was at the hospital, she tried unsuccessfully to contact Prime Minister Burnham by a walkie-talkie that was given to her for such a purpose. She then drove the car with the corpse to the Prime Minister's residence, where she spent the night. Early the following day, Dr. Walker was taken to the airport by Shirley Field-Ridley, wife of Minister Hamilton Green. There she was put on the flight which left for the United States.

Dr. Walker was the only known witness to the shooting of Mr. Teekah, but her hasty removal from Guyana meant that the police could not question her. According to Andrew Morrison, writing in his book, *Justice*, stated:

> The police should certainly have wanted to know how a shot fired from outside the car could have entered Teekah's right hip and travelled horizontally across his body and how the body could have been cold on arrival at the hospital if it had been brought there in about fifteen minutes after the shooting. Watchmen in the area where the shooting was supposed to have taken place reported that they heard two shots fired in rapid succession at about 11.30 p.m. that night, that a car had been parked in that area for some time and it started and moved off in great haste after the shots were fired. The hustling out of the country of the only reported witness and the silence of the police, apart from ruling out death by accident, drew widespread charges of yet another deliberate cover-up by the authorities.

The police ruled out accidental death by his gun since the bullet that killed him was not from his pistol, which was found on him.

On October 24, 1979, Mr. Teekah was a guest speaker at the Bladen Hall science and technology exhibition. After that event, he telephoned Dr. Walker to schedule an appointment for a bleeding tooth. Dr. Walker couldn't fit him into her schedule until after work. She had a complete program that included Mr. Burnham at 4:00 p.m. She suggested that she can see him later in the evening.

In the evening, Minister Hamilton Green telephoned Mr. Teekah's home and was told that he went to see the dentist. Since no inquiry or investigation was conducted on the death of Mr. Teekah, there have been many versions of what may have happened. Also, the only witness is no longer in the country, and no attempt was made to have her returned to tell what happened.

One version is that at Dr. Walker's clinic at the GDF headquarters, Camp Ayangana, a quarrel intensified over jealousy that rival lovers had for the same woman. At that time, Mr. Teekah was shot. A bullet entered his right hip, traveled diagonally, and exited above the left hip. He was not taken to the hospital immediately. Instead, at 11:00 p.m., the body was taken to the Ruimveldt Industrial area in the vicinity of Lyson's Knitwear. A gun was fired twice to give the impression that the car was being attacked. Dr. Walker then drove the vehicle to St. Joseph's Mercy hospital. At the hospital, the nurses refused, despite the insistence of Dr. Walker, to take the body to the ward. The nurses noticed the body was already cold. The body was merely put in a chair and pushed aside in the corner of the reception room. It was also noticed that the arms were very pale, an indication that there was no blood in the body. Dr. Walker tried to contact Prime Minister Burnham with the walkie-talkie given to her for the purpose, to no avail. She tried using the telephone but still to no avail. She left in Mr. Teekah's car for Mr. Burnham's residence, where she spent the night.

In the early morning hours, Mr. Teekah's wife received

a telephone call from Mr. Burnham asking her to come to his residence immediately. The Commissioner of Police, Mr. Barker; Crime Chief, Roberts; Chief of Security Lewis, and Head of the Army, McLean, were at Mr. Burnham's residence when she arrived. She requested the body be handed over for a quiet family funeral, but that was denied. Prime Minister Burnham called the Chronicle newspaper and instructed that the word "Assassination" must appear in headlines and the first paragraph of Mr. Teekah's murder article. The BBC was also contacted and fed the same "Assassination" line.

Later that morning, Dr. Walker kept her appointments with top-ranking officials of the People's Militia without showing any effects of being involved in such a serious incident earlier in the morning. In addition, she phoned a medical colleague to discuss a mutual patient and carried on the conversation with the utmost calmness. The same Thursday morning, Minister Hamilton Green presented himself at the post-mortem.

Dr. Walker never returned to her suite at the Pegasus hotel where she had checked in on Wednesday. After her appointments and telephone call that morning, she was taken to the airport by Mrs. Shirley Field-Ridley, wife of Hamilton Green.

Guyana's history during this period was replete with duplicity and unexplained occurrences. Some have been directly linked to covert CIA operations and those whom they trained. In addition, Guyana's Prime Minister Burnham, and his People's National Congress party, became accomplished at the arts of keeping themselves in power and privilege. The majority of the Guyanese people have borne the burden of violence and manipulation. They have lashed out at each other under the CIA and government-backed racial manipulation; been disenfranchised by vote fraud and election rigging; have been disgraced by the Jonestown affair; suffered from extreme poverty as a result of secretly negotiated deals between the ruling party and international lending agencies such as the IMF and World Bank; been set upon by thieves and thugs comprising the paramilitary arm of the House of Israel religious cult, and faced steadily escalating official repression.

Guyana's economic crisis deepened considerably, accompanied by the rapid deterioration of public services, infrastructure, and overall quality of life. Blackouts occurred almost daily, and water services were increasingly unsatisfactory. The litany of Guyana's decline included shortages of rice and sugar (both produced in the country), cooking oil, and kerosene. While the formal economy sank, the black-market economy in Guyana thrived.

The Working People's Alliance declared itself a political party to remove the PNC from power. Dr. Walter Rodney was recognized as the leader. He worked very closely with the PPP in organizing the referendum boycott and agitation against the PNC, even though the WPA expressed tactical differences with the PPP in carrying out the struggle against the regime.

On July 11, 1979, the building housing the Ministry of National Development and the Office of the General Secretary of the PNC and the GUYSUCO building were destroyed by fire. The Government claimed that the fire was deliberately set and that the watchmen had been tied up and transported across Georgetown to a suburb on the East Coast by men dressed in army uniforms.

Dr. Rodney and other WPA members Bonita Harris, Kwame Apata, Maurice Odle, Omawale, Rupert Roopnaraine, Karen, de Souza, and Davo Nandlall were questioned by police and subsequently charged with arson. On July 14, 1979, the WPA leaders appeared at the Georgetown Magistrate Court in Brickdam to answer the charge. A WPA-organized protest demonstration was outside the court, and numerous press photographers were observing and snapping pictures. Among them was Bernard Darke, a Roman Catholic priest who also took photos for the weekly *Catholic Standard*. He was also a high school teacher at St. Stanislaus College, located just across from the Magistrate Court. Darke took shots of the WPA demonstration outside the Magistrates' Court and returned to the college.

Shortly after, the WPA leaders were granted bail and transported in a police van to the Camp Street prison, where the police planned to release them away from the crowds. The WPA demonstrators marched with their pickets along Brickdam behind the van, and as they passed the college, Darke came out on the street to snap more photographs. Suddenly, as the demonstrators passed the Brickdam Police Station, they were attacked by a group of young men carrying sticks, daggers, and knives. The assailants were all members of the House of Israel. The demonstrators ran in all directions to escape the brutal attack, with many running into yards opposite the Police Station.

As the House of Israel members attacked people, Darke took photographs of what was happening. Then three of the gang members turned on him and beat him with sticks. As he tried to run away, one of them stabbed him with a bayonet in the back. Mike James, a journalist, and Jomo Yearwood, a bauxite worker, were also seriously wounded in separate attacks. Plainclothes police officers appearing on the scene fired two shots in the air to scare off the attackers and quickly made some arrests. The police took Darke to the Georgetown Public Hospital, where he was given immediate attention. He was later transferred to the St. Joseph's Mercy Hospital and operated on by two surgeons to repair his damaged lung. However, he died at around 6:00 p.m.

Members of the House of Israel were convicted in court

for carrying dangerous weapons during the attack. However, they were given barely minimum fines. One of them, Bilal Ato, who stabbed Darke, was charged with murder. His trial came up three years later. He pleaded "not guilty of murder" but "guilty of manslaughter." Justice Pompey eventually sentenced him to eight years in prison.

The Working People's Alliance, founded in 1973, became an official political party in 1979 and evolved as an alternative to Mr. Burnham's PNC and Dr. Jagan's PPP. The WPA was a multi-ethnic combination of politicians and intellectuals that advocated racial harmony, free elections, and democratic socialism opposed Mr. Burnham's authoritarianism.

> They have lived for these many years by putting on certain masks, by trying to fool the outside world and even some Guyanese who live right here, with the mask of democratic Government because they have a joke institution called a parliament. In this mask they have something called a free press, free judiciary, *etc.*, but we know that when we lost the right to choose our own Government in free elections, we lost all other rights. It is just a matter of time - they take when they want to take, they give when they want to give until the time when the people intervene. Unmask them and show them that power belongs to the people. - Dr. Walter Rodney, Georgetown, Guyana August 1979.

A Marxist historian and one of the most vociferous opponents of Mr. Burnham, Dr. Walter Rodney was the voice of a younger generation frustrated with the racial bitterness. He said:

More than one political party has been responsible for the crisis of race relations in this country. I think our leadership has failed us on that score. I think external intervention was important in bringing the races against each other from the 50s and particularly in the early 1960s. But I am concerned with the present. If we made that mistake once, we cannot afford to be misled on that score today. Neither ordinary Afro-Guyanese nor ordinary Indo-Guyanese can today afford to be misled by the myth of race. Time and time again it has been our undoing.

Opposition claims of electoral fraud were upheld by a team of international observers headed by Britain's Lord Avebury. According to Dr. Walter Rodney, Mr. Burnham's "style of rule has many similarities with that of the late Nicaraguan dictator, Anastasio Somoza," who not only oppressed the working class but those in the upper echelons of the society who refused to go along with his domination. Walter Rodney was assassinated on Friday, June 13, 1980. He was killed in a mysterious explosion in Georgetown. Many believed because he stridently opposed Mr. Forbes Burnham and the PNC had a hand in his demise. Dr. Walter Rodney was killed by a bomb concealed in a walkie-talkie that he had been tricked into testing. Ironically, his murder, designed to silence his eloquent opposition, has ripped the mask of respectability from the Guyana government of Mr. Burnham. In an interview, two years later, with *New York Times* journalist Richard J. Meislin, Mr. Burnham asserted: "We had nothing to do with Rodney's death; Rodney was up to mischief - to blow up the jail. He picked the wrong frequency for the device and blew himself up."

CHAPTER 33

The Administration of Mr. Forbes Burnham -1980

ELECTIONS WERE HELD ON DECEMBER 15, 1980, under proportional representation for 65 Members of the National Assembly. The WPA refused to participate in an electoral contest regarded as fraudulent. A new constitution was promulgated in 1980. The old ceremonial post of President was abolished. The head of Government became the Executive President, chosen, as the former position of Prime Minister had been, by the majority party in the National Assembly. Mr. Burnham became Guyana's first Executive President and promised elections later in the year.

The PNC claimed 77 percent of the votes and forty-one seats of the popularly elected seats in the elections, plus the ten chosen by the regional councils. The PPP and UF won ten and two seats, respectively.

The National Assembly of the Fourth Parliament of Guyana 1980-1985

The 65 seats were allocated as follows:
PNC 53
PPP 10
UF 2

From the General Elections, 53 to be elected by and from the National Congress of Local Democratic Organs 2 to be elected by and from the ten Regional Democratic Council, 1 Member each.

The PNC formed the Government. The following were the first Members of the National Assembly:

Speaker

Sase Narain

Members of the Government – People's National Congress (69)

Dr. Ptolemy Alexander Reid, *Prime Minister*

Other Vice-Presidents (4)

Shiw Sahai Naraine, *Works, and Transport*
Hugh Desmond Hoyte, *Economic Planning and Finance*
Hamilton Green, *Public Welfare*
Bishwaishwar Ramsaroop, *Parliamentary Affairs and Party/State Relations*

Senior Ministers (10)

Ranji Chandisingh, *Higher Education*
Oscar Eleazer Clarke, *Regional Development*
Robert Herman Orlando Corbin, *National Development*
Franklin Eleazar Hope, *Trade and Consumer Protection*
Hubert Oliver Jack, *Energy*
Dr. Mohamed Shahabuddeen, *Attorney General*
Rashleigh Esmond Jackson, *Foreign Affairs*
Joseph Adolphus Tyndall, *Agriculture*
Stanley Alfred Moore, *Home Affairs*
Jeffrey Ronald Thomas, *Education*

Ministers (13)

Joshua Peter Chowritmootoo, *Environment and Water Supply, Ministry of Public Welfare*
Urmia Eleanor Johnson, *Co-operatives*
Jean Narinee Maitland-Singh, *Consumer Protection, in the Ministry of Trade and Consumer Protection*
Seeram Prashad, *Crops and Livestock, in the Ministry of Agriculture*
Sallahuddin, *Finance, in the Ministry of Economic Planning and Finance*
Robert Edward Williams, *Fisheries, in the Ministry of Agriculture*
Christopher Anthony Nascimento, *Mechanical Equipment, in the Ministry of Works and Transport*
Frank Ulan August Campbell, *Information*
Fitz Uriel Alexander Carmichael, *Forestry, in the Ministry of Agriculture*
Yvonne Veronica Harewood-Benn, *Public Service*
Harun Rashid, *Office of the President*

Ralph Chesterfield Van Sluytman, *Drainage, and Irrigation,* in the Ministry of Agriculture

Richard Alexander Van West-Charles, *Health, in the Ministry of Public Welfare*

Ministers of State (3)

Malcolm Corrica, *Culture, in the Ministry of Education*

Roy Clifton Fredericks, *Sport, and Youth, in the Ministry of National Development*

Conrad Egerton Wright, *Construction, in the Ministry of Works and Transport*

Parliamentary Secretaries (3)

Agnes Winifred Bend-Kirton, *Women's Affairs, and Housing*

Philomena Ameena Rayman, *Office of the Prime Minister*

Edith Myrtle Bynoe, *Office of the Prime Minister*

Other Members (23)

Donald Alfred Nicholas Ainsworth
Mohamed Ally
Milton Armogan
Bissoondai Beniprashad
Basdeo Bhagwan
Joseph Bernard Caldeira
Allan Albert Chin
Elaine Beatrice Davidson
Harry Doobay
Abel Benjamin Felix
Eugene Hugh Allan Fowler

Patricia Fredericks
Eugene Fitzpatrick Gilbert
Joyce Gill
Albert McRae
Joyce Myrtleen Munroe
Ryburn Nathaniel Primo
Chintaman Gowkarran Sharma
Harold Lall Bahadur Singh
Sydney Hansel Sukhu
Bidiawattie Tiwari
Calvin Vandenburg
Huldah Benomi Walcott, Government Chief Whip

Members from the National Congress of Local Democratic Organs (2)

Rudy Bishop
Bhagmatee Latchminarayan

Members from the Regional Democratic Councils (10)

Kenneth Nathaniel Jones, *Region 1 - Barima/Waini*
Khelanand Vishvaykanand Jairam, *Region 2 - Pomeroon/Supenaam*
Cora Agnes Singh, *Region 3 - Essequibo Islands/West Demerara*
Walter Bipat, *Region 4 - Demerara/Mahaica*
Howard Ivan London, *Region 5 - Mahaica/Berbice*
Isaac Chowritmootoo, *Region 6 – East Berbice/Corentyne*
Nellie Rowena Charles, *Region 7 - Cuyuni/Mazaruni*
Dianne Abraham, *Region 8 - Potaro/Siparuni*
Abel Dorrick, *Region 9 – Upper Takutu/Upper Essequibo*
Denzil Hinds, *Region 10 - Upper Demerara/Berbice*

Members of the Minority (12)

People's Progressive Party (10)
Cheddi Jagan, *Minority Leader*
Ram Karran, *Deputy Speaker*
Janet Jagan
Reepu Daman Persaud, *Minority Chief Whip*
Narbada Persaud
Clinton Collymore
Sheik Feroze Mohamed
Isahak Basir
Cyril Calvin Belgrave
Dalchand
United Force (2)
Marcellus Feilden Singh, JP
Michael Anthony Abraham

The Fourth Parliament of Guyana commenced when the National Assembly first met on January 30, 1981. The National Assembly elected Sase Narain to be Speaker of the National Assembly, and Ram Karran was elected to be Deputy Speaker of the National Assembly. The Ceremonial Opening of the Fourth Parliament took place at the second sitting of the National Assembly on February 9, 1981. The President, Linden Forbes Sampson Burnham, addressed the National Assembly.

For the 28 years that Mr. Burnham's party governed the country, the British described him, "an opportunist, racist and demagogue intent only on personal power," as quoted by Arthur M. Schlesinger, Jr. He held power through force and fraud until he died in 1985. He ran up a foreign debt of more than $2 billion, a sum more than five times Guyana's Gross Domestic Product (GDP). Interest in that debt consumed 80 percent of its revenue and more than half of its foreign earnings. That led to a disastrous economic situation which can still be felt in Guyana. No one in Guyana believed that Mr. Burnham's prescription for economic success was working. Emigration continued to increase, with the remaining Guyanese overseeing a pitifully diminished private sector. In its state-controlled economy, the Government was the country's largest employer, and Afro-Guyanese held most jobs. The Government controlled the media, and television broadcasting still had not arrived in the nation by 1983, except in unreliable pirate stations.

Political dissent was nonexistent when the Government controlled all media, and it was further suppressed by economic means. Dr. Jagan and other foes of Mr. Burnham claimed that most employed Guyanese remained politically inactive for fear of losing their jobs. Again, Mr. Burnham stated that he ruled legitimately, with the support of the majority. "An oppressive Government cannot last this long," he declared to New York Times's Meislin. "We don't have the financial accouterments for a police state."

Guyana had little financial resources left after the costs of maintaining the army and other instruments of control were funded. The country was saddled with massive foreign debt, and the continuing import restrictions made some types of items, such as toilet paper, extremely hard to obtain. Furthermore, Mr. Burnham's odd alliances with fringe groups had not diminished after the Jonestown disaster. "On the streets, people speak fearfully of the House of Israel," wrote Meislin, who described the group as "a religious sect of several thousand Guyanese headed by a man who calls himself Rabbi Washington but is really a fugitive from the United States named David Hill." The New York Times report continued, "There is a widespread belief among Guyanese that the group operates as a paramilitary squad for the Government."

Hill was wanted on corporate fraud charges and had gained some eight thousand Afro-Guyanese followers with a doctrine asserting that blacks were the original tribes of Israel and that Christianity was a tool of oppression.

In October of 1983, US military forces invaded the Caribbean island nation of Grenada and assassinated "Marxist dictator" Maurice Bishop, who had been in power since 1979. President Burnham had close ties to Prime Minister Bishop and denounced the maneuver. In an interview with the *New York Times,* Mr. Burnham scoffed at the stated justification for the invasion as Grenada's ties to Cuba. Through it, the Soviet Union posed a threat to democracy in the Caribbean. "The threat," Mr. Burnham told Meislin, "was that if the Grenadians succeeded in transforming their economy, other countries in that position might say that this ideology or that economic tactic on the part of Grenada must be good. There's nothing in international law that says that's a good reason for invading."

Amid the turbulent period, Mr. Burnham underwent surgery for a throat ailment. On August 6, 1985, while in the care of Cuban doctors, Guyana's first and only leader since independence died. Mystery and intrigue surrounded the death and burial of Forbes Mr. Burnham. Now that he had been declared the father of social cohesion in Guyana, it is perhaps a good time to set the record straight to the causes of Mr. Burnham's death.

After the death of Mr. Forbes Burnham, the then ruling PNC wanted to elevate him to a demi-God status, and as soon as he was entombed, the mourners were rushed out of the Botanic Gardens, where his body was laid to rest. Mr. Burnham's body was retrieved from the tomb and taken back to the funeral parlor. It was later shipped out to the Soviet Union. The PNC wanted to make Mr. Burnham a political idol. The party wanted him to be compared to the likes of

Mao Tse Tung of China and Lenin of the Soviet Union, whose bodies were embalmed and placed on permanent display.

At the time, Guyana didn't have enough electricity, and there were constant blackouts. Reports were circulating that the long funeral service which the PNC organized to eulogize Mr. Burnham had caused deterioration of the body. There were also suggestions that Mr. Burnham's remains further deteriorated because of a power outage where it was being held before it being shipped to the Soviet Union.

The theory about the deterioration of the body after the funeral must be examined in the context of the time that the body was in the Soviet Union. If the body had deteriorated en route to the USSR, the Soviets would not have kept it so long. There is another theory that the body never reached the Soviet Union. It was said that what came back to Guyana was a wax model made in Madame Toussaint's museum in England. One unconfirmed report had stated that Mr. Burnham's body was so badly decomposed en route to the Soviet Union that it had to be disposed of in England.

It was questioned, why would the Government bury the body after it was returned from Russia? One possible explanation was the changing ideological stance of Mr. Desmond Hoyte, who, it was said, was not keen to have the presence of Mr. Burnham hanging over his presidency. Mr. Burnham was buried a second time after it was said that his family agreed that he should be buried in keeping respect for the sensitivities of the Guyanese people.

If Mr. Burnham's life was shrouded in controversy, so was his death. Mr. Burnham died on the operating table while undergoing surgery at Georgetown Hospital. Mr. Burnham had gone for a throat operation. Cuba had flown in two specialists for the operation. Mr. Burnham never woke up from the anesthesia. It was said that his heart gave out.

In 1977, the United States received reports that Mr. Burnham had suffered a heart attack. US embassy sources had reported that he missed a significant address to the nation that year. When he was seen months later by an embassy official at his home in Belfield, he seemed far thinner. Declassified documents also reveal that a Trinidadian doctor had told US embassy sources in Guyana that Mr. Burnham had throat cancer. Mr. Burnham was a known chain smoker.

Burnham's replication of certain Soviet-style customs continued, even after his death. According to his instructions, he was to be enclosed in a tomb made of purple glass and modeled after Soviet leader Vladimir Lenin. A glass coffin installed in the Georgetown botanical garden and exposed to the sun in a near-equatorial climate quickly proved to be an unwise idea: Even though a refrigeration unit was used, Guyana's electrical capacity was so inconsistent that the cooling unit often shut down. A mausoleum was later constructed at the site.

Most around the world, Burnham's rule is remembered for his transaction with the People's Temple cult that eventually committed mass suicide in November 1978. Burnham's internal control is more memorable for events such as the June 1980 assassination of Walter Rodney, one of the world's great progressive thinkers on economics and development strategies.

CHAPTER 34

The Administration of Mr. Desmond Hoyte -1985

F OLLOWING BURNHAM'S DEATH IN 1985, PRIME Minister Hugh Desmond Hoyte acceded to the Presidency and was formally elected in the December 1985 national elections.

Prime Minister Hugh Desmond Hoyte inherited an impoverished nation with the lowest standard of living in the Caribbean and a per-capita income less than that of Haiti. Despite concerns that the country was about to fall into a period of political instability, the transfer of power went smoothly. As the new Executive President and leader of the PNC, Mr. Hoyte's initial tasks were threefold: To secure authority within the PNC and national Government, take the PNC through the December 1985 elections, and revitalize the stagnant economy. Mr. Hoyte gradually reversed Burnham's policies, moving from state socialism and one-party control to a market economy and unrestricted freedom of the press and assembly. He declared his intention to speed up "the pursuit of socialist construction" in Guyana and re-emphasized this assertion after reinforcing his power at grossly rigged elections four months later. However, within less than a year, he began to find his pursuit untenable as Guyana continued to experience a severe economic crisis, a spill-over from the Burnham administration.

President Hoyte quickly accomplished his first two goals. The new leader took advantage of factionalism within the PNC to quietly consolidate his authority. The December 1985 elections gave the PNC 79 percent of the vote and forty-two of the fifty-three directly elected seats. Eight of the remaining eleven seats went to the PPP; two went to the UF, and one to the WPA. The opposition boycotted the December 1986 municipal elections. With no opponents, the PNC won all ninety-one seats in local Government.

Revitalizing the economy proved more complicated than the President anticipated. Mr. Hoyte gradually moved to embrace the private sector, recognizing that state control of the economy had failed. President Hoyte's administration lifted all curbs on foreign activity and ownership in 1988. The Government did not completely abandon the authoritarianism of the Burnham regime, but it made some political reforms. Hoyte abolished overseas voting and the provisions for widespread proxy and postal voting. Greater freedom was given to independent newspapers, and political harassment abated considerably.

Faced with a steady decline in production levels and an acute shortfall in the balance of payments, Hoyte ordered a cut in public spending in attempts to encourage foreign investment. He also curtailed all policies geared towards cooperative socialism to attract investment from North America and Western Europe and win financial support from the multilateral financial institutions. The International Monetary Fund (IMF), since 1983, had curtailed all further lending to Guyana because payments on previous loans were long overdue. In 1985, the country was declared ineligible for additional credit and loans.

The IMF decisions caused Mr. Hoyte to declare during his address to the PNC's sixth biennial congress on August 19, 1985, that "we have concluded that the standard IMF prescription is not only palpably irrelevant and useless, but also positively dangerous and counter-productive in our particular situation. We must resist with all our might the pressures that might be exerted to force us on to the IMF's Procrustean bed."

Real GDP had declined by an average of 10 percent in 1982-83 due to sharp contractions in the bauxite sector and decline and stagnation in most other productive sectors. Economic decline eased up in 1984, but the economy remained stagnant through 1987. With a *per capita* gross domestic product of only US$500, Guyana became one of the poorest countries in the Western Hemisphere.

Confronted with these stark economic realities, Mr. Hoyte was forced to depart from Burnham's economic policy. He realized that *Cooperative Socialism* was a failure. At the time, the country was burdened with an oppressive foreign debt and a large payment of arrears that the PNC regime had accumulated. The arrears by 1988 were more than US$885 million, approximately four times Guyana's annual exports. Mr. Hoyte feared that all credit to the country would be completely cut off by international donors. In that situation, he was propelled to carry out negotiations in 1988 with the IMF, which quickly arranged with the World Bank an Economic Recovery Program (ERP) to re-introduce a pro-capitalist market economy in place of the failed cooperative socialist program of the past eighteen years.

The PNC government introduced the ERP with a great deal of publicity. Its specific objectives for 1989-1991 were:

Achieving real GDP growth of 4 percent annually.

Reducing the rate of inflation from 50 percent to 10 percent.

Reducing the public sector deficit to 20 percent of GDP.

Eliminating the external and internal payments arrears on the debt.

Building a net international reserve.

Incorporating the parallel economy into the official economy, and normalizing Guyana's financial relations with its foreign creditors.

The ERP was to be carried out in three phases: The *Stabilization* phase was planned for March to November 1989, the *Rehabilitation* phase for 1990-1991, and *Recovery and Growth* for 1992 and beyond. During the stabilization period, the Government, with the support of an IMF-monitored program, undertook the following measures:

An initial 70 percent devaluation of the currency.

Price increases resulting from the devaluation.

A 20 percent ceiling on public sector wage increase.

An increase of the prime interest from 14 percent to 35 percent and the reduction of all foreign exchange retention accounts to 10 percent of export proceeds except for bauxite.

As part of the ERP program to encourage economic growth, the Government freed up the foreign exchange regulations. For the first time in many years, this allowed exporters to retain part of their foreign currency earnings for future use. Before this change, only the Bank of Guyana could hold foreign currency. Soon after, price controls were removed on many consumer items, but they were retained for petroleum, sugar, and rice. The removal of price controls was followed by lifting import restrictions on almost all items other than food. Individuals were also allowed to import goods without government intervention.

To encourage private investment, the Government promised a rapid approval of projects and offered incentives, including tax holidays. The laws affecting mining and oil exploration were improved, and tax reforms designed to promote exports and agricultural production in the private sector were enacted. The Government also announced an end to its nationalization policy to provide a solid assurance to foreign investors.

Concerning the absorption of the parallel market into the legal economy, this was necessary since the similar market was causing the Government to lose tax revenues. It also boosted inflation through uncontrolled currency trading while encouraging illegal activities.

By freeing foreign exchange, the Government began to restrict some aspects of the illegal economy. In 1989, it introduced the Foreign Currency Act, which allowed licensed dealers to exchange Guyanese dollars for foreign currency at market-determined rates. Several foreign currency exchange operations were licensed, but illegal currency traders continued their operations.

At the same time, the Government began a steady devaluation of the Guyanese dollar for the official exchange rate to match the market rate. From the beginning of the ERP to 1991, exchange slid at the rate of 250 percent annually. The Guyana dollar was also systematically devalued; the exchange rate of $US1 in 1986 was G$4.37; in 1987 - G$10; 1989 - G$33; and 1990 - G$45. This devaluation process was an essential feature of the ERP on the belief that it would destroy the parallel economy and improve the country's export competitiveness.

As the central tool of economic management, the exchange rate policy was negatively affected by all forms of exchange management over a relatively short period. They included a fixed exchange rate, *crawling peg*, *currency basket* mechanism, *managed float*, and *secondary foreign exchange window* (during 1985-1987) and *free floating* or *cambio* (in 1990). Those proved to have little success.

In early 1991, the Government adopted a floating exchange which removed the distinction between the official and the market exchange rates. By mid-year, the exchange rate stabilized at G$125. All of those devaluations and an accompanying wage restraint policy proved to be very harsh on the general population.

Public finances worsened throughout the 1980s. The overall budget deficit - the difference between actual expenditures and revenues - widened from 17 percent of recorded GDP in 1980 to 59 percent in 1985. After experiencing a short-level reduction during 1987-1988, the deficit jumped back to an estimated 55 percent of GDP in 1989. That deficit was rooted in increases in central government expenditure, increased domestic interest payments, decreased revenues due to economic decline, and the shifting of many activities into the parallel economy.

The deterioration of the state enterprises also contributed to the budget deficits. Up to 1980, the combined account surplus had partially financed the deficit. But the surplus turned into a deficit from 1981-1987 due to devaluations and a steady drop in the production of export commodities.

The ERP sought to get rid of the internal and external payment arrears. Half of the expenditures for 1989 were put aside for interest payments to bridge the gap. In addition, the Government cut public spending, which included delaying salary increases and eliminating some civil service positions, and ceasing funding to the state corporations, except the Guyana Electricity Corporation. Since many of these corporations were a burden on the economy, it became clear that the IMF, through the ERP, wanted the Government to privatize them.

The Government eventually sold 15 of the 41 government-owned businesses. The telephone company and assets in the timber, rice, and fishing industries were privatized. International corporations were hired to manage the State sugar company, Guysuco, and the largest State bauxite mine, Linmine. An American company was allowed to open a bauxite mine, and two Canadian companies were permitted to develop the largest open-pit gold mine on the South American continent.

With the new privatization policy, the PNC regime departed significantly from its previous hard-line position on nationalization. Only four years before, Hoyte, in his address to the PNC's sixth biennial congress, had emphasized very firmly:

> We have seen, within recent times, a document being circulated which alleged that every conceivable problem we are facing, economic or otherwise, has stemmed from nationalization. The inference was that we should denationalize. And it is not without significance that this document surfaced at a time when a campaign was mounted externally to coerce us into accepting a policy of denationalization - or privatization, as it is called...but let me make our position clear on this issue. While the People's National Congress remains in office, the bauxite industry, the sugar industry and the other strategic industries which we have nationalized in this

country will never, never, never be denationalized. For one thing, to do this would be an admission that we are abandoning the socialist ideal, and we have no intention of doing that.

The IMF and the World Bank were worried about the deficit in Guyana's balance of payments. By 1986, the country was importing more goods and services from the rest of the world than exporting. It was experiencing serious problems in making payments to international creditors. Part of the payments was made from the reserves, including stocks of gold, but when the funds dried up, the Government found itself in no position to continue paying. Guyana thus became a bad credit risk and faced problems in acquiring even short-term credits from international lenders. By 1988, the external payment arrears amounted to almost three times Guyana's GDP.

To solve the problem, the Government tried to increase exports and reduce imports. But this did not help much since production of rice, sugar, and bauxite seriously declined. Exports suffered a setback in 1988-1989, and the arrears further increased in the wake of a deepening crisis in the sugar industry. By the end of 1989, the economy had plummeted to such an extent that the actual levels of GDP and export earnings were respectively 23 percent and 50 percent lower than in 1980.

To finance the budget and the overall deficit, the Hoyte administration resorted to heavy borrowing. There was a sharp increase in commercial arrears, US$1.2 billion, in mid-1989. The total public sector external debt reached almost US$1.9 billion by 1989, more than double the level at the beginning of the 1980s. Measured by the usual indicators of debt to GDP and debt to exports, Guyana became one of the most heavily indebted developing countries globally.

By 1989, the Government convinced the IMF and the World Bank that it was committed to rebuilding the economy. As a result, the multilateral institutions organized an eight-member *Donor Support Group*, led by Canada and the Bank for International Settlements, which subscribed US$180 million to enable Guyana to repay arrears. That amount was refinanced by the World Bank and the Caribbean Development Bank and thus became another loan. However, that *bridging finance* - borrowing money to pay debts - re-established Guyana's international creditworthiness and allowed the Government to negotiate new international loans and reschedule other external debts.

As part of the ERP stipulations, taxation was steeply increased - almost doubling yearly for income and consumption tax. This resulted in increased revenue from $3.3 billion in 1989 to $5.3 billion in 1990 and $11.27 billion in 1991. On the other hand, the series of devaluations also led to a massive increase in debt payments, from G$1 billion in 1989 to G$4.9 billion in 1990 and G$12.67 billion in 1991, which was more than the total current revenue collected. In 1990, debt service payments and interest amounted to 140 percent and 53 percent respectively of export earnings. Guyana's foreign debt by the end of 1991 amounted to US$2.1 billion, with debt service payments amounting to 105 percent of current revenue. As a result of the PNC regime's incompetence and mismanagement, the Current Account Consolidated Fund showed a vast deficit, increasing from G$6 billion in 1989 to nearly G$18 billion in 1991.

An October 1989 report of the Commonwealth Advisory Group (the McIntyre Report) on Guyana's economic and social situation emphasized that this state of affairs was clearly unsustainable. With the country's crisis, the opposition PPP constantly criticized the ERP and noted that the recovery program failed to consider social development. The Party further declared that the refusal of the PNC regime to embrace democracy was the main detrimental factor since the majority of the people had no confidence and trust in the Government. Up to 1991, the ERP reforms showed little progress. Instead of stabilization and progress, there was retrogression - a negative instead of a positive growth rate. For 1988, the GDP fell by 3 percent. A policy framework paper prepared by the Government in cooperation with the World Bank and the IMF predicted that real GDP would grow by 5 percent in 1989; instead, real GDP fell by 5 percent. The economic performance continued to decline in the early 1990s. Changes in government policy failed to alleviate the economy's difficulties: a massive foreign debt, emigration of skilled persons, and the lack of infrastructure. In that year, the GDP fell by a further 3.5 percent.

Guyana rescheduled its debt, making the country eligible for international loans, assistance, and foreign investment. As a result of foreign investment and the sale of many government enterprises, Guyana's GDP increased by 6.1 percent in 1991, the first increase after 15 years of decline.

The economy, however, had not shown much success. There was a drastic decline in the production levels of the key exports - bauxite, sugar, and rice. Sugar production declined from 220,995 tons in 1987 to 129,900 tons in 1990. Rice production was 131,700 tons in 1987 but dropped to 94,000 tons in 1990. Bauxite dropped from 1,486,000 tons in 1987 to 1,321,000 tons in 1990. As a result of the decreased production, Guyana could not supply sufficient bauxite to Venezuela for the existing bauxite/fuel deal.

Sugar and rice, accounting for nearly 16 percent of the GDP, contributed almost half of Guyana's foreign exchange earnings while employing 40 percent of the labor force. Those two industries, which were net foreign exchange-earners, were experiencing a severe production crisis through mismanagement. Sugar production since 1988 had fallen to such an extent that the Government was forced to import sugar for domestic consumption from Guatemala. Because of this drop in production, Guyana failed to meet its export quotas for markets in the European Economic Community and the United States. In 1990, rice production was the lowest in 14 years. The general shortfall led to the loss of the lucrative markets in the Caribbean. The country received a gift of rice from Italy that year to supplement the local market.

In what has been described as an attempt to save foreign exchange, the Government banned importing wheat flour, split peas, and other basic foods, and there were chronic shortages of many items, including cooking oil and milk. In an interview, Mr. Hoyte suggested that the country's economic difficulties had been exaggerated. "More people are better off now than they were 10 years ago," he said. Speaking to a crowd of supporters in New Amsterdam, Mr. Hoyte declared that "progress has never ceased in this country under his Party's rule." And, he added," It will never cease."

In addition, the country's underdeveloped and decaying infrastructure seriously handicapped economic development. Many of the basic facilities and services deteriorated severely during the 1980s. No reform of Guyana's productive sectors was possible without a significant level of investment in electricity, transportation, communications, the water system, and sea defenses. The entire country was also plagued with an unreliable electricity supply and blackouts of sixteen hours per day were common.

Concerning the high-interest rate policy, this was intended to encourage savings and control the excess liquidity in the financial system, which contributed to inflationary and balance of payments pressures. In trying to curb inflation and the parallel market in currency trading, the high interest rate at the same time squeezed the local entrepreneurs, thus defeating one of the significant ERP objectives - increased production for export and foreign earnings.

But the greatest obstacle to rehabilitation was the currency devaluation and wage restraint policy. The sharp devaluations from 1988, and particularly in 1991, impacted most adversely against consumers and producers. The accompanying rampant inflation drastically reduced the quality of life, and by 1991 more than 60 percent of the population was living below the poverty line.

Inflation, which had generally remained within the 20 percent range after 1981, rose to 40 percent in 1988 and doubled to 80 percent in 1989. In 1991, it stood at between 110 percent and 125 percent. Prices, measured by the official Consumer Price Index (CPI) constructed on a 1970 base year, increased by 13 percent annually.

Wages and salaries lagged seriously behind inflation. Between 1981 and 1991, the Guyana currency was devalued by more than 4,333 percent while the national minimum wage rose by 508 percent. In 1991, workers were given a 50 percent increase in wages and salaries, raising the daily minimum wage from $43.03 offered in 1990 to $65.56; the lowest in Latin America and the Caribbean. That was inadequate to meet the cost of living and well below the $193.77 per day demanded by the TUC in 1989 and the $307.07 for 1991.

On May Day 1991, the General Secretary of the TUC, Joseph Pollydore, stated that workers were in a state of near destitution and incapable of buying "even basic food"; that Government "has left children breadless and homes rice-less because of the inability of bread-winners to buy even minimum quantities for their families." TUC President Frank Andrews attacked the Government's policy of removing subsidies and price controls while imposing utterly inadequate wages and salary levels. To illustrate the effects of the harsh cost of living, workers on May Day 1991 carried placards declaring that the ERP brought them, *Empty Rice Pots!* The purchasing power can gauge the workers' desperation level at the daily minimum wage of $64.56 in 1991. This amount could buy about one and a half pounds beef, six eggs, or two and a half pounds sugar. It was insufficient to purchase a pound of chicken.

Noting the marked deterioration in economic and social conditions, the McIntyre Report had observed two years earlier:

> But perhaps the even greater loss has been the deterioration in the physical quality of life of the population. Since 1980, average incomes have fallen by 50 percent, unemployment has doubled to 40 percent of the workforce; health and educational services are minimal, and many of the best doctors, nurses and teachers have emigrated.

Interestingly, Carl Greenidge, who during the Hoyte administration held the post of Minister of Finance, alluded in his 1991 budget presentation that several economic indicators were in poor shape. So serious was the situation that in 1990, GDP had declined to less than US$370 *per capita*. However, the leaders of the PNC government adamantly refused to admit that the causes of this decline were mismanagement, bad policies, rampant corruption, and the lack of confidence by the people through the absence of democracy.

As the elections scheduled for 1990 approached, Dr. Jagan went to The Carter Center. He claimed that previous elections had been fraudulent and asked for help to ensure that the next one would be honest and fair. The center agreed, provided the ruling Party would also accept the presence of observers. Mr. Carter visited Georgetown and had extensive discussions with President Desmond Hoyte. For several months, President Desmond Hoyte objected strongly. Finally, as Mr. Carter was preparing to leave the country and declared that he could not participate, President Hoyte accepted all of the provisions. The election was delayed until October 1992, and government officials invited observers of the British Commonwealth, with whom they had enjoyed a close and friendly relationship.

One of the changes attributed to Mr. Hoyte has been a voter registration list that his opponents declared to be fairly and accurately composed. It contained some 372,000 names. Gordon Todd, the President of one of the leading unions in Guyana and a co-chairman of the Guyana Human Rights Association, said he had been encouraged by the steps taken by Mr. Hoyte. But, he said, "I wouldn't be so naive as to say I think the elections will be totally fair."

On election day, it became apparent that Dr. Jagan's Party was winning. Riots erupted in Georgetown, with buildings being burnt and several people killed. A mob attacked the central election headquarters, but Mr. Carter remained there with four Secret Service agents. Mr. Carter said it was, "the most personal danger I have felt since leaving the White House was in Guyana in 1992." Eventually, he called on the White House to intercede. President George H.W. Bush then prevailed on President Hoyte to provide police protection, and order was finally restored.

David de Caires, a prominent conservative lawyer, said he believed most Guyanese were totally disenchanted with the country's course under the ruling Party. Critics said that mainly because of mismanagement, Guyana's main products, bauxite, sugar, and rice, have fallen 30 to 50 percent in 10 years. Per-capita income is estimated to have plunged in about the same proportion. With more than $2 billion in debt, the International Monetary Fund and most other lenders, including the United States, have refused to give Guyana more money.

Guyana accumulated massive debts, increasing stagflation, the enormous rise in crime, and rigging of elections until the 1992 election overseen by former USA President Jimmy Carter. In the 2000s, both the British and United States of America formally apologized for their contribution to the destabilization.

CHAPTER 35

The Administration of Dr. Cheddi Jagan -1992

I N 1992, THE ELECTIONS SCHEDULED FOR 1990 EVENTUally took place. One hundred international observers, including a group headed by Mr. Carter and another from the Commonwealth of Nations, monitored the elections. Both groups issued reports saying that the elections were free and fair, despite violent attacks on the Elections Commission building on Election Day and other irregularities.

Guyanese were free to join or support political parties of their choice. The 1992 general elections were considered free and fair, if not entirely unflawed, by foreign observers. They brought the major opposition party to power while turning the current governing party into the main opposition. Despite constitutional provisions, elections were still not held on schedule or in a consistent manner. Municipal elections, scheduled for December 1992, were not held until the end of 1993.

The National Assembly of the Sixth Parliament of Guyana 1992 - 1997

The following seats were won by the Political Parties: PPP/C 36, PNC 26, WPA 2, and UF 1

On October 9, 1992, Cheddi Jagan was elected and sworn in as President of Guyana at the State House in Georgetown. In addition to the 65 Elected Members of the National Assembly, six persons who were not elected Members of the Assembly were appointed by the President to be Ministers and became Members of the Assembly. The Public Building was, from that time, placed under the administration of Frank A. Narain, Clerk of the National Assembly. Frank A. Narain, requested that the building be used only for Parliament matters. On December 16, 1992, the President informed him that his request had been granted.

The Sixth Parliament commenced when the National Assembly met on December 17, 1992. Mr. Derek Chunilall Jagan was elected Speaker, and Mr. Arthur A. Alexander was elected Deputy Speaker. President Cheddi Jagan addressed the National Assembly that comprised of the following 72 Members:

Speaker of the National Assembly

Derek Chunilall Jagan

Members of the Government (42)

Samuel A Hinds, *Prime Minister*

Reepu Daman Persaud, *Senior Minister of Agriculture (Leader of the House)*

S. Feroze Mohamed, *Senior Minister of Home Affairs, (Government Chief Whip)*

Harripersaud Nokta, *Senior Minister in the Ministry of Public Works, Communications and Regional Development*

Asgar Ally, *Senior Minister of Finance*

Ramnauth D.A. Bisnauth, *Senior Minister of Education and Cultural Development*

Bernard C. DeSantos, *Attorney General and Minister of Legal Affairs*

Henry B. Jeffrey, *Senior Minister of Labor, Human Services and Social Security*

Moses V. Nagamootoo, *Senior Minister in the Office of the President*

Clement J. Rohee, *Senior Minister of Foreign Affairs*

Gail Teixeira, *Senior Minister of Health*

M. Shree Chan, *Senior Minister of Trade, Tourism and Industry*

Janet Jagan

Clinton C. Collymore, *Minister in the Ministry of Agriculture*

Indranie Chandarpal, *Minister in the Ministry of Labor, Human Services and Social Security*

F. Vibert DeSouza, *Minister in the Ministry of Public Works, Communications and Regional Development*

George E. Fung-On, *Minister in the Office of the President*

Cyril C. Belgrave

Brindley H. Benn

Fazil M. Ali

Husman Alli

Shaik K.Z. Baksh

Komal Chand
Shirley V. Edwards
Randolph Evans
Hughley H. Hanoman
Una James
Alston A. Kissoon
Moti Lall
Khemraj Ramjattan
Donald Ramotar
Lawrence E. Rodney
Pauline Sukhai
Winslow M. Zephyr
Khadim Bacchus
Samad A. Baksh, *(Region 2 – Pomeroon/ Supenaam)*
Harrinarine Baldeo, *(Region 5 – Mahaica/Berbice)*
Joseph M. DeSouza, *(Region 1 – Barima/ Waini)*
Eugene La Cruz, *(Region 9 – Upper Takutu/Upper Essequibo)*
Bagot Paul, *(Region 8 – Potaro/Siparuni)*
Kum Karan Ramdass, *(Region 6 – East Berbice/Corentyne)*
Ramrattan a/k Balkarran, *(Region 3 – Essequibo Islands/ West Demerara)*

Members of the Minority (29)

People's National Congress (26)
Hugh Desmond Hoyte, *Minority Leader*
Sase Narain
Robert H. O. Corbin
Winston S. Murray
Patrick L. McKenzie
Clarissa S. Riehl
Kenneth F.S. King

Deryck M.A. Bernard
Faith A. Harding
Amna Ally
Jean M.G. Persico
Arthur A. Alexander, *Deputy Speaker*
Simon H. Ng-See-Quan
Dunstan Barrow
David Subnauth
Reynold David, *(Region 7 – Cuyuni/Mazaruni)*
Jennifer A. Ferreira
Aftabuddin Ahamad
Kenrick Tyndall
Phillip Bynoe, *(Region 10 – Upper Demerara/Berbice)*
Andy Gouveia
Hukumchand a/k Parag
Joan Richards
Gwenneth A. Brouet
John Fredericks
Ivan Peters, *(Region 4 – Demerara/Mahaica)*
Working People's Alliance (2)
Clive Y. Thomas
Matheson Williams
The United Force (1)
Manzoor Nadir

Dr. Jagan's political life, which began in 1946, reached its peak in 1992 when he was elected President of Guyana. He occupied a special place in Caribbean politics. His commitment and dedication to Guyana's poor and working people; his vision for a *New Human Order* were his ideas for a people-centered path to development. George Lamming remembers him best:

There is no Caribbean leader who has been so frequently cheated of office; none who has been so grossly misrepresented; and no one who, in spite of such adversity, was his equal in certainty of purpose and the capacity to go on and on until his time had come to take leave of us.

Through the struggle, Dr. Jagan defended his beliefs:

I believe that my first charge is to raise my people from the mire of poverty in which, for too long, they have suffered. I have never made any secret of my views. I have been thrown out of Office. I have been subjected to violence, indignity and jail. I am willing to face these things again, and gladly, in the fight to free my people and aid them. Here I stand. Here I will stand until I die.

No progress was made on reforming or replacing the Constitution, which grants excessive power to the President. Constitutional reform requires a two-thirds majority in Parliament, which could only be achieved through the co-operation of the ruling party and the opposition. Only one constitutional amendment was proposed during the 1993 parliamentary session to change the composition of the National Elections Commission, and that was eventually agreed to after extended negotiations among the four parties represented in Parliament.

There are no legal impediments to women or minorities participating in the political process, but historically neither women nor Amerindians were encouraged to participate, other than by voting. Any Guyanese citizen 18 years or older can register to vote, and about 80 percent of those registered cast votes in the 1992 election. President Jagan's Cabinet included:

Two women.
Two persons of Portuguese heritage.
One of Chinese ancestry.
Eight Indo-Guyanese.
Four Afro-Guyanese.
One Native Guyanese.

The new 65-member Parliament includes 13 women and 8 Natives, representing both major parties.

Following the 1992 elections, Canada, the United Kingdom, and the United States increased their aid to Guyana. The U.S. assistance had ceased in 1982 due to economic and political differences with the Burnham regime. In 1986, the United States began to supply humanitarian food aid to the country, to a total value of nearly $500 million in 1986-93. The economy made dramatic progress after President Hoyte's 1989 Economic Recovery Program (ERP). As a result of the ERP, Guyana's GDP increased 6% in 1991 following 15 years of decline. Growth was consistently above 6% until 1995 when it dipped to 5.1%. The Government reported that the economy grew at 7.9% in 1996, 6.2% in 1997, and fell 1.3% in 1998. The 1999 growth rate was 3%, which declined to 0.5% in 2000 and 2001.

From 1986 to 2002, Guyana received its entire wheat supply from the United States on concessional terms under a PL 480 Food for Peace program. PL 480 wheat was eliminated for F.Y. 2003. The U.S. and Guyana Governments mutually agreed on using Guyanese currency generated by the sale of the flour made from the grain. As with many developing countries, Guyana is heavily indebted. Reduction of the debt burden has been one of the present administration's top priorities. In

1999, through the Paris Club "Lyons terms" and the Heavily Indebted Developing Countries Initiative (HIPC), Guyana negotiated $256 million in debt forgiveness.

Guyana's economy depends on agriculture and mining, with sugar, rice, bauxite, and gold being the major export earners. Despite an estimated growth rate of 8.2 percent in 1993, Guyana's *per capita* gross domestic product was only about $465 in 1992. The economy suffers from high external debt, shortages of skilled labor, and a deteriorating infrastructure.

Human rights problems in Guyana in 1993 continued to include extrajudicial killings by police, police rape, and other abuse of detainees and prisoners. Police generally were able to commit these abuses with impunity. Societal violence against women and children and discrimination against the Indigenous Amerindians continued. There were still limitations on workers' rights, but political control of union activity diminished somewhat.

A 1992 U.N. Children's Fund (UNICEF) report on children and women in Guyana stated that "the rights of children and women to survival and development, to protection, and to participation have not been adequately met." An estimated 65 to 86 percent of Guyana's population lives in poverty, and children are more severely affected than any other group. The severe deterioration of the public education and health care systems has stunted children's futures and often cut short their lives. For many children, health care has become unaffordable. Children are often denied access to education because their families cannot afford school fees or because their families need the children to run the household by working or providing child care for other children.

The worst effects on children's lives come from migration. Over 3 percent of Guyana's population emigrates every year in search of a brighter economic future. As parents migrate, they often leave behind their children to be raised by other family members, friends, or other children. Children under the age of 14 head nearly 1 percent of Guyana's households.

In 1992 the Government distributed land titles to some Amerindian communities. The APA charged that the titles were distributed just before the elections to win votes and criticized the allocations because they were smaller than recommended by the Government Lands Commission in 1968 and did not include mineral rights.

The Government still holds title to 90 percent of the land claimed by Amerindians. The Amerindian Act retains the ability to repossess the land titles already distributed if it determines that it is in the Amerindians' interest. Several large leases and concessions were granted, allowing mining and timber companies to operate on traditional Amerindian lands, often under contracts and terms never made public. Amerindians displaced by timber and mining operations in such cases have no legal recourse.

In 1993 the foreign-owned Barama Company began timber operations on 4.2 million acres of primary tropical forest where five Indigenous communities were located. Of the 1,200 Natives living within the Barama concession, only 550 live in government-recognized Indigenous villages. The rest are scattered along the rivers and have no legal protection for their homesteads. The APA claimed that the traditional hunting, fishing, and farming lands of the Indigenous communities are being destroyed. Nine families living inside the Barama concession were removed from their land. The APA also claimed that Barama denied Natives access to their traditional forest paths and waterways within the Barama concession. Barama officials rejected the claims, saying that a total of four families relocated voluntarily to new housing built at Barama's expense. Barama further claimed that it respected the boundaries of Indigenous communities and that environmental damage in these areas was often caused by gold miners operating without supervision in the region.

In late 1992, the new Government appointed an Indigenous person to the new position of Minister of Amerindian Affairs. The Minister considers himself a liaison between the Native peoples and the Government. However, as a junior minister in the Ministry of Public Works, Communications, and Regional Development, he has no staff and no separate budget. The APA and the Guyanese Organization of Indigenous Peoples complained that he is consequently ineffective in the position.

Prisons continued to be severely overcrowded. According to the Ombudsman, Guyana had 267 prison inmates per 100,000 populations in 1992. The GHRA cited poor diet, inadequate medical attention, underpaid and poorly trained staff, and lengthy trial delays as problems facing the prison system. The Ombudsman reported 33 complaints from prisoners in 1992. Prisoners complained of prison conditions, unreasonable charges, mail delays, and censorship. Suraj Persaud, a teenage boy, was beaten to death in Brickdam jail in Georgetown. The GHRA complained to Police Commissioner Laurie Lewis that fellow prisoners beat Persaud for several days with no attempt by police to intervene.

The Constitution provides that no person may be deprived of personal liberty except as authorized by law and requires a judicial determination of the legality of detention, a mandate that was generally respected in practice in 1993.

An arrest does not require a warrant issued by a court official, only an assessment of guilt by the police officer. The law requires that a person arrested and held for more than 24 hours be brought before a court to be charged. Chief Magistrate K. Juman Yassin publicly complained that suspects are often detained for more than 24 hours but never charged.

Bail is generally available except in capital cases. In narcotics cases, magistrates have discretion in granting bail before trial but must send all persons convicted on narcotics charges to custody, even if an appeal is pending.

Although the laws of Guyana recognize the right to legal counsel, in practice, except for capital crimes, it has been limited to those who cannot afford to pay. A group of lawyers is working to begin a Legal Aid Clinic. The Government has provided a small cash grant for the clinic and the services of a lawyer from the Attorney General's Office. The clinic was expected to open early in 1994 after the Government provided office space. Due to resource constraints, the clinic initially will limit its activities to certain civil cases in Georgetown.

On February 14, 1997, President Jagan suffered a heart attack, and despite treatment at the Walter Reed Army Medical Center in Washington DC, he died there on March 6, 1997. Prime Minister Samuel Hinds assumed the Office of and became the Fifth President of Guyana. On March 17, 1997, Janet Jagan was appointed President; Samuel Hinds was sworn in as Prime Minister and First Vice-President.

In September 1997, President Samuel Hinds requested the Secretary-General of the Organization of American States (OAS), Dr. Cesar Gaviria Trujillo, to send a mission to that country to observe the national and regional elections that were to take place on December 15. It was the first time that the OAS had been invited to observe elections in the country. The Secretary-General accepted the invitation and dispatched a Mission to Guyana from September 28 to October 10, 1997, to seek agreement on the terms of the Mission and privileges and immunities for the observers. The two agreements were signed on October 20, after which the Secretary-General designated Dr. Joseph Edmunds as Chief of Mission. The Mission was further strengthened by Assistant Secretary-General

Christopher R. Thomas, who joined the Mission in Guyana on December 12, 1997.

The OAS Mission consisted of 28 observers from 20 countries. On Election Day, the Mission visited 457 polling stations, approximately 25% of the total number. The Mission noted with satisfaction that the Elections Commission members worked together to assure that all eligible citizens of Guyana were allowed to vote. It exercised considerable flexibility in the electoral process when required, before and during the election. On Election Day, while some areas of concern were caused by a lack of training, poor communications and faulty logistics, the Mission observed no widespread hindrance to the balloting. Votes were cast for the most part in a climate of calm and freedom.

In contrast to the situation before the elections and during the voting, the Mission noted significant weaknesses in the organization, management, and administration of the collection, transmittal, verification, and announcement of results. That situation, coupled with substantial delays in the announcement of results from crucial polling districts, created a climate in which some have questioned the electoral process and results. Nevertheless, despite allegations of intentional manipulation of the results and other objections to the process, no substantiated claims were brought to the attention of the OAS Mission.

National elections were held on December 15, 1997, and Mrs. Janet Jagan was elected President with her PPP party winning a 55% majority of seats in Parliament. She was sworn in on December 19, 1997.

CHAPTER 36

The Administration of Mrs. Janet Jagan -1997

AS WAS THE CASE DURING NATIONAL ELECTIONS IN 1992, local and foreign independent observers judged the election to be free and fair. However, the leader of the PNC stated that his party would not accept the election results, alleging that the elections were rigged. The PNC initiated court action and called on its supporters to demonstrate in the streets. In October, the court began hearing testimony in the PNC case. It had not reached a verdict by year's end. Mr. Desmond Hoyte accused President Janet Jagan of election fraud and appealed to the Guyana Supreme Court to nullify the legislative elections. The court refused to annul the legislative elections.

CARICOM sent a three-member conciliation commission headed by Henry Forde of Barbados to Guyana on January

14, 1998. The CARICOM commission mediated the signing of the *Herdmanston Accord* on January 17, 1998, which provided for constitutional reforms and presidential elections within three years. CARICOM established a seven-member commission (Barbados, Grenada, Jamaica, Saint Lucia, Trinidad, and Tobago) and two staff observers headed by Ulric Cross of Trinidad and Tobago to audit the 1997 legislative elections on February 13, 1998.

On April 8, 1998, the Organization of American States (OAS) mission reported that the 1997 legislative elections were free and fair. On June 2, 1998, the CARICOM mission noted that the 1997 legislative election results were not fraudulent. The Government banned street protests in Georgetown on July 1, 1998. On July 2, 1998, CARICOM heads of state mediated an agreement between President Jagan and Desmond Hoyte in St. Lucia after several weeks of political violence in Guyana. The PNC ended their boycott of the National Assembly on July 15, 1998.

In a stunning decision, Justice Claudette Singh said several critical institutions in the country, most notably the 65-member Parliament that acted illegally in making the possession of a voter identification card a prerequisite for voting in the elections. As a result, she ruled that the December 1997 general elections were conducted under rules that contradicted the Constitution.

In previous elections, the production of a national passport or the regular national identification card was enough identification for a voter, whose name appeared on the official voter's list, was required to vote. In the election, persons were denied the right to vote because they did not have voter identification cards issued by the elections commission. The court found that about 30,000 persons, almost ten percent of the total eligible voters, were denied the chance to exercise their franchise. The judge ruled that the elections were null and void because the act that made identification cards the only voting prerequisite had breached several statutes in the Constitution, the supreme law of the land. The ruling plunged the country into further political and constitutional turmoil about two months before elections set for March 19.

Doodnauth Singh, who presided over the last elections as Chairman of the National Elections Commission, called the decision "unprecedented." "This means that Parliament and the Cabinet have been constituted illegally," he said. "This is unprecedented in that I have never heard in the Commonwealth of a judge declaring an entire national election as null and void. Usually they do so in a region or constituency, but not in a national election. This is unprecedented and has serious implications for the country," said Singh.

PNC Leader and former President Desmond Hoyte complained that the additional two months in office would give the administration invaluable access to State resources to campaign against its political opponents. He wanted the country to be run by a caretaker administration, a suggestion that was dismissed based on the relatively short period. After that, the court voided the elections; Mr. Hoyte claimed victory and argued that the ruling vindicated his position that an illegal government was running the country. "We are in a constitutional crisis," said Hoyte.

In the second part of her ruling, Justice Singh said that there were dozens of obvious fraud cases: switching of numbers to favor one party over another, disappearances of ballot boxes, and other acts of collusion by officials, but they were not enough to overturn the elections. There were irregularities reported as well. Georgetown mayor and former presidential candidate for the Good and Green Guyana party Hamilton Green and his wife voted at the same polling station. When results were announced, Green's party had only one vote, giving rise to jokes that his wife voted for another party. Manzoor Nadir, a presidential candidate for the United Force party, had a similar experience. He, his wife, and their three grown children also voted at the same place. But only one vote was registered for his party.

Close to 300 witnesses gave evidence ranging from ordinary polling day clerks to the chief elections officer. Most corroborated opposition claims that some poll forms were forged and that false entries were made on commission computers producing election results. One key area of concern is that voters in the upcoming elections will have to pay special identification cards again to vote. "But now that the judge has ruled, it means that Parliament would have to amend the act, but since the Parliament is illegal I am not sure how it is going to be done," said Doodnauth Singh.

On January 14, the PNC organized a massive, peaceful march in direct defiance of this government order. In late January, a high-level Caricom delegation brokered an end to the civil unrest by striking a deal between the leaders of the PPP/C and the PNC. The accord called for institutional changes, including constitutional reform and new elections within 3, rather than the standard five years. Also, as part of this agreement, a Caricom team conducted an independent audit of the election results. Its report, released in June, found no evidence of electoral manipulation or fraud, similar corroborating appraisals from several international observer teams. Nevertheless, the PNC remained unmoved by CARICOM's findings and returned to the streets.

The demonstrations became violent, with PNC supporters committing abuses of other citizens' rights. For several days in January and again in June, the PNC organized a series of unauthorized protests that intimidated citizens and disrupted business and government operations. Security forces made responsible attempts to contain these illegal gatherings, but on January 12, the protests turned violent. PNC supporters smashed shop windows, looted, and beat Indo-Guyanese citizens. The Government responded by placing a moratorium on public gatherings and marches.

When the June protests also turned violent, CARICOM again intervened to broker a second truce. By agreements signed in January and June by President Jagan and PNC leader Desmond Hoyte, an extra-Parliamentary Constitutional Reform Commission (CRC) presented a new draft constitution to Parliament and the public no later than July 1999. However, it took Parliament nearly eight months to agree on a formula to determine the CRC's composition, and members had not yet been named by year's end, casting doubt on its ability to meet the deadline.

Several opposition parties filed the petition in early 1998, weeks after the country was gripped by daily opposition-organized street demonstrations that necessitated tear gas and pellet guns by police. Worried that the riots and protests could have spilled over into full-scale anarchy, Caribbean Community leaders forced the governing People's Progressive Party and the prominent opposition People's National Congress to sign an agreement bringing forward elections to later in the year instead of 2002.

The ruling came at the time for the Bharrat Jagdeo administration. The PNC and other opposition parties were calling for an interim administration to run the country until elections in March. The special accord was agreed on January 17, 2001, as the outer limit for elections. Still, the Elections Commission said it was unable to meet that deadline and postponed the polls to March 19, 2001, instead.

The following seats were allocated for the 65 Elected Members of the National Assembly:

PPP 36, PNC 25, UF 2, and AFG 2.

On December 19, 1997, Mrs. Janet Jagan was sworn in as President. The Seventh Parliament of Guyana commenced when the National Assembly met on February 26, 1998. Ten persons who were not elected Members of the National Assembly were appointed by the President to be Ministers and became Non-elected Members of the Assembly. President Janet Jagan addressed the National Assembly.

The 25 Members from the PNC who were declared elected did not attend the first and subsequent Sittings of the Assembly. Under Articles 54 and 156(1) (b) of the Constitution and Standing Order No. 77, they vacated their seats in the Assembly. Their names were extracted from the lists, and they were again declared elected on July 13, 1998. They attended and subscribed to the Oath on July 15, 1998.

The following were the First Members of the National Assembly of the Seventh Parliament:

Speaker (1)

Derek C. Jagan

Members of the Government (46)

Samuel Hinds, *Prime Minister*

Reepu Daman Persaud, *Minister of Agriculture and Parliamentary Affairs*

Clement J. Rohee, *Minister of Foreign Affairs*

Bharrat Jagdeo, *Minister of Finance*

Charles R. Ramson, *Attorney General and Minister of Legal Affairs*
Ramnauth D.A. Bisnauth, *Minister of Education*
M. Shree Chan, *Minister of Trade, Tourism and Industry*
Indranie Chandarpal, *Minister of Human Services and Social*
Clinton C. Collymore, *Minister in the Ministry of Local Government*
F. Vibert DeSouza, *Minister of Amerindian Affairs*
George E. Fung-On, *Minister of the Public Service*
Henry B. Jeffrey, *Minister of Health and Labor*
Moses V. Nagamootoo, *Minister of Information*
Harripersaud Nokta, *Minister of Local Government*
Satyadeow Sawh, *Minister of Livestock and Fisheries*
Gail Teixeira, *Minister of Culture, Youth, and Sports*
C. Anthony Xavier, *Minister of Transport and Hydraulics*
Shaik K.Z. Baksh, *Minister of Housing and Water*
S. Feroze Mohamed
Cyril C. Belgrave
Donald R. Ramotar
Fazil M. Ali
Husman Alli
Komal Chand
Navindranauth O. Chandarpal
Bernard C. DeSantos
Shirley V. Edwards
Hughley H. Hanoman
Cheddi B. Jagan
Alston A. Kissoon
Moti Lall
Odinga N. Lumumba
Khemraj Ramjattan
Hari Narayen Ramkarran
Leslie S. Ramsammy

Lawrence E. Rodney
Philomena Sahoye-Shury, *Parliamentary Secretary, Ministry of Local Government*
Pauline R. Sukhai
Winslow M. Zephyr, *Deputy Speaker*
Joseph M. DeSouza, (Region 1 – Barima/Waini)
Heeralall Mohan, (Region 2 – Pomeroon/Supenaam)
Ramratan, (Region 3 – Essequibo Islands/West Demerara)
Geoffrey A. Fraser, (Region 5 – Mahaica/Berbice)
Ramsundar Sankat, (Region 6 – East Berbice/Corentyne)
Eustace S. Rodrigues, (National Congress of Local Democratic Organs)
Kumkaran Ramdas, (National Congress of Local Democratic Organs)

Members of the Minority (29)

People's National Congress (25)

H. Desmond Hoyte, *Leader of the Opposition*
Winston S. Murray
Dunstan Barrow
Clarissa S. Riehl
E. Lance Carberry
Faith A. Harding
Ivor Allen
Kadim A. Khan
Jean M.G. Persico
Aubrey C. Norton
Cyrilda A DeJesus
Andy Goveia
Deborah J. Backer
John S. DeFreitas

Raphael G.C. Trotman
Dalgleish Joseph
Volda A. Lawrence
Joseph L. Hamilton, (Region 4 – Demerara/Mahaica)
Sherwood A.J. Lowe
Andrew Hicks
Neaz Subhan
Colin Bynoe
Sandra M. Adams, (Region 10 – Upper Demerara/Berbice)
Kelly Andries, (Region 7 – Cuyuni/Mazaruni)
Milton L. Ganpatsingh

The United Force (2)
Manzoor Nadir
Matthew R. Charlie, (Region 9 – Upper Takutu/Upper Essequibo)

Alliance for Guyana (2)

Rupert Roopnaraine
Albertino Peters, *(Region 8 – Potaro/Siparuni)*

Maurice King of Barbados, representing CARICOM, facilitated inter-party dialogue between the PPP and PNC. The PPP and PNC ended the inter-party exchange on March 1, 1999. Chief Emeka Anyaoku, Secretary-General of the *Commonwealth of Nations* (CoN), mediated negotiations between Government and PNC representatives on May 6-9, 1999, and the parties agreed to resume inter-party dialogue. The PPP and PNC resumed inter-party conversation on June 14, 1999. Bharrat Jagdeo was appointed Prime Minister on August 9, 1999. President Janet Jagan resigned for health reasons, and Bharrat Jagdeo was sworn in as President on August 11, 1999. On January 15, 2001, the Guyana Supreme Court invalidated the results of the 1997 legislative elections and called for new legislative elections in March 2001.

On April 19, 2000, the non-governmental Members of the National Assembly, under the Chairmanship of the Speaker of the National Assembly, Hari Narayen Ramkarran, elected Hugh Desmond Hoyte to be Leader of the Opposition. On August 27, 2000, the name of the People's National Congress was changed to People's National Congress/Reform (PNC/R).

On September 3, 2000, a new political movement, Rise, Organize and Rebuild Guyana (ROAR), was launched by Ravi Dev.

CHAPTER 37

The Administration Mr. Bharrat Jagdeo -1999

As Guyana was wrestling with the ethnic and political tensions, Mr. Jagdeo ascended to the Presidency in 1999, not by election, but rather through the anointment of his predecessor, Janet Jagan, thus taking the helm with no electoral mandate.

Legislative elections were held on March 19, 2001, and the PPP won 35 out of 65 seats in the National Assembly. More than 150 international observers representing six international missions witnessed the polling. The European Union (EU) sent eight election experts and 29 short-term election observers headed by Mark Stevens of Britain to monitor the legislative elections between October 13 and April 5, 2001. The Organization of American States (OAS) sent 34 observers from eleven countries led by Ambassador Colin Granderson

611

of Trinidad & Tobago to monitor the legislative elections from March 1 to April 8, 2001. The Commonwealth of Nations sent eleven observers headed by Sir Ieremia Tienang Tabai of Kiribati to monitor the legislative elections beginning on February 26, 2001. CARICOM sent ten observers from ten countries led by R. Carl Rattray of Jamaica to monitor the legislative elections. The Carter Center/Council of Freely Elected Heads of Government (CC/CFEHG) sent six medium-term observers and 37 short-term observers from 10 countries headed by Jimmy Carter, Rosalyn Carter, and Lloyd Erskine Sandiford of Barbados to monitor the legislative elections from February 5 to April 6, 2001. The observers pronounced the elections fair and open, although marred by some administrative problems. As in 1997, public demonstrations and some violence followed the election, with the opposition PNCR disputing the results.

Mr. Jagdeo of the PPP was elected President by the National Assembly, and on March 31, 2001, he was inaugurated as President. The 25 Geographical seats and the 40 National Top-Up seats, for a total of 65 Elected Members of the National Assembly, were allocated as follows:

Geographical National Total Top Up

PPP/C 34, PNC/R 27, GAP/WPA 2, UF 1, and ROAR 1.

The PPP/C 34 Members, together with UF 1 Member, formed the Government. The First Sitting of the National Assembly was held on May 4, 2001.

Speaker (1)

Hari Narayen Ramkarran

Members of the Government (37)

Samuel Hinds, *Prime Minister and Minister of Works and Communications*

Reepu Daman Persaud, *Minister of Parliamentary Affairs*

Clement James Rohee, *Minister of Foreign Trade and International Cooperation*

Harripersaud Nokta, *Minister of Local Government and Regional Development*

Gail Teixeira, *Minister of Culture, Youth and Sport*

Henry Benfield Jeffrey, *Minister of Education*

Saisnarine Kowlessar, *Minister of Finance*

Shaik K. Z. Baksh, *Minister of Housing and Water*

Navindranauth Omanand Chandarpal, *Minister of Agriculture*

Ronald Gajraj, *Minister of Home Affairs*

Ramnauth Dale Arlington Bisnauth, *Minister of Labour, Human Services and Social Security*

Clinton Carlton Collymore, *Minister in the Ministry of Local Government and Regional Development*

Satyadeow Sawh, *Minister of Fisheries, Other Crops, and Livestock*

Samuel Rudolph Insanally, *Minister in the Office of the President with responsibility for Foreign Affairs*

Doodnauth Singh, *Attorney General and Minister of Legal Affairs*

Jennifer Reginalda Ann Westford, *Minister of the Public Service*

Carl Anthony Xavier, *Minister of Transport and Hydraulics*

Bibi Safora Shadick, *Minister in the Ministry of Labor, Human Services and Social Security*

Manzoor Nadir, *Minister of Tourism, Industry, and Commerce*

Carolyn Rodrigues, *Minister of Amerindian Affairs*

Leslie S. Ramsammy, *Minister of Health*
Sheik Feroze Mohamed, *Government Chief Whip*
Cyril Calvin Lewis Belgrave
Donald Rabindranauth Ramotar
Husman Alli
Komal Chand
Indranie Chandarpal
Bernard Celestino DeSantos
Shirley Veronica Edwards
Odinga N. Lumumba
Heeralall Mohan
Ramesh Chandra Rajkumar
Kumkaran Ramdas, JP
Khemraj Ramjattan
Bheri Sygmond Ramsaran
Philomena Sahoye-Shury, *Parliamentary Secretary, Ministry of Housing and Water*
Pauline R. Sukhai

Members of the Opposition (30)

People's National Congress/Reform (27)

Hugh Desmond Hoyte, *Leader of the Opposition*
Robert Herman Orlando Corbin
Winston Shripal Murray
Clarissa Sabita Riehl, *Deputy Speaker*
Everette Lancelot Carberry
Ivor Allen
Deborah Jan Backer
Deryck Milton Alexander Bernard
Cyril Stanley Ming
Raphael Gregory Conwright Trotman

Vincent Luther Alexander
Andy Goveia
Volda Ann Lawrence
Dalgleish Joseph
Amna Ally
Sandra Michelle Adams
Jerome Khan
George Aubrey Norton
Myrna Elizabeth Neomi Peterkin
James Kennedy McAllister
Lurlene Anita Nestor
Abdul Kadir
Ricky Khan
Rajcoomarie Bancroft
Nasir Ally
Judith David
Genevieve Purvesta Roxanne Allen

Guyana Action Party/Working People's Alliance (2)

Sheila Holder
Shirley Juliana Melville

Rise, Organize and Rebuild Party (1)

Ravindra Dev

At the First Sitting, the National Assembly elected Hari Narayen Ramkarran to be Speaker and Clarissa Sabita Riehl to be Deputy Speaker. President Bharrat Jagdeo addressed the National Assembly.

The political disturbances following the election partially

overlapped and politicized a major crime wave that gripped Guyana from 2002 through May 2003. By summer 2003, the worst of the crime wave had diminished, and agitation over the election had subsided. In the spring of 2002, citing the failure of the PPP/C Government to fulfill agreements made through an inter-party dialogue process, the PNC/R began a boycott of Parliament.

Through the first part of 2003, the leaders of the PPP/C and PNC/R made an effort to restart the dialogue, resulting in the return of PNC/R to Parliament in May 2003. The parties appeared to be on the path to a constructive engagement, with some slippage of dates and commitments, until late 2003. Since then, a general lack of trust resulted in a return to the political impasse between the parties.

Agriculture and mining were Guyana's most important economic activities: sugar, bauxite, rice, and gold, accounting for 70% - 75% of export earnings. However, the rice sector experienced a decline in 2000, with export earnings down 27% through the third quarter of 2000. Ocean shrimp exports, which were heavily impacted by a 1-month import ban to the United States in 1999, accounted for only 3.5% of total export earnings that year. Shrimp exports rebounded in 2000, representing 11% of export earnings through the third quarter of 2000. Other exports include timber, diamonds, garments, rum, and pharmaceuticals. The value of these other exports is increasing.

Guyana's extremely high debt burden to foreign creditors has meant limited availability of foreign exchange and reduced capacity to import necessary raw materials, spare parts, and equipment, thereby further reducing production. The increase in global fuel costs also contributed to the country's decline in production and growing trade deficit. The decline of production has increased unemployment. Although no reliable statistics exist, combined unemployment and underemployment are estimated at 30%. Emigration, principally to the United States and Canada, remains substantial. After years of a state-dominated economy, the mechanisms for private investment, domestic or foreign, were still evolving. The shift from a state-controlled economy to a primarily free market system began under Desmond Hoyte and continued under PPP/C governments.

The foreign exchange market was fully liberalized in 1991, and the currency was freely traded without restriction. The rate was subject to change daily; the Guyana dollar depreciated 17.6% from 1998 to 2000. The Guyanese economy, which was heavily dependent on the export of six primary commodities: rice, timber, gold, bauxite, shrimp, and sugar, expanded at an average rate of 3 percent over the past decade. Despite the incremental improvement, the government officials have been either unwilling or unable to share the modest prosperity with the average Guyanese citizens.

Indicative of that trend was that the allocation for education as a percentage of government spending was significantly lower than it was ten years ago. Public spending on education dropped to 6.1 percent of total GDP in 2007, down from 8.5 percent in 2000. Because of that lack of investment in public education, the percentage of primary school entrance-age children enrolled in schools dropped from 91.8 percent to 62.0 percent. It is difficult to speculate what effect the substantive budget cuts have on children's education and childhood literacy rates in the country, owing to a lack of data collected by Government officials.

There were some positive results in healthcare, including an increase in life expectancy and a notable decrease in infant mortality. Many difficulties, however, remain unaffected. For instance, about a fifth of the Guyanese population still lacks access to clean sanitation facilities. The World Health Organization estimated that Guyana had one of the highest prevalence rates of HIV/AIDS in Latin America and the Caribbean.

Mr. Jagdeo's tenure can also be remembered for the spike in violent crimes experienced throughout the country, a situation exacerbated by repeated extrajudicial killings on the part of State authorities. Since 2001, the phantom or death squads, with alleged connections to government agencies referred to as *Black Clothes Police*, have been linked to 400 murders. "A clear pattern is emerging," said a member of the opposition People's National Congress Reform (PNC/R). "The Black Clothes Police have constituted themselves as accusers, judges, jury and executioners, and have been gunning down people with impunity."

The Jagdeo administration shocked the region by rejecting a request by the United States, Britain, and Canada to do an independent probe of what amounted to repeated human rights violations. "We are very concerned about the allegations and we believe that the integrity of the government is something that is at question here," said British High Commissioner Stephen Hiscock. Amnesty International wrote an open letter to President Jagdeo in 2001 demanding prosecution of any officials involved in extrajudicial violence and saying that the Guyanese Government had "repeatedly failed to ensure the protection of the internationally recognized fundamental right to life, and to take measures to prevent such killings." Although several officers were indicted for their participation in extrajudicial killings in 2004, none were convicted.

Assassins killed Satyadeow Sawh, Minister of Agriculture, and three other individuals on April 22, 2006. CARICOM foreign ministers condemned the assassinations on April 26, 2006, and Commonwealth of Nations (CoN) Special Envoy

Paul Reeves condemned the assassinations on April 27, 2006. Eight individuals were killed in political violence in Bagotstown and Eccles on August 8, 2006. The Organization of American States (OAS) Inter-American Commission on Human Rights (IACHR) condemned the killings on August 14, 2006.

Some have responded in kind to the state violence, such as in the notorious Rondell Rawlins case. Rawlins, who accused the Government of kidnapping his girlfriend, waged a campaign of terror in Guyana, seeking her return. That resulted in the shocking deaths of 23 people.

Jagdeo's tumultuous Presidency was also beset by a series of fatal bombings, including one attack on the Ministry of Health in 2009 and two additional assaults in 2011. One at the Stabroek Market and the other at the residence of Philomena Sahoye-Shury, a leading member of President Jagdeo's People's Progressive Party. As one editorial in Guyana's Stabroek News put it, "The security situation grows murkier by the day and it is in this milieu that there has been a rash of dangerous events." Guyana's motto, One People, One Nation, One Destiny, only seems a cruel joke in the face of the stark division that seized the country, a division that Jagdeo did almost nothing to address.

Crimes in Guyana took on a racial dimension, reflecting the continued perception of the longstanding Afro-Guyanese exclusion under the PPP. In 2007, Andre Douglas, an alleged Afro-Guyanese murderer, who was eventually killed by police after escaping from jail, placed his crimes in the context of social marginalization and inequality. He called himself a freedom fighter and said, "Look into innocent black Guyanese problems or unrest will not end." In other words, Douglas would keep terrorizing Guyana until the social problems of the Afro-Guyanese were alleviated. The large turnout at Douglas' funeral showed that his frustration resonated with the country's

Afro-Guyanese community. Thus, the ethnic division remains a challenge that disrupts quotidian life in Guyana, and that President Jagdeo has not effectively taken steps to resolve. Stagnation, violence, corruption, arch-sectarianism, and unfettered crime seem to be the heritage President Bharrat Jagdeo will bequeath to his country.

Chosen by former President Janet Jagan to succeed in the office and supposedly held in high esteem by Dr. Jagan, Jagdeo could only receive the lowest marks from any independent evaluation. Through his tolerance of crime, racism, and dismal social progress, President Jagdeo turned in a fifth-rate performance as President of one of the poorest countries in the hemisphere. As the Guyanese use every strategy, legal and illegal, to flee the dysfunctional country, Jagdeo will go down in history as a man who did almost nothing for his nation while in office. It is the hope of the Guyanese people that whoever inherits Jagdeo's position must work to tackle the persistent issues and clear the air of hopelessness when it comes to improving life in one of the hemisphere's most impoverished and most forlorn countries.

Minister of Home Affairs, Mr. Ronald Gajraj, denied involvement in the *Phantom Gang* which allegedly killed criminal suspects. "I wish to be cleared categorically," said Mr. Gajraj in a televised speech. "I've never acted contrary to the laws of Guyana." He said he was acting "to end this smear campaign against me and to thwart a concerted campaign to bring the entire government into disrepute." There was no indication as to whether President Jagdeo would accept his resignation and open the inquiry. The country of 770,000 people has been experiencing a severe crime wave. There were more than 160 killings in 2002 and 210 in 2003, compared to an average previously of about 50 killings a year.

Opposition groups say The Phantom Gang has gunned

down several well-known criminals over the last year, at the behest of the Government. The opposition walked out of Parliament, vowing not to return until an independent investigation was set up. Opposition parties have written to UN Secretary-General Kofi Annan asking for assistance in getting an inquiry under way. The United States and Canada have revoked Mr. Gajraj's tourist visa and called for an impartial investigation.

United States Ambassador Roland W. Bullen issued a statement that Roger Khan threatens to control the fragile Guyanese state akin to Pablo Escobar's erstwhile control over Colombia. Khan was active in drug trafficking, money laundering, and arms smuggling. His economic interests include construction and forestry. DEA developed a plan in 2004 to establish a counter-narcotics operation in Guyana. An informant leaked details about the project. After the leak, Khan threatened to blow up the operation site and threatened the lives of the Ambassador and the then RSO. Those threats forced the operation's abandonment.

Khan surrounds himself with a coterie of former police tactical squad members for security. He was a principal in the *Phantom Squad* (aka death squad) that former Minister of Home Affairs Gajraj employed to crack down on crime from 2002 to 2004. The Minister of Home Affairs reported that Khan regularly travels to Suriname and Trinidad and meets with Desi Bouterse. Khan bought off countless people in Guyana. Through that patronage, he was able to operate with impunity. It was clear that the Government of Guyana (GoG) was compromised to such an extent that it would not pursue Khan, despite paying lip service to the fight against narco-trafficking. Multiple sources have expressed fears to the Ambassador that not only has Khan penetrated almost every level of Guyanese Government and society, but that he exerted ever more significant influence over the political scenes. Most respected commentators believe that Guyana was already a narco-state, and if Guyana was a narco-state, then Khan was its leader. The Ambassador had spoken with GoG to little avail about Khan's drug activities and unaccounted wealth. The GoG has adopted a head-in-the-sand approach to Khan and narco-trafficking in general. The GoG asks for hard evidence and pretends not to know how Khan acquires his means.

Mr. Khan had close ties to the then People's Progressive Party/Civic, with the late ex-Home Affairs Minister, Ronald Gajraj, acting as a conduit for a *Phantom Squad*. The squad was accused of murdering several criminals, competitors, and others. Although the PPP government had sought to distance itself from Khan, he stated publicly in an advertisement in local newspapers that he had been fighting crime on behalf of the Bharrat Jagdeo government. Khan also implicated the Minister of Health, Dr. Leslie Ramsammy, in his escapades and documents bearing the Minister's signature authorizing the purchase of a sophisticated wire-tapping device. Jagdeo was President of Guyana from August 11, 1999, to December 3, 2011. There were three massacres: Lusignan, where 11 people were killed; Bartica, where 12 were killed; and Lindo Creek, where seven miners were slaughtered. There were countless extrajudicial killings, with an estimate of around 400 males gunned down.

Guyanese police investigated the circumstances surrounding the bombing of the Ministry of Home Affairs. - reported by Jarryl Bryan.

Police said that three channa bombs - bottles filled with petrol-soaked chickpeas - were hurled by three men who were seen standing under a tree outside the Ministry before the incident. The fire caused damage to the upper and middle floors of the Ministry but did not affect work at the Ministry.

The Ministry of Home Affairs was at the center of controversy since Minister Ronald Gajraj was accused of being linked to death squads. Since then, supporters of the country's main opposition party, the People's National Congress, have picketed the Ministry on a daily basis and were calling on the Minister to step down and for an independent inquiry into his alleged links to death squads. The PNC claimed that the Ministry was also involved in gross irregularities in issuing firearms licenses and that too should be investigated.

Minister Gajraj noted that while he is not sure of the motive for the attack, it must be seen within the context of all three charges which have been leveled against him. "What might be the reason or the motive for such criminal acts, I am not sure," said Minister Gajraj. "But of course you would know that within recent times, the minister has been the target of vitriolic attacks being levelled against him by the main opposition party and other parties." PNC leader Mr. Robert Corbin told BBC Caribbean Service he noticed that since the present Government assumed office, the fire had mysteriously destroyed or seriously damaged at least three ministries when they were under investigation. "We have waged a campaign in past weeks in a peaceful and orthodox manner that has astounded the government and it is strange they have been predicting all along that there'll be violence that has not materialized," he said. "I would not put it beyond the imagination that someone is trying to create some diversions." He added that his party would not be diverted from mounting peaceful protests.

Former Home Affairs Minister, Ronald Gajraj, sued Gail Teixeira, a senior member of the People's Progressive Party, over her alleged statements contained in leaked US Embassy cables.

Gail Teixeira, the Parliamentary Chief Whip for the Opposition, was also a former Home Affairs Minister. Excerpts of the WikiLeaks US Embassy cables quoted Teixeira as saying that Gajraj was corrupt. Gajraj, who was Guyana's High Commissioner to India, moved to the court, suing both Teixeira and a Guyana newspaper for libel. The lawsuit was filed in the Supreme Court by Gajraj's Attorney-at-Law, Arun Gajraj, who is claiming more than $30M in damages. Teixeira and the Guyana Chronicle were also reportedly served with the writ.

Gajraj was claiming damages in excess of $10M for "defamation of character as a result of certain callous slanders spoken by Teixeira and published by the Chronicle."

Gajraj was also claiming in excess of $10M for Libel, which the Guyana Chronicle allegedly published. More than $10M was also contended for Aggravated and Punitive Damages. In addition, Gajraj is seeking an injunction restraining the Guyana Chronicle or "their servants, agents or whosoever otherwise from repeating or republishing said or similar libel of plaintiff." Gajraj was also seeking the cost of the proceedings and any further sums the court may award. According to the writ, both defendants are commanded to appear before the court to answer the suit.

The lawsuit stems from the Chronicle publication headlined "WikiLeaks cable... Teixeira accused Gajraj of visa racketeering." The cables quoted in the article had reportedly been sent from the Charge d'Affaires at the US Embassy, Michael Thomas, to his Headquarters in the US. In the cable, the conversation between Thomas and Teixeira was dated December 28, 2005. According to the cable, she had requested a consular briefing on trends in fake civil documents detected by the Embassy's consular section. Teixeira acknowledged that there "is quite a lot of corruption in the immigration division." She was quoted as saying that former Home Affairs Ministry Security Policy Coordinator, Sultan Kassim, was "very closely linked to a number of networks, particularly the Chinese." She also revealed that a slush fund was financed by Brazilian fees for work permits that "Gajraj and Kassim had run." She was criticizing Gajraj for the direct control held over the Home Affairs Ministry.

Gajraj vacated his portfolio as Minister of Home Affairs in 2005, following his involvement in the activities of a phantom death squad, which hunted and killed criminals and suspects during the crime wave of the early 2000s. Gajraj was then sent on a diplomatic posting by President Bharrat Jagdeo, and Teixeira was then appointed Home Affairs Minister. When the A Partnership for National Unity/Alliance for Change (APNU+AFC) came to office, Gajraj returned to Guyana. Several ex-phantom death squad members had alleged that Gajraj knew about the squad's activities, while telephone records had reportedly linked him to some members. Gajraj has consistently denied the allegations.

The PPP held a press conference to deal with parliamentary and sectoral matters. Teixeira, when questioned, acknowledged that there was a conversation between her and embassy officials at the time, and she had requested evidence of civil document racketeering but noted that many statements attributed to her were Thomas's interpretation. "In relation to what is stated in the Chronicle, I have not had a look at the WikiLeaks (referred to in the article) but as is (the case of) all of these cables any foreign missions send briefings of every single meeting they have with Government officials, NGO, anybody. That's a responsibility." "In those cables, they put their own personal assessments," she stated. "(However) the way in which the Chronicle's article was written, as if certain things in the Charge d' Affaires' opinion is being put over as if I said that...I did not."

She recalled that her Government received numerous reports from the US embassy about fraudulent passports and birth certificates. She said that immigration, under the law, came under the police force. "(General Registry Office) GRO (and) the issuing of birth certificates came under the Ministry of Home Affairs. The US embassy was asked by me to provide evidence of these fake documents. Now, the GRO ones were particularly disturbing because they were actually authentic." She related that the birth certificates came with the watermark of the GRO. There were also signatures of persons working at the GRO, but the information was false. "Those persons (to whom birth certificates were issued didn't exist. And from that false document, they then created other fake documents (fake passports). The passports were genuine, but the persons on them were not real." She said that it was that evidence that she requested, as well as fictitious marriage certificates. She stated that those were being issued to persons who were nowhere around when they were issued in the case of the marriage certificates. "As a result of this, action was taken to have investigations opened. Police investigations were held and a number of people in the GRO were recommended to be charged. However, the police under Felix's stewardship did nothing."

Teixeira also called into question the overall accuracy of the WikiLeaks cables, noting that there had been cables detailing conversations she had between December 2005 and July 2006. Those cables, she said, became public knowledge in 2011 but contained some inaccuracies. For instance, she recalled one conversation attributed to her. In the conversation, she had allegedly called into question former Police Commissioner Henry Greene's suitability for the post. She made it transparent that the conversation, in fact, never took place. "In December 2005, Felix was the Commissioner of Police and at no point was there any discussion as his retirement did not come up until June/July 2006," Teixeira said, "The Commissioner of Police is a prerogative of the President (at the time Bharrat Jagdeo) and therefore there would be no inclination on my part to enter into such discussions."

The US was concerned by Guyana's Decision to Reinstate Former Home Affairs Minister Ronald Gajraj.

The United States was deeply concerned by Guyana's decision to reinstate former Home Minister Ronald Gajraj. A Guyanese commission of inquiry looking into his links to the so-called "Phantom Death Squad" has found severe procedural irregularities in his official conduct related to his involvement with individuals who allegedly carried out extrajudicial killings. Significant questions remain unanswered regarding his involvement in serious criminal activities. The United States and the Government of Guyana enjoy close, cordial relations and share a crucial bilateral agenda. However, Gajraj's resumption of a key Ministry with direct authority over law enforcement activities in Guyana undermines law in that country. The USA asserted that it would be looking at the range of assistance it provides the Government of Guyana to protect the integrity of that plan, particularly in the areas of governance and law enforcement.

Party affiliation in Guyana continued along ethnic lines.

Jagdeo's PPP overwhelmingly receives the vote of the Indo-Guyanese, while the opposition PNC garners the support of the country's Afro-Guyanese. One study of the 2001 elections called the crossover votes between ethnic groups "insubstantial" and concluded that "PPP is still, for all practical purposes, an Indian-dominated party." After the 2006 election, Jagdeo's efforts to diminish the trend were nowhere to be seen. One editorial in the Stabroek News in 2010 commented that the two main parties remain within their ethnic platform. It said, "Both the PPP and PNC follow an unwritten rule that their leader must be from a particular ethnic group and both derive a high percentage of their support from a single ethnic group."

Under the Jagdeo PPP/C Administration, Guyana earned the reputation of being among the most corrupt countries in the hemisphere, coupled with widespread discrimination, nepotism, and high levels of unemployment, particularly among young people.

CHAPTER 38

The Administration of Mr. Donald Ramotar - 2011

IN NOVEMBER 2011, MR. DONALD RAMOTAR OF THE PPP was elected President. His party and its junior coalition partner, the Civic Party, lost their majority in the National Assembly when A Partnership formed a coalition for National Unity (APNU) - an alliance comprising the People's National Congress Reform (PNCR; a reconstituted PNC, including the former Reform Party) and several smaller parties - and the Alliance for Change (AFC) party. APNU-AFC's single-vote majority, combined with the PPP's continued control of the presidency, resulted in a period of legislative gridlock.

The Organization of American States (OAS) Electoral Mission Final Report, which referenced the Mission with observers from 14 countries, applauded significant efforts made by the Guyanese Electoral Commission (GECOM) to execute an overall inclusive and clean electoral process. The report mentioned the "high level of training and dedication exhibited by GECOM staff in the polling centers." The Commonwealth observation team also endorsed those views. The report also noted areas of improvement to make subsequent elections more efficient and fair.

In that election, the APNU and the AFC fielded candidates separately and won 33 seats. That was one more than the PPP/C, which failed to secure a parliamentary majority for the first time in 19 years. Mr. Ramotar subsequently formed a minority PPP/C Government since Guyana gained independence from the United Kingdom in 1966.

On May 15, 2012, President Donald Ramotar at the General Council Meeting of the Organization of American States (OAS) in Washington DC.

The region should put poverty eradication at the top of its agenda. Democracy cannot be safeguarded without reducing poverty; neither can poverty be effectively combated without addressing inequality. Job creation should be an essential aspect of whatever model of social and economic development is pursued. For Guyana, no priority is greater than combat poverty, extreme poverty, inequality, and social exclusion. This can be done through policies that promote economic growth, access to education, health care, and housing in order to achieve sustainable development with social justice. A critical component of these efforts is initiatives to promote social protection and economic development among vulnerable groups.

It was, however, unfortunate that the President, as demonstrated by the 2012 National Budget proposals, did not pursue the agenda that he theoretically promoted. Donald Ramotar's

PPP/C Administration was immediately confronted with the following challenges:

A 2% Reduction of the VAT from 16%. The Opposition proposed that the oppressive 16% VAT should be reduced by 2% to relieve the impact of the high cost-of-living which has intensified the ravages of poverty visited on large segments of the Guyanese population. The Opposition pointed out that, since the VAT is a regressive tax, its impact is most significant on the poor. Therefore, the 2% reduction would be a beneficial poverty relief measure. The Government countered this with the argument advocated by the Minister of Finance that the poor will benefit very little from reducing the VAT rate.

Double the Old Age Pension to $15,000/month. The Opposition pointed out that Pensioners are among the most vulnerable groups in Guyana. After strong representation by the Opposition, the Government reluctantly agreed to increase the Old Age Pension to $10,000/month.

The drastic reduction, by $210.4Mn, of the 2012 Budget allocation for Social Services within the Ministry of Labor, Human Services & Social Security. Given the large and growing number of Guyanese existing in conditions of dire poverty, it is a matter for deep concern that the 2012 Budget allocation for Social Services has been reduced by $210.4Mn, mainly since the Ministry is responsible for administering the vital social safety-nets, including the Old Age Pension and Public Assistance.

Increase Public Sector pay by 10% across-the-board while re-establishing effective Collective Bargaining. The Public Service pay has been woefully depressed by the Government through the arbitrary annual imposition of increases below the cost-of-living while subverting the Collective Bargaining process for Public Servants. The Government has ignored this call.

Restore the subvention agreed by the National Assembly to the Critchlow Labor College. As part of its vendetta against the Guyana Trade Union Council (GTUC), the Government continues to deny the Trade Union educational institution the subvention which was agreed by the National Assembly.

Freeze the proposed electricity tariff increase to the depressed Region 10 communities while introducing measures to create economic growth, employment, and incomes. The Government remains adamant that their proposed electricity tariff increases will be immediately implemented, even though it is evident that the depressed conditions in that region have driven a large segment of the population into poverty.

Reduce the Berbice River Bridge toll from $2,000 to $1,000. The high toll has created hardships, particularly for families with school-age children needing to cross the bridge daily. In addition, it is inhibiting the movement of produce from Berbice to markets in Georgetown.

Stop the abuse of the mechanism of contract employees to undermine the Public Service Union and bypass the jurisdiction of the Public Service Commission. The Government continued to use every possible device to skip the Public Service Commission's jurisdiction and weaken the bargaining strength of the Public Service Union. Implement the recommendations for the reform and modernization of the Public Service. The Government continued to ignore the long outstanding requests contained in the several studies undertaken to reform and modernize the Public Service.

Pay over the substantial financial assets belonging to the people of Guyana, which were being misused by National Industrial and Commercial Investments Limited (NICIL), into the Consolidated Fund to ensure National Assembly oversight. The Government, as the sole shareholder, while avoiding oversight by the National Assembly, was misusing the substantial public assets held by NICIL as "slush funds" through the convoluted, self-serving argument that this was a "private company."

Immediately implement the constitutionally mandated Public Procurement Commission to stem the widespread corruption in the issuing of construction and other publicly funded contracts. There was a clear indication that the Government intends to continue using every device to impede the establishment of an independent and autonomous oversight Public Procurement Commission.

Increase the subvention for the University of Guyana. The Government continued to manipulate and undermine the autonomy of the nation's highest institution of learning, the University of Guyana, by devices such as ensuring that it remains cash-strapped and its physical plant and equipment remain in a state of decrepitude.

Stop treating constitutional offices - such as the Parliament Office, Guyana Elections Commission (GECOM), and the Service Commissions, *etc.* as Budget Agencies under the President's Office and, thereby, undermining their independence and autonomy. Those entities should receive their subvention directly from the Consolidated Fund.

Stop the misuse of the publicly funded Government Information Agency (GINA) and National Communications Network (NCN) as propaganda mouthpieces of the PPP Administration. Since the passage of the amended 2012 Budget, the Ramotar PPP/C Administration has mounted an intense propaganda assault, through the continued misuse and abuse of GINA and NCN, against the Opposition because they insist that those entities should be managed in a non-partisan and transparent manner in the service of the nation. President Donald Ramotar must ensure that the words uttered to impress the international community mirror his deeds in Guyana.

While delivering the feature address at the opening ceremony of the Police Officers' Conference held at the Police Mess Annex, Eve Leary, President Ramotar explained that the police force's effectiveness is not measured by the number of arrests made but by the lack of crime. He mentioned the recent findings of the Latin American Public Opinion Project (LAPOP), which found that Guyana has the lowest level of trust in the Police than anywhere else in the region. According to the President, while persons may have their respective views on the methodology and analysis used for the survey, it does not take away from the fact that the findings have been published and disseminated widely as such an objective approach is needed to address the issues raised by LAPOP.

The survey found that between 2012 and 2014, the public's trust in the Guyana Police Force has decreased by 10 points on a zero to a hundred scale, from 45.8 in 2012 to 35.4 in 2014. That, according to the President, was worrying and should not be acceptable. Ramotar proposed to restore confidence in the country's Police Force. One of the President's measures was the reopening of cold cases and unsolved crimes to improve the clear-up rates in homicide, shootings, robberies, larceny, and sexual offenses. "If criminals don't think that they will be caught, they will continue to commit crimes," he pointed out. The President's call comes in the wake of the steep increases in murder and the alarmingly high rates of unsolved crimes.

President Ramotar chose to investigate the death of Dr. Walter Rodney, which took place thirty-four years ago. According to declassified documents, there was evidence that the end of the internationally-known historian and activist Dr. Walter Rodney in Georgetown was a political assassination. Dr. Rodney was a popular opposition figure known for his disapproval of the US-backed Government of President Forbes Burnham. Dr. Rodney was killed when a bomb exploded in the car he was sitting in with his brother. The Government claimed Rodney himself and his brother, Donald, were responsible. President Donald Ramotar appointed a commission to investigate the death. The investigation was terminated early after the new Government of Mr. David Granger came to power. Nonetheless, the Commission's report concluded that state authorities were behind the operation.

Commission of Inquiry into the death of Dr. Walter Rodney

Dr. Walter Rodney met his death in violent and controversial circumstances at John's Street, close to the Georgetown Prison, on the night of June 13, 1980. Thirty-four years later, on February 6, 2014, the President of Guyana appointed a Commission of Inquiry according to the Commission of Inquiry Act, Chapter 19.03. The Commissioners appointed were Sir Richard L. Cheltenham, KA, Q.C., Ph.D. Chairman; Mr. Seenath Jairam, S.C., and Mrs. Jacqueline Samuels-Brown, Q.C.

The Terms of Reference of the Commission were:

To examine the facts and circumstances immediately prior, at the time of, and subsequently, the death of Dr. Walter Rodney to determine, as far as is possible, who is or what was responsible for the explosion resulting in the death of Dr. Walter Rodney. To enquire into the cause of the explosion in which Dr. Rodney died; whether it was an act of terrorism and, if so, who were the perpetrators.

To specifically examine the role, if any, which the late

Gregory Smith, Sergeant of the Guyana Defense Force, played in the death of Dr. Walter Rodney and if so, to inquire into who may have counseled, procured, aided, or abetted him in doing so, including facilitating his departure from Guyana after Dr. Walter Rodney's death.

To examine and report on the actions and activities of the State, such as the Guyana Police Force, the Guyana Defense Force, the Guyana National Security, the Guyana People's Militia, and those who were in command and superintendence of those agencies; to determine whether they were tasked with the surveillance of and carrying out of actions and whether they did execute those tasks and carried out those actions against the Political Opposition for the period January 1, 1978, to December 31, 1980.

To examine, review, and report on earlier investigations and inquiries done into the death of Dr. Walter Rodney.

Before the appointment of a Commission of Inquiry, there was no official public inquiry into the circumstances surrounding the death of Dr. Walter Rodney, which occurred some thirty-four years ago. There was, however, a coroner's inquest into his death which took place some eight years after his death. There was also an inquiry into his death which was carried out by the International Commission of Jurists.

The Commissioners were determined to build public support for the task by meeting with persons and organizations that may have been able to assist the public inquiry directly or indirectly. Accordingly, they held meetings with the following persons: The President of the Co-operative Republic of Guyana, Chief of Staff of the Guyana Defense Force, The Leader of the Opposition and leaders of the main political parties, The Chancellor of the Judiciary, The Commissioner of Police, The Private Sector Commission, The head of the Chamber of Commerce, The head of the Trades Union

Congress, Heads of major religious organizations and head of the main interreligious organization.

The Commissioners drafted the Rules governing the procedure to be followed during the inquiry. The Rules were published in the Official Gazette on April 22, 2014. The Commission held 66 sessions on the following dates: April 28, 2014 to May 2, 2014; May 27, 2014 to June 6, 2014; June 23, 2014 to July 2, 2014; July 29, 2014 to August 7, 2014; August 25, 2014 to August 29, 2014; October 20, 2014 to November 7, 2014; January 26, 2015 to January 30, 2015; February 9, 2015 to February 20, 2015; March 23, 2015 to March 27, 2015; July 27, 2015 to July 31, 2015; September 28, 2015 to October 2, 2015.

They heard the oral evidence of some 31 witnesses, 29 of whom were examined, cross-examined, and re-examined where necessary. Among them, two witnesses were heard on video at the witnesses' request. In addition, they listened to the incomplete evidence of two other witnesses, namely, Major General Norman Mc Lean and Holland Yearwood, also called Jomo. Mr. Denbow of the Commission Secretariat, assisted by Counsel to the Commission and investigators, went about the task of identifying, contacting, and interviewing potential witnesses. It was helpful that they had the record of the coroner's inquest proceedings and the record of the trial of Donald Rodney before the magistrate court. Also available to them was the International Commission of Jurists report, which visited Guyana during the period of March 14, 1995, to March 17, 1995, and produced its report dated May 2, 1995. Even though many individuals who played important roles in this event died, many were still alive and were willing to testify. Even though some were prevented from doing so by the premature termination of the Commission, statements were provided by them and made available to the Commission. A large number of witnesses who had not given evidence came forward voluntarily and offered to testify.

The Rodney Commission adjourned its sittings on Friday, March 27, 2015, and set no date for its resumption as the general election was imminent. That election was held on Monday, May 11, 2015, and resulted in a change of Government. The new administration, led by President David Granger, determined that the Rodney Commission would be given two more days of public hearings on July 27, 2015, and July 28, 2015. Those two days were devoted to receiving submissions from Commission counsel and Counsel representing interested parties.

The premature termination of the inquiry implicated the thoroughness and completeness of the report. There were at least ten witnesses still to be heard and who will not be heard. In addition, the fairness of the information will be impacted as well. Some individuals who were adversely criticized by witnesses in the 17 hearings have not been provided an opportunity to answer and/or comment on those criticisms. No adverse findings can, in the circumstances, be made against those individuals. The Commission, however, was obliged to observe that it was wholly within the competence of the Executive arm of the Government to terminate the public hearings of a Commission.

The Commission was given until November 30, 2015, to deliver its report to the President. For an assortment of reasons, some Commissioners and others related to the Commission itself requested extensions of the dates for the delivery of the report, and their requests were granted, the last of which is to end on February 8, 2016. Secretary to the Commission, Mr. Hugh Denbow was appointed as head of the Commission's Secretariat and later Secretary to the Commission following the departure of Nicole Pierre. His task involved identifying and sourcing literature and documentation relevant to the period. He was also responsible for placing and requesting individuals who would be of help to the inquiry.

Evidence was obtained from Senior Supt. Leslie James, head of the Criminal Investigations Department (CID), entered the Guyana Police Force (GPF) on February 8, 1987. Mr. James produced some files to the Commission but, significantly and perhaps unsurprisingly, did not produce all the relevant files though, apparently, not his fault. He produced three files, which the GPF labeled as WPA8; WPA9, and WPA10 (meaning Working People's Alliance 8, 9, and 10). Those files came from the Special Branch, which is a branch of GPF. Mr. James said that those three files covered the period 1980, the same year Dr. Rodney was killed.

Mr. James told the Commission that two of those files reflect "Re: Death of Dr. Walter Rodney," and the third is a murder file of the accused person, "Gregory Smith." That witness could not account for the missing files, namely WPA 1, 2, 3, 4, 5, 6, and 7. On the first day of the hearing, Mr. James accepted that the "Walter Rodney" files were a matter of continuing interests but could not account for their absence. Also, Mr. James, whose role before the Commission was to produce and comment as best as possible on the police files relevant to Dr. Walter Rodney and his death and Gregory Smith. Those files were at one point within the custody of the Special Branch. Mr. James could give no account for the disappearance of the files.

One explanation was that there was a serious flood in Guyana in 2005, and many of the files may have been destroyed. That was a matter of some speculation, and there was no hard evidence that the missing files from the Special Branch were the victims of the flood. There were also files missing from the GDF concerning Gregory Smith, and there was similar speculation that the missing Gregory Smith file might have been the result of the flood. Snr. Supt. Leslie James expressed great surprise at the disappearance of the Special Branch files and said that in his experience, it was the first time he had ever heard of such a thing happening.

Elsewhere in the report, it discussed the impact and implications of paramountcy on the civil service and the State corporations. As Mr. Danns pointed out in his book, the police force was seriously impacted by the civil service bureaucracy. In support of that contention, Mr. Danns refers to an address delivered by Prime Minister Burnham to middle-level management of the Police Force at a training course. He said, among other things:

> You cannot enforce law and order in vacua. Law and order have to be enforced within a particular context of values and objectives. Incidentally, I would prefer to drop the word 'enforce' and its derivative 'enforcing' and use instead assisting fellow citizens to have a greater regard for the law and its norms. I say without apology because there are still some who would say that the Police Force must be apolitical; it must merely enforce the law. Policemen are citizens first and then vocationally policemen. You will be judged by your performance not only professionally but as a citizen, as a man, as a builder of a new society. I have hope, nay a conviction that out of those series of courses there will come many real leaders in terms of the definition I have attempted to set out.

Minister Clement Rohee testified about the impact of

paramountcy on public service and the military. He was referring to Sallahuddin's book, Guyana: The Struggle for Liberation 1945-1992. He wrote on pages 308-309:

> Significant numbers of public servants and the military were expected to pledge allegiance to the PNC. They did, under the practice of party paramountcy, a policy that placed the PNC over and above all other organizations and agencies and relegated the Parliament and the Government to a position of subservience in relation to the PNC.

The Commission also received evidence stating that there was also in circulation among police officers a Recognition Handbook. A U.S. journalist who was shown it at a press conference said, "Oh, a hit list." The booklet carries the following under the *Foreword*:

> These notes are designed to provide a guide to the easy recognition of personnel of the Working People's Alliance and vehicles that are associated with the organization's activities. It must be appreciated that vehicle numbers and color may change from time to time as is now a regular practice with that organization.

A copy of the Recognition Handbook was presented to the Commission. In addition to the photographs of high-profile members of the WPA contained therein, biographical data and passport numbers were also included. These would generally be outside of the knowledge and reach of ordinary persons. In the circumstances, it was concluded that the handbook was compiled by an agency of the State which had access to personal and privileged information of those WPA members mentioned in the handbook. That handbook was in regular use among police officers at that time.

Burnham's grip and absolute control over the Guyanese society were so firm and extensive that he de-humanized and belittled many Guyanese by compelling them to clean "trenches," canals, or drains, thus giving credence to the slogan, "Trench or be retrenched." Mr. Chase reflects the experience on page 158 of his book:

> The jobs done were basically unskilled work such as cleaning trenches, drains, canals, weeding and under-brushing, picking up coconuts, fetching goods. The crux, however, was that while the various activities were taking place, he would strut around on his horse, stirrup, whip, from one field to another over the estate. In this overseer role, instructions were shouted to the unfortunate to do or do over this or that task. The whip whacked and cracked in terrorem at some of these unfortunate victims.

We next turn to our consideration of Burnham's speech in his capacity as Commander-in-Chief, Prime Minister, and leader of the PNC, in his address at the Third Biennial Congress of the People's National Congress Vol 2, August 22-26, 1979, at the National Exhibition Park. 6.30 - At that time, Rodney and the WPA were attracting increasing numbers of all ethnicities at their public meetings. The office of the General Secretary of the PNC, located in the Ministry of National Development, had suffered damage due to a fire on

July 11, 1979. The stature of Rodney on the political scene, already considerable, was multiplying.

The WPA led by Rodney in association with the PPP and organizations across the country were seen to be united against Burnham and the PNC administration. That was the context in which Burnham made the below-mentioned remarks at the conference, and I quote:

> We are a party of peace, but we are not pacifists, and literally and metaphorically, we promise to match steel with steel and fire with fire. So, comrades, let us deal now with another of them - the Worst Possible Alternative. That is what they must be known by. What does WPA stand for? Comrades, they had better make their wills, because so far as we are concerned, we are not asking them for a quarter and we will not give them any.

Burnham concluded his address to the conference after describing the WPA as the Worst Possible Alternative, with the following words:

> The People's National Congress will never start violence. The People's National Congress did not ask for a confrontation. But, Comrades, as I said on Thursday, the battle is joined, no holds are barred. Comrades, we are now in the Roman amphitheater. The lion and the gladiator cannot both survive; one must die, and we know that the People's National Congress will live.

There has been much debate whether the words used by Mr. Burnham represented rhetorical excess or whether they were harsh and threatening words reflecting the extent to which Rodney and the WPA had become a matter of grave concern to him.

The following day when he went home, his brother informed him that members of the YSM had come to the home during the night looking for him. That incident took place about two to three months before Rodney's death. The YSM's roles were described by Mr. Joseph Hamilton, who testified that there was a lot of coordination between the YSM cadet corps and the House of Israel. The House of Israel, he said, had several points of coordination in the relationship with the PNC. He named Mr. Hamilton Green, Mr. Robert Williams, and Mr. Emerson Simon, who worked at the PNC headquarters.

The four investigations which were relevant to the inquiries into the death of Dr. Walter Rodney are as follows:

Coroner Edwin Pratt conducted the inquest from February 4 – 15, 1988.

The post mortem report of Dr. H. R. M. Johnson, a consultant pathologist, and Reader in Forensic Medicine, was attached to the Forensic Medicine Unit, Department of Morbid Anatomy, St. Thomas Hospital. Medical School, London, England, dated June 30, 1980.

An investigative report dated July 23, 1980, from Dr. Frank Skuse, Forensic Scientist at the Home Office Forensic Science Laboratory, Lancashire, England.

A report issued by the International Commission of Jurists (ICJ), dated May 2, 1995, visited Guyana from March 14 through March 19, 1995.

According to the Coroner's Act, Chapter 4:03 of the Laws of Guyana, it was an unnatural death warranting the holding of an inquest with urgency. However, even though Snr. Supt. James testified that an inquest is typically held within two months of the death; in the case of Dr. Rodney, it was held almost eight years after his death. No explanation was provided for the long delay. The police file did reveal that ASP Gentle requested the inquest to the coroner on October 26, 1987.

There was significant material irregularities in the inquest as the reports of the foreign experts, Drs. Johnson and Skuse were not tendered into evidence at the inquest or the trial of Donald Rodney. Additionally, Sergeant Trenton Roach was a witness at the inquest but was not called at the trial of Donald Rodney. He conducted a critical examination of the electronic equipment, which consisted of three domestic radio receivers, one very high-frequency monitor, four walkie-talkies - two Midland and two Lafayette. They were all seized from No. 40 Russell Street, Charlestown, Gregory Smith's former residence. Since he was carrying out his examination on June 14, 1980, the day after Rodney was killed; he thought that "these were WPA equipment." However, after his investigation, he wrote a statement of his findings and appended his signature thereon.

Notwithstanding the preceding, the typed and unsigned statement which was produced to the Commission from the police file contained material discrepancies and differed from the handwritten note found by Sergeant Roach on the monitor which had read, "Remember to work on the 14th" and then written over the "4" was the number "3". Both the date and month on the typed statement produced said, "Remember to work on January 14, 1980 but the number four (4) was overwritten on the number two (2)". The significance of the discrepancies was intended to distort the record as it relates to Smith's role on June 13, 1980.

The other significant discrepancies were: the date of the

statement given as June 27, 1980, and the signature listed as June 30, 1980. Sgt. Roach vehemently denied that the information on the typed record was correct. Included in the file was a typed document signed by ASP Gentle, dated 88-02-03. He and a party of policemen executed a search warrant at 40 Russell Street and seized the equipment on June 19, 1980. That, however, was another attempt to cover up the true identity of the killer by the Police relating to Dr. Rodney's death. Sgt. Roach maintained that his examination was on the day after Rodney died.

Another attempt to hide evidence by the Police was that they never disclosed or made public the reports of the foreign experts who provided forensic support to show that Dr. Rodney was murdered. The stated position of the Government was that it would make all forensic reports related to his death public. That, they never did. The ICJ's statement alluded to several shortcomings by the Police in their investigation into the death of Dr. Rodney. Having examined the 92 pieces of evidence before them, the Commission agreed that there were several shortcomings.

Captain Gouveia, a Lt. in the GDF, admitted that on the morning of June 14, 1980, he flew his airplane 8RGER from Timehri to Kwakwani. On that flight, he took Gregory Smith, his girlfriend Gwendolyn Jones, and their children. He left at 9:08 a.m. and arrived at Kwakwani airstrip at 9:57 a.m. At the time, Captain Gouveia testified that he had not realized that the adult male passenger was Gregory Smith. He claimed that a few days later, he saw a photograph in the Catholic Standard, and he then realized that he had flown the same person to Kwakwani. Given the chain of command, he did not use that aircraft of his own volition but had been instructed by his superiors to do so. He further stated that his commander 1980 was Lt. Col. Godwin McPherson, but he assumed that in June 1980, his commanding officer was Captain Baker.

Captain Gouveia testified that at that time of the events, the State-controlled the flow of news, implying that he had not seen or heard anything on the government-controlled media that Gregory Smith was wanted in connection with the death of Walter Rodney.

Captain Gouveia's arrival at Kwakwani on June 14, 1980, with Gregory Smith and his family, did not go unnoticed. Several witnesses who lived and worked at Kwakwani saw the GDF aircraft 8RGER when Captain Gouveia said he landed. Those Kwakwani witnesses were: Avril Bourne, aged 38 years old, being the reputed wife of Robert Vanconten, who lived at Kwakwani, Park, Berbice River. Her witness statement was dated July 16, 1980. Joel Southwell, a supernumerary constable with Guyana Mining Enterprise Ltd. at Kwakwani, dated July 15, 1980. Robert Vanconten was a corporal attached to Guyana Mining Enterprise security department at Kwakwani who lived on the security compound with his reputed wife (Avril Bourne) and family and dated July 14, 1980. Anita Thom, a supernumerary constable, employed by the Guyana Mining Enterprise Ltd. at Kwakwani gave her witness statement dated July 15, 1980. Egerton Causeway, a supernumerary constable, attached to the Guyana Mining Enterprise Ltd. security department at Kwakwani and dated July 15, 1980. Those witnesses gave signed statements to Sgt. Winston Saigo.

What is significant is that of the five witnesses who saw Captain Gouveia and Smith and his family on June 14, 1980, three of them also saw when his aircraft arrived on June 17, 1980. They all stated that they saw his aircraft land at about 9:24 a.m. on that day and left at 10:05 a.m. taking on board Gregory Smith alone. On that very day, Captain Gouveia returned to Timheri at 11:36 a.m.

When that account was put to him, Captain Gouveia denied that he flew Gregory Smith from Kwakwani to Nickerie, Suriname. In attempting to explain the destination of his flight on June 17, 1980, he testified that he could not recall based on his memory. However, on examining his pilot's logbook, it was clear to him that he left Timehri, went to Tacama, and returned to Timehri on June 17, 1980. On the evidence before the Commission, it was found that Gregory Smith was a passenger on the said aircraft on June 14, 1980, and June 17, 1980. More importantly, Captain Gouveia admitted that the time stated in his pilot's logbook was sufficient for him to have gone to Kwakwani and taken Gregory Smith to Nickerie, provided that all governmental approval was granted.

On the evidence, there was no conflict between the Kwakwani witnesses and Captain Gouveia concerning the movement of Gregory Smith on June 14, 1980. There were also statements in the police file from Gregory's younger brother, Aubrey Smith, stating that he saw Gregory in a GDF uniform and confirmed that Gregory Smith was enlisted in the GDF. Also, Pamela Beharry gave full details of Gregory Smith being in the GDF, where he lived, and with whom. Ms. Beharry knew these details because she had lived in the same house as Gregory, his wife, and his children.

The police file also had a witness statement from Joan Melvin, a former civil servant, who became a diplomat and posted abroad shortly after Rodney's death. She had described Gregory as her fiancé and kept two photographs of him in her locked desk drawer at work. Those photographs were removed without her knowledge, and she has never seen them again. In light of the facts, matters, and events, it was concluded that any well-functioning Police Force would have pursued all leads to locate and bring Gregory Smith in for questioning at least as the prime suspect in the killing of Dr. Walter Rodney. On the facts, the inevitable inference indicated a collaborative effort by agents of the State to conceal and keep Gregory Smith from the long arms of the law. There were too many unexplained events that point irresistibly to the conclusion:

The swift removal of Gregory Smith, his girlfriend, Gwendolyn Jones, and their children from Timehri to Kwakwani by Capt. Gouveia on a GDF aircraft on June 14, 1980, with the approval of the High Command of the GDF.

The removal of Gregory Smith from Kwakwani on June 17, 1980, from Kwakwani to Nickere, Suriname, or some other destination by the GDF aircraft, was relied on from the statements of Kwakwani constables on the police file.

The sudden disappearance of Gwendolyn Jones and their children, and the removal to New York, United States of America.

The unauthorized removal of Gregory Smith's 2 [two] photographs from the locked desk drawer of Joan Melvin, coupled with her immediate promotion as a diplomat in the Ministry of Foreign Affairs. Her post on July 6, 1980, to New York and later ended up in Toronto, Canada. She subsequently disappeared.

Denial by the Chief-of-Staff of the army at the time, Major General Norman Mc Lean, that Gregory Smith was a member of the GDF or a serving member of the maritime branch of the GDF. The unexplained disappearance of Gregory Smith's file(s) with the GDF, coupled with the unexplained disappearance of the WPA files 1-7 (inclusive), kept by the Special Branch of [the] Police Force in its private registry was, in the Commission's judgment, deliberate. It found: Gregory Smith being allowed to return to Guyana at least twice without being arrested or even stopped. The granting to Gregory Smith of 2 [two] inconsistent birth certificates with different and contradicting particulars and facilitating him with passports, especially Guyana passport No. 0890057 issued on May 21, 1999, authorized by Commissioner of Police Chief Immigration Officer of Guyana, Mr. Laurie Lewis. In that context, the following was noted: A true copy of the extract of the Birth Register of District Georgetown for the year 1964 under the hand of the Registrar dated 2014-11-04, which showed that at Entry No. 99 the child [Gregory Smith] was born on June 5, 1946, at Public Hospital Georgetown; whose given name at birth was William; father's name given as Cecil Smith (Mixed) of 64 Hunter Street, mother's name given as Anita Smith formerly Berry of 64 Hunter Street. It was concluded as an accurate and true record of Gregory Smith's birth particulars.

A true copy of the extract of the Birth Register of District 8 Plaisance for the year 1982 [after the killing of Dr. Rodney] under the hand of the said Registrar dated as well 2014-11-04 which showed at Entry 87 the child was born on June 5, 1946, at 17 Barr Street, Kitty [not Public Hospital Georgetown] whose given names [not name] at birth were Cyril Milton [not William], father's name given as Cecil Adolphe Johnson [not Cecil Smith]; mother's name given as Anita Johnson nee Simpson [not Anita Smith, nee Berry].

Starting with the Appendices in the book Assassination Cry of a Failed Revolution by William Gregory Smith and his sister Anne R Wagner, the alleged birth certificate for Cyril Milton Johnson corresponds to that set out above for Gregory Smith. The completed Application Form for A Guyana Passport dated December 17, 1975, followed the particulars set out with a height of 5' 8", which was signed by William Smith and had a copy of his photograph thereon and his occupation was given at that of an Electronic Technician; that passport was issued in the name of William Smith. The completed Application Form for A Guyana Passport followed the particulars and was unsigned by the applicant Gregory Smith and has a copy of

Gregory Smith's photograph. Still, this time his date of birth was stated as June 5, 1943 and not June 5, 1946; his occupation was changed to Carpenter from Electronic Technician, and his height had increased to 5' 9", although he was much older. That was the form approved by Mr. Laurie Lewis on May 21, 1999, and a Guyana passport was issued in the name of Cyril Milton Johnson.

The copy of the passport on the 3rd page of the book's Appendices over the by-line, "Passport Cyril Johnson provided by the WPA," is a copy of a previous passport issued to Gregory Smith. The knowledge of the Police about Gregory Smith's involvement in the killing of Dr. Walter Rodney, as borne by the evidence of ASP Mc Rae. The acceptance by Snr. Supt. James that the police investigation was unprofessional. The combination of the unassailable facts and circumstances point irresistibly to official involvement in removing all traces of Gregory Smith and persons closely connected to him prior and subsequently to the killing of Dr. Rodney. Those in turn point to a conspiracy and collaboration in the killing of Dr. Walter Rodney by, between or among the State officials, the GPF, the GDF, and Gregory Smith.

When considering all the pieces of evidence in determining who was responsible for killing Dr. Rodney, it was clear that the Police had actual possession of the post mortem report dated June 30, 1980, from Dr. H. R. M. Johnson and investigative report dated July 23, 1980, from Dr. Frank Skuse. Those reports point to the involvement of Gregory Smith in the death of Dr. Walter Rodney. It was difficult to understand why the Police took no active steps to find or apprehend Gregory Smith, apart from the police posting on its Wanted Men Board that Gregory Smith was a wanted person.

At Dr. Rodney's inquest, when Mr. Jainarine Singh, attorney-at-law, was cross-examining Snr. Supt. Gentle, the

Counsel asked him if he went with police officers to search the premises at Lot 40 Russell Street, Charlestown, Georgetown, where Gwendolyn Jones lived, and whether he was looking for Gregory Smith. Mr. Gentle amazingly answered, "At that time, no." That prompted Counsel to ask him the further question, whether he was saying up to this day [February 10, 1988] his investigations did not show that Gregory Smith resided at 40 Russell Street, and his answer was: "My investigation did not include looking for Gregory Smith." On that evidence, Mr. Vernon Gentle and the Police were clearly implicated in the conspiracy to conceal and distort the truth relating to the killing of Dr. Rodney and events immediately following his death.

The pattern of distortion and concealment did not stop with Snr. Supt. Gentle. It transcended or infected the highest echelon of the Guyana Police Force. An example of statements made by police officers are as follows: At the trial of Mr. Donald Rodney for being in "possession of explosive without lawful authority" before Magistrate Norma Jackman, Deputy Superintendent Ignatius Mc Rae being sworn on February 11, 1982, stated as follows: "I do not know that Gregory Smith had a girlfriend working at the Ministry of Health. I do not know that immediately after the incident she was transferred to the Ministry of Foreign Affairs. I do not know if she lived in Ruimveldt. I do not know if she was subsequently posted to the Guyana High Commission in Canada. During investigation I might have heard the name Gwendolyn Jones. I do not know that she had several children with Gregory Smith. I heard that Gwendolyn Jones was interrogated by the Police and I do not know if she gave a statement. I do not know who interrogated Gwendolyn Jones. I do not know where Gwendolyn Jones is now. What I have told the court about Jones is true . . . On one occasion Mr. Roberts [Mr. Cecil *Skip* Roberts, the Deputy Crime Chief who had supervision and control of the investigation, called all members of the investigating team for consultation." Except for the last part, the above statements were untruthful because of what we have set out above.

At the same trial Mr. Mc Rae in answer to cross-examination to Mr. Doodnauth Singh, attorney-at-law, said: "I would not recognize the handbook WPA was circulated among the members of the Guyana Police Force. I have seen a copy of this book. I know that this booklet has been published but I do not know that it was circulated among the security forces. And as the booklet sets out, it is a guide to personnel of the WPA. The first paragraph is of Rodney, Roopnarine and Omawale. I know that these three leaders were charged for arson of a building in Camp Street. I do not know if the building is the office of the General Secretary of the People's National Congress but I know it is the Ministry of National Development." The above statements by Mr. Mc Rae were inaccurate or untruthful because of the fact that judicial notice can be taken of them that the *raison d'etre* for the Recognition Handbook was to assist the Police in their surveillance of the members/leaders of the WPA. It was established that the building on Camp Street had housed both the Ministry of National Development and the Office of the General Secretary of the People's National Congress.

In the end, it was clear that the Police were unprofessional, extremely inefficient, and turning a blind eye to the obvious, or deliberately botched the investigation in Dr. Rodney's death, or were complicit with others, including the GDF in hiding or shielding Gregory Smith from facing the brunt of the law for having murdered Dr. Walter Rodney.

Given all the relevant facts, events and circumstances set out in the report, it was unhesitatingly concluded that Gregory Smith was not acting alone but had the active and full support, participation and encouragement of, and/or was aided and abetted by the GPF, the GDF, agencies of the State, and the political directorate in the killing Dr. Walter Rodney.

Dr. Walter Rodney was a man of large and significant stature both in Guyana and beyond at the time of his death. He could only have been killed in what we find to be a State organized assassination with the knowledge of Prime Minister Burnham. It was a controlled society, and Burnham had an extensive and detailed understanding of whatever was being done by the State and its agencies.

Mr. Laurie Lewis, then head of Special Branch and later Commissioner of Police, is dead. However, there is *prima facie* evidence that he, along with Major General Norman McClean, then Chief of Staff of the GDF, and Mr. Cecil *Skip* Roberts, the Deputy Commissioner of Police and Crime Chief, had significant roles to play in the conspiracy to kill Dr. Walter Rodney and the subsequent attempt to conceal the circumstances surrounding his death.

Further, given how the country was run, coupled with the threats issued by Prime Minister Burnham to the members of the WPA and the evidence of Mr. Robert Allan Gates, it was concluded that Prime Minister Burnham knew of the plan and was part of the conspiracy to assassinate Dr. Walter Rodney. Relying on the testimony of Robert Allan Gates and on the relevant circumstances and events described in the report for that finding resulted from the premature termination of the Commission. None of those alive and herein identified was given the opportunity to testify and to resist the discovery. The result is that there was no firm and specific determination concerning their roles beyond what is indicated here.

It was accepted that Gregory Smith gave Donald Rodney a remotely controlled explosive in what appeared to be a walkie-talkie, a communications device. At the time, Gregory Smith was a sergeant in the Guyana Defense Force in the marine department. It's accepted that Gregory Smith was encouraged in providing that device by prominent members of State agencies. It was found on the balance of probabilities that Walter Rodney had intended the walkie-talkie to be a communications device that would have permitted him to be in relatively easy contact with fellow WPA activists and for no other purpose.

At that time, telephones were not readily available. There was discrimination in the distribution controlled by a State agency, which would have been denied the WPA in all likelihood. It was further found that Donald Rodney, whose testimony was accepted, on the night of June 13, 1980, was doing nothing more than accompanying his brother, Walter, to collect what they thought would have been a walkie-talkie. There was no evidence to suggest that the reason for collecting the device was other than indicated by Donald.

Satisfactory evidence was presented that Smith was protected by the State, and the inference was strengthened when it was revealed that within hours after the explosion, which resulted in the death of Dr. Walter Rodney, Smith was taken to Kwakwani in a Guyana Defense Force aircraft. He was given a passport, not in the name of Gregory Smith, which name he carried as a member of the Defense Force, but in the name of CYRIL MILTON JOHNSON. The investigators were told that the change of name was intended to conceal the true identity of the killer of Dr. Walter Rodney and that it could only have been achieved with the cooperation and support of the Passport Office, which was part of the Police Force.

It was significant that the head of the Immigration Department at the time was Mr. Laurie Lewis. It was accepted that Mr. Gregory Smith, renamed Cyril Milton Johnson, received State assistance in going to French Guiana. The choice of country was deliberate and was undoubtedly informed by the fact that the French Government, of which French Guiana was a Department, had a policy opposed to the death penalty. It would have been difficult, virtually impossible, to secure the extradition of Smith/Johnson from French Guiana.

According to the evidence of Woman Police Sergeant Alexis Adams, Gregory Smith returned to Guyana on more than one occasion and received a new passport on one such visit. It was also accepted that on occasion, the Passport Office was acting on instructions from the then Commissioner of Police, Mr. Laurie Lewis. The inspection of the passport form produced before the inquiry revealed that Smith renamed Johnson was not required to sign the form and fill in the necessary particulars required. Mr. Allan Gates was an important witness to the findings in relation to Gregory Smith/Cyril Johnson. Mr. Gates' testimony was that he and Gregory Smith grew up in neighboring districts and knew Gregory for years. He further testified that Gregory Smith told him that once Dr. Rodney was dead, he would receive US$1 million and that he and his wife/girlfriend and child would be facilitated in being relocated out of the country. Mr. Allan Gates, a former policeman and an instructor in security matters, was at the time of his testimony serving a period of imprisonment for several offenses of obtaining money by pretenses.

At the heart of the offenses for which he was convicted was dishonesty. There is no rule of evidence or human experience that because a man is in prison or has been convicted, his testimony must be rejected. Nevertheless, it was considered whether to accept Mr. Gates' evidence and what weight should be attached to it. After corroborating the evidence, it was confident that Mr. Gates' testimony should be accepted. He was unruffled in the course of testifying; he looked the Commissioners straight in their eyes; he was unshaken in cross-examination, and his evidence is supported by events that occurred after Dr. Rodney's death. That series of coincidences was not accidental, and it was found that Mr. Allan Gates was a witness of the truth. Also, no evidence was produced by anyone contradicting his testimony.

A book was purportedly written by Gregory Smith and his sister, Anne Wagner, entitled *Assassination Cry of a Failed Revolution: The Truth about Dr. Walter Rodney's Death* is a self-serving account of what took place on the night of June 13, 1980. In the words of the publication itself, it was intended to present Gregory in a good light in the eyes of history. In Anne Wagner's words on page 17, "My brother's one unfulfilled wish was to clear his name. Hence my solemn promise to him and to myself to let the world know the truth, even if it kills me." Unfortunately, her account as set out in the book does not harmonize with the evidence presented at the inquiry.

The suggestion that Dr. Walter Rodney was killed on his party's initiative, WPA, has no support on the evidence. In any event, Dr. Rodney was highly respected, if not idolized, by WPA members who had difficulty traveling and could not have arranged Smith's sudden and disguised exit from Guyana. They could not do so. They often had to resort to what has been called the "backtrack" to exit Guyana themselves. It is inconceivable that a party whose executive members had difficulty traveling could either have secured a passport for Gregory Smith in the name of Cyril Johnson and/or secure the services of a Guyana Defense Force aircraft to support his exit from Guyana with his family.

There was no hesitation in holding Gregory Smith responsible for Dr. Walter Rodney's death on June 13, 1980. In doing so, he acted as an agent of the State, having been aided and abetted to do so by individuals holding positions of leadership in State agencies and committed to carrying out the wishes of the PNC administration.

Gates further testified that three days before Dr. Rodney's death, President Burnham met with *Skip* Roberts, Laurie Lewis, and Norman McClean to be briefed on the plot to kill Rodney. His evidence is that President Burnham insisted that Carl Ram Doobay be present. Doobay was close to the President, and the President rode horses with *Skip* Roberts. Mr. Gates further testified that he spoke with several persons to satisfy himself as to who killed Dr. Rodney and how he died. He said that Sgt. Mark Johnson informed him that the meeting took place at the President's official residence three days before Rodney's death. He said that as part of his investigation into Dr. Rodney's death, he looked at intelligence clippings and spoke to Sgt. Liverpool and Sgt. Saigo. He concluded that he judged that "Rodney's death was State sponsored and to Burnham's knowledge." He said that President Burnham and the PNC administration were concerned with the increasingly large crowds which were attracted to WPA meetings; and which were seen as a threat to the Government. Dr. Rodney's infiltration of the intelligence and security forces and his activities were seen as interfering with the smooth function of the State.

After Smith/Johnson was in Cayenne, Anton Barker was sent there to keep watch on him. That assignment was given to Barker by Major General Norman McClean (Ret'd.). He gave Norman McClean's code name as *Moon River*.

Resulting from the findings of the Commission, the following recommendations were made:

Every effort should be made to have a well-trained and highly professional Police Force with a thorough appreciation of its duty to serve impartiality regardless of ethnicity or party affiliation and loyal to the country's best interests and the constabulary.

That would, in turn, call for heavy investment in training at every level and on an ongoing basis with attention to appropriate values in addition to proper policing techniques.

The army must be professional. Nothing is worse than an army in a country striving to be an ideal functioning democracy partial to any political party, whether in Government or otherwise. An army, by definition, has a near-monopoly of the legitimate instruments of violence and must be trained to act responsibly at all times.

The coroner: In this case, there may have been more than one coroner over the eight-year period that elapsed before the coroner's inquest into the death of Dr. Rodney started. That delay did nothing to assist in maintaining confidence in the justice system. Every inquest hereafter should commence within six months of death in unnatural circumstances or any circumstances warranting an inquest. That is the goal to which all coroners should aspire. The coroner should be encouraged to exercise his or her discretion/judgment in such instances. It should be added that ACP Ignatius McCrae did describe Dr. Rodney's death "as unnatural."

The Police should be aware of the need to act with reasonable dispatch in these matters. They should be preparing their investigative files to meet the timeframe indicated with oversight from the office of the DPP.

In the course of the inquiry, the Police conceded that a thorough investigation was not done into Dr. Rodney's death. The evidence is that the Police did not act with professionalism, thoroughness, or speed. The recommendation is that the department in the Police Force tasked with the responsibility to investigate serious crimes, like murder, should strive to do so with thoroughness and urgency, without compromising the investigations and those in authority should make it their duty to so ensure. Failure to pursue their investigations professionally, as in the Dr. Rodney case, may be regarded as an adverse reflection on society's regard for the right to life, one of the hallmarks of a civilized society.

Some critical records, including files with evidence relating to the Walter Rodney case and in the custody of the Police and the army, were not made available to the Commission as requested. The explanation provided was that they could not be found: That is a negative commentary on the thoroughness, efficiency, and security of their record-keeping systems.

The recommendation was that a thorough and prompt review of the systems be undertaken to ensure that an improved, efficient and reliable method of record-keeping is provided to both the army and the Police. Such a system will call for adequately trained personnel to manage and maintain it. A secure computerized system could go a long way in achieving this objective.

The commission handover of the inquiry result was tentatively set for 12:30 p.m. Still, when no confirmation came, and persons who should have made the confirmation could not be reached, a decision was made to go ahead and be at the President's office for the handover at the scheduled time.

> We were keen to discharge our obligation and hand over the report. At 12:45 p.m. with no word from the President, the Chairman instructed Mr. Denbow (Commission Administrator) to alert our security personnel and the Police that we were going to the President's office at 1:00 p.m. to hand over the report. On arrival at the President's office we identified ourselves to the security at the front gate and stated that we were

there to deliver the report. The security officers called someone and in short order a lady came and asked that we follow her. We were taken to a room where we waited for the President. After about twenty-five (25) minutes a lady (whom we assumed to be the President's Secretary) came and informed us that the President would not be able to see us as he was otherwise engaged. She added that he had instructed that we should take the report to the Secretary to the Attorney General and leave it with her. That we did just before 2:00 p.m.

Sir Richard Cheltenham said he took photographs all along the way and of the handover to the Attorney General's Office. Regarding the Commission not being able to print the entire report on Monday because of running out of ink, he said when the typed version of the information was being published at the hotel through private printing facilities, the Chairman received word that the ink had run out. The Secretariat was contacted for a replacement, and the Commissioners were advised that the Secretariat had no ink. It would have to be procured by the Administrator of the Commission Secretariat, Mr. Denbow. "We were further advised that the Secretariat had tried and failed to reach Mr. Denbow. The Chairman tried to reach Mr. Denbow without success. At 11:15 a.m. on that said morning he came to see us at the Marriott Hotel and explained that he had been meeting with aviation officials visiting the country and apologized for being out of reach. He said further that he had provided ink days before in anticipation of the printing and was surprised that it had run out. He, however, left the hotel and returned at 11:45 a.m. with the additional ink which he purchased personally. We then re-commenced the printing of the report". He explained that the Commission wanted to hand over the report the same day, but the Commissioners were told that the President would not have been available for the rest of the day on Monday, and that was the reason behind the decision to move the hand over to Tuesday.

Mr. Cheltenham also sought to clear the air about the Commissioners not having a signed contract for their work and the need for them to be paid for the report's writing. "The terms and conditions under which the Commissioners' services were engaged were settled with the former Attorney General, Mr. Anil Nandalal, who, at all times, was acting on behalf of the President. There was no signed contract which is not uncommon in Commissions of inquiry. The Chairman was careful, however, to send a letter dated February 10, 2014, to Attorney General Nandalal reflecting the terms of our engagement which had been agreed with the Chairman and the other Commissioners at the Amaryllis Hotel in Barbados on February 8, 2014." He said before that letter was dispatched to the then Attorney General, the Commissioners agreed to reduce their fees with Attorney General Nandalal and were paid in accordance with the agreed reduction. "One of the elements of our engagement included a writing fee for the Commissioners, as is the norm. A writing fee is a standard part of the engagement of Commissioners. It reflects the reality that Commissioners have to spend considerable time, separate and apart from hearing the evidence, in analyzing and writing up the report. It is the fee paid to Commissioners for the final phase of their responsibilities." He said the writing fee was due to be paid in full ten (10) days before the delivery of the report.

A letter from the Chairman setting out the terms concerning writing fees was provided to the Administrator, at his request, during the last sitting of the Commission in

August 2015. The Chairman reminded the Attorney General in writing on January 20, 2016, that a writing fee was due to the Commissioners. "Notwithstanding that, none of the writing fee was paid, the Commissioners went to Guyana determined to discharge their responsibilities under the Terms of Reference and have done so."

President David Granger described the report of the Dr. Walter Rodney Commission of Inquiry as deeply flawed, and he believes that it has left Guyanese still starved for the truth. The President's statement came two weeks after he refused to accept the report and suggested it be taken to the Secretary at the Attorney General's office.

Speaking to members of the media, President Granger said the Commission's report does not address the mandate for which it was established. He told the Commissioners depended on hearsay and gossip instead of pursuing means through which the truth could be found. The President said:

> I would like to say that the report is very badly flawed in many respects. From the start we realised that the Commission was paying a lot of attention to hearsay evidence and the most glaring example of the flaw in the Commission's report is the fact that they decided to accept the evidence of a convict. They brought a convict, who at the time was a constable in the Guyana Police Force. He reports verbatim on a conversation between the President of Guyana, the Chief of Staff of the Guyana Defence Force and two assistant commissioners of Police and he was not present. How does he know what was going on? And why should the Commission believe that he knew what was going on?

He told the media that a key witness, who was available to the Commission and had knowledge of what would have possibly transpired, was not allowed to testify. "The Commission brought one of the persons who was present at that meeting into this country for ten days, kept him at a hotel and then sent him back to the United States without asking him a single question. Why should the Commission accept the word of a convict and refuse to bring unto the stand, the Deputy Commissioner of Police, who in fact was supposed to be at that meeting with Former President Burnham and was also the Chief investigator into the circumstances surrounding the death of Dr. Rodney? So, when you look at details of the evidence provided it is clear that the report itself is very badly flawed and we intend to challenge the findings of the report and the circumstances under which that report was conducted," he noted.

He further added that while the Government has expended large sums of money on the Commission and its work in pursuit of truth and closure, none of these has been achieved despite the handing over of the report. The President expressed:

> It has cost the Guyanese taxpayers a tremendous amount of money. We could have built ten schools with the money that was spent on that Commission. They are just gobbling up money and at the same time they are not providing the Guyanese people with the truth. We supported the Commission's pursuit of truth but the Commission has varied from its mandate and has accepted a lot of hearsay evidence and not given the Guyanese people what they deserve. That is to say, what were the circumstances under which Dr. Rodney acquired a certain device

and how did that device come to be detonated? That is what we want to know.

The report was initially supposed to be handed over to President David Granger at midday on February 8 but was not submitted because the Chairman of that Commission, Sir Richard Cheltenham, informed the Attorney General, Basil Williams that he had run out of ink while printing the document. This call was made even as President Granger had already arrived at the Ministry of the Presidency to facilitate the handing over of the report. While President Granger has discredited the Commission's report, former President Donald Ramotar has praised the report as giving justice to the family of Walter Rodney.

The following are declassified documents from the United States Department of State that features a substantial biographical sketch of Dr. Rodney. Ambassador George Roberts and members of his staff followed information as they emerged about Dr. Rodney's death. The American diplomats seemed genuinely interested in finding out what happened but were troubled at growing evidence that the U.S.-backed regime covered up the existence and whereabouts of an active-duty sergeant of the army who allegedly gave the booby-trapped walkie talkie to Dr. Rodney.

The picture looked bleaker when sources indicated that a senior military officer, Guyanese Defense Force Chief of Staff Norman McLean, may have helped the sergeant, Gregory Smith, escape the country and set him up with a shrimp fishing company. Embassy sources included articles in government-controlled and Opposition newspapers, government officials, and unnamed individuals.

Of particular interest among those records are Ambassador Roberts' lengthy summary of "opinions" and the account by former Deputy Chief of Mission Dwyer of his interview with a shrimp fishing executive in Martinique who gave detailed information about the bombing but, in the end, may only have clouded the issue further.

"Interview with Guyanese Opposition Leader Dr. Walter Rodney," Secretary of State Washington, D.C., December 14, 1979.

On December 5, a meeting was requested by Dr. Walter Rodney to meet 'discreetly' with James L. Adkins, who was the embassy's political officer. Dr. Rodney had briefly met Adkins earlier in 1979 and was comfortable talking with him. Dr. Rodney would not have known that Adkins was a CIA employee attached to the embassy. The conversation covered the increasingly repressive tactics the Government of Guyana (GoG) was using against opposition groups, leaving the WPA, in Rodney's view, no alternative but violence, which Rodney predicted could result within the next year. Rodney said while he "abhorred terrorism, the WPA may be forced to it." Relations with and opinions on Grenada, Cuba, and Suriname were covered. Adkins' Comment section concluded that Rodney "intensely" wanted to convince him that he was favorable to the U.S. and no threat to its national security. He added that the WPA "recognized that Guyana could only be saved by a government which represented all interest groups and races." Then, the conversation assumed a dark side when Rodney predicted that because violence might result within the year, he asked for Adkins' assistance in obtaining permanent resident alien status for his family to go to the U.S. if he was killed.

"Interview with Working People's Alliance Leader Dr. Walter Rodney," American Embassy Georgetown to Secretary of State Washington, D.C., April 29, 1980.

The embassy had a third meeting with Dr. Walter Rodney in December 1979. Other documents revealed that Ambassador Roberts knew Rodney from when they were in Dar es Salaam in the 1960s, and embassy Political Officer James L. Adkins had met with Walter Rodney twice in 1979 and knew Mrs. Rodney. Embassy officials were well informed about Rodney's international reputation as a scholar and WPA leader. In this meeting, the focus was on his views on how the U.S. treated Guyana compared to its regional neighbors, and the subjects of potential violence and terrorism were covered.

Rodney was described as "being in good spirits" and said while active in WPA administrative work. He had also continued his academic career by completing a book on Caribbean history to be published by Johns Hopkins University Press. Rodney claimed U.S. funding for Guyana was not being used to promote social services but instead abetting GoG control over opposition parties by freeing funds for surveillance technology and military equipment. He asked why the U.S. praised human rights progress in Barbados while criticizing Grenada but ignored Guyana's human rights abuses.

He was unwilling to agree that the refugees fleeing Cuba meant its economy had failed but said Cuba needed to free itself from the Soviet "yoke," meaning that Soviet aid had prevented Cuba from developing a successful economy. He described the WPA's relationship with the Maurice Bishop regime in Grenada as being quite good. Regarding violence, Rodney said the WPA was willing and able to defend itself if one of its leaders should be killed by the Government, but he was opposed to terrorism and harming innocent people.

American Embassy Georgetown to Secretary of State Washington, D.C., Springtime Politics – Notable for Their Absence, May 12, 1980.

"But overall, Forbes Burnham seems confident, even arrogantly in control, and remains the only individual who makes the important decisions." Relying on embassy observations, an unidentified "reliably good source," and rumors, the tranquil political situation at the time was mainly due to the GoG's delay in establishing the new Constitution with no definite date being set for national elections. Residents' concerns include the upcoming trial of three WPA leaders for arson, set for June 3, what might occur if one or all of them are found guilty, including the possibility of terrorist attacks against the Government by more radical WPA members. In addition, poor economic conditions, increasing use of automatic weapons by criminals, and the number of suspects killed by police in the course of arrests result in a "fragile calmness," presumably the calm before the storm.

"According to the Government Owned Guyanese Chronicle Newspaper, On June 1 The Guyanese Police Arrested Sixteen Persons 'Involved in Training of the use of Arms with the intent of overthrowing the government of Guyana'." American Embassy Georgetown [Deputy Chief of Mission Dwyer] to Secretary of State Washington, D.C., June 3, 1980.

An article from the GoG-owned newspaper Guyana Chronicle about the June 1 arrests of 23 individuals. Sixteen were reported to be "involved on training of the use of arms with the intent of overthrowing the government of Guyana," and seven in New Amsterdam were arrested for "defacing public buildings." GoG-controlled radio broadcasts indicated the latter were WPA activists accused of placing anti-government slogans on buildings. The arrests were likely intended to intimidate because they occurred just two days before the June 3 scheduled trial on arson charges of the three WPA leaders.

The embassy repeated its plans to send an observer to the trial of Dr. Rodney, Dr. Omawale, and Dr. Roopnarine, although space would be limited. Great Britain was sending former Labor Attorney-General Sam Silken, and Amnesty International would be represented by David Weissbrodt, a University of Minnesota law professor. He had previously worked as a consultant on political trials for the State Department. The trial opened on June 3 but was adjourned until late August, according to a June 14, 1980 document.

Note: A lengthy article by Sam Silkin, the U.K. Parliamentary Human Rights Group observer to the June 3, arson trial provided an eye witness account of the events inside and outside the court, including the prosecutor's demeanor, conversations with Dr. Rodney, and the other defendants, and listening to Dr. Rodney addressed the crowd of two to three thousand who waited outside to greet the defendants after the trial was adjourned.

"WPA Leader Rodney Dies in Car Explosion," Death and Allegations of CIA Involvement. American Embassy Georgetown to Secretary of State Washington, D.C., June 14, 1980.

There was shocking news of Dr. Rodney's death in a car explosion on the evening of Friday, June 13. Although the GoG deputy police commissioner for crime, Cecil *Skip* Roberts, told the embassy that Rodney's identity had not been immediately confirmed, the embassy had already heard about a WPA press release issued early that morning that said he had been murdered and added, "informed sources state that it [press release] accuses the Guyanese government and the CIA of murdering Rodney."

Family members and then the Guyanese police soon confirmed that Dr. Walter Anthony Rodney was the deceased individual. Who was responsible for his death quickly evolved into two arguments: the GoG claimed Rodney caused his death by accidentally switching on an illegally obtained bomb concealed in a walkie-talkie. In contrast, the WPA claimed a bomb had been hidden in the walkie-talkie given to Rodney and his brother Donald by an undercover government agent. The WPA alleged the bomb was then remotely detonated by that agent, who immediately left the country on a flight arranged by the Government.

A 35-year struggle to find an answer has been pursued by Dr. Rodney's widow, Patricia Rodney, and culminated in a formal Commission of Inquiry held in 2014. The commission decided the Forbes Burnham PNC government had been responsible, and Gregory Smith was the Government's agent. As of June 12, 2020, only an unofficial printed copy of the report became available, as explained in an Editorial Note on the last page of the Commission of Inquiry. There is no explanation for the Government's delay in releasing the official report to the public.

"GOG Requests USG Assistance in Obtaining Forensic Pathologist for Rodney Death," American Embassy Georgetown to Secretary of State Washington, D.C., June 16, 1980.

Deputy Chief of Mission Dwyer provides some reassurance about the reported WPA claim against the CIA. He wrote, "We have now seen a report allegedly issued by the Working People's Alliance (WPA) on the Rodney death. It does not repeatedly accuse the CIA of involvement as the first reports of the WPA reaction (reported REFTEL) had alleged. Nonetheless, further suggestions of USG involvement from the WPA would not be surprising."

"Brother Gives Version of Death of Dr. Walter Rodney," American Embassy Georgetown to Secretary of State Washington, D.C., June 17, 1980.

Additional reassurance was provided for U.S. officials, stating that Donald Rodney's story did not mention the CIA or the United States. The name Gregory Smith appears here for the first time in a cable as the provider of the walkie-talkie that contained a bomb. The identity of that person and his disappearance were significant factors leading to embassy officials becoming suspicious of GoG involvement.

"GOG Request for USG Assistance in Obtaining Forensic Pathologist," Secretary of State Washington, D.C. to American Embassy Georgetown to, June 17, 1980.

The decision by the Department of State not to grant a GoG request for the U.S. to provide expert advice since the WPA has allegedly accused the CIA of complicity in Rodney's death. The Washington office has also learned that the GoG had requested similar assistance from the British, who indicated a favorable response.

"Further Reactions to Death of Guyanese WPA Political Activist Dr. Walter Rodney," American Embassy Georgetown to Secretary of State Washington, D.C., June 18, 1980.

A report in the GoG-owned newspaper, The Guyana Chronicle, about Rodney's death focuses more attention on a series of WPA releases reproducing statements of "outrage and sympathy" from Caribbean leaders that should be "undoubtedly more worrying for the regime of Prime Minister Burnham." The statements came from the Prime Ministers of Grenada and Jamaica, the Government of Zimbabwe, and various organizations in the Caribbean, Europe, and the United States. The last section of the cable notes another WPA release entitled "Walter Rodney's Assassination: A Cold-Blooded Plot of the PNC State," which claimed, "It was a carefully designed bomb, a bomb probably designed with the aid of 'foreign experts' like the CIA." The same release alleged that Guyana Defense Force (GDF) Chief of State Norman McLean was involved. Regarding the GoG request for U.S. and British experts to aid their investigation, the WPA release states: "We can have no confidence in the verdict of highly reactionary police forces [sic] from imperialist capitals in a highly political incident in which they may have been involved at an earlier stage."

"Message of Condolence to Rodney Widow," American Embassy Georgetown to Secretary of State Washington, D.C., June 19, 1980.

The Deputy Chief of Mission Dwyer revealed that Ambassador Roberts was out of the country and needed to be consulted before the embassy sends a message of condolence to Mrs. Rodney. The cable revealed that Ambassador Roberts and Walter Rodney had met several years earlier when both resided in Tanzania and that embassy political officer Adkins was acquainted with Mrs. Rodney. Dwyer considers the propriety of sending a condolence note and how it might be used by the WPA and interpreted by the GoG.

"Message of Condolence to Mrs. Walter Rodney," American Embassy Georgetown to Secretary of State Washington, D.C., June 23, 1980.

A "personal note of condolence from the charge" (the acting senior official at the embassy in the ambassador's absence) to Mrs. Rodney. A memorial Mass for Rodney was held in the Roman Catholic Cathedral on June 21, before the police released his body. The cable anticipates a large funeral procession on June 23, leading to his burial in Le Repentir Cemetery in Georgetown.

"Two Weeks After Rodney Death: How Things Stand," Updates on Complicity for Rodney's Death. American Embassy Georgetown to Secretary of State Washington, D.C., July 1, 1980.

The "GoG and its critics remain as far apart as ever" in their versions of Rodney's death. One of the main points in dispute was the role or even the existence of Gregory Smith, who Donald Rodney identified as a former Guyana Defense Force (GDF) sergeant who gave him the walkie-talkie that contained an explosive that killed Walter Rodney. The GOG "ridicule[d]" the idea and claimed no one named Gregory Smith in the GDF. The cable cites a WPA handout alleging that Forbes Burnham had Rodney murdered because the WPA would be "in the way" of another "rigged election."

The document goes on to reference an article in The Guardian (U.K. newspaper) by Sam Silkin, the former Labor U.K. Attorney General who represented the U.K. Human Rights Group at the June 3 arson trial in Georgetown, who writes that Rodney was a man who did not believe in violence except when all other forms of opposition had been exhausted. Finally, the cable cites a "well-placed source" who told the embassy that the preliminary British forensic results indicated the bomb that killed Rodney was resting in his lap and that it was a sophisticated device but "of a type generally available to terrorist organizations around the world." The embassy offered no comment on that information.

"Location of Person Implicated in Walter Rodney Killing," American Embassy Georgetown to Secretary of State Washington, D.C., July 29, 1980.

An anonymous source informed the embassy's political officer Adkins about a late-night request by Guyanese Defense Force Chief of Staff Norman McLean to an old friend to secretly transport Gregory Smith, a suspect in Rodney's death, out of Guyana to French Guiana, where he would be employed for a year under an alias in a shrimping company. The friend complied, according to the source, apparently without knowing the identity of the individual he was harboring, but later realized that it was the person accused of killing Rodney. Of significant concern to the embassy was the U.S. citizenship of the friend and the company owner, which would give the appearance of U.S. "complicity in a GoG cover-up." The cable ends with the comment: "Moreover, if it is true that McLean assisted Smith ... it represents another strong implication [*sic*] of GOG guilt in planning and carrying out Rodyney's [*sic*] assassination."

Rodney Death- The Case against the GOG, American Embassy Georgetown to Secretary of State Washington, D.C., August 15, 1980.

In a lengthy cable, Ambassador Roberts details the strong, although the admittedly circumstantial case for GoG responsibility for Rodney's death. He starts with his February 6 meeting with Prime Minister Forbes Burnham. He ends with a series of recommendations, including avoiding being closely identified with the GoG, to provide a "frank" treatment of the matter in the State Department's annual Human Rights Report, and to delay any new U.S. aid to Guyana. He points to some risks with this approach, including possibly strengthening the position of a long-time leftist politician and future President Cheddi Jagan, who remains "unacceptable to the U.S."

"Alleged Killer of Walter Rodney Identified by Opposition Press," American Embassy Georgetown to Secretary of State Washington, D.C., August 19, 1980.

The embassy in Guyana reports on the latest developments, including stories in the Catholic Standard, a small weekly opposition newspaper containing a photo of Rodney murder suspect Gregory Smith, confirming that he was a former Guyana Defense Force member and a radio electronics expert. The document also reveals that the embassy secretly obtained a copy of a British bomb expert's report specifying the frequency used on the walkie-talkie that killed Walter

Rodney and asserting "it should be possible to identify which person or persons or services operate on [that] frequency." The embassy suggests there has been "foot-dragging by the Guyanese authorities" on the matter. The Catholic Standard had a special interest in uncovering information to assist the WPA in finding the truth behind Rodney's murder. The paper's photographer, Bernard Darke, had been assaulted and killed on July 14, 1979, while taking photos during a WPA demonstration.

Ambassador Roberts continued to pursue leads and meetings with GoG officials. He commented that GoG Police Chief Cecil *Skip* Roberts' approach to the Rodney case was plausible, although he was known for his loyalty to Prime Minister Burnham. The problem was obtaining conclusive evidence that Rodney's death was not the result of an accident. GoG officials whom Ambassador Roberts met repeated the same reasoning – that Rodney's death was "justifiable self-defense by the GOG since he had been planning the violent overthrow of the government." The ambassador advises continuing "our low-profile policy and our avoidance of new initiatives which might be interpreted as supportive of the GoG."

Richard Dwyer, formerly the DCM in Georgetown, became American consul in Martinique in early July 1980, pursued the Rodney investigation, and visited the Cayenne location of a seafood company where Rodney murder suspect Gregory Smith believed to be an employee. The company's manager, Bill Charron, proved eager to talk about the case and indicated he was a friend of GDF Chief of Staff Norman McLean, who was reported to have orchestrated Smith's covert departure from Guyana. Sources whose names he could not reveal told Charron that Smith was a GoG double agent responsible for giving the Rodney brothers an explosive device. The plan, he claimed, was to alert GoG security forces that the Rodney brothers were in possession of a bomb and then arrest them. However, the device reportedly went off accidentally. Why the Rodney brothers wanted Charron did not explain the device. Dwyer told Charron that various accounts, including ones similar to his, were circulating in Georgetown but always "seemed to depend upon the motives of the teller." Charron insisted his sources "knew the facts of the matter."

The Human Rights report for Guyana for 1980 prepared by the U.S. Embassy in Georgetown, first introduced by the Carter administration, received careful review and revision before being published and presented to Congress and the public. Often a draft version will include information that is later eliminated. However, due to the ongoing investigation and source information on Walter Rodney reported to the embassy, the published version of the case was more definitive, stating, "Available information indicates that the government was implicated in the June 13 death of WPA activist Walter Rodney and in the subsequent removal of key witnesses from the country." (Country Reports on Human Rights Practices 1980, p. 56). By comparison, in the draft report, the phrase "may have been involved" was used.

On November 4, 1980, U.S. Ambassador to Guyana, Roberts made a courtesy call on President Forbes Burnham at Burnham's request. Roberts saw it as an opportunity to explain the new human rights policy of the U.S. introduced by the Carter administration. However, while Roberts later reported that the meeting was "non-contentious," Burnham was not having any of it and "launched into a defense of Guyana's human rights situation," declaring the "United States had too many beams in its own eye to make accusations about human rights and democratic processes in Guyana." Roberts noted that concerns raised by the State Department's Bureau of Human Rights and Humanitarian Affairs, "along with other offices in the Department," included "various reports about the death of Dr. Walter Rodney" and issues surrounding elections in the country. Burnham believed that U.S. complaints reflected that Guyana had never been forgiven for nationalizing the bauxite industry. Burnham said the late activist had been up to "no good" and had blown himself up with his bomb regarding Rodney's death.

The printing of the commission's 155-page report has not been made public or presented to the Guyana legislative body. President David Granger, a former commander of the Guyana Defense Force, held that position at the time of Rodney's assassination and was a leading figure in the PNC at that time.

The Justice for Dr. Walter Rodney Committee has demanded that President Granger "must recognize the historical significance of this inquiry, not only as a means of bringing closure to an aspect of Guyana's sad history over the last 50 years, but as a measure that, if dealt with properly, can aid the beginnings of the long awaited and lofty ideal of reconciliation, and the expectations of Guyanese at home and abroad for a new beginning."

The major electoral issues were measures to tackle the high crime rate, unemployment, corruption, and drug and human trafficking. The early elections followed the prorogation of Parliament by the President in November 2014, in an apparent attempt to avoid a vote of no confidence against his minority government. A motion had been tabled in August by the AFC, which accused the PPP/C of corruption, mismanagement, and lack of transparency. A successful vote would have seen the dissolution of Parliament and early elections. In January 2015, the President announced the holding of early parliamentary elections, stating that the prorogation of Parliament had not eased tensions between the parliamentary parties.

Similar sentiments came from Opposition Leader David

Granger, who said it was "a dark day for democracy in Guyana." Granger, who leads the majority in Guyana's Parliament, bemoaned that President Ramotar's executive decree had engineered a "constitutional crisis." The Caricom Secretariat noted that the Council of Ministers, during their 35th meeting last year, was "satisfied that the prorogation of Parliament was in keeping with the provisions of the Guyana Constitution and did not constitute a breach of the Commonwealth Charter." But on the international front, Guyana's allies in the Commonwealth, the Union of South American Nations (UNASUR), and the United States, Canada, and the United Kingdom were dissatisfied with the move. They called for President Ramotar to rethink his position.

Although Local Government elections are slated to be held every three years, the PPP Government has not called an election since 1994. Instead, the Government exercised its power to dissolve local Government, replacing them with PPP appointees, which has sparked tensions between citizens and their local government representatives. Since gaining the majority in Parliament, the political opposition had proposed four bills to reform the system. President Ramotar approved three of the bills but withheld his assent to the Local Government Bill, which would have stripped the power of the Local Government Minister to dissolve local government authorities and instead vest that power in a Local Government Commission. Twenty-one years later, there is still no indication of when Guyanese will go to the polls to elect their local representatives since the country's laws prohibit National and Local Government elections from being held in the same year.

Led by President Donald Ramotar, the PPP Government has been stained by allegations of corruption, abuse of state resources, and state victimization of dissenters, among other things. Observers have further accused the PPP of subverting democracy due to a failure to hold Local Government elections in over two decades and a perceived failure to consent to Opposition-approved bills to protest its party's reduced influence in the legislature.

President Ramotar, fearing an unprecedented parliamentary motion of no-confidence against his PPP Government, prorogued all sittings of the National Assembly, dissolved the Parliament, and called elections for May 11, 2015. The idea that triggered the confidence motion was the decision by Finance Minister Ashni Singh to authorize spending in 2014 of GY$4.5B (US$21M) after the Opposition-controlled Parliament disapproved of the spending of those monies. Opposition members called for Singh to be taken before Parliament's Privileges Committee and for the Guyana Police Force to investigate what they deemed "illegal spending." The motion was introduced by the Alliance For Change (AFC).

The PPP Government's 32 seats in the 65-seat House were not enough to overpower support for the motion. After his suspension from Parliament, President Ramotar could not convince the broader public that the decision was in their best interest. Protesters rallied outside the Parliament Building in Georgetown as the Guyana Police Force blocked the gates and secured the perimeter. Speaker of the National Assembly, Raphael Trotman, called the action more distasteful than the suspension of Guyana's Constitution in 1950 by the British Government. He added that "the illegality of the President's decision is compounded by the fact that no certain date has been given to the restoration of the affairs of Parliament."

CHAPTER 39

The Administration of Mr. David Granger - 2015

G ENERAL ELECTIONS WERE HELD ON MAY 11, 2015, alongside regional elections. The Partnership for National Unity/Alliance for Change coalition (APNU/AFC), led by David Granger, narrowly won both parliamentary and presidential elections, ending the People's Progressive Party/Civic (PPP/C) 23-year rule. Outgoing President Donald Ramotar, who lost to Mr. Granger, claimed the elections had been rigged and demanded a recount. International observers said the elections were free and fair. On May 16, Mr. Granger was sworn in as the new President.

On May 26, 2015, Mr. David Granger was sworn in at the eleventh Parliament opened with the Speaker of the House, Dr. Barton Scotland. Prime Minister and Leader of the House, Mr. Moses Nagamootoo took his oath. The APNU+AFC

Government obtained 33 of the 65 seats in the National Assembly, and the Opposition PPP obtained 32. The PPP was absent from the opening ceremony.

The 36 APNU+AFC members in the 11*th* Parliament were:

Moses Nagamootoo, *Vice President and Prime Minister*
Joseph Harmon, *Minister of State*
Simona Broomes, *Minister within the Ministry of Social Protection*
Raphael Trotman, *Minister of Governance*
Basil Williams, *Attorney General and Minister of Legal Affairs*
Winston Jordan, *Finance Minister*
Khemraj Ramjattan, *Minister of Public Security*
Cathy Hughes, *Minister of Tourism*
George Norton, *Minister of Public Health*
Karen Cummings, *Minister within the Ministry of Public Health*
Volda Lawrence, *Minister of Social Protection*
Amna Ally, *Minister of Social Cohesion*
Ronald Bulkan, *Minister of Communities*
Rupert Roopnaraine, *Minister of Education*
Nicolette Henry, *Minister within the Ministry of Education*
Valerie Garrido-Lowe, *Minister within the Ministry of Indigenous People's Affairs*
Keith Scott, *Minister within the Ministry of Communities*
Jaipaul Sharma, *Minister within the Ministry of Finance*
Noel Holder, *Minister of Agriculture*
Dominic Gaskin, *Minister of Business and Investment*
Annette Ferguson, *Minister within the Ministry of Public Infrastructure*
David Patterson, *Minister of Public Infrastructure*
Sydney Allicock, *Minister of Indigenous People's Affairs*
Winston Felix, *Minister of Citizenship*

Carl Greenidge, *Minister of Foreign Affairs*
Dawn Hastings, *Minister within the Ministry of Communities*
Charandass Persaud
Michael Carrington
Richard Allen
Audwin Rutherford
Jermaine Figueira
John Adams
Jennifer Wade
Haimraj Rajkumar
Rajcoomarie Bancroft
Valerie Patterson

Technocrat Ministers

Mr. Sydney Allicock, *Minister of Indigenous People's Affairs*
Mr. Keith Scott, *Minister in the Ministry of Communities*
Mr. Winston Felix, *Minister of Citizenship*

The schools in Guyana never taught Guyana's history or post-independence history. Students were never taught the origin of their ancestors and fraudulent elections or racial strife. Mr. Granger said that historical accounting might not be what the nation needs to heal. "People have spoken about truth and reconciliation," he said. "I always tell them that the truth doesn't always bring reconciliation. You can discover the truth about something, but it doesn't always mean that you're reconciled to the perpetrators of misdeeds. Sometimes, it can do more damage." As the army commander at the time of Dr. Rodney's death, Mr. Granger was asked to testify before the commission, but without a subpoena, he refused to testify.

The commission of inquiry in the death of Dr. Walter Rodney didn't issue the official findings in the wake of the election. Although the WPA joined the opposition coalition, the PPP implicated David Granger, who was a commander in the GDF at the time of Dr. Rodney's death. The evidence painted a grim picture as to how the country was run. The Term of Reference limits the period that should be investigated from January 1, 1978, to December 31, 1980. There was no hesitation in concluding that the political directorate under the leadership of Mr. Burnham was the supreme authority and Commander-in-Chief of the Republic's armed forces. He was the head of the Guyana Defense Force Board and was also head of the National Security Committee and, from all the evidence, kept a very tight rein on all aspects of the country's business.

Mr. David A. Granger recorded in his book, *National Defense: A Brief History of the Guyana Defense Force 1965-2005*, (2005) at pages 186-187 stated that:

> Paramountcy: The increasing involvement of the Defence Force in party politics, a marked departure from the apparent non-partisan stance taken in the immediate post-independence period, raised public concern about the direction being taken by civil-military relations. This pattern of politicization became more evident after the promulgation of the Declaration of Sophia on December 14, 1979 exactly 10 years after the PNC had first come to power. As a consequence of this thinking, political participation was positively promoted and many officers and soldiers were encouraged to become members of the PNC in the ensuing period. Similar ideas had been embraced by the GDF high command for several years and in 1977 the Chief of Staff,

Clarence Price, appeared in military uniform before the PNC's 2nd biennial congress and pledged publicly our loyalty and dedication to the Comrade Leader of the People's National Congress and Prime Minister, Forbes Burnham committing the Defense Force to following the road mapped out by the party and government. This ritual pledge of loyalty was repeated in succeeding congresses up to Burnham's death in 1985, although not by the Chief of Staff in person. As a result of these measures, the civil administration was able to establish and maintain its control over the GDF. It was not felt that there was a need to install civilian political agents in military units as it was thought that there was already significant support for the PNC party in the force. This interest was fostered by the attitude of the Prime Minister who, as Minister responsible for defence, started to appear regularly at official military functions, dressed in uniform. The significance of this symbolism was not lost on the public or the troops.

That analysis, given by Granger, was accepted. It harmonized with the evidence with Paramountcy's effect on the military and paramilitary organizations of the country. A career soldier of the Guyana Defense Force and the son of a policeman, Mr. Granger embraced Mr. Burnham. In an interview, he praised the former leader for building schools and roads. He spoke of him as "the father of modern Guyana who brought Guyana out of the colonial era and gave us a sense of pride and dignity in the international community."

Mr. Granger said, "It's impossible for any statesman to be faultless," and added that closer scrutiny of Dr. Jagan's record would reveal "some grievous errors or mistakes." Asked about rigged elections during Mr. Burnham's rule, he replied that "all of Guyana's elections had been flawed and that he has publicly called for an investigation of the past five."

In election years, PPP campaigners frequently invoked the Ballot Box Martyrs, even suggesting that Mr. David Granger, who was an army officer in 1973, had blood on his hands for those deaths. At a concert commemorating Indian indenture on a sugar estate a week before the election, Mr. Donald Ramotar said, "We must never forget their sacrifices, but [the PNC] now are saying that those things never happened before. They want to forget the past. We must never forget that past."

In 2018, Guyana ranked third to last on the perceived corruption in the Caribbean, according to Transparency International's Corruption Perceptions Index (CPI), only ahead of Haiti and the Dominican Republic. The country scored 37 out of a possible 100 index points. Barbados, Bahamas, and St. Vincent & the Grenadines rounded out the top three countries. At the same time, Guyana, the Dominican Republic, and Haiti were perceived to have the highest levels of public corruption in the sub-region. The CPI is based on surveys and assessments that seek to gauge the extent of bribery, the diversion of public funds, the use of public office for private gain, nepotism in the civil service, and the influence of personal interests in a state's decision-making process. It also considers measures to combat corruption such as integrity legislation, effective prosecution of corrupt officials, and financial disclosure laws. The index is not without its critics. Perception is not always reality, and experts such as Prof. Dan Hough at the Sussex Centre for the Study of Corruption have long considered the CPI to be misleading, he said: "Corruption is complex, multifaceted and riddled with nuance, and this makes aggregate indicators, such as the CPI, problematic."

No-confidence vote in the Parliament

On December 21, 2018, a vote of no confidence against the ruling A Partnership for National Unity + Alliance for Change coalition government shocked the country. The vote was expected to follow along party lines, stripping the People's Progressive Party opposition to get such a motion through. Expectations crumbled when the opposition was able to win the vote on a narrow 33-32 margin, made possible by a single defector, Charrandass Persaud of the AFC, within the incumbent alliance coalition government. The vote would set the stage for new elections to be held within 90 days, with the winner of the latest elections gaining hold of the Presidency.

The legal challenges to the motion remained throughout the first half of 2019, with various courts either validating or invalidating the vote of no confidence. It would not be until the second week of June of 2019 that the motion would be upheld by the Caribbean Court of guaranteeing that new elections would be held in Guyana.

There were further delays for elections in 2019, as the Guyana Elections Commission (GECOM), the statutory body responsible for overseeing the electoral process, faced its series of challenges, including a change in Chairperson. The CCJ's required a new GECOM Chairperson appointed by incumbent President David Granger and agreed by the opposition leader Dr. Irfan Ali. Justice Claudette Singh was announced as the new Chairperson on July 26, 2019. In September, GECOM clarified that it could not conduct credible elections until the end of February 2020. Elections were scheduled and carried out in March of 2020.

The most notable feature of the election was a vigorous challenge to the declared result for Region Four, which includes the country's capital. "The lure of petroleum revenue made these elections more exciting, perhaps more contentious than ever," President Granger admitted. But it also fueled a divisive election campaign that played mainly along ethnic lines.

Election of March 2, 2020

Originally due at the end of President Granger's term in September 2020, Guyana held national elections on March 2, 2020. A legal challenge to the motion delayed elections until after the Caribbean Court of Justice, Guyana's highest Court of Appeals, ruled in June 2019 that it was valid. Running for re-election, Granger was the presidential candidate of the APNU/AFC coalition, and the PPP/C's candidate was Dr. Irfan Ali, who previously served as Minister of Housing. Final election results have not been released because of fraud allegations.

On March 6, international election observer missions from the Organization of American States, the Carter Center, the European Union (EU), and the Commonwealth maintained that the tabulation of results was interrupted and incomplete. Legal challenges delayed a recount, but it was finally held between May 6 and June 8, overseen by a three-member CARICOM team. Preliminary recount results showed the opposition PPP/C secured enough votes to win. The CARICOM team concluded that the recount, despite some irregularities, reflected the "will of the voters." In contrast, Guyana's chief election officer (CEO) maintained that the vote was not free or fair because of numerous irregularities.

Further hurdles have delayed the release of final election results. On June 16, the Chairperson of the Guyana Elections Commission (GECOM), Ms. Claudette Singh, directed the CEO to prepare a final election report based on the recount, but another legal challenge ensued. On June 22, Guyana's Court of Appeal ruled that the winner could be declared only based on "more valid votes cast." That led the CEO to submit a report to GECOM on June 23, removing more than 115,000 votes cast, resulting in an APNU/AFC victory. Another legal challenge to the CCJ led to a July 8 decision invalidating the Guyana Court of Appeal ruling on the CEO's June 23 report. On July 11, the CEO submitted another report to GECOM showing a victory for the ruling coalition, contrary to the recount results.

After the March 2020 elections, U.S. Ambassador Sarah-Ann Lynch joined the heads of mission from Canada, the United Kingdom, and the EU to issue a March 6 joint statement expressing "deep concern over credible allegations of electoral fraud." The ambassadors called on President Granger to avoid a transition of government, maintaining it would be "unconstitutional" because the tabulation process "lacked credibility and transparency." On June 5, the ambassadors commended Granger and opposition leader Dr. Ali, for supporting the recount and their commitment to abide by its results.

In a June 24 statement, the ambassadors said that "election results are long overdue" and expected GECOM to meet "its constitutional duty" to issue an electoral declaration based on the recount "to ensure the democratic choice of the people is fulfilled." In a July 1 press briefing, Secretary of State Mike Pompeo stated that he instructed the State Department "to ensure those who undermine Guyana's democracy are held accountable."

Guyana received assistance since 2004 to combat HIV/AIDS and since 2009 to help combat the drug trade and improve citizen security through the Caribbean Basin Security Initiative. Before the suspension of a Peace Corps program due to COVID-19, Guyana had over 60 volunteers working on education, health, and environmental projects. Among other U.S. aid spigots, the United States also provided almost $4.8 million in humanitarian assistance from FY 2017 to FY 2020 through international organizations for some 22,000 Venezuelan refugees and migrants in Guyana. The United States provided service to help respond to the COVID-19 pandemic through a portion of $2.2 million in health funding for the Caribbean and $350,000 in humanitarian assistance for Venezuelan refugees and host communities.

Granger, however, refused to acknowledge the ruling of the Court yet, in the same breath, told his supporters that "our Coalition is committed to the rule of law". He told his supporters that the CCJ "made no coercive orders… they have not given any instructions to what GECOM is empowered under the laws of Guyana to do", deliberately leading them to believe that the CCJ ruling was of no consequence. Granger repeated the entirely false claim that there has been "massive" fraud and irregularities during the elections and that his party will continue to fight for only "valid votes to be counted." Again, Granger chose to ignore the very specific rejection by the CCJ of the Court of Appeal's unnecessary insertion of the word "valid" which, the Court pointed out, "invited the CEO to engage unilaterally in an unlawful validation exercise."

David Granger had known from the very day after March 2 that a majority of Guyanese voted to elect the PPP/C in an open, freely contested, internationally monitored, and closely observed election. Granger knew that from the published Statements of Poll in his party's possession, but he consistently and dishonestly refused to accept the result. Granger, instead, first from behind the scenes, but now openly, had led his party to believe that they could cheat the counting process, cheat the Recount result, and, when that failed, depend upon a biased judiciary to keep him in power.

The official election results didn't come in for days. Doctored poll statements were discovered in time to be discounted but discovered nonetheless at election commission headquarters, and the PPP demanded a wholesale recount. While Guyana waited, its capital was a ghost town, shops shuttered and streets desolate.

Being entered into the Guinness Book of Records is usually for a remarkably deserving event. Guyana has now been inscribed in its pages for the unworthy event of having achieved the longest delay, in the world's history, between an election and the declaration of a result.

The unfortunate behavior of the APNU+AFC leadership has been to criticize everyone who urged that they concede defeat and allow the Guyanese people to move on and transform the country from being the second poorest in the Caribbean to the richest. Whether ill-advised by their lawyers or ill-instructing their lawyers, the APNU+AFC have indulged in the worst form of abuse of the legal system to delay the delivery of democracy in Guyana.

In democracies, leaders step aside when they are voted out of office. That is the importance and strength of institutions, not individuals, to the power of the people and not those who would usurp their authority. Senior U.S. officials, including the Secretary of State, have made numerous public statements about Guyana since the March elections. Elections must be free, fair, credible, and transparent. Secretary Pompeo stated that there would be consequences for individuals who seek to undermine democracy. On July 15, he announced visa restrictions on individuals responsible for, or complicit in, undermining democracy in Guyana. Those could include members and their families. The action came after months of warnings and expressions of concern. The measure was intended to send a clear message of the consequences of subverting democracy and the rule of law. The CARICOM chair said that the entire world knows a small group is trying to hijack Guyana's elections. Canada demanded a swift and transparent conclusion to the election process and held accountable those who prevented it. Brazil called on Guyana's leader to respect the popular will. The United Kingdom initiated the process of imposing sanctions against culpable officials.

There was no way to minimize how flagrant the actions of Guyana's leaders have been. The United States said that there was no preference in favor of one or the other party, as long as it is selected through a free, fair, and credible electoral process. That is why the work of the OAS remains so crucial throughout the region. The OAS called upon President David Granger to honor the results of democratic elections. If the stalemate continues, however, it will only be the Guyanese people who suffer. Guyana was facing choices of either wanting to have a functioning executive and legislature to pass the laws it needs to encourage the development of its people or remain a country whose leaders cannot travel and are subject to sanctions. The urgent meeting of the OAS reflects the severity of Guyana's predicament.

By all credible measures, as indicated by local and international observers like GECOM and CARICOM, the APNU + AFC alliance coalition lost the March 2, 2020 elections. Yet, four months after the elections, the APNU + AFC coalition government leaders refused to cede power. Instead, some APNU + AFC leaders maintain that the results of the March 2, 2020 elections, which showed a PPP/C win, were still under judicial review. The longer the APNU + AFC alliance coalition takes to admit defeat, the more likely political divisions within Guyana will increase. Such social and political dynamics can undermine the cohesiveness necessary for the full exercise of national sovereignty by Guyana.

Allegations of election rigging are a theme of Guyana's elections every election year, even though it is the case that these allegations are consistently unfounded by observers. Elections and election results in Guyana were always contested between the politicians and the people due to blind party loyalty. President Granger has been a consistent critic of Guyanese elections except for the 2015 elections, in which the alliance coalition won the election. The 2015 election was not without its allegations of electoral fraud, as the PPP alleged Western interference, rigging, and ballot stuffing for their 2015 loss.

If this sounds familiar in 2020, it's because the same playbook has been utilized at every election cycle in Guyana since 1964. The 2020 elections are unique given the extremely high stakes in this election for Guyana and for the geopolitics of the region, which provided more urgency for these claims. These stakes include the discovery of oil in Guyana that is expected to enrich the country and allow the party that rules over the oil to gain political supremacy.

Given the high stakes for 2020, Guyana and its elections are receiving intense scrutiny by some Western states, which before were largely uninterested in the small, impoverished country. The United States, Britain, Canada, and the European Union, collectively referred to as the ABCE countries in the region, uniquely weighed in on the 2020 elections, given the allegations of election rigging. They asserted that the incumbent APNU + AFC alliance coalition must step down, lest they and Guyana be met with sanctions and interventions against

Guyana's sovereignty. The U.S. has couched its intent to violate international law under the broader concern for democracy (ironically). This concern was notably absent during prior election years in Guyana, where allegations of rigging were also rampant. For instance, in 2015, when the PPP lost the election and pushed for a recount, the U.K. and other international observers made it clear that they were not interested in conducting a recount, stating that elections were free and fair.

That was far from the case of the 2020 elections, where multiple recounts were implemented, supported by ABCE countries that expressed "concern for democracy." That concern was undoubtedly linked to Guyana's newfound oil reserves and wealth. Exxon Mobil has already secured a lucrative contract with the Guyanese government after discovering the oil in 2015. Guyanese newfound crude oil is expected to gross billions of dollars for the country, Exxon Mobil, and the other oil corporations.

Guyana's highest Appellate Court, the Caribbean Court of Justice (CCJ), pronounced authoritatively on the matter. Dr. Ralph Gonsalves, a lawyer on constitutional issues and the current Chairman of CARICOM, said, "any attempt, however ingeniously clothed, to litigate all over again this or that matter upon which there has been a final determination or upon which the CCJ has pronounced authoritatively, is tantamount to an abuse of process of the court or is frivolous and vexatious," In other words, democracy delayed is democracy denied.

The ethnic divide in Guyanese society constitutes a fragile fault line. General elections always produce an atmosphere that puts that fault line under severe stress.

BIBLIOGRAPHY

1. A Partnership for National Unity + Alliance for Change Coalition, (Manifesto Elections 2015).
2. A. R. Wallace, *A Narrative of Travels on the Amazon and Rio Negro.* (London: Ward lock & Co. 1853).
3. Anara Khan, *Guyana's First Female GECOM Chair Sworn in.* (Guyana Department of Public Information, July 29, 2019).
4. Andrew Levy, *The First Emancipator: Slavery, Religion and the Quiet Revolution.* Robert Carter. (2005). New York, Random House, 2005).
5. Arthur M. Schlesinger and David Bruce, *White House Memo, British Guiana,* February 27, 1962 (*declassified July 2001*). (John F. Kennedy Library: Arthur M. Schlesinger, Jr. Papers, b.28, f.: British Guiana, 1962).
6. Arthur M. Schlesinger, Jr. *A Thousand Days: John F. Kennedy in the White House.* (Boston: Houghton Mifflin, Company, Boston, 1965).
7. Ashley Davis, *Posttraumatic Stress Disorder DSM-IV™ Diagnosis & Criteria.* (Mental Health, 2000).
8. *Associated Press* (AP), December 13, 1997; December 20, 1997; January 15, 1998; July 2, 1998; March 21, 2001; Banks and Muller, 1998, 385-389; Beigbeder, 1994, 246, 286.
9. Associated Press. Politics. *Trump to Meet with Caribbean Leaders at Mar-a-Lago.* (Sun Sentinel, March 20, 2019).
10. BBC News, *Columbus Sparked a Genocide.* (BBC News. October 12, 2003).
11. Benjamin Quarles and Sidney W. Mintz, *Black Histiry Unbound, in Slavery, Colonialism, and Racism.* (New York, W.W. Norton 1974).
12. Brian G Dias and Kerry J. Ressler. (2014). *Parental olfactory experience influences behavior and neural structure in subsequent generations.* (Nature Neuroscience, 2014 volume 17, 89–96).
13. British Broadcasting Corporation (BBC), December 10, 1997; December 18, 1997; January 2, 1998; January 5, 1998; January 6, 1998;

January 12, 1998; June 29, 1998; July 1, 1998; July 2, 1998; August 9, 1999; August 12, 1999; March 19, 2001; March 20, 2001; April 22, 2006; August 29, 2006; September 1, 2006; January 27, 2008; January 28, 2008; February 1, 2008; February 18, 2008; November 28, 2011; December 2, 2011; July 19, 2012; September 30, 2012.

14 C. Barrington-Brown, *Canoe and Camp Life in British Guiana*. (London: E. Stanford, 1877).

15 C. H. Eigenmann, *The freshwater fishes of British Guiana, including a study of the ecological grouping of species and the relation of the fauna of the plateau to that of the lowlands*. (Memoirs Carnegie Museum No. 5, Pittsburgh 1917).

16 C. Lahaye et al., *Human occupation in South America by 20,000 BC: The Toca da Tira Peia site, Piaui, Brazil*. (Journal of Archaeological Science 2013).

17 Caribbean Community (CARICOM) Press Release, January 15, 1998; January 17, 1998; January 20, 1998; February 16, 1998; March 10, 1998; March 31, 1998; July 2, 1998; July 3, 1998; July 16, 1998; March 1, 1999; March 19, 1999; September 4, 1999; December 17, 1999; March 15, 2001; March 26, 2001; August 25, 2006; August 29, 2006.

18 Caribbean Life. *Homestretch for Guyana Elections*. (Caribbean Life News, Guyana, December 30, 2019).

19 Caribbean Net News, April 26, 2006; August 11, 2006; August 14, 2006; August 25, 2006; August 28, 2006; August 30, 2006; September 1, 2006; September 5, 2006; September 7, 2006.

20 Carter Center Press Release, January 23, 2001; March 16, 2001; March 20, 2001; March 21, 2001; August 31, 2006; (Carter Center report, February 15, 2007).

21 Cecil *Skip* Roberts, *Guyana: The Faces Behind The Masks* No. 10 Aug. – Sept. 1980 pp. 18 -25 as receiving INPOLSE training in the U.S.A. (USAID's Office of Public Safety program, 1980).

22 Christopher Fyfe, *Review of Roger Anstey, The Atlantic Slave Trade and British Abolition, 1760-1810*. (Journal of African History, XVII/I 1976).

23 Christopher Hull, *Going to War in Buses: The Anglo-American Clash over Leyland Sales to Cuba*, (Diplomatic History 1963-1964, v. 34, no. 5, p 810).

24 CIA Memo, *Addendum, Phase II, Operation MONGOOSE*, August 31, 1962 (*declassified May 8, 1998*), Task 25. (Digital National Security Archive, CIA Set III 1962).

25 CIA Memo, *Minutes of Special Group Meeting*, March 22, 1962 (*declassified March 17, 2006*). (Digital National Security Archive, 1962).
26 CIA Memo, Richard Helms for the record, *Meeting on CA Matters with the Panel of the President's Foreign Intelligence Advisory Board*," July 25, 1962 (*declassified November 6, 1995*) in (Digital National Security Archive, CIA Set no. III. John Prados, Safe for Democracy, 1962)
27 Claudia Mitchell-Kernan, *Troubled Little Guyana's Problems Extend Far Beyond Jonestown*. (Los Angeles Times, August 26, 1979).
28 Colin A. Palmer, *Cheddi Jagan and the Politics of Power*. (The University of North Carolina Press, Chapel Hill, 2010).
29 Commonwealth of Nations (CON) press release, December 2, 1997, May 9, 1999, February 27, 2001, March 12, 2001, March 20, 2001, August 29, 2002, September 6, 2006, September 22, 2006, November 18, 2011; Degenhardt, 1988, 144-145.
30 Congressional Research Service, *Indigenous Peoples in Latin America*. (Statistical Information Updated July 16, 2020).
31 David Attenborough, *Zoo Quest to Guiana*. (London, Lutterworth Press 1956).
32 Denis Chabrol, *Jagdeo Rejects Granger's Nominees for GECOM Chairman*. (Demerara Waves, July 17, 2019).
33 Derwayne Wills, *Backgrounder on Guyana's 2015 Parliamentary Elections*. (Antillean Media Group, Politics, May 10, 2015).
34 E.I. Daes, E.I., *Explanatory note concerning the draft declaration on the rights of Indigenous peoples*, (UN Doc. E/CN. 4/Sub.2/1993/26/Add.1).
35 Edmund Heward, *A Biography of William Murray 1st Earl of Mansfield 1705–1793, Lord Chief Justice for 32 years*. (Chichester: Barry Rose Publishers Ltd. 1985).
36 Elisabeth Meier Tetlow, "*Sumer*". *Women, Crime and Punishment in Ancient Law and Society*: Volume 1: The Ancient Near East. Women, Crime, and Punishment in Ancient Law and Society. 1. (New York: A & C Black, 2004).
37 Eric Alden Smith, K. Hill, F. Marlow, D. Nolin, P. Wiessner, M. Gurven, S. Bowles, M. Mulder, T. Hertz, and A. Bell, *Wealth Transmission and Inequality Among Hunter-Gatherers*". (Current Anthropology, 2010).
38 Eric Williams and Andre Deutsch. *Inward Hunger: The Education of a Prime Minister*. (Fredric Warburg, 1969).
39 Eric Williams, and Andre Deutsch, *British Historians and the West Indies*. (Fredric Warburg, 1966).

40 Eric Williams, *Britain and the West Indies*. (Longmans, University of Essex 1969).
41 European Union (EU) Bruxelles Statements, March 21, 2001, June 3, 2002.
42 Facts on File, May 26-June 1, 1966, December 19-25, 1968, January 30-February 5, 1969, July 29-August 4, 1973, April 5, 2001.
43 Francis C. Assisi, *First Indian-American Identified: Mary Fisher, Born 1680 in Maryland*, (2003).
44 G. Haynes, D.G. Anderson, C.R. Ferring, and S.J. Fiedel, *Redefining the Age of Clovis: Implications for the Peopling of the Americas*, (Science 2007).
45 Gaiutra Bahadur, *CIA Meddling, Race Riots, and a Phantom Death Squad*. (Foreign Policy, 2015).
46 Global Slavery Index, *Inaugural Global Slavery Index Reveals more Than 29 Million people Living In Slavery*. (Walk Free, 2013).
47 Guyana Chronicle. *Prime Minister Moses Nagamootoo*, (Editorial, February 29, 2020).
48 Gyanendra Pandey, *The construction of communalism in colonial north India*. (Oxford University Press, 1990).
49 Hamba Wanzola, *Rediscovering the Hidden World: The Changing Human Geography of Kongo*. (Xlibris Corporation. November 30, 2012. p. 72).
50 Hearings before the Subcommittee of the Committee on Foreign Affairs. (1980). House of Representatives. Ninety-Sixth Congress. Second Session. *Impact of Cuban-Soviet Ties in the Western Hemisphere*. March 26, 27; April 16, 17, and May 14, 1980.
51 Herbert S. Klein, III and Ben Vinson, *African Slavery in Latin America and the Caribbean* (2nd Ed.). (New York: Oxford University Press 2007).
52 INews Guyana. (2013). *AFC Defectors Wanted Coalition with APNU for next General Elections*, (Local News, September 25, 2013).
53 International Bank for Reconstruction and Development/World Bank. *Indigenous Latin America in the Twenty-First Century*: (The First Decade 2015).
54 International Foundation for Election Systems (IFES) Press Release, December 11, 1997, December 16, 1997; Jessup, 1998, 265-267.
55 Jamaica Observer, *2019 Was a Mixed Year for the Caribbean*. December 28, 2019.
56 James Hollis, *The Middle Passage, From Misery to Meaning in Midlife*. (Inner City Books, 1993).
57 James L. Adkins, *Final Report of the Independent Counsel for Iran/Contra Matters*. Volume 1 August 4, 1993.

58 Jean LaRose and Fergus MacKay, *Our Land, Our Life, Our Culture: The Indigenous Movement in Guyana*. (Cultural Survival Quarterly Magazine 1999).
59 Jo Loosemore, *Sailing Against Slavery*. (British Broadcasting Corporation 2014).
60 Joe Minihane, *The Grim Truth behind Britain's Stately homes*. (CNN, September 27, 2020).
61 John Dryden and Anthony de Verteuil, *Pas de Six Ans! In: Seven Slaves & Slavery*: Trinidad 1777 - 1838, (Port of Spain, 1992, pp. 371-379).
62 John Prados, *Safe for Democracy: The Secret Wars of the CIA*, 2009.
63 Julian H. Steward and Louis C. Faron, *Native Peoples of South America*. (The McGraw-Hill Book Company, Inc. 1959).
64 K. Kempadoo, *Bound Coolies' and Other Indentured Workers in the Caribbean: Implications for debates about human trafficking and modern slavery*', (Anti-Trafficking Review, issue 9, 2017, pp. 48-63).
65 K.M. Brow et al., *Regarding Colliers and Salter. The Records of the Parliaments of Scotland to 1707*. St. Andrews: (University of St. Andrews, 2007).
66 Keesing's Record of World Events, March 1-8, 1969; October 1, 1976; September 4, 1981; February 1986; December 1997; January 1998; June 1998; Langer, 1972, 1251.
67 L. Anselmo and F. MacKay, *Indigenous Peoples, Land Rights and Mining in the Upper Mazaruni*, forthcoming, (Nijmegen: Global Law Association, 1991).
68 L. Tuhiwai Smith, *Decolonizing Methodologies. Research and Indigenous Peoples*. (London: Zed Books, 1999).
69 L. W. King and Richard Hooker, *Mesopotamia: The Code of Hammurabi. Prologue, the shepherd of the oppressed and of the slaves*, (Code of Laws No. 307.1910).
70 Lisa Ann Vasciannie, *International Election Observation in the Commonwealth Caribbean: Race, Aid and Democratization*. (Springer International Publishing. Volume 40, Issue 6, June 2013, Pages 2840-2847).
71 Luc Cohen, Julia Payne, and Ron Bousso, *Large Oil Traders Vie for Guyana Marketing Deal despite Price Plunge*. (Reuters, Commodities 2020).
72 Luis Felipe Duchicela, Svend Jensby, Jorge Uquillas, Jelena Lukic and Karen Sirker, *Our People, Our Resources: Striving for a Peaceful and Plentiful Planet*. (World Bank, Washington, DC, 2015).

73 M. Colchester, *Guyana Fragile Frontier: Loggers, Miners and Forest Peoples.* (London: Latin America Bureau & World Rainforest Movement 1997).
74 Madhavi Kale, *Fragments of Empire. Capital, Slavery, and Indentured Labor Migration in the British Caribbean.* (Philadelphia, University of Pennsylvania Press 1998).
75 Michael R. Pompeo, *U.S. Department of State Imposes Visa Restrictions on Guyanese Individuals Undermining Democracy.* (U.S. Department of State, 2020).
76 Michael Swan, *The Marches of El Dorado, British Guiana, Brazil, Venezuela.* (Beacon Press, 1958).
77 Michelle Bosquet Enlow, Katrina L. Devick, Lianna R. Lipton, Brent A. Coull, and Rosalind J. Wright, *Maternal Lifetime Trauma Exposure, Prenatal Cortisol, and Infant Negative Affectivity.* (Infancy 2017, 22(4): 492–513).
78 Moshe Szyf, *Lamarck revisited: epigenetic inheritance of ancestral odor fear conditioning.* (Nature Neuroscience, 2014, volume 17, 2–4).
79 National Archives of Scotland, *Slavery, Freedom or Perpetual Servitude? - The Joseph Knight Case,* 2010.
80 National Security Council. *British Guiana,* (*declassified May 16, 1983*). John F. Kennedy Library: Kennedy Papers: National Security File: Meetings and Memoranda series, b. 335R, f.: NSAM-135, British Guiana, 1962).
81 Neil Marks, *Guyana Government to Challenge No-Confidence Vote in Court.* (Reuters, World News, January 3, 2019).
82 Norman McLean, *Guyana: The Faces Behind The Masks* No. 10 Aug. – Sept. 1980 pp. 18 -25 as receiving INPOLSE training in the U.S. (USAID's Office of Public Safety program 1980).
83 Organization of American States, Press Release, January 12, 1998; January 13, 1998; April 8, 1998; March 17, 2001; October 1, 2001; August 29, 2006; November 25, 2011; November 29, 2011; December 8, 2006.
84 Paul Heinegg, *A Concise Chronicle History of the African-American People.* (Google Books 1999-2005).
85 Paul Mtubani, *African Slaves and English Law.* (PULA Botswana Journal of African Studies Vol 3 No 2, Nov, 1983).
86 Perry Mars, *Ethnic Conflict and Political Control: The Guyana Case, Social and Economic Studies,* 1990. vol. 39 (3), pp. 65-94.

87 Peter P, Hinks, John R. McKivigan and R. Owen Williams, *Encyclopedia of antislavery and abolition*. (Greenwood Publishing Group 2007, pp 643).
88 R.W.G. Hingston, *A Naturalist in the Guiana Forest*. (London: Ed Arnold 1932).
89 Reuters. October 7, 1992; December 13, 1997; January 13, 1998; January 15, 1998; January 18, 1998; June 2, 1998; March 28, 2001; March 20, 2001.
90 Richard A. Dwyer, *Oral History Interview for Foreign Service Institute by Charles Stuart Kennedy* on 12 July 1990, pp. 58 -59. (The Association for Diplomatic Studies and Training Foreign Affairs Oral History Project, 1990).
91 Richard Helms, *White House Meeting on British Guiana*, (June 21, FRUS 1961-1963).
92 Richard Schomburgh, (trans W.E. Roth), *Travels in British Guiana 1840-1844*. (Georgetown: Daily Chronicle, 1922).
93 Ro McConnell, *Land of Waters, Explorations in the Natural History of Guyana, South America*. (The Book Guild Ltd. Sussex, England, 2000).
94 Robert A. Waters, Jr. and Gordon O. Daniels, "When You're Handed Money on a Platter, It's Very Hard to Say, 'Where Are You Getting This? The AFL-CIO, the CIA and British Guiana," op. cit. Phillip Agee, *Inside the Company: CIA Diary*. New York: Bantam Books, 1976, p. 635.
95 Robert A. Waters, Jr. and Gordon O. Daniels. *When You're Handed Money on a Platter, It's Very Hard to Say, Where Are You Getting This?* The AFL-CIO, the CIA and British Guiana. (*Revue belge de philologie et d'histoire*, v. 84, no. 4, 2006, pp. 1075-109).
96 Robin Winks, *Blacks in Canada: The Journal of Negro History*. (The University of Chicago Press, 1972).
97 Sam Silkin, *The Match at Guyana's Powder Keg*, (The Guardian (*London*), 16 June 1980, page 9).
98 Special National Intelligence Estimate 87.2-61, *Prospects for British Guiana*. March 27, 1961 (*declassified 1997*), p. 1. CIA electronic reading room. Cf. John Prados, *Safe for Democracy: The Secret Wars of the CIA*. Chicago: Ivan R. Dee (now Rowman and Littlefield).
99 Staff Reporter, *Parliament to Be Dissolved on Monday*. (Guyana Chronicle, December 27, 2019).
100 Stanley J. Tambiah, *Leveling Crowds, Ethnonationalist Conflicts and Collective Violence in South Asia*, 1997.
101 State Department Cable, Deptel 4426, Rusk-Bruce, February 19, 1962.

102 State Department Memo 303 Committee, s*upport to Anti-Jagan Political Parties in Guyana*. March 17, 1967, in *Foreign Relations of the United States, 1964-1968, v. XXXII*. (Washington, DC: Government Printing Office, 1964-68).
103 State Department Memo, Dean Rusk-John F. Kennedy. *Memorandum for the President: British Guiana*. Rusk's supporting documents form parts of the Digital (National Security Archive, CIA Set no. III. 1962)
104 State Department Memo, *Possible Courses of Action in British Guiana*, March 15, 1962. (FRUS 1961-1963, v. XII).
105 State Department Memo, William R. Tyler-Dean Rusk, *British Guiana*, February 18, 1962 in *Foreign Relations of the United States, 1961-1963, v. XII: American Republics*. (Washington, DC: Government Printing Office, 1996).
106 Stephen Tomkins, *Keeping it under their Hats*. (BBC NEWS Magazine, March 2007).
107 Steven G Rabe, *U.S. Intervention in British Guiana, A Cold War Story*. The University of North Carolina Press, (Chapel Hill, North Carolina, USA, 2005).
108 Steven M. Wise, *Though the Heavens May Fall: The Landmark Trial That Led to the End of Human Slavery*. (Hachette Books 2005).
109 Stuart Fiedel, *Origins of the first Americans: Before and after the Anzick genome*. (Reviews in Anthropology 2018).
110 Stuart Fiedel. *Initial Human Colonization of the Americas: An Overview of the Issues and the Evidence*. (Radiocarbon 2006, 44(02).
111 T. D. Dillehay, Steve L. Goodbred, Mario Pino, Victor Vasquez and Teresa Rosales Tham, *A late Pleistocene human presence at Huaca Prieta, Peru, and early Pacific Coastal Adaptations*. (Cambridge University Press 2017).
112 T. D. Dillehay, C. Ocampo, J. Saavedra, A.O. Sawakuchi, R.M. Vega, M. Pino, et al., *New Archaeological Evidence for an Early Human Presence at Monte Verde, Chile*. (PLoS ONE 10(12): e0145471, 2015).
113 T. D. Dillehay, *From Foraging to Farming in the Andes*. (Cambridge University Press, Cambridge 2011).
114 T. D. Dillehay, *The Settlement of the Americas: a New Prehistory*. (Basic Books, 2000).
115 Tamanisha John. *Caribbean sovereignty and politics, economic imperialism, race, financial exclusion, and Canadian multinational banks in the Caribbean*. (Council on Hemispheric Affairs, 2020).

116 The Subcommittee of the Committee on Foreign Affairs. *Impact of Cuban-Soviet Ties in the Western Hemisphere, Spring 1980*, House of Representatives. Ninety-Sixth Congress. Second Session. March 26, 27; April 16, 17 and May 14, 1980. Note: mentions of Guyana are on pages: 34, 59, 64, 65 73, 80, 81, 91, 92, 94, and 101. See pages 115-116 for the answers Dr. Edward M. Collins, vice director for foreign intelligence, (Defense Intelligence Agency, 1980).

117 The World Bank, *How much do you know about the Indigenous populations of Latin America?* November 22, 2016.

118 Thomas Erskine May, *Last Relics of Slavery. The Constitutional History of England (1760–1860)*. II. (New York: A. C. Armstrong and Son, 1895, pp. 274–275).

119 Tim Weiner, *A Kennedy-C.I.A. Plot Returns to Haunt Clinton*, (New York Times, October 30, 1994, p. A10).

120 TIMES INT'L. *Key NY Backers Leave AFC for APNU*. (Guyana Times International, Top Stories, September 20, 2013).

121 United Nations. *The State of the World's Indigenous People*: Implementing the United Nations Declaration on the Rights of Indigenous Peoples, 4th volume, (ST/ESA/371, 2019).

122 US Department of State, *"Slavery, Abduction and Forced Servitude in Sudan."* (2002).

123 US Senate, Committee on Foreign Relations and US House of Representative Committee on Foreign Affairs, *Country Reports On Human Rights Practices*. (US Government Printing Office, Washington DC, 1981).

124 V. A. Funk, M. Fernanda Zermoglio, and Naseem Nasir. (1999). *Testing the use of specimen collection data and GIS in biodiversity exploration and conservation decision making in Guyana.* (Biodiversity and Conservation, 1999, 8: 727-751).

125 Walter Rodney, *A History of the Guyanese Working People, 1881 to 1905.* Baltimore and London. (The Johns Hopkins University Press 1981).

126 Walter Rodney, *A History of the Upper Guinea Coast 1545 to 1800.* (London: Oxford University Press, 1970).

127 Walter Rodney, *How Europe Underdeveloped Africa.* (Howard University Press, Washington, D.C. 1972).

128 Walter Rodney, *The Groundings with My Brothers.* (London: Bogle-L'Ouverture Publications, 1969; London and New York: Verso Press, 2019).

129 Walter Rodney, *The Russian Revolution: A View from the Third World*. (United Kingdom: Verso Books, 2018).
130 Walter Rodney, *Walter Rodney Speaks. The Making of an African Intellectual.* [*transcripts of 1975 conversations*]. Atlanta, GA: Africa World Press. (Institute of the Black World, 1990).
131 Wazim Mowla, *Guyana's Incumbent APNU+AFC Coalition Puts Its Future at Risk*. (Global Americans, sec. Democracy & Elections July 2, 2020).

CPSIA information can be obtained
at www.ICGtesting.com
Printed in the USA
LVHW100201231221
706811LV00011B/98